QUESTIONING
AUTHORITY

QUESTIONING AUTHORITY

Justice and Criminal Law

BY

DAVID L. BAZELON

WITH A FOREWORD BY

Supreme Court Justice William J. Brennan, Jr.

ALFRED A. KNOPF   NEW YORK   1988

For my dear family,
each of whom gave so much to me:
Mickey, Jim, Rick, Eileen, Emily, Lara, Jill, Dana

THIS IS A BORZOI BOOK
PUBLISHED BY ALFRED A. KNOPF, INC.

Copyright © 1966, 1982, 1984, 1987 by David L. Bazelon
All rights reserved under International and Pan-American Copyright Conventions.
Published in the United States by Alfred A. Knopf, Inc., New York,
and simultaneously in Canada by Random House of Canada Limited, Toronto.
Distributed by Random House, Inc., New York.

Library of Congress Cataloging-in-Publication Data
Bazelon, David L. (David Lionel).
Questioning authority.
Bibliography: p.
Includes index.
1. Criminal justice, Administration of—United States.
2. Insanity—Jurisprudence—United States.
3. Criminal liability—United States.
4. Crime and criminals—United States. I. Title.
KF9223.B36 1988   345.73'05   87-45253
ISBN 0-394-55304-7   347.3055

Manufactured in the United States of America
First Edition

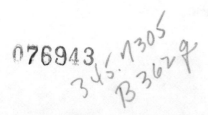

PERMISSIONS ACKNOWLEDGMENTS

"The Morality of the Criminal Law: Rights of the Accused" was originally published in Vol. 72, no. 4, Winter 1981 issue of *The Journal of Criminal Law and Criminology*.

"The Dilemma of Criminal Responsibility" was originally published in Vol. 72 of the *Kentucky Law Journal*, p. 263 (1983–84). "Has the Court Left the Attorney-General Behind?—The Bazelon-Katzenbach Letters on Poverty, Equality, and the Administration of Criminal Justice" was originally published in Vol. 54 of the *Kentucky Law Journal*, p. 464 app. (1966).

Grateful acknowledgment is made to the following for permission to reprint previously published material:

American Psychiatric Association: "Report to the Board of Trustees, American Psychiatric Association, From the Ad Hoc Committee on the use of Psychiatric Institutions for the Commitment of Political Dissenters." Reprinted from the papers of the Board of Trustees, the American Psychiatric Association, Washington, D.C.; from the collections in the archives of the American Psychiatric Association. Reprinted by permission.

Columbia Law Review: "Institutionalization, Deinstitutionalization and Adversary Process" by David L. Bazelon. Copyright © 1975 by the Directors of the Columbia Law Review Association, Inc. All rights reserved. This article originally appeared at 75 Colum. L. Rev. 897 (1975). Reprinted by permission.

New York University Law Review: "Civil Liberties—Protecting Old Values in the New Century," 51 N.Y.U.L. Rev. 505 (1976). Reprinted by permission.

Southern California Law Review: "The Morality of the Criminal Law" by David L. Bazelon, from Vol. 49 of the S. Cal. L. Rev., 385 (1976). Reprinted by permission of the *Southern California Law Review*.

University of Cincinnati Law Review: "The Defective Assistance of Counsel" by David L. Bazelon, from the *University of Cincinnati Law Review*. Reprinted by permission.

Vanderbilt Law Review: "The Crime Controversy: Avoiding Realities" by David L. Bazelon, from Vol. 35 of the *Vanderbilt Law Review*. Copyright © 1982 by David L. Bazelon and the *Vanderbilt Law Review*. Reprinted by permission.

Contents

Foreword

David L. Bazelon is among the great judges in American judicial history. His recent retirement from active service as a federal judge marked the end of a legendary career on the United States Court of Appeals for the District of Columbia Circuit. In his thirty-five years on the court, with over fifteen years as chief judge, he authored an extraordinary number of distinguished opinions. This book contains the writings of Judge Bazelon on criminal law and responsibility, the field in which his work has received the most widespread attention.

Judge Bazelon served on a court that was ideally situated to influence the development of criminal law. The District Court of Appeals has a well-deserved reputation for its intelligent and illustrious judges; and its rulings and opinions often have significant influence on federal and state courts throughout the country. During most of Judge Bazelon's tenure—particularly prior to the Reorganization Act of 1970—the court served as the court of last resort on issues of local law in the District of Columbia. By virtue of this special jurisdiction, it heard an unusual number of criminal law cases. If Judge Bazelon has written more opinions on the insanity defense than any other federal judge, it is largely because his court has confronted a larger number of insanity defense cases than all the other courts of appeals combined.

The "Bazelon Court" (as it was often referred to during his years as Chief Judge) had powers and responsibilities that disposed it to safeguard rigorously the fundamental rights of defendants in the criminal justice system. The jurisdiction of the court over local law permitted reliance on supervisory power, whereas other federal courts could intervene only pursuant to constitutional command. A federal court is more likely to exercise its authority if it can rely on its supervisory power, since this power can be used at the court's discretion without necessarily creating precedents of wide-ranging impact. Moreover, prior to the establishment of District of Columbia home rule, the Bazelon Court shouldered the special responsibility of protecting the rights of citizens who had no voice in the passage of laws that governed the District. As a result, there is hardly an issue of importance in criminal law on which Judge Bazelon has not written one of the leading opinions.

I first became acquainted with Judge Bazelon's views on criminal responsibility and the insanity defense in July 1954, when I attended, as a member of the New Jersey Supreme Court, a conference on prison administration. The principal speaker was a psychiatrist from St. Elizabeths Hospital, a large public mental institution located in the District of Columbia. A few days earlier, Judge Bazelon had issued his seminal opinion *Durham v. United States,* which established a new formulation of the insanity defense in the District. The speaker abandoned his prepared remarks to talk about this opinion and its author. So excited was the psychiatrist about both that he literally tripped over his words. He regarded the decision as one of the most momentous in the history of jurisprudence. It opened the courthouse door, he proclaimed, to expert evidence from scientists of human behavior; it transformed criminal justice from a system focused upon retribution to one focused upon correction of the causes of crime and rehabilitation of offenders. The speaker was equally enthusiastic in his appraisal of *Durham*'s author: In his view, the opinion showed the then-young federal judge to be a luminary of the rank of Holmes, Cardozo, or Brandeis. After I read *Durham,* I could well understand his enthusiasm for both the opinion and its author.

Two years later, I met Judge Bazelon when I came to Washington, D.C., to become an associate justice of the United States Supreme Court. A close friendship ensued that has lasted to this day. Over the years I have become familiar with the devotion and passion that he brings to his craft. Most striking is the audaciousness of his thought. He has heeded Justice Brandeis' admonition: "If we would guide by the light of reason, we must let our minds be bold." In *Durham,* for instance, Judge Bazelon challenged the wisdom of the *M'Naghten* rule, which had been the leading precedent with regard to the insanity defense since its formulation by an English court in 1843, and was then still followed by a majority of courts in this country. He never refuses to ask a question merely because it has never been asked. Nor does he shy away from proposing an answer merely because it has never before been proposed. As this book discloses, he often takes positions that he knows will generate substantial criticism from his colleagues, legal scholars, and the general community.

The boldness of Judge Bazelon's approach is tempered by a willingness to subject his views to rigorous rethinking and, where necessary, to abandon a view that proves untenable in practice. In *Brawner v. United States,* he stepped away from the approach taken in *Durham.* He wrote *Durham* because he felt that judges and juries, in evaluating a defendant's mental condition at the time of the crime, ought to have the candid and comprehensive advice of experts in the behavioral sciences. When the experts disappointed his expectations, he did not hesitate in *Brawner* to voice his disappointment. The significance of Judge Bazelon's judicial legacy is not fairly measured by the number of courts that have adopted his positions on specific issues, but by the extent of the debate and reexamination of fundamental issues of criminal law that his questions have provoked.

Central to his writings is the theme that judges must perfect the adversary process as the essential tool for evaluating the performance of disciplines to which a modern society must look for aid in resolving complex legal controversies. He has sought to establish a means by which the expertise of all disciplines may illuminate criminal law. More than any other judge, David Bazelon has struggled to open the doors of the nation's courts to the insights of the social sciences regarding the vagaries of human behavior. These insights come not only from psychiatrists and psychologists, but also from economists, political scientists, anthropologists, social workers, and others in a position to shed light on the nature and etiology of crime.

David Bazelon has not confined this approach to the field of criminal law. His philosophy is reflected in the more than one thousand opinions he has written, most in areas far removed from the insanity defense and the criminal law. These opinions concern momentous issues of modern society: the powers and responsibilities of administrative agencies in evaluating scientific evidence, broadcasters' rights under the First Amendment, prison administration, the rights of institutionalized mental patients, and many, many more. While it was his opinions on the insanity defense that first brought him prominence, I suspect that ultimately his reputation will rest on a much broader base: his long and continuing struggle to break down artificial barriers to the free flow of information, and to establish a means by which the expertise of countless disciplines may illuminate the imponderable dilemmas that courts must daily confront.

WILLIAM J. BRENNAN, JR.,
Associate Justice,
Supreme Court of the United States

Acknowledgments

Because of declining health, my husband has not been able to complete the formal recognition of those who have contributed to this book. I am certain he would regard this as a very important, and a most difficult, task, for he is given to strong feelings of affection and appreciation toward those with whom he has shared his professional life. As acknowledgments are so personal, I know I may not be including here all those whom David himself would wish to thank. But I cannot let this opportunity pass; so I take the responsibility, in the hope of "doing justice" to those whose contributions are manifest throughout this book.

The preparation of the book and its guidance to completion were possible only through the invaluable aid and dedication of Leslie J. Scallet, one of David's former law clerks, who has gone on to a distinguished career in the mental health field. Creative and thoughtful editorial suggestions along the way were given freely and generously by Professors Martha Minow and Alan Dershowitz of the Harvard Law School, by Judge Abner Mikva and Chief Judge Patricia M. Wald of the Court of Appeals, and by our son Richard L. Bazelon, Esquire. Initial preparatory research was done by Dean Hashimoto, Eric Hamburg, and Michael Michaelson. Ashbel Green, of Alfred A. Knopf, has provided consistent support and editorial guidance. I know how grateful David is for their stellar contributions.

In the early part of David's legal career, the late Rabbi Joshua Loth Liebman, the late David K. Niles, and Professor Leon

Green were significant influences on his ideas. From law school to the present time, the Honorable Arthur J. Goldberg has been an esteemed friend. Many distinguished jurists served with my husband during his long tenure on the U.S. Court of Appeals. Among those with whom he shared a special collegial and personal relationship during their lifetimes were Henry White Edgerton, Charles Fahy, and George Thomas Washington. He would wish as well to recognize his longstanding and close relationship with J. Skelly Wright.

David's friendship with Justice William J. Brennan, Jr., deserves special mention. It began in the early 1950s and has grown deeper with the passing years, through long hours of sharing ideas with mutual respect and affection. We have learned that Justice Brennan is no less remarkable as a human being than he is as a jurist.

David has valued most highly his relationship with his law clerks. His work with these exceptional men and women knew few limits in dedication, time, commitment, intellectual challenge, and camaraderie. His "family" of law clerks are very special to him, and he takes great pride in their contributions to his work, and as well in their personal growth and subsequent careers. Each will identify his or her role in this collection.

1949–51: Abraham Goldstein; 1951–52: William R. Perlik; 1952–53: Joseph Goldstein; 1954–55: Howard Adler, Jr.; 1956–58: Harold Ungar*; 1958–59: Robert Basseches; 1959–60: Alan Wurtzel; 1960–61: Neil Adelman; 1961–62: George B. Driesen; 1961–65: Patricia Weinberg; 1962–63: Alan Dershowitz; 1963–64: Robert Burt, Armand Derfner, James Flug; 1964–65: Peter Strauss; 1965–66: Stephen M. Goodman, John Koskinen; 1966–67: Stephen Weiswasser, Peter Zimroth; 1967–68: Robert Goldberg, Joseph Onek; 1968–69: Russell H. Carpenter, Jr., William D. Iverson; 1969–70: Alexander M. Capron; 1969–71: Barbara Underwood; 1970–71: Michael Helfer, John T. Rich; 1971–72: Loftus Becker, Ron Gilson, Gerald Rosberg; 1972–73: Bernard Carl, Thomas Reid, Eleanor Swift; 1973–74: Ronald Carr,

---

* Deceased.

Steven Goldberg, Joel Klein, Joseph Perpich; 1974–75: Jonathan Cannon, Peter Hoffman, Leslie J. Scallet, Daniel Segal; 1975–76: Lynn Bregman, Don Elliott, David Silberman; 1976–77: Douglas Dworkin, James Harris, Jay Spears*; 1977–78: Richard Kaplan, Thomas W. Merrill, Robert Post; 1978–79: James Steinberg, David Stewart, Frederic Woocher; 1979–80: Martha Minow, Jonathan Schwartz, John Sexton; 1980–81: Douglas Rosenberg, Gerson A. Zweifach; 1981–82: Perry Dane, Jeffrey Kindler; 1982–83: Richard Bartlett, Charles Curtis; 1983–84: Eric Lewis, Rebecca Matthews, Sherryl Michaelson; 1984–85: Dean Hashimoto, Michael Michaelson.

My husband also has always been especially grateful to those law firms and those members of the Bar who provided high-quality legal counsel at the request of the court, as amicus curiae or as counsel for indigents. Without them, the development of legal ideas would have been a far more difficult task.

As this book reflects, the author took a broad view of his role as a jurist. He enjoyed dialogue with judges from other courts around the country. And he especially valued his friendships with distinguished social and physical scientists, with whom he could explore the interrelationships of their respective disciplines with the law. Some of these latter merit particular mention, because of their contribution over many years to the development of his ideas, as represented in this book: the late Albert Deutsch, the late Dr. Philip Handler, Dr. Alexander Leaf, Dr. Jerrold Zacharias, Dr. Jerome Weisner, Dr. David Hamburg, Dr. Joseph Perpich, Dr. Harold Visotsky, and Dr. Jonas Salk and many scientists at the Salk Institute, on whose board David has served since its founding.

The constant support and affection over some twenty years of Judge Abner Mikva, Dr. Julius Schreiber, and Dorothy L. Levinson will always be deeply appreciated by my husband, and by myself and our family. There were secretaries during his judgeship—Agnes Johnson, Mary Commisso, Evelyn Rocklein—whose assistance and devotion were exceptional.

* Deceased.

And John Griffis, his aide since 1949, continues to earn his—and our—gratitude.

Over the course of many years I was witness to a public servant growing, inquiring, adapting, opening his mind to all aspects of the life and problems of society—concerned, dedicated, courageous, committed to his perception of his role. The late Judge Charles Fahy wrote the following inscription in a book of memoirs of Chief Justice Warren that he gave to my husband:

To David Bazelon, who uses the law to the limit of the good it can do but who realizes the vast area of good to be done beyond the limit of the law and enters upon that area.   (Sept. 3, 1977)

MIRIAM K. BAZELON
July 1987

Introduction

Judges are invested with considerable authority in our society. Not least is their authority to question, to probe behind the carefully constructed arguments and counterarguments in an effort to reach the truth. After thirty-five years on the bench, I am now left with even more questions than when I began— a condition to be appreciated, not deplored. For it is the advance of knowledge that stimulates each new round of questions.

The judge's role entails constant dialogue, confronting problems and forcing others to confront them—our contribution to the open inquiry and vigorous debate so vital to a democratic society. Just as important, the questions are meant to elicit information, "to inform" the judges' decisions. Thomas Jefferson saw such education as underpinning broad participation in democratic decision-making.

> I know no safe depository of the ultimate powers of society but the people themselves; and if we think them not enlightened enough to exercise their control with a wholesome discretion, the remedy is not to take it from them, but to inform their discretion.[1]

In our political system, judges, on behalf of other citizens, have the authority to make many important decisions balancing individual and societal rights. In so doing, judges bear an obligation to exercise "informed discretion." The knowledge with which a judge approaches decisions is the product of his learning and his experience.

In this book I have collected some of my writings on one important area—the criminal law and criminal responsibility. Its purpose is not to provide an authoritative statement of what the law is or should be. Such a book soon would be obsolete. Rather, it is intended to provide readers with an opportunity to understand more fully how judges do their work, and particularly how the hundreds of cases a judge may decide over the course of his career form an incremental and evolving approach to an area of law. Instead of focusing on my conclusions, I hope that readers will allow themselves to experience the development of these ideas as I did—responding to individual cases as they came before the court, as well as through the extrajudicial writing and committee work that form an integral part of my conception of a judge's role. The selections are drawn from the scores of articles, letters, and speeches through which I have sought to explore and refine ideas, as well as opinions written either to support or dissent from decisions of our court.

As an appellate judge, I could have chosen to ignore the harsh reality behind the cases that came before the court and focused on the complex abstract principles that arise in legal appeals. But I firmly believed that it was essential to infuse my consideration of legal principles with the passion and pain of life in our society. Obviously, this does not mean that criminal convictions should be overturned because an appellate judge feels sympathy for the defendant. A desire to understand the people who commit crimes, and compassion for them, should not be mistaken for being "soft on crime." Put simply, if we wish to prevent crime, and not merely to punish it after the fact, we must first know why some people behave this way.

A judge does not often have the luxury of knowing everything he would like to know about a case, or even everything he should know to make a fully informed decision. But nevertheless he must decide, based on the law and the facts provided through the adversary process of a trial.

Speaking of his colleagues, who—like judges—must sift a

multitude of facts and theories in a search for truth, the eminent historian C. Vann Woodward has said:

> Questions have to be asked before they can even be wrongly answered, and answers have to be ventured even before we are sure that they are addressed to the right questions. Errors have to be made before they can be corrected and contrary answers provoked. All of which leads to controversy, to be sure, but controversy is one of the ways we have of arriving at what we assign the dignity of truth.[2]

The role of an advocate is to narrow the issues and frame them to support his client's cause, even if this requires obscuring problems or squeezing them into a doctrinal closet. Nevertheless the issues are there, and it is the role of the judge to search them out. People often wondered why the late Justice Benjamin Cardozo seemed to get all the most interesting cases. What they seldom recognized was that he enriched otherwise typical cases by exploring all the issues that others might have missed.

In a criminal case, that exploration includes a moral dimension. Good decisions often require framing the moral choice as starkly as possible. The judge, and the public, should see clearly what is at stake. A judge can properly decide only the relatively narrow legal issue before the court. But he can draw attention to many related concerns through his opinions, his dissents, and his participation in extrajudicial writing and professional activities. In my view, a judge has an obligation and an opportunity to place important issues and moral choices on the public agenda. It is then for others to explore and elaborate them.

One way for a judge to encourage fuller understanding of issues is to dissent from majority opinions with which he disagrees. By challenging the court's reasoning or result, dissenters force the majority to consider carefully, to weigh other evidence and interpretations. Sometimes a dissenter or the reasoning in a written dissenting opinion convinces a later majority in a similar case, and the first decision is overturned. Certainly that pattern is discernible in my career. In the early years I dissented often from the decisions of the court on which I served, and then for a number of years my opinions represented the majority, and later I found myself frequently in the minority again.

This constant questioning may at times infuriate people who want to get on with the solution. But only by opening the judicial process to a full exploration of relevant information can we hope to make informed decisions. In this process I believe that judges should be willing to consider new approaches even though there can be no assurance of success. If this is what is meant by an "activist judge," then I must stand guilty.

Another charge often leveled against "activists" is that they usurp the roles of other decision-makers. Some may challenge what I consider one of the most important tools an appellate court has to force a full examination of the issues: sending a case back for further development by the lower court or the government agency responsible for making the initial decision. This questioning of the earlier process is not a usurpation of the role of the first decision-maker. Rather it is the responsible exercise of the appellate duty to hold those decision-makers accountable for fulfilling their roles properly.

Nothing we do in public life can be more important than debating the governing principles of our society. Many fundamental issues have remained remarkably consistent over the years— the role of government in economic life, the role of state and national governments in a federal system, the relationship between individual rights and liberties and the common stake in security and order. These and other issues arise repeatedly in differing contexts during our history; the balance struck and the terms of discussion have altered, and will alter again.

Today, for example, one central debate in constitutional law involves whether the courts' role is to recapture and apply the "original intent" of the Constitution, or to apply the principles embodied in the Constitution, as best we can, to the current situation. I agree with Justice William J. Brennan, who rejects the theory that we can know the framers' original intent, with respect to issues they never could have imagined, as "arrogance cloaked as humility" or "facile historicism."[3] Even if it were possible to figure out the framers' intent with regard to today's issues, deciding cases solely on that basis would deny our Constitution its inherent genius, the creation of a dynamic experiment in self-government.

Indeed the genius of self-government includes the constitutional significance of two hundred years of living experience since adoption of the document. Authority in our system rests not on the past alone but the present, not the elites alone but the people. It is remarkable to consider that we are governed by a document written before the explosion of science, technology, and knowledge that otherwise shapes so much of our daily existence. How can we know what the framers would have thought about the risks and benefits of nuclear power plants? The framers aimed to establish essential principles which could accommodate inevitable change, not to straitjacket their descendants. We may differ from the framers not only in our answers to certain questions but even in the questions we think to ask. Today's decisions are in the hands of people living today, and must be informed by the best knowledge and the fullest experience of today's society. That experience must include the ever-changing heterogeneity of our people, and our evolving sensitivities toward distinctions based on race or gender or age or handicap.

I have sought throughout my career as a judge to follow that imperative—to open the legal process to the widest possible array of information. The most direct way to obtain information is to ask questions. In some instances, the questions I raised represented a break with tradition. That these attempts did not produce permanent solutions, and may have raised new questions, was inevitable. I am reminded of the story so often told about Gertrude Stein's dying words. A close friend leaned over her deathbed and whispered to her, "What is the answer?" The barely audible reply as Gertrude Stein passed away was: "What is the question?"

Any selection from thirty-five years of writing is necessarily incomplete. In focusing on one area—the criminal law—which has been central to my career and my thinking, this book is intended to illustrate how a complex set of legal and moral issues evolves over time, and inevitably spills over to other equally complex domains. Some repetition of ideas is inevitable, and even intentional, to demonstrate how ideas nourish one another.

My judicial career has been as a member of the United States Court of Appeals for the District of Columbia Circuit, often called the nation's second most important court. As do all federal appeals courts, this court reviews cases decided by the district (trial-level) judges in its jurisdiction. Since the District of Columbia is home to the federal government, many of the most important cases—those that challenge national law and require interpretation of it—are brought here.

Generally, appellate cases turn on interpretation of the law. In the lower courts, the judge (and a jury, if there is one) sees the evidence and hears all the witnesses. On appeal, we do not hear witnesses. We read briefs, hear arguments, research the law, consider, discuss and debate among ourselves, then decide. The only appeal is to the Supreme Court, but since the number of appeals that court agrees to consider is small, in practice circuit decisions are often final.*

Judges, especially appellate judges, do not simply make decisions. They also write *opinions* explaining how they reached their conclusions. These not only enable other courts and lawyers to assess the reasoning behind a decision, but help assure that judges do base their decisions on the law and the facts, not on whims or prejudice, and may provide an educational tool for the entire community.

Opinions here have been edited to eliminate most legal references and to summarize the main points of an argument, but

---

* Some of the terms that recur throughout this book pertain to the range of appellate decision-making responsibility. In most cases, a *panel* of three judges hears a case and makes the decision for the court. Sometimes the entire court (*en banc*) will reconsider the decision of the panel. We can *reverse* (overturn) or *vacate* (void) a decision and *remand* (send it back) to the lower court for reconsideration. We can interpret federal law and overrule our own precedents on issues that have not been decided by the Supreme Court. The district courts in our jurisdiction are bound in future cases by our decisions.

no wording has been changed. Readers who wish a complete version are encouraged to read the published opinion. Articles and speeches have been edited, and in some instances combined, to enhance the themes and organization of the book and to avoid unnecessary duplication of points or examples. For those familiar with my style of reworking and recombining ideas over the years, it will be no surprise to see that the most recent version incorporates and builds upon those that came before. While some details or references have been added to relate ideas more clearly to recent developments, I have sought to maintain the integrity of arguments made in the original article or speech, and have not attempted to soften points of view in hindsight.

Part I, "The Dilemma of Criminal Responsibility," explores the central question of the relationship between morality and crime. The insanity defense, which has played a pivotal role in my consideration of criminal responsibility, from the *Durham* case in 1954 to the present, provides a similar focus here. Part II, "The Roots of Crime," addresses the factual realities that underlie crime, including the undeniable poverty and injustice that infuse the childhoods of so many who later commit crimes. Part III, "Equality Under the Law," considers the implications of our constitutional promises and the distance between rhetoric and practice in the criminal justice system. Part IV, "What Is the Question?," was perhaps the most challenging. It relates the principles on which the first three parts rest to the larger universe of legal and social problems, and it connects my experience with the criminal law with my views and work in widely divergent areas.

It will be clear that the selections advance a distinct point of view. The argument is not a popular one at this time, nor for that matter was it twenty years ago. But the problems I have attempted to address over the years remain with us today. My message is that we must never give up the search for solutions. By opening decision processes to new information and knowledge, by being willing to explore the tough questions, we gain an opportunity to find better answers.

I

THE DILEMMA OF CRIMINAL RESPONSIBILITY

Through the courts, society decides whether a person is guilty of a crime, and, if he is, punishes him for violating the law. The moral underpinning of this process is so integral that it too often goes without saying. But it is this moral dimension that fuels the outrage of society against criminals and justifies the measures we take against them.

In our society, the vast majority believe that people are free agents who choose to do right or wrong and are responsible for what they do. But most do not wish to punish where we cannot impose blame.

And therein lies the dilemma. The criminal law is not simply a method to determine "who did it." What happens when an individual breaks the law, perhaps kills someone, but is not "blameworthy"? There may be many reasons for our not "blaming" him for what he did. He may have been defending himself and his family from an intruder (or may have thought, mistakenly, that he was). He may have been threatened with bodily harm unless he helped others commit a crime. Or he may have been mentally disturbed and convinced that the victim was the devil.

In any of these cases, someone may be dead, his family bereft. Society has been injured not only by the insult to its peace and tranquillity but perhaps by the loss of a productive member. Yet we are not comfortable imposing the same blame (and punishment) on the person who committed the act as we do on someone who cold-bloodedly plans and carries out a brutal murder. It would not be "fair" or "decent." We therefore have

1

created legal defenses to cover such situations as self-defense, duress, and insanity. But deciding when these defenses exculpate a defendant is no easy task.

These difficult cases, in my view, are vital to the criminal law and to its most basic notions of morality and responsibility. They mark the boundary of condemnable behavior, enabling us to unite the concepts of guilt and responsibility without violating our own consciences. By declaring a small number not responsible, we emphasize the responsibility of all others who commit crimes. By cultivating our understanding of these limits, we illuminate and strengthen the moral authority of the criminal law.

Concern with the boundaries does not in any way diminish concern for holding the guilty responsible and protecting society. It does not lessen outrage at heinous acts or sympathy for the victims and their families. Far from it. Most victims as well as most of the criminals discussed here share the same deprivations and obstacles in life. Their problems are integrally related, and can be understood and addressed only in that light.

To understand is not to excuse. And to understand is not to be certain what to do. Should we prosecute and punish family members who "end the misery" of a loved one suffering a painful, lingering death? Should we jail a young child who sets a fire? Most defendants found not guilty by reason of insanity make us similarly uncomfortable. We do not fully understand why they behave as they do or how to modify that behavior. We do not want to punish them, or at least not in the same way we punish someone who committed a crime to enrich himself or to take revenge. But we do want to protect ourselves against them, and we don't want others to believe they can commit similar acts with impunity. What should society do with a person found not responsible for an act proscribed by law? There is no simple answer.

Such questions do not even arise until the legal and moral finding of guilty or not guilty has been made. In this section I discuss my approach as a judge to making these choices. Of all these boundary questions, the insanity defense has occupied me—some would say preoccupied me—throughout my career on the bench. It has been a prism through which to focus the questions of morality and responsibility. Starting with the opinion in *Durham v. United States,* which I wrote in 1954, the U.S. Court of Appeals for the District of Columbia attempted to define and apply a more open approach to the insanity defense than courts traditionally had taken. Our experience in the ensuing years provides a vivid illustration of the dilemma of criminal responsibility, and a court's struggle to resolve it in a long line of individual cases.

Recent changes in the law have narrowed the insanity defense, and some states have sought to abolish it entirely.[1] The United States Supreme Court has not addressed the fundamental issue directly, but has consistently recognized the role of the defense, most recently by underscoring the importance of assuring expert witnesses to assist defendants in insanity cases and by prohibiting the execution of prisoners who become insane after conviction for a capital offense.[2] The issues of criminal responsibility, as exemplified in the insanity defense, remain controversial. They invoke the deepest questions about our society's willingness to pay the price of our moral principles. Neither we nor other courts nor legislatures have found a fully satisfying solution. If, during my tenure, our court's contribution was to draw attention to these crucial questions, and encourage their full exploration, our time and efforts were well spent.

1

Morality and the Criminal Law[1]

The late Justice Felix Frankfurter once wrote to me: "What ties men in friendship is not identity of opinion but harmony of aims."[2] The goals of criminal justice are to punish the guilty and to protect the community, while guarding the values and individual rights embodied in the Constitution. How we simultaneously balance these shared goals is often the subject of debate.

The thesis for this chapter was presented as the first J. Edgar Hoover Foundation Lecture, which I was asked to deliver in 1975. Hoover always felt criminal justice and social justice could and must be separated. I did not share that belief, and I still do not. There can be no truly just criminal law in the absence of social justice. In a way, the following examination of the morality of the criminal law is my side of a discussion that J. Edgar Hoover and I should have engaged in when he was alive, but never did.

In the years since I wrote the two articles on which this chapter is based, the language we use to discuss the crime problem has changed somewhat. Terms like "retribution" and "punishment" are employed far more freely now, though it is not clear that the actions described by those words reflect much change from "corrections" or "rehabilitation," the terms formerly used. The language of economics now more fully pervades discussion of criminal responsibility (and many other areas of law) than it did when I criticized the "cost-benefit" argument. The external constraint view described here can be roughly equated with today's "utilitarian" or "economic efficiency" school of thought.[3]

The rising crime rate appears to have moderated—at least for the time being—though remaining at historically high levels. Terrorism has added a frightening element of random violence to our lives. Many have lost faith in rehabilitation, and victims' rights rather than prisoners' rights inspire today's reformers. Calls for mandatory sentencing and prison construction escalate, and the death penalty has returned.

As H. L. Mencken once said, for every complex problem in our society, there is a solution that is simple, plausible—and wrong. The questions remain because we have not yet solved the problem. Our answers today may differ from those twenty years ago, or twenty years from now. Swings of the pendulum are only to be expected, but moral dilemmas remain. The framework suggested here has helped me to contend with the formidable complexities of crime and criminal justice.

* * *

There are two distinct approaches to the criminal law. Each begins with the premise that establishing some sort of order is a moral imperative in civilized society. Each asserts that there can be no moral development in a world in which the mighty prey on the weak. What separates the two positions are the means they would employ to achieve order and, ultimately, the types of order they seek.

The first view, which enjoys the greatest currency today, holds that achieving order is so important that there is little room for concerns of social justice in devising the means to that end. An essentially amoral process is justified by a high moral end. This view then can endorse what is apparently the easiest means to achieving order—the imposition of strong external constraints. It demands that the criminal law punish disorder and make the cost of violating the law so great that few will dare to violate it. I have called this view, and the cluster of beliefs associated with it, "law as external constraint."

The alternative concept is that the law's aims must be achieved by a moral process which recognizes the realities of social and economic injustice. This philosophy sees externally imposed order—repressive order—as suffering from the same basic defect as "disorder": both lack moral authority. It asserts that an order built on fear of punishment cannot long endure. As the poet Wallace Stevens wrote: "A violent order is a disorder."[4] To be truly moral and lasting, order must derive from the internalization of control. Members of society must obey the law because they personally believe that its commands are justified. This view demands that the law facilitate internalization by becoming a moral force in the community.

I associate myself with the latter view. When I talk of moral force or morality in the law, I am not speaking of a righteous certitude or a mystical sense of authority. Rather, I refer to elements of human decency such as are embodied in the words "Do unto others as you would have them do unto you." Whether phrased in religious or philosophical terms, this essential concept of reciprocal decency is what I mean by morality.

The Moral Basis of Criminal Sanctions

One arena of conflict between the two views is the debate over the question of what acts should be made criminal. Proponents of the law-as-external-constraint philosophy translate this question into cost-benefit terms. They ask whether the resources that would be required to enforce the law are justified by the social benefits that would be reaped. Thus, proposals to decriminalize so-called victimless offenses such as gambling, prostitution, homosexuality, fornication, and public drunkenness stand or fall on the proposition that decriminalizing such conduct would free policy, prosecutorial, and judicial resources to concentrate on more serious offenses.

Rather than posing the issue in these terms, I would ask: is the conduct in question viewed by the society as both a moral wrong and a breach of some minimum condition of social existence? In other words, although not every act regarded as immoral by the dominant community should be made criminal, no act should be made criminal if it is not viewed as immoral. The criminal code should define only the minimum conditions of each individual's responsibility to the other members of society, in order to maximize personal liberty.

There will be times, no doubt, when some will vehemently disagree with, and perhaps even be morally offended by, the community's decision as to what it should condemn. But unless we are willing to allow the community the freedom to reach even "wrong" decisions, there is no hope of making the criminal law a statement of moral principles to which all can aspire.

Moral considerations are equally implicated in determining what should be done with people who engage in proscribed conduct. Those who look to the law for external control seek sentences which will maximize order; their primary concern is to determine how harsh sentences can be without becoming so harsh that juries will stop convicting, or police and prosecutors stop charging.

Those in favor of internal controls, however, see sentencing as a weighing of safety considerations against the dictates of what I call the "sixth sense"—the moral sense. The "internalists" may disagree whether the sixth sense would be better served by individualization and mercy on the one hand, or by uniformity and equality of punishment on the other. But at least their disagreement is over what social justice would require.

This disagreement, they believe, must be resolved before embarking on the necessary consideration of what community safety demands. Those who subscribe to the internal model do not think that sentencing policy should be used to achieve repressive order.

Moral considerations intrude even earlier in the process of deciding what to do with people who engage in proscribed conduct. Those who see the law as a moral force insist that the law should not convict unless it can condemn. According to this view, a decision for conviction requires the following three determinations: (1) a condemnable act was committed by the actor-defendant; (2) the actor can be condemned—that is, he could reasonably have been expected to have conformed his behavior to the demands of the law; and (3) society's own conduct in relation to the actor entitles it to sit in condemnation of him with respect to the act he committed.

To some extent the law already inquires into at least the first two of these factors. In England, starting in the late thirteenth century, the law went beyond its prior exclusive focus on physical acts which violated the penal code, to consideration of why the acts occurred. Through the element of intent or *mens rea,* and the defenses of mistake, duress, and, most important, insanity or lack of criminal responsibility, the modern law has sought to punish only what Roscoe Pound termed "the vicious will."[5]

But the law, like the rest of us, "promises according to its hopes but performs according to its fears."[6] Although it has been asserted repeatedly that only a free choice to do wrong will be punished, in practice the law presumes, almost irrebuttably, that proscribed behavior is the product of "a free agent confronted with a choice between doing right and doing wrong and choosing freely to do wrong."[7]

In *The Common Law,* Justice Oliver Wendell Holmes recognized the conflict between certain moral pretenses and practices when he observed that if punishment

> stood on the moral grounds which are proposed for it, the first thing to be considered would be those limitations in the capacity for choosing rightly which arise from abnormal instincts, want of education, lack of intelligence, and all other defects which are most marked in the criminal classes.[8]

In other words, if moral condemnation were the basis for criminal sanctions, we would have to consider—to take some examples from cases that have come before me—whether a free choice to do wrong can be found in the acts of a poverty-stricken and otherwise deprived black youth from the central city who kills a marine who taunted him with a racial epithet,[9] in the act of a "modern Jean Valjean" who steals to feed his family,[10] in the act of a narcotics addict who buys drugs for his own use,[11] or in the act of a superpatriot steeped in cold war ideology who burglarizes in the name of "national security."[12]

We are uneasy in contemplation of these situations and of

the issues Holmes raises. But we dare not shy away from them simply because they are difficult or the answers unsettling. The questions must be faced if the criminal law is to be an instrument for the reinforcement of moral obligations.

Goals of the Criminal Process

The "externalists" assume that most criminal acts are the products of the actor's free choice. They contend that the criminal justice system can deter these "rational" actors by assuring swift and certain consequences for unlawful behavior. As James Q. Wilson explains, "if the expected cost of crime goes up without a corresponding increase in the expected benefits, then the would-be criminal—unless he or she is among that small fraction of criminals who are utterly irrational—engages in less crime."[13]

In order to achieve the deterrent effect, the criminal process must identify and punish the guilty with speed and surety. Herbert Packer compares the process to an assembly line.[14] For the externalist, then, the measure of the process lies in its efficiency and finality. Criminals must be identified, apprehended, tried, convicted, and punished as rapidly as possible. Once we are reasonably sure we have identified the guilty, the need for certainty demands that we cut off opportunities to challenge the process.

In this model, attention to procedural niceties—before, during, and after trial—must be carefully restrained, lest they clog up the system. The externalists believe that the primary purpose of constitutional safeguards is "to ensure that the innocent are not wrongly convicted."[15] Procedures are important mainly as a means of accomplishing the overriding goal of the criminal law—swift and certain separation of the guilty from the innocent.

This is not to suggest that the externalists have little solicitude for the rights of the accused. But in their model, the costs of procedural safeguards (delay and uncertainty) cannot outweigh their benefit (protecting the innocent). When an expansion of constitutional requirements advances the determination of guilt only marginally, externalists contend that belief in the efficacy of the system of justice declines, a point of diminishing returns is reached, and procedures must give way to efficiency and finality.

Thus, externalists believe that convictions should not be reversed for procedural irregularities if the defendant-appellant was "guilty anyhow." Attacks on unfair procedures should not be entertained unless the petitioner makes a supportable claim of innocence. In short, the goal of an ordered society—which it is thought will be achieved through deterrence—must transcend procedural means.

Those who feel that the law must encourage internalization of control do not view questions of criminal procedure as requiring a choice between the rights of defendants and the rights of society. In the long run, society requires a genuine, lasting order. That kind of order, I am convinced, can better be built on respect for the law than fear of punishment.

Stopping Crime

The final and most important arena in which the tension between the two polar positions on the criminal law can be felt has nothing—and everything—to do with the criminal justice system per se: What do we do with those who commit crimes? The internalists urge actions designed to alleviate the social and economic causes of crime. The externalists call for mandatory incarceration of convicted criminals in order to remove from the streets persons who would otherwise commit crimes and to deter other would-be criminals from violating the law.

I do not wish to enter the debate over whether mandatory incarceration could have a significant impact on the crime rate; the evidence on the question is far from clear. If mandatory imprisonment proves ineffective, however, other repressive measures could certainly be devised that would be horribly effective. A tap on every phone, a bug in every house, and a cop on every corner might well do the trick. If not, we could always imprison every potential criminal or perhaps mercifully put them to sleep, thereby writing off all such persons as beyond rehabilitation.

In the short term, it may well be that mandatory incarceration or some other form of repression will have to be adopted to respond to the public demand for security. But such measures would be accompanied by the painful awareness that any resulting order will be immoral, or at best amoral. It is simply unjust to place people in dehumanizing social conditions, to do nothing about those conditions, and then to command those who suffer, "Behave—or else!" The overwhelming majority of violent street crimes, which worry us so deeply, are committed by the ignorant, the ill-educated, and the unemployed and often unemployable.

I don't believe that this is coincidental. We cannot produce a class of desperate and angry citizens by closing off all means of economic advancement and personal fulfillment for a sizable part of the population, and thereafter expect a crime-free society.

What concerns me about the wave of proposals for getting tough with criminals is that those who offer them often have no awareness of the underlying causes of crime. Three intellectual justifications can be offered for the externalists' attempt to divorce criminal justice from social justice and to rely on "get tough" solutions to crime.

First, it is argued that this society cannot afford social justice. At a time when the largest city in America reaches the brink of bankruptcy, notwithstanding its extremely high rate of taxation, this argument is understandable. Some localities cannot even afford adequate police protection, let alone measures to provide the educational and economic opportunities which are lacking for an alarming number of their citizens. Moreover, the experience of the 1960s teaches that the costs will be high, for we have learned the hard way that halfway measures will not work. Nevertheless, these costs must be borne, for there is no alternative consistent with the survival of a truly free democracy. A nation whose gross national product hovers at the $1 trillion mark can find the resources.[16]

Second, it is suggested that we do not truly know the causes of crime. In a very narrow sense, this is true. We do not understand why some poor people commit crime and others do not, why crime increases in periods of economic growth as well as in periods of decline, or why some cities with high unemployment experience less crime than other cities with lower unemployment. We do not understand the effect of population growth and density on crime, and there is respected opinion suggesting that increases in population affect not only the degree but also the very nature of the problem. We do not understand the effect of age, sex, geography, race, or genetics on crime—and each of these factors may be of some relevance.

As I have already stated, we do know that most violent crime is committed by the disadvantaged and deprived. We know that the family is the most effective child-developing and child-socializing agent available. We know, or think we know, that the crucial period for personality formation is during infancy. And we certainly are aware that grinding poverty wreaks destruction on the family unit and makes it very difficult for parents to convey a sense of order, purpose, and self-esteem to their children. In short, poverty appears to be intimately related to the occurrence of most violent crime though it is not the sole condition.[17]

The real problem is that because of our limited knowledge the only apparent solution to the poverty-and-crime problem is to alleviate the suffering of all deprived people, including noncriminals. If physical order is the goal, this solution is undeniably wasteful since it directs resources to persons who pose no danger of physical disorder to society. But if moral order is the aim, this solution is a necessity. The fact that some persons are resigned to their plight and that their miseries cause us no trouble is hardly a justification for allowing them to continue to suffer. And the fact that some individuals or some cultures are less likely than others to react to poverty by becoming criminals should be a cause for admiration and a stimulus to learn how and why they respond this way—not an excuse to condemn those who don't live up to the loftier standard.

The third justification that is offered for divorcing crime

control from social reform is one of cost-effectiveness. It is argued that precisely because poverty is the root cause of crime, it is also the most difficult to deal with. Therefore, it would be wiser to concentrate on less deep-seated causes. This position is deficient in two respects.

The application of cost-benefit analysis to crime control is dangerous. Costs include tangible, quantifiable elements such as money spent on a trial or imprisonment; they also include matters less often mentioned by the advocates of the approach, such as welfare for the prisoner's family. Intangible sums are often omitted from such analyses simply because they are not quantifiable: the impact on a young child of a father's incarceration, or the impact on the community's quality of life when greater numbers of (perfectly innocent) people are stopped by police.

The more repressive the criminal law becomes, the more likely it will be to hide its costs. Every time the criminal law erroneously confines someone on the basis of a mistaken assumption that he will commit another crime unless confined, there is obviously a significant cost (both tangible and intangible); but it is a hidden cost, since society rarely, if ever, learns about the error. Every time there is a wiretapping or mail opening, the invasion produces significant costs; but they, too, tend to be hidden, since victims who are innocent seldom complain.

The costs of nonrepression, on the other hand, are often cited in detail. When the system erroneously releases an individual who commits a new crime, we usually learn about it. When the search that turns up a criminal is determined to be illegal and as a result the criminal's conviction is reversed, we learn about that as well. Thus, aside from questions concerning the propriety of cost-benefit analysis for the kinds of issues dealt with by the criminal law, such analysis, if not appropriately formulated, will provide an inadequate basis on which to make decisions regarding crime control measures.

But even if one were to make the heroic assumption that cost-benefit analysis could work and the even more heroic assumption that the most cost-effective method of crime control is repression, the argument would hardly be ended. What ultimately is at issue in the debate over alternative responses to the crime problem is a question of the goal to be pursued: repressive order or moral order. On that question, cost-benefit analysis has nothing to offer. Moral order is a long, painful, and costly process. The only less appealing option I can imagine is not to choose it. Creating order through repression will not be easy, and maintaining it, as the frustrations of the deprived grow, will be more and more difficult. As the poet Langston Hughes warned:

> What happens to a dream deferred?
>> Does it dry up
>> like a raisin in the sun?
>> Or fester like a sore—
>> And then run?
>> Does it stink like rotten meat?
>> Or crust and sugar over—
>> like a syrupy sweet?
>> Maybe it just sags
>> like a heavy load.
>> *Or does it explode?*[18]

A Moral Criminal Law

By trading off the rights of the accused in favor of immediate safety, the externalists may embrace procedures that cannot command, and do not deserve, voluntary compliance. Ever-increasing repression may be necessary to maintain a fragile order based on fear.

In contrast, the criminal process must strive to attain a moral force that entitles it to respect. With Judge Elbert Tuttle, I believe that "the only way the law has progressed from the days of the rack, the screw and the wheel is the development of moral concepts. . . ."[19] A truly moral criminal law must be guided by three fundamental principles. First, the criminal process must always remain sensitive to the social realities that underlie crime. Second, it must make meaningful the claim of "equal justice under law." Third, it must, through a process of constant questioning, force the community to confront the painful realities and agonizing choices posed by social injustice. These principles are *reality, equality,* and *education.*

THE REALITY PRINCIPLE   Former Justice Arthur Goldberg has observed that the Supreme Court's criminal procedure decisions should be judged, in part, by asking "whether the Court has dealt in realities, and not in legal fictions."[20] My experience has confirmed the importance of this reality principle. Truly moral judgments cannot rest on philosophical abstractions, but must be derived from the facts which generate human behavior in the real world.

An effort to understand these realities must begin by precisely identifying the problem that terrifies Americans. The emotionalism and near-desperation that attend contemporary discussions about criminal justice do not, after all, derive from a generalized concern about all types of crime. White-collar crime, for instance, costs society untold billions of dollars—far more than street crime. Yet, understandably, it does not instill the kind of fear reflected in the explosion of get-tough proposals. Those sorts of crimes, committed by the middle and upper classes, do not, by and large, threaten our physical safety or the sanctity of our homes.[21]

Nor does organized crime scare most Americans. Hired guns generally kill each other. The common citizen does not lock his doors out of fear of becoming the object of gang warfare. Organized crime unquestionably contributes to street crime, most obviously through drug-trafficking; but, however much it should, organized crime does not produce the demands for tough sentences. Similarly, crimes of passion, no matter how celebrated, do not cause people to bolt their doors at night: to do so would be to lock the fox inside the chicken coop.

It is the random assaults of violent street crime that Americans fear. The muggings, the rapes, the purse snatchings, and the knifings that plague city—and, lately, suburban—life are what put us in mortal fear of our property and lives.

The reality principle requires identification of the criminals we fear. This is not a pleasant task. The real sources of street crime are associated with a constellation of suffering so hideous that society cannot bear to look it in the face. Yet, as Emerson said, "God offers to every mind its choice between truth and repose." However painful it may be, we cannot aspire to a genuinely moral society unless we choose truth.

Nobody questions that street criminals typically come from the bottom of the socioeconomic ladder. Unemployment leads to higher arrest rates.[22] Current get-tough programs are aimed at offenders who come from an underclass of brutal social and economic deprivation.

The circumstances that lead some of these people to crime are no mystery. They are born into families struggling to survive—if they have families at all. They are raised in deteriorating, overcrowded housing. They lack adequate nutrition and health care. They are subjected to prejudice and educated in unresponsive schools. They are denied the sense of order, purpose, and self-esteem that makes law-abiding citizens. With nothing to preserve and nothing to lose, they turn to crime for economic survival, a sense of excitement and accomplishment, and an outlet for frustration, desperation, and rage.

The *Washington Post* once profiled a young armed robber who made the capital a city of fear. He is sadly typical. Elton Smith, black and eighteen years old, lived—when not in jail—in a public housing project wedged between the Anacostia River and an interstate highway in a part of Washington few tourists ever visit. Most of his fellow residents were on welfare. *Post* reporter Thomas Morgan described Smith's home this way:

> The hallway to his family's two-bedroom apartment, a pastiche of soul food smells, mildew and trash, bustles with activity. Two teenagers, seeking privacy from noisy overcrowded apartments, huddle in a corner sharing secrets. A girl with pigtails sprawls across the stairway using a step as a desk to do homework as stereos inside several apartments blast music into the hall.[23]

Elton Smith's mother explained that the family lived in these surroundings because they could not afford to go anywhere else. She told the reporter that her boy had had problems with the law ever since she and his father had separated when he was thirteen years old. He had no skills, other than as a robber, and had been unable to retain a steady job. In his neighborhood, Elton Smith was a hero and a role model to kids who regarded academic achievers as "sissies." And Smith himself offered a simple explanation for his criminal activities: "I know the money does not belong to me," he says. "But the only way I can survive is [by] taking money from someone else."*

THE EQUALITY PRINCIPLE   The equality principle follows logically from the reality principle. Once we acknowledge the squalid conditions that breed crime, we can tolerate inequities in the criminal process only by donning moral blinders. Of course, the ideal of equal justice before the law is as old as the republic itself. But the reality principle requires us to recognize how far short we fall of the ideal. Reginald Smith's comments of more than sixty years ago remain disturbingly accurate:

> The administration of American justice is not impartial, the rich and the poor do not stand on an equality before the law, the traditional method of providing justice has

---

* In 1985 a D.C. grandmother, Catherine Fuller, was brutally assaulted, robbed, and beaten to death. A group of young men from her neighborhood was convicted of murder. Another *Washington Post* article described the life of the recognized leader:

> If Rouse acted like a big man as a young adult, his childhood was the stuff of a Dickens novel: Rice three times a day when the food stamps ran out; the children gathering dimes and quarters from odd jobs to buy milk and cereal; a home with no kitchen or stove or father; constant shifting from house to house; a box of old toys from the Salvation Army for Christmas; staying in the fifth grade an extra year because he was afraid of the bigger boys in sixth grade. . . . When their oldest sister Jeanette Drew was found dead in a trash dumpster in June 1980, [a family friend] said, the family fell apart. [The mother] moved to Norfolk and her sons began to pop in and out of jail. . . . By the time he dropped out of his special education classes in 1982, he was in 10th grade but reading at only the third grade level.[24]

operated to close the doors of the courts to the poor, and has caused a gross denial of justice in all parts of the country to millions of persons.[25]

Externalists regret, even deplore, these inequities. But under that model, the criminal law must punish the guilty with a maximum of efficiency and finality; social and economic inequality is simply irrelevant to that process. Thus, even Attorney General Nicholas Katzenbach, who enthusiastically and admirably administered many of the civil rights and antipoverty programs of the mid-sixties, characterized as "ridiculous" my suggestion that criminal procedures should take steps (such as assuring counsel at all stages of prosecution, from detention through sentencing) to compensate for the disparities that produce unequal access to constitutional rights.[26]

The criminal law, of course, is now closer to the ideal of equal justice than it was in Reginald Smith's day. At one time the law, in its majestic equality, permitted the rich as well as the poor an equal opportunity to retain private counsel, to hire investigators and expert witnesses, to purchase trial transcripts, and to pay fines. The middle-class majority puts a set of rights at its own eye level but ignores the fact that the growth of others has been stunted by many circumstances, including the accident of birth. Gradually, we have come to realize that "[t]here can be no equal justice where the kind of trial a man gets depends on the amount of money he has."[27] With this reminder from Justice Hugo Black, we have sought to give the stunted a box to stand on to reach our own eye level.

Yet, for many, the criminal process, while promising equal justice under law, continues to deliver only justice for those who can afford it. The deprived know from bitter experience that when a crime is committed, most anyone in the neighborhood might be suspected and arrested. And once they have entered the criminal justice system, they are unlikely to receive the considerate treatment and light punishment so frequently enjoyed by the well-to-do. The powerful, but not the weak, have effective assistance of counsel from the earliest stages of the process, enjoy freedom from confinement pending their trials and appeals, receive respectful treatment from judges, prosecutors, policemen, and probation officers, and undergo incarceration in the least restrictive prisons available.

The externalists often argue that the criminal system has spent too much effort perfecting justice and too little in creating swift and certain punishment of wrongdoers. I have always found this argument rather puzzling. If allowing rich defendants certain rights does not interfere with the efficient operation of the system, how can ensuring poor defendants the same rights place an intolerable burden on it? Those who fear that too much effort has been expended perfecting the quality of justice are living in a world of make-believe. Since most cases are either dismissed by police or prosecutor or else disposed of by guilty pleas, the criminal process is often nothing more than a series of discretionary, and often arbitrary decisions.

But my disagreements with the attitudes on criminal procedure of the externalists extend to an even more fundamental level. The proponents of that thesis downgrade and even ignore the important role that respect for the law—as distinguished from fear of the law—can play in achieving order. As Charles Evans Hughes warned over fifty years ago:

> A petty tyrant in a police court, refusals of a fair hearing in minor civil courts, [or] the impatient disregard of an immigrant's ignorance of our ways and language, will daily breed Bolshevists who are beyond the reach of your appeals.[28]

The manner in which we treat those accused of crime is important as an end in itself, and not simply as a means to convicting the guilty, if only because "the guilty are almost always the first to suffer those hardships which are afterwards used as precedents against the innocent."[29]

Charles Silberman has stated, "[T]he double standard that lower-class people see applied produces a deep-rooted cynicism about government, business, and indeed, American society as a whole."[30] There can be no doubt that this conviction on the part of the disadvantaged that "the system" is against them contributes substantially to the sullen, defiant hostility which flashes out in urban crime. The rules which govern the relationship between the disadvantaged and the official power of the state cannot perpetuate this unfairness. Criminal procedures should be a haven of equality for those whose life history—of poverty, discrimination, callous disregard—teaches them that they are not equal. Without a meaningful commitment to the equality principle, we cannot begin to aspire to a moral order grounded in the will and hearts of the people rather than in fear of punishment.

In short, a criminal process worthy of moral respect must always follow the commandment of Judge Learned Hand: "Thou shalt not ration justice."[31]

THE EDUCATION PRINCIPLE   Without a vigorous dedication to the equality principle, the rules of criminal procedure cannot earn the moral respect of those who now suffer inequities in the administration of justice. But the reality principle demands that we acknowledge that sole reliance on the criminal law, however nobly conceived, will not solve violent street crime. In the end, the institutions of criminal justice act as mere janitors, tidying up the human and social wreckage that happens to end up in a courtroom. They cannot begin to cure the conditions that drive people like Elton Smith to crime.

But these institutions can help society pursue a moral order by pushing those conditions into high public visibility. By probing the sordid realities that underlie its cases, the criminal justice system can force society to confront and address the facts about crime. And by articulating constitutional rights in ways that clearly and constantly reaffirm our fundamental values, the criminal law can keep those values at the forefront of social consciousness—thus encouraging humane and intelligent responses to the crime problem. This is the education principle.

I differ fundamentally with the externalists in what I expect from the criminal law. The exclusionary rule (preventing the use at trial of illegally obtained evidence), the *Miranda* rule (requiring suspects to be informed of their rights prior to questioning), and aspects of habeas corpus (allowing people to challenge their imprisonment) have all come under attack in the name of swift and certain punishment. But in relying on reform of the criminal process to deter crime, the externalists travel a superhighway leading to a cow path. A relatively modest percentage of street crimes are reported to the police and thus enter the criminal justice system. Of that group, only a small portion result in arrest. It is utter folly to expect changes in the procedures that govern those cases meaningfully to affect the crime rate.

More important, even if the criminal process could achieve the threat of certain punishment, it would have little impact on the people at the bottom of society's ladder. As Diana Gordon of the National Council on Crime and Delinquency has noted, prison must pose an empty threat to one whose urban environment is itself a prison.[32] Elton Smith candidly admitted that punishment would not stop him from committing future robberies. "They can't keep me in jail forever," he told the *Washington Post.* "If they let me out tomorrow, I might be tempted to do the same thing all over again to survive if I don't have a job. I really believe that."

Thus we court disaster if we persuade ourselves that changing the criminal process will provide the answer to street crime. Moreover, if we expect miracles from such reforms, we may put far more important tasks on the back burner. Repairing the machinery of criminal procedures cannot substitute for a substantial attack on the uninhabitable housing, insufficient food, medieval medical care, and inadequate educations suffered by people who commit street crimes. No matter how we modify criminal procedures, we cannot rely upon the criminal justice system as the primary agency to solve these problems. Other institutions, better adapted to broad-scale programs and more responsive to changing conditions, must address the grinding oppression around us. These conditions cannot be ignored simply because the great majority of those who endure them do not disturb our sleep and threaten our lives.

What the criminal process can do is bring the submerged

realities of crime to the surface so that the responsible institutions will address them. By incessantly asking questions—in court, in judicial opinions, and in public dialogue—courts can accomplish a substantial amount to ensure that the agencies which are supposed to be dealing with a particular problem are actually looking for answers, instead of simply taking action out of prejudice or ignorance. And courts, by constantly reminding society of the constitutional values that underlie specific decisions, can help ensure that the responsible institutions take action consistent with our best moral instincts. Like Justice William O. Douglas, I believe that "[t]he judiciary plays an important role in educating the people as well as in deciding cases."[33]

Our best hope of achieving a truly moral social order lies in seeking out the causes of the criminal act. The criminal process—from arrest to sentencing—resembles a postmortem: a postmortem cannot revive the dead, and the criminal process cannot undo a heinous act. But in each procedure we can attempt to discover the cause of failure. Of course, eliciting the information necessary to understand the forces that drive people to commit crime will not cure the disease. Once we enlighten our understanding, we will still need to decide whether the costs of grappling with the roots of crime are more than we are willing to pay. But society can never hope to achieve a just and lasting solution to crime without first facing the facts that underlie it. For, as Justice Benjamin Cardozo once wrote, "[t]he subject the most innocent on the surface may turn out when it is probed to be charged with hidden fire."[34]

2

The Insanity Defense:
Symbol and Substance[1]

For those who view the criminal law as an embodiment of society's moral vision, the problem of assigning criminal responsibility is profoundly disturbing. Finding a defendant guilty is not only a factual judgment; it also constitutes a moral condemnation of the person. In our tradition, moral blame cannot attach where an act was not the result of a free choice. The verdict of not guilty by reason of insanity is nothing more than an expression of that moral intuition.

The disturbing problems arise, however, in trying to put this simple imperative into effect. There is no easy or mechanical way to draw the line between free and unfree choices. And although determinations of legal "insanity" are indispensably illuminated by scientific observations about both human behavior in general and particular defendants' mental conditions, those same scientific findings always threaten to usurp the ultimate decision-making function, which must remain a matter of moral rather than scientific judgment.

Many people seem to think that to find someone NGRI (not guilty by reason of insanity) is the same as saying "he didn't do it." That is simply a misunderstanding of the law. A whole nation watched the televised replay of John Hinckley's attempted assassination of President Reagan. The fact that Hinckley was later found NGRI did not mean that anyone doubted he pulled the trigger. It simply meant that the jury found him not guilty of the act—not deserving of moral condemnation. Hinckley did not get off or go free; he will remain in a secure hospital facility not appreciably distinguishable to the eye from a prison, for as long as the doctors and the judge decide is necessary, which is likely to be a long time. Judges, lawyers, and the news media have an obligation to help the public understand this.

The *Durham* rule was one attempt to grapple with the insanity defense dilemma. In 1954 our court announced, in an opinion I wrote, a new test of criminal responsibility which governed trials on the issue of insanity in our jurisdiction, until we changed it again in 1972. The *Durham* case and its successors represented perhaps the most thorough examination of the insanity defense ever undertaken in a single jurisdiction, and engendered considerable controversy and debate in legal and psychiatric circles. While the other federal courts of appeals and the state legislatures did not adopt the *Durham* rule, its impact nevertheless was widespread.[2] The rule provoked endless discussion and reaction, and was a major impetus for the American Law Institute to develop the liberalized insanity test that was adopted through most of the country—including the District of Columbia in 1972. Today the pendulum has swung back, and we hear more insistently the call to abolish the insanity defense.

In fact I was attracted for a time to the idea of shifting the question of responsibility from a separate defense of insanity to the consideration of the defendant's "intent" to commit the crime—his "*mens rea*" or "guilty mind"—which is an element that must be proved in virtually all crimes. I thought this might be a way to make the assertion of insanity an integral part of the inquiry into criminal responsibility, rather than a peripheral special case, and was willing to consider a variety of options so long as all the information bearing on the issue could be brought before the court. But I've concluded that outcome was unlikely, and that a separate defense in some form is needed.

While the insanity defense does not solve problems, it does far more good than harm. It reminds us that the people who commit crimes are individuals, and that the reasons for their actions are individual. It illuminates the complex moral judgments we make in finding guilty a person who commits a criminal act. And it provides an opportunity to educate ourselves about the people who commit crimes, so that we can begin to do more than strike back at them, one at a time.

That the *Durham* experiment did not fully succeed in achieving all its goals is perhaps less important than that it fueled a debate which uncovered a vast range of perplexing and previously hidden questions. Its most enduring legacy was to change the terms of that debate. No particular form of words can be as important as assuring that the essential questions continue to be asked.

* * *

There are no simple answers to the terrifying problem of violent crime. And no element of criminal law has been subjected to more abuse in the name of simple solutions than the insanity defense. But after all the emotion-charged cases and all the law review articles, what do we know? Changing a word here and a word there in the insanity test will not effect any great metamorphosis. The much-touted "guilty but mentally ill" alternative[3] will do little but reassign people from grossly underfunded mental hospitals to prisons with their all-but-nonexistent psychiatric services. Eliminating the defense entirely will similarly reallocate from hospitals to prisons those least likely to survive in the savage jungle that is our prison system.

Some believe that the insanity defense should be abolished because it hasn't worked. But the defense is integral to the moral foundation of the criminal law. It is our nemesis, and it is our hope.

The insanity defense debate is part and parcel of the larger dispute about crime and punishment in our society. John Hinckley's 1981 shooting of President Reagan was the latest in a long line of highly visible cases in which a defendant who clearly had committed the act in question was found "not guilty by reason of insanity." In the wake of the *Hinckley* case, the insanity defense has emerged as a scapegoat for the failures of the entire criminal justice system. Critics argue that the defense is an integral part of the crime problem and that its elimination is an integral part of the solution.

What underlies the abolitionist position is a rejection of an individualized approach to criminal justice. Who are these people committing crimes? The answer, it is argued, must be "We don't care!" The insanity defense is worth fighting for precisely because individualization is a prerequisite to a moral system of criminal justice.

In the meantime, the criminal justice system must operate. We have to conduct this searching inquiry into the criminal's life history, not to excuse, but to appreciate the conditions that inevitably attend and may lead to criminal behavior. Focusing on the individual offender is not part of the problem of crime; it is part of the solution.

It is, at first glance, puzzling that the insanity defense occupies such a central place in the pantheon of right-wing demonology. Why should anyone care about the insanity defense, let alone vilify it? The defense is raised in, at most, between 1 to 2 percent of cases that go to trial. Of those cases where it *is* raised, only 10 percent result in not-guilty-by-reason-of-insanity verdicts. And the defendant who is acquitted is likely to spend as much or possibly even more time in a mental institution than he would have in a prison had he been convicted and sentenced.[4]

As an empirical matter, the net result of abolition of the insanity defense would be the transfer of one of every 10,000 criminal defendants from a hospital to a prison. A 1978 survey reported that of 20,000 admissions of "mentally disordered offenders" to public institutions, only 1,625 were defendants found not guilty by reason of insanity. (In 1977 over 300,000 inmates resided in state and federal prisons.) Another 6,400 were incompetent to stand trial, and 1,200 were committed as mentally disabled sex offenders. The remainder (more than 10,000) had been convicted of crimes and were serving regular prison sentences until transferred from prison to a mental health facility.[5]

Is this the goal for the war on crime? I would submit that the attack on the insanity defense does not concern the realities of the criminal justice system, but is rather an attack on a way of thinking about crime and about criminals.

The insanity defense starts from the simple proposition that a moral society is unwilling to impose condemnation and punishment where it cannot impose blame. This view has been basic to our legal tradition. Condemning the act does not require condemning the action (or the actor) if the action was not the product of a free choice to do wrong. The defense acknowledges that a variety of factors can impair that volition, that ability to choose.

Today we are told we can no longer afford to embrace this view of criminal responsibility. Crime can be controlled, but only if those who violate society's norms, for whatever reason, are quickly apprehended and subjected to swift, certain, and severe punishment. Free will, in this view, is not merely assumed; it is an irrebuttable presumption.

The insanity defense is now under more sustained attack than at any time since I wrote the opinion for our court in *Durham v. United States.*[6] Congress has recently considered proposals to eliminate the defense, and has curtailed it dramatically. The American Medical Association, the American Psychiatric Association, and the American Bar Association have all gone on record to restrict it.[7]

The defense is said to be not working very well. Juries are confused, it is claimed, by the spectacle of competing psychiatric experts. More important, our society, plagued as it is by street crime, can no longer afford the luxury of a test of criminal responsibility. When we are fighting for our survival, we cannot be too humane to the enemy within our gates.

The insanity defense provides a tempting target on which to pin the failures of the entire criminal justice system. Many of the most sensational criminal cases involve well-publicized insanity pleas. Run-of-the-mill muggings by street toughs are too common for the front pages, but even the most banal burglary is newsworthy if committed by someone with a psychiatric history. Each new insanity acquittal brings cries of outrage that criminals are, literally, getting away with murder. The law itself is seen as an enemy of social order rather than a safeguard.

This may be what Senator Mack Mattingly was driving at when he said: "[S]ociety has a right to be protected from the likes of John Hinckley, [whether] sane or insane."[8] Or Presidential Counselor Edwin Meese, when he suggested that with the abolition of the insanity defense, "[w]e would do a lot better as far as ridding the streets of some of the most dangerous people that are out there, that are committing a disproportionate number of crimes."[9]

The insanity defense has in fact not worked very well and there is a connection between the terrible problem of street crime and our tests of criminal responsibility. But this failure and the problems of street crime have been caused not by too much compassion, but by too little—by a failure of our moral imagination, not an excess.

Curtailing or even abolishing tests of criminal responsibility will not stem the persistent flow of street criminals into our courts. Such measures betray a complete misunderstanding of the problem. It is only through an expansion of our tests of criminal responsibility that we can hope to alert the community to the root causes of crime, and, in turn, to move toward solutions.

Some might view our grappling with these questions of criminal responsibility as a failed experiment—full of sound and fury, signifying nothing. But law is not a static order built on certitude, it is a dynamic order built on process.

Courts do their work through cases, actual conflicts which must be resolved whether or not all the information we might wish to have is available. Facts and values in the world are ever changing; every decision is made in that terrible period known as meanwhile. What is more, the world changes as a result of our decisions. How the world will be reshaped through law is never predictable with certainty.

So we must peer out and see the consequences—or the wreckage—of our handiwork. In the thirty-year experiment with the insanity defense in the District of Columbia, we have witnessed a lot of wreckage. But the process has been as illuminating as it has been frustrating.

On the eve of the *Durham* decision, we were optimistic that the young and promising discipline of psychiatry would open up new vistas in our inquiry into the causes of human behavior. That hope was not realized. Over the years I have grown disillusioned in many ways with the application of psychiatry to the criminal law.

At first, I was troubled that psychiatrists were not candidly sharing their knowledge with the courts. In time, I came to realize that the difficulty was more profound. The problem was not that psychiatric medicine wouldn't give us all the answers; it simply didn't have them. We have learned from the *Durham* experiment that the bedrock issue in the law of criminal responsibility is not medical but societal; and the scale of the solution must match the scale of the problem.

When I was appointed to the bench in 1949, defendants who raised the insanity defense in the District of Columbia were subject to a slightly modified *M'Naghten* test, the revolutionary piece of judicial lawmaking of another era. In 1843, Daniel M'Naghten, convinced that British Prime Minister Peel, the Pope, and the Jesuits were all conspiring to kill him, decided to launch a preemptive strike and kill Peel. Upon his arrival at 10 Downing Street, M'Naghten murdered Peel's secretary, Drummond, in the mistaken belief that the poor fellow was Peel. M'Naghten was acquitted by a jury on grounds of insanity, and his case created a furor in Parliament.

The issue was referred to the common law judges, who set out the famous formulation that an accused could not be found criminally responsible if it was shown that he was suffering from such "a defect of reason, from disease of the mind, as not to know the nature and quality of the act he was doing; or, if he did know it, that he did not know what he was doing was wrong."

The new rule expressed the simple principle that it is both wrong and useless for society to impose punishment where it cannot attribute blame. *M'Naghten* was, of course, met with outrage. A popular poem of the time foreshadowed the American public's response over a century later in the Hinckley case:

> Ye people of England: exult and be glad
> For you're now at the will of the merciless mad.

The heresy of one age often becomes the orthodoxy of another. In the early 1950s *M'Naghten* was the prevailing rule in almost every American jurisdiction. The more cases I reviewed, however, the more strongly I felt that *M'Naghten* required that behavioral scientists confine their testimony to a single narrow issue: whether the defendant knew what he was doing and knew whether it was right or wrong.

M'Naghten seemed to ignore the modern dynamic theories of the human personality as an integrated whole. It concentrated on a single aspect of that personality—cognitive reason—as the sole determinant of human behavior. Psychiatrists who testified under *M'Naghten* were engaging in a charade. They were supplying answers under the guise of expert medical opinion to questions that were essentially metaphysical. Juries did little more than decide which expert was more credible.

Psychiatrists implored us to free them from the straitjacket of *M'Naghten* and permit them to present a more adequate account of psychic realities. If psychiatrists were to testify meaningfully as experts on the issue of criminal responsibility, they had to be allowed to address that issue in terms appropriate to their medical discipline. They argued that, freed from the traditional tests, they could provide extensive insights into aspects of behavior highly relevant to the issue of responsibility.

I have always felt strongly that the question of guilt or innocence was not a medical question, but a moral one. Valid moral judgments, however, required the best information available about every aspect of the defendant's functioning, and psychiatrists promised a wealth of facts about human behavior. To obtain these facts for the jury, I wrote the opinion in the *Durham* case, holding that an accused is not criminally responsible if it is shown that "his unlawful act was the product of mental disease or defect."

The new rule was a challenge both to behavioral scientists and to juries. It challenged the scholars because it subjected their discipline to full and searching inquiry. They had to let us know everything that their discipline could tell us about the accused, and perhaps more important, everything it could not. We needed to learn both the known and the unknown about human behavior. *Durham* was also intended to inspire juries to reach informed moral decisions themselves, without relying on the conclusions of experts.[10]

Some have said *Durham* was intended to give over the question of moral responsibility to doctors. But our goal in broadening the scope of their testimony was to present to the jury a more complete picture of why the accused had acted as he had. It was up to the jury to decide for legal, not medical, purposes whether a mental disease or defect was present and, if so, whether the act was the product of that disease or defect. These questions were intelligible only in the moral sphere, not in medical science. The experts would provide information and opinion; the jury would draw the conclusions.

It didn't work out that way. Law in action is very different from law in theory. For while better decisions required candor from psychiatrists and initiative from jurors, easier decisions did not. And easy decisions were what we got. Psychiatrists continued to use labels without explaining the origin, development, or manifestations of a disease in terms meaningful to the jury. Instead of testifying about the defendant's capacity to discern right from wrong, they spoke about new ultimate conclusions: the existence of mental disease and whether the act was its product.

Psychiatrists are not unprincipled, and the failure of *Durham* was not entirely their fault. Partisan lawyers wanted certain, not equivocal, answers; the legal process has trouble with ambiguity. Indeed, psychiatrists were only responding to the conclusory questions put to them. They also were unaccustomed to having their diagnoses, and even the integrity of their discipline itself, subjected to the often hostile scrutiny of the adversary process. Finally, judges and juries often preferred to delegate weighty responsibilities to experts.

But psychiatrists had promised candor and had a special obligation to make good their promise. Their obligation was to disclose that a proper examination required time and resources that they did not possess. Dr. Winfred Overholser, superintendent of St. Elizabeths Hospital in Washington, was one of the early champions of the *Durham* decision. Yet after *Durham,* St. Elizabeth psychiatrists continued to give the same testimony in court as before. After a few years I asked Overholser why his staff still clung to their boilerplate testimony. He told me not to blame the psychiatrists. A sanity examination that would fulfill the *Durham* requirements would take up to a hundred hours of interviews and investigation, and such examinations were impossible, given the hospital's meager resources. State hospitals like St. Elizabeths could manage only a few hours at most with each defendant.

I did not blame the staff psychiatrists, but I felt that Overholser had not obtained from Congress the necessary resources to perform proper examinations, nor had he instructed his staff to point out in their testimony the patent inadequacy of their data. State psychiatrists had an obligation as well to acknowledge that their appraisals were often influenced by the bedspace they had available, by their willingness or unwillingness to have certain defendants as patients after acquittals, by political pressure, and by their own ideas about criminal responsibility. They also had a duty to reveal the uncertainties in their diagnoses and the disagreements among the staff in official hospital reports. Often the final report that appeared in court reflected only the majority view at the staff conference.

As a result, attorneys and their clients, as well as judges and juries, were left unaware of minority viewpoints that might have shed a very different light on their inquiries. For years I tried unsuccessfully to obtain records or tapes of staff conferences at St. Elizabeths where official diagnoses were made. I believed that juries had a right to see the practice of psychiatry as it was: not as science dealing with absolute physical laws, but as a diagnostic art based on educated, but nonverifiable, hypotheses.

Durham was a simple contract between law and medicine. Doctors could offer candor and insight if the law would free them from *M'Naghten.* We accepted. For eighteen years we tried to avoid the conclusion that the contract had been breached.

We tried in a long series of cases to work with the *Durham* formulation to evolve a way of gaining the benefit of all relevant information, while avoiding conclusory expert testimony. Nothing worked. Finally, in 1972, we admitted that our best-laid plans had gone awry, and unanimously decided to abandon the *Durham* rule.

The court substituted a new test proposed by the American Law Institute. The rule provides that "[a] person is not responsible for criminal conduct if at the time of such conduct as a result of mental disease or defect he lacks substantial capacity either to appreciate the wrongfulness of his conduct or to conform his conduct to the requirements of the law." Mental disease or defect was limited to medically recognized conditions characterized by a broad consensus that free will was absent.

Looking for Law in All the Wrong Places

While the *Durham* approach had failed in operation and had to be abandoned, I believe that, at best, the new alternative has done nothing to address the problems, and may have aggravated them. I concurred in overruling the old rule, but not in the new test adopted. As I said in my opinion, "while the generals are designing an inspiring new insignia for the standard, the battle is being lost in the trenches."[11]

The court seemed to assume that the infirmities of *Durham* could be cured by manipulation of the language of the test. But the problem of experts giving their conclusions about the issue of "productivity," rather than providing information from which the jury could draw its own conclusions, could not be altered by magically changing the word "product" to the word "result." Both embody the ultimate question of causality. Neither is suitable for resolution by experts. One term is as liable as the other to be abused. If we learned anything at all from *Durham*, it was that the problem of administering the defense could not be solved by a verbal trick.

Nor did the new test (based on the 1972 case *United States v. Brawner*) solve the problem of domination by medical experts.

In effect, it limited the range of testimony to medically recognized conditions. The battle over the validity of diagnoses was merely diverted to one over medical recognition. This greater reliance on acceptance in the medical community flew in the face of the critical lesson of *Durham:* that psychiatrists did not have a monopoly of knowledge about human behavior, and that much of what we were beginning to know was coming from sources other than psychiatrists.

Neuroscientists, for example, are making gigantic strides in solving the mysteries of the human brain and, in turn, of human behavior. Anxiety, depression, and aggression can all be enhanced or diminished by the action of certain chemicals in the brain. Behavior is, of course, a highly complex phenomenon and is at least in part socially determined. Science may never provide complete answers. Moreover, the possibilities of biochemical alteration of behavior will present new challenges for law.

There is more that remains hidden about the wellsprings of human behavior than we ever thought. Our moral judgments of other human beings must reflect the humility borne of self-doubt.

The insanity plea has been criticized as a rich man's defense. Sensational cases like that of John Hinckley create the impression that a successful insanity defense requires vast resources. This is largely true, because a proper insanity defense costs money. It requires a good lawyer, as well as extended examinations by independent experts, neither of which are usually available to indigent insanity defendants. Lawyers representing indigents are often overworked and inexperienced. In addition, a defendant raising the insanity defense presently has no right to an independent expert in most jurisdictions.[12] Most often, the accused who gives notice that he intends to raise an insanity defense is sent to a state hospital for examination.

Psychiatry is not a value-free discipline. Psychiatrists in state hospitals often have a hidden agenda, whether conscious or not—the institutional pressure and personal biases that cause them to serve interests other than the therapeutic needs of their patients. In one case, a government psychiatrist, informed by an assistant United States attorney that the case was "one of major significance," actually changed his diagnosis of the accused from "chronic undifferentiated schizophrenia" to "without mental disease."[13]

Although cases involving such direct prostitution of the diagnostic process are rare, forensic psychiatrists are often at least indirectly influenced by external demands. Years ago the superintendent of the Napa State Hospital in California told me with commendable candor that the state government at Sacramento was always looking over his shoulder on internal decisions. While most hospitals are probably not so closely monitored, it is clear that state psychiatrists have institutional needs and perspectives which make them less likely to support the defendant's insanity plea. Since insanity trials fail to elicit the institutional biases that lead to particular results, the indigent defendant, as a result of his inability to secure an independent expert, is fundamentally prejudiced in his attempt to raise this affirmative defense provided by law.

What is more, while at the state facility, the defendant is on alien ground, without the procedural protections afforded at other stages of the criminal process. A recent case decided in our circuit, *United States v. Byers*,[14] is illustrative. Byers was arrested for murder and committed to St. Elizabeths for examination. The psychiatrists found that he had been afflicted with delusions at the time of the murder, believing himself under a spell that could be broken only by killing the victim. The government did not accept this diagnosis and so committed Byers, over defense objections, to a government hospital in Springfield, Missouri.

Byers spent eight weeks there without a lawyer, without any warning that the psychiatrists encouraging a free flow of communication could be adversaries at trial, and without any records kept of the interviews. At trial, a psychiatrist dropped a bombshell. He stated that Byers had told him that the story of the spells had been suggested to him by his wife after his arrest. No record of this disclosure was in the psychiatrist's notes or anywhere else. The trial judge called his testimony "devastating" to Byers' defense.

The *Byers* case points out fundamental problems with the administration of the insanity defense. The constitutional protections against self-incrimination, as well as the Fifth and Sixth Amendment guarantees of due process and effective assistance of counsel, all require, at a minimum, the presence of counsel or a taped record of psychiatric interviews.

The American Psychiatric Association has opposed such measures on the ground that they would undermine the therapeutic relationship between the psychiatrist and the defendant. But the state hospital is an institution where a therapeutic facade masks a real divergence of interests between doctor and patient. Psychiatrists cannot have it both ways. They can't invoke the sanctity of the doctor-patient relationship to justify the unimpeded collection of information that may then convict a patient. The protections I have suggested would assure that insanity verdicts will not come down to the defendant's word against the unverifiable word of the expert.

While any criminal defendant raising the insanity defense can be ordered to a state hospital, it is the indigent who are almost always forced to rely on state doctors for their own defense. Greater procedural protections could be assured if an independent pool of defense psychiatric experts were attached to each public defender's office.

We must also assure that the indigent's sanity or insanity does not hinge on a psychiatrist's or factfinder's stereotyped view of life in poverty. Psychiatric experts have speculated whether the defendant would have committed the act in question had he not been mentally ill. Such speculation is rife with potential for the articulation of social prejudices in the guise of medical science.

I was once told by the judge in question of the case of a sixteen-year-old black girl who had literally sliced her boyfriend to ribbons with a piece of broken glass. Although the child had a previous history of mental health problems, the judge, relying on the testimony of a psychiatrist, found that the girl's behavior was not "sick" because such conduct was "normal" in her ghetto subculture. Thus, to the limited degree that this offender's background was taken into account, it was used to convict an indigent person, for whom violence was seen to be "normal." In these terms, then, someone from a more affluent background might have been acquitted of the same offense on grounds of insanity because violence is presumed not to be part of her environment. Such discriminatory conjectures must not be permitted to affect the decision-making process.

Procedural protections are nothing more than tentative first steps. They represent our commitment to inquiry, to examining why this particular individual committed an act we define as a crime. How we fulfill that commitment is the real question.

3

Durham v. United States[1]

As a new, young judge in the early 1950s I became intrigued with the insanity defense cases that occasionally came before us. Nothing in my earlier career as a commercial lawyer and Justice Department official (in the areas of U.S. lands and alien property) presaged such an interest. But something about these cases and the window they opened into lives so different from my own demanded my attention. In those days before the random assignment of cases, judges, especially very junior ones, had little say about the cases they were assigned. But I approached Chief Judge Henry J. Edgerton and asked for a chance to handle some of the insanity matters. He readily agreed, probably happy that someone was willing to take an interest in cases that were not among the most coveted. By the time of *Durham* I had some experience with such cases.

A key element was that the cases had to be well argued, and their then-novel issues fully illuminated. The two very able lawyers assigned Monte Durham's case were Abe Fortas, later a Supreme Court Justice, and Abe Krash, still a highly respected Washington attorney. Another key element was the availability of new information and insights from behavioral science. I had long been interested in psychiatry and its potential contribution to understanding human behavior.

Durham coincided with revolutionary developments in psychiatry, most importantly the discovery of effective drug treatments for the major symptoms of mental illness. It was a time of ascendancy for our faith in science and technology. In the wake of the discovery of atomic energy, the prestige of scientific experts was at a new high. It rose even higher after the Soviets in 1957 launched *Sputnik,* the first satellite, and the Space Age began. The new drugs enabled psychiatrists to claim membership in this scientific elite. Some began to argue that most patients could be discharged from the warehouses known as mental hospitals, to be treated more humanely in community settings. Soon the deinstitutionalization movement was underway, with results that failed to match expectations any more closely than our expectations about expert testimony.[2]

The case coincided, too, with the beginnings of the civil rights movement, which focused attention on individual as against majority rights. It was not mere chance that *Durham* was decided during the same month as *Brown v. Board of Education.*[3] In some ways we were responding to the same general awakening of social concern. The insanity defense had been seen as a "whites only" defense, available exclusively to one seen as suffering from a certifiable illness. By expanding it to examine human behavior more broadly, we were in practice opening it to minorities and the poor, whose aberrations had seldom been regarded in the sympathetic light of sickness. I later received some criticism from Dr. Thomas Szasz, who gained prominence arguing that mental illness is a "myth," for imposing the insanity defense on poor blacks like Monte Durham.[4] The irony, of course, was that Durham was white. He, too, was unhappy with me, not for the decision but because he thought the case should have been named after me rather than himself. He had been, he complained, tarred forever as "Durham the nut."

Durham also benefited from a then-recent exploration of responsibility issues by Britain's Royal Commission on Capital Punishment. On receiving a copy of our decision, the chairman wrote that he was "gratif[ied] to find that what my colleagues and I took so much trouble over is not without its effect on the trend of judicial thought." He noted that he had been "shocked to realize how large a section of the public there is here whose attitude might be described without great exaggeration as being that the madder a murderer is the stronger is the case for hanging him."[5] He was right to point out the underlying ambivalence that so often characterizes society's feelings about the insanity defense. These questions continue to trouble us. The Supreme Court recently defined an important line of demarcation, holding unconstitutional the execution of a convicted murderer who had become insane while on death row.[6]

The unique political status of the District of Columbia gave our court a role unusual for federal appellate jurisdictions. In the federal system, the great majority of criminal cases are handled through state law and state courts. However, for many years the District of Columbia was subject to direct federal authority. It had an appointed executive, Congress was its legislature, and our court acted as the District's "state supreme court." We thus had responsibility for reviewing criminal cases from the local trial courts, as well as the federal cases with which all U.S. courts of appeal are concerned. We also could see the direct impact of our decisions on a local community.

This circumstance was of critical importance in providing both the stimulus and the opportunity to cultivate an emerging interest in criminal law and responsibility. No other federal appellate court would have offered a comparable range and number of criminal cases. This was still more true of cases involving such rare issues as the insanity defense. Like all large cities, Washington has its share of mentally unstable citizens, some few of whom are prosecuted for crimes. The presence of the federal government and its huge St. Elizabeths mental hospital, and the unique role of the Congress as both the city and state legislature for the District, enhanced the visibility and newsworthiness of such crimes and trials and made District laws and practices models (for good or ill) for the states. At the same time, the Supreme Court tended to treat our court's decisions as if they were those of a state supreme court, deserving great deference in the federal system, rather than as federal cases with potential national application. This gave us much the same latitude as a state, then, to be a laboratory of democracy.

On the other hand, typical disputes among legislative, executive, and judicial branches simply did not exist as they did in the states. During the period of *Durham,* the District was largely, in effect, a fiefdom of Congress. A powerful Congressman was said to have described the city (openly and with impunity) as an ice cream sundae—80 percent chocolate, 20 percent vanilla, and sprinkled all over with nuts and flakes. District citizens had no elected representatives. The courts, including ours, were cast in the special role of protecting the dispossessed.

Since the passage of home rule for the District, these roles have changed. Nevertheless, the legacy of federal involvement still dominates the criminal law in this jurisdiction. At this writing, St. Elizabeths is undergoing a long-awaited transfer from federal to District control. But Congress still oversees District legislation. The presence of the federal government assures that a certain number of "White House cases"—ranging from people making a disturbance at the gates to those attempting violence against officials—will be patients at the hospital. And what happens in the nation's capital remains uniquely the business of the nation.

BACKGROUND   Monte Durham had a long history of imprisonment and hospitalization. In 1945, at the age of seventeen, he was discharged from the Navy after a psychiatric examination had shown that he suffered "from a profound personality disorder which renders him unfit for Naval service." In 1947 he pleaded guilty to motor theft and was placed on probation for one to three years. He attempted suicide, was taken to the Gallinger Hospital for observation, and was transferred to St. Elizabeths, from which he was discharged after two months.

In 1948, after Durham was convicted of passing bad checks, the District Court revoked his probation. His behavior within the first few days in jail led to a "lunacy inquiry" in which a jury found him to be of unsound mind. He was committed to St. Elizabeths and diagnosed as suffering from "psychosis with psychopathic personality." After fifteen months, he was discharged as recovered and returned to jail to serve the balance of his sentence.

In June 1950 he was conditionally released, but violated the conditions by leaving the District. After he was found, a jury again decided he was of unsound mind, and he was readmitted to St. Elizabeths in February 1951. This time the diagnosis was "without mental disorder, psychopathic personality." He was discharged for the third time in May.

The housebreaking which led to this case took place two months later. After his indictment, he was once more found of unsound mind, committed to St. Elizabeths for the fourth time, and given subshock insulin therapy. This commitment lasted sixteen months, until he was released to the custody of the District jail as "mentally competent to stand trial and . . . able to consult with counsel to properly assist in his own defense." He was brought to trial and convicted. On appeal, the case came before the U.S. Court of Appeals for the District of Columbia.

The following is an excerpt from my 1954 opinion for the court, establishing the *Durham* rule, which was applied in insanity cases for eighteen years.

* * *

It has been ably argued by counsel for Durham that the existing tests in the District of Columbia for determining criminal responsibility, i.e., the so-called right-wrong test supplemented by the irresistible impulse test, are not satisfactory criteria for determining criminal responsibility. We are urged to adopt a different test to be applied on the retrial of this case. This contention has behind it nearly a century of agitation for reform.

The right-wrong test, approved in this jurisdiction in 1882, was the exclusive test of criminal responsibility in the District of Columbia until 1929 when we approved the irresistible impulse test as a supplementary test in *Smith v. United States*.[7] The right-wrong test has its roots in England. There, by the first quarter of the eighteenth century, an accused escaped punishment if he could not distinguish "good and evil," i.e., if he "doth not know what he is doing, no more than . . . a wild beast."[8] Later in the same century, the "wild beast" test was abandoned and "right and wrong" was substituted for "good and evil." And toward the middle of the nineteenth century, the House of Lords in the famous *M'Naghten* case[9] restated what had become the accepted "right-wrong" test in a form which has since been followed, not only in England but in most American jurisdictions as an exclusive test of criminal responsibility:

. . . the jurors ought to be told in all cases that every man is to be presumed to be sane, and to possess a sufficient degree of reason to be responsible for his crimes, until the contrary be proved to their satisfaction; and that, to establish a defense on the ground of insanity, it must be clearly proved that, at the time of the committing of the act, the party accused was labouring under such a defect of reason, from disease of the mind, as not to know the nature and quality of the act he was doing, or, if he did know it, that he did not know he was doing what was wrong.

As early as 1838, Isaac Ray, one of the founders of the American Psychiatric Association, in his now classic *Medical Jurisprudence of Insanity,* called knowledge of right and wrong a "fallacious" test of criminal responsibility.[10] This view has long since been substantiated by enormous developments in knowledge of mental life. In 1928 Mr. Justice Cardozo said to the New York Academy of Medicine: "Everyone concedes that the present [legal] definition of insanity has little relation to the truths of mental life."[11]

Medico-legal writers in large number, The Report of the Royal Commission in Capital Punishment 1949–1953, and The Preliminary Report by the Committee on Forensic Psychiatry of the Group for the Advancement of Psychiatry present convincing evidence that the right-and-wrong test is "based on an entirely obsolete and misleading conception of the nature of insanity." The science of psychiatry now recognizes that a man is an integrated personality and that reason, which is only one element in that personality, is not the sole determinant of his conduct. The right-wrong test, which considers knowledge or reason alone, is therefore an inadequate guide to mental responsibility for criminal behavior. . . .

Nine years ago we said:

> The modern science of psychology . . . does not conceive that there is a separate little man in the top of one's head called reason whose function it is to guide another unruly little man called instinct, emotion, or impulse in the way he should go.[12]

By its misleading emphasis on the cognitive, the right-wrong test requires court and jury to rely upon what is, scientifically speaking, inadequate, and most often, invalid and irrelevant testimony in determining criminal responsibility.

The fundamental objection to the right-wrong test, however, is not that criminal irresponsibility is made to rest upon an inadequate, invalid or indeterminable symptom or manifestation, but that it is made to rest upon *any* particular symptom. In attempting to define insanity in terms of a symptom the courts have assumed an impossible role, not merely one for which they have no special competence. As the Royal Commission emphasizes, it is dangerous "to abstract particular mental faculties, and to lay it down that unless these particular faculties are destroyed or gravely impaired, an accused person, whatever the nature of his mental disease, must be held to be criminally responsible. . . ." In this field of law as in others, the fact finder should be free to consider all information advanced by relevant scientific disciplines.

Despite demands in the name of scientific advances, this court refused to alter the right-wrong test at the turn of the century. But in 1929, we reconsidered in response to "the cry of scientific experts" and added the irresistible impulse test as a supplementary test for determining criminal responsibility. Without "hesitation" we declared, in *Smith v. United States*, "it to be the law of this District that, in cases where insanity is interposed as a defense, and the facts are sufficient to call for the application of the rule of irresistible impulse, the jury should be so charged."

We find that as an exclusive criterion the right-wrong test is inadequate in that (a) it does not take sufficient account of psychic realities and scientific knowledge, and (b) it is based upon one symptom and so cannot validly be applied in all circumstances. We find that the "irresistible impulse" test is also inadequate in that it gives no recognition to mental illness characterized by brooding and reflection and so relegates acts caused by such illness to the application of the inadequate right-wrong test. We conclude that a broader test should be adopted.

The rule we now hold must be applied on the retrial of this case and in future cases is not unlike that followed by the New Hampshire court since 1870.[13] It is simply that an accused is not criminally responsible if his unlawful act was the product of mental disease or mental defect.

We use "disease" in the sense of a condition which is considered capable of either improving or deteriorating. We use "defect" in the sense of a condition which is not considered capable of either improving or deteriorating and which may be either congenital, or the result of injury, or the residual effect of a physical or mental disease.

Whenever there is "some evidence" that the accused suffered from a diseased or defective mental condition at the time the unlawful act was committed, the trial court must provide the jury with guides for determining whether the accused can be held criminally responsible. We do not, and indeed could not, formulate an instruction which would be either appropriate or binding in all cases. But under the rule now announced, any instruction should in some way convey to the jury the sense and substance of the following: If you the jury believe beyond a reasonable doubt that the accused was not suffering from a diseased or defective mental condition at the time he committed the criminal act charged, you may find him guilty. If you believe he was suffering from a diseased or defective mental condition when he committed the act, but believe beyond a reasonable doubt that the act was not the product of such mental abnormality, you may find him guilty. Unless you believe beyond a reasonable doubt either that he was not suffering from a diseased or defective mental condition, or that the act was not the product of such abnormality, you must find the accused not guilty by reason of insanity. Thus your task would not be completed upon finding, if you did find, that the accused suffered from a mental disease or defect. He would still be responsible for his unlawful act if there was no causal connection between such mental abnormality and the act. These questions must be determined by you from the facts which you find to be fairly deducible from the testimony and the evidence in this case.

The questions of fact under the test we now lay down are as capable of determination by the jury as, for example, the questions juries must determine upon a claim of total disability under a policy of insurance where the state of medical knowledge concerning the disease involved, and its effects, is obscure or in conflict. In such cases, the jury is not required to depend on arbitrarily selected "symptoms, phases or manifestations" of the disease as criteria for determining the ultimate questions of fact upon which the claim depends. Similarly, upon a claim of criminal irresponsibility, the jury will not be required to rely on such symptoms as criteria for determining the ultimate question of fact upon which such claim depends. Testimony as to such "symptoms, phases or manifestations," along with other relevant evidence, will go to the jury upon the ultimate questions of fact which it alone can finally determine. Whatever the state of psychiatry, the psychiatrist will be permitted to carry out his principal court function which, as we noted in *Holloway v. U.S.*, "is to inform the jury of the character of [the accused's] mental disease [or defect]." The jury's range of inquiry will not be limited to, but may include, for example, whether an accused who suffered from a mental disease or defect did not know the difference between right and wrong, acted under the compulsion of an irresistible impulse, or had "been deprived of or lost the power of his will. . . ."

Finally, in leaving the determination of the ultimate question of fact to the jury, we permit it to perform its traditional function which, as we said in *Holloway*, is to apply "our inherited ideas of moral responsibility to individuals prosecuted for crime. . . ." Juries will continue to make moral judgments, still operating under the fundamental precept that "[o]ur collective conscience does not allow punishment where it cannot impose blame." But in making such judgments, they will be guided by wider horizons of knowledge concerning mental life. The question will be simply whether the accused acted because of a mental disorder, and not whether he displayed particular symptoms which medical science has long recognized do not necessarily, or even typically, accompany even the most serious mental disorder.

The legal and moral traditions of the Western world require that those who, of their own free will and with evil intent (sometimes called *mens rea*), commit acts which violate the law, shall be criminally responsible for those acts. Our traditions also require that where such acts stem from and are the product of a mental disease or defect as those terms are used herein, moral blame shall not attach, and hence there will not be criminal responsibility. The rule we state in this opinion is designed to meet these requirements.

4

The Experiment: 1954–1972

Although *Durham* was widely praised for opening a reexamination of the insanity defense, implementation of the rule ran into serious difficulties. The test never suffered a shortage of critics, but virtually all of them missed what I consider the crucial failure which emerged in its operation. The critics assumed that our ruling would generate far-reaching changes, and they questioned or condemned the changes they foresaw. But the first few years' experience dispelled any illusion that the decision would alter the insanity defense in any fundamental way.

Two closely entwined problems emerged. First, as already pointed out in Chapter 3, expert witnesses on the issue of insanity generally did not live up to their promise to share all they knew, and even more important, what they didn't know, with the jury. They continued to make conclusory pronouncements, simply to put a psychiatric label on the defendant, rather than offering useful explanations of his behavior. Part of the fault lay with attorneys who failed, out of either ignorance or a desire to simplify matters, to dig beneath the experts' boilerplate.

Secondly, the participants in the decision-making process mistakenly tended to see the crucial variables "mental disease or defect" and "product" as technical scientific terms about whose meaning expert opinion was not only necessary but the final word. To the extent that this required experts to make value judgments beyond their expertise, it perpetuated expert dominance of the decision, and usurped the jury's proper role as the moral voice of the community.

The D.C. court struggled with these problems in a long line of cases, over one hundred in the first decade alone. In some the insanity defense prevailed, in others the defendant was convicted, but all tried to breathe life into the goals of *Durham.* Leading cases included *McDonald v. United States,*[1] in which the court attempted to rescue the term "mental disease or defect" from the grip of expert witnesses by clarifying its legal significance, and *Washington v. United States,*[2] in which the court barred any expert testimony on the issue of when an act was the "product" of mental disease. Throughout this period, the court continued to insist that expert testimony not be a vehicle for personal value judgments presented as scientific truth, and that the jury be required to determine for itself, from all the available evidence, whether the accused should be held morally responsible.

Nevertheless, the misuse of the *Durham* test continued. Finally, in the 1972 *Brawner* case, our court unanimously agreed to overrule *Durham.* The majority decided that the *Durham* rule should be replaced with the standard developed by the American Law Institute, and fairly characterized as a more subtle and less restrictive combination of the "knowledge of right and wrong" and the "irresistible impulse" tests that had obtained prior to *Durham.* I agreed that the *Durham* formulation should be abandoned, but argued in a separate opinion that the majority opinion in *Brawner* concentrated on form rather than substance and failed adequately to confront the lessons learned from our efforts to implement *Durham.* Nothing has changed my mind about that.

My opinion in the case, excerpted here,[3] illustrates some of the main points in controversy, as well as the process that occurred among the judges on the court as we struggled with these issues. Our experience with *Durham* had taught me that valid moral judgments of offenders required information from any and all sources about their lives. The tragedy of the approach adopted in *Brawner* was that it remedicalized the problem. I suggested a new approach.

I proposed that the jury be instructed that a defendant is not responsible "if at the time of his unlawful conduct his mental or emotional processes or behavior controls were impaired to such an extent that he cannot justly be held responsible." This test, if properly administered, frees the law of criminal responsibility from a medical model. It allows anyone with knowledge of the offender's life—psychologists, sociologists, teachers, ministers, neighbors—to tell the jury about the defendant and his environment. The test, moreover, candidly informs the jury that it is their function to apply the moral standards of the community to what they have learned about the offender.

It could be said of my view in *Brawner,* as Judge Learned Hand said of *Durham,* that it creates more problems than it solves. I would only change that to read: it recognizes more problems than it solves. If, in a given case involving criminal responsibility, social and economic deprivation is a substantial component of behavior, evidence as to this personal history should not be categorized as "irrelevant" and therefore excluded. The issue of criminal responsibility, like other subjects in the criminal law, does not permit us to ignore the relationship between antisocial conduct, on the one hand, and poverty and social injustice, on the other.

BACKGROUND   After spending an afternoon drinking wine, Archie Brawner went to a party at the apartment of three friends. During the evening several fights broke out. Brawner was hit in the jaw and knocked down; he left the apartment immediately. In the next hour he was seen by several friends, who described him as dizzy, unclear of speech, and bleeding from the mouth. He refused to go to a hospital for medical attention, and told his friends he had been jumped. Pounding on a mailbox with a fist, he said that someone—perhaps himself—was going to die. Returning to the building in which the party had been held, he fired five shots through the closed door of the apartment. Two struck and killed one of the occupants. Brawner was arrested nearby shortly afterward.

At his own request, Brawner was committed to St. Elizabeths Hospital for observation. The standard commitment order asked the hospital to report on both his competence to stand trial and his responsibility at the time of the act. With respect to responsibility, the hospital was asked "whether the defendant, at the time of the alleged criminal offense, committed on or about September 8, 1967, was suffering from a mental disease, or defect which substantially affected his mental or emotional processes and substantially impaired his behavior controls, and if so, whether his criminal act was the product of his mental condition. . . ." The hospital's summary report stated that Brawner was competent for trial; that he was mentally ill at the time of the act; and that the act was not causally related to his illness.

At trial, four expert witnesses from the hospital staff testified on the issue of responsibility. All agreed that Brawner was mentally ill at the time of the shooting. They used various labels, but in general they concurred that he had an organic brain pathology and an associated explosive personality disorder. The organic damage was indicated by a history of epileptic seizures, an abnormal electroencephalogram test, and a pattern of responses to psychological tests characteristic of persons with organic impairment. The explosive personality disorder was indicated by psychological testing and by psychiatric interviews and observations.

All four experts went into commendable detail in describing the nature of Brawner's disorder and its effect on his behavior. Each in turn stated that the disorder was manifested in an inability to deal with provocation. He was said to possess severe feelings of inadequacy, and to be easily threatened. He would respond to a felt threat without control; his behavior would be explosive, and out of proportion to the situation.

The only conflict in the expert testimony arose in the course of an inquiry into whether the act was a "product" of the disorder—an inquiry in which expert conclusions had been banned since the *Washington* case. Two doctors testified that Brawner's unlawful act was the product of his explosive epileptoid personality disorder. Two other physicians said that shooting through the closed door of an apartment was not the product of his illness but rather one of a normal desire to retaliate for a broken jaw. That is, even if Brawner had not been ill, he would have retaliated in this way. One testified that

"I think I would, too, under the same circumstances want to get even with somebody who broke my jaw." The jury found Brawner guilty of second-degree murder. Our court remanded the case to the District Court to consider whether, in view of a new standard for the insanity defense, the original judgment should be sustained or, instead, a new trial held.

*   *   *

In place of *Durham,* juries are now instructed in terms of the American Law Institute test that a person is not responsible for a criminal act if as a result of mental disease or defect he lacks substantial capacity either to appreciate the wrongfulness of his conduct or to conform his conduct to the requirements of law. But the adoption of this new test was largely an anticlimax, for even though *Durham*'s language survived until the *Brawner* decision, the significant differences between our approach and that of the ALI test vanished many years ago. As described in Judge Leventhal's scholarly opinion (for the majority), the ALI test may make possible an improvement in the adjudication of the responsibility issue. But on the whole I fear that the change has been primarily one of form rather than of substance.

The principal question is whether the adoption of the ALI test is responsive to the lessons we learned from the efforts to implement *Durham,* and whether it offers any promise of resolving the difficulties that have always troubled us. Plainly, we did not fail for want of trying. . . .

The experts were able to retain their influence in part because of the manner in which *Durham* was construed. The term "mental disease or mental defect" was saddled with an unintended and astringent medical meaning. And the "productivity" requirement was perversely viewed as a locked door which could only be opened by an expert's key. But most important, the court failed to deal with crucial practical obstacles that operate under any formulation of the test to impede the flow of information to the jury.

The first of these difficulties was the subject of our 1962 decision in *McDonald v. United States* where we attempted to rescue the term "mental disease or defect" from the grip of the expert witnesses. The definition of mental disease adopted in *McDonald* rendered our test, in almost every significant respect, identical to the ALI test. Yet *McDonald*, no less than *Durham*, left the power of the experts intact. Expert witnesses still testify in misleading and conclusory terms about the medical or psychiatric definitions of mental disease.

The second source of difficulty concerns the productivity requirement—the albatross of the *Durham* decision. This court's frustration with the conclusory expert testimony on the issue of productivity culminated in our decision in *Washington v. United States* which barred such testimony altogether. And yet, in the face of our prohibition, the experts have continued to testify in conclusory terms, as the records in *Brawner* and dozens of other cases attest. A reiteration of our ban will not be effective, and the Court held that the issue of productivity must henceforth be eliminated from the instructions to the jury. In my view, we can prevent encroachments on the jury's function only by adopting an instruction that candidly describes its power and responsibility. Since we have no simple, scientific formula that will provide a clear-cut answer to every case, we have no choice, in my opinion, but to tell the truth: that the jury, not the experts, must judge the defendant's blameworthiness; that a calibrated, easily applied standard is not yet available to guide that decision; and that the jury must resolve the question with reference to its own understanding of community concepts of blameworthiness.

The third source of difficulty—and to my mind the paramount cause of *Durham*'s failure—is the cluster of practical obstacles that stand in the way of the full disclosure of information that *Durham* hoped to secure. Here too the court's decision shed no new light. For no matter how felicitous its phrasing, a responsibility test cannot, single-handed, overcome these practical obstacles.

Neither *Durham* nor *Brawner* lets slip our well-guarded secret that the great majority of responsibility cases concern indigents, not affluent defendants with easy access to legal and psychiatric assistance. In a long line of cases we have been asked to confront difficult questions concerning the right to an adequate psychiatric examination, the right to psychiatric assistance in the preparation of the defense, the right to counsel at various stages of the process, the role and responsibility of a government expert who testifies on behalf of an indigent defendant, the burden of proof, the right to treatment during postacquittal hospitalization, and many more. If the promise of *Durham* was not fulfilled, the primary explanation lies in our answers, or lack of answers to those questions.

I fear that it can fairly be said of *Brawner*, as well as *Durham*, that while the generals are designing an inspiring new insignia for the standard, the battle is being lost in the trenches. In fact, our obligation to confront the practical problems now is greater than it was in 1954, if only because our efforts to implement *Durham* have brought many of these problems to first light. . . .

Eighteen years ago this Court formulated a new test of criminal responsibility for the District of Columbia. In *Durham v. United States* we held that "an accused is not criminally responsible if his unlawful act was the product of mental disease or mental defect." The *Durham* test was formulated in response to the widespread complaints of psychiatrists that under traditional tests of responsibility the law asked them to go beyond their professional competence; the traditional tests seemed to saddle them with the job of deciding which defendants were guilty and which ones should be excused for lack of criminal responsibility. The *M'Naghten* rule and the various "irresistible impulse" tests attempted to define the types of illness that the law would regard as exculpatory, and asked the psychiatrist whether the particular defendant suffered from such an illness at the time of his unlawful act. Thus, under *M'Naghten*, the psychiatrist was asked whether the defendant could tell right from wrong, and under the irresistible impulse test he was asked whether the defendant had the capacity to refrain from doing the unlawful act. The psychiatrist's answer was the whole answer to the question of responsibility. The only function of the jury was to choose which expert to believe in case of a conflict.

Psychiatrists vociferously criticized that approach to the

problem of criminal responsibility on the ground that it did not correspond to the state of psychiatric knowledge. In their view few if any persons could be said to be totally lacking in the capacity to distinguish right from wrong or to control their actions. At the same time psychiatrists believed that they could provide extensive insights into other aspects of behavior that were highly relevant to the problem of responsibility. Since the traditional tests were deemed too narrow to allow consideration of such insights, many psychiatrists sought to include them under the cover of psychiatric labels and legal conclusions. The expert treated a neutral scientific question about the defendant's mental condition as one addressed to the legal significance of that condition. He was often allowed to do so because the factfinder [judge or jury] was happy to be relieved of a difficult and troubling task, namely, deciding whether the defendant's illness was severe enough to excuse him. The psychiatrist performed this task simply by fitting, or refusing to fit, the defendant into one of the categories of exculpatory mental illness. But even if psychiatric diagnosis is sufficiently flexible to permit this kind of manipulation, it does not provide a satisfactory solution from a legal standpoint. The difficulty of deciding the issue of responsibility may not be avoided by turning it over entirely to the experts.

One solution might have been to formulate a new and broader definition of "exculpatory mental illness," in order to retain *M'Naghten*'s goal of offering the psychiatrist a limited role, i.e., ascertaining whether the defendant suffered from such an illness. But we found it impossible to formulate a general definition which would eliminate the need to evaluate blameworthiness in each individual case. Our problem, therefore, was to make it clear that evaluation was to be made not by the experts but by the jury. On the basis of past experience we feared that any concrete definitions we might offer the jury for guidance would promptly find their way into the standard repertoire of psychiatric testimony, capable again of yes-or-no answers, thereby returning the ultimate issues to the keeping of the psychiatrists.

For inspiration we turned to a model long familiar to the

law, the method of assessing fault in negligence cases. We articulated no precise definition of responsibility, as the law articulates no precise definition of negligence. Instead in each case we allow the jury to hear all relevant information and ask it to decide whether by prevailing community standards the defendant was at fault. Thus the jury not only makes the factual determination that the defendant behaved in a certain manner, or that his mental condition was of a certain character, but also fixes the legal norm against which the mental condition and its relationship to the behavior must be measured. The role of the expert is to tell the jury anything he can about the relationship between the defendant's behavior and his state of mind. The jury decides in the light of that information whether the defendant can justly be held responsible for the harmful consequences of his act, or whether, on the contrary, the harm should be attributed to chance, for example, or to mental disorder.

The principle of *Durham* was to impose responsibility only if an act was the product of a free choice on the part of the defendant, and not of a mental disease or defect. In adopting the term "product" we borrowed again from the law of torts. In negligence cases the law is concerned with the relationship between the defendant's conduct and the resultant injury. Even when it is possible to establish some sort of causation, the requirement of "proximate cause" permits the jury to decide that the negligence was too slight or the causal connection too remote to have legal significance. *Durham* uses the term "product" not to limit liability but to limit its avoidance. Nevertheless, the function of productivity is similar to the function of proximate cause. In criminal cases the law is concerned with the relationship between the defendant's mental condition and his unlawful conduct. Even though it is usually possible to establish some sort of causal relationship between almost any mental illness and the unlawful conduct, the requirement of productivity permits the jury to decide that the illness was too slight or the causal connection too remote to have legal significance.

Critics of *Durham* said the product requirement was illusory, because no psychiatrist would be able to deny the possibility of a causal connection between the illness and the act. Consequently, it was argued, responsibility would turn solely on the question of mental disease, a question clearly within the scope of psychiatric expertise. Thus *Durham* would increase the power of the expert to decide legal and moral questions, rather than cut it down. We intended, however, that the inquiry into productivity would define the moral determination inherent in any determination of responsibility, and commit it to the judgment of the jury rather than that of the experts. We expected that if a mental illness was present, and the experts could not exclude causation entirely, the issue would ordinarily go to the jury as a question of degree.

Ever since this court announced its new test of responsibility in 1954, we have been struggling with the problem of distinguishing between the uniquely psychiatric elements of the determination of responsibility, and the legal and moral elements of that determination. We have repeatedly urged psychiatrists to avoid using the conclusory labels of either psychiatry or law. Testimony in terms of the legal conclusion that an act was or was not the product of mental disease invites the jury to abdicate its function and acquiesce in the conclusion of the experts. Testimony in terms of psychiatric labels obscures the fact that a defendant's responsibility does not turn on whether or not the experts have given his condition a name and the status of disease.

Since *Durham* we have been engaged in a continuing process of refining and explicating the rule of that case. *Carter v. United States*[4] defined the term "product" in broad terms designed to restrict conclusory expert testimony and expand the basic factual information available to the jury. Later *McDonald v. United States* sought to do the same for the term "mental disease or defect" by discouraging the use of psychiatric labels which often served to hide the fact that the experts were providing virtually no information about the defendant's underlying condition. The point in both cases was to invite all the information that modern knowledge could provide, to guide the jury's consideration of the moral, legal, and medical elements in the issue of responsibility. But most psychiatrists declined the invitation and continued to decide themselves when an illness should relieve a defendant of responsibility. Therefore in *Washington v. United States* we reluctantly took the step of prohibiting all psychiatric testimony in terms of the issue of productivity, on the ground that such testimony was particularly likely to usurp the jury's function of resolving the ultimate question of guilt. We said that the existence of disease was a medical question which psychiatrists could properly answer, but the question of productivity was the ultimate question for the jury, involving a mixture of medical information and moral judgment.

The reason for the *Washington* rule was to reserve exclusively for the jury one part of the determination of criminal responsibility. By prohibiting testimony in terms of the ultimate question of productivity we sought to focus on the need for testimony in depth concerning the nature, extent, and manifestations of the defendant's disability. The purpose was to give the jury an adequate basis for deciding whether the disability was such that it would be unjust to condemn the defendant for his conduct.

In practice, however, under *Durham* and its progeny psychiatrists have continued to make moral and legal judgments beyond the proper scope of their professional expertise. Even after *Washington,* the District Court continues to commit defendants to the public mental hospital for examination under a standard order that asks for a conclusion on productivity. And the doctors who perform most of the examinations have shown little reluctance to answer that an illness was present but the act was not its product. The testimony takes a form which indicates that the psychiatrists are in fact making a moral judgment, that they are finding an illness which in their view is not *sufficiently* serious or *sufficiently* related to the act to warrant acquittal. And that, of course, is precisely the judgment that we have entrusted not to the experts but to the jury.

Moreover, the productivity requirement tends to focus the attention of expert witnesses and the jury on extraneous and inappropriate issues, and to divert them from the core of the question of responsibility. *Durham* suggested that the government could establish criminal responsibility either by proving freedom from illness or by proving that the illness did not cause the act. And one way to prove that the illness did not cause the act is to prove that the defendant would have done it anyway. *Carter* even more explicitly than *Durham* invited the government to establish responsibility by proving that the defendant would have committed the act even if he had not been ill. *Carter* stated that productivity amounted to causation of the "but for" variety: an act is the product of mental disease if "the accused would not have committed the act he did commit if he had not been diseased as he was." This approach invited experts and juries to speculate about the defendant's character, and convict him on the ground that he would have been "bad" if he had not been sick.

The abuses of the productivity inquiry are strikingly illustrated by the record in this case. Since the expert witnesses agreed that appellant suffered from a substantial disorder, his conviction would seem to depend on the jury's resolution of the question of productivity. The government's two expert witnesses both found mental illness without productivity. The testimony of these two witnesses is open to at least two interpretations. It may be that they regarded appellant's illness as highly specific in its operation: that its only effect on appellant's behavior was to produce an occasional reflex-like explosive reaction following instantly on the heels of the triggering event rather than an hour or two later; that the illness could have no relation to behavior of the type that resulted in appellant's prosecution. Putting aside the conclusory parts of their testimony, the balance of their testimony so understood could support a jury finding of criminal responsibility.

But it is not clear whether the conflict among the experts related to the scope of the illness or to its legal significance. In other testimony the government witnesses seem to reject such a tightly compartmentalized view of appellant's mental and emotional processes. There is reason to suspect that their conclusion was based not on a professional judgment about the scope of the illness but rather on the view that the illness was irrelevant because appellant would have committed the crime in any event.

Their testimony suggests that they regarded appellant's act as a normal response for someone in his circumstances.

Clearly, firing a shotgun through a closed door is not a normal response for everyone who is hurt in a fight, though it may well be for some people. The criminal law assumes that there is a spectrum of "normality," and that some "normal" people commit crimes while others do not. We cannot allow either the experts or the jury to speculate about where on that spectrum the defendant would belong if he were not mentally ill. That sort of speculation is especially pernicious because it is likely to discriminate systematically against inner-city slum residents like appellant, since violent unlawful behavior is more common in the slums than in middle-class neighborhoods. To regard behavior as the product of illness in the suburbs but "normal" in the slums is to establish an odious double standard of morality and responsibility.

The insanity defense is based on the premise that it is unjust to convict a man for behavior he could not control. There is a high incidence of mental illness in inner-city slum areas, and we are bound to give it the same significance in dealing with their residents as we do in dealing with other people. If appellant's behavior controls were substantially impaired by mental illness, he should not be held responsible on the ground that it is "normal" for those in his environment to behave that way, or even because the examining psychiatrist believed that "under the same circumstances I would want to get even with somebody who broke my jaw."

. . . The effort to preserve the jury's function from encroachments by the experts must begin with a clear understanding of what that function is. In determining the responsibility issue, a jury has two important tasks:

> In the first place it measures the extent to which the defendant's mental and emotional processes and behavior controls were impaired at the time of the unlawful act. The answer to that question is elusive, but no more so than many other facts that a jury must find beyond a reasonable doubt in a criminal trial.

The second function is to evaluate that impairment in light of community standards of blameworthiness, to determine whether the defendant's impairment makes it unjust to hold him responsible. The jury's unique qualification for making that determination justifies our unusual deference to the jury's resolution of the issue of responsibility.[5]

Nothing in the Court's opinion today suggests a departure from our long-standing view that the second of these two functions—the evaluation of the defendant's impairment in light of community standards of blameworthiness—is the very essence of the jury's role.

Against this background it is clear that *Durham* focused the jury's attention on the wrong question—on the relationship between the act and the impairment rather than on the blameworthiness of the defendant's action measured by prevailing community standards. If the ALI test is indeed an improvement, it is not because it focuses attention on the *right* question, but only because it makes the *wrong* question so obscure that jurors may abandon the effort to answer it literally.

Instead of asking the jury whether the act was caused by the impairment, our new test asks the jury to wrestle with such unfamiliar, if not incomprehensible, concepts as the capacity to appreciate the wrongfulness of one's action, and capacity to conform one's conduct to the requirements of law. The best hope for our new test is that jurors will regularly conclude that no one—including the experts—can provide a meaningful answer to the questions posed by the ALI test. And in their search for some semblance of an intelligible standard, they may be forced to consider whether it would be just to hold the defendant responsible for his action. By that indirect approach our new test may lead juries to disregard (or at least depreciate) the conclusory testimony of the experts, and to make the "intertwining moral, legal, and medical judgments" on which the resolution of the responsibility question properly depends. The Court's own opinion hints at this approach. . . .

The Court's approach may very well succeed and encourage

jurors to look behind the testimony and recommendations of the experts. But, as I have tried to demonstrate above, there is also a significant possibility that our new test will leave the power of the experts intact—or even make possible an enlargement of their influence. In my opinion, an instruction that tells the jurors candidly what their function is, is the instruction most likely to encourage the jurors to resist encroachments on that function. . . .

Our instruction to the jury should provide that a defendant is not responsible *if at the time of his unlawful conduct his mental or emotional processes or behavior controls were impaired to such an extent that he cannot justly be held responsible for his act.* This test would ask the psychiatrist a single question: what is the nature of the impairment of the defendant's mental and emotional processes and behavior controls? It should leave for the jury the question whether the impairment is sufficient to relieve the defendant of responsibility for the particular act charged.

The purpose of this proposed instruction is to focus the jury's attention on the legal and moral aspects of criminal responsibility, and to make clear why the determination of responsibility is entrusted to the jury and not the expert witnesses. That, plainly, is not to say that the jury should be cast adrift to acquit or convict the defendant according to caprice. The jury would not be instructed to find a defendant responsible if that seems just, and to find him not responsible if that seems just. On the contrary, the instruction would incorporate the very requirements—impairment of mental or emotional processes and behavior controls—that *McDonald* established as prerequisites of the responsibility defense.

The proposed instruction has the additional advantage of avoiding any explicit reference to "mental disease" or "abnormal condition of the mind." As used in our prior tests, these terms were never intended to exclude disabilities that originate in diseases of the body, but simply reflect the fact that the defense of non-responsibility has traditionally been associated with mental illness, or in the language of an earlier day, "insanity."

I would adopt an instruction based on the language of

McDonald, which seems to me more comprehensible than the language of the ALI test. The capacity to appreciate the wrongfulness of conduct and capacity to conform conduct to the requirements of the law are, I fear, concepts with little meaning to experts or to jurors. But for the present purpose, the critical aspect of the proposed jury instruction is not the use of the *McDonald* terminology or the omission of any reference to an "abnormal condition of the mind." If the Court is convinced that the terminology of the ALI test would illuminate the jury's inquiry, or that the terms "mental disease" or "abnormal condition of the mind" should, for whatever reason, be retained, it is still possible to draft an instruction that clearly describes the jury's role in deciding when the defendant's incapacity is sufficient to warrant exculpation. In fact, a minority of the ALI draftsmen (along with Professor Wechsler, the reporter of the Model Penal Code) proposed a test providing that a person

> is not responsible for criminal conduct if at the time of such conduct as a result of mental disease or defect his capacity either to appreciate the criminality of his conduct or to conform his conduct to the requirements of law is *so substantially impaired that he cannot justly be held responsible.*

By contrast, the majority ALI test, now adopted by his Court, provides that·a person

> is not responsible for criminal conduct if at the time of such conduct as a result of mental disease or defect he lack substantial capacity either to appreciate the criminality of his conduct or to conform his conduct to the requirements of law.

The difference between the two approaches does not pertain to the type of showing a defendant must make. Both require the defendant to demonstrate a particular form of incapacity. The approaches diverge in establishing a standard to determine when the incapacity is sufficient to exculpate the

defendant. Under the ALI majority view, the jury must acquit
if the defendant's capacity is *substantially* impaired. The ALI
minority would require acquittal where the defendant's
capacity is *so substantially impaired that he cannot justly be held
responsible.*

The ALI ultimately rejected the minority approach because
"[s]ome members of the Council deemed it unwise to present
questions of justice to the jury, preferring a submission that *in
form, at least,* confines the inquiry to fact."[6] The Court apparently shares this view, and rejects an instruction "overtly cast in
terms of 'justice' " on the grounds that such an instruction
"cannot feasibly be restricted to the ambit of what may properly be taken into account but will splash with unconfinable
and malign consequences." That argument seems to present
two separate justifications for pretending that the inquiry is
confined to fact.

First, the argument apparently reflects a concern that adoption of the "justice" approach would permit the introduction at
trial of extraneous information. But under the approach urged
by a minority of the ALI Council, a defendant must still demonstrate that proferred evidence is relevant to an impairment
of capacity. The test does not provide him with a license to
introduce evidence merely for the purpose of engendering
sympathy for him in the jury. Adoption of the "justice" approach would still leave standing all of the traditional obstacles
to the introduction of irrelevant evidence.

The Court's second ground of objection is apparently that
an instruction cast in terms of justice would permit the jury to
convict or acquit without regard to legal standard. The Court
points out, for example, that

> [i]t is one thing . . . to tolerate and even welcome the jury's
> sense of equity as a force that affects its application of
> instructions which state the legal rules that crystallize the
> requirements of justice as determined by the lawmakers of
> the community. It is quite another to set the jury at large,
> without such crystallization, to evolve its own legal rules
> and standards of justice.

I take it that in the Court's view the majority version of the ALI test offers the jury "legal rules that crystallize the requirements of justice as determined by the lawmakers of the community," and that the minority version sets the jury adrift without such crystallized rules. What, then, are these crystallized rules? I pointed out above that while the minority version asks the jury to measure the impairment in terms of its own sense of justice, the majority version requires acquittal if the incapacity is *substantial,* and requires conviction if the incapacity is *insubstantial.* Can we seriously maintain that the majority ALI instruction is preferable because its determination that the impairment must be "substantial" reflects a crystallization of the requirements of justice by the lawmakers of the community? Naturally, we would all prefer a rule that could, as a matter of law, draw a bright line between responsible and nonresponsible defendants. But the ALI test adopted by this Court is plainly not such a rule. It offers the jury no real help in making the "intertwining moral, legal, and medical judgments" that all of us expect. In fact, because it describes the question as one of fact it may lull the jury into the mistaken assumption that the question of responsibility can best be resolved by experts, leaving the jury at the mercy of the witness who asserts most persuasively that, in his expert judgment, the defendant's capacity was or was not *substantially* impaired.

It is not at all clear that the approach I have suggested— whether based on the terminology of the ALI test or *McDonald*—would finally bar encroachments on the jury's function. Nevertheless, this approach—unlike the majority ALI test adopted by the Court—comes directly to grips with the problem of expert domination in a manner that is at least responsive to our experience under *Durham.* The majority ALI test merely reshuffles and obfuscates the *Durham* components; it does nothing to sort out for the jury the difference between its function and the function of the expert witnesses. Our instruction should make clear that in order to convict a defendant the jury must first determine, on the basis of expert opinion and the factual background disclosed by the experts, the extent to which the defendant's mental and emotional processes and behavior controls were impaired, and then find, on the basis of community moral standards, that the degree of impairment was sufficiently slight that the defendant can fairly be blamed and held responsible for his act like any other person.

To expand the scope of the inquiry in this way would not invite a significant increase in the number of acquittals. It would, however, encourage greater commitment to the effort to understand how each criminal defendant came to act as he did. Even if juries were consistently to set the standard of responsibility so low that virtually every defendant would meet it, they would still have to confront the causes of criminal conduct in a way that might teach us all something about human behavior. And they would be giving defendants the kind of careful, individual study that should precede any decision as consequential as the imposition of moral condemnation on another human being.

In a distressing number of recent cases this Court has been asked to consider questions unrelated to the substantive test of responsibility, but which have, as a practical matter, far greater impact on the operation of the defense than the language of the rule. . . . If our paramount goal is an improvement of the process of adjudication of the responsibility issue, our attention should be focused on these questions rather than on the ultimate definition of the test. Obviously, these questions cannot all be resolved by one opinion. But the Court's approach to the disposition of this case offers some indication of the manner in which these questions will be handled in the future.

The one consistent note in the Court's analysis of our experience under *Durham* is the objection to domination by the experts accomplished through the productivity requirement. We attempted to deal with that problem in *Washington v. United States* by barring conclusory, expert testimony on the issue of productivity. Virtually all of the expert witnesses at Brawner's trial agreed that he was suffering from an abnormal condition of the mind. The issue in dispute was productivity—the ultimate issue for the jury. And the transcript is riddled with conclusory, expert testimony on that issue. It is hard to imag-

ine a case which could make a stronger appeal for enforcement of the *Washington* rule. . . .

I suggested above that the abandonment of the term "product" may have some beneficial effect in reducing the mystique
that surrounds the causality question in this jurisdiction. But I
also noted that the Court has made available a new handle for
conclusory testimony on the issue of causality—"result"—and
at the same time it has lifted the ban on conclusory testimony
on this issue. The transcript of Brawner's trial offers a glimpse
of what we can expect from responsibility trials under the ALI
test. The Court's unwillingness to reverse Brawner's conviction
on this ground makes clear that this Court and the trial courts
no longer have any weapons to combat the problem of
conclusory testimony and the resulting domination by experts.

Since 1895 the federal courts have taken the position that if
the defendant introduces "some evidence" of insanity, the issue will be submitted to the jury and the government will bear
the burden of proving responsibility beyond a reasonable
doubt.[7] Yet as the responsibility defense has developed under
our case law, it has become increasingly clear that the defendant carries an overwhelming practical burden which is not
acknowledged in the traditional rule. As a practical matter, the
defendant often has very great difficulty obtaining adequate
expert assistance to gather the information necessary for the
presentation of a significant defense. If he can obtain such
information, his defense will often prove vulnerable to attack
unrelated to the real merit of his responsibility claim. And
even if the attack is very weak the defendant will rarely be
entitled to a directed verdict.

With limited access to expert psychiatric assistance, indigent
defendants normally rely on the government to provide an
adequate psychiatric examination at the hospital to which the
defendant is committed for observation. In a large number of
cases the government's experts are called to testify on behalf of
the defense, and their testimony has often proved inadequate.
In one recent case, for example, the trial court concluded that
the testimony of a government expert testifying for the defense was completely unacceptable under the principles of

Washington v. United States, and he struck the testimony as inadmissible. Yet the trial court refused to grant the defendant's motion for a mistrial or a new mental examination by experts capable of explaining their findings to a court. And this Court affirmed that ruling.[8] If an indigent defendant relies on the government for assistance in preparing his case and if there is no remedy when the government's assistance is legally inadequate, it will be little consolation to the defendant that the government still carries the burden of persuasion on that issue.

The practical burden on the defendant is greatly enhanced by the ease with which defense testimony can often be torn to pieces on cross-examination. Where a psychiatrist testifying for the government asserts that the defendant did not suffer from any abnormal condition which could impair his mental processes or behavior controls, defense counsel must have considerable expertise in psychiatry to pick out the weak points in the analysis. . . . Even where the defendant has obvious symptoms of mental disorder, defense counsel is frequently helpless to rebut the suggestion by government psychiatrists that the defendant is malingering. If he produces testimony from a private psychiatrist that the defendant is not a malingerer, he is almost sure to find that the government and its expert witnesses will disparage that testimony on the grounds that it was based on an insufficient period of observation. . . .

The defendant might be able to cope with these obstacles to the successful use of the defense if he were willing to set aside jury verdicts unsupported by the evidence. In fact, we have been extremely reluctant to overturn a jury verdict even in the face of substantial evidence that the defendant's act was the product of a condition which impaired his mental or emotional processes and behavior controls. If the burden of proof does rest on the government, then acquittal should be required not only when non-responsibility is proved, but also when there is a reasonable doubt about responsibility.

This Court's search for a new set of words to define the elusive concept of responsibility has a distinctly archaic quality. The arguments for and against the *Durham* wording, the wording of the majority and minority versions of the ALI test, and the wording of *McDonald* were clearly articulated many years ago. What should by now be clear is that the problems of the responsibility defense cannot be resolved by adopting for the standard of the jury instruction any new formulation of words. The practical operation of the defense is primarily controlled by other factors, including the quality of counsel, the attitude of the trial judge, the ability of the expert witnesses, and the adequacy of the pretrial mental examination. If the adoption of the ALI test produces some improvement in the quality of adjudication of the responsibility issue, that, of course, is all to the good. But we cannot allow our search for the perfect choice of words to deflect our attention from the far more important practical questions. For it is on those questions that the rationality and fairness of the responsibility defense will ultimately turn.

5

Reprise: United States v. Byers[1]

Although *Brawner* marked the end of the *Durham* experiment, it did not terminate our court's efforts to implement the insanity defense. In recent years the law relating to mental health and mentally ill offenders has become an integral part of legal decisions and scholarship.[2] The Supreme Court, in the criminal justice arena, has considered the constitutional standards for admissibility of psychiatric testimony,[3] standards for initiating commitment and continuing hospitalization of defendants acquitted as mentally nonresponsible,[4] psychiatric expert testimony on dangerousness at capital penalty hearings,[5] and defendants' due process rights to psychiatric assistance if insanity will be a significant factor in the trial.[6]

A recent comprehensive exploration of the entire area of criminal responsibility was undertaken by the American Bar Association in formulating its Criminal Justice Mental Health Standards.[7] These standards have no official effect, but they will be the most important reference point for courts and legislatures that examine the issues in the future.

The ABA recommends narrowing the insanity defense to read: "A person is not responsible for criminal conduct if, at the time of such conduct, and as a result of mental disease or defect, that person was unable to appreciate the wrongfulness of such conduct." This is, essentially, the "cognitive" half of the old American Law Institute test we adopted in *Brawner*. It leaves out the "volitional" half of the test, which turns on the accused's ability to control his actions, even if he "knows what he's doing."

71

The standards endorse placing the burden of pleading insanity and introducing evidence to that effect on the defendant, but only place the burden of proof or persuasion (by a low, "preponderance of the evidence" standard) on the defendant where the old, broader insanity defense remains in effect. If the new, narrower "cognitive test" is in force, the burden should be on the prosecution to prove responsibility "beyond a reasonable doubt," as with all other elements of the crime.[8]

The ABA standards clearly endorse the view that experts leave ultimate issues to the trier of fact. Experts "should not express or be permitted to express an opinion on any question requiring a conclusion of law or a moral or social value judgment properly reserved to the court or jury." This position was also adopted for federal courts in the Comprehensive Crime Control Act of 1984. A problem remains, of course—defendants and judges often demand just such conclusions. One experienced expert witness has written that in six hundred trials in which he has testified, he was always asked for his conclusion on the ultimate issue.[9]

The ABA standards do authorize court-ordered evaluation of a defendant by the prosecution's expert where the defendant has claimed nonresponsibility, but only where the defendant intends to rely on expert evidence. The standards also set out stringent requirements for responsibility evaluations and qualifications for an evaluator. They require him to inform the defendant of the purpose and nature of the evaluation, the potential uses of the information obtained, and the consequences of refusal to cooperate—in essence a special *Miranda* warning for defendants undergoing psychiatric examination. They also require prosecutor-initiated evaluations to be audiotaped and if possible videotaped, and require the presence of counsel in certain circumstances.[10] These same protections, reflecting an appropriate sensitivity to the Fifth and Sixth Amendments, are contained in the Uniform Law Commissioners' Model Insanity Defense and Post-Trial Disposition Act, which was approved by the National Conference of Commissioners on Uniform State Laws in 1984.

That same year Congress enacted the Comprehensive Crime Control Act of 1984. That bill defined insanity legislatively for the first time, as an "affirmative defense" which can be raised by the defendant, who then bears the burden of proving that he was insane by "clear and convincing evidence."[11] This means that in federal insanity defense cases it is the responsibility of the defendant to submit evidence on his insanity, and if he fails to convince the jury, he loses. Previously, federal prosecutors had the burden; once the question of the defendant's sanity was raised it was the prosecutor's responsibility to submit evidence and convince the jury beyond a reasonable doubt that the defendant was not insane.[12] In cases tried under state laws (by far the majority of cases), thirty-eight states already put the burden on the defendant— but thirty-six of these require only that he meet a modest "preponderance of the evidence" standard. That is, the jury need only find that it is more likely than not that the defendant was insane, in order to find him NGRI.[13]

The newly enacted definition of insanity for federal criminal trials is that the defendant "as a result of a severe mental disease or defect, was unable to appreciate the nature and quality or the wrongfulness of his acts." It is too soon to tell whether this new form, and more important, the shift of the burden of proof, will make any difference either in the operation of the insanity defense or in public perceptions about it.[14]

Videotaping, at written request, was also authorized. And in another section of the new law, rule 704 of the Federal Rules of Evidence was amended to provide: "No expert witness testifying with respect to the mental state or condition of a defendant in a criminal case may state an opinion or inference as to whether the defendant did or did not have the mental state or condition constituting an element of the crime charged or of a defense thereto. Such ultimate issues are matters for the trier of fact alone." I concur. But the controversy is likely to continue.[15]

Although I have serious concerns about a solely cognitive test for nonresponsibility, I am firmly convinced that the words are less important than the availability at trial of the relevant information about the defendant's mental condition. No set of words can assure that this will happen in the real world. Procedural requirements are designed precisely for that purpose. This is the approach adopted in the ABA standards and the Uniform Law Commissioners' model law, both of which reflect requirements similar to the recommendations I set out in *U.S. v. Byers*, for applying Fifth and Sixth Amendment rights in the situation of the defendant pleading nonresponsibility.

BACKGROUND   Billy Byers admitted that he had killed his former girlfriend. In fact, after the shotgun shooting, he had called the police himself and told them he did it. He pled not guilty by reason of insanity. After a comprehensive psychiatric examination at St. Elizabeths found that he "probably lacked substantial capacity to appreciate the wrongfulness of his conduct," the government decided to seek a second opinion. Over defense objections, the court agreed to a new exam, conducted in Springfield, Missouri, at the Department of Justice's medical center for federal prisoners.

That examination came to a conclusion more to the liking of the prosecution, which then took Byers to trial. He was found guilty. Our court heard the case on appeal, and in a plurality decision (where there was no clear majority for any one opinion, but there was a majority for the result) affirmed the conviction. I dissented, for the following reasons.

*   *   *

. . . In this custodial environment one thousand miles from home, Billy Byers spent eight weeks under the probing supervision of government psychiatrists. From those eight weeks there emerged one brief, ambiguous statement from one interview which, when presented at trial, proved "devastating" to Byers' defense. One psychiatrist testified that Byers had told him that the crux of his insanity defense was a *post hoc* rationalization invented by Byers' estranged wife and communicated to him after the homicide. . . .

No recording of the interview was made. No third party witnessed the admission. The doctor's notes of the session were destroyed when he dictated his report to the court one week later. This report, . . . contains no reference to Byers' alleged admission. Nor was this admission included in the staff evaluation report. Nor did the doctor share his discovery with any of the other psychiatrists assigned to the evaluation. Rather, for nearly a year, the sole repository of this statement which would, in the words of the trial judge, "torpedo the [defendant] out of the water," was the memory of this one psychiatrist. . . .

This extraordinary background to a murder conviction vividly illustrates the grave potential for abuse that inheres in the court-ordered psychiatric examination. . . . The Fifth Amendment bars compulsory self-incrimination in "any criminal case." It is clear, and the plurality [those judges joining the court's opinion] agreed, that the privilege against self-incrimination has presumptive application in criminal cases where sanity is the only issue in dispute. It is clear as well that the values underlying the privileges against self-incrimination are uniquely threatened by the compelled psychiatric examination. The court conceded that the traditional rationales for excluding the compelled examination from the protections of the Fifth Amendment are mere "devices" and do not withstand analysis. Rather than rely upon such artifice, the plurality instead contrives a controversy. It assumes incorrectly that protection of the right requires sacrifice of important state interests. The plurality then denies the privilege in the name of "fundamental fairness." I cannot accept the plurality's needless balancing away of this essential privilege. . . .

The privilege against self-incrimination is not violated every time the government compels the criminal defendant to provide incriminating evidence. The Supreme Court has found that the defendant may be required to take part in a lineup, to speak for voice identification, to submit to a blood test, and to give handwriting exemplars. These practices were held not to violate the privilege because they secure "real" as opposed to "testimonial" or "communicative" evidence. The Fifth Amendment is only implicated when the state compels active, conscious communication from the defendant. . . .

The products of psychiatric examinations fall along the entire continuum from real to testimonial evidence. On one end of the spectrum are the clearly physical parts of the examination: x-rays; blood and urine tests; and electroencephalograms. Standardized psychological tests, which probe patterns of association, require vocal responses and more active cooperation from the individual examined. The interview portion of the examination at issue in the instant case falls squarely at the testimonial end of the spectrum.

A number of courts have analogized this interview portion to the physical part of the psychiatric examination. In this view, statements are elicited not for their substantive meaning, but rather to allow the psychiatrist to discern patterns of association and to divine subconscious significance. The defendant's words, it is argued, are mere symbols, communicating a wholly separate code of meaning. While some statements are used purely as diagnostic inputs, others are used to establish the truth of the matter asserted. When a statement is used in the latter fashion, it is clearly testimonial and within the scope of Fifth Amendment protection. In *Estelle v. Smith*, the Supreme Court drew this distinction between uses of statements made to psychiatrists. The Court held that "[t]he Fifth Amendment privilege, therefore, is directly involved here because the state used as evidence against respondent the *substance* of his disclosures during the pretrial psychiatric examination."[16]

The privilege is designed to prevent the state from delving into the private sanctum of the human mind. It "reflect[s] the concern of our society for the right of each individual to be let alone." Its foundation "is the respect a government—state or federal—must accord to the dignity and integrity of its citizens." . . .

The compelled psychiatric examination significantly intrudes into the "private enclave" of the human personality. The very goal of the examination is to discover and to analyze the intricacies of the individual's thought processes. . . .

The privilege is also designed to ensure that the state has no incentive to use coercive tactics in extracting confessions. In *Miranda v. Arizona*,[17] the Supreme Court held that incommunicado police interrogations were "inherently coercive" and therefore violative of the Fifth Amendment privilege against self-incrimination. The Court emphasized that it was guarding against the risk of coercion that "is psychologically rather than physically oriented." It focused specifically on a number of police practices that contributed to the psychologically oppressive atmosphere: isolation of the accused, removal of the accused from familiar surroundings, and the interrogator's feigned friendliness and concern toward the accused. The Court stated: "An individual swept from familiar surroundings into police custody, surrounded by antagonistic forces, and subjected to . . . techniques of persuasion . . . cannot be otherwise than under compulsion to speak."

The compelled psychiatric examination is, at the very least, as "inherently coercive" as the custodial police interrogation proscribed in *Miranda*. Like the custodial interrogation, the court-ordered examination requires the defendant to submit to government inquiry directed toward issues that will be contested at trial. The examination often takes place over a period of weeks in the "unfamiliar surroundings" of a government institution far from the defendant's community. During this stay, the defendant is under the total control of his examiners. They control what he does, when he eats, when he sleeps, and whether he is to be given psychotropic drugs. A series of examinations, some with a single psychiatrist and others with the entire staff, are conducted entirely in secret.

The government psychiatrist who conducts the exam is a complex and threatening adversary. Some government psychiatrists may use trickery to gain information. Some may consciously deceive defendants about their true role. Some may slant their diagnoses to suit the prosecution's wishes. In the main, however, the problem is not bad faith. Rather, the difficulty is inherent in the relationship between the institutional psychiatrist and the defendant-patient.[18] . . .

Unlike the policeman, whose goals and methods engender wariness in the defendant, the government psychiatrist in the state hospital engenders trust. But this trust is unwarranted. The psychiatrist's aim is diagnosis, not therapy. His primary commitment is to his institution, not to his patient. Given these concerns, I must conclude that the court-ordered psychiatric examination poses a threat of coercion similar to that in the interrogation deemed unconstitutional in *Miranda*.[19]. . .

As Judge Frank wrote, "[t]o put an individual . . . in a position where his natural instincts and personal interests dictate that he should lie . . . and then punish him for lying is . . . intolerable."[20] The Fifth Amendment privilege allows a third option, silence, which avoids the "cruel trilemma" of self-accusation, contempt, or perjury. . . .

The compelled psychiatric examination forces the accused into precisely that situation which the privilege is designed to prevent. Most defendants will realize that what they say will significantly affect the likelihood of a successful insanity defense. The pressure on defendants to lie or to feign what they conceive of as insane symptoms will be intense, even for those whose insanity defenses are legitimate. Even the truly mentally ill person is likely to have some stereotyped conception of what distinguishes sanity from insanity and to manifest symptoms of the latter. The defendant cannot alleviate this pressure to dissemble by refusing to cooperate. Such a refusal is likely to precipitate sanctions which, in effect, forfeit the accused's insanity defense. Thus under current law, the defendant is faced with an analogous cruel trilemma: confessing responsibility, feigning insanity, or forfeiting the affirmative defense.*. . .

The privilege against self-incrimination also seeks to safeguard a fair balance of advantages in the criminal process. As Mr. Justice Stewart noted, the privilege is directed "to preserving the integrity of a judicial system in which even the guilty are not to be convicted unless the prosecution 'shoulder the entire load.' "[21] By requiring the state to produce independent evidence of guilt, the privilege discourages oppressive

---

* Such confessions, however, may be unreliable psychological self-assessments. It is a symptom of certain mental diseases that the individual guards against disclosing his disorder. *See Rollerson v. United States*, 343 F.2d 269, 274 (D.C. Cir. 1964); J. Katz, J. Goldstein, and A. Dershowitz, *Psychoanalysis, Psychiatry & Law* (1967), p. 599.

tactics and encourages the production of more trustworthy evidence. . . .

The compelled psychiatric examination threatens this structural integrity of our accusatorial system. The examination compels the defendant to be the prime source of the government's evidence. Because the psychiatrist is purportedly interpreting and relating the defendant's own statements, his testimony is likely to be accorded substantial weight. Given the availability of such evidence, the state is unlikely to seek out other, perhaps more probative evidence of the defendant's mental state. Thus the fair state-individual balance is subverted; the state has an incentive to ignore independent evidence and rely on the "cruel, simple expedient of compelling [testimony from the defendant's] . . . own mouth."[22] . . .

The inquiry into whether a right exists is prior to and separate from consideration of the means of enforcing that right. If the right exists and the sole means of its enforcement conflicts with important state interests, then the court must resolve the difficult dilemma. In this case, however, safeguarding the right does not require any sacrifice of important state interests. Many intermediate safeguards are available which protect the values underlying the privilege against self-incrimination while still permitting the purportedly necessary compelled examination. Since I believe that the Fifth Amendment is applicable and can be safeguarded without prejudice to the state, I can see no reason why these protections should not apply. . . .

Rational accommodation of the Fifth Amendment values implicated here can begin with the recording of all psychiatric interviews.* The very presence of a tape would help ensure that overreaching does not take place. It would quiet our con-

---

* Judge Edwards would not mandate a full transcript or tape or video recording of the psychiatric examination. While he believes that a full and adequate record of the interview is required under the Fifth Amendment and the supervisory power, he would allow the district court in its discretion to determine in each case the appropriate method of obtaining that record. While he regards taping as one alternative method of assuring procedural fairness, he believes that, in some cases, taping may be inhibiting and not effective in deterring overreaching. It is his opinion that in many cases it would be adequate for a psychiatrist to maintain and produce complete notes of the interview.

cern that psychiatrists might manipulate or intimidate the defendant in an *in camera* interview. A complete record would also help inform the court's judgment regarding the voluntariness and reliability of the defendant's statement. Self-deprecatory statements are distrusted because of the possibility of coercion or dishonesty on the part of the interrogator. A recording of the examination would mitigate these causes for distrust. . . .

The government and one of the *amici* suggest that even this alternative safeguard may prove disruptive or "inhibiting" to the clinical interview. As I read the empirical evidence, however, it is decidedly mixed (as well as sparse). Indeed, there is a strong argument that, to the extent that recording frees the interviewer from constant note-taking, its net effect may be to improve the free flow of communication.[23] In addition, the defendant may well be less apprehensive about the examination if he knows that his lawyer will have an opportunity to monitor the fairness and accuracy of the interviewer. . . .

I dare to venture that a criminal defendant subject to a court-ordered clinical interview, knowing that none of what he says will be kept in confidence in any event, will be less likely to be "inhibited" by the presence of a recording device than a patient or client who fears an intrusion into an otherwise private and trusting relationship. A recent study notes that "[t]he wish to protect the sanctity of the therapeutic relationship is a major force opposing the use of [recording]."[24] No such relationship exists in the court-ordered examination. . . .

In my view, the defendant has a right to be alerted to the realities of this inherently deceptive situation, wherein "pressures which work to undermine the individual's will to resist" are not apparent. If we are going to compel a defendant to talk to a professional who may testify against him at trial, we must, at the very least, inform him of that fact. . . .

Mental health professional organizations believe that there is an ethical obligation to inform a defendant in advance of the interviewer's conflictual roles and of the absence of confidentiality. In view of the Fifth Amendment's concern for voluntariness, I believe that there is a constitutional obligation as well. . . .

I believe that when a court considers denying the privilege in a situation where it would otherwise apply, it must acknowledge that the source of the limitation is not the Fifth Amendment itself. Rather, the court must admit that it is weighing an important individual right against a state interest—not rooted in the privilege—that is incompatible with the assertion of that right. In striking that balance, the court must be "ever mindful of its critical role as the protector of the citizen." The court must also make certain that the government interest is truly fundamental and that its accommodation is irreconcilable with meaningful exercise of the right. While I firmly believe that no such balancing test needed to be conducted in this case, I feel that the balancing test that the plurality did conduct failed to articulate and consider the serious interests at stake.

The plurality denies application of the privilege on the ground that refusal to undergo the examination would deprive the government of necessary information. The safeguards described above, however, allow the government to obtain what it needs while furthering the core purposes of the privilege. The plurality's dismissal of these safeguards as "exotic" reflects a crabbed construction of the privilege wholly at odds with the unambiguous pronouncements of the Supreme Court. As the Court has said of the privilege, "[t]his constitutional protection must not be interpreted in a hostile or niggardly spirit." In constructing a false dichotomy between a completely unmonitored psychiatric interrogation, on the one hand, and the absence of any compelled evaluation on the other, this court has manifestly failed to heed the Supreme Court's precepts.

The Sixth Amendment guarantees an accused the right to the assistance of counsel in connection with any "critical stage" of the proceedings against him. A "critical stage" is any . . . pretrial "confrontation" with the government . . . occurring at or after the start of "adversary judicial proceedings," . . . for which the assistance of counsel is necessary to prevent "potential prejudice to defendant's rights."

There is no requirement, however, that "confrontations" be themselves formal proceedings. Indeed, lineups and unwitting conversations with government informants are two quintessential examples of informal but nevertheless crucial "confrontations" between the accused and the state. . . .

A court-ordered clinical interview is clearly a "confrontation" in the sense that the accused is present and is the object of the inquiry. The plurality attempts to delineate far more restrictive criteria for a confrontation, and then exclude the psychiatric examination from Sixth Amendment protections for failing to meet those criteria.

Whatever doubts there once may have been on this point are, I believe, completely eliminated by *Estelle v. Smith.*[25] In *Smith,* the Court unequivocally held that the competency examination at issue "proved to be a 'critical stage' of the aggregate proceedings against respondent," in connection with which he was entitled to the assistance of counsel. This holding logically required the Court to find both (a) that the examination was a "confrontation" and (b) that the assistance of counsel was necessary to preserve the defendant's rights. The *Smith* decision's first finding clearly controls in this case. With regard to whether a clinical interview constitutes a "confrontation," I see no relevant distinction between defendants who plead insanity and those who do not. Indeed, although the "confrontation" finding was only implicit in the *Smith* decision's Sixth Amendment discussion, I find strikingly relevant to the instant issue the portion of *Smith's* Fifth Amendment discussion in which the Court spoke explicitly about the adversary nature of a clinical examination. The Court stated that, to the extent that an examination aids the prosecution, it is a species of "official interrogation" in which the role of the interviewer is "essentially like that of an agent of the State." It then concluded what should also be obvious in this case: the accused subject to such an examination "assuredly was 'faced with a phase of the adversary system' and was 'not in the presence of [a] perso[n] acting solely in his interest.' "

In the plurality view, the psychiatrist is not an adversary because at the time of the examination he has not yet decided to testify for the prosecution and is therefore neutral. Witnesses for the state, however, are often neutral at the time of their contact with the defendant and only later decide to aid the state. Indeed, police officers and prosecutors should be neutral when they first confront the defendant. Sides are taken on the basis of the information gathered in the interviews. It would clearly be senseless to withhold protection in situations likely to provide the substance of a prosecution witness's testimony and then confer protection once the information has been extracted and the neutral observer declares himself for the prosecution. . . .

I do not presume to assess the precise significance of the phenomena I have described, nor do I intend to cast a disparaging light on the general utility of clinical interviews and expert testimony in helping juries decide the enormously difficult issue of criminal responsibility. I do conclude, however, that the phenomena I have described may pose a serious risk to the reliability of expert testimony in a significant number of cases. I also think it obvious that the threats to a fair trial posed by these effects are of the same type as those identified in *United States v. Wade*.[26] If defense counsel had an accurate, complete record of the clinical interview he could, with the aid of his own experts, attempt to identify the distortions and interactions that may have affected the substance of the interviewer's reports and testimony. But such a complete, accurate record cannot, by virtue of the very effects I have described, be expected to be forthcoming from the interviewer. The accused, moreover, whatever his mental state, cannot be relied upon to fill in the gaps necessary for a complete and accurate assessment. It is therefore clear that—in the absence of safeguards that will afford to counsel the ability effectively to reconstruct at trial the events of the clinical interview—counsel may be unable to detect distortions or to cross-examine meaningfully the government's expert and rebut his conclusions. The accused is therefore deprived of his right to the assistance of counsel in connection with that interview. . . .

In this opinion I have focused on the constitutionally required need to have counsel *monitor* the court-ordered clinical interview. The essence of this role is to equip counsel with the ability "effectively to reconstruct at trial" the possible distortions and suggestive influences present in the interview. If the presence of counsel were the only means to achieve that goal, we would—in light of both *Smith* and other earlier cases—be left with a difficult dilemma. But fortunately there are alternative safeguards that are less disruptive (and perhaps even more effective) than the actual presence of counsel. A complete tape recording or videotape of the interview would provide counsel with exactly the sort of objective and precise record that, as I have previously discussed, is often a prerequisite to detection of distortions and to effective cross-examination or rebuttal at trial. As discussed above, such a taped record would facilitate constitutional aims without impairing the interview process itself.

In light of the above discussion, I would hold that, in the absence of waiver, the fruits of court-ordered clinical interviews conducted after the initiation of "adversary judicial proceedings" should not be admitted at trial unless counsel was either allowed to be present or was provided with a complete and accurate taped record of the interview. Because the testimony of the government experts was admitted in this case without such a record having been provided, Billy Byers was deprived of his right to the assistance of counsel under the Sixth Amendment. . . .

As courts have long recognized, a trial court's obligation to the defendant and to the judicial process cannot end with the signing of the commitment order. Having exercised its authority to send a defendant to a government-run, custodial mental hospital, the court must order procedures which protect the accused's rights and which assure reliable and verifiable results. In the absence of such procedures, evidence from the interview should not be admitted.

The abuses in Billy Byers' case are emblematic of this court's failure to exercise its supervisory authority over the administration of the insanity defense. We presently condone a process in which conviction can hinge on a recollection by a government psychiatrist with potentially conflicting loyalties of a secret interview conducted far in the past. . . .

Thirty years ago, with the opinion that I wrote for the court in *Durham v. United States*,[27] this circuit undertook to transform the role of the psychiatric expert from moral oracle to modern behavioral scientist. We acted largely in response to the psychiatrists' representations that they did not want to resolve ultimate questions of right and wrong, but wanted only to report their findings as scientific investigators. We challenged mental health professionals to disclose to us their intermediate observations and inferential processes. . . .

We were sorely disappointed. . . . Twelve years ago, in *United States v. Brawner*,[28] we unanimously abandoned the *Durham* formulation for a new test of insanity. At that time, I noted that the real problem with the insanity defense lay in the fairness of its administration, not in its verbal formulation. . . . And so too it must now be said of *Byers*. Byers' experience in the system of institutional psychiatry was a grotesque catalogue of what we have been decrying for three decades. The government psychiatrist offered a conclusory pronouncement of responsibility based on an unverifiable and ambiguous statement allegedly made by Byers during an *in camera* examination, the details of which are unknown. Once again, this court has failed to intervene in a system with such demonstrated capacity to abuse, distort, and degrade.

I am aware that today the insanity defense is not at all popular. Its purposes, its prevalence, and its consequences are poorly understood. We must be mindful, however, that the insanity defense is integral to the moral foundation of the criminal law. We cannot ignore our obligation to assure that the defense is administered fairly, that the inquiries conducted are thorough, that the data is scrutinized, and that the rights of those who assert the defense are guarded zealously. I fear that this court's failure to protect the rights of defendants permits the conversion of the insanity defense from a moral bulwark into a trap for the ignorant and unwary.

II

THE ROOTS OF CRIME

In the attempt to end the nightmare of violent crime, we must choose between two highly divergent strategies. We can lock more people up for a longer time—which would entail relaxing protections for criminal defendants as well as enormous outlays for police, courts and prisons. Or we can assure a more decent start in life and a real safety net for all who need it— which would entail some compromise in the values we place on individual responsibility and self-sufficiency as well as equally enormous costs.

Of course, the choice is rarely posed as either/or: it is more a matter of which strategy is emphasized, and this can become an inadvertent decision. Nevertheless, we do not make our choice easier by ignoring it. Tough talk and promises of a fast cure merely hide the choice from view. Unless we face the harsh realities of crime and confront the difficult alternatives for ending it, crime will grow, and the pressure to adopt ever harsher measures will increase. We will inexorably pick a strategy for fighting crime, although we may not realize it. In the process, we will also pick the kind of society we want. Our choices about the means are as important as our choices about the ends.

Speaking before the nation's police chiefs in 1981, President Reagan said, "The frightening reality is that for all the speeches by those of us in government—for all the surveys, studies, and blue ribbon panels—for all the fourteen-point programs and the declarations of war on crime—crime has continued its steady, upward climb and our citizens have grown more and more frustrated, frightened, and angry."[1] More recently, we are told that there has been a decrease in crime rates; some attribute this to locking up more career criminals for longer periods of time, others to a demographic shift that has reduced the number of young men in the population. But the assumption that a statistical softening of the crime rate demonstrates anything about the incidence of crime, much less the effectiveness of punitive enforcement, is unproved. In any event, there is little new here. These are the same issues we were debating in the 1960s.

A more hopeful sign is the growing public concern about family breakdown, teenage pregnancy, and the culture of poverty. President Reagan has blamed "misguided welfare programs . . . [that] ruptured the bonds holding poor families together. . . . But the waste of money pales before the sinful waste of human potential—the squandering of so many millions of hopes and dreams."[2] Others point out that the trends which some blame on Great Society programs actually were present before those programs were enacted.[3]

I don't think we know enough about either the causes of poverty or the impact of welfare programs to support a single cause/effect statement. It would be simply too convenient if the solution to poverty turned out to be eliminating public spending for the poor. I disagree profoundly with a philosophy that abdicates responsibility and concern for the plight of millions of people locked in a cycle of deprivation and despair. If government programs share the blame for a situation that encourages poverty, does not the government have a responsibility to remedy its error? Simply terminating programs would not, in the legal analogy, make the victim whole. As fellow human beings, we have an obligation to help those less fortunate. As fellow citizens, we recognize the mutual benefit of helping others to live productive and satisfying lives.

Clearly, current government programs have not solved the problems of poverty and family disintegration. Whether this is because they actually exacerbate the problem or whether—as I believe—they were imperfectly designed as well as inadequately funded, the answer is not to abolish them and let market forces operate. The vast majority of poor are elderly or women with children; and the upward trend in the poverty rate for children is truly frightening. If the current system doesn't work, for our own good as well as theirs, we must find ways to do better.

Even in an era of shrinking public dollars—especially at such a time—we must find the resources to continue to research the problem, to evaluate the programs we are supporting or cutting. Anything else is simply imprudent and irresponsible, in light of the billions of dollars and millions of lives at stake. If today's programs are no good, we must get rid of them and try something different. Yet in the 1980s the new reformers have sought relentlessly to cut back on efforts to examine the questions they raise about the effects of government spending. The only reason for not wanting to find out the truth is fear that the studies will show the need for more resources and more change.

Some argue that I am out of place in the hardheaded world of the 1980s. Today we are told that crime can be controlled only if those who violate society's norms, whatever the reason, are quickly apprehended and subjected to swift, certain, and severe punishment. This emphasis makes it more important that we retain, somewhere on our social agenda, a counterbalancing concern. What if the punitive approach does not work?

It is easy to concede the inevitability of social injustice and find the serenity to accept it. The far harder task is to feel its intolerability and seek the knowledge and strength to change it.

6

Avoiding Realities[1]

We are confronted today by a class of people being left behind
in an increasingly affluent society—the losers in a Hobbesian
universe, a constant war of all against all and each against the
other. We see them—defendants and victims—every day in
our criminal justice system. Our society ignores these facts only
at its peril. If we fail to acknowledge the reality of crime, if we
insist on viewing defendants as mere objects to be acted upon,
we will be doomed to a vicious circle of crime and repression
and more crime.

Most proposals for getting tough on crime mask the painful
facts and difficult choices our country must face before we can
meaningfully address the crime problem. We cannot frame
the issues—let alone resolve them—until we develop and consider all the relevant facts and competing considerations. First,
we must identify the precise kinds of crime that we mean to
attack. Second, we must seek to understand and confront the
realities underlying those crimes. Only then—with all the facts
before us—can we make an informed judgment about the various proposals. All of us must, of course, be prepared for a
conflict between reality and our most cherished assumptions.
As Kingman Brewster, former president of Yale University,
has said,

> There is great danger, though, that fascination with pun-
> ishment will seem to relieve us of the burden of all re-
> sponsibility for doing something about the conditions
> which fostered the crime. This is always the shortcoming

of the "law and order" sloganeers. If order were the sole purpose of law, then the police state would be just fine. But justice is the ultimate purpose of law. Therefore, the social and psychological roots of criminal conduct are at least as important, indeed more important, than the tactical response to crime once committed.[2]

Too often a false dichotomy is created between those who care about the rights of criminal defendants and those who care about victims of crime. Reality is complicated, not black or white. Most offenders and most victims share a common background, come from the same neighborhoods; where the defendant is devalued and the facts of his experience ignored, so also is the victim likely to be treated. In order to devise effective solutions to the problem, we must understand and address the problems that lead both to the criminal court. This does not require that we be blind to danger or allow criminals to prey upon us. It does require that we not succumb to comforting slogans.

*   *   *

Politicians and journalists speak rather generally about crime in America without specifying exactly what they mean. There are, in fact, diverse types of crime, each of which poses particular problems and requires particular remedies.

White-collar crime does not, by and large, threaten our physical safety or the sanctity of our homes. That dubious distinction belongs to violent street crime—the robberies, rapes, and other forms of violence that plague our daily life. Current proposals to keep violent offenders off the street will have little impact on the chieftains who direct mob activities from executive suites. Moreover, ending organized crime will not necessarily eradicate street crime. Although the mob provides at least part of the supply of drugs and weapons which helps street crime flourish, the demand for these items seems so great that if one source is cut off, another is likely to take its place. To understand the reasons for that demand, we must

look closely at the people who terrify city—and suburban—
dwellers across the country.

The causes of violent street crime are complex and, of course,
not completely understood. Nevertheless, only the blind or the
willful can deny the clear association of this kind of crime with
the culture of poverty and discrimination that is still tolerated
in every American city.

No intelligent effort to deal with street crime can ignore
these stark realities. It is in this respect that I differ most fundamentally with the approach of the current leadership. President Reagan, like many of his predecessors, seems to ignore
that virtually all the people who commit this kind of crime
come from the same culture of grinding oppression: "[I]t's
obvious . . . that deprivation and want don't necessarily increase crime. . . . The truth is that today's criminals, for the
most part, are not desperate people seeking bread for their
families. Crime is the way they've chosen to live."[3]

The President based his explanation on what he called "absolute truths"—namely, that "individuals are responsible for
their actions," and that "men are basically good but prone to
evil." Crime, the President said, is a problem of the human
heart: "Only our deep moral values—and strong social institutions—can hold back that jungle and restrain the darker
impulses of human nature." He also observed that institutions
like the family, the neighborhood, the church, and the school
play an important role in providing young people with moral
guidance and support.

But the President does not seem to account for a fundamental reality: some segments of our society have no "strong social
institutions" upon which to rely. I cannot improve on the comments of *Chicago Sun-Times* columnist Mike Royko on the President's speech:

> You take some teen-ager in an affluent suburb. He has
> just returned from playing tennis or football after
> school. . . . He walks into a seven- or eight-room house in
> which he has his own room, equipped with a stereo and

maybe his own TV set, and a closet full of nice clothes. . . .

. . . [A]fter having dinner with his father, who has a well-paying job, and his mother, who might work but might also be home every day, he goes in his room, looks in the mirror and asks himself:

"What is in my heart? Do I want to join a gang and go out and mug somebody on the street and pursue a life of violence and crime? Or do I want to go to college and become a CPA?"

Goodness, thank goodness, usually prevails over evil. So the lad does not go out and join [a street gang].

. . . [A] similar decision is made by a youth in one of the city's many slum areas. His home is a dismal flat or a congested housing project. Income is his mother's welfare check. School is a place where the most important thing you learn is not to turn your back on strangers. Security and social life are the other kids on the street—the gang. . . .

So he looks in the cracked mirror and asks: "What is in my heart? Do I want to become a CPA, or a physician, or a lawyer? Do I want to someday make $50,000 or more a year? Do I want to go to Northwestern or Georgetown or maybe Yale? Hell no. I *want* to pursue the life of crime and violence. I *want* to go out and mug somebody. I *want* to wind up doing 10 to 20 in [prison] so I can be with my friends. I want this because it is in my heart and has been there since I was born."[4]

I do not suggest, of course, that poverty or racism equals crime. As a matter of fact, only a small percentage of those who endure these social evils violate the law. What is amazing is that so many deprived Americans accept their lot without striking out. It seems fair to say that violent crime among these people would be much more prevalent but for influences such as religion, welfare, and perhaps alcohol. I am astonished by those who point to the docile deprived and say, "Their conditions do not force them to break the law; why should those conditions force others to?" Society should be as alarmed by the silent misery of those who accept their plight as it is by the violence of those who do not. We should try to understand and celebrate whatever it is that enables some to overcome the appalling odds, not castigate others for failing to accomplish the nearly impossible. In any event, it is essential to acknowledge who the offenders are and where they come from.

I believe that there are two ways of approaching the problem of street crime. One consists of short-term programs for curbing its rise. These programs generally propose changes in legal procedures and moderate expenditures on the criminal justice system. The long-term approach, on the other hand, requires a major and fundamental commitment to a more permanent solution.

The short-term approach reflects an understandable desire for immediate, concrete results. Superficially, this approach can be justified as buying time needed to look for more humane and enduring solutions. Although the need is pressing, we must not be tempted to embrace measures whose superficial allure obscures their demonstrated ineffectiveness. Adopting these measures may result in compromising important constitutional values to no avail and—because of a failure to recognize the limits of the measures—in dangerously postponing the search for meaningful and lasting approaches.

The 1981 report of the Attorney General's Task Force on Violent Crime[5] typifies the short-term approach. The proposals primarily are based on the theory that an increased certainty of punishment will deter criminals. The report, however, fails to achieve its goals because the principal recommendations—modifying legal procedures and spending some money on prisons—will have little effect on the certainty of punishment.

Today, the criminal justice system prosecutes, convicts, and incarcerates a larger proportion of those arrested for felonies than it did fifty years ago. Yet crime continues. Clearly, the uncertainty about punishment derives from the great unlikelihood of arrest. As the task force itself acknowledged, "[o]nly a small fraction of all crimes known to the police are solved by an arrest." Justice Department studies indicate that only about

21 percent of crimes are "cleared" through arrest or other means.[6] We cannot realistically expect to reduce crime by changing the machinery with which we process that small group of offenders.

For example, modifying the exclusionary rule—the doctrine that prohibits the use of illegally obtained evidence—may or may not be advisable for symbolic or other reasons. I take no position on the constitutional issues that such a modification would raise. Nevertheless, we defraud ourselves if we think we can meaningfully affect crime by changing a rule that, according to the General Accounting Office, makes a difference in little more than 1 percent of the cases.[7]

The task force also endorsed preventive detention—a rule that would allow judges to deny bail to dangerous defendants to prevent them from committing offenses while awaiting trial. This proposal is the kind that tries men's souls. It has enormous appeal: we are all familiar with horrendous instances of crimes committed by individuals out on bail. But preventive detention, which has now become law, will have serious costs.[8]

A policy of incarcerating individuals before they have been duly convicted raises basic questions about our dedication to the presumption of innocence. My experience—and all that I have read on this subject—convinces me that it is well-nigh impossible to predict dangerousness with any accuracy. Some studies have estimated that to be sure of jailing a single individual who would engage in violence while on bail, we would have to detain as many as four to ten people who would not. Before we incur the substantial financial and constitutional costs of preventive detention, we should at least consider less onerous measures. For example, one possibility worth exploring is to establish adequate supervision of individuals who are out on bail.

Ultimately, however, bail reform—like other changes in the criminal justice system—is not likely to affect the rate of violent crime significantly. Despite the celebrated horror stories, the fact is that relatively few defendants are arrested for serious crimes of violence while on bail. A recent major study of the problem found that although about 16 percent of those released on bail were rearrested before their trial date, only 2 percent were people who initially had been charged with violent crime and who were picked up during their pretrial period for either a property or a violent crime.[9]

The principal recommendation of the Attorney General's task force was to spend $2 billion on construction of prisons and jails. Governor James Thompson of Illinois, co-chair of the task force, said that this proposal is based on the panel's conclusion that " 'we have to lock up more violent offenders and we have to keep them locked up.' "[10] Unfortunately the facts are that the proposal would not accomplish that aim; even if it could, violent crime would not be significantly reduced; and the cost of a genuine commitment to an "incapacitation" policy would far exceed $2 billion.

Diana Gordon, president of the National Council on Crime and Delinquency, determined that the $2 billion which the task force proposed, at best, would reduce the current overcrowding by paying for some 38,000 new cells. Those cells would house less than two-thirds of the increase in the inmate population experienced in the past three years. More than half the states are now operating some prisons that have been declared unconstitutional.[11]

A Department of Justice study reported that the state prison population increased by 54 percent from 1972 to 1978.[12] The study predicted that the demand for space would continue to outstrip capacity. Some state prisons now house about twice their rated capacity.

The combined number of inmates in federal and state prisons has risen from 300,024 in 1977 to 463,866 in 1984, an increase of 55 percent in only seven years. By June of 1985, there was another increase of 26,000.[13]

Even if the necessary funds were spent to build new prisons, and even if every prison were filled with violent offenders, the rate of violent crime would barely diminish. A 1977 study in Ohio predicted that only about 4 percent of violent crime could be prevented by imposing mandatory sentences of five years on all persons convicted of felonies.[14] The same study demonstrated why tougher sentencing policies cannot be relied on to reduce crime: not quite 8 percent of the reported crimes of violence resulted in convictions and thus even reached the sentencing stage.

One alternative is to make the cost of violating the law so great—and the prospect of punishment so certain—that would-be offenders, whatever their circumstances, would not dare to commit crime. As I have suggested, however, the assurance of swift and certain punishment cannot be achieved merely by changing rules of procedure or by spending $2 billion on prisons. When one remembers who the offenders are, one sees how difficult it will be to deter them.

Thus, if we are to deter these people effectively, arrest must be made nearly certain and punishment frighteningly severe. Maurice Cullinane, former chief of police of the District of Columbia, who has never been accused of being "soft on crime," presided over a force with more policemen per capita than any other in the country. Moreover, he said that this statistic does not include the several thousand park, Capitol, and other federal police visible all over Washington. The chief told me that to achieve a real certainty of arrest, he would have to amass an enormous concentration of patrolmen in one particular area. He believes that most of his counterparts across the country would agree with him.

Only the presence of a policeman on virtually every block could create the possibility of keeping crime under control. Furthermore, as Cullinane said, crime suppressed in one neighborhood necessarily would burgeon in other, unguarded parts of the city. Of course, society could employ curfews, limit people's movements, and require identification. It could, in short, impose a regime akin to martial law.

If we succeed in apprehending most offenders, we must then be sure to keep them off the street long enough to neutralize the threat to our daily lives. This kind of incapacitation would not be cheap. In New York, for example, it has been estimated that a 264 percent increase in state imprisonment would be required to reduce serious crime by only about 10 percent. In New York alone this would cost about $3 billion just to build the necessary cells and another $1 billion a year to operate them.[15]

Aside from being extremely costly, a strategy based on increased incarceration is fundamentally cruel. Despite the efforts of the corrections profession, the nation's prisons continue to be dangerous and squalid. The homicide rate inside prisons is more than seven times greater than it is on the outside. The evidence consistently demonstrates that prison sentences are followed by higher rates of recidivism than are nonprison sentences.[16]

After a year and a half on the Commission for Accreditation for Corrections, I concluded that genuine prison reform would continue to elude us as long as the prisons remain invisible.[17] Corrections professionals labor mightily with little or no public support. As the report of the New Mexico Attorney General concluded after that state's bloody prison riot in 1981, "elected officials have turned their attention to the ugly problems of the penitentiary only when the institution has erupted in violence and destruction."[18] At least until the public is prepared to support fundamental changes in prison conditions, it is grossly inhumane for the attack on crime to rely on massive incarceration.

In short, it may be possible to deter some street criminals and to permanently lock up the undeterred. This path, however, should be chosen only after confronting the enormous financial and social costs it would require. Nor would such a program be a temporary expedient. Even as we put one generation of offenders behind bars, another will emerge from the hopeless subculture, ready to follow the model that their fathers and brothers have set. As time progressed, there would be no choice but to turn the screw tighter, to spend more money, to move closer to a police state.

The other basic path for attacking crime would consist of an effort to determine the causes of crime and a commitment to eradicating them. The fact that not enough is known about the sources of criminal behavior should only encourage further investigation.

Seeking answers will be costly and time-consuming. The price of changing the relevant conditions may prove more than society is willing to pay. If the roots of crime lie in the breakdown of the heretofore private preserves of family, church, or school, we may have to reconsider our traditional ideas about the role of the state. It is possible that crime can never be solved without countenancing substantial government intervention in private institutions.

Accepting the full implications of what we know about street crime might require us to provide every family with the means to create the kind of home all human beings need. It might lead us to afford the job opportunities that pose for some the only meaningful alternatives to violence. It might demand for all children a constructive education, a decent place to live, and proper pre- and postnatal nutrition. It might require proper day care or foster care for those children who suffer from inadequate family environments. More fundamentally, it might compel the eradication of racism and prejudice. These goals may be "utopian"—not only in aiming at more than our society can realistically provide, but also in the sense that they would require a society organized to assure everyone's material needs, raising serious concerns about the social and human consequences of a highly structured, controlled society.[19]

In sum, changing legal procedures or building more prisons simply will not work. If we really wish to do something about the problem, we must put polemics aside and choose between two basic paths. Both are costly; both might jeopardize important social values; and neither can assure success. No simple solutions are available.

7

United States v. Alexander and Murdock[1]

My interest in the roots of criminal behavior intensified during the years of the *Durham* experiment. As it became apparent that psychiatrists could not provide all the answers, I looked for other explanations.

The *McDonald* case in 1962 marked a transition in which our court tried to break through the confines of the medical model of behavior and enable juries to consider additional factors in weighing criminal responsibility. In that case we defined mental disease in legal terms as "any abnormal condition of the mind which substantially affects mental or emotional processes and substantially impairs behavior controls."[2]

Of course, this formulation proved to be no panacea. But it did encourage exploration of environmental factors beyond mental illness in the lives of people who committed criminal acts. Whether such factors should excuse the acts or not, I firmly believe that we must examine and, in time, understand them if we are to learn how to prevent crime.

Our court pursued this exploration through the cases that came before us. *Alexander and Murdock* provides an unusual wealth of detail that enables us to experience some of the reality that lies behind crime. It raises also the very troubling fact that there is no necessary relationship between culpability or non-culpability and our ability to provide effective treatment or modify behavior. What should the community do with an individual found not responsible, probably dangerous, but not amenable to mental health treatment? We can seek to avoid the issue by constraining the concept of non-responsibility, as the court did in this case. But in doing so we are really making an implicit choice—and avoiding our own responsibility.

BACKGROUND   On the evening of June 4, 1968, five men and a woman—all white—walked into a Washington, D.C., hamburger shop, stood by the take-out counter, and ordered some food. The men were United States Marine lieutenants in formal dress-white uniforms; the woman was a friend of one of them. They noticed three black men sitting at the other end of the counter; these were appellants Alexander and Murdock and Cornelius Frazier. (Actually, "Murdock" is the given name of the defendant, Murdock Benjamin; a mistake was made in the trial record, which it is now easier to perpetuate than to correct.)

During a dispute in the restaurant, both Alexander and Murdock drew guns on the other group; shots were fired that left two of the marines dead and another and the woman seriously wounded. At a joint trial by jury in February 1969, Alexander and Murdock each were found guilty of carrying a dangerous weapon and of four counts of assault with a dangerous weapon. Murdock, in addition, was guilty of two counts of second-degree murder. A separate hearing for Murdock on the issue of insanity was held in November 1969, at the close of which the jury returned a verdict of guilty on all counts. The defendants received sentences totaling five to twenty-three years for Alexander and twenty years to life for Murdock.

The defendants' conviction was upheld by our court. The facts of the case illustrate well the realities of a trial in which insanity is at issue, and the lives of the people involved.

According to the prosecution witnesses, Lieutenant Kramer realized that Alexander was staring at him, and he returned the stare. No words were exchanged between the two men, and Kramer soon turned and faced the counter. Murdock and Frazier left the shop, but Alexander stopped in the doorway. He tapped Kramer on the shoulder. When the marine turned around, Alexander poked his uniform nametag and said, "You want to come outside and talk about it more?" When Lieutenant Kramer replied, "Yes, I am ready to come out," Alexander added, "I am going to make you a Little Red Ridinghood." At this point, Lieutenant King stepped up beside Lieutenant Kramer and made a remark variously reported by the prosecution witnesses as "What you God-damn niggers want?"; "What do you want, you nigger?"; "What do you want, dirty nigger bastard?"; and "Get out of here, nigger."

Alexander abruptly drew a long-barreled .38 caliber revolver, cocked it, and pointed it at the group or directly into Lieutenant King's chest, saying, "I will show you what I want."

The marines possessed no weapons whatsoever. As they stood there, shocked at the sight of the gun, Murdock reentered the shop at Alexander's left and rear, and drew a short-barreled .38 caliber revolver. A series of shots suddenly rang out, and the marines and Miss Kelly fell or dived to the floor. None attempted to retaliate because they all were taking cover and trying to get out of the line of fire. Alexander and Murdock withdrew from the shop, but one of them stuck his arm back into the shop and attempted—unsuccessfully—to fire his weapon several times more.

Lieutenants King and Lesnick were mortally wounded in the fusillade; they died within minutes. Lieutenant Kramer was wounded in the head, but he remained conscious, as did Miss Kelly, who had been shot in the hip.

Alexander, Murdock, and Frazier fled to Alexander's automobile and drove off rapidly in the wrong direction on a one-way street. Alexander was driving, and Murdock fired three more shots from the window of the car, at the door of the hamburger shop and at people in the street. A nearby scout car raced after the fleeing vehicle and stopped it within a few blocks.

In their defense, Frazier and Murdock testified that the marines in the restaurant had been drunk and loud. Frazier said that they had obstructed his exit as he left. He walked around them and left the restaurant just ahead of Murdock, but when he looked back Murdock had gone back inside. He then heard shots and ran to Alexander's car.

Murdock said that when he realized Alexander had not followed him out of the restaurant, he returned, and as he entered he heard someone say, "Get out, you black bastards." He then saw a marine advancing toward him. Murdock called to Alexander to leave with him, and Alexander turned as if to go. Murdock then heard a "sound like all the feet in the place were moving," turned around, and saw Alexander's drawn gun. Murdock pulled his own gun, as a reflex, and testified that he "commenced firing about the time one of them was actually right up on me. . . . [M]aybe a foot away." He said that the other marines were advancing toward him fast, and he felt they were going to kill him. On cross-examination he admitted that he emptied his fully loaded revolver at the marine group in the restaurant, said that he didn't know if Alexander had fired, and admitted that he fired three shots from Alexander's gun from the window of the car as it was driven off.

The court of appeals affirmed the convictions (but over-turned Alexander's conviction on three of the four assault charges). While the court issued only a brief order without an opinion, my concerns led me to write a lengthy dissent.

* * *

At issue here are much more than technical rules of law devoid of any significance outside a courtroom or law school lecture hall. A racial epithet hurled at appellants by one of their victims touched off an explosion of violence and bloodshed, an explosion that reverberates the traumas of our entire society. We cannot rationally decry crime and brutality and racial animosity without at the same time struggling to enhance the fairness and integrity of the criminal justice system. That system has first-line responsibility for probing and coping with these complex problems.

The tragic events which gave rise to this appeal might possibly have been avoided by various means. Proponents of legislation for the effective control of firearms will find powerful ammunition here. But such measures can never reach the root causes of crime so long as we remain in ignorance of the mental agonies that produce bizarre and violent behavior. Criminal trials—and, above all, the responsibility defense—compel us to explore these problems, and thereby offer some slight hope that we will learn, in the course of deciding individual cases, something about the causes of crime. Not only the defendant but the criminal justice system as a whole has a vital interest in insuring that trials are conducted without significant error and in a manner that guarantees the ventilation of all the pertinent issues and information. We cannot afford to obscure the difficult questions for the sake of speed and efficiency in obtaining convictions, since efficiency of that order yields a specious economy. Appellate courts must scrutinize carefully the record of trial, and expose—where necessary with opinions as lengthy as this one—the difficulties that plague our efforts to improve the quality of the criminal justice system. . . .

The evidence offered by the Government is insufficient to disprove the hypothesis—strongly suggested by the testimony of all the witnesses—that Alexander was acting entirely on his own when he tapped Lieutenant Kramer on the shoulder and asked him to step outside, that it was entirely for his own protection that he drew his gun when Lieutenant King stepped forward, and that he had every intention of backing out of the restaurant and leaving. At that point Murdock reentered the restaurant, drew his own gun, and commenced firing. The Government's evidence is insufficient to prove that this was not a complete and horrifying surprise to Alexander. No evidence shows that Alexander even knew Murdock had a gun, much less expected him to fire it at insulting strangers. To refer to the Government's own theory, there is insufficient evidence of a "criminal venture." The Government does not suggest that [Alexander and Murdock] entered the restaurant intending to wait for Marines who had not yet arrived, and it would be sheer speculation for the jury to find that they hatched a plan of assault or murder after the Marines came in. . . .

Another argument—one that appealed to the trial judge below [the judge who tried the case in the original or lower court]—is that in some sense Alexander incited the behavior that resulted, since it was he who precipitated the confrontation with Lieutenant Kramer. The difficulty with this argument is that Alexander's "inciting" words and action were directed to the wrong person—to Lieutenant Kramer, not to Murdock, who was apparently already outside when Alexander's "inciting" began. . . .

Without [his] claim [of self-defense], the evidence that Alexander was guilty of at least one of the counts of assault with a dangerous weapon would indeed be overwhelming. [This claim], however, raises the possibility that some members of the jury allayed their doubts about Alexander's justification for drawing his gun by reminding themselves that they had been instructed that they could find him guilty of aiding and abetting Murdock's assaults. . . . Since the evidence should not, in my view, support a conviction on the theory that Alexander aided and abetted Murdock in the killing of Lieutenant King— much less on the theory that Alexander himself killed King— it is clear to me that the count charging murder in the second degree was improperly submitted. [Even though Alexander was acquitted on this count, its submission to the jury could have been a significant factor in the jury's mind as it was deliberating what to do.]

Alexander's able defense counsel, in turn, felt obliged to devote nearly twice as much to the murder counts as he did to Alexander's self-defense claim to assault. Finally, the major portion of the trial judge's instructions necessarily concerned the murder and manslaughter counts. . . . Since the evidence that Alexander was guilty of the offense of assault with a dangerous weapon was not overwhelming—because of the presence of the self-defense claim—the possibility that the verdict was reached as a result of a compromise is a real one. . . .

It is our responsibility to insure not only that Alexander is guilty, but also that his guilt is determined by a process which is conducive to a full and fair ventilation of the pertinent facts and issues. Even outstanding trial counsel, such as Alexander's, cannot provide his client with the best possible defense if he is compelled, through no fault of his own, to tilt at windmills. I am unable to say that the result of trial would inevitably have been the same if Alexander's counsel and the jury had been able to focus their attention on the questions genuinely in issue. I am unable to say that the claim of self-defense would not have been accepted if counsel and the jury had not been sidetracked by an improperly submitted count. Under these circumstances, I would conclude that the instruction on aiding and abetting was prejudicial error. . . .

Prior to trial, Murdock filed a notice of intent to rely on the insanity defense, as required by statute. Alexander moved for severance, partly on the ground that he would be prejudiced by Murdock's insanity defense. The court responded by bifurcating [holding separate trials on whether Murdock committed the act and on whether he could sustain an insanity defense] Murdock's trial, in order to permit the trial on the merits of both defendants to go forward promptly without severing the trial of Murdock from that of Alexander. Only after Murdock had been provisionally "convicted" at the first part of the bifurcated trial was he committed to St. Elizabeths Hospital for a mental examination.

Murdock's confinement in the hospital was unusually long, apparently because the facility was overcrowded. During that time, he was examined by various members of the hospital staff, and also by a private psychiatrist of his selection. Subsequently, he was examined at the jail by another private psychiatrist, appointed by the court at the request of the government. Nine months after the original trial, Murdock finally had the opportunity to submit his claim of mental disorder to a jury. The jury found that he was criminally responsible for the acts charged, and accordingly convicted him. . . .

At the first part of the trial, the jury found that Murdock had committed the acts that constitute second-degree murder. That is, they found he had killed two people unlawfully and with the state of mind known to the law as "malice." In reaching that conclusion, the jury had before them only the evidence concerning the objective circumstances of the crime, and not the psychiatric evidence bearing on Murdock's mental condition.

Murdock contends that the information subsequently presented by the expert witnesses at the insanity hearing was relevant not only to the insanity defense, but also to the issue of malice. Accordingly, after the experts had testified at the insanity hearing, Murdock asked for an instruction permitting the jury to reopen the question of malice. He proposed to tell the jury:

> [M]ental unsoundness, though insufficient to entitle the accused to an acquittal under the legal test of responsibility, may nevertheless be sufficient to prevent the accused from forming malice aforethought, and thus diminish the defendant's responsibility or reduce the grade of the offense. . . . If you find that the accused's mental condition resulted in a failure to formulate malice aforethought, you must find the accused guilty of only manslaughter.

The trial court rejected the proposed instruction, and this court today finds no error in that ruling. The majority relies primarily on prior decisions of this court, in which we rejected the doctrine of "diminished responsibility" in seemingly broad terms. In my view, however, there are several reasons why those precedents should not control the decision here.

It should go without saying that Murdock ought not to suffer for the inadequacy of the government psychologist's testimony. Apparently it does need saying, however, since he is made to suffer by this Court's conclusion that he can be tried and convicted without adequate expert assistance.[3] This case is only one among a great many which clearly demonstrate that the responsibility defense is nothing more than a public ritual, maintained to satisfy the public's need for the image—and only that—of fairness and justice. It is still another indication that we have junked the defense in practice. Honesty requires us to do the same with its theory and rhetoric. . . .

Murdock relied primarily on the testimony of Dr. Williams, a board-certified psychiatrist, and professor at Howard University Medical School. Dr. Williams had examined Murdock on two occasions during his confinement in St. Elizabeths Hospital. According to the testimony of Dr. Williams, Murdock was strongly delusional, though not hallucinating or psychotic; he was greatly preoccupied with the unfair treatment of Negroes in this country, and the idea that racial war was inevitable. He showed compulsiveness in his behavior, emotional immaturity, and some psychopathic traits. Since his emotional difficulties were closely tied to his sense of racial oppression, it is probable that when the marine in the Little Tavern called him a "black bastard" Murdock had an irresistible impulse to shoot. His emotional disorder had its roots in his childhood, in the Watts section of Los Angeles; particularly important was the fact that his father had deserted his mother, and he grew up in a large family with little money and little love or attention.

Dr. Williams stated firmly that in his view Murdock was suffering from an abnormal mental condition that substantially impaired his behavior controls. But he stated just as firmly that the condition did not amount to a mental illness. . . .

This court has made it perfectly plain for purposes of the insanity defense, "mental illness" is a legal term of art. A criminal defendant's responsibility cannot turn on the label attached to his condition. The insanity defense is neither expanded nor contracted by changing fashions in psychiatric terminology. In particular, mental illness for our purposes is not limited to psychosis; it includes any "abnormal condition of the mind that substantially affects mental or emotional processes and substantially impairs behavior controls."[4]

Defense counsel was thus confronted with a serious dilemma, arising from the fact that "mental illness" meant one thing to his witness, and another to the law. It was clear that the law would permit a jury to find mental illness on the basis of Dr. Williams' testimony about Murdock's "abnormal condition." In practice, however, a jury might well be reluctant to look beyond the doctor's statement that the condition did not amount to mental illness as he understood the term.

Counsel's strategy was to bypass the troublesome term "mental illness," and invite the jury to focus directly on the legal definition of that term. He conceded to the jury that Murdock "did not have a mental disease in the classic sense," i.e., he did not have a psychosis. But, counsel argued, the expert testimony showed that at the critical moment Murdock did not have control of his conduct, and the reason for that lack of control was a deepseated emotional disorder that was rooted in his "rotten social background." Accordingly, he asked the trial court to omit the term "mental disease or defect" from the jury instructions. I think his proposal was ingenious; the trial court might well have framed a suitable instruction asking the jury to consider whether Murdock's act was the product, not of "mental illness," but of an "abnormal condition of the mind that substantially affects mental or emotional processes and substantially impairs behavior controls."

While the trial court denied the requested instruction, we cannot say that ruling was error. The judge carefully instructed the jury to resolve the question of mental illness in accordance with its legal definition; he told them they were not bound by medical conclusions as to what is or is not a mental disease, and he told them to ignore defense counsel's concession that Murdock was without mental disease. In this respect the instructions conform to the requirements set forth in our cases.

But the judge injected into the instructions a special note of caution, in response to the testimony and argument presented in this case. He told the jury:

> We are not concerned with a question of whether or not a man had a rotten social background. We are concerned with the question of his criminal responsibility. That is to say, whether he had an abnormal condition of the mind that affected his emotional and behavioral processes at the time of the offense.

Defense counsel had objected to that instruction before it was given, because his theory of the case was that Murdock had an abnormal mental condition caused in part by his "rotten social background." The trial court overruled his objection, deeming the instruction necessary to counteract what he saw as an attempt by defense counsel to appeal to the jurors on the basis of sympathy, or passion, or prejudice.

It may well be that the trial judge was motivated by a reasonable fear that the jury would reach its decision on the basis not of the law but of sympathy for the victims of a racist society. Nevertheless, I think that the quoted instruction was reversible error sufficiently serious to justify reversing the court's finding. It had the effect of telling the jury to disregard the testimony relating to Murdock's social and economic background and to consider only the testimony framed in terms of "illness." Such an instruction is contrary to law, and it clearly undermined Murdock's approach to the insanity defense in this case. For Murdock's strategy had two parts: first, he sought to convince the jury to disregard Dr. Williams' finding of no "mental illness," and then he sought to persuade them to find mental illness in the legal sense of the term. The jury could hardly consider the issue of mental illness without considering Murdock's background, in view of the fact that all the witnesses traced such disabilities as they found at least in part to his background.

No matter what the trial judge intended, his instruction may have deprived Murdock of a fair trial on the issue of responsibility. But even if that instruction had not been offered, Murdock could argue that he was denied a fair opportunity to present his particular responsibility defense. While the language of our responsibility test theoretically leaves room for such a defense, our experience reveals that in practice it imposes illogical constraints on the flow of information to the jury and also on the breadth of the jury's inquiry. Our test demands an "abnormal condition of the mind," and that term carries implications that may mislead counsel, the court, and the jury.

McDonald defined mental illness for purposes of the responsibility defense as an abnormal condition of the mind that "substantially affects mental or emotional processes and substantially impairs behavior controls." The thrust of Murdock's defense was that the environment in which he was raised—his "rotten social background"—conditioned him to respond to certain stimuli in a manner most of us would consider flagrantly inappropriate. Because of his early conditioning, he argued, he was denied any meaningful choice when the racial insult triggered the explosion in the restaurant. He asked the jury to conclude that his "rotten social background," and the resulting impairment of mental or emotional processes and behavior controls, ruled his violent reaction in the same manner that the behavior of a paranoid schizophrenic may be ruled by his "mental condition." Whether this impairment amounted to an "abnormal condition of the mind" is, in my opinion, at best an academic question. But the consequences we predicate on the answer may be very meaningful indeed.

We have never said that an exculpatory mental illness must be reflected in some organic or pathological condition. Nor have we enshrined psychosis as a prerequisite of the defense. But our experience has made it clear that the terms we use— "mental disease or defect" and "abnormal condition of the mind"—carry a distinct flavor of pathology. And they deflect attention from the crucial, functional question—did the defendant lack the ability to make any meaningful choice of action— to an artificial and misleading excursion into the thicket of psychiatric diagnosis and nomenclature.

It does not necessarily follow, however, that we should push the responsibility defense to its logical limits and abandon all of the trappings of the medical or disease model. However illogical and disingenuous, that model arguably serves important interests. Primarily, by offering a rationale for detention of persons who are found not guilty by reason of "insanity," it offers us shelter from a downpour of troublesome questions. If we were to facilitate Murdock's defense, as logic and morality would seem to command, so that a jury might acquit him because of his "rotten social background" rather than any treatable mental illness, the community would have to decide what to do with him.

If acquitted because he lacked responsibility, Murdock would automatically have been committed to St. Elizabeths Hospital for further examination. He could then obtain an unconditional release only upon the certification of the hospital superintendent "(1) that such person has recovered his sanity, (2) that, in the opinion of the superintendent, such person will not in the reasonable future be dangerous to himself or others. . . ." Plainly, the hospital would find it difficult to justify holding Murdock on the grounds that he was insane in any conventional sense. None of the psychiatrists who testified at trial, including those from St. Elizabeths, suggested that his "sanity" had ever been lost.

Nevertheless, Murdock may well be dangerous. We have no carefully crafted technique for resolving the complex of legal, moral, and political questions concealed in the determination of dangerousness. Regrettably, those questions are now decided, at least in the first instance, by psychiatrists. We can only speculate on the outcome of their inquiry.

They might conclude that Murdock's rage and resentment were burned off by the explosion in the restaurant; the cathartic effect of his violent outburst may have made its repetition unlikely. On the other hand, the crime Murdock committed is a prototype of the crimes that arouse the greatest public anxiety. He seems to be a man whose bitterness and racial hostility have turned into blasting powder which can be touched off by a spark. Since there is no obvious way to insulate him from further sparks, and since the powder is not being deactivated, further explosions may be unavoidable. It would not be surprising if the psychiatrists took the view that Murdock is now, and is likely to remain, extremely dangerous.

However accurate the prediction of dangerousness, it is not at all clear that the statute would permit Murdock's confinement. Read literally, the statute seems to establish a return to sanity and an absence of dangerousness as independent preconditions of unconditional release. That reading would require the hospitalization of a dangerous person who lacked any mental illness whatsoever. Our cases have made it clear, however, that "dangerousness" refers to "dangerousness by reason of mental illness." Thus, a defendant who was dangerous but no longer insane could not be involuntarily hospitalized. If Murdock cannot be considered insane, the hospital would have to release him.

We are left, therefore, with an obligation to choose among four unattractive alternatives:

A. We can impose narrow and admittedly illogical limitations on the responsibility defense to insure that a defendant like Murdock will not be acquitted on the theory that he lacked responsibility. By confining such a defendant in a penitentiary, we can avoid the difficult questions presented by the effort to hold him in confinement following a successful use of the responsibility defense.

B. If we remove the practical impediments to Murdock's defense and he is, in fact, acquitted for lack of responsibility, he could be released from custody in spite of his apparent dangerousness. That result would conform with the principle that civil commitment is ordinarily barred where a defendant is dangerous but not mentally ill. And there are even precedents for the acquittal and release of dangerous defendants who have been brought to trial on a criminal charge. The Fourth Amendment exclusionary rule, for example, effectively precluded conviction of some defendants who appear to be dangerous. But that rule has been subjected to heavy assault even though it serves important, extrinsic interests—the redress and deterrence of unconstitutional action and the preservation of judicial integrity. Acquitting a defendant like Murdock and returning him to the street might also protect our integrity. But it would probably be more difficult to obtain public support for, or even unfriendly acquiescence in, Murdock's release than to defend the operation of the exclusionary rule. It could be said, after all, that acquittal would result not in spite of Murdock's dangerousness, but precisely because of it. Thus, while there may be no reason in logic why Murdock could not be returned to the street, as a practical matter that is probably an unfeasible result.

C. If the community will not tolerate Murdock's release we can strive to find a vaguely therapeutic purpose for hospitalization. Skinnerian-like techniques may be available to reprogram his behavior. We might conclude that they should be used and that their use justifies his confinement. But that will require us to stretch the medical model substantially so that new techniques can be applied to many persons not conventionally considered "sick."

I do not mean to suggest the existence of a bold line which segregates the orthodox, universally admired techniques from the techniques which are unconventional, morally and legally troublesome, and as yet unaccepted. Some commentators have insisted that the most traditional techniques, including psycho-therapy, should never be imposed on an unwilling subject. And some of the techniques which raise the most profound moral and legal questions are already being put to use. Still, there does seem to be a continuum running from the less controversial to the more controversial techniques. Without suggesting that we can blink at the techniques that are now widely used, it seems clear to me that we must, at the very least, scrutinize with care the implications of advancing further along the continuum.

D. Finally, if there are no known or foreseeable techniques for "curing" someone like Murdock (or if we are unwilling to utilize the techniques that may be available), and if the inca-pacitation of the defendant is a practical imperative, we will have to confine him in exclusive reliance on a prediction of dangerousness. That confinement would be nothing more or less than unadorned preventive detention.

The options that would permit us to acquit Murdock but hold him in custody nonetheless—preventive detention and a stretching of the medical model to permit the use of new tech-niques—raise profound moral and legal questions. Resolution of those questions would require a prolonged and thorough public debate. But however they are resolved, it is at least clear that each of these options requires an expansion of the bound-aries of the civil commitment doctrine. We could strive to limit the expansion by applying the new rationale only to persons who have undergone a criminal trial and been acquitted for lack of responsibility. But as a practical matter it seems very unlikely that the expansion could be so confined. The new rationale would permit—perhaps demand—that all persons who are rendered dangerous by a "rotten social background" should be preventively detained. Or that all persons who ex-hibit antisocial behavior patterns should have their behavior reconditioned. We cannot escape the probability, if not abso-lute certainty, that every effort to diminish the class of persons who can be found criminally responsible will produce a con-comitant expansion in the class of persons who can be sub-jected to involuntary civil commitment. The implications in this context are staggering. The price of permitting Murdock to claim the benefit of a logical aspect of the responsibility doctrine may be the unleashing of a detention device that operates, by hypothesis, at the exclusive expense of the lowest social and economic class.

That result can certainly be avoided—even if we are unwilling to return the defendant to the street—by reading the responsibility doctrine so narrowly that the issue of post-acquittal custody rarely arises. We could, for example, redefine the concept of responsibility so that it would approximate the concept of self-defense. All civil and criminal sanctions on the nonresponsible defendant would be barred, and the test would be reformulated to ask explicitly which defendants should escape all state-imposed sanctions. Alternatively, we could retain the medical model and acknowledge its illogic as a significant virtue. Psychosis may be an irrational test of criminal responsibility, but it does have a recognizable symptomatology. In the civil commitment context it may provide the only manageable stopping point short of a full-fledged scheme of preventive detention. These limitations on the responsibility defense permit an avoidance—perhaps to the good—of a confrontation with the difficult questions posed by preventive detention and the various forms of behavior control.[5]

On the other hand, we sacrifice a great deal by discouraging Murdock's responsibility defense. If we could remove the practical impediments to the free flow of information we might begin to learn something about the causes of crime. We might discover, for example, that there is a significant causal relationship between violent criminal behavior and a "rotten social background." That realization would require us to consider, for example, whether income redistribution and social reconstruction are indispensable first steps toward solving the problem of violent crime. . . .

Each of these approaches to the responsibility doctrine has significant advantages and disadvantages. No one can fault us for choosing the wrong approach. We can be faulted, however, for refusing to make any choice at all—or at least for refusing to confront the implications and shortcomings of our de facto choice. It is a critical responsibility of courts, legislatures and commentators to undertake a purposive analysis of the responsibility defense, instead of merely paying it lip service in deference to its historical significance and our "liberal" consciences. Under each of the prevailing tests of criminal responsibility, the operation of the defense has been haphazard, perfunctory, and virtually inexplicable. If we cannot overcome the irrational operation of the defense, we may have no honest choice but to abandon it and hold all persons criminally responsible for their action.

8

Justice and Juveniles[1]

Even those who demand harsh justice are troubled when children are involved. The law is reluctant to blame children as we blame adults. With children, the question of "why" is even more pressing. And resistance to pursuing that question may be more easily relaxed. The causes of their problems are so obvious. With adults, the forces shaping behavior are obscured with the passage of time. We do not have that cop-out with children. And we feel more responsibility where children are concerned.

We established a separate juvenile court system early in this century in the belief that we could prevent delinquency, or at least prevent delinquent children from turning into adult criminals, by taking a caring and rehabilitative rather than a punitive approach. This rationale justified more informal legal procedures in which juveniles' rights were held less important than their need for help.

In the 1960s we began to face up to the problems this had created. (The same approach caused us trouble with the mentally disabled.)[2] Rather than helping young people, the absence of formal procedural safeguards exposed them to serious risks. It became impossible to ignore the abysmal treatment juveniles were accorded both in court and in training schools. Not only that, it was apparent that their main training was in how to be more effective criminals.

During the late 1960s and early 1970s, the Supreme Court overhauled juvenile law, focusing on the establishment of children's right to due process of law.[3] The next step was to establish standards for the juvenile justice system, the most prominent being those developed by the American Bar Association and Institute for Judicial Administration.[4] An Office of Juvenile Justice and Delinquency Prevention was formed in the Department of Justice, to assist states to improve their systems. Federal law required that children could not be incarcerated for actions that would not be crimes for an adult, and that children could not be held in adult jails.[5] The intent of this movement was to divert as many children as possible away from the adult criminal community.

Today we are witnessing a backlash—toward treating children as adults. In March 1986 there were eighteen people on death rows in the United States for crimes committed while they were under the age of eighteen. Of thirty-six jurisdictions with capital punishment, twenty-six set a minimum age, ranging from eighteen to ten.[6] The Administration has sought to terminate federal juvenile justice funding on grounds that the statute's purpose has been met.[7] From 1980 to 1985, federal education spending has dropped by one-third, while the total federal budget went up 21 percent.[8] A nationwide study by the Children's Defense Fund found that of three million seriously disturbed children in the United States, two-thirds are not getting the services they need, and many others are receiving inappropriate services.[9]

The children who come through the courts are living evidence of the failures of our society to provide the basic necessities of a healthy mental and physical life for all too many of those we call society's most precious resource. If we refuse to invest in our children, we can only expect more of the same.

This article, originally published in 1975, raises concerns that are equally compelling today.

* * *

Our juvenile court system was originally based upon the assumption that society should take responsibility for children's behavior and attempt to prevent misbehavior in the future by understanding its causes. But there is a movement afoot today to change this purpose, to give juveniles a dose of swift and prolonged punishment. For example, to solve the problem of juvenile crime in the District of Columbia, the proponents of law and order reduced the number of juvenile offenders overnight by simply lowering the upper age limit of children eligible for juvenile court jurisdiction.

I have spent most of my professional life, to paraphrase Socrates, learning what I do not know about the problems of children. What do we really know about treating disturbed children? I've learned from my years of interaction with people in the behavioral disciplines how much we don't know about human behavior and human problems. My awe of the behavioral scientists disappeared when I discovered what I should have realized all along: the professionals have no secret wisdom or answers about the causes of behavior. Although that gives me some confidence to venture my own views, it also scares me that no one may know a great deal more than I do.

It is a rude awakening for us nonexperts to realize that the professionals have no easy prescription to treat the social and mental ills that surface so regularly in and out of the courts. But once I had this realization I began to express my doubts about expert pronouncements. These experts seemed to reach most of their conclusions without benefit of facts. I couldn't evaluate their opinions and conclusions until they told me what they actually knew and, more important, what they didn't know. Some behavioral scientists misinterpreted this as an attack on their integrity and values. But I'm not the little boy shouting that the emperor has no clothes; I'm merely pointing out that someone with so many holes in his clothes should not claim to have a monopoly on the fashion industry.

Few honest experts will claim that they know how to treat a misbehaving child. We don't have the slightest notion of what really works, except in the most commonsense way. We feed our children, comfort them, play with them, call the doctor for them, talk to their teachers, lecture them, swat them once in a while, and most of all warm them with our love and pride. Not many of us subject them to repeated batteries of tests and interviews, isolate them for weeks for misbehavior, make them account for every five minutes of their time, deny them privacy, censor their mail, and refuse them all contact with the opposite sex. Yet in most justice systems, this is what passes for treatment.

We hold out the promise of treatment, and juvenile courts are operated on the assumption that we can help children with difficult problems. Perhaps we need to look again at what it is we are attempting to treat and to reconsider the extent to which our present arsenal of services is appropriate for the children we see in juvenile court—or for any other child.

My own experience with delinquents and criminals is that their lives on the street have destroyed their ability to empathize with other human beings. It does not take an expert to guess that some children reared in the ghetto, where acknowledgment of one's own identity and worth is problematic, will develop at best a hard insensitivity to other humans. Such individuals feel nothing but hatred toward their victims and society as a whole. This lack of connection to the majority's culture and values may have nothing to do with mental disease, unless not being able to see or to feel beyond resentment and rage is classified as such. I suspect that our providers of treatment services—psychiatrists, psychologists, or social workers—lack the know-how to implant middle-class sensibilities into youngsters who have been actively neglected twenty-four hours a day, every day. There is no magic humanizing pill for these youths to swallow.

The way these children think we feel about them determines how they feel about us. I have a particularly vivid memory of one incident. Many years ago I was visiting a prison in California in order to observe certain kinds of group therapy being practiced by prison psychiatrists. A young man about nineteen years old spoke about all "those people out there," meaning the world at large, who hate him.

"Why," I asked, "do you think they hate you?" He quickly replied, "Because they hate all of us in here—that's why they put us in here like animals." Then I asked, "Do you think 'they' have cause to hate you for what you've done?" To which he replied, "Maybe they have and maybe that's why their hatred is harder for me to bear." Then he admitted that the only way he knew of living with that hatred was to return it—to hate "them." At first, he thought his pent-up hate was making him psychotic. He developed a ritual which saved him—when his cell door was locked each night and he was alone, he would as quietly as possible discharge his rage by shaking his fists at the window of his cell to the world outside and repeating the obscenities, "F—— you! F—— you! Just wait until I get out of here!" He kept this up until he was tired enough to fall asleep. That was his way of dealing with what he saw as his total rejection by the outside world.

Children on all levels of society are acutely sensitive to rejection, as was this young man. It is not hard to understand why they would react in much the same way when they feel unwanted or unloved—either in reality or in their imaginations—by their parents, the school, the society.*

I can best explain my concerns by describing the experience of a young psychiatrist with whom I have worked closely—an experience that parallels my perspective with cases in the juvenile justice system. He worked in a community mental health center in Washington serving primarily poor, predominantly black families living in public housing projects. What touched

---

* A recent case in the District of Columbia (already referred to in Chapter 1) revived my memories of this case. A *Washington Post* article describes several of the young men convicted of a brutal murder as follows:

> ... Rouse emerges still as an enigma. There is the insecure and troubled youth who attempted suicide when he was 12 after being caught shoplifting, and whose oldest sister was beaten, strangled and thrown in a trash receptacle to die.... There is "my baby," the youngest child ... [who] dropped out of high school to get a job to help ... pay the bills.... In the next few years, Rouse had three children by three different women and worked short-term jobs as a cook or a parking lot attendant.... Christopher, 20, the only high school graduate among the murder case defendants, is routinely described by acquaintances as "sweet" and smart. He tutored youngsters, sometimes held two jobs, and often played the adult in a family where the father spent much of his life in and out of jail and the mother smoked drugs with her children.... Catlett, with his pathetic nickname of "Snot Rag," which he would write in big, ornate letters, [recalled bitterly that] "I was teased about being a foster kid.... People would say, 'You don't know your father.' That makes you very confused and angry.... When I was smaller, I held the anger inside."... Catlett found ... a father figure in Levy Rouse, who bought him clothes and gave him money. "Levy my daddy," he liked to tell friends.[10]

him most deeply was the effects of poverty on the children. As he described it to me, he saw the two- or four-year-old black child—eyes alert, warm and open—loving to be read to, to be played with, to be talked to. There was a zest and unquenchable curiosity. The potential was evident and, with love and care, would flourish.

But, with unmitigated poverty, havoc was wreaked on this child of promise. With each succeeding year the attributes of humaneness and interest slowly died and withered away. Without nurturance the dream was aborted. My friend observed the personality change from openness to distrust, from interest to apathy, from warmth to hostility. By adolescence the attendant curses of drugs, alcohol, and delinquency led down the dismal road to the door of the juvenile court or the mental institution. The "man-child in the promised land" was lost, probably forever.

I have seen the battered, deprived child of today become tomorrow's vengeful, brutal, and callous adult criminal. Behavioral science has made explicit what many of us nonexperts have known intuitively—the battered child becomes the battering parent. Spiritual and physical mutilation in childhood cannot be washed away. We can't expect a viable adult to arise like a phoenix from the ashes of an aborted childhood.

What does one do in such a situation? My friend's first response was to help strengthen the home—find better living quarters, provide for comprehensive health care, and ensure that the mother was receiving the maximum amount of public assistance to which she was entitled.

He next became involved in the schools. And here he was faced with the conflict between the needs of the school—besieged with problems and overcrowding—and the needs of the children. The schools sought psychiatric evaluation and diagnosis. Children labeled "hyperkinetic" or "unsocialized aggressive reaction" obviously must be treated: according to the school authorities, treatment in a hospital would be preferable. Rather than focusing on how the school might fashion a program to meet the needs of the child, or eliminate conditions creating the child's problems, the focus invariably was on the problem child.

If he refused to diagnose and label a child and prescribe medication, the schools' response was to refer the child to the juvenile court. There the child was shown to have a poor school record—truancy, bad grades, misbehavior with teachers and classmates. His miserable record had followed him from teacher to teacher and become its own self-fulfilling prophecy.

In light of the record, the juvenile court referred the child for an evaluation to the mental health center. He was observed once again by my psychiatrist friend. Only now it was the interests of the court, not the school, which dominated the situation.

Armed with a psychiatric evaluation and now given a legal label as well—"person in need of supervision"—the court might place the child on probation. Coming full circle, the probation officer recommended psychiatric evaluation and treatment, and the child was sent back to the psychiatrist. This time it was the interests of the probation department that he was supposed to implement.

The score on this referral game of child disposal was Institutions 3, Child 0. We looked to psychiatry to resurrect the innocence and love of the three-year-old who is run through the educational, legal, and psychiatric gauntlet and then pummeled beyond recognition. In every case, the institutions created to serve the child rejected those who could not fit in the assembly line or conveyor belt and left it to the expert to deal with the rejects.

The experts admit that they do not know what to prescribe for the disturbed child and the institutions which could help that child struggle from under the burden of a brutalizing environment can seemingly do nothing but refer the child to court or back to the experts. Our promise of treatment and the assumptions of the juvenile court are thus doubly unfulfilled. I am reminded of a certain gubernatorial candidate who made plainly impossible campaign promises to enlist election workers. When he won the election his aides asked him how they should respond to demands that he fulfill his promises. The governor's face fell for a moment. Then he suddenly brightened and exclaimed: "I have it! Just tell them I lied!" We lie to children who have never been "habilitated," much less rehabilitated.

So where do we go from here? I have my doubts about a single-minded therapeutic approach and whether that approach can ever really deliver as much as we expect of it. We simply do not know enough about treatment. I do not mean to turn my back on our long tradition of providing goods and services to society's victims and to its rejects. But if we want to make sure that our efforts are really constructive we must examine our expectations much more carefully. Many agencies make children the initial priority, not only because it seems right to help children first, but also because it's sensible to try to prevent problems before they start, or at least catch them before they become serious.

But in the attempt to demonstrate compliance with public priorities, figures showing increases in services for children may be inflated to convince the public that children are getting priority treatment. Staff may be classified as child psychiatrists and social workers specializing in children when in actuality most of their time is spent with adults. Every time an inquiry is received from a school, it may be counted as a "patient care episode" for a child, and used to swell the total figure.

But even if services are provided, the question would remain: What do children really need? Before we scrap our helping efforts or redouble them, we must have a better understanding of this question. We must reappraise our efforts, no matter how painful that may seem. But in the end such reappraisal will be cheaper and less painful than plunging headlong down the path of treatment. A better understanding of what children need will help us answer my final question: where should we be spending our money and directing our energies to come most effectively to grips with the problems of children?

The only thing that my expert colleagues know for sure is that the family is the most effective child-developing agent around. Out of the plethora of studies of day care and early intervention, one thing stands out: a child needs most a family—it is there that he finds his roots and his education. Mothers and fathers who spend time with their child are better at it than are most organized group care arrangements.

But the parents of children under the poverty mark often have less time and energy for their families. They may be easily overwhelmed simply by the struggle for survival. A frantic and harassed mother simply may not provide the attention and security a child needs. A father who is filled with failure and desperation and cannot put food on the table often can't convey to his child a sense of order, purpose, or self-esteem, and he may not even stay around long enough to try. The poor are confronted by the same problems which confront the rich, and more of them. The difference is that they simply do not have the resources or the time to cope. And when they slip, they find it all the harder to come back.

Something is just plain wrong with asking our juvenile courts or mental health care institutions to straighten out young lives already twisted by the effects of poverty. Our first priority in distributing justice to children ought to be distributing income to their families. It is simply not right that children in this country grow up in poverty. Families should receive an income which allows them to make choices for their children. There is a wide consensus on this principle, and programs implementing it have been proposed by both political parties. Commission after commission on crime, race, violence, or children has recommended some form of income redistribution as the only way to begin to solve our toughest social problems.[11]

The advantage of distributing income directly is that government intervention in private lives should diminish. The resources and options provided by money should allow families to function without agency oversight or official intervention at every turn. An adequate income will give them the self-respect to ask for advice instead of having it gratuitously heaped on.

The system gone wrong is, of course, a major focus of what attorneys call family law. Family law has taken on ever-increasing importance in recent years because of explosive social and economic changes that have rocked the foundations of the nuclear family. More and more we hear of the dissolution of the conventional family unit. By 1976, 10 percent of the children in the United States lived with only one parent. Divorce rates doubled between 1965 and 1975. Changing social conceptions of the rights and responsibilities of parents and children place increasing pressure on already strained family bonds.[12]

Of course, there are obvious limits to what an increased income can do for the family mired in poverty or the child who is sick or in trouble. The immediate and visible effects may be few, although the lessening of the income gap between the very poor and the mainstream of society should siphon off a great deal. It may be that an adequate family income won't guarantee a stable family life, won't eradicate the effects of bigotry, or stop crime cold, or solve the problem of schizo-phrenia. But I am convinced that nothing else can begin to work without it.

It is difficult to quarrel with the proposition that, in certain circumstances, the state must substitute for the parent or other family authority. The day has long passed when, as a society, we can tolerate child neglect or wife-battering in the guise of preserving the family's autonomy. Indeed, the rapid growth of family law in recent years has occurred predominantly in the area of the rights of individual family members against those of other members. Questions such as the legal right of a minor child to obtain contraceptives against the parents' wishes or without their consent were virtually unthinkable twenty years ago, yet such issues now occupy a central place in our family jurisprudence.

In 1929 Bertrand Russell observed that

[t]he substitution of the State for the father, so far as it has yet gone in the West, is in the main a great advance. It has immensely improved the health of the community, and the general level of education. It has diminished cruelty to children, and has made impossible such sufferings as those of David Copperfield. It may be expected to continue to raise the general level of physical health and intellectual attainment, especially by preventing the worst evils result-ing from the family system where it goes wrong.[13]

But state intervention is not without its perils, as Lord Russell himself acknowledged. Especially in an ostensibly pluralist society, the state's protective jurisdiction may come into sharp conflict with nonconforming political and religious beliefs. At the same time, the authoritarianism of the family may be even more repressive of individual liberties than the state.

9

Kent v. United States

Significant changes occurred in juvenile law as well as other areas of criminal law during the 1960s. The first of the major Supreme Court cases was *Kent v. U.S.*[1], holding that juveniles have a right to due process of law before being transferred from juvenile to adult court. It was soon followed by *In re Gault*,[2] declaring that children accused of delinquency have due process rights to counsel and protection against self-incrimination, and *In re Winship*,[3] stating that charges against juveniles must be proved by the same "beyond a reasonable doubt" standard used in adult trials. Changes in juvenile law owe their origin, in some measure, to these landmark cases.

More recently, the rights of juveniles have experienced some erosion. For instance, the Supreme Court has upheld the preventive detention of juveniles accused of being delinquent.[4] And courts' exercise of discretion to transfer children to adult court for trial is a growing phenomenon.[5]

The *Kent* case arose in the District of Columbia. Our court's original decision was appealed to the Supreme Court. That Court agreed with my dissenting opinion, and the case was sent back to the district court for reexamination. The finding also was appealed to our court, leading this time to a majority decision following the new Supreme Court precedent.

The following excerpts from my two opinions—in dissent and then for the later majority—illustrate the role of appellate courts (both the circuit courts of appeals and the Supreme Court) in the evolution of law, and the varied legal and human responses of the judges charged with this responsibility.

BACKGROUND   At the age of sixteen, Morris Kent was accused of committing several robberies and rapes. The juvenile court waived jurisdiction, allowing him to be tried in adult court. He was indicted on three counts of housebreaking, three of robbery, and two of rape. A jury returned a verdict of guilty of housebreaking and robbery and not guilty by reason of insanity of rape. The district court sentenced him to thirty to ninety years, with credit for the time he had spent in St. Elizabeths while awaiting trial.

Kent appealed his conviction, contending that the juvenile court had waived jurisdiction in his case without an adequate hearing. Our court affirmed his conviction (over my dissent) in 1964. The Supreme Court reversed (in 1966), directing the District Court to hold a full-dress hearing to determine whether Kent should have been waived to adult court in 1961. At the new hearing, the District Court found that the 1961 waiver was "appropriate and proper."

On the subsequent appeal, we reversed that decision, concluding (in 1968) that because of inaccuracies in several of the District Court's findings, and because Kent was suffering from a serious mental illness, waiver was inappropriate. Not all the judges on the court agreed. Judge Warren Burger (later Chief Justice of the United States) dissented, arguing that district courts should have wide latitude in granting waiver, and that in any event the result (Kent's going to St. Elizabeths for treatment) was the same no matter how the case was decided.[6]

In Dissent (1964)[7]

As Judge Washington's concurring opinion recognizes, "It is a fair inference from the record before us that one of the reasons why the Juvenile Court waived jurisdiction was because appellant was seriously disturbed and the Juvenile Court lacked facilities adequately to treat him." I think it shocking that a child was subjected to prosecution and punishment as a criminal because he was thought to suffer from a serious mental or emotional disturbance. I can think of no stronger reason for not doing this.

Waiver of the Juvenile Court's jurisdiction over a child amounts to a proposal that he be prosecuted in the District Court as a criminal. A prosecution is an attempt to impose punishment. The Juvenile Court has no reason and in my opinion no right to assume that this attempt will fail. In the present case the attempt resulted in a sentence of thirty to ninety years.

If the Juvenile Court cannot find within its purview the means to rehabilitate children and to contain them during the treatment process, it is futile to look to the criminal courts for help. When the Juvenile Court washes its hands of a child, it throws him on the scrap heap of a prison and it gains nothing by employing euphemisms to describe this tragedy. . . . As long as the Juvenile Court practices the self-deception that allows it to believe in the existence of facilities "elsewhere," it will not face squarely the need to develop for itself the tools it requires to care for these children.

When this court affirmed appellant's conviction, a majority took the position that it did not know why the Juvenile Court had waived jurisdiction over appellant but would trust to "the skill and experience of the specialist judge. . . ." Accordingly this court made no use of its statutory authority to review the "social records" of the Juvenile Court concerning the appellant. In effect, this court set up an irrebuttable presumption that a waiver of jurisdiction by the Juvenile Court is proper. This conflicts with the Juvenile Court Act, with our previous opinions, and with the court's observation in this very case that waivers must not be "arbitrary or capricious."

Though our reviewing authority is of limited scope, it exists. There can be no intelligent review of the Juvenile Court's waiver of jurisdiction unless the reasons for it are *stated on the record*. Without the benefit of such statement, the child's counsel is duty-bound to pursue by inquiry and challenge every matter conceivably affecting the waiver decision in order to make a record for review. This will formalize and burden the Juvenile Court procedures and necessarily accentuate the adversary role of counsel.

On Reconsideration (1968)[8]

The Supreme Court has recently revolutionized the procedural aspects of juvenile court proceedings. Today we face the more fundamental issue of the substantive role of juvenile courts. In particular we must determine what obligations juvenile authorities, acting as *parens patriae* [in place of the parent], have with respect to mentally disturbed adolescents.

Many of the findings below are incontestable. Morris Kent had "engaged in extensive criminal activity characterized by aggressiveness and violence" and had not responded satisfactorily to his previous contacts with the Juvenile Court. He "was suffering from a psychosis known as schizophrenic reaction, chronic undifferentiated type" and "there was reason to believe that a period of time beyond the limits of the Juvenile Court's jurisdiction was required for reasonable prospects of rehabilitation." Moreover, the Juvenile Court's long-term confinement facilities could not provide adequate psychiatric treatment for psychotic children.

Because of the obvious inadequacy of the juvenile detention facilities, Kent urged that the Juvenile Court should have taken steps to civilly commit him to St. Elizabeths Hospital. The District Court found that Kent was indeed civilly committable in 1961. But it determined that "because of the defendant's potential danger to himself and/or others his civil commitment in 1961 was an inappropriate alternative to waiver in the District Court." This finding turns civil commitment law on its head. Under D.C. [law] a person may be involuntarily committed *only* if "he is likely to injure himself or other persons" due to mental illness. Dangerousness does not make civil commitment "inappropriate"; it makes civil commitment appropriate.

In rejecting civil commitment, the court relied on a series of Government-proposed findings to the effect that civil commitment did not provide adequate protection for society. The reliance is misplaced since these findings are based on erroneous assumptions and unwarranted speculations. One finding divined that on civil commitment, St. Elizabeths Hospital would have committed defendant to a nonsecurity facility from which he could elope, rather than to the maximum security facility, John Howard Pavilion. But the record does not convince us that St. Elizabeths would be so negligent and incompetent as to knowingly place a person who needed a secure setting in a nonsecure one. Another finding was that a "person who is civilly committed to St. Elizabeths Hospital may be released by the doctor in charge of the case without any prior court authorization," the implication being that the doctor may act negligently or ignorantly. Pursuing this speculation further, the court found that if the defendant were released before age twenty-one the Juvenile Court could not have reinstated charges because "as a matter of practice" it would drop charges against a child committed to St. Elizabeths. There is no support in the record for a determination that St. Elizabeths doctors will prematurely recommend release for criminally dangerous psychotics. And if they did release Kent before age twenty-one, the Juvenile Court could have reinstated charges. The fact that charges had been dropped in a few cases in the past does not mean they had to be dropped in Kent's case.

Since the District Court's decision that waiver "was appropriate and proper" was based heavily on these defective findings, the decision must be vacated and set aside.

Both the Supreme Court and this court have stated that "[I]t is implicit in [the juvenile court] scheme that noncriminal treatment is to be the rule—and the adult criminal treatment, the exception which must be governed by the particular factors of individual cases." We believe that on the facts of this case waiver was inappropriate.

It is true that the Juvenile Court has "a substantial degree of discretion" in determining whether to retain jurisdiction over a child. But this discretion must be exercised in accordance with the spirit of the Juvenile Court Act. As the Supreme Court said in *Kent*:

The theory of the District's Juvenile Court Act, like that of other jurisdictions, is rooted in social welfare philosophy rather than in the corpus juris. Its proceedings are designated as civil rather than criminal. The Juvenile Court is theoretically engaged in determining the needs of the child and of society rather than adjudicating criminal conduct. The objectives are to provide measures of guidance and rehabilitation for the child and protection for society, not to fix criminal responsibility, guilt and punishment. The State is *parens patriae* rather than prosecuting attorney.

Congress had made clear that the waiver provision is not excluded from this fundamental philosophy of *parens patriae*. [The relevant D.C. law] states:

> Sections 11-1551 to 11-1554 . . . shall be liberally construed so that, with respect to each child coming under the court's jurisdiction: . . . (3) when the child is removed from his own family, the court shall secure for him custody, care and discipline as nearly as possible equivalent to that which should have been given him by his parents.

Parens patriae requires that the Juvenile Court do what is best for the child's care and rehabilitation so long as this disposition provides adequate protection for society. In the instant case, no concern was shown for Kent's care and rehabilitation, and mechanisms by which society could be protected were ignored.

The juvenile authorities who waived Kent knew that he was seriously ill and in need of treatment. The Government argues, however, that their decision to waive does not indicate a lack of concern for Kent's care and rehabilitation. It emphasized that "if a waived juvenile is found not guilty by reason of insanity, the psychiatric facilities of the distict court are, of course, at least as adequate as those available to the Juvenile Court. . . ." The argument is, at best, disingenuous. It overlooks the fundamental point that waiver is a judgment that an adult criminal prosecution should be instituted against the juvenile. The purpose of this exercise is to obtain a conviction for which the juvenile may be penalized as an adult. The exercise succeeded when the jury convicted Kent on several counts even though it recognized full well that he was suffering from a serious mental illness.

Treatment of a sick juvenile is not a concern of an adult criminal proceeding. Kent's case bears this out. Before trial the District Court sent him to District of Columbia General Hospital and then to St. Elizabeths Hospital for mental examinations, not treatment. Upon completion of these examinations, he spent eleven months in a prison prior to trial without any psychiatric attention.

To all intents, psychiatric care was withheld from this schizophrenic juvenile for eighteen months from the date of his arrest while he was undergoing the trauma inherent in the incidents of a criminal prosecution. When he finally entered a hospital for treatment, a thirty-to-ninety-year prison sentence loomed over him, undoubtedly impairing his chances of recovery. It seems clear that the chief reason for waiver was that the Juvenile Court could retain jurisdiction over Kent for only five years and that he was unlikely to recover within this period. The paradoxical result is that the sicker a juvenile is, the less care he receives from the Juvenile Court. Since it may not be possible to guarantee that a very sick adolescent will recover by the time he is twenty-one, he will invariably be subjected to all the strains and stresses of a criminal prosecution, with only the hope that the Government will not succeed in its effort and that he may ultimately receive treatment pursuant to D.C. [law].

Perhaps even this harsh result might be justified if there is no other way to protect society. But it is clear that society can be protected without departing from civilized standards for the prompt and adequate care of disturbed children. The Juvenile Court can institute civil commitment proceedings against the youngster. If commitment ensues, he will be confined and treated until he is no longer dangerous due to mental illness. If not, the Juvenile Court will be free to follow its usual procedures.

Since waiver was not necessary for the protection of society and not conducive to Kent's rehabilitation, its exercise in this case violated the social welfare philosophy of the Juvenile Court Act. Of course, this philosophy does not forbid all waivers. We only decide here that it does forbid waiver of a seriously ill juvenile.

Since Morris Kent should not have been waived in 1961, the subsequent criminal proceedings were invalid and must be vacated. This does not mean, however, that he will be released from St. Elizabeths Hospital. The Government can institute civil commitment proceedings against Kent to ensure that he remains in the hospital. We think the institution of commitment proceedings is demanded by appellant's long history of serious illness accompanied by sordid behavior. Such proceedings will assure his confinement for treatment for as long as the public safety requires. And to avoid any gap in Kent's confinement, we stay our mandate in this case until the commitment proceedings have been completed, provided they are instituted within thirty days.

III

EQUALITY UNDER THE LAW

One reality that must be faced is the chasm between our criminal justice system and the ideal we profess of "equal justice under law."

The problems of criminal justice cannot be equated with the problem of crime. It has been fashionable in recent years to suggest that reforming the criminal courts—particularly speeding up their work—is the key to reducing crime. I find this extremely doubtful.

The frame of reference for my discussion of the criminal justice system is its application to street crime, the crime bred by poverty and racism, the crime committed by the dispossessed, disadvantaged, and alienated of our society. These offenders almost always lack the intellectual or financial means to invoke the rights and considerations which are guaranteed to all persons by the Constitution. Most important, they need counsel who will effectively invoke those rights in their behalf. Throughout my tenure on the bench, I encouraged the finest lawyers in Washington to work on these cases. As Justice Schaefer of the Illinois Supreme Court put it: "Of all the rights that an accused person has, the right to be represented by counsel is by far the most pervasive, for it affects his ability to assert any other rights he may have."[1] For a comprehensive examination of the issues involved here, the American Bar Association's *Standards for Criminal Justice,* including commentary, are an indispensable resource. The *Standards* have been cited over twelve thousand times by appellate courts, and continue to be used by legislators and administrators seeking guidance on law and policy.[2]

The criminal courts of our urban jurisdictions have been inundated with a caseload reaching crisis proportions. The burden of moving these cases puts tremendous pressure on everyone in the system to dispose of each case as rapidly as possible. But no matter how we improve our judicial machinery, we are not likely to make significant inroads on crime, since so few criminals ever reach the courts. More sobering, by advocating criminal justice reforms solely in the interest of crime reduction, we lose sight of our legitimate interest in justice for its own sake. Civilized society must have a humane criminal justice system which treats defendants with understanding and insight—regardless of how much or how little that system affects the crime statistics. For the system we create expresses our values and stands as our legacy long after we're gone.

Many judges believe that it would be better to preserve the illusion that nothing is wrong. Whatever value this illusion may have, I am more than uneasy with the notion that appellate courts should paper over a widespread deprivation of constitutional rights to preserve the pretense that justice is being done. It might be argued that the illusion is a necessity because the problems it hides can never be solved. But branding a problem insoluble to avoid facing it, or a solution utopian to avoid trying it, turns doubts into self-fulfilling prophecies.

The exclusionary rule, for example, burdens a criminal trial only as a result of official misconduct. Its purpose is to deter illegal actions by government; evidence illegally obtained cannot be used in the trial. The cases which come to public attention often involve defendants who did have something to hide, making it appear as if the only purpose of the exclusionary rule is to help the guilty. The Supreme Court has recently opened a "good faith exception" that allows illegally obtained evidence to be admitted at trial if the violation was "technical."[3] And some would do away with it entirely. Attorney General Edwin Meese, for example, has said: "The exclusionary rule has never helped an innocent person. It only helps the guilty, and I think it is a bad rule."[4]

But if we condone illegal law enforcement activity, we encourage the police to be less careful of constitutional rights. This will affect not only their approach to searching the apartment of a guilty drug dealer but also their search of the apartment of an innocent citizen who is wrongly suspected. Only the person found possessing drugs is prosecuted, so that is the only case we hear about—especially if he goes free because of an illegal search. The innocent citizen, though, must deal with the consequences of such a search. His peace and privacy were rudely invaded, his door may be broken down, and his neighbors may forever after be suspicious of him.

Every innocent citizen has at least as great a stake in the exclusionary rule as do criminal defendants. The way to make the rule less burdensome is not to abandon it without providing a viable alternative, but to decrease the incidence of official misconduct giving rise to its application. Remedies like class action injunctive suits, damage actions, and declaratory judgments are means of deterring practices amounting to official misconduct.

Notions such as "guilty anyway" serve as rationalizations for refusing to admit the deprivations of constitutional rights that occur at trials. This failure to admit what we are doing does not, however, alter the fact. Appellate courts cannot correct errors in past trials to prevent their recurrence in future trials unless we reverse convictions. Incidental observations and nonbinding dicta are just not sufficient. When we allow a conviction to stand despite violations of the Constitution, we conceal a serious problem and nourish the mistaken euphoria that our justice system is alive and performing well. The cost of this concealment is paid in the loss of fairness to individual defendants and in the absence of guidance for police, lawyers, and judges in future cases.

I am always puzzled by the moral fervor with which some proponents of judicial restraint attack my emphasis on individual rights and on the rights of the minority as a pernicious example of judicial activism. It seems to me that it is those attempting to overrule decades of Supreme Court precedents in the name of today's popular majority who are the proponents of radical change.

The judicial branch is a profoundly conservative institution. Unlike the elected executive and legislature, the independent judiciary was designed, in the words of Alexander Hamilton, the leading conservative of his day, "to guard the Constitution and the rights of individuals from the effects of those ill humours which the arts of designing men, or the influence of particular conjunctives, sometimes disseminate among the people themselves, and which, though they speedily give place to better information and more deliberate reflection, have a tendency in the meantime to occasion dangerous innovations in the government, and serious oppressions of the minority party in the community."[5]

10

Fair Play in Criminal Justice[1]

On all sides we hear the clamor for judicial reform, which too often looks like a euphemism for dealing with more defendants in less time. Why allow men and women who are "guilty anyway" to clutter the courts with all sorts of difficult legal and constitutional questions? This "guilty anyway" syndrome underlies much of the current push for greater "efficiency" in the criminal courts. Indeed, we have even seen a kind of "guilty anyway" exception emerging for all our cherished constitutional protections, especially those embodied in the Fourth, Fifth, Sixth and Fourteenth Amendments. These amendments were adopted specifically to guard individual liberty against overweening government authority. They protect against unreasonable search and seizure, self-incrimination, and deprivation of liberty without due process of law, and guarantee equal protection of the law and the right to counsel to help individuals protect their precious rights.

Many of the pervasive issues of modern criminal procedure can be analyzed in terms of the two contrasting philosophies outlined in Chapter 1. By assigning very different purposes to the criminal process, these two approaches offer distinct ways of resolving some of the recurring dilemmas posed in the adjudication of constitutional rights. The choices in Fourth, Fifth, and Sixth Amendment cases often embody tensions between the values we espouse and those we are prepared to fulfill.

This article, originally written in 1981, explores these tensions. The law in this area is undergoing constant change, but the underlying clash in values has remained largely the same.

* * *

Over the years, the painful lessons I learned from dealing with individual cases was that doing my job required a complex balancing act. Laws are fashioned to make individuals and organizations behave in certain ways. I might reach a conclusion that was impeccable on the narrow issue raised in a case, but clearly counterproductive in relation to what society and the law were trying to achieve, or the way the individual or company or government agency actually would respond to the decision might negate its purpose. I had to recognize also that the information I could bring to bear on the facts and law before me was inevitably limited—and that I might be wrong.

These concerns have led me to place great value on the constitutional rights that protect all of us from arbitrary government action and from law enforcement mistakes. This value cannot be quantified. Judge Edmund B. Spaeth, Jr., has pointed out: "When a court purports to quantify the values at issue, it evades the need to articulate its vision of the sort of society to which we should aspire."[2] One of the essential responsibilities of the courts is to keep ever before us the ideals embodied in the Constitution.

Search and Seizure

A few years ago, Justice Lewis Powell called the Fourth Amendment a "benighted area of the law."[3] Some might think this characterization too kind. Perhaps more than in any other aspect of criminal procedure, the complexity and confusion surrounding the rules of search and seizure persistently cloud understanding. I have no desire to usurp the Court's unenviable struggle to develop a body of sound and stable doctrine in this area. Rather, I wish to demonstrate the ways in which that struggle reflects a conflict between the two philosophies I have described.

Much of the bewildering quality of Fourth Amendment jurisprudence derives from the necessity of drawing lines that give content to the prohibition against unreasonable searches and seizures. For example, does the use of a telescope constitute a search, but not the use of binoculars? Can the police enter the hallway of an apartment building uninvited but not the hallway of a one-family home? Under any view of the purposes of criminal law, these lines must be drawn with enough clarity to permit comprehension by citizens, police, and lower courts. Thus, I take as common ground the importance of establishing relatively "bright lines."

But there are bright lines and bright lines. The externalists [those who view the role of law as imposing external constraints on behavior] seek lines that will further the goals of efficiency and finality and thus advance the cause of swift and certain punishment. Law enforcement, they fear, will be slowed or inhibited if policemen must wrestle with vague and unpredictable constitutional requirements at the scene of each search and seizure. For those who see the law as encouraging the internalization of control, on the other hand, bright lines can enhance the morality of the criminal process to the extent that they reflect the reality, equality, and education principles. These different approaches will, in many cases, produce differences in determining how to draw the line.

Two companion cases decided in 1981 by the Supreme Court illustrate this point. Both *Robbins v. California* and *New York v. Belton*[4] involved a familiar pattern. In each case, patrolmen stopped a car on the highway, detained the occupants, smelled marijuana, and searched the car. The California officers found "two packages wrapped in green opaque plastic" in the trunk of the automobile; upon unwrapping them, the police discovered fifteen pounds of marijuana subsequently used to convict Robbins. The New York police went no further than the backseat, where they came upon, in a zippered pocket of Belton's leather jacket, some cocaine. Both defendants asked the Court to order suppression of the drugs. Robbins won; Belton lost.

The two cases greatly divided the Court, together producing ten opinions. Justice Potter Stewart wrote the prevailing view in both decisions. In *Robbins,* he held that the "automobile exception" to the Fourth Amendment's warrant requirement does not justify a warrantless search of a closed container found inside an automobile. Justice Stewart reasoned that the basis of the automobile exception—the inherent mobility of cars and the lesser expectation of privacy in their contents—does not apply to closed pieces of luggage. He further decided, principally in order to establish a bright line, that the Fourth Amendment protects closed containers of whatever sort and wherever found.

In *Belton,* the question concerned the "arrest exception" to the warrant requirement. Here, Justice Stewart concluded that the purpose of that rule—the need to prevent arrestees from escaping, or from harming or destroying evidence—applied to the passenger compartment of an automobile, since that area generally falls within the immediate control of the arrestee. Once again seeking to articulate a bright line, he determined that the Fourth Amendment does not protect anything found within that area, including closed containers.

For the externalist, cases like these pose a conflict between the needs of law enforcement and the freedom of innocent citizens. Thus, the line should be drawn at a point that will maximize efficient police work without seriously threatening legitimate privacy interests. Searches that produce marijuana or cocaine are clearly efficient means of identifying drug offenders. And there can be little legitimate privacy interest in contraband—or in evidence of a crime, for that matter. Thus, in those situations where warrants are not required, if the police have probable cause to believe the defendant is guilty of something, there should be virtually no limit to the scope of the search. The officer should be allowed to inspect everything on the scene, "including the glove compartment, the trunk, and any containers in the vehicle that might reasonably contain the contraband."[5]

The innocent have nothing to fear, on this view. Subsequent judicial review of "probable cause" determinations will discourage indiscriminate invasions of privacy, permitting searches only of the possessions of people who are probably guilty. Thus, a line drawn far from the original purposes of the rule serves both efficient law enforcement and the externalist goals of the Bill of Rights. This appears to be the analysis adopted by the Justices who would have sustained the searches in both cases. Indeed, Justice William Rehnquist advocated the next logical step. Since there need be no relationship between the reason for the warrant exception and the scope of the search, he argued, there is no need for a warrant at all once the police reasonably suspect guilt.

The line-drawing efforts of internalists like myself, in contrast, do not focus on promoting the efficiency principle. Nor would the internalist accept protection of the "probably innocent" as justification for line-drawing, both because the argument itself (subsequent judicial review of probable cause is sufficient protection) is highly dubious and because it does not address the fundamental values which underlie the Fourth Amendment. Instead internalists seek bright lines which exert moral force—and therefore encourage compliance with the law both by officers and citizens—because they reflect the realities of police-suspect confrontations, promote equality in the treatment of suspects of all types, and speak clearly to the community of the values at stake in such confrontations. Since those who wish to encourage internalization of control have little faith in the ability of the criminal justice system to cure crime, they are less concerned if the lines produced by these standards somewhat retard the efficiency of the police.

The three Justices who would have struck down the searches in both *Robbins* and *Belton* seem to have been guided by some of these considerations. They recognized that rules of criminal procedure worthy of moral respect must be based on the facts which generate behavior in the real world. In *Robbins* where they prevailed, Justice Stewart's majority opinion observed that luggage simply does not exhibit the characteristics of cars that justified the automobile exception:

While both cars and luggage may be "mobile," luggage itself may be brought and kept under control of the police. . . . [Furthermore, no] diminished expectation of privacy [such as attends cars] characterizes luggage; on the contrary, luggage typically is a repository of personal effects, the contents of closed pieces of luggage are hidden from view, and luggage is not generally subject to state regulation.

Similarly, in *Belton,* Justices Brennan and Marshall rejected as "fiction" the majority's assumption that everything inside a car lies within the control of an arrestee and thereby falls within the intent of the arrest exception. As Justice Brennan's opinion put it,

[u]nder the approach taken today, the result would presumably be the same even if Officer Nicot had handcuffed Belton and his companions in the patrol car before placing them under arrest, and even if his search had extended to locked luggage or other inaccessible containers located in the back seat of the car.

These three Justices did not adopt fictitious portraits of police-suspect confrontations as a means of "providing police officers with a more workable standard for determining the permissible scope of searches. . . ." As Justice Brennan noted, "the mere fact that law enforcement may be made more efficient can never by itself justify disregard of the Fourth Amendment." The warrant requirement itself reflects a constitutional choice to sacrifice some degree of efficiency in law enforcement in favor of strong protection for individual privacy. The education principle requires that exceptions to that requirement be constructed in a way that reaffirms the underlying policy. Thus, Justices Brennan, White, and Marshall drew the necessary line nearest to the core of the relevant exception; the purpose of the doctrine defined its reach. This approach announces clearly that autos and arrests are special cases. Limiting those exceptions to situations where they are strictly justified therefore reminds society of the fundamental rule: searches must ordinarily be authorized by warrants.

Robbins also posed a question implicating the equality principle, although none of the Justices wrote about it in those terms. California argued that the two plastic bags of marijuana deserved less protection than, for example, "sturdy luggage, like suitcases." The plurality rejected this contention on two grounds. First, the Fourth Amendment protects people's "effects whether they are 'personal' or 'impersonal.' " When items are placed in "a closed, opaque container," the owner has "manifested an expectation that the contents would remain free from public examination." Second, there is no principled basis for distinguishing the variety of containers people use to hold their belongings.

Before *Robbins* was decided, our court confronted a case involving a similar question. Like Robbins and Belton, Albert Ross was properly asked by police to stop his car. After spotting weapons on the front seat, the officers arrested and handcuffed Ross and then searched the rest of his vehicle. In the trunk, they found "side by side a closed brown paper sack about the size of a lunch bag and a zippered red leather pouch." The paper bag, police discovered, contained heroin; there was $3,200 in cash in the leather pouch. The contents of the two receptacles helped convict Ross of a federal narcotics offense.

Under the Supreme Court's decision in *Arkansas v. Sanders,*[6] a precursor to *Robbins,* the police could not constitutionally search "luggage" found in properly stopped and searched automobiles without a warrant. Regarding Ross's red leather pouch as a form of luggage, all of the judges who originally heard the case agreed that the $3,200 in currency must be suppressed because the police had not obtained a warrant. The court divided, however, on whether the paper bag fell within the *Sanders* rule. The majority of the initial three-judge panel concluded that Ross did not have a reasonable expectation of privacy in his paper bag, partly because "a reasonable man would [not] identify a paper bag as a normal place to entrust his intimate personal possessions." My dissent, and the subsequent opinion of the full court, concluded that the paper bag was equivalent to the red leather pouch for Fourth Amendment purposes.[7]

Ross thus posed a classic Fourth Amendment line-drawing problem. The amendment clearly protected luggage. The panel majority drew the line there and excluded paper bags from that protection. While this line can be faulted for lack of precision, I felt its greater difficulty lay in its failure to reflect reality and insure equality.

The simple fact is that in some of our subcultures paper bags are often used to carry intimate personal belongings. And, the sight of some of our less fortunate citizens carrying their belongings in paper bags is too familiar to permit such class biases to diminish the protection of privacy.

In *Robbins,* Justice Stewart also rejected a " 'worthy container' rule encompassing bags of leather but not of paper." Yet, consistent with his general approach in both *Robbins* and *Belton,* he seemed to base this conclusion more on the efficacy of a bright, formal line than on questions of reality and equality:

[The] Amendment protects people and their effects, and it protects those effects whether they are "personal" or "impersonal". . . . Once placed within [a closed, opaque] container, a diary and a dishpan are equally protected.

[Moreover,] it is difficult if not impossible to perceive any objective criteria by which [a distinction between suitcases and other containers] might be accomplished. What one person may put into a suitcase, another may put into a paper bag. . . . And as the disparate results in the decided cases indicate, no court, no constable, no citizen, can sensibly be asked to distinguish the relative "privacy interests" in a closed suitcase, briefcase, portfolio, duffel bag, or box.

Thus, proponents of the two philosophies of criminal procedure can arrive at the same bright line for very different reasons. For Justice Stewart, a "worthy container" rule would simply be incapable of sensible application; it would violate the efficiency principle. For me, there is no moral basis for a Fourth Amendment line, however bright, that makes "the level of constitutional protection available to a citizen dependent on his ability to purchase a fancy repository for his belongings."

The Constitution is not for sale to the highest bidder; neither is it a special preserve for those with more material goods to protect. The private spaces where belongings are kept are not less—and are perhaps more—important to the person who has only a paper bag to carry his worldly goods than to the man who carries matched, designer luggage.

Miranda and Self-incrimination

Some of the most difficult issues in modern criminal procedure concern the privilege against self-incrimination. In particular, *Miranda v. Arizona*[8] continues to spawn a series of complicated questions. When is interrogation "custodial"? What is the functional equivalent of questioning? What constitutes sufficient waiver? Again, my purpose is not to plumb the details of these questions. Rather, I hope to demonstrate the ways in which the continuing controversy about *Miranda* implicates choices between the two philosophies of criminal law I have described.

Critics of the criminal justice system often reserve their sharpest attacks for the *"Miranda* revolution." In an article entitled "Abolish the 5th Amendment," Mickey Kaus contended that the amendment's "natural constituency" consists of sex murderers, "assorted mafiosi, drug smugglers, tax cheats, and labor racketeers."[9] For him, *Miranda* and its progeny seem to have as their hidden purpose the maximizing of the number of times when the Fifth Amendment will be employed by the guilty to frustrate the police.

Kaus' comments are consistent with the "law-as-external-constraint" hypothesis. An externalist might argue that confessions provide the police with a fast and easy way of obtaining reliable evidence of crimes; that "innocent" people have nothing to confess and therefore cannot be harmed by the practice; that *Miranda* inhibits the acquisition of this valuable evidence without any compensating benefit to the truly innocent; and therefore that the decision diminishes the threat of swift and certain punishment without advancing the guilt-determining process.

For many years, this approach governed the Supreme Court's evaluation of confession cases. Physical torture obviously offends due process, as the Court recognized early on. Beyond that, the Court's principal concern seemed to be the risk that confessions derived from questionable police methods might be unreliable. Out of this concern arose the standard which prevailed for many years: if the totality of the circumstances indicated that the suspect's admission was not voluntary, then the confession might be false. In that event, the interrogation frustrated the externalist goal of separating the guilty from the innocent. If it were demonstrated that a particular police practice did not reliably identify the guilty, and caused suffering among the innocent, it would be prohibited.

Beginning in 1961, however, the Supreme Court excluded coerced confessions "not because such confessions are unlikely to be true but because the methods used to extract them offend an underlying principle in the enforcement of our criminal law: that ours is an accusatorial and not an inquisitorial system."[10] In one case from that period, the Court excluded a confession obtained after the suspect had swallowed a truth serum. The shift in emphasis effectively placed a higher priority on the internalist goal of giving moral force to criminal procedures. This paved the way for *Miranda*.

There may be no better example of a criminal procedure decision that follows the reality, equality, and education principles than *Miranda v. Arizona*. Until then, the law, like people generally, simply ignored the grim facts about the gatehouse of American criminal procedure—the police station "through which most defendants journey and beyond which many never get."[11] This violation of the reality principle made the law of confessions fundamentally amoral:

[S]ociety, by its insouciance, has divested itself of a moral responsibility and unloaded it on to the police. Society doesn't want to know about criminals, but it does want them put away, and it is incurious about how this can be done provided it is done. Thus, society in giving the policeman power and wishing to ignore what his techniques must be, has made over to him part of its own conscience.[12]

In *Miranda,* the Supreme Court confronted the grim facts. In order to arrive at an "understanding of the nature and setting of . . . in-custody interrogation," the Court undertook an extensive examination of reports, cases, and police manuals. Based on its assessment of the facts, the Court "concluded that without proper safeguards the process of in-custody interrogation of persons suspected or accused of crimes contains inherently compelling pressures which work to undermine the individual's will to resist and to compel him to speak where he would not otherwise do so freely."

Miranda also reflected the equality principle. Those most likely to suffer coercive police practices behind closed stationhouse doors are the poor and uneducated perpetrators of street crime. Educated, respectable suspects ordinarily know of their rights to be silent and to retain a lawyer. By insisting that the disadvantaged be informed of those rights, by demanding that all suspects be treated with dignity, and by refusing to admit confessions extracted through police tactics usually reserved for the deprived, *Miranda* promised genuine equal justice before the law.

Finally, the *Miranda* decision conformed to the education principle. As Professor Yale Kamisar has noted, before that case the salient features of stationhouse confessions were

the invisibility of the process—"no other case comes to mind in which an administrative official is permitted the broad discretionary power assumed by the police interrogator, together with the power to prevent objective recordation of the facts"—and the failure of influential groups to identify with those segments of our society which furnish most of the raw material for the process.[13]

Miranda recognized that "[p]eople are willing to be complacent about what goes on in the criminal process as long as they are not too often or too explicitly reminded of the gory details." The decision forced the previously hidden world of the "gatehouse" into the open. It thus reminded society both of the importance of meaningful constitutional guarantees and of the fact that the people most in need of those rights are most often denied them. *Miranda*'s success as an instrument of education is marked by the fact that every television viewer is familiar with the required litany of station-house rights.

Miranda, then, represents the potential of the law of criminal procedure to exert moral force. Today, the challenge is to ensure that its promise is fulfilled. There is evidence that many defendants do not understand the *Miranda* warnings. Externalists might regard this as proof that *Miranda* is inefficient, that its costs to aggressive law enforcement outweigh its benefits in protecting the innocent. But I believe that this evidence only requires us to work harder at making *Miranda* effective. The standards for finding waivers of the right to counsel and the right to remain silent have become crucial.

A number of years ago, a case in our court underscored the importance of effective *Miranda* warnings.[14] The police arrested Eugene Frazier for the robbery of Mike's Carry Out. After they advised him of his rights and let him read a copy of the *Miranda* warnings, Frazier signed a "Consent to Speak" form and told an officer that he understood his rights and did not want a lawyer. When an officer started questioning him about Mike's Carry Out, Frazier interrupted and admitted to robbing High's Market. The policeman started to transcribe Frazier's remarks, but the defendant stopped him, saying, "Don't write anything down. I will tell you about this but I don't want you to write anything down."

The officer put down the pad and continued listening in silence as Frazier went on about the High's robbery. After about five minutes of this, Frazier confessed to the robbery of the Meridian Market. Two hours or so later Frazier ended the questioning, stating, "That's it; that's all I know and that's all I am going to tell you." When the police asked the defendant to write out his confession or to sign a typed summary, Frazier refused. "No, I'm not going to sign anything," he said.

When the case first came to us on appeal from Frazier's conviction for the Meridian Market robbery, we were troubled by "[t]he strong implication . . . that appellant thought his confession could not be used against him so long as nothing was committed to writing." We therefore doubted whether the Government had carried its heavy burden of establishing that the defendant had "intelligently and knowingly" waived his rights. We remanded the case to the lower court, in order to give the Government an opportunity to present evidence that the waiver was nevertheless valid. On remand, the trial court concluded that the Government had carried its burden. On a second appeal, the full court affirmed. I dissented.[15]

I emphasized *Miranda*'s teaching that a confession made in the absence of counsel "can stand if, but only if, the accused *affirmatively* and *understandingly* waives his rights." The evidence developed on remand suggested that, far from admonishing Frazier that an oral confession could be as damaging as a written one, the police "elected not to risk any clarification for fear [he] would stop talking." The majority recognized that the defendant might not have understood his rights but held, nonetheless, that the Government can meet its burden by showing that the warnings were given and "if the issue is raised that the person warned was capable of understanding the warnings."

In my view, the majority's approach made of *Miranda* a "preliminary ritual." By ignoring the realities of police interrogation, it denied people like Frazier genuinely equal treatment before the law:

> Of course, the problem posed by this case would not exist if the warnings were so clear that no one possessing even minimal intelligence could possibly misunderstand them. But capacity to understand the warnings does not by any means guarantee that they will actually be understood.

The available empirical evidence clearly indicated that many, if not most, defendants do not understand the warnings, even where the defendants are intelligent and well-educated. The likelihood of understanding is necessarily reduced where, as here, the 28-year-old defendant has been afflicted with sickle cell anemia for many years and used narcotic drugs to mitigate his pain. . . .[16]

Where the police officers are dealing with ill-educated and uncounseled suspects, they have a special obligation to be alert for signs of misunderstanding or confusion.

Miranda continues to pose substantial challenges to the development of a moral criminal law. For many poor and uneducated people, for example, a variety of confrontations outside of "custodial interrogation" are inherently coercive. Indeed, state investigations conducted by officers other than the police—such as psychiatrists examining defendants for sanity—may pose some of the same dangers. To fulfill the promise of *Miranda*, we must always be guided by the reality, equality, and education principles that formed the foundation of that decision. I continue to believe what I wrote in my *Frazier* opinion:

> [T]he *Miranda* rule reflects a principle fundamental to a democratic society. The Fifth Amendment protects *all* persons; it ensures that no individual need incriminate himself "unless he chooses to speak in the unfettered exercise of his own will." *Miranda* is designed to make that protection meaningful for the man who has neither the education, the experience, nor the counsel that would enable him to make an informed decision. Far from being a mere technicality, it touches the heart of a system of justice that purports to treat all of its citizens equally under the law.

The Right to Counsel

More than 170 years after the adoption of the Sixth Amendment, *Gideon v. Wainwright*[17] breathed life into the right to counsel by assuring representation for indigents in state trials. *Gideon* recognized the reality that for the poor and uneducated who need lawyers the most, the Sixth Amendment had offered only barren rhetoric. The decision promoted genuine equality by requiring the state to furnish counsel to those who could not afford it. It served the education principle by alerting society both to the importance of legal representation in our adversary system and to the plight of the disadvantaged. Like *Miranda, Gideon* stands as a statement of our highest moral aspirations.

Yet, as with *Miranda,* the legacy of *Gideon* continues to demand further effort. What I wrote many years ago remains sadly true: "[A]lthough we generals of the judiciary have designed inspiring insignia for the standard, the battle for equal justice is being lost in the trenches of the criminal courts where the promise of *Gideon* . . . goes unfulfilled."[18] Time and again, the cases that came before my court revealed that the indigent's lawyer is unequipped to provide even the most basic protection for the defendant's rights. Too often, the lawyer is either unaware of or totally indifferent to the client's fate.

The reality principle demands that we acknowledge the woefully inadequate representation received by the poor. The equality principle requires that we lift the burden of defective advocacy that falls largely on a single subclass of society. The education principle insists that the courts stimulate a renewed commitment to equal justice by the bar and by the public. In short, the fundamental Sixth Amendment challenge today is to ensure effective representation of counsel for all members of society.

Externalists might offer a variety of reasons why a serious effort to remedy ineffective assistance of counsel should not be undertaken. Too broad a reading of the right to counsel might impair our ability to assure swift and certain punishment. Justice Felix Frankfurter, for instance, feared that recognizing claims of ineffective assistance "would furnish opportunities hitherto uncontemplated for opening wide the prison doors of the land."[19] Furthermore, guaranteeing all defendants diligent advocates might so impede the courts that the criminal justice system would grind to a halt. And, at bottom, externalists might believe that ineffective assistance is unimportant unless it results in the punishment of an innocent person. This may be why many appellate courts require claimants to show not only that their constitutional right to effective counsel was denied but also that the denial was prejudicial.

No amount of rhetoric from appellate courts will assure defendants effective representation unless trial judges, the bar, and the public at large recognize the fundamental importance of enforcing the Sixth Amendment. The Supreme Court has stated that trial judges must zealously "maintain proper standards of performance by attorneys who are representing defendants in criminal cases in their courts."[20] And the bar must increase its efforts to monitor the performance of its members and to take appropriate disciplinary action against attorneys who fail to fulfill their obligations to their clients. In the end, of course, there can be no substitute for legislative action. Money is needed to attract more experienced appointed lawyers and public defenders, to make public defender positions economically viable career posts, to provide initial and ongoing training for inexperienced lawyers both in and out of defender offices, and to create more defender positions.

The fact that the ultimate solution may not be within the powers of the criminal law, however, does not entitle us to ignore the situation or to accept it as immutable. In the Sixth Amendment, as elsewhere in criminal procedure, the law must be guided by the education principle. It must alert the public to "the sordid reality that the kind of slovenly, indifferent representation provided Willie Decoster is uniquely the fate allotted to the poor."[21] It must constantly impress upon society the importance of effective assistance of counsel.

Criminal procedures can be neither moral nor effective unless they at least encourage people to internalize the commands of the law. Ultimately, however, no amount of tinkering with the criminal justice system will provide a meaningful and lasting solution to crime. As long as the conditions that breed that kind of crime continue, our efforts to solve the problem amount to a tragic charade. The criminal law cannot change social conditions but it can force those conditions onto the public consciousness. By remaining constantly sensitive to the realities of social and economic deprivation, to the promise of genuine equality, and to the fundamental values underlying the Bill of Rights, the law can help society see the imperative of linking criminal justice with social justice. Society might then pursue an enduring social tranquillity worthy of our highest moral aspirations.

11

The Bazelon-Katzenbach Letters[1]

Although often portrayed as a "liberal," I have had profound disagreements with administrations of all political stripes. But no matter the depth of the disagreement, it is important to maintain a dialogue among opposing views.

More than two decades ago I had a rather celebrated dispute with Lyndon Johnson's chief law enforcement official, Attorney General Nicholas Katzenbach. This discussion took place during the last generation of criminal justice reform. The identical issues were, of course, central to the recent lengthy deliberation that culminated in passage of the Comprehensive Crime Control Act of 1984. The new legislation improves the criminal justice system in many ways. However, in my view its defects unfortunately include allowing preventive detention—authorizing judges to consider whether a defendant poses a danger to the community in deciding whether to grant bail.

President Reagan called his version of the legislation "a long overdue protection to law-abiding Americans that would help put an end to the era of coddling criminals."[2] But proposals to get tough on crime are nothing new, nor are they unique to conservative administrations. Just how far the liberal Johnson Administration was from coddling criminals is evident in the views expressed here. Fighting crime is something on which all parts of the political spectrum agree. Our differences lie in how we propose to do it.

On reading this correspondence, Professor Anthony G. Amsterdam wrote me a letter which is briefly excerpted following my letter and Katzenbach's. I agree heartily with his conclusions. My views of the Johnson and Reagan Administrations' policies on crime control are much the same: both represent a simplistic approach to a complex problem. The following correspondence probably did not change anyone's mind, but it did ventilate the issues.

June 16, 1965

Dear Mr. Katzenbach:

In light of our recent discussions about the administration of criminal justice, it was with particular interest that I read your very fine speech to the University of Chicago Alumni. You have rightly pointed to the needs to examine how theoretical legal rights work in practice and to "reevaluate the divergence of ideal and practice." In line with this concern, I believe you may share my misgivings about Articles 1, 2, and 3 of Preliminary Draft Number 1 of the proposed American Law Institute Model Code of Pre-Arraignment Procedure.

The Code proposes twenty-minute detention of a citizen to "aid in the investigation or prevention of a crime" and dragnet arrests where "it is likely that only one or more but not all of the persons arrested may be guilty of the crime." The Code also approves police questioning of a suspect from four to twenty-four hours after his arrival at a police station. These provisions would, in my experience, primarily affect the poor and, in particular, poor Negro citizen. I doubt that police would, for example, arrest and question the entire board of directors of a company suspected of criminal antitrust violations although it might be "likely that only one or more but not all . . . may be guilty of a crime." It is not apparent to me, however, that prosecuting authorities have had notable success in detecting or combatting such "white collar crimes" as antitrust violations or tax frauds. I cannot understand why the crimes of the poor are so much more damaging to society as to warrant the current hue and cry—reflected in the proposed Code—for enlarging police powers which primarily are directed against those crimes.

It is also likely that, in some instances, professionals who engage in organized crime may be held and questioned by police. But these suspects know their rights and counsel is ordinarily available to them. Thus the discriminatory working of the proposed Code is most graphically revealed in the provisions regarding availability of counsel during police interrogation.

The proposed Code permits a suspect to retain counsel during interrogation but it deliberately fails to provide counsel for those who cannot afford it, or for those too ignorant or inexperienced to understand their rights and their need for counsel. The Code provides that retained counsel may be present during police interrogation, though the *Reporter* suggests, as an alternative proposal, that retained counsel may be excluded from the interrogation though he would be permitted to consult with his client prior to the interrogation.

In the teeth of *Gideon, Griffin, Coppedge* and *Hardy*,[3] the *Reporter's* Commentary argues that neither proposal regarding counsel works an invidious discrimination between rich and poor on the ground that the state has no "affirmative obligation to insure that persons in custody will not incriminate themselves" but rather that the "state must remain neutral." But the proposed police detention and interrogation are not "neutral" state acts. Their primary effect, unless counsel is provided, is to elicit damaging admissions from suspects. (The Commentary suggests that detention and interrogation may also permit the suspect to exculpate himself. But the presence of counsel would aid rather than inhibit this purpose.) If the state subjects all suspects to detention and interrogation, it is only a pretense of "neutrality" to permit those able to retain counsel to protect their rights effectively while refusing to provide equal protection to the poor and inexperienced.

The Code's alternative proposal—that retained counsel be excluded from the interrogation—would partially eliminate one blatant discrimination between rich and poor by impeding the ability of the rich to protect their rights. But a major distinction between rich and poor would remain: those who could afford it would have some support from counsel; the poor have none.

In any event, elimination or curtailment of counsel's role in the interrogation procedures raises grave doubts about the fairness of those procedures. The source of these doubts is revealed in the Commentary's rationale for the Code's refusal to appoint counsel during police interrogation:

> the expenditure of large public funds is not justified to assure that in *all* cases in-custody interrogation can be effective only for the purposes of exculpation and *never for inculpation.*

The clear premise of this argument is that no one, if advised by counsel, would volunteer inculpatory statements. Since the Commentary cannot assume that counsel would coerce a suspect to remain silent, I think this argument is an implicit admission that counsel's presence militates against the confusion or fear or insufficient understanding of his rights which prompt a suspect to speak.

Indeed, the Commentary itself admits that the "atmosphere [of a police station] tends to be one of confusion and indeterminacy" and it is, I think, coercive to many who are accustomed to view the police as hostile. In such atmosphere, the Code's intricate provisions for police warning of rights will be ineffective. Counsel, unlike the police, has no transparent interest in eliciting self-incrimination, and he ordinarily is more detached and knowledgeable than a relative who may, according to the Code, be present or consulted during interrogation. Since the Code refuses counsel to those most likely to be detained and interrogated, its claims ring hollow that "the suspect retains a meaningful choice as to whether and how much he will cooperate in the inquiry" and that it "provide[s] equal access [for rich and poor?] to sufficient information to make choices meaningful."

Moreover, these Code provisions fail to take account of a vital consideration set out by the Allen Committee in its *Report on Poverty and the Administration of Federal Criminal Justice:*

> The essence of the adversary system is challenge. The survival of our system of criminal justice and the values

which it advances depends upon a constant, searching, and creative questioning of official decisions and assertions of authority at all stages of the process. The proper performance of the defense function is thus as vital to the health of the system as the performance of the prosecuting and adjudicatory functions. It follows that insofar as the financial status of the accused impedes vigorous and proper challenges, it constitutes a threat to the viability of the adversary system. (at p. 10)

The police interrogation procedure approved by the Code requires "constant, searching, and creative questioning" to insure its fairness and even its compliance with the elaborate Code provisions. The Code's failure to see the need for counsel "at all stages" of the criminal process is at sharp variance with the philosophy of the Criminal Justice Act of 1964, and with the Allen Report and the policies of the Department of Justice which led to that landmark Act.

The proposed Code would in practice diverge greatly from the ideal that the administration of criminal justice should avoid invidious discrimination based on wealth. But the Code and the *Reporter*'s Commentary fail to follow your injunction in the University of Chicago speech: that we must "admit what we are doing . . . not merely for the sake of symmetry, but for the sake of social honesty—and, indeed, for the sake of better controlling crime." I hope you share my concern and I welcome your comments in the same spirit of open-minded investigation which characterized your University of Chicago speech and our recent conversations.

Unless you see some objection, I would like to furnish a copy of this letter to some of those with whom I have discussed this problem from time to time and to the interested people at the American Law Institute.

Cordially,
David L. Bazelon

June 24, 1965

Dear Judge Bazelon:

The kind reference in your recent letter to my remarks in Chicago was most gratifying. I am happy you agree that we cannot continue public discussion of problems in the administration of the criminal law without recognizing our actual practices and inquiring into the reasons for them. A viable resolution of the issues we face is indeed possible only if we pull all the considerations into the open and honestly attempt to balance the competing goals of our society.

The underlying assumption of your approach appears to be some conception of equality. No one, of course, would argue with "equal justice under law" or any other formulation. Nor do I propose to argue that purely formal conceptions of equality may have unequal impact in law as they do in virtually every aspect of our life. The poor are disadvantaged in many ways as against the rich; the ignorant as against the educated; the sick as against the healthy; etc. To what extent and by what means legal processes should take into account such inequalities raises difficult questions. I would suppose the answers, insofar as we can discover them, lie in other values which are sought within our system. It would be ridiculous to state that the overriding purpose of any criminal investigation is to insure equal treatment. Obviously, criminal investigation is designed to discover those guilty of crime. We limit both investigation and criminal prosecution in various ways both to protect the innocent and the personal rights (for example, privacy, freedom of movement and speech) we enjoy in our society. It is entirely proper to limit what the police may do in the course of an investigation, even if those limitations result in some of the guilty avoiding conviction. For example, we do not permit confessions to be tortured or beaten out of people, rich or poor—not because such confessions are necessarily unreliable but because these things are incompatible with decent law enforcement, and because— inevitably—the rack would be used on the innocent as well as the guilty. All this is obvious. But what may be forgotten is that each such decision to impose a limitation involves a balance of the values thus promoted against the value of discovering those guilty of crime.

In recent years we have taken steps to make the process fairer to the poor—by providing counsel, by revising bail procedures, etc. But in none of these efforts has equality been our overriding objective—nor should it be. We provide counsel in order to ensure that the innocent are not wrongly convicted, that they may raise defenses which help preserve the integrity of the judicial process. We do it for our sake, not for theirs. And we are providing bail procedures because we believe that in many instances financial condition is irrelevant to the purposes sought to be promoted by bail. Again, it is not a welfare program, but one designed to better effectuate the purposes of bail.

In short, I do not believe that regulation through judicial decision or statute of investigatory procedures should have as its purpose to remedy all the inequalities which may exist in our society as a result of social and economic and intellectual differences to the exclusion of all other purposes and values sought to be achieved in the criminal process. I do not believe that any decision of the Supreme Court, nor of any Court of Appeals, has been explicitly based on such a premise of equality. The courts have been attempting, in the cases before them, the same difficult balance of goals, a balance all the more difficult for lack of an adequate public and legislative discussion of the issues.

In general, over the past quarter-century, appellate decisions marking off broad new areas of reform in criminal procedure have gained public acceptance and the full support of law enforcement officers, prosecutors, and judges alike. But as the cases have presented more and more difficult questions of fairness and propriety, I believe the judges have left the public behind, and, even among judges, the margins of the consensus have been passed. The most basic investigatory methods have come to be questioned in the context of specific cases and unique factual situations, rather than after review of all of the considerations which might be thought relevant in designing rules for the system as a whole. As a result, policemen, district attorneys, and trial court judges have become increasingly unsure of the law with respect to arrest and post-arrest procedures, often differing vigorously among themselves. In your own court of appeals, the result is too often determined by the particular panel which hears a case. Thus the consistency, the efficiency, and consequently the fairness of justice have suffered.

Your suggestion that police questioning will primarily affect the poor and, in particular, the poor Negro, strikes me as particularly irrelevant. The simple fact is that poverty is often a breeding ground for criminal conduct and that inevitably any code of procedure is likely to affect more poor people than rich people. For reasons beyond their control, in Washington many poor people are Negroes; in Texas, Mexicans; in New York City, Puerto Ricans. A system designed to subject criminal offenders to sanctions is not aimed against Negroes, Mexicans, or Puerto Ricans in those jurisdictions simply because it may affect them more than other members of the community.

There are, of course, inequities in our society resulting from differences in wealth, education, and background, and these inequities are sometimes reflected in the outcome of the criminal process. Poverty, ignorance, and instability produced by wretched living conditions may make an individual's criminal acts more susceptible to discovery and proof. But, I am sure you will agree these same conditions are major causes of crime. So long as they exist and lead an individual to victimize his fellow citizens, government cannot and should not ignore their effects during a criminal investigation. Otherwise, so many persons guilty of crime would be insulated from conviction that our system of prevention and deterrence would be crippled.

This would in fact increase the suffering of the less favored in our society, for it is they who live in the high-crime areas and they who are the usual victims of crime. Investigation is not a game. It is a deadly serious public responsibility, whatever the crime. Losses and injuries which may appear small are often crushing to the victims involved. We are not so civilized that we can afford to abandon deterrence as a goal of our criminal law.

Thwarting detection and prosecution would also close the door to the rehabilitative correctional system, which is appropriately designed to ameliorate the effects of social injustice.

Indeed, it is questionable whether similarity of outcome is even relevant to the design of a process which seeks to separate out the innocent before charge and to make possible the trial of those who appear guilty. The elimination of disabling discrimination is the primary goal of the Poverty Program, the Civil Rights Act, and numerous and expanding services in vocational rehabilitation, school assistance, and medical care. It is one of the goals of the Criminal Justice Act, which recognizes that counsel make a positive and essential contribution to the further separation of the innocent from the guilty in adversary proceedings and to appropriate dispositions. Society gains in all these. But absolute equality of result could be achieved in the investigatory stage—after a crime has been committed and before a trial is possible—only by deliberately forgoing reliable evidence and releasing guilty men. Acquittal of the guilty does not promote social justice.

Moreover, acquittal of the guilty in the name of equality of treatment may prevent our achieving other, more fundamental goals also contained in the ideal of equal justice. Fairness is owed to those who obey the law, and to those guilty who are convicted. Many undergo hardship and rigorous self-discipline while observing the restraints of the law, and are unjustly disadvantaged if some are permitted to break the law with impunity. And to a man convicted because he was careless in leaving a fingerprint, or too poor to change his telltale clothes after a crime, there is no more galling governmental act than the release of one who betrayed himself because he was careless in answering a question. Furthermore, in the elimination of questioning a high price would be paid by the innocent who are exculpated early in the criminal process by police questioning, and by those who appear at first to deserve a more serious charge than is eventually filed after questioning. The introduction of counsel at this early stage would not, as you suggest, promote this screening, for there must be the possibility of an incriminating as well as an exculpatory outcome if there is to be imaginative and energetic investigatory questioning.

The interests are subtle and complex. When analyzing our system in terms of the concept of equality, it seems to me wholly arbitrary to choose as groups for comparison only some of the poor guilty and some of the rich guilty.

In any event, I do not think the dissimilarities in outcome for rich and poor are so great as you suggest. The failure to arrest a Board of Directors for questioning about an antitrust violation does not strike me as an example of unequal treatment. The investigations of antitrust violations and of violent urban crime are simply not comparable, and the anonymity and mobility of modern urban life often do not permit postponement of arrest when crimes of violence are involved. Moreover, when any crime is in issue those who have respectability at stake, and who could have a lawyer at their command, cannot afford to appear guilty. Calling a lawyer for protection from investigation, or refusing to answer questions, does often give the appearance of guilt, and as a consequence the rich will often talk, and, if guilty, will often provide incriminating evidence.

You are right, I fear, that "professionals who engage in organized crime" frequently succeed in avoiding conviction under our system. But I have never understood why the gangster should be made the model and all others raised, in the name of equality, to his level of success in suppressing evidence. This is simply the proposition that if some can beat the rap, all must beat the rap. I see no reason to distort the whole of the criminal process in this fashion. Because we cannot solve all crimes and convict all criminals is no reason to release those guilty whom we can convict.

Discussions such as ours, now stimulated by the American Law Institute's draft code, are being generally undertaken with regard to the design of our whole system of criminal law. My chief concern is that in seeking to achieve the freedom, security, legal and social justice that are at stake in our conclusions, we do not permit the real issues to be obscured. If the issue is conviction of the innocent, then we must specifically examine that. If it is the coercion of the socially disadvantaged, then we must discuss that carefully and realistically. If it is the meaning of the privilege against self-incrimination, or the likely effect, and proper function of counsel, then we must turn to that on its merits. But we cannot afford merely to draw out the logic of unexamined assumptions. The stakes are too high.

I have no objection, of course, to your releasing your letter to anyone you wish, and should you desire you may append this reply to it.

> Sincerely,
> Nicholas deB. Katzenbach
> Attorney General

July 2, 1965

[Dear Judge Bazelon:]
. . . I sadly fear that the Attorney General is selective in the assumptions he will and those he will not examine. . . .

The obvious generalizations which he does state—for example, "I do not believe that regulation . . . of investigatory procedures should have as its purpose to remedy all the inequalities which may exist in our society . . . to the exclusion of all other purposes and values . . ."—are neither responsive to your letter nor adequate to support the General's reasoning from them unless they mean something cruder than they say. I take them to mean what they must mean in order to take the General where he goes. And this is, in short, that equality is a pretty unimportant value in the criminal process. . . .

The General's proposition is that it is unimportant that these protections are unavailable to those too ignorant to claim them and too poor to engage a lawyer for their vindication. That makes them unavailable, by the General's own admission, to the classes of persons most likely to be prosecuted for crime, unavailable, in short, in most of the cases in which they were designed to operate. I am not yet so cynical as to believe that the statesmen and judges who expressed the high aspirations of our society in these guarantees meant them only as window-dressing for a system in which the accepted and ordinary practice was that they were to be lost by ignorant and involuntary waiver. Nor can I forget that equality of procedure is synonymous with regularity of procedure and that in a world where even the best of men (among whom I shall include *arguendo* the police of Chicago, Illinois, of Philadelphia, Pennsylvania, and of Philadelphia, Mississippi) sometimes surrender to the delusion of infallibility, regularity of procedure is all that protects the citizen against conviction of crime by the policeman and imposition of punishment through "investigatory" detention and brow-beating interrogation. . . .

The [desired] end is a safe, secure society for all of us who live in it. That end is more efficiently attained, I am sure the General would agree, by encouraging citizen cooperation to law than by perfecting the means for apprehending and punishing the disobedient. For the most part, encouraging obedience and punishing disobedience are mutually consistent, even mutually supporting means.

They cease to be consistent when the powers given officials to apprehend and punish the disobedient are so unconstrained that their exercise arouses citizen resentment and contempt for law. Nothing so much arouses resentment and contempt for law as arbitrariness and inequality of treatment at the hands of officers of the law. . . .

Best regards,
Anthony G. Amsterdam

12

Counsel and Conscience[1]

The constitutional guarantee of "effective assistance" of counsel is a guarantee with a purpose. That purpose is not, as some people believe, to shift the balance against the "peace forces" in favor of the "criminal element." It is to assure that our adversary system of justice really is adversary and really does justice.

The adversary system assumes that each side has adequate counsel. That is the predicate for the truth-seeking function of the courts, a role that accords with a fundamentally democratic nation that rejects inquisitorial government. But what I have seen from the bench leads me to believe that a great many— if not most—indigent defendants do not receive the effective assistance of counsel guaranteed them by the Sixth Amendment.

Good defense work may well take more of the court's time. That is the price we pay for constitutional protections. If society believes in those protections, it will have to pay the price in terms of increased expenditures and time for the criminal justice system. If the price of a truly constitutional trial becomes too great, we have two alternatives: we can reduce the number of trials by limiting the scope of the criminal sanction, or we can make the defendant pay the price by denying him protections that the Constitution guarantees. When we tolerate ineffective assistance of counsel, we are actually choosing the second alternative.

Counsel, as the defendant's advocate, is the one who must prod the system's conscience to insure that the man or woman is not lost for the crime. Counsel must see to it that his client's individual needs will not be overwhelmed by the system's pressing need for administrative efficiency. Counsel must be the medium of reconciliation. While counsel's protection of his client's legal rights and his role in the adversarial process are essential to his constitutional responsibilities, these functions should not be the limit of counsel's advocacy for his client. We should also examine an expanded role for counsel which can serve the interest of the defendant and society; I discuss this in the last section of this chapter.

Only recently have we even recognized that the lack of effective counsel inevitably deprives the poor of the right to a fair trial. One hundred and forty-one years after the adoption of the Bill of Rights, the Supreme Court first held, in *Powell v. Alabama*,[2] that due process requires the appointment of counsel for an indigent defendant in a capital case. Not until *Gideon v. Wainwright*,[3] more than thirty years later, did the Court acknowledge that the "noble ideal" of equal and fair justice could not be realized "if a poor man charged with crime has to face his accusers without a lawyer to assist him," and extend the right to counsel to all state felony prosecutions. And not until 1972, in *Argersinger v. Hamlin*,[4] did the Court affirm the right to counsel in all criminal prosecutions that could result in deprivation of liberty for the accused.

The Supreme Court's effort to eliminate second-class justice for the poor has not been confined to providing counsel for the indigent. But the right to counsel is most essential in assuring fair and equal justice, for without the conscientious and knowledgeable advice of a trained legal advocate, an accused can secure none of the safeguards of the criminal process intended to protect all defendants. To the extent that the indigent defendant receives inadequate representation, markedly inferior to that available to a defendant who can afford "competent and conscientious counsel," a dual system of justice endures.

Inevitably there will be disparities in the quality of representation; some lawyers are simply more competent or more conscientious than others. What offends the Constitution, however, is not merely that there are variations in the quality of representation, but that the burden of less effective advocacy falls almost exclusively on a single subclass of society—the poor. In constructing standards for assessing the ineffective assistance of counsel, we must consider not only what measures are necessary to assure a fair trial in the case of any particular defendant. We also must structure our approach to eliminate the gross disparities of representation that make a mockery of the adversary process in pursuit of truth, and our commitment to equal justice. We must institutionalize and enforce standards of attorney competence designed to assure adequate representation for all defendants.

The article that follows was written in 1973. The problem it deals with, unfortunately, remains essentially unchanged.

* * *

For criminal defendants with court-appointed attorneys and for those defendants who can beg, borrow, or steal a hundred dollars or so to pay for a lawyer, the right to counsel too often means little more than pro forma representation.

There are no statistics to illustrate the scope of the problem, because, as I shall demonstrate, the criminal justice system goes to considerable lengths to bury the problem. But no one could seriously dispute that ineffective assistance is a common phenomenon. A very able trial judge once described some of the counsel coming before the courts as "walking violations of the Sixth Amendment."

I came upon these "walking violations" week after week in the cases I reviewed. I have seen trial records, for example, in which:

• Defense counsel did not know that the court kept records of prior convictions;
• Defense counsel advised the judge that he could take only a few minutes for summation because he had to move his car by five o'clock;
• Defense counsel invited the jury to draw an inference from

the fact that there were no witnesses to corroborate his client's alibi defense;

• Defense counsel told the jury he had done the best job he could "with what I have had to work with";

• Defense counsel based his case on an 1885 decision; when the judge asked for a later precedent, the attorney said that he couldn't find a Shepard's citator [a reference book lawyers use routinely to identify cases on the same issue].

Perhaps this is surprising to many. After all, any law student is familiar with the series of Supreme Court decisions, from *Powell v. Alabama* to *Argersinger v. Hamlin*,[5] which have guaranteed the right to counsel for anyone facing loss of liberty. The Court has repeatedly recognized, in an often-quoted phrase from Justice Sutherland in *Powell*, that a criminal defendant "requires the guiding hand of counsel at every step in the proceedings against him." To implement these judicial pronouncements, the Federal Criminal Justice Act[6] and similar provisions in the states have required the courts to establish mechanisms for the appointment and compensation of counsel for indigent defendants.

As a result, we have today what appears to be a sound and effective guarantee of every defendant's Sixth Amendment right. Appearances can be convincing. In a fit of optimism brought on by the Court's decisions in *Gideon v. Wainwright* and *Escobedo v. Illinois*,[7] I once made a rosy prediction: "No doubt in ten years the right to counsel will be another area which we can view with satisfaction, finding in it a high degree of rationality and protection of individual rights."[8] So it seemed to me in 1964.

Now, I am not so optimistic. I must concur with Chief Justice Burger's observation that:

our "delivery" of justice, to borrow a term from experts in medical care, is faltering and inadequate. The means of "delivery" . . . [include] an effective legal profession. . . . Surely an effective system of justice is as important to the social, economic and political health of the country as an adequate system of medical care is to our physical health.[9]

Much like the provision of medical care to the poor, the assignment of legal counsel to the indigent is a nonprestigious activity that the public and the profession would rather not think about. Just as we assume that medical responsibility is met when we provide poor people a hospital, no matter how shabby, undermanned, and underfunded, so we pretend to do justice by providing an indigent defendant with a lawyer, no matter how inexperienced, incompetent, or indifferent.

The American Bar Association's Project on Minimum Standards for Criminal Justice used the metaphor of the three-legged stool to depict the criminal justice system— justice balanced on a tripod consisting of the trial judge, the prosecutor, and the defense counsel.[10] If any one of those three is shorter, or weaker, than the other two, there is an imbalance that can result in injustice. Chief Justice Burger, who chaired the ABA project, stated not long ago that the most common cause of imbalance and injustice in the system is the weakness of defense counsel. To see why this is so, it might be valuable to focus on each leg of the tripod and its role in the criminal trial.

Defense Counsel—Public Defender, Regulars,
Uptown Lawyers, Neophytes

Most of my own experience is in the District of Columbia, where representation for indigent defendants comes from a number of sources. About one-fourth of these cases are handled by a public defender service. I am well aware that the quality of public defenders varies tremendously and that those in the District of Columbia are certainly among the best. Our Public Defender Office controls its own caseload; with adequate support staff, one of its lawyers handles an average of about sixty felonies and misdemeanors each year. In contrast, with little control over their caseload and inadequate support staff, public defenders in other major American cities have annual felony case loads of up to 500 per attorney.*

Our public defender is not directly governed by the local courts, but is accountable to a Board of Directors, the members of which are selected by the chief judges of the District's local and federal courts. The agency depends on Congress for appropriations. There is the danger that the agency will fall under pressures inconsistent with the interests of its clients. In the District, but even more so where agencies operate under the direct control of trial judges, public defenders may be torn between their duty to the client and their duty to the court and its crowded calendar. I have been reliably informed that a director of one such agency periodically checked with trial judges to determine whether his staff attorneys were too aggressive or took too much of the courts' time. Criticism by a trial judge was passed on to the offending lawyers. Such practices may be conducive to rapid and efficient processing of cases but do not promote diligent and conscientious advocacy.

There is a continuing awareness in the public defender agency of the need to protect against subordinating the goal of criminal defense to the requirements of the system. The majority of the indigent defendants in Washington, as in other cities, are represented by private attorneys, who fall into three broad categories: the regulars, the uptown lawyers, and the neophytes.

The bulk of these cases are handled by a relatively small coterie of what are commonly called "courthouse regulars." These attorneys were depicted by the ABA Criminal Justice Project as "a cadre of mediocre lawyers who wait in the courtroom in the hopes of receiving an appointment" and have "more expertise at extracting a fee . . . than in defending a criminal case."

* There has been some improvement since the mid-1970s; however, the average caseload in the District is still 70 to 80 per year, while that in other major cities is 150 or even 300.[11]

The Criminal Justice Act provides for payment on a per-hour basis with a statutory per case maximum. It is, in effect, a piecework system of compensation. The more cases a regular handles, the more income he receives. The essential element in the regulars' practice is volume—and a number have been able to earn $30,000 to $50,000 per year, with fees averaging about $150 per case. Thus, each of these lawyers handled from 250 to 350 cases. [For the sake of comparison, the National Legal Aid and Defender Association has proposed standards fixing a maximum of 150 felony cases per year for an experienced attorney who has adequate support and investigative resources at hand, and there is considerable feeling that even this figure is too high.][12]

Although the high-volume regulars are relatively few, they are assigned a percentage of appointed cases far out of proportion to their numbers. The result of their high-volume practice is that they often have little or no time to prepare a case or even to talk to their clients. The investigative services of the public defender are available to all appointed counsel, but the regulars rarely bother. They often investigate a case by questioning the arresting officer for a few furtive minutes in the corridors of the courthouse, filling in the gaps through examination of witnesses during the trial.

Why do we tolerate this type of representation? Some argue that the regulars get better results for their clients than more zealous lawyers. A federal judge once warned me that the tenacious new breed of defense attorneys would only aggravate judges, resulting in fewer dismissals and longer sentences for their clients. The regulars probably justify their type of representation on the basis of just such a view.

Their rationalization, however, has serious implications. To the extent the quality of justice depends on an incestuous relationship between judges and attorneys, the adversary quality of the system is corrupted; but that alone is too simple a response. This rationalization is not necessarily a matter of bad faith; it may be a result of system maintenance pressures. When nonassertive lawyers get better deals for their clients, the system is rewarding them for saving the court's time. This was borne out by a study in Massachusetts showing that defendants who waive counsel generally get lower sentences than those who do not.[13] The system evidences its need for efficiency by pressuring defendants into not cluttering up the system with lawyers at all. That obviously strikes at the very heart of the adversary system, the Sixth Amendment, and the right to trial itself.

From the regulars' point of view, any trial is uneconomical: it limits their availability for other appointments. The quickest way to turn over a case is to induce a client to plead guilty, and up to 90 percent of criminal cases are disposed of by such pleas. A Georgia case, which I hope is unusual, indicates the potential for abuse.[14] A defense attorney was handling some five thousand cases a year. He had one ten-to-fifteen-minute interview with his client before pleading him guilty to a capital charge. His only response to three letters from the client suggesting exculpatory witnesses was a warning that an extra fee would be required if the case went to trial. To make his point, the lawyer informed the defendant that copies of his prior record would be circulated among the jury and that the judge had promised the electric chair if the defendant were found guilty at trial. Fortunately, the plea was held involuntary on collateral attack. But, in many cases, the decision to cop a plea evolves from a procedure invisible even to the trial judge. There is no way of knowing how many thousands of pleas each year are engineered by the guiding hand of lawyers such as that Georgian.

The District of Columbia has made efforts to circumvent some of these problems by assigning cases to "uptown" lawyers—corporate, labor, securities, or patent attorneys—who are rarely seen in the vicinity of the courthouse. Most do not want anything to do with the criminal justice system; they may share the attitude of the Carl Sandburg character who was asked whether there was a criminal lawyer in his town. "We think so," he replied, "but we haven't been able to prove it on him." These attorneys accept appointments only as a matter of public duty and, on the whole, do fairly well, particularly if they have had some criminal law experience. But many others, including leaders of the bar in other fields of law, do not. In spite of the myth that all lawyers are generalists, criminal defense is a specialty. It requires a skilled trial advocate who is familiar with not only the criminal code but also police and prosecutorial practices, the availability of local experts and private crime labs, and the informal norms of the criminal courts. Certainly any self-respecting prosecutor would be familiar with these aspects of the system. Is it fair to saddle a defendant with counsel who is not?

Some experienced lawyers tell me that any competent trial attorney can learn how to try a criminal case. This may be true, but even so, the cost in time and money would be immense. Any reasonably bright lawyer can search out the existing law on bail, for example, but all the time he is learning his client waits in jail. A personal injury lawyer who is assigned a criminal case may have trial experience, but he will have to rediscover the wheel on every substantive issue of criminal law and procedure, particularly any complicated issue such as entrapment. Further, uptown lawyers often have a serious communication problem in dealing with an indigent defendant. They are not prepared for the cultural shock of learning that their client is neither middle-class nor cast in their image of the deserving poor.

These difficulties raise serious questions about reliance on uptown lawyers as a panacea for the problem of representing indigent defendants. It might profit us more to search for approaches which will attract attorneys into taking continuing interest in criminal defense work.

Another mode of providing counsel, one that is prevalent in many parts of the country, is assigning the most junior members of the bar to criminal appointments. This approach, too, is troublesome. Defense of an indigent is not an extension of law school. If criminal representation is too complex for the uptown practitioner, it is obviously beyond the grasp of a lawyer with no experience at all. You may have heard the familiar refrain "'I got experience—my client got jail." I would not like to be the defendant whose trial is the vehicle for some young lawyer to gain trial practice. The medical profession is often accused of letting new doctors get their training by practicing on the poor without the close supervision they need. The charge applies with equal force to the law.

Our inability to provide every defendant with an effective defense is also due to the failure of legal education. Law schools do not teach students how to try criminal cases. The typical law school graduate trying his first criminal case not only does not know what to do next, he does not know what to do first. Unlike his Wall Street counterpart, whose firm provides a closely supervised apprenticeship period, the neophyte criminal lawyer is not apt to find such on-the-job training programs. (An exception is the new defense counsel who spent a few preliminary years as an assistant district attorney, but he started there as an inexperienced graduate.) The Wall Street litigator may take three years to argue his first motion. He may never try a case entirely on his own. The criminal lawyer could have his first solo case a few weeks after passing the bar.

A common fear is that a neophyte will compensate for his inexperience by engaging in unnecessarily vigorous and hostile advocacy. But the supervisors of the leading legal internship programs believe that the opposite is the case; the unsupervised junior attorney is more apt to bury his anxiety by copping a plea or falling into the pattern of docility that he sees in the practice of the criminal court regulars. The law schools have begun to deal with both of these dangers through clinical programs which provide the absolutely essential element of supervision at a critical juncture in the student's socialization process. Because of the need for close supervision, good clinical programs are expensive. As one would expect, some programs are good and some not so good. Without provision for careful supervision, they can become just another way of throwing the neophyte into the water where either he will swim or his client will sink.

The Prosecutor

The prosecutor also contributes to the problem of ineffective representation. Too often he views the courtroom as a marketplace where he must buy a bargained plea for the best price he can obtain.

In one case, a soldier was charged under both the misdemeanor and the felony sections of the Controlled Substances Act. If prosecuted under the misdemeanor provision, the soldier could avoid a dishonorable discharge and be entitled to probation and eventual expungement of his record. At trial, the soldier's appointed counsel conferred for a minute with his client—apparently for the first time—in the corner of the courtroom, and then agreed to a guilty plea to the felony charge. When the judge inquired into the basis for this plea, it became obvious that the proper charge was the misdemeanor; accordingly, the judge offered the prosecutor time to draw up the necessary papers for the misdemeanor. However, the prosecutor said that was unnecessary and thereupon pulled the document from his folder. He had come to court ready to drop the felony charge in return for a plea on the misdemeanor—but the defense counsel was too ignorant, or too indifferent, to seek that bargain. And—what is at least as shocking—the prosecutor was perfectly willing to let the defendant be victimized by his lawyer's inadequacy.

The problem is that the prosecutor has no incentive to police the quality of his adversary. We all know the theory that a prosecutor's goal should be to do justice rather than to gain a victim. With notable exceptions, however, a prosecutor's incentive is to win cases, or at least to dispose of them quickly, so he is not always sensitive about taking advantage of a defense counsel's weakness. A former assistant United States attorney told me that he once asked a fellow prosecutor why he was bothering to pursue a particularly weak case. The answer was that the case was weak, but the defense counsel was even weaker. Prosecutors might well think twice in such circumstances if there were a serious risk of the conviction being reversed owing to ineffective assistance of counsel for the defense, but this is rarely a serious threat.

The Trial Judge

The power of appointment and payment of defense counsel generally is entrusted to the trial judge. To the extent that the lawyers who represent indigent defendants are dependent for their livelihood on these judges, there is a great incentive for them not to rock the boat. These lawyers know that many judges are preoccupied—and understandably—with keeping their overcrowded dockets moving. Consciously or not, many judges are looking for, as the labor cases put it, a "sweetheart" lawyer. They do not want attorneys to present a lot of motions or to put on a lengthy trial. Some are not only willing but insistent on papering over the inadequacy or indifference of the lawyers practicing before them. Others do so inadvertently because they focus on the defendant's guilt and ignore his counsel's performance. Even the most conscientious judge will feel the pressures of his overloaded calendar, and this concern will be evident to the perceptive attorney. When defense counsel's earnings flow from the pen of the trial judge, the principle of independent advocacy that is essential to the adversary system of justice is undermined.

Judges can, and many do, take steps to protect a defendant who is represented by inadequate counsel. They discuss waivers with a defendant himself instead of relying on the attorney. It is not uncommon for a judge to vacate the appointment of a lawyer he believes will render ineffective assistance. Judges grant recesses so that lax lawyers can do the research they should have done in preparation for trial. Judges will sometimes steer attorneys onto an effective line of defense either at bench conferences or through their own questioning of witnesses. Sometimes a judge will call in a public defender lawyer to assist obviously floundering defense counsel. In one case, where the attorney was proving himself incapable of handling a complex insanity defense, the judge pressured him into moving for a mistrial.

All these measures put the trial court in a difficult position. While no conscientious judge wants to sit silently while an attorney butchers his case, the judge cannot take over the defense's case altogether. Moreover, the steps he can take are stopgaps; they are inefficient and open to abuse. Clearly, it would be unreasonable to rely on the trial judge alone to deal with the problem of ineffective counsel.

Because of the pressure of numbers, there is often a unanimity of interest among defense counsel, trial judge, and prosecutor in pushing criminal defendants through the system as quickly as possible. The goal of mass-production justice is rapid processing of cases. The most common mechanism to satisfy this goal is the guilty plea. When the defendant pleads guilty, defense counsel collects one more fee and moves on to the next case; the trial judge removes one more trial from his calendar; the prosecutor reduces his caseload and adds one more "guilty" to his list of courtroom triumphs. It may be true that most defendants would plead guilty even with the best of counsel. But in today's high-pressure system, a genuine calculation of defendant's interests is unlikely. There is no way to assure those interests have been served unless the plea has resulted from proper preparation and analysis of the case.

Traditional Remedies and New Approaches

Traditionally, the legal profession has borne the responsibility for disciplining lawyers. Unfortunately, the bar associations, like most professional societies, have shown themselves unable, or at least unwilling, to police their own members. Our vaunted Code of Professional Responsibility has not served as a means of policing the quality of defense counsel. The ABA Project on Standards for Criminal Justice developed some valuable standards for the defense function, but they are merely guidelines and have not been implemented. Today, even as minimums, these guidelines are honored as much in the breach as in the observance.

There are traditional legal approaches to this problem. One is the private malpractice suit brought by a defendant who has suffered because of his attorney's inadequacy. When standards that clearly articulate counsel's duty to his client are developed, such suits may become more practical, but whatever it may become, this form of action is not at all significant now.

Any after-the-fact policing will be expensive and unwieldy. After-the-fact remedies, by their very nature, do not change the game of Russian roulette played by a defendant whenever counsel is appointed for him. They come into effect only after a defendant has been assigned one of the loaded cylinders the system tolerates. What we should be looking for are preventives. Rather than engaging in a mud-slinging contest after a failure occurs, we should be developing criteria to be met before appointment.

The linchpin of any screening mechanism is certification. Defense counsel must possess basic skills and stay on top of a rapidly changing area of law. The medical profession, which is also struggling with the obligation to keep up, provides an example for dealing with our own problem. Medicine has faced up to the fact of specialization. To become board-certified as a specialist, a doctor must demonstrate an acceptable level of competence in his field. The Ford Foundation has expressed interest in a similar certification of criminal law specialists. Certification of attorneys on a periodic basis for separate felony, misdemeanor, and juvenile court panels could be a prerequisite for Criminal Justice Act appointments to such cases. This suggestion presents issues too complex for complete discussion here—questions as to the criteria for certification, and the role of the bar, government, and community in the process—but these are problems that our profession must begin to consider.

If we are going to demand that criminal lawyers demonstrate a specialist's expertise, we must provide them with some means to achieve it. Since we want to keep the field open to lawyers who are not in full-time criminal practice, criminal law institutes and continuing legal education should be available, and possibly mandatory, for certification. Service as co-counsel is another educative device. For law students and the neophyte lawyer, we need to provide a way of obtaining adequately supervised experience. Law school clinical programs are a step in this direction, but many current programs are too limited. Students should be moved out of the classroom and into supervised programs of internship in the criminal justice system. We should begin to experiment with various other means of introducing lawyers to criminal defense work. Postgraduate residencies, such as public defender training programs or Reginald Heber Smith fellowships, are such options. Participants in all these programs who do not remain in criminal law practice will be a resource within the private bar on which the courts can later draw.

Insuring initial competency is a step toward insuring effective representation, but competency is not the equivalent of effectiveness. The institutional pressures which produce ineffective representation must be alleviated so that lawyers who are competent are not forced into patterns of docility or inadequacy.

If these institutional pressures are to be alleviated, perhaps the power of appointment might best not be given to trial judges. The ABA project on criminal justice standards observed that "an assigned lawyer . . . may not have the same freedom of action in defending his client before the judge responsible for the assignment that retained counsel would have." Is there any more reason for judges to control the selection of counsel for indigents than for nonindigents? Rather, the power of appointment should be lodged in a public agency, independent of the courts, but deeply committed to the defense of indigents. Some trial judges in my jurisdiction, concerned about the competence of the lawyers appearing before them, have opposed this reform. But assigning the power of appointment to a public agency capable of developing and enforcing clear standards for eligibility does seem a better means of insuring competence and diligence than ad hoc judgments of individual trial judges. As the commentary to the ABA Standards for Providing Defense Services observed, "ad hoc assignment does not fulfill either the objective of quality or of equality," and the committee reserved particular condemnation for the common practice of appointing lawyers who happen to be in the courtroom or are waiting around the courthouse for an assignment.

Also proposed is a system in which the defendant "appoints" his own lawyer. These are so-called judicare plans in which the defendant hires the lawyer of his choice and the government pays the fee. While in theory this would duplicate a wealthy man's options, in reality it may accomplish far less. Wealthy defendants get better representation not only because they choose their own lawyers but also because they have the resources to pay large fees and are apt to be viewed differently by everyone in the system. Judicare might do little more than put the indigent in the same shoes as defendants able to buy an inexpensive defense now. For such questionable improvement, the plan would involve immense practical problems. Surely, many of these problems could be resolved, but for the immediate future, I believe, appointment by a public agency is preferable.

I would seriously consider placing the responsibility for a continuing review of indigent criminal defense work with the same public agency. Supervising agency attorneys could investigate complaints and, where necessary, spot-check or assist lawyers in their cases. Not every lawyer requires supervision or assistance, but it is clear that many, particularly the neophytes, do. The agency would not only be a supervisor but an educator, providing up-to-date information on legal issues and guiding attorneys to agency and community resources of which they might not be aware.

In warning that the Sixth Amendment guarantee of effective assistance of counsel is in danger of becoming a dead letter in our major urban courts, I have concentrated on the problem at the trial level, but the appellate courts must share the responsibility. One of the major reasons that the problem of ineffective assistance has remained hidden is the appellate courts' remarkable propensity to ignore the issue altogether and to paper over the cracks in the house that *Gideon* built.

Appellate courts expound at great length on questions of evidence or procedure without touching on the cause of those errors—the inadequacy of counsel. My court once unanimously reversed a murder conviction because the trial judge erroneously excluded certain evidence.[15] The majority failed to mention the many instances in which defense counsel demonstrated abject ignorance of law and procedure. The time has come for appellate courts to directly confront this source of error. Such failure to ventilate the issue of ineffectiveness cuts off both public discourse of a serious shortcoming in our system of justice and efforts to provide guidance for future cases.

There are several reasons why appellate courts, like the other participants in the system, so rarely face up to the problem of inadequate representation of indigent defendants. Some courts avoid the issue for practical purposes. I have often been told that if my court were to reverse every case in which there was inadequate counsel, we would have to return half the convictions in the jurisdiction.

It frightens me to hear the suggestion that we should respond to a problem by ignoring it. If the problem is that widespread, our responsibility to confront it is all the more urgent. When we evade the constitutional claim on such pragmatic grounds, we are like the man in the Buddha's parable of the burning house. A bystander told him to flee because his house was ablaze. But the man was too practical; before he left home, he had to discover whether it was raining outside and whether he could find a new place to live. So it is with the courts. While we wait to confront the problem of ineffective assistance, our system of criminal justice crumbles around us.

There is also a common fear that the criminal justice system would collapse for the lack of enough competent lawyers to provide an effective defense for every indigent defendant. Burgeoning law school enrollments and growing interest in criminal litigation among students cast substantial doubt on these predictions.

Then it is argued that if there were enough conscientious lawyers the criminal courts would be so impeded by their efforts that the system would grind to a halt. In short, good lawyers would make the courts inefficient. On the contrary, providing skillful and diligent defense attorneys might do much to alleviate the real inefficiencies in criminal trials. A lawyer who has prepared his case and knows what to do at trial can handle cases far more efficiently than incompetents who conduct investigation at the witness stand and require a recess to research every significant point.

I think it is also a misplaced concern for efficiency that has led to criticism of my practice of appointing new counsel on appeal. The argument is that appointing the original attorney will save both the time a new attorney would need to review the record and the expense of a transcript. Frankly, I agree with Justice Arthur Goldberg that no attorney worth his salt, no matter how familiar with the trial, would bring an appeal without reviewing the transcript and the record.[16] The "inefficiency" in appointing new counsel is that the new lawyer is more apt to identify difficult questions—including inadequate representation—that trial counsel would not raise. We can hardly expect an attorney to argue matters which reflect his own inadequacy. Actually, a lawyer in Arkansas once did raise this issue. The Eighth Circuit accused him of attempting to fabricate a defense for a client who had no other. If the defendant does have a colorable claim of ineffective assistance which is not raised on appeal, it is apt to be raised on collateral attack, resulting in more, not less, litigation. If the claim is never raised at all, our concern for efficiency may have cost a defendant his Sixth Amendment right.[17]

Another reason appellate judges maintain a hands-off policy is their reluctance to soil the reputations of appointed counsel by labeling their work ineffective. I once issued an opinion in which I pointed out eight substantial errors made by defendant's trial counsel. When the newspapers reported the case, the big news was not the attorney's inadequacy but rather the fact that a judge had mentioned it.[18]

We must come to realize that the issue in effectiveness of counsel cases is not the culpability of the lawyer but the constitutional right of the client. There will, no doubt, be many ill-founded claims of ineffectiveness—there are such now—but such claims are an occupational hazard of the profession. My colleague Judge Charles Fahy once said:

> Embarrassment caused counsel by an unjust charge of ineffectiveness is a price that unfortunately must be paid at times for careful judicial administration. And where the charge is just the remedy is not to save counsel from embarrassment but to save his client from unjust conviction or sentence.[19]

A lawyer necessarily must—and I think he safely can—rely on the good sense of an appellate tribunal. In any event, we cannot let our concern for his feelings stop us from considering the issue of his effectiveness.

The final reason why judges are reluctant to reverse convictions on grounds of inadequate assistance is particularly disturbing to me. It is the belief—rarely articulated, but, I am afraid, widely held—that most criminal defendants are guilty anyway. From this assumption it is a short path to the conclusion that the quality of representation is of small account. This may be why appellate courts commonly require appellants to show not only that their constitutional right to effective counsel was denied but also that the denial was prejudicial.

The Second Circuit once considered a case in which defense counsel was observed to be sound asleep during the examination of prosecution witnesses.[20] The Court found that there was not ineffective assistance because "the testimony during the periods of counsel's somnolence was not central to [the accused's] case and . . . if it had been, [the trial judge] would have awakened him rather than [waiting] for the luncheon recess to warn him." If the lawyer had not been present, there would have been a reversal without a showing of prejudice; but because the lawyer was merely asleep, an entirely different standard was applied. The Court found that the presence of a warm, albeit sleeping, body at the defense table satisfied the defendant's Sixth Amendment right. It is difficult to accept the Court's distinction between the right to the presence of counsel and the right to his assistance. Adding a consideration of overall fairness to a Sixth Amendment guarantee dilutes that amendment's independent vitality and impairs its deterrent purpose. A defendant should be relieved of the burden of showing prejudice. Once he has proved ineffectiveness, the government should have the burden of showing no resulting prejudice.

It will doubtless be said of this suggestion that I am again striving for a perfect trial, which everyone knows is impossible. The impossibility of perfection is hardly grounds for complacency about a shabby status quo and it does not excuse the failure to perform better.

Whatever the standard, it should address the real issue, which is not a lawyer's gross incompetence, or his experience, or good intentions, or whether he was at fault. We are not trying counsel for a crime. The real question should be whether counsel did everything that a diligent lawyer could reasonably be expected to do, whether he filled the role imposed on him by the rigors of the adversary system. The articulation of specific duties would help the courts define that role. When counsel fails in those duties, his representation has been ineffective, no matter how honest or well-intentioned he may have been. Stating the issue in this way also makes it clear that effective assistance is not a static concept; it is one that changes with the development of new resources and the recognition of new obligations.

In a Fifth Circuit case,[21] the defendant argued that his guilty plea was the result of ineffective assistance of counsel. He maintained that his lawyer should have asked for a competency hearing and pursued a responsibility defense rather than recommending a plea. The court majority found that the decision to advise that plea was "strategical" and thus "not open to question."

From the dissenting opinion, however, it appears that the lawyer's decision was not so much strategy as ignorance or indifference. The attorney had one fifteen-to-twenty-minute interview with his client, during which the defendant said he had twice previously been committed to a mental institution. Had the attorney investigated this point, he would have discovered that his client had a history of masochistic behavior and suicide attempts. Two months before the crime, a psychiatric examination had found the defendant suffering from "manic depressive pyschosis." At the time the crime was committed, the defendant was an escapee from the state mental institution. Without the benefit of this information, the lawyer "bargained" a plea by which his twenty-five-year-old client was sentenced to seventy-five years in prison.

My dissent in *United States v. Simpson*[22] dealt with the need for procedures which "assure that a defendant is adequately advised by his attorney before pleading," and noted that adequate advice requires counsel have a full grasp of the facts and law of the case. When his client pleads guilty, however, no record is kept of counsel's performance and he is not required to demonstrate any preparation. Accordingly, I proposed that the trial judge require the attorney to indicate for the record the extent and results of his investigation of the facts of the case and a concise breakdown of its preparation.

With such information we could return to the approach of establishing specific duties for defense counsel in guilty-plea cases. Prescriptive norms of conduct will give lawyers notice of their obligations and provide courts with a concrete basis for determining whether a defendant really did receive effective assistance of counsel at the time of his plea.

A significant problem with the concept of delineating specific duties for defense counsel is the matter of trial tactics. Any checklist of duties must include enough flexibility to take into account the peculiarities of a particular trial. But flexibility can go too far. Appellate courts have been so willing to excuse questionable decisions and omissions as "trial tactics" that almost any error can be ignored under that rubric. It reminds me of our early right-to-treatment cases in the mental health area; the government's answer in every case was that the patient was receiving "milieu therapy," which meant in practice that few patients were getting any treatment at all.

My own court invoked the possibility of "trial tactics" in a rape and assault prosecution.[23] A doctor who examined the victim on the night of the alleged attack reported that he found no indication of rape or of a struggle—but he was never called to testify for the defense. The majority refused to remand to explore the issue of ineffective representation. It speculated on circumstances in which the failure to call the doctor might have been reasonable. No case should be decided on the basis of mere surmise. Procedures must be found to provide the information necessary to determine whether or not the defense's action—or inaction, in this instance—is an informed, deliberate, and rational choice.

To make this kind of judgment about a lawyer's tactics, or to evaluate his preparation for entering a guilty plea, the appellate courts will require information which is often unavailable from the trial record. A number of mechanisms are available to provide a hearing in the trial court, thus supplementing the record, on the ineffectiveness issue. An appellate remand is one such device but is rarely used.

It might, of course, be more efficient for an appellate court to hear the appeal after rather than before such supplementation of the trial record. An attorney on appeal, who intends to raise an ineffectiveness claim but has an inadequate record, can assert the claim first on a motion for a new trial. If the district court is inclined to grant the motion, it would so indicate to the appellate court, which would then remand the case for that purpose. If the district court were unwilling to grant the motion, the record thereby compiled could nonetheless serve to supplement the record on appeal. Collateral attack, allowing defendants to raise on appeal constitutional issues that counsel overlooked at the original trial, also provides a means to supplement the record on the issue of ineffectiveness, but here a petitioner must often make an even stronger showing than on appeal.

It would be preferable to obviate a hearing as often as is possible by having the necessary information in the original record. To meet this need, it has been proposed that appointed lawyers file reports on their preparation and investigation, either at the conclusion of trial or when their client enters his plea. Such reports would not only provide a valuable record on appeal, but might also be a means to develop some basic norms of defense counsel responsibility.

Trial judges can also make defense counsel's decisions more visible to the appellate courts. In the plea context, a judge should make, for the record, a searching inquiry into the factual basis for the plea and the elements of the agreement between prosecutor and defense attorney. He might also inquire into counsel's preparation and investigation.

When the defendant goes to trial, the judge can ask at the arraignment, the beginning of trial, or the close of evidence whether the client is satisfied with his appointed lawyer. Obviously this would not provide a sophisticated legal appraisal of counsel's performance, but it might bring into the open such problems as the failure to call a witness.

But no matter how careful the trial judge is in constructing a record, the effort will be of little value as long as appellate courts are unwilling to confront demonstrated ineffectiveness. If trial records more accurately reflected counsel's blunders, it might be harder for appellate courts to ignore the issue as frequently as they do today.

The New Defense Counsel:
Representing the Whole Person

I have made it clear that any Sixth Amendment renaissance will require a concerted effort on the part of trial judges, appellate judges, prosecutors, defense counsel, and the bar. To make sure that no one escapes the onus, I shall discuss defining the role of counsel by reference to the law schools' part in that process. Law schools should take the lead in a reappraisal of the role of defense counsel—what it is and what it should be. They are best fitted to engage in the comprehensive, long-range analysis that the question demands, and to do so on a continuing basis to take account of new problems. Clinical education in the law schools is at the interface of legal theory and practice. It could be an important tool for the development of standards and the identification of resources and skills defense counsel needs to do the job. It may well be that the way we define the role of counsel will, itself, cause the development of new resources.

Both the Supreme Court and the ABA have recognized that

defense counsel has an important role in sentencing. With the vast majority of criminal cases disposed of by guilty pleas, sentencing is the crucial part of the trial for most defendants. Certainly paid defense lawyers who represent white-collar defendants put a major emphasis on sentencing. They even concern themselves with the question of which prison facility their client will be sent to. An indigent should not be deprived of the same concern as a wealthier defendant. Yet there is a common notion among appointed defense lawyers that their responsibility ends with conviction; after that the defendant is a problem for the social worker or penologist. A few vague mutterings about the quality of mercy cannot constitute effective assistance of counsel.

The effect is shown by one case that came before my court. The appellant had been suffering from sickle-cell anemia for nearly a decade and relied on heroin to ease the pain of his illness. That pain, his addiction, and the helplessness of knowing he was fatally ill clearly pervaded the man's entire life. In the portion of the presentence report dealing with the accused's physical and mental health, the investigating officer observed only: "He claims and appears to be in good health. He states that he suffered from 'sick cells' which he describes as a blood disease." The loss not only to the defendant but to society resulting from such cursory and inadequate attention to the individual is obvious.[24]

The expanded role of defense counsel also demands active representation prior to the trial. Statements of defendants in court and the "jail mail" received by judges and the public de-fender service indicate that many appointed attorneys fail to seek pretrial release or to file bond review motions. As a consequence, the defendant stays in jail, sometimes as long as a year or more, awaiting trial. If he is convicted, the damage may be compounded. Studies show that defendants who are incarcerated before trial tend to receive longer sentences. There is some feeling that pretrial incarceration also affects the determination of guilt.

It falls on the defense attorney to put together a reasonable program—including residence, employment, and other conditions—to convince the judge that his client's appearance can be assured without incarceration. But it is rarely done.

Efforts to place the burden as to pretrial incarceration somewhere in the system other than with counsel are simply no substitute for the watchful eye of a concerned advocate. Most important, counsel is the defendant's advocate. If the system is to be humanized and individualized—made to accommodate the individual needs of the defendant—then counsel must bring those needs to the attention of the court. There are many things counsel might do if equipped with the appropriate kind of information and redefined sense of obligation.

Counsel may have a role in diverting the accused from the criminal justice system altogether. There are certainly cases where the process of criminal stigmatization—the finding of guilt—serves neither society's nor the individual's best interests. Diversion does raise problems of its own, but counsel should be capable of proposing alternatives to prosecutions—drug addiction treatment, or merely job training—with the assent of his client.[25]

Plea bargaining is probably the most ritualized, mechanistic aspect of the criminal justice system. It is commonly viewed by defense counsel and prosecutor alike more as a sales contract—a test of negotiating acumen—than as a determination of a man's future. Clearly, an attorney in a civil case would come to a negotiation session with complete knowledge of his client's case. If defense attorneys were to bring to plea bargaining adequate knowledge about the defendant as an individual, his problems and needs, that process might well be both rationalized and humanized.

The need to deal with the defendant as an individual goes beyond the trial. The accused may require assistance with personal relationships, disrupted by his arrest, with his job, landlord or creditors. And if the defendant is convicted, his attorney should be prepared to discuss long-term rehabilitation programs as an alternative to a shorter sentence. Such decisions must ultimately be the defendant's but they should be informed decisions, made after a full exploration of the alternatives with counsel. Even if the defendant is acquitted, his lawyer might suggest that his client is in need of available social services like mental health programs, family counseling or job training. The accused's problem, his alienation, his needs, do not end with the conclusion of trial.

I might best focus my remarks about redefining the role of defense counsel by contrasting the role with the criminal justice system I described earlier. The system is production oriented, a picture well summarized by the President's Commission on Law Enforcement and Administration of Justice: "[F]or most defendants in the criminal process, there is scant regard for them as individuals. They are numbers on dockets, faceless ones to be processed and sent on their way."[26] Only if counsel becomes a "counselor" is there any hope for making the system's goal humanistic rather than mechanistic.

The late legal philosopher Edmund Cahn noted that the criminal justice system treats defendants as fragments rather than whole men.[27] The courts find it too easy to limit their inquiry to whether or not a man is a burglar or a thief. But the same man may also be the father of a sick child for whom he cannot secure medical care. He may be a school dropout unable to find work. And despite the fact that the system is concerned with only part of the man, it puts the whole man in jail. It is not unlike a medical specialist who treats a particular condition. If the patient dies a week later from another ailment, what service has the doctor rendered? Someone in the justice system must be concerned with the whole man, rather than just with whether he committed a particular act. That person is counsel. This is not to say that counsel must be a social worker, psychologist, job counselor, or the like. Rather, by being sensitive to a client's needs, concerned with him as a person and aware of available resources, counsel can bring the client to those resources.

We must also remember that the criminal trial represents a failure of society. From it we can learn something about why crime occurs. But that will only be true if the system is responsible for prodding us to look beyond the criminal act to the man or woman who committed it. Where can we turn except to counsel?

13

United States v. Willie Decoster[1]

Soon after I wrote the preceding article, our court was faced with a situation illustrating in pungent detail all of the issues addressed there in more theoretical guise. The *Decoster* case also shows how an appellate court works and reworks its views on an important area of law. Over nearly ten years, this case provided both an egregious example of inequality of representation and a learning experience for our court system.

The evolution of the Sixth Amendment right to the effective assistance of counsel reflects a growing awareness of the barriers faced by an indigent defendant seeking a fair trial, and of the challenge these obstacles pose to our ideal of justice without regard to wealth. By any reckoning, the barriers are formidable. The street crime that clogs our courts most often is committed by those who need the advice of a trained advocate. In the words of Justice Sutherland: "Even the intelligent and educated layman has small and sometimes no skill in the science of law. . . . He requires the guiding hand of counsel at every step in the proceedings against him. . . . If that be true of men of intelligence, how much more true is it of the ignorant and illiterate, or those of feeble intellect."[2]

The cruel irony, of course, is that the indigent are the very people who are least able to obtain competent representation. For the most part, "you get what you pay for" in legal representation. Of course, reversing Decoster's conviction would not have remedied the pervasive problem of ineffective representation of the indigent. The disparity between representation of the poor and of the well-to-do reflects the larger inequality of riches in our affluent society. The imbalance in the quality of legal assistance is one of a host of inequities.

The judiciary has neither the means nor the competence to redress all of society's imbalances. But the court acts on a premise of equal justice. It must not betray the community's trust that it will adhere to and enforce the basic guarantees of the Constitution. We do have the duty, entrusted to us by the Bill of Rights, to assure that no individual is deprived of liberty by our courts of law without a constitutionally adequate trial. We violate this duty when we place our imprimatur of "Equal Justice Under Law" on the incompetent performance of court-appointed counsel.

An appellate court's role is limited. We can promulgate standards that specify the minimum requirements of the constitutionally mandated competent performance. We can closely scrutinize the records of those cases in which effectiveness is at issue, carefully monitoring trial counsel's performance to ensure that the attorney's obligations have been fulfilled. When substantial violations are uncovered, we can enforce the Sixth Amendment's guarantee by vacating the defendant's conviction and remanding for a new trial in which effective assistance of counsel will be provided.

The real battle for equal justice, though, must be waged in the trenches of the trial courts. While reversing criminal convictions can have a significant deterrent effect, an appellate court necessarily depends upon the trial courts to implement the standards it announces. No amount of rhetoric from appellate courts can assure indigent defendants effective representation unless trial judges—and ultimately defense counsel themselves—fulfill their responsibilities. The Sixth Amendment means more than exhortation. It requires not only articulation of standards, but a commitment to meet them.

What the Decoster case did was to encourage the right kind of ferment, the right kind of questions. It can provide a framework for courts and legal scholars to use in examining the right to effective assistance of counsel. No defendant can be said to have had his day in court unless he had effective assistance of counsel on that day.

BACKGROUND   In 1971, Willie Decoster was convicted of assault with a deadly weapon and aiding and abetting an armed robbery. Decoster's court-appointed counsel neither filed a timely application for bond review nor obtained a transcript of the preliminary hearing. Furthermore, he failed to interview a single witness—including three prosecution witnesses—before the trial.

In a 1973 panel decision, *Decoster I,* the Court of Appeals ordered a rehearing on the issue of defense counsel competency, and granted Decoster a new trial. Our decision and my opinion for the court articulated a revised standard to govern appellate review of ineffective assistance claims: "A defendant is entitled to the reasonably competent assistance of an attorney acting as his diligent conscientious advocate." To give practical content to this rule, we employed specific guidelines based on the ABA's Standards for the Defense Function as the minimal components of "reasonably competent assistance":

(1) Counsel should confer with his client without delay and as often as necessary to elicit matters of defense, or to ascertain that potential defenses are unavailable. Counsel should discuss fully potential strategies and tactical choices with his client.

(2) Counsel should promptly advise his client of his rights and take all actions necessary to preserve them. . . . Counsel should also be concerned with the accused's right to be released from custody pending trial, and be prepared, when appropriate, to make motions for a pretrial psychiatric examination or for the suppression of evidence.

(3) Counsel must conduct appropriate investigations, both factual and legal, to determine what matter of defense can be developed. . . . [I]n most cases, a defense attorney, or his agent, should interview not only his own witnesses but also those that the government intends to call, when they are accessible. The investigation should always include efforts to secure information in the possession of the prosecution and law enforcement authorities. And, of

course, the duty to investigate also requires adequate legal research.

We expressly recognized that these requirements provide only a "starting point for the court to develop, on a case-by-case basis, clearer guidelines for courts and for lawyers as to the meaning of effective assistance."

Since merely specifying the requirements for defense counsel will not alone give force to the Sixth Amendment, we further held that once a substantial and unjustified violation of any of defense counsel's duties is shown, the court must reverse the conviction unless the government can demonstrate that the violation did not prejudice the defendant's position. We thus established a three-step inquiry: (1) Did counsel violate one of the articulated duties? (2) Was the violation "substantial"? (3) Has the government established that no prejudice resulted?

After the new hearing, the District Court denied the motion for a new trial. In 1976, in *Decoster II,* our panel of three again reversed the lower court, concluding that Decoster had been denied the effective assistance of counsel. The full court vacated that decision and reopened the matter for hearing. In *Decoster III,* the court then upheld Willie Decoster's conviction. The plurality held that for a conviction to be reversed for ineffective assistance, the defense counsel must demonstrate "a serious incompetency [falling] measurably below the performance ordinarily expected of fallible lawyers." It further held that the sufficiency of defense counsel's pretrial investigation must be judged on a case-by-case basis and may be viewed in the light of the strength of the government's case. The plurality of the full Circuit Court thus rejected the application of categorical standards, characterizing the ABA criteria as partially "aspirational." With respect to prejudice, the plurality required the defendant to show that his counsel's performance was likely to have affected the outcome.

I dissented, adhering to the standards I had developed in my opinion for the court in *Decoster I.* In my view, the court's new standards violated both the reality and equality principles: "[M]y colleagues condone callous, back-of-the-hand representation by dismissing the basic duties of competent lawyering as 'aspirational.' "

*   *   *

Willie Decoster was denied the effective assistance of counsel guaranteed by the Sixth Amendment because he could not afford to hire a competent and conscientious attorney. His plight is an indictment of our system of criminal justice, which promises "Equal Justice Under Law," but delivers only "Justice for Those Who Can Afford It." Though purporting to address the problem of ineffective assistance, the majority's decision ignores the sordid reality that the kind of slovenly, indifferent representation provided Willie Decoster is uniquely the fate allotted to the poor. Underlying the majority's antiseptic verbal formulations is a disturbing tolerance for a criminal justice system that consistently provides less protection and less dignity for the indigent. I cannot accept a system that conditions a defendant's right to a fair trial on his ability to pay for it. Like Justice Black, I believe that "[t]here can be no equal justice where the kind of trial a man gets depends on the amount of money he has."[3] The Constitution forbids it. Morality condemns it. I dissent. . . .

Because my colleagues in the majority divorce their analysis from the economic and social reality underlying the problem of ineffective assistance of counsel, their decision leaves indigent defendants nothing more than an empty promise in place of the Sixth Amendment's commitment to adequate representation for all defendants, rich and poor. At best, the majority's approach might help to rectify a few cases of blatant injustice. But their standards do nothing to help raise the quality of representation provided the poor to a level anywhere approaching that of the more affluent. . . . The majority thus provides no incentive or structure to improve the caliber of defense advocacy. By focusing exclusively on the consequences of counsel's dereliction, their approach encourages an attorney who believes that his client is guilty to "cut corners," with little risk that he will be held accountable for the inadequacies of his representation. . . .

In its holding, the majority turns its back on the evolution in this circuit of the standard for evaluating claims of ineffective assistance. In the earliest cases, we approached the problem solely from a due process–fundamental fairness viewpoint, re-quiring a defendant seeking relief to show that the proceed-ings were a "farce and a mockery of justice."[4] We later explained that the "farce and mockery" requirement was not to be taken literally, but was meant only to demonstrate that in order to obtain relief the accused bears a heavy burden of showing that "there has been gross incompetence of counsel and that this has in effect blotted out the essence of a substan-tial defense. . . ."[5] In our original opinion in this case, *United States v. Decoster* (*Decoster I*), this court adopted a standard for direct appeals consistent with the Sixth Amendment's "more stringent requirements": *"a defendant is entitled to the reasonably competent assistance of an attorney acting as his diligent conscientious advocate."*

Decoster I represented a major advance in this court's recog-nition of the realities of ineffective assistance. In that case, this court shifted the focus of judicial inquiry away from the prej-udice to the defendant in any particular case and toward the task of articulating basic duties counsel owes his client. This approach, for the first time, gave content to what previously had been empty verbal formulations. Even more importantly, it recognized that the very lack of effective trial counsel might preclude a defendant from later establishing prejudice. Thus the court concluded that the only way to assure that every defendant receives a fair trial is to promulgate and enforce standards of adequate representation that apply across-the-board. Underlying *Decoster I*, therefore, was a commitment to the basic principle that every defendant—rich or poor, inno-cent or guilty—is entitled to the reasonably competent assis-tance of an attorney acting as his diligent conscientious advocate. . . .

On appeal, this court was troubled by a number of actions taken by Decoster's court-appointed counsel which, taken together, suggested that Decoster may not have received the effective assistance of counsel. . . . [S]everal months after [the] arrest, the trial judge received a letter from Decoster in which he requested new counsel because his attorney was not providing adequate representation. . . .

We also noted that events at the beginning of trial raised serious questions about the adequacy of counsel's pretrial preparation and communication with his client. As the trial was about to start, and after counsel had asserted that he was prepared to proceed, appellant himself stepped forward and asked if the court would subpoena his two codefendants, explaining that he "didn't have a chance" to discuss the matter with his lawyer. Defense counsel then told the court that he had considered the possibility of issuing subpoenas, "except for the fact that we have no address for the other defendants." The prosecutor immediately volunteered that codefendant Eley was in jail with Decoster; an address for Taylor was subsequently provided from the court records. The court thereupon ordered defense counsel to "take care of the situation."

Moments later, after defense counsel again announced that he was ready for trial, the prosecutor informed the court that the Government had not received any response to its alibi-notice demand. Defense counsel replied that although he might rely on an alibi defense, no response was needed because the Government had not given the twenty days' notice required by the local rules. The trial judge ordered the defense to provide the names of alibi witnesses anyway, whereupon defense counsel relented and stated, "We will proceed without the alibi witnesses."

Defense counsel then informed the court that his client wished to waive jury trial. When asked if he was aware that the trial judge already had heard evidence concerning Decoster's case while presiding over the trial of his codefendants, counsel responded that he was not. After attempting unsuccessfully to find another judge who could hear the case at such a late date, the trial judge ruled that he could not hear the case himself but would instead preside over a jury trial. Appellant's case thereupon proceeded to trial before a jury.

In the midst of all this confusion, Decoster again complained to the court about his attorney's efforts on his behalf. . . .

Defense counsel then requested to withdraw from the case "because apparently I have caused some dissatisfaction to the defendant. . . ." The district judge, however, did not inquire into the basis of the defendant's complaints. Instead, after receiving counsel's assurances that he had prepared the case and was ready to go to trial, the court denied the request for a continuance and refused to appoint new counsel. . . .

[I]n our original opinion we remanded for supplementary hearings on the adequacy of trial counsel's representation and granted leave for appellate counsel to move for a new trial. At the hearings on remand, . . . counsel admitted that he had not interviewed the robbery victim or either of the police officers. He also admitted that he had made no attempt to contact or interview the hotel desk clerk or, for that matter, anyone else at either the D.C. Annex hotel or the Golden Gate bar.

As for the codefendants, counsel conceded that he had not interviewed Taylor, but claimed that he had talked with Eley in the cellblock behind the courtroom on the second day of the trial. Counsel also admitted that he never obtained a transcript of the preliminary hearing, but stated that since he had conducted most of the cross-examination at that hearing, he saw no need for the transcript. Moreover, counsel testified that the U.S. Attorney's office usually makes a copy of the transcript available during discovery. Although he did not specifically remember Decoster's case, counsel said he assumed that the government's copy had been available and that he had read it. . . .

Counsel also was asked at the remand hearing to explain the reasons underlying certain "tactical decisions" he had made. He could not recall why the motion for bond review was filed in the wrong court. . . . With respect to the waiver of jury trial, counsel said that although he opposed the idea, he had requested a bench trial at his client's insistence. Finally, counsel stated that he gave no opening statement because he had felt it to be unnecessary, and not because he had no defense theory at the time the trial started. However, counsel could not recall why he had concluded that an opening statement was unnecessary. . . .

The analysis of this case should be guided by the principles established in *Decoster I*. We there held that upon showing a substantial violation of any of counsel's specified duties, a defendant establishes that he has been denied effective representation and the burden shifts to the government to demonstrate that the violation did not prejudice the defendant. Thus, *Decoster I* prescribed a three-step inquiry for determining whether a claim of ineffective assistance of counsel warrants reversing a conviction:

1) Did counsel violate one of the articulated duties?
2) Was the violation "substantial"?
3) Has the government established that no prejudice resulted?

The heart of this approach lies in defining ineffective assistance in terms of the *quality of counsel's performance,* rather than looking to the effect of counsel's action on the outcome of the case. If the Sixth Amendment is to serve a central role in eliminating second-class justice for the poor, then it must proscribe second-class performances by counsel, whatever the consequences in a particular case. Moreover, by focusing on the quality of representation and providing incentives in all cases for counsel to meet or exceed minimum standards, this approach reduces the likelihood that any particular defendant will be prejudiced by counsel's shortcomings. In this way, courts can safeguard the defendant's rights to a constitutionally adequate trial without engaging in the inherently difficult task of speculating about the precise effect of each error or omission by an attorney. Although the question of prejudice remains part of the court's inquiry, it is distinct from the determination of whether the defendant has received effective assistance. Rather, prejudice is considered only in order to spare defendants, prosecutors and the courts alike a truly futile repetition of the pretrial and trial process.

In *Decoster I*, this court attempted to give substantive content to the Sixth Amendment's mandate by setting forth minimum requirements of competent performance. The obligations were described as "duties owed by counsel to client," and thus were not offered as merely "aspirational" guidelines to which attorneys should strive. Indeed, the duties announced in *Decoster I* represent the rudiments of competent lawyering guaranteed by the Sixth Amendment to every defendant in a criminal proceeding.

The duties set forth in *Decoster I* were derived from the American Bar Association's *Standards for the Defense Function*.[6] These ABA Standards summarize the consensus of the practicing Bar on the crucial elements of defense advocacy in our adversary system. . . . Naturally, given the complexities of each case and the constant call for professional discretion, it would be a misguided endeavor to engrave in stone any rules for attorney performance. Nonetheless, preserving flexibility is not incompatible with establishing minimum components of effective assistance. . . .

In *Decoster I* this court was sensitive to these concerns and so did not attempt to prescribe categorical standards of attorney performance. Instead, we took pains to note that the articulated duties were "meant as a starting point for the court to develop, on a case by case basis, clearer guidelines for courts and for lawyers as to the meaning of effective assistance." We recognized, however, that there were certain tasks, such as the ones we enumerated in our decision, that can never be ignored: conferring with the client without delay and as often as necessary; fully discussing potential strategies and tactical choices; advising the client of his rights and taking all actions necessary to preserve them; and conducting appropriate factual and legal investigations. I submit that no one can dispute that a reasonably competent lawyer, absent good case, would or should do less. . . .

In the present case, Decoster's attorney did none of these things. Although the failure to interview a particular witness, by itself, may not rise to the level of inadequate assistance, defense counsel's investigation and preparation for this case was so perfunctory that it clearly violated his duties to his client. . . .

Surely, many of the problems that developed at and just prior to trial could have been eliminated had counsel more fully prepared himself and discussed the case with his client. . . .

In sum, counsel violated each of the duties enunciated in *Decoster I* as the prerequisites of a reasonably competent performance. Appellant's court-appointed attorney provided the kind of shoddy representation that none of us would tolerate for ourselves—a slovenly, slipshod job, almost totally lacking in preparation, characterized by repeated failures to protect his client's rights and an obvious indifference to his client's fate.

Contrary to the intimations of the majority, we do not contend that the slightest departure from a checklist of counsel's duties establishes ineffectiveness and requires reversal. Since counsel's decisions must be adapted to the complexities of a given case, the proper performance of an attorney's obligations necessarily entails considerable discretion. Moreover, the human animal is too fallible and the task of defense counsel too complex to expect that every action taken by an attorney will prove correct on hindsight. . . . The Sixth Amendment demands that counsel's conduct be conscientious, reasonable, and informed by adequate investigation and preparation; it does not demand that counsel's performance be flawless.

Thus, like the majority, we recognize that counsel's conduct must be evaluated in the context of a particular case and that not every deviation from a perfect, or even average performance makes out a claim of ineffective assistance. Instead, counsel's violations must be substantial to offend the Sixth Amendment right to effective assistance of counsel.

Perhaps counsel concluded from this limited information that his client had no alibi defense and was guilty, and that therefore counsel was excused from conducting any investigation. But the suggestion that a client whose lawyer believes him to be guilty deserves less pretrial investigation is simply wrong. An attorney's duty to investigate is not relieved by his own perception of his client's guilt or innocence. I can think of nothing more destructive of the adversary system than to excuse inadequate investigation on the grounds that defense counsel—the accused's only ally in the entire proceedings—disbelieved his client and therefore thought that further inquiry would prove fruitless. The Constitution entitles a criminal defendant to a trial in court by a jury of his peers—not to a trial by his court-appointed defense counsel. . . .

In the end, the majority's conclusion that appellant was not denied the effective assistance of counsel rests on their perception that the record contains overwhelming evidence of appellant's guilt. "[U]ltimately, there was a total failure of appellant to show that it was likely that counsel's deficiencies had any effect on the outcome of the trial." The logic of their position seems to be as follows: If the accused was probably guilty, then nothing helpful could have been found even through a properly conducted investigation. Thus, any violation of that duty—no matter how egregious—was inconsequential and hence excusable.

Even on its own terms, such reasoning is faulty. It assumes that the value of investigation is measured only by information it yields that will exonerate the defendant. Yet, even if an investigation produces not a scintilla of evidence favorable to the defense—an unlikely hypothesis—appellant still will benefit from a full investigation. One of the essential responsibilities of the defense attorney is to conduct an independent examination of the law and facts so that he can offer his professional evaluation of the strength of the defendant's case. If this full investigation reveals that a plea of guilty is in the defendant's best interest, then the attorney should so advise his client and explore the possibility of initiating plea discussions with the prosecutor. It is no secret that in the majority of criminal prosecutions the accused is in fact guilty, notwithstanding any initial protestations of innocence. It is also no secret that the vast majority of criminal prosecutions culminating in conviction are settled through plea bargaining. Indeed, the Supreme Court has recognized that plea bargaining will remain "an essential component of the administration of justice" in this country until the courts' resources are greatly expanded.[7] In many cases, therefore, perhaps the most valuable function that defense counsel can perform is to advise the defendant candidly that a thorough investigation—conducted by his own representative and seeking any glimmer of exonerating evidence—has turned up empty. Only then can the defendant truly evaluate his position and make an informed decision whether to plead guilty or whether to continue to assert his innocence at trial.

More importantly, the majority's position confuses the defendant's burden of showing that counsel's violation was "substantial" with the government's burden of proving that the violation was not "prejudicial." The former entails a forward-looking inquiry into whether defense counsel acted in the manner of a diligent and competent attorney; it asks whether, at the time the events occurred, defense counsel's violations of the duties owed to his client were justifiable. In contrast, the inquiry into "prejudice" requires an after-the-fact determination of whether a violation that was admittedly "substantial," nevertheless did not produce adverse consequences for the defendant.

All that the accused must show to establish a Sixth Amendment violation is that counsel's acts or omissions were substantial enough to have deprived him of the effective assistance of counsel in his defense. He need not prove that counsel's violations were ultimately harmful in affecting the outcome of his trial. Quite simply, the inquiry into the adequacy of counsel is distinct *from the inquiry into guilt or innocence.* The Constitution entitles every defendant to counsel who is "an active advocate in behalf of his client." Where such advocacy is absent, the accused has been denied effective assistance, regardless of his guilt or innocence. The majority opinions nevertheless force the appellant to shoulder the burden of proving that counsel's acts or omissions actually or likely affected the outcome of the trial. To thus condition the right to effective assistance of counsel on the defendant's ability to demonstrate his innocence is to assure that only the constitutional rights of the innocent will be vindicated. Our system of criminal justice does not rest on such a foundation. . . .

On the record before us in the present case, I would conclude that the government has failed to discharge its burden of proving that no adverse consequences resulted from counsel's gross violations of his duties to his client. Several important questions on the matter of prejudice remain unanswered, and in the absence of any evidence on these critical issues, I am unable to find that counsel's violations were "so unimportant and insignificant" that reversing appellant's conviction would be a futile exercise. No inquiry was made, for example, on the relationship between counsel's failure to investigate and Decoster's decision to go to trial rather than to seek and possibly accept a plea bargain comparable to that of his codefendants. Nor was there exploration of whether counsel's failure to offer any allocution at the sentencing hearing had any bearing on the trial judge's decision to sentence Decoster to a prison term of 2–8 years, while his codefendants received only probation.

In *Decoster I,* the court expressly stated that reversal would be required "unless the government '*on which is cast the burden of proof once a violation of these precepts is shown,* can establish lack of prejudice thereby.' " Thus, any doubts about the harmlessness of counsel's violations in this case would ordinarily be resolved against the government, and the case would be reversed and remanded for a new trial. Yet, despite our prior remand, it is not clear that the government was ever required to satisfy its burden of proving that the denial of Decoster's right to the effective assistance of counsel was harmless beyond a reasonable doubt. . . .

Because, as this case demonstrates, ineffective representation is often rooted in inadequate preparation, a first step that a trial judge can take is to refuse to allow a trial to begin until he is assured that defense counsel has conducted the necessary factual and legal investigation. The simple question "Is defense ready?" may be insufficient to provide that assurance. Instead, we should consider formalizing the procedure by which the trial judge is informed about the extent of counsel's preparation. Before the trial begins—or before a guilty plea is accepted—defense counsel could submit an investigative checklist certifying that he has conducted a complete investigation and reviewing the steps he has taken in pretrial preparation, including what records were obtained, which witnesses were interviewed, when the defendant was consulted, and what motions were filed. Although a worksheet alone cannot assure that adequate preparation was undertaken, it may reveal gross violations of counsel's obligations; at a minimum, it should heighten defense counsel's sensitivity to the need for adequate investigation and should provide a record of counsel's asserted actions for appeal.

The trial judge's obligation does not end, however, with a determination that counsel is prepared for trial. Whenever during the course of the trial it appears that defense counsel is not properly fulfilling his obligations, the judge must take appropriate action to prevent the deprivation of the defendant's constitutional rights. "It is the judge, not counsel, who has the ultimate responsibility for the conduct of a fair and lawful trial."[8]

My colleagues fear that judicial "inquiry and standards . . . [may] tear the fabric of our adversary system." *But for so very many indigent defendants, the adversary system is already in shreds.* Indeed, until judges are willing to take the steps necessary to guarantee the indigent defendant "the reasonably competent assistance of an attorney acting as his diligent conscientious advocate," we will have an adversary system in name only. The adversary system can "provide salutary protection for the rights of the accused" only if both sides are equally prepared for the courtroom confrontation.

Some of my colleagues are also concerned that a wide-ranging inquiry into the conduct of defense counsel would transform the role of the trial judge. . . . Yet this is the very role that the Constitution has assigned the trial judge. His is the ultimate responsibility for ensuring that the accused receives a fair trial, with all the attendant safeguards of the Bill of Rights. It is no answer to say that defense counsel will fulfill the function of protecting the accused's interest; the very essence of the defendant's complaint is that he has been denied effective assistance of counsel. The trial judge simply cannot "stand idly by while the fundamental rights of a criminal defendant are forfeited through the inaction of ill-prepared counsel. . . ."[9]*

However vigilant the judge, the problem of inadequate representation of the indigent cannot be solved by the courts alone. The bench, bar and public must jointly renew our commitment to equal justice. The bar certainly must increase its efforts to monitor the performances of its members and to take appropriate disciplinary action against those attorneys who fail to fulfill their obligations to their clients. Additional funding is needed to increase the number of public defender positions and to provide those organizations with better support services. We must increase the compensation of court-appointed counsel to attract high-quality legal talent and to ensure that those who represent the indigent on a regular basis do not have to sacrifice all economic security to perform this vital role. We must reduce the caseloads of both public defenders and court-appointed counsel to manageable levels. And we must establish procedures to insulate appointed counsel from the pressure to curry favor with the judges who appoint them and fix their compensation.

* In light of Judge Leventhal's repeated charges [in the court's plurality opinion] that our approach will produce a "thorough reordering of the adversary system," I must emphasize that I am not proposing to transform the adversary system into one "more inquisitorial in nature." Indeed, nothing could be farther from the truth. The purpose of our approach is merely to assure that our "adversary system of justice" really is adversary.

Judge Leventhal frequently expresses his fears that the approach outlined in this opinion will undercut the adversary system and seriously disrupt the administration of justice. Yet nowhere does he elucidate the exact nature of the predicted dire consequences. The approach adopted in this opinion does not require that defense counsel reveal—at each stage of the proceedings—the precise information and reasoning that prompted him to pursue a given course; it only requires that he be able to assert that his actions have in fact been based upon informed tactical decisions. And if counsel is eventually called upon to justify his conduct in a post-trial inquiry, it is enough for him to defend his actions by articulating the reasoning behind them; the reviewing court will not substitute its own judgment as long as counsel's decisions are informed and rational. I thus cannot understand how the adversary system will be "tortured out of shape" if the defense counsel must contemplate from the beginning that he may be called upon to justify his conduct at some future date. And I fail to see how requiring defense counsel to fulfill the most rudimentary obligations of pre-trial investigation and preparation will disrupt the administration of justice.

That the ultimate solution does not lie exclusively within the province of the courts does not justify our ignoring the situation nor our accepting it as immutable. The people have bestowed upon the courts a trust: to ensure that the awesome power of the State is not invoked against anyone charged with a crime unless that individual has been afforded all the rights guaranteed by the Constitution. We fail that trust if we sit by silently while countless indigent defendants continue to be deprived of liberty without the effective assistance of counsel.

IV

WHAT IS THE QUESTION?

The way questions are asked frequently has a lot to do with how they are answered. During the long debate leading up to passage of the Comprehensive Crime Act of 1984, one Senator polled his constituents about whether Congress "should eliminate release on bail for dangerous criminals awaiting trial." A *New York Times* editorial pointed out: "When the question is put that way, it's hardly surprising that many reply with a hearty yes. But put it another way: Should Congress require that a person charged with a crime but still presumed innocent prove that he won't commit 'another crime' if allowed to remain free pending trial?"[1] For many people, the answer this time would be no.

It is a distressing task for a judge to sift daily through official records detailing what we call "behavior problems," the wreckage of human lives. They occur not only in criminal cases, but in cases of child abuse and neglect, welfare eligibility, civil commitment, and many others.

The one thing that makes this task tolerable is the hope that we can learn something about the reasons for this human wreckage that will help us to avert it in the future and terminate the seemingly endless cycle of pain and despair. Each case necessarily focuses public attention on a piece of human behavior. What better laboratory can one expect?

Why do some people break the law? For the most part, the question of why is deemed irrelevant by the law. It is enough that a man robs a liquor store—it doesn't matter that his family is hungry. The law tends to avoid looking into the why of behavior because such questions are seen as undermining the order and symmetry of the law. Decisions become vastly more complicated; facts and relevant considerations are much harder to pin down. And any qualification of the principle of individual responsibility is seen as risking erosion of a fundamental assumption of our system of justice. Years ago when I was on a radio program about criminal responsibility with Senator Paul Douglas, he remarked, "Apparently you believe in the French maxim that to understand all is to forgive all." I replied that I didn't know it was a French maxim, but since it's hardly likely that we'll ever understand all, we're not in much danger of being called on to forgive all.

One traditional exception to seeing the why of behavior as irrelevant seemed to be the case of a defendant who claimed he was insane when he committed a crime. It was simply too barbarous to hold someone responsible for actions he plainly couldn't control. But only the most obvious cases of uncontrollable behavior came within the scope of the insanity defense. Essentially, a man was considered to know what he was doing as long as he knew that the gun in his hand was not a toothbrush. Of course, most people who are that far out of touch with reality are identified long before they can do any harm. It was the less obvious cases that gave us trouble.

The potential of the insanity defense to focus on the question of why people behave as they do has never been realized. But as a judge—and as a human being—I was led beyond my original interest in the extreme forms of behavior we designate as aberrant. It was as if my experience in viewing the drama of the courtroom had opened a window onto the whole world of troubled people.

The problems we confront in the courtroom are not simply the problems of "other people." They are the problems of all of us, and are not very far removed from the rest of society's life and experience. The behavior we scrutinize through the public, dramatic focus of the courtroom reflects truths that apply to everyone and can provide an understanding of ourselves and those about us. And the behavior of our courts both reflects and shapes who we are as a society, and who we will become.

But maybe we don't really want to learn that much. Maybe it would be too painful to look closely. Maybe we don't want to understand that there are no simple solutions to social problems—not if we really believe in western civilization's fundamental value of individual human dignity. In sum, maybe we don't want our noses rubbed in odorous reality, and perhaps for that reason we cover it up with the deceptive perfume of slogans like "law and order."

The courts can provide an unparalleled education, to the benefit of judges and our whole society. If we allow it, what we learn in one area also spills over into many others. By participating in a wide range of activities, a judge risks the "activist" label. But I have felt that my responsibility as a judge included educating myself, following the questions wherever they led, and contributing my views and experience, wherever I properly could do so, to the many forums beyond the courtroom where people struggled with pressing social problems.

In the following section, the lessons of my experience with the criminal law are applied to other, but related, problems: the prison system, Soviet psychiatry, mental health law, the First Amendment. In some areas, like corrections and the right to mental health treatment, the outgrowth was almost inevitable once we began to question the reality of equal justice. In others, such as Soviet psychiatry, my examination of the social-control role played by psychiatrists in our criminal justice system led to some uncomfortable questions for both American psychiatrists and their Soviet counterparts.

I can only begin to suggest the power released when we dare to question expertise and long-standing assumptions. During the last decade, for example, my attention has been drawn ever more strongly to the challenges and questions presented by advances of science and technology.[2] Dr. Donald Fredrickson, then director of the National Institutes of Health, oversaw the bitterly controversial struggle to bring up to date NIH guidelines for research involving recombinant DNA molecules. He has written about the difficulty, and the importance, of airing "in an open and public manner the scientific and social issues"[3] when letting loose a new technology whose risks are not known with certainty. He was kind enough to note that he had heeded my advice to this effect.

As we confront the perils and promises of this scientific age, both democracy and human dignity demand that we be told of the risks, uncertainties, and value choices that are made in our names. It will be argued that society would balk if it knew just how blindly we march into the future—and at what cost. But false reassurances, unjustified confidence, and hidden agendas will only create cynicism and destroy credibility. Our people have always been prepared to accept risks and to pursue the larger good of the society. Progress can hardly be achieved in any other way. Choices will be made despite uncertainty and despite the social disruptions and dislocations. To choose rationally, however, society must be informed about what is known, what is feared, what is hoped, and what is yet to be learned.

14

Correcting Corrections

An important element of my career has been the opportunity it offered me to participate on professional committees and commissions which sought to include a judge's viewpoint. Those extending the invitations may not always have known what they would be getting. I have always regarded such activities as a serious and integral part of my responsibility as a judge to improve the administration of justice and the many areas of public activity our decisions affect. My obligation, as I saw it, was to contribute to the process my experience, my views, and the benefits of my approach to problems.

In turn, I had a chance to learn and to relate judicial decisions with their practical implementation. I had to be consistent, to say the same things in the less formal context of professional activities as I did in court—to ask the same types of uncomfortable questions and demand the same adherence to honesty in facing realities.

My experience with the corrections commission—one of the many professional committees and commissions on which I have served—was certainly an education for me, and I hope for the others involved. This chapter demonstrates the type of dialogue I tried to foster, in a forum where the issues could be discussed far more informally and candidly than in judicial opinions.

The field of corrections has been a neglected sector of public policy. Those advocating that we lock up more criminals and throw away the key are seldom to be found struggling with how to fund and administer a prison system that is responsible for at least minimum levels of decency in conditions of confinement and if possible preventing inmates from emerging even more dangerous than when they entered. Until quite recently, most judges never even visited the prisons to which they consigned people. For the outsider, the realities of our correctional system may be shocking—even for a judge with prior background dealing with criminal defendants and the criminal process.

Just like judicial standards, professional standards for correctional facilities, adopted by the American Correctional Association in 1977, had to be implemented in practice if they were to have any meaning. The role of the Commission on Accreditation for Corrections was simply to determine whether individual prisons met those standards. One acute observer noted that if notoriously substandard prisons receive approval,

> then accreditation will become meaningless and an innovative idea for upgrading conditions will have been lost, subverted by the short-term needs of administrators trying to deflect public criticism and to ward off lawsuits. If this happens, it could even damage the credibility of the standards themselves. . . .[1]

As a member of the commission, I saw it as my responsibility to assure that the goals of the standards received more than lip service. The material in this chapter is not presented as a finished consideration of the issues discussed, but to let the reader observe a process in action. Since 1982 the commission has continued to have organizational problems. It is currently, as I predicted, under the auspices of the American Correctional Association.

The memoranda included here further illustrate how the approach I've espoused can be applied in forums beyond the courtroom. My role, as I saw it, was to raise difficult questions and force others to address them. I had more success at the former than the latter, but at least I can be sure that important issues were ventilated.

The successive memoranda are given in chronological order, to show graphically how such bodies operate, and how difficult and discouraging it can be if one takes seriously their assurance that they truly want an outside colleague's active participation. The self-protective instincts of corrections professionals are, of course, no different or more egregious than those of dozens of other professional groups—all the more reason for requiring the sort of open dialogue and public access for which I argued, to little avail in this instance.

Those responsible for hospitals, mental institutions, and nursing homes, or nuclear power plants and space programs, must be questioned in the same way. A cartoon once depicted a witness interrupting the oath he was about to take and protesting to the judge: "Is this really necessary, Your Honor? I'm an expert." The answer, of course, is yes.

The positions of trust experts hold in our society require that the rest of us, for our own safety and well-being, find a way to hold them accountable. This need not and should not mean, as it usually does here as in the criminal justice context, punishing or criticizing people after the fact. Rather, we should encourage and compel a more open process for their original decisions. Certainly, there is a place for expertise, but in questions of social choice and moral values, the professionals are no more expert than anyone else.

May 13, 1981

MEMORANDUM TO: Commission on Accreditation
for Corrections
FROM: David L. Bazelon

My six months of service on this Commission have provided me with an opportunity to consider our procedures and our common goals. Of course, I have not had time to develop technical expertise in the operation of prisons. I suspect that I was asked to serve on this body not for my technical expertise but instead because I have spent much of my professional life concerned with the role of our penal system in society. And it is from that perspective that I would like to open up certain areas for reflection and discussion at our next meeting.

In the decade since this accreditation process was conceived, we have witnessed drastic change in the prison system. For example, from 1972 to 1978, our state prison population jumped from approximately 175,000 to almost 270,000. According to the National Institute of Justice, that rise caught prison planners and officials by surprise. Almost every major prison system now suffers from appalling overcrowding, which breeds idleness, tension, and apocalyptic riots.

The overcrowding is due partly to the ascendancy of incapacitation as the guiding light of corrections. Few will admit to a belief in rehabilitation. This may be because rehabilitation is unsound in theory or because we never invested the necessary resources. Nor is there much faith in deterrence. Incapacitation at least promises some safety for the community. Put less politely, it translates as "lock the bastards up"—at least they won't hurt us while they're behind bars. It can take many forms—preventive detention, isolation of "career criminals," stricter parole release. The ultimate result, however, is the same: more people stuffed into our already overcrowded institutions.

Another crucial, new factor is the national Administration's commitment to cutting federal funds. According to our own Annual Report, many of the systems interested in accreditation rely on LEAA money. Those funds will be cut off. Some states may use their own funds to stay in the program. But that option will be most difficult for those systems most in need of serious change. In this fiscal crunch, the competing claims will increase and, if history is any guide, corrections will be at the bottom. How will state and local prisons make the needed changes? The scandal of prison medical care has troubled me deeply for over a decade. But improvements will not be without cost. Where will the money come from?

Some fear that the new Administration may abdicate its responsibilities in corrections. For example, the inmate grievance guidelines and procedures developed by the Department of Justice may be weakened and watered down. If true, the absence of federal leadership will make far more difficult the job of moving the prison system forward.

These developments seem to raise some fundamental questions about our goals and possibilities. What can we hope to accomplish? Where will systems get the resources to meet our standards? Will our guidelines be demanding, or will we bend them to accommodate inadequacies in funding? If only a few systems are involved—last December we had only 151 of 500–600 adult institutions and only 20–25 of our wretched jails—what does accreditation mean? Can we evaluate our role without considering developments in the law? If the courts, like the federal government, lose interest in penal reform, we may well be the only game in town. Recent signals from the Supreme Court suggest that this scenario cannot be dismissed. Are we equipped to handle that responsibility?

Corrections is obviously public business of the highest order. This introduces a major issue which troubles me—the quasi-private nature of our activities. In 1973, the National Advisory Commission on Criminal Justice Standards and Goals found:

> Correctional systems have hidden themselves and their problems behind walls, legal procedures, and fear tactics for many years. To the maximum possible extent, citizens have been systematically excluded.

I am afraid that those remarks are not inappropriate for our accreditation process as well. Too many of our processes and activities are out of the public eye. We do not involve community and other interest groups in what we do, whether it be a specific audit, a Commission meeting, or the development of standards and procedures.

I have no evidence that our decisions will be improved by enlisting the public. But if we show our warts and willingness to receive outside help, we will add to our credibility, and we will enhance the public perception of corrections. My experience with government in general, and with governmental agencies in particular, has convinced me that, as Mr. Justice Brandeis said, sunlight is the best antiseptic.

Finally, no system of decision-making, whether it be accreditation or anything else, can be better than its fact-finding procedures. I must confess to serious reservations about our procedures, and would like to share them with you. In order not to make this letter excessively long, I have set out these questions in an attached memorandum. I welcome your reactions.

In view of all this, I think we should take stock of where we are going. And we should do this not by ourselves, but with the help of some of the many individuals and groups who remain deeply committed to the Commission's role in prison reform. We must initiate an exchange of views with citizen groups, legislators, and state and federal officials responsible for the various correctional systems.

Our prison system has occupied our ablest and noblest minds for almost two hundred years. I have no illusions that we will be able to solve our intractable problems. But the accreditation process can offer a means for achieving vital change. We cannot ignore fiscal and political realities. But neither can we afford to trade-off our most valuable resource: the noble vision of a humane correctional system. For that reason I urge that, at this time of flux, we undertake a serious self-examination. As with individuals, so with organizations—the unexamined life is not worth living.

Procedural Issues

The success of accreditation depends on three factors: people, procedures, and standards.

PEOPLE   Much obviously rests on the qualities and skills which members of visiting committees bring to their work. I have these questions concerning those people:

1. Do we have a sufficient cadre of trained auditors to assure:—that sites visits can be scheduled promptly when candidates are ready?

—that the experience and views of a small group do not unduly influence accreditation decisions?

2. Do we recruit in such a way as to assure that the cadre of auditors is appropriately heterogeneous in experience and opinion to reflect such diversity as may exist concerning sound correctional practices?

3. Are we able to assign people with appropriate backgrounds or expertise to assure that standards compliance can be fairly and accurately assessed? What is the basis for our conclusion that laymen can adequately determine an institution's compliance with medical and health care standards?

4. Do we take adequate precautions to assure that auditors are free of bias concerning accreditation in general (i.e., that it should be generally awarded or withheld) and in the particular case (e.g., do we routinely determine that assigned auditors have no actual or potential disposition to accredit or deny accreditation to a program, agency, or institution as a result of familiarity with personnel of the candidate, or previous employment by the candidate or in the system of which it may be a part)?

PROCEDURES Imagine the consequences of sending auditors on accreditation visits armed only with an appropriate *Manual of Standards,* and you will know the role and value of sound procedures. I hope the following questions will help us decide whether our procedures are meeting our needs.

1. Are our procedures sufficiently clear and simple so that a common understanding will be developed by the many different individuals and types of people who must work with them?

2. Do the procedures clearly spell out *what* constitutes compliance with standards and *how* it must be proven? I imagine our standards which require "written policy and procedure" (some 220 out of 465 Adult Correctional Institution standards) are the most difficult type to assess. It is our intention, I believe, to exact unfailing compliance as a precondition to accreditation. Auditors must rely on sampling of some kind to determine compliance. Do our procedures adequately guide this crucial process by stipulating acceptable sampling proto-

cols and indicating the number of files, interviews, or observations which must be assessed in each case?

3. Do our procedures allow/require auditors to interview
individually the head of each line division of a candidate
agency, program, or institution to help measure the context
and intensity of that division's current compliance efforts?

4. Do our auditors have enough time to do a thorough and
exacting job on-site? I understand that we normally assign, in
the case of a major institution, three people for three and
sometimes four days. That works out to about eleven or twelve
minutes for each standard—assuming no time lost to meals or
breaks or briefing and debriefing or general conversation with
staff, inmates, and others with relevant knowledge.

5. Are there procedures which assure that instances of doubtful compliance are referred to the Commission for assessment
and resolution? If so, how much uncertainty triggers our involvement? Is a mere scintilla sufficient or must there be more?

6. Does the Commission have a procedure for referring
compliance-related information from sources other than the
candidate to audit teams for review as part of their site work?
Do we routinely (or under any circumstances) seek such information from ombudsmen or other grievance mechanisms,
from organizations that deal with the agency, program, or
institution (such as AA), from inmates or their representatives,
or from litigators?

7. Does the Commission have guidelines which assist auditors to determine whether plans of action are acceptable? Do
we require—and monitor—fulfillment of plans of action in
accordance with their terms? What are the consequences of a
failure to perform? Of a refusal to perform?

8. What are the consequences of the failure of an accreditation holder to maintain the compliance level determined by
the original audit? Suppose compliance with a mandatory standard ends. So what? Imagine that compliance with essential
standards falls from 96 to 91 percent. What happens? If it goes
from 94 to 89 percent? How do we know that accreditation
holders tell us about declining compliance and failed plans of
action?

9. Has the Commission validated its audit procedures by using a second team of auditors to verify audit findings? Have we used another procedure?

10. Does the Commission verify claims of continuing compliance with accreditation standards? Do we spot-check compliance?

11. In general the Commission's relationship with participants in the accreditation system is a confidential one. Is this approach consistent with the philosophy which underlies such standards as 146, 151, 1109, 110, and 2015? Are the Commission's confidentiality policies consistent with Principle XI of the Statement of Principles? Does confidentiality significantly advance any Commission goal?

STANDARDS   The American Correctional Association recently completed revision of the accreditation standards. I have these questions about the standards we have been and will be using.

1. Are the standards as written sufficiently clear and unambiguous so that the reader of a standard, knowing that an agency, program, or institution has been found to be in compliance with it, knows how the accreditation holder is performing?

2. During the operation of the accreditation programs, standards have been applied to more numerous and more diverse situations than were encountered during field testing. Have the specificity, breadth, and requirements of the standards been adjusted to reflect this broader experience?

3. It might be generally supposed that a program, agency, or institution which had been accredited was operating in accordance with best contemporary correctional practices. I am informed that in at least one case, accreditation has been awarded to an institution which a court has found does not operate constitutionally. If this is accurate, it implies that best contemporary practice may fall below constitutional minima. Can sound professional standards be standards which do not meet the Constitution?

4. We are charged with enforcing these standards. Do we have enough of a say as to their content?

August 4, 1981

MEMORANDUM TO: Commission on Accreditation
for Corrections
FROM: David L. Bazelon

The development of basic standards for decent prison administration stands as a major breakthrough in the history of
American corrections. In the decade since the American Correctional Association adopted its *Plan for Accreditation,* the concept of judging institutions against tough and evolving criteria
has earned growing acceptance among criminal justice professionals. The ACA, the Commission and Dr. Fosen and his staff
deserve considerable credit for establishing a framework for
systematic improvement and review of our nation's correctional institutions. The vehicle of accreditation offers the hope
of genuine reform of our society's treatment of criminal
offenders.

Today, however, that structure faces a grave crisis that
threatens the fulfillment of its noble promise. Driven by an
understandable terror over alarming crime rates, the public
increasingly demands a criminal justice system that will put
those who endanger our safety out of our way and in their
"place." In the current political climate, a meaningful attack on
the roots of crime seems unlikely. Instead, decision-makers call
for "incapacitation" programs that will confine more people
into our already overcrowded institutions. As a result, corrections may suffer the greatest burden in its history. In four
years, the United States will probably keep nearly half a million adults behind bars. . . .

As the money dries up, the courts retreat, and incapacitation puts an unbearable strain on the institutions, we can
only hope to fulfill the promise of accreditation by directly
engaging the understanding and support of the public. My
experience reviewing the work of Washington's administrative
agencies persuades me that opening up the accreditation

process to public scrutiny and participation is critical to enhancing our credibility and influence. As I have said of other organizations charged with a public trust, "the healthiest thing that can happen is to let it all hang out, warts and all, because if the public doesn't accept it, it just isn't worth a good damn." Today, a veil of secrecy surrounds prisons that lifts only when the institutions erupt in bloodshed and destruction. As a result, the public naturally harbors deep suspicions and fears about what goes on behind the walls. By revealing both the good and the bad in corrections, the accreditation process can improve society's respect and understanding for the agonizing work of the corrections professional. Corrections could thereby attain the substantial public support it needs and deserves. . . .

As a Commissioner, I cannot be confident that our procedures guarantee full development and exploration of all the facts needed to determine whether a program or facility complies with the relevant standards. In this respect, I believe our deliberations could benefit from the approach my court takes when reviewing the actions of regulatory agencies. I have no more expertise in the substantive scientific questions raised at many of these agencies than I do in the technical operations of prisons. But, as a judge, I *can* monitor the fairness and reliability of the agencies' decisions. To withstand judicial review, the agencies must provide fair notice so that comments and criticisms can be raised. The record of the agency decision must also disclose all evidence heard, policies considered, and reasoning relied upon. The agency must point to evidence and policy arguments which support and which detract from its conclusions—*and* it must state the basis for its resolution of those conflicts. In sum, the court requires an *open* agency process with full and clear disclosure. I am confident that the Commission's decision-making can be substantially improved by applying the same principles. . . .

I repeat, unless we tell the public about the good *and* the bad in corrections, we can never hope to enlist their support and understanding—and we will not deserve it.

I recognize that opening up the accreditation process to public scrutiny will not be easy for corrections professionals trying earnestly to satisfy the conflicting demands of a variety of constituencies. But I believe complete disclosure of our work serves the long-run best interests of all those dedicated to humane prison administration. Corrections professionals do not need the tenth anniversary of Attica or the recent episode in New Mexico to recognize the urgency of prison reform. I must believe that most of those who have chosen corrections as a career genuinely seek to treat prisoners with decency and compassion. It may be true, as the *Chapman* court said, that "the Constitution does not mandate comfortable prisons." But the moral imperative of "do unto others as you would have them do unto you" requires that a civilized society provide prisoners with the basic human dignity that criminals deny the innocent victims of crime. Human beings, whether in prison or out, deserve physical necessities, medical and mental health services, a measure of privacy, and opportunities to improve themselves.

Yet the conscientious corrections professional has enough trouble just getting through the day. Society hands him its worst casualties and demands that he reform them or at least "warehouse" them quietly and invisibly. With shrinking budgets, overcrowded cell blocks, undertrained staffs, hostile inmates, and no glory, he faces an almost hopeless task. It is hardly surprising that, in some states, annual guard turnover reaches 75 percent. How long can a corrections professional maintain a humane vision when he must confront the sordid conditions of the institution every day? He knows that rehabilitation can only be a distant ideal in the hell of today's prisons. And he knows that, as the pressures on the system increase, the fear, bitterness, and frustration that pervade the world "inside" will inevitably explode in violence.

Speaking out about these things will not endear the corrections professional to the politicians and the agencies that hold the purse strings. Nor will it enhance his job security. When individuals at the top of the profession try to force the public to face the ugly realities and painful limitations of corrections, they do not stay at the top very long. How much harder must it be for those "on the line" to call society's attention to the necessity of drastic prison reform? In order to survive in an exceedingly tough profession, they understandably restrain their sense of the possible.

As a judge with life tenure, I have no right to condemn the natural instinct to protect one's career and livelihood. But I am convinced that corrections professionals will never get the public understanding and support they deserve if they keep the ugly realities of prisons hidden from view. As Herbert Packer noted, "[p]eople are willing to be complacent about what goes on in the criminal process as long as they are not too often or too explicitly reminded of the gory details." The public has always turned away from the "gory details" of the prisons. As the Attica Commission noted ten years ago, "prisons, prisoners, and the problems of both are essentially invisible in the United States. We Americans have made our prisons disappear as if by an act of will." And little had changed by the time New Mexico's attorney general evaluated the causes of that state's recent riot:

> Throughout its history the Penitentiary of New Mexico has suffered from neglect. The New Mexico prison has always waited at the end of the line for public money, and elected officials have turned their attention to the ugly problems of the penitentiary only when the institution has erupted in violence and destruction.

Meaningful and lasting reform will continue to elude us as long as the prisons remain invisible. Unless the profession summons the courage to force the problems of prisons onto the public consciousness, the noble promise of a humane and effective system of corrections will never be achieved.

REMARKS OF JUDGE DAVID L. BAZELON
Before the Commission on Accreditation for Corrections
January 20–22, 1982

As you know, I have tried, since May of last year, to bring to the Commission's attention several matters that I believe pose fundamental challenges to the success and value of our efforts. At the last meeting, which I was unable to attend, the Key Issues Committee, having apparently reviewed my suggestions, proposed for the full Commission's consideration "a four-point program as a first step in expanding public awareness of the Commission's purpose, goals, and operational policy and procedure." The Commission adopted the recommendations, noting that "[t]hey were intended to identify broad areas in need of work, and reflect a cautious approach towards disclosure." I understand that the purpose of tonight's meeting is to take another look at the recommendations adopted in August.

In my view, the Commission—as well as the corrections profession and the public—can no longer afford a "cautious approach" to opening up the accreditation process. As I observed in my August memorandum, the American prison system is, quite simply, in extremis. The political pressure to solve the problem of crime by increasing incapacitation of offenders is matched only by the public's indifference to the sordid facts about prison life and to the nearly impossible task facing the most conscientious administrators. In this climate, corrections professionals have no higher duty than to force society to recognize the ugly realities and painful limitations of the prison system. As I have said time and again, to do so is demanded by their self-interest as professionals, their responsibilities as public officials, and their moral obligations as citizens.

The Commission must advance the effort to enlist the understanding and support of the public, and it must do so now. We do not have the luxuries of time and public indulgence: the crisis facing corrections grows more acute every day. In order both to discharge its responsibility to the public and to improve the quality of its decision-making, I believe the Commission must immediately commit itself to a substantial increase in the public's awareness of and participation in the accreditation process. And it must dedicate itself to achieving the strength and credibility that can only come through independence from the corrections professionals whose work it seeks to evaluate. To these ends, I urge the Key Issues Committee and the Commission to reconsider their decision of August and to adopt the specific proposals. . . .

August 6, 1982

MEMORANDUM TO: Commission on Accreditation
                          for Corrections
FROM: David L. Bazelon

I will soon complete two years of my five-year term on the Commission on Accreditation for Corrections. During my tenure, I have repeatedly called on the Commission to make some fundamental reforms in its fact-finding procedures and in its relationship with the corrections community. Although it has taken a few tentative steps in the right direction, the Commission has repeatedly refused to take meaningful steps to guarantee its independence and to insure the integrity of its decisions. The Commission has therefore broken faith with the public and has betrayed the promise of accreditation.

Specifically:

1. The Commission has repeatedly refused to open up the accreditation process to public scrutiny and participation.

2. The Commission's audit techniques and deliberative procedures are inherently unreliable.

3. The Commission is unwilling to accommodate constructive criticism and the possibility of meaningful change.

4. The Commission's priorities are fundamentally flawed.

5. The Commission has pervasive conflicts of interest with the facilities it is charged with monitoring.

6. The Commission has permitted the accreditation movement to be transformed into a propaganda vehicle for corrections authorities.

The attached memorandum details these failures in depth. Copies of my previous memoranda and statements to the Commission are also attached as appendices.

It is clear to me that the Commission will continue to resist efforts to change course. I cannot, therefore, continue to support its work, and I resign from the Board of Commissioners effective immediately.

MEMORANDUM OF RESIGNATION

A. The Promise of Accreditation

The promise of the accreditation movement in corrections could not have come at a more critical time. The history of corrections in America, I believe, is best characterized as a conspiracy of silence between corrections officials and the public. In the words of the Attica Commission, "prisons, prisoners, and the problems of both are essentially invisible in the United States. We Americans have made our prisons disappear as if by an act of will."[2] This conspiracy has intensified in recent years. Terror over alarming crime rates has grown. The public increasingly demands that offenders be "put in their place." More and more politicians cater to this "lock 'em up" hysteria. More and more offenders are being packed into our already over-crowded institutions. At the same time, however, federal and state appropriations for corrections have been slashed. Facilities continue to deteriorate. And even the federal courts have begun to back away from enforcing the Eighth Amendment's ban against cruel and inhumane prison conditions.[3]

In this climate, the concept of accreditation is especially vital, for it offers one of the few hopes for rational and humane reform in corrections. The real promise of accreditation is that the conspiracy of silence between corrections officials and the public can be replaced with a partnership for reform.

When I was asked to join the Commission on Accreditation for Corrections ("Commission" or "CAC") two years ago, I believed that its accreditation program was fulfilling this noble promise. Working with the American Correctional Association ("ACA"), the Commission was developing national standards for juvenile and adult correctional facilities. The compliance of applicant facilities with these standards was to be measured through a rigorous "quality control process."[4] An applicant would first perform a self-evaluation to determine how it measured up to the standards. A team of independent auditors would then investigate the facility, and its report would be reviewed, standard by standard, by a Commission panel. If the panel accepted the team's report, it would award a three-year certificate of accreditation. Once accredited, the facility would submit annual reports detailing its progress toward meeting standards it had failed, and it would be subject to follow-up monitoring visits. The entire process would be one of "continuous review and growth consistent with the experiences of new knowledge, skills, and methods."[5]

I was particularly impressed with the apparent commitment of the ACA and the Commission to openness and public involvement in the accreditation process. In its *Declaration of Principles,* for example, the ACA declares that "[t]he success of the corrections process in all its stages can be greatly enhanced by energetic, resourceful and organized citizen participation."[6] This emphasis on openness was important, the ACA noted, because "[i]n a democracy the success of any public agency, including corrections, depends in the final analysis on public assistance and support. . . ."[7] Similarly, the Commission's *Statement of Principles* pledged "the further development of public participation and understanding" and "performance in the public interest."[8] The process of accreditation, the Commission emphasized, would "provide to interested citizens the opportunity to view their correctional agencies and systems within the framework of nationally-recognized standards."[9]

The Commission's apparent commitment to public scrutiny and participation, I believed, was of central importance to the future success of accreditation for three fundamental reasons:

a. The Commission would have a fiduciary obligation to be candid with the public. Citizens and their organized representatives would rightfully demand that they review claims made by public institutions seeking the Commission's seal of approval.

b. Public involvement would be essential to the integrity of the Commission's fact-finding and decision-making. By opening its activities to public scrutiny and participation at every stage of the accreditation process—from self-evaluation, to on-site audit, to panel deliberations, to announcement of its decisions—the Commission could be more confident that its procedures guaranteed full development and exploration of all the facts needed to determine whether an applicant complied with the relevant standards. Many people would have information of direct relevance to the Commission's work—community leaders, medical, religious, and architectural authorities, local citizens, inmates and their families, public interest groups, professional critics, law enforcement representatives, judges, and so forth. By actively soliciting their input, the Commission could insure full ventilation of all relevant information.

c. By opening up the accreditation process to the public, the Commission could improve society's respect for and understanding of the agonizing work of the corrections professional. By candidly revealing both the good and bad in corrections, the Commission could educate the public about the excessive demands made of corrections officials. Candor would encourage the public to confront the real causes of crime and to support innovations in corrections.

B. The Reality of the Accreditation Process

1. The Commission has repeatedly refused to open up the accreditation process to public scrutiny and participation.

Shortly after joining the Commission, I discovered that the *Statement of Principles'* promise of "public participation" in the accreditation process has not been kept. The public is systematically excluded from every stage of the Commission's work.

Specifically:

a. The Commission and the ACA make no effort to seek out public comments in the development of their standards.

b. Agency applications and self-evaluations are kept secret.

c. The on-site auditing process includes no substantial, systematic efforts to elicit information from sources other than the applicant.[10]

d. The Commission's deliberations are secret and provide no meaningful opportunity for public input.

e. The Commission does not release the results of standards-compliance evaluations to the public.

It is difficult to imagine resistance to disclosure except from those who distrust the public. Yet from its inception in 1974 until 1981, the Commission never formally considered the compatibility of these secret procedures with its public-interest mandate. Beginning early last year, I have made intensive efforts to persuade my fellow Commissioners to open the accreditation process up to the public.

The result: my proposals twice have been rejected out of hand. In response to adverse publicity, the Commission in recent months has accepted recommendations to "encourage" applicants to involve independent individuals and organizations in the accreditation process, to "encourage" applicants to forward adverse comments, to "require" applicants to submit "relevant" independent information, and to "recommend" that applicants disclose the results of the standards-compliance audits.[11] Similarly, the Commission has gone on record that it will "consider" outside information brought to its attention.[12] These changes are in line with the "cautious approach toward disclosure" adopted by the Commission last year.[13]

The public must see these changes for what they are. In presenting them to the Commission for its approval, the chairman of the drafting committee stated that "the thrust of the Task Force recommendations is to 'encourage,' not require, agencies to disclose information. The agency retains the option to determine what is relevant for submission to the Commission."[14] This statement, and the wording of the changes themselves, demonstrate that the Commission's "cautious approach" is thoroughly ineffectual and misses the mark entirely. Public scrutiny and participation must not be left to the discretion of applicants. To get all relevant information for its decision, the Commission must require the involvement of independent individuals and organizations. Rather than passively wait for random information to filter in, the Commission's staff should aggressively pursue all relevant sources, and the determination of "relevance" must be made by the Commission. And to serve the public faithfully, the Commission must require that its findings be released for public scrutiny.[15]

The credibility of these recent gestures is further undermined when they are compared with the recurrent statements by Commission and ACA officials categorically rejecting public scrutiny and participation. Here are the arguments that have been made:

a. Openness will destroy the Commission. At the Commission's January 1982 meeting in Las Vegas, Anthony Travisono, executive director of the ACA, warned that "the commission will fold in one year's time if this opening of the process is permitted to exist."[16] Similarly, Commissioner B. James George warned that openness would be "sheer suicide."[17] The premise of these remarks—that either accreditation is run the way that prison officials want it to be run, or else—is an insult to the public. If Travisono and George are correct, then the Commission had better stop claiming that it is an "independent," "professional" organization. Unless every effort is made to consider all relevant information, and unless the Commission shares all aspects of its work with the public, the "certificates of excellence" that it awards will not be worth the paper they are printed on.

b. Openness will destroy the integrity of the accreditation process. Robert Fosen, the Commission's executive director, has argued that if "information [about prison conditions] is to be broadcast willy-nilly about the land," then "all kinds of persons will be critical," and this "will simply upset . . . the integrity of the process."[18] History has repeatedly taught, however, that the integrity of fact-finding and decision-making processes depends on public scrutiny and participation. Only by opening its work to the public can the Commission be confident that its judgments will be fair, thorough, and unbiased.

c. Only corrections professionals can make a positive contribution. A former president of the ACA has argued that "[t]oo often, the laymen defer to the professionals and thereby become co-opted. Professional corrections people are less likely to be co-opted by other professionals than many outsiders are."[19] Similarly, one of my fellow Commissioners advised me that whereas "[i]nterested citizen groups too often have only special interests," and "politicians far too often have political interests," "corrections professionals" are the only group that can "bring about meaningful and continuous improvements in the criminal justice system."[20] But although most corrections professionals are honest and conscientious, their values and ideas—like those of any professional group—are necessarily limited by their training, experience, and job constraints.[21] Moreover, many groups have important information about prison conditions: prisoners and their families, public-interest and community groups, lawyers, judges, architects, doctors, religious leaders. Finally, the chance that outside testimony will sometimes be biased is no reason to refuse to consider it in the first place. Assessing the credibility of witnesses and verifying the truth of accusations should be an integral part of the Commission's business.

d. The contractual nature of the Commission's relationship with applicants requires secrecy. This reasoning is circular: if the Commission's contracts with applicant agencies provide for the systematic exclusion of public scrutiny and participation, then it should change the contracts. The Commission's first duty is to the public and not to the administrators of corrections facilities.

e. Other accrediting bodies do not require openness. It has been argued that the Commission is similar to accreditation agencies for hospitals and schools, and that the work of those bodies is not open to the public.[22] There are several answers to this argument. First, to the extent that other accrediting bodies do exclude the public, that is no excuse for the Commission to follow along. Second, hospitals and schools are much more open to the public, and there are a variety of other ways in which the public is able to monitor their performance. Third, hospitals and schools do not so completely circumscribe the lives of their constituents in ways that can threaten fundamental constitutional rights. Fourth, hospitals and schools do not have such sorry histories. Finally, the premise of the argument is inaccurate: accrediting bodies for hospitals and schools have opened up their processes to the public in a variety of ways.[23]

In light of these statements defending secrecy, it is ironic that the Commission's recent policy statement on public relations is entitled *Public Information: Open and Accountable.* In reality, the process is neither. There is no excuse for not opening up the Commission's work to public scrutiny and participation. The Commission must affirmatively involve the public at every stage of the accreditation process. It cannot wait for outside information to filter in in a haphazard and piecemeal fashion. Until the Commission takes corrective action, its fact-finding and decision-making processes will be seriously flawed, and its work will not deserve the public's respect or support.[24]

2. The Commission's audit techniques and deliberative procedures are inherently unreliable.

The accreditation process has many other flaws in addition to secrecy. The Commission has taken a few steps in the right direction, but they are not nearly enough.

The Commission's auditing procedures, for example, do not insure accurate, complete, and unbiased truth-finding. Specifically:

a. The Commission has no sampling protocols to guide auditors in verifying the extent to which an applicant's performance matches the language of his written documentation.

b. The Commission's guidelines for evaluating the adequacy and implementation of an applicant's plan of action are inadequate.

c. The Commission has performed no replication studies to

determine the extent to which audit findings can be accepted with confidence.

d. There are no assurances that the Commission recruits in such a way as to assure that the cadre of auditors is appropriately heterogeneous in experience and opinion.

e. Applicants may peremptorily reject proposed auditors. Although applicants should be able to notify the Commission of possible conflicts of interest, the Commission should not automatically disqualify challenged auditors. It should be the ultimate decider of audit team composition.[25]

f. The Commission does not conduct unannounced on-site pre-accreditation or post-accreditation inspections to verify compliance with its standards. Prison officials are informed of impending visits months in advance, thereby enabling them to put on a "one-day shine" for auditors.[26]

g. Auditors have neither the time nor the resources to perform thorough inspections. For a major institution, the Commission normally assigns three auditors for three and sometimes four days. It has been reported that this works out to be about twelve minutes for each standard—assuming no time is lost to meals, breaks, briefing, and general conversation.[27] This brevity precludes exacting scrutiny, and the Commission therefore cannot be confident that its teams are able to uncover violations and gaps between the applicant's policy on paper and its actual practices.

h. There have been repeated instances where audit teams refused to consider critical information. For example, there have been extensive charges in the media about official tolerance of "Goon Squads" at the Union Correctional Facility in Florida. Yet the audit team that visited Union refused to interview key witnesses who had made these charges: "The committee had neither the resources, the authority nor the desire to determine the accuracy of the allegations," the team noted in its report.[28] In another case, the audit team that inspected Menard Correctional Facility in Illinois failed to contact the federal judge who had found conditions at Menard to be unconstitutional or the special master he had appointed to oversee improvements. The audit team apparently even misrepresented the special master's assessment of conditions at Menard.[29]

In addition to unprofessional investigatory practices, the credibility of the Commission's findings also suffers from the brevity and narrow focus of panel proceedings. With a few exceptions, I have found that, instead of demanding full development and exploration of all the relevant facts needed to determine the accreditability of applicants, Commission panels function more like rubber stamps.[30] For example:

a. Panels typically spend only one hour evaluating and deliberating the accreditability of each applicant.

b. The only evidence a panel typically considers is the applicant's self-evaluation and the audit team's report.[31]

c. The only parties permitted to testify are representatives of the applicant and members of the audit team.[32]

3. The Commission is unwilling to accommodate constructive criticism and the possibility of meaningful change.

The Commission's response to my reform proposals demonstrates that its promise of "continuous review and growth"[33] has not been kept. From my experience, the Commission's response to reform efforts is typically one of rationalization and justification.

For example, after I circulated my first memorandum in the spring of 1981, urging the Commission "to take stock of where we are going,"[34] the Commission discussed it only briefly at the May 1981 meeting. I received only three responses from individual Commissioners, and none from the Commission as a group, from its staff, from the "Key Issues Committee," or from the ACA. After I circulated a follow-up memorandum the following August,[35] focusing particularly on the issue of disclosure, the staff issued a response to the questions I had posed in my May memorandum. That response was a grave disappointment, for the "questions" the staff answered were not, in many cases, those that I had asked.[36]

My proposals received equally short shrift at the August 1981 meeting. The only known consideration of my memoranda by the Key Issues Committee occurred on August 14, and the full Commission devoted all of a few minutes' consideration the following day, after which it hurriedly passed a resolution defending secrecy on the ground that "full public disclosure may inhibit agencies from participating in the accreditation process."[37]

My final effort to put the issue of disclosure before the Commission occurred at the Las Vegas meeting last January.[38] The Commission's response was two-pronged. On the one hand, it adopted a series of public-relations resolutions "encouraging" and "recommending" disclosure by applicants. At the same time, out of the public eye, it bowed to implied threats that public disclosure would be "sheer suicide" and would cause the Commission to "fold in one year's time."[39]

The Commission has recently decided to schedule annual meetings "for the purpose of reviewing and updating existing policy and for consideration of new policy positions by the full Board."[40] In light of the history of my own efforts to obtain meaningful consideration of new policy proposals, I fear that this step will be but another cosmetic gesture.

4. The Commission's priorities are fundamentally flawed.

The Commission's 1980 annual report states that "[i]t is the rigor of the process that promotes and sustains credibility. . . ."[41] The Commission's priorities run directly counter to this premise, however, and have put it on the path of least—or no—resistance. The Commission's "first priority," according to Executive Director Fosen, is to encourage as many facilities to join the accreditation process as possible; at some unspecified future date, it can then begin to "tighten" its standards and procedures.[42] Under this "seduction" theory, the Commission's long-term credibility depends on the number of institutions that participate in accreditation, thereby justifying a short-term relaxation of its scrutiny and a lowering of its expectations.

This strategy must be rejected. The Commission is destroying the promise of accreditation before it has had any meaningful opportunity to prove its worth. Hard decisions may not

be popular ones within the profession, but they must be made—
and enforced—now. I am well aware that the Commission is
relatively new and is struggling for an independent life. But is
it a life worth living if it must sacrifice its credibility and the
integrity of the accreditation process? The Commission is not
an end in itself. Our institutions do not exist merely to be
accredited, and accreditation does not exist merely for the
benefit of institutions. Rather, both exist for the purpose of
serving the public by achieving the most rational, humane, and
effective correctional system possible.

The one form of authority this Commission has is the power
to award accreditation. If this power is to mean anything, it
must be exercised responsibly. Yet there is a large gap between
the award and the reality of many of the institutions the Commission has voted to accredit.[43] Rather than affix the label of
"excellence" to facilities that meet only the minimal standards-
compliance level, the Commission should use several levels of
accreditation.[44] Rather than rely solely on the facility's plan of
action to achieve unmet standards—a practice the Commission's own task force found subject to "major weakness[es]"[45]—
the Commission should institute a program of conditional accreditation.[46] Most of all, the Commission must do more than
merely seduce compliance; it must *demand* it.[47] If it does not,
then the promise of accreditation will fail no matter how many
correctional facilities participate.

5. The Commission has pervasive conflicts of interest with the
facilities it is charged with monitoring.

Independence is the cornerstone of the Commission's credibility. However, although the Commission insists that it is an
"independent" organization, it has numerous conflicts of interest with the agencies it evaluates.

For example, the Commission depends for its financial survival on the fees it receives from applicant facilities. Applicants
pay an "accreditation fee" ranging from $3,000 to $12,000,
depending on their size and nature. Executive Director Fosen
has estimated that the Commission needs 1,000 fee-paying ap-

plicants in order to survive.[48] In the words of the Commission's own former chairman and treasurer, Gary Blake, "[i]f we did [take a more active role in investigation], I think we could kiss the whole process of accreditation goodby."[49] The conflict of interest is manifest. How can the Commission in good conscience represent itself as "independent" and "unbiased" while being financially dependent on the objects of its scrutiny? If the Commission is in fact nothing more than a (well-paid) private consulting organization, it at least owes it to the public to say so.

The Commission has another, equally disturbing, conflict of interest that is undermining the credibility of accreditation. The ACA is made up of state and federal corrections officials—the group whose performance the Commission is charged with evaluating. In theory, the Commission became independent of the ACA in April 1979. In reality, the Commission continues to be seen in the field as an arm of the ACA, if any distinction is made at all. Indeed, many accredited institutions claim that they are "ACA accredited," not "CAC accredited." My impression, in fact, is that the Commission has been moving *closer* to the ACA.

The Commission has a number of specific conflicts of interest with the ACA:

a. The ACA exerts too much control over the writing of the Commission's standards. There can be no doubting the importance of professional experience and knowledge in the development and application of the standards. The objects of the Commission's scrutiny must not, however, be given the power to veto its standards.

b. The ACA appoints fifteen of the twenty-one Commission members. The Commission *itself* should make these decisions rather than permit the ACA to determine its composition.[50] Moreover, while recognizing the importance of having several representatives of the ACA on the Board, the Commission should draw the majority of its members from other groups—including representatives of offenders, medical providers, governments, business, and the citizenry at large.

c. The ACA apparently controls the Commission's most basic policy decisions. At the recent meeting in Las Vegas, for example, representatives of the ACA played the decisive role in defeating efforts to open the accreditation process up to the public. Anthony Travisono, executive director of the ACA, warned that the proposal "may have to go to the parent agency. The Commission can't do this on its own."[51] He then issued a thinly veiled threat that the ACA would remove its support for the accreditation movement if the Commission voted in favor of public disclosure.[52]

In light of such ultimatums, how can the Commission in good conscience advocate anything *but* complete independence from the professional group whose interests it affects? Until the Commission weans itself from the ACA, its claims of "independence" can have little credibility.

6. The Commission has permitted the accreditation movement to be transformed into a propaganda vehicle for corrections authorities.

As a result of the above-described flaws—secrecy, shoddy procedures, resistance to reform, flawed priorities, and pervasive conflicts of interest—the Commission's noble promises have been subverted and its accreditation awards have become meaningless. Time and time again I have seen or heard of instances in which corrections officials have used the Commission for their own needs. They have used it to deflect public criticism and scrutiny of their management, to boost their standing with governors and legislators, to ward off judges and lawsuits, and to pat themselves on the back.[53] They have used it to paper over the crises in corrections with certificates of "excellence." They have used it, in short, for their own propaganda needs.

In permitting itself to be used in this way, the Commission has betrayed the very purpose of its existence. The Commission was organized to serve the public through open, unbiased, comprehensive, thoroughly scrutinizing investigation and review of the state of our correctional facilities. It has failed this purpose, and in doing so it has seriously damaged the future of prison improvement in this country.

C. *Conclusion*

We must never forget that the quality of the Commission's decisions cannot be any better than the quality of the processes from which they are derived. I have great respect for many of the staff and my fellow Commissioners. In common with most corrections personnel, they are a dedicated and hardworking group. I know that many of them share my concerns for the direction that the accreditation movement is taking. But all the dedication, all the hard work, and all the shared concerns will amount to very little so long as the Commission's structure and processes remain the same. Its structure is unsound. Its processes are unreliable.

My efforts to persuade the Commission to make meaningful reforms have been unsuccessful, and I cannot continue to support its work. The Commission has broken faith with the public and has betrayed the promise of accreditation. In resigning, I urge my fellow Commissioners to change their present course. If they do not, this country will have lost one of the last, best hopes for reforming the human wasteland that is our prison system.

15

The Soviet Parallel

In 1967, I visited the Soviet Union as a member of the first United States Mission on Mental Health. The seven-member mission was concerned with a broad overview of Soviet mental health services; as the only legally oriented member, my particular concern was with the Soviet approach to criminal responsibility, the criteria for compulsory treatment of various kinds, and the procedures by which mental illness is diagnosed for legal purposes.

Our report[1] was later described by leading experts as "generally enthusiastic and uncritical. . . . The book revealed no awareness of psychiatry's use for political purposes . . . partly because the mission had taken place just before solid evidence began to reach the West on a regular basis." But the authors were kind enough to say that my contribution "stood out because of the questions it posed concerning the absence of judicial review in civil commitment."[2]

As an outgrowth of that mission, I was later named to an American Psychiatric Association task force to study case reports, smuggled out of the Soviet Union, bearing on the psychiatric commitment of political dissidents. Assuming that the reports were authentic, they revealed obviously improper uses of psychiatry. The evidence supporting findings of psychopathology was tenuous at best; there were no behavioral manifestations of the alleged pathology which might justify a conclusion of "social danger"; the facilities to which the dissidents were committed belied the asserted goal—treatment. In short, the medical label "sick" had been used by Soviet psychiatrists to serve the political purposes of the state.

I had a *déjà vu* feeling on reading these reports; I had seen similar situations in my own court, and found it troubling that our task force might issue a report condemning Soviet practices while ignoring a related problem in the United States. My position was not shared at first by the other members of the committee, so I undertook to advance my views separately in a statement to the APA Board of Trustees.[3] The committee report and my separate statement, proposing a study to examine the problem in the United States as well, are included here. As in other contexts, my goal was not to present the definitive analysis, but to raise questions and draw attention to issues others may have preferred to avoid.

It has been pointed out that accepting the Ad Hoc Committee's recommendations and my proposal "conveniently exempted" the APA from further exploration of Soviet abuses.[4] However, the later history of APA leadership on these issues within the World Psychiatric Association is much to its credit. It was the APA's promise to examine its own house that went unfulfilled.

The APA board authorized our committee to formulate a research project to study the ways in which various conflicting loyalties are dealt with in the practice of psychiatry in America. Our proposed project then was rejected by the board as an "adversarial muckraking investigation."[5] Six years later, a beginning was made with an APA-sponsored conference on "the psychiatrist as double agent."[6] Yet the basic institutional role conflict remains largely unspoken and unresolved in the United States.

As for the Soviet Union, reports of abuse have continued to proliferate. During the 1970s the World Psychiatric Association was the scene of angry debate over the Soviet use of psychiatry to contain dissidence. The question was whether Soviet psychiatrists went along with hospitalization while knowing the patient was "well," or whether there was something even more chilling at work. One American expert notes: . . . "because of the nature of political life in the Soviet Union and the social perceptions fashioned by that life, dissenting behavior really does seem strange there and . . . this strangeness has, in some cases, come to be called schizophrenia. . . . [N]ot only the K.G.B. and other responsible officials but the psychiatrists themselves really believed that the dissidents were ill."[7]

In 1983, anticipating suspension from the WPA, the Soviets resigned from that body. The charges and the controversy continue.

REPORT TO THE BOARD OF TRUSTEES,
AMERICAN PSYCHIATRIC ASSOCIATION, FROM THE AD HOC
COMMITTEE ON THE USE OF PSYCHIATRIC INSTITUTIONS
FOR THE COMMITMENT OF POLITICAL DISSENTERS

The committee was appointed by the Board of Trustees of the APA with the assigned task of studying a set of documents, supplied largely by the journal *The New York Review,* which pertain to the alleged use of psychiatric facilities in the Soviet Union for the purpose of suppressing political dissent. The members of the committee have read and examined these documents. While the committee manifestly cannot make a definitive judgment on their authenticity and accuracy, its members were impressed by the scope and quality of the material reviewed. Assuming the reliability of the documents, the committee is of the opinion that they support the above allegations.

The committee also discussed, at length, the perplexing human and legal problems inherent in any society that finds it necessary on occasion to determine whether the behavior of an individual, by reason of mental illness, constitutes a danger to himself or others and if so, to confine him in a psychiatric hospital without his consent. The power of making such a decision clearly puts the profession of psychiatry in a position where it is peculiarly vulnerable to pressure, both explicit and covert, from the value system prevailing in the society in which it functions and from the institutions embodying those values. Such value systems vary from one cultural context to another and it may be presumed, for example, that highly visible political dissidence would more readily be judged as "sick" in the Soviet Union than in our own country. This does not mean that the U.S. is immune from such judgments and, in fact, it is the view of the committee that improper commitments to psychiatric facilities for political reasons may occur in all countries where such facilities are available. Correction of the problem lies in constant awareness that it can happen and in vigilance in preventing it.

The Board of Trustees of the American Psychiatric Association has gone on record as "opposing the misuse of psychiatric facilities for the detention of persons solely on the basis of their political dissent, no matter where it occurs." The committee interprets the word "facilities" to mean the totality of psychiatric knowledge, practice and institutions. The committee concurs with the principle expressed in the APA resolution and hopes that it will prove acceptable to all psychiatrists.

It is specifically recommended to the trustees:

a) That the President of the World Psychiatric Association be asked to circulate the APA position statement to all national societies which are members of the World Psychiatric Association requesting their endorsement of the principle expressed in the APA resolution.

b) That an appropriate international organization (for example the World Psychiatric Association, the World Federation for Mental Health, the World Health Organization, or an appropriate body of the United Nations) be urged to establish a properly staffed agency to formulate internationally acceptable standards and guidelines to safeguard involuntary hospitalization from political influences as far as possible, to receive complaints from any individual or appropriate national body alleging the enforced use of psychiatric facilities for political purposes, and to make investigations of such complaints.

Raymond W. Waggoner, M.D., Chairman
Paul Chodoff, M.D.
John Fisher, M.D.
Hon. David L. Bazelon (HF-APA)

STATEMENT OF CHIEF JUDGE DAVID L. BAZELON

I want to state at the outset my reason for submitting a separate statement to the Board of Trustees. It is not that I deeply disagree with the general conclusions and specific recommendations which the Ad Hoc Committee report contains. But it seems to me that the Ad Hoc Committee mistakes its mandate in confining its observations to the Soviet Union, and to the suppression only of the political activists around the world. We were asked to comment on the existing evidence that psychiatric facilities (interpreted broadly to mean the totality of psychiatric knowledge, techniques and institutions) are used to confine political dissenters (also interpreted broadly to mean those who are running against the political and social currents of the day). Hence I take it that the Trustees are interested in the reasons for the widespread potential abuse of psychiatric facilities to label, treat, confine and commit individuals who, although not "highly visible political dissidents," in their own way defy the public or social order.

I think we can learn much from the Russian experience if the materials are authentic. These documents illustrate that the medical model of "sickness" has been substituted for legally relevant criteria of what is socially and politically unacceptable behavior. Most of the Russian materials we have seen involve persons accused of crimes but who have nevertheless been removed from the criminal process. In place of a trial and a finding of "guilty," these individuals were found "not accountable" for whatever actions they might or might not have committed.

However, the point which should be noted now is that the Soviet psychiatrists involved were not acting on behalf of their individual "patients" but were using psychiatric terminology and techniques on behalf of the state to serve the state's political purposes. Several factors compel me to reach this conclusion. First, although obviously we cannot vouch for the authenticity of these documents, if we admit [for the sake of argument] that the cases reveal clear-cut indications of psychopathology, the behavioral manifestations of this pathology in no way support the finding of "dangerousness" which is necessary to justify the compulsory commitment of an individual to any kind of mental institution. I cannot accept that the belief in, or advocacy of, ideas could ever constitute such a showing. Second, the majority of these cases were confined in "special" or prison hospitals, in conditions so severe as to belie any suggestion that the patients were receiving "treatment" appropriate for their particular diagnoses.

However, the abuse of psychiatric facilities revealed in these materials would still exist were the patients incarcerated in less severe surroundings; left unconfined but given compulsory treatment; or left untreated but labeled "mentally ill." All of these actions would constitute the use of psychiatric "facilities" to suppress political dissent—that is, employment of the medical label of "sick" behavior to serve political purposes.

This type of *abuse* of the psychiatric discipline is not confined to the suppression of highly visible political activists. Abuse is imminent whenever psychiatrists abandon their role as the patient's ally and use their skills to serve institutional purposes. The Soviet practices are only an extreme example of the dangers for the individual "patient."

The first step in combating these dangers is to identify those practices which contain the seed of abuse and then develop safeguards appropriate to the situation.

The definition of "psychiatry" in the usual dictionaries is: "the medical treatment of mental illness." Psychiatry began to be practiced as an outgrowth of neurology and followed very closely the medical model in which an individual would seek out a physician, complaining of certain symptoms, discomfort or ailment, and request treatment. The physician was hired as the patient's ally or agent, and with the patient would do battle using his techniques and technology to combat the illness or discomfort. Thus in the traditional psychiatric relationship, an individual driven by inner discomfort would seek out a psychiatrist, who would attempt to help him alleviate or deal with his discomfort.

Within this voluntary relationship, the psychiatrist can act in several ways, broadly categorized as (1) intra-psychic intervention or (2) extra-psychic intervention. While these modes of action have different results, the doctor is basically acting as the patient's agent. I elaborate on these terms only to clarify for myself the tools which a psychiatrist may employ.

Intra-psychic intervention, based on the analytic model, encourages the patient to look into himself and his past history, to see whether the difficult he is experiencing is related to his past and to examine what he does to provoke or promote his difficulty. This encourages the individual to change himself, to adapt better to his situation. Incidentally, this also encourages the individual to accept society and the status quo and to consider the difficulty as his own rather than that of his total marital, familial, or societal situation.

Extra-psychic intervention should also help alleviate an individual's inner discomfort, but the approach is different. It follows from a community mental health model, in which the psychiatrist agrees with and supports the patient's contention that his situation is other than optimal. The psychiatrist presents or provides alternatives for action which the individual may follow. For example, the doctor may contact or influence a social agency or some other institution which directly affects his patient's life. This intervention may not promote perpetuation of the status quo, but rather may encourage the individual to try to change his situation.

In the first type of intervention the individual is more clearly seen as "sick" while in the second his social condition may also be seen as "sick." What remains constant is that the psychiatrist is motivated to act only as the individual's agent and not on behalf of any other individual or institution. Even if payment is funded through an insurance or other type of plan, if the patient is unhappy with the situation he can relinquish the voluntary contract and seek out other help at any time.

We trust the psychiatrist who practices within this model to evaluate mental illness—that is, to ascertain the difference between symptomatology which reflects adequate coping mechanisms, and symptomatology which makes coping difficult and would benefit from treatment. Of course, the psychiatrist's personal values, interests and emotional makeup influence his medical decisions and may cause him to abuse the patient's interests. More should be done to counteract this potential for abuse, but basically we rely on the training and traditions attached to the medical model of the doctor-patient relationship and trust that because the doctor is the agent of the patient, he at least will "do no harm."

When the psychiatrist's posture toward a patient is altered, however, the underpinnings of our trust vanish. Over the last seventy-five years, a vast body of scientific and technical information has been accumulated about how people think, why they think and act the way they do, and how their thoughts, values and actions can be modified. Psychiatrists have applied this knowledge at the request of local communities or of a variety of public and social institutions—military, political, judicial, and penal, among others. The task set for them by these institutions is to diagnostically label and treat individuals for institutional purposes—generally to retain the status quo and suppress deviance which is detrimental to the institution.

There are clear-cut distinctions which separate the use of psychiatric knowledge and methodology in these settings from the traditional practice of "psychiatry" discussed above.

First, the psychiatrist is no longer only the agent of the patient, but acts on behalf of the institution which employs him.

Second, the patient enters the relationship under compulsion and may eventually be forced to receive involuntary treatment.

Third, the ambiguity which necessarily arises over the psychiatrist's primary alliance, or commitment to interests, is not clarified for the patient.

These distinctions are so significant that it is both inaccurate and dangerous for us to continue to consider the use of psychiatric methodology in these settings to be within the traditional definition of psychiatry—"the medical treatment of mental illness." There are two dangers implicit in these situations—the first to the psychiatrist and the second to the patient.

The psychiatrist, trained in the medical model according to which he is the patient's agent, is hired, or perhaps thrust, into the employment of an institution which naturally assumes that he will promote its interests and implement its goals. Conflicts are inevitable. For example, a psychiatrist in a state hospital may feel pressured to release fewer patients from commitment than the law actually permits, for fear one mistake will cost his institution dearly. At other times, administrative or economic pressures encourage a rapid turnover in patient population. A military psychiatrist is pressured to diagnose and discharge soldiers who defy military authorities, and to do so at the least cost to the military. A psychiatrist evaluating a person accused of a crime may be influenced by demands for "law and order" from not only social but also political groups.

A psychiatrist initially faced with these conflicts is most likely to be deeply troubled about what decision to make, or whose interests to put first. But in an institutional setting, he is also likely to be overcome by the intense pressures to conform and identify with institutional goals. The patient is, after all, not "his" patient but an identified troublemaker. Resolution of the conflict in favor of the institutional goals may be very subtle, so that the psychiatrist still feels he is acting in perfectly good faith and doing "the best for the patient."

Protestations of good faith are simply not enough. Recognition of the conflict of interest undermines the trust we place in the psychiatrist. Psychiatrists are only human, as subject to pressures of public and social authority as we all are. The louder they protest that they are able to benevolently exercise their neutral expertise in the most conflict-laden circumstances, the more it must be feared that the seeds of abuse will sprout.

When they do, the dangers for the individual are obvious. The psychiatrist will overstate rather than minimize the patient's inner discomfort; may incorrectly and unjustifiably label him "sick"; remove him from society and/or subject him to sophisticated techniques to encourage him to conform to institutional or social authority. The paradigm of such dangers is, of course, brainwashing or the Soviet method of suppressing political dissent which is revealed in the documents before us. These tactics make use of psychiatric knowledge and techniques, but few would argue that they fall within an acceptable definition of psychiatric practice.

The psychiatric profession has an interest in identifying those settings in which it is asked to label and treat deviant behavior on behalf of, and in the interest of, public institutions—be they hospitals, prisons, courts, military or prosecuting authorities. Otherwise, the profession runs the risk of someday being justly accused of prostituting its discipline in the Soviet fashion, or perhaps in the vein of our own McCarthyism. The profession must ask itself whether it wants to assume both the janitorial function, and responsibility, of helping to sweep some of society's most troublesome problems under the rug.

That public institutions today need to use psychiatric professionals to help them suppress unacceptable behavior may or may not be true. That the medical model is relied on to cover up our reluctance to create adequate legal criteria and standards to deal with "society's problems" is not the fault of the psychiatric profession. At any rate, I am not saying that psychiatrists should never use their knowledge and techniques outside of the traditional doctor-patient relationship. I do ask the profession not to blind itself to the dangers which exist in these different settings.

The profession must also help "distill" the information which its members can provide to assist public institutions and help remove the impurities of institutional bias, pressures and interests which color psychiatric judgments. The profession should also leave it squarely to public authorities to accept responsibility for "treating" or "punishing" those who are considered problems.

I have a few suggestions to initiate this process. First, psychiatrists must be able to understand and identify those situations in which they assume an alliance with a public or social institution rather than with the patient. Recognition of the inevitable conflict of interest must be legitimized rather than silenced by rote repetition of the Hippocratic Oath.

Second, the conflict of interest must be made explicit to the patient. It is nothing short of dishonest to encourage a patient to communicate freely by allowing him to assume that the psychiatrist is acting solely as his agent. The patient is entitled to at least one statement, like the *Miranda* warnings, of the risks involved in the relationship.

Third, the profession should encourage forms of third-party review of its most critical decisions. This already exists in the case of judicial review of involuntary commitments, and review by the Veterans Administration of military psychiatric discharges and disability awards. Of course, the value of third-party review depends on many factors—the objectivity and expertise of the reviewer; the process of review within which he functions; and the nature of the task he is assigned.

Review will not eradicate the potential for abuse of psychiatric facilities. What is more urgently needed is for the psychiatric profession to stop sweeping its own problems under the rug and to conduct an in-depth inquiry into the use of psychiatric discipline in the institutions of our own society.

Nothing in this statement should be read to mitigate our condemnation of the practices which the Soviet documents, if authentic, reveal. The Trustees should utilize every means within the American Psychiatric Association's disposal to protest the hospitalization of these Soviet citizens and to aid in securing their freedom.

16

Institutions and Adversaries[1]

The social-control role played by psychiatrists is just as troubling in our country as in the Soviet Union. Here, at least, the law does have oversight responsibility. How well has the legal system discharged that responsibility? If my experience with the criminal justice system is any indication, not very well.

Concern about how our society and the law dealt with criminal defendants found not responsible because of mental illness led me inevitably to wonder about how we dealt with all those we considered mentally disturbed. I soon found that the legal system had taken very little interest.

In the mid-1960s "mental disability law" was still an esoteric adjunct to criminal law, dealing primarily with the insanity defense and competency to stand trial. Since then, a revolution has occurred. Today, there is a substantial legal industry devoted to protecting the legal rights of mentally ill and mentally retarded people. Federal and state statutes establish patients' bills of rights and specialized advocacy programs. The *Mental and Physical Disability Law Reporter* catalogues over six thousand cases.[2]

In the mid-1960s I wrote two opinions that addressed for the first time the right of mental patients to appropriate treatment. The *Rouse* case recognized a right to appropriate treatment under the relevant D.C. statute, and the subsequent *Lake* opinion held that the right to appropriate treatment meant treatment in the least restrictive alternative setting.[3] I would never have imagined all that would follow. Since most of the people concerned were poor, powerless, and often incarcerated for life in mental hospitals, they had neither the money nor the credibility to focus attention on the legal issues they faced. All of that was to change with the entry of public interest attorneys. We may debate the merits of increasing legal involvement in any sector of society. But few doubt that the recognition of mental patients' legal rights has precipitated far-reaching changes in attitudes and in the mental health system.[4]

The first decade of the mental disability rights movement (roughly 1965–1975) coincided with the height of public concern for civil rights. Legal attention turned to discovering other groups of disadvantaged and disenfranchised citizens, among them mentally ill and mentally retarded people. The first effort was to establish that they had rights at all, in the sense assumed for other citizens. A series of federal court cases— *Rouse* and *Lake,* along with such landmarks from other courts as *Wyatt v. Stickney*[5]—and the Willowbrook case[6]—began to recognize that persons committed to mental institutions had rights protected by statutes and by the Constitution. The Supreme Court held in 1975 that persons who are civilly committed, not dangerous, not receiving treatment, and able to survive in the community could not be held against their will.[7]

Since the mid-1970s, attention has shifted from establishing rights to implementing them, a far more complex endeavor. It was, bluntly, far easier to convince states to release patients than to provide funds to serve them in the community. Here in the District of Columbia, a case brought to enforce the *Lake* promise of less restrictive alternatives is still mired in the courts, over ten years after the plaintiffs "won."[8] The inability or unwillingness of government to provide adequate community-based mental health care has contributed to a situation that has become scandalous, as many former mental patients join the army of homeless people in our city streets. Patients' lawyers now spend more time fighting to get or keep their clients on the Social Security disability rolls than to obtain treatment for them.

Why are these issues and "these people" so troublesome? Despite evidence that the great majority of mental patients are no more dangerous than anyone else, we continue to regard them with fear.[9] Did "deinstitutionalization" fail? Should we have known better? This article, written just as the legal focus shifted from establishing rights in law to implementing them in practice, touches on these questions, which we face still.

* * *

What are we to do with persons we decide to excuse from normal concepts of responsibility? Much of the debate concerning the proper scope of the insanity defense centers on this unstated problem. Many assume that whatever is done, the defendant should be confined to an institution. But what is the purpose of the confinement?

The problem is really more basic: what should we do with both the nonresponsible criminal offender and the more general class of those we label as mentally disturbed? Both groups make the rest of us uncomfortable. On the one hand, we want to protect ourselves from these individuals and thereby allay our discomfort. But, on the other hand, we want to protect them and ameliorate their suffering by helping and treating them. Too often the types of custody that make us feel more comfortable are not the best for these individuals. The greatest danger we fear, then, is to let our desire to help disturbed or disturbing individuals become a rationalization for confining or institutionalizing them in order to protect ourselves.

Maryland's Patuxent Institution for "defective delinquents" provided perhaps the best example of the conflict between our ideal of humanitarian aid to disturbed or disturbing individuals and our desire to protect ourselves from them. To some degree I shared the dreams of those who designed it. They were genuine humanitarians who thought they were replicating in the field of corrections the reform that Dorothea Dix and others had wrought in the field of mental health. If good intentions were controlling, Patuxent would have been a revolutionary advance that would at last have brought us out of the dark ages of revenge and retribution into the enlightened era of humanitarian treatment and care. But implicit in their efforts was an element of self-protection. The Patuxent reformers sought to "treat" a person who (in the words of the statute) demonstrated "persistent aggravated antisocial or criminal behavior," and who had "such intellectual deficiency or emotional unbalance . . . as to clearly demonstrate an actual danger to society so as to require . . . confinement and treatment. . . ."[10] On Humpty Dumpty's premise that "a word means just what I choose it to mean," the humanitarian reformers called for indeterminate sentences, to run until the individual was sufficiently "treated" or "rehabilitated" to be released. But how can we know what rehabilitation is if we don't even know what habilitation is?

The reality of Patuxent was no Sunnybrook Farm. It actually served as a vehicle for increasing state intervention in the lives of offenders. The flower planted by these humanitarian reformers starved on the meager fare of standardized treatment, and withered into lengthy prison sentences for minor offenses and constant resort to punitive measures in the name of social protection.

There is a dangerous tendency today to justify retributive or punitive measures as treatment, and not on their own ground as punishment. This confusion of purposes must be unraveled. The social justification for a particular confinement must be forthrightly recognized. Only then can we think clearly about the conditions and extent of confinement, and rationally evaluate our societal response to disturbing behavior. Of course, more than one purpose may be served by a particular confinement. But we should be clear as to which purpose justifies which punitive or rehabilitative action.

Revenge (or retribution) and deterrence are, of course, the prime justifications for use of the criminal sanction, despite much scholarly talk of the rehabilitative ideal. But these two rationales are generally thought inappropriate to justify confinement of nonresponsible criminal defendants or the general class of those we label as "mentally disturbed." We may surely doubt, however, whether in practice the law successfully excludes retribution from its interventions in their lives.

The two overt justifications for control are: first, that the individual presents such a danger of future misconduct that he might injure others; and, second, that the individual can be treated or rehabilitated both to ease his suffering and to prevent any further antisocial behavior. Two cases illustrate the practical difficulties inherent in these two justifications.

In the first case, a boy named Tom Cross was committed to St. Elizabeths Hospital at the age of eighteen because of a persistent tendency to indecently expose himself in public. He was never charged with any physical molestation. Indecent exposure is ordinarily punished by a jail sentence of not more than ninety days. After spending fifteen years in St. Elizabeths, Cross was rearrested several months after his release for six new acts of indecent exposure, and again was committed to the hospital. Only then did he begin the litigation which resulted in our court's 1969 opinion in *Cross v. Harris.*[11]

Of particular interest is the debate between Judge, later Chief Justice, Warren Burger in dissent, and myself, writing for the court. Was Tom Cross being confined for perhaps another fifteen years because of his acts or because of his "dangerousness"? Is confinement on the basis of "dangerousness" alone constitutional? Recent studies indicate that the accuracy of predictions of future dangerousness is less—far less, to put it mildly—than the requirement of "beyond a reasonable doubt" which is our legal standard to justify criminal confinement.[12] Indeed, to accept commitments on the basis of present predictions of dangerousness, we must virtually reverse Blackstone's immortal formulation of the presumption of innocence: instead of freeing nine guilty persons to avoid convicting one innocent person, we must confine nine nondangerous persons to avoid freeing one dangerous person.

The major difficulty resulting from the limitations of present predictions of dangerousness is, then, the large number of so-called "false positive" predictions—that is, persons who are in fact not dangerous are predicted to be dangerous. Institutional psychiatrists and other behavioral professionals generally seem to err on the side of overprediction, and their errors may be traced to a disturbing extent both to the nonconformity of the offender to middle-class values and to the desire to avoid the consequences of a "false negative" prediction.[13]

The main thing I've learned about predictions of dangerousness, from attending innumerable meetings of our experts
on crime and violence, is that an offender who has committed
ten prior antisocial acts is more likely to commit another than
is an individual who has committed only one, two, or three
prior antisocial acts. This suggests that the findings underlying
dangerousness and repeat offender statutes are very similar.

A further problem is the definition of what is "dangerous."
Some people considered Tom Cross dangerous because he
exposed himself in public. Prior to the *Cross* case, my court
held that an individual who wrote bad checks was dangerous.[14]

Several problems suggest themselves for our consideration:
(a) Are such findings of dangerousness any more than a determination that a particular individual is presently disturbing
us because of a form of mental disability? (b) If so, and if our
desire is to rid ourselves of nuisances, is total incarceration of
the nuisance necessary? (c) When we assess the potential dangerousness of a past offender, do we consider only the harmful nature of the previous acts he committed or the harmful
nature of much more serious acts that could be predicted from
the prior acts? In other words, is Tom Cross' dangerousness
based on the harm of indecent exposure or the projected harm
of more serious acts of sexual deviancy? (d) For some projected harms, would a form of custody less onerous than total
incarceration be sufficient to protect us from the harm?

Turning to the other justification for confinement—institutionalization because of a "need for treatment"—an example
may be drawn from the case of Catherine Lake. She was committed to St. Elizabeths because she was prematurely senile
and tended to forget numbers and wander about. She was also
indigent. The trial court found that she was not competent to
care for herself and therefore was in need of treatment because she presented a danger to herself. But what exactly was
her need for treatment and why was she not able to provide it
for herself?

Our court found that the then new D.C. Hospitalization of
the Mentally Ill Act, written after extensive hearings by Senator Sam Ervin's Subcommittee on Constitutional Rights, re-

quired an exploration of less restrictive alternatives before resorting to total incarceration.[15] We directed that the trial court consider whether Catherine Lake "and the public would be sufficiently protected if she were required to carry an identification card on her person so that the police or others could take her home if she should wander, or whether she should be required to accept public health nursing care, community health and day care services, foster care, home health aid services, or whether available welfare payments might finance adequate private care."

But necessary as such questions are, they can never provide complete solutions. When Mrs. Lake's case went back to the trial court for a full investigation of alternative forms of care, none was found. Although her case became something of a landmark—if selection for law school curricula is any measure—Mrs. Lake remained at St. Elizabeths.

Can indigency render a person incompetent to care for herself and for that reason "in need of treatment"? Soon after the *Lake* decision, our court ruled in another case that welfare residency requirements were unconstitutional. Three weeks later, I saw a newspaper item announcing that as a result of this decision over seventeen hundred patients would be released from St. Elizabeths. This puzzled me; I wondered what possible connection there could be. On inquiry, I learned that under a long-standing rule of the welfare administration, residents of St. Elizabeths were not considered residents of the District of Columbia, where the hospital is located. Under the old rule, after release they would have to establish residency for a full year before becoming eligible for benefits. As a result, many patients had been kept in the hospital long after they might have been released—not because they still needed treatment, if they ever had needed it, but simply because they had no other means of support. Once the residency requirement was struck down, the hospital could in good conscience release seventeen hundred such persons who would now be eligible for welfare.

My point about these cases is not to condemn any particular result but only to suggest that we overtly, explicitly, clearly correlate a particular social intervention with a particular social justification. This same point applies to decisions about custody and treatment within an institution. The logical extension of the treatment rationale for confinement is the "right to treatment." But attempts to enforce that right soon exposed the central failure of the closed institution that had been hidden for so long under the cloak of benevolence and professionalism: its standardized response to the multitude of individual disabilities herded into the institution.

The *Rouse v. Cameron* case, which my court decided in 1966, is usually remembered for its recognition of the "right to treatment."[16] However, a little-noticed fact about the decision in Charles Rouse's case was that he was being provided some treatment—loosely termed "environmental" therapy—from which he withdrew prior to litigation. Our court found that this "treatment" was inadequate because there was no showing of any attempt to see whether it met Rouse's individual needs. The need for an individual treatment plan cannot be overemphasized. Unless there is such a plan—refined and improved on the basis of experience with the patient—there is no guarantee that the promise of treatment will take root in reality.[17]

The Supreme Court decided, in 1975, in the case of *O'Connor v. Donaldson*,[18] that people may not be confined "without more" if they are not dangerous, are able to survive in the community with the help of family or friends, and are not receiving treatment. In point of fact Donaldson was a Christian Scientist who refused drug treatment and shock therapy. There was evidence that he could have lived with a longtime friend, who on four occasions had asked that Donaldson be released to his care. There was further evidence that he could have gone to live in a halfway house for mental patients, which had also asked for his release to its care. The requests were refused, apparently because of a hospital rule that patients could only be released to their parents.

Much of the legal argument was devoted to the problem of whether judicially manageable standards exist for defining the right to treatment. The Supreme Court concluded that "[w]here 'treatment' is the sole asserted ground for depriving a person of liberty, it is plainly unacceptable to suggest that the courts are powerless to determine whether the asserted ground is present." I agree. As I believe *Rouse* makes clear, the requirement of an individualized treatment plan, officially recorded and utilized in prescriptions, is a manageable standard.

Of course, courts cannot make psychiatric judgments, just as they cannot make many judgments which are entrusted to expert administrative agencies. What they can do is insure that such judgments are in fact made, rationally, on an individualized basis, and recorded for future reference and scrutiny. This requires that professionals be held accountable for their decisions, and that they present facts and conclusions drawn logically from those facts to justify treatment decisions. Donaldson's case is easy when one takes this perspective, since there was evidence that he received only "milieu" therapy—the same brand as did Charles Rouse—and spent but four hours with his attending psychiatrist during nine years of his confinement. The jury was able to find, "based on abundant evidence," that, if mentally ill, Donaldson had not received treatment.[19]

The most difficult problems arise in connection with the form of institutional custody and care of persons committed by reason of their "dangerousness" alone. A psychiatric hospital faces a serious confusion of purposes whenever an individual is committed for this reason: the finding of dangerousness indicates that social protection is at least a partial justification for the confinement, but conceptually a hospital should not be governed by principles relating to social protection. The situation is complicated greatly when the hospital must attempt to treat someone who is found dangerous but not mentally ill.

In the case of Murdock Benjamin,[20]* who killed two white marines in response to being accosted with a racial epithet, it was agreed that the killing was a product of an extreme and compulsive hatred for whites gained through Benjamin's experiences in the Watts ghetto. I had doubts as to Benjamin's criminal responsibility, but became concerned with the problem of what to do with him if he was found nonresponsible. If

---

* Discussed in Chapter 7.

he was committed, what could we rightfully expect of those who would treat or help him? If we gave up on the possibility of treatment to alleviate his hatred, either because treatment wouldn't work or because successful treatment would amount to questionable behavior modification, would our choice be between punitive incarceration or total freedom? I suspect the hospitals are presently handling this dilemma for many individuals who are dangerous and untreatable without any guidance from social policymakers. This is a major, largely unanalyzed question which must be seriously confronted if we are to make rational choices about the nature and extent of societal intervention in the lives of disturbed or disturbing individuals.[21]

Many failures of institutional treatment and the general problem of a standardized institutional response are centrally linked to certain requirements of the closed institution—order, administrative efficiency, discipline, bureaucratic routine. These factors are all too often countertherapeutic. Trying to accommodate the needs of the individual to the needs of the institution is often like trying to fit a square peg in a round hole. This problem is the source of the much-discussed "conflict of loyalty" which is inescapable for institutional professionals. Is their first loyalty to the institution or to the patient? Should the professional prescribe a heavy dose of Thorazine to quiet a confined person and thereby preserve order—or should he let a patient cause trouble, act out, confront human situations, if that will help the patient?

When reviewing the use of psychiatric facilities in the Soviet Union, I was exposed to the most serious conflicts in loyalty among institutional professionals. The medical model of "sickness" could be and was perverted to conform to a judgment of what the managers of the institution considered politically unacceptable behavior. We do not like to compare ourselves to the Soviet Union in this regard, but I am sad to say that psychiatrists in the United States, wittingly or unwittingly, react to the institutional pressures of their employers in a manner which is analogous in principle, at least, to behavioralist professionals in the Soviet Union.[22]

Deinstitutionalization

Some institutional reformers have sought to enforce the right to treatment and the right to the least restrictive alternative by demanding more resources, setting high standards for confinement and treatment, and seeking to expose the hidden punitive element in what passes for treatment or protective custody. Others have turned 180 degrees—and in their disillusionment with the panacea of institutionalization, have demanded the abolition of institutions. Just as the right to treatment began to make headway in the courts, cases involving the right to resist it began to appear. Deinstitutionalization threatened to become a new cure for dealing with the problems of institutional abuses.

But if there is anything we should have learned from our experience with institutions, it is that there can be no single solution for the complex problems of human behavior. Deinstitutionalization poses many of the same dangers as the closed institutions—and some new ones besides. The promise of freedom may be just as chimerical as the promise of treatment.

The advocates of deinstitutionalization comprise a wide spectrum, from civil libertarians to rigid economizers, all of whom pay insufficient attention to the nascent problems of deinstitutionalization. In concentrating on the money that will be saved in the long run, the economizers neglect to consider the larger sums that will be required in the short run to establish a network of community support systems. Without them, communities are unable to absorb the harmless, much less the dangerously deviant individual. Recent articles and editorials in the *New York Times* demonstrate the folly of premature release of mental patients without follow-up services.[23] They provide a glimpse of the backlash that could be expected—from restrictive zoning laws to editorial demands for the establishment of "rural havens" for the mentally disabled. This solution sounds suspiciously like the institutional refuges of the nineteenth century.

Civil libertarians in their proper concern with limiting state intervention in the lives of disturbed or disturbing individuals may fail to account for the reality of mental disability. How real is the promise of individual autonomy for a confused person set adrift in a hostile world? The benevolent purpose of institutionalization may be perverted into excessive state intervention, but there is no guarantee that the benevolent purpose of deinstitutionalization will not itself be perverted into a justification for excessive neglect. Are back alleys any better than back wards?

The real problem is that deinstitutionalization also represents a standardized response to a multitude of individual problems. Just as all patients cannot be helped by "environmental" or "milieu" therapy, not all patients will be helped by autonomy in the community.

Both the civil libertarians and the economizers stand implicitly on the same foundation as the advocates of institutions—the reliance on expert techniques of behavior control. Deinstitutionalization would never have been politically acceptable without psychoactive drugs. We rely on these drugs as a new form of custody and treatment.

This last point brings us to an interesting impasse. Will drugs and electrode implants, psychosurgery and behavior modification, become instruments of state intervention far beyond the wildest imagination of those who attacked closed institutions? We stand today on the threshold of a revolution in our understanding of the brain and human behavior. Will we allow this awesome power to change, shape, and mold human behavior to create new closed institutions without walls?[24]

Perhaps I am too critical of the deinstitutionalization movement. Many criticisms of institutions—the experimentation, behavior modification, punitive and barbaric conditions—go to the need for clear thinking about the purposes of social intervention. If we intervene to help or treat an individual, why do we confine that individual in a modern-day dungeon, under truly primitive conditions, and provide virtually no medical treatment? If we are confining individuals to control their dangerousness, why do we not tailor the confinement to the extent of the dangerousness? What is the justification for behavior modification and experimentation with confined human beings?

But deinstitutionalization proponents may have their own confusion of purposes. Implicit in their proposals may be the assumption that confinement on the basis of a prediction of dangerousness or a determination of a need for treatment constitutes an invalid occasion for social intervention. Indeed, the assumption may also be that there is no such thing as mental illness and hence all treatment is really political behavior modification. Proponents of deinstitutionalization should forthrightly argue the validity or invalidity of these justifications for social intervention.

I have no answers to the many serious and awesome questions raised by government intervention in the lives of mentally disturbed individuals. I am only aware that well-informed, conscientious citizens strongly disagree about the proper occasion and extent of that intervention. The law's contribution to a resolution of this conflict is to suggest a model for handling individual cases—the adversary process. The law cannot wait for experts or society as a whole to resolve the various conflicting points of view. It must deal with individual cases as they arise.

In individual cases, the law and the adversary process do not seek final solutions to perennial questions about the legitimacy of particular state interventions in the lives of disturbed individuals. The law in theory, if not in practice, recognizes the continuing nature of such deep-rooted conflicts. Courts and other social agencies review and fashion criteria for resolving each case as it comes. The criteria are made known to the public in written opinions; the competing values are ventilated. Consequently, the judgments are never fixed or frozen—they can be altered in response to new information, new understanding, or new public demands.

Individualization is the key to the law's approach. But even if it is not a constitutional requirement, individualization is a policy whose practical wisdom recommends itself. It not only accords each citizen recognition of individual dignity, but it prevents overgeneralization.

Unfortunately, the law does not always live up to its principle of individualization. Rather than confront difficult, virtually insoluble problems that threaten current rules and policies, some would retreat behind invocations of expertise and "justiciability," thus sweeping the problem safely under the rug and out of view.

To the contrary, there is a central but limited role for courts in this system. That role is to guide professional decision-making, and may be best described by the familiar model of judicial review of administrative decision-making. Courts must determine whether there has been a full exploration of all relevant facts, opposing views and possible alternatives, whether the results of the exploration relate rationally to the ultimate decision, and whether constitutional and statutory procedural safeguards have been faithfully observed. Our function is not to determine whether the decisions taken by those charged with handling disturbed or disturbing individuals are correct or wise, but whether they are rational in the manner I have just described.

The challenge we face is not so much to resolve these sensitive issues but rather to confront them, to open the door to a portion of human experience that had previously been decreed irrelevant. *Rouse* and *Lake* are a response to this challenge. I would consider those decisions meaningful if they only lead the law to address seriously the manifold problems raised by the institutionalization—or deinstitutionalization—of disturbed or disturbing individuals.

There are some who still say that we should leave these delicate questions of state intervention to the behavioral experts. But I would remind those who suggest this—both outside and within the legal profession—that state intervention involves a serious component of individual rights and hence a difficult balancing of power between the state and the individual, where the stakes are highest for human and personal rights. Courts have traditionally been the protector of individual rights against state power, and there is no reason why the particularly difficult problems in the area of government intervention are any different.

We cannot delegate our responsibility for protecting individual rights to the medical professions. Those disciplines are, naturally enough, oriented toward helping people by treating them. Their value system assumes that disturbed or disturbing individuals need treatment, that medical disciplines can provide it, and that attempts to resist it are misguided or delusionary.

But in order for courts to monitor intelligently the decision-making process of the medical disciplines, and to ensure accountability for decisions, they must constantly seek increased understanding of individual problems and needs. In the *Lake* case, the court attempted to force the experts to confront directly the individual treatment and custody needs of mental hospital patients. Only then can the experts and administrators learn what they and what we as a society are not providing. And only with this heightened awareness will any of us be moved to seek improvement.

The courts will not be successful in these roles without the cooperation of the professionals who have the practical responsibility for state intervention in individual lives. These professionals must take the lead in questioning their own roles. The law has a standard stock of tools to recommend. Decisions must be open, at least to colleagues, and based on stated reasons; records must be kept on staff conferences and treatment decisions. Factual issues can be subject to an internal adversary scrutiny. When institutional interests may conflict with the duty to the patient, they must be noted and discussed. Criteria for resolving such issues will be flexible if they are out in the open. Decisions may approach wisdom if they are incorporated into a learning process.

Some medical professionals reject out of hand any attempt to apply legal techniques to their internal operations. But they should understand that these tools can be doubly helpful to them. First, they give the decision-maker an opportunity to rectify any mistaken decisions without either outside interference or the pressure to defend decisions solely to avoid admitting a mistake. But equally important, these techniques can help professionals make better decisions in the first instance, and defend them should they be challenged.

This sort of scrutiny is becoming more and more an integral part of decision-making in the realm of social deviance. Trial courts, parole boards, and psychiatrists alike are gradually— very gradually—being pressed to explain the reasons behind their decisions. The process of accountability, then, which the courts must guarantee, starts with self-scrutiny and includes ongoing oversight by peers, by other concerned disciplines, by the legislature, and ultimately by the public at large. In this way, decisions will never be embedded in concrete.

What I am suggesting is not novel. It is the same account-ability envisioned in the concept of peer review that has long received lip service from professions of all kinds. The law is uniquely equipped to participate in structuring such scrutiny. And through this process of open decision and review we might possibly develop the knowledge and experience to avoid the pitfalls of both institutionalization and deinstitutionalization.

17

Not Guilty by Reason of Insanity: The Right to Treatment

Most histories of the right to treatment begin with the case of *Rouse v. Cameron.*[1] Although based on D.C. statutory law, not the Constitution, the case did raise the possibility of a constitutional right to treatment. (The fact that D.C. statutes were enacted by Congress added to the authoritative impression.) Both *Rouse* and *Cross v. Harris* illustrate what really happens after the not guilty by reason of insanity (NGRI) verdict, as well as the interplay on the court as we struggled with a new set of issues.

It was clear that Rouse, Cross, and others were held at St. Elizabeths Hospital far longer than they would have been imprisoned had they been convicted of their crimes. Were they receiving the treatment the statute prescribed as the justification for their indefinite confinement?[2]

Once we started looking at the treatment of insanity acquittees, it was impossible to ignore the parallel issues for patients who were confined under civil commitment statutes. These patients had not committed any crime; they were hospitalized as mentally ill and in need of treatment. Our statute clearly contemplated that they would receive appropriate treatment. What were they actually receiving?

Since those early days, the "right to treatment" has remained a powerful force for change in the mental health system. Once more, we have to call things by their right name. If we take away someone's liberty because he needs help, the least we can do is provide help.[3]

Rouse v. Cameron (1967)[4]

BACKGROUND   In November 1962, Charles Rouse was found not guilty by reason of insanity of carrying a dangerous weapon, a misdemeanor for which the maximum sentence (if he had been convicted) is one year. As an insanity acquittee, he was committed to St. Elizabeths Hospital for treatment. After more than four years, he filed a habeas corpus action challenging his continued confinement on grounds that he was not receiving treatment.

The District Court held a hearing and denied relief in habeas corpus. It refused to consider Rouse's contention that he had received no psychiatric treatment, the judge noting, "My jurisdiction is limited to determining whether he has recovered his sanity. I don't think I have a right to consider whether he is getting enough treatment." The Court of Appeals reversed that decision, for the reasons discussed in my opinion.

* * *

The principal issues raised by this appeal are whether a person involuntarily committed to a mental hospital on being acquitted of an offense by reason of insanity has a right to treatment . . . , and if so, how violation of this right may be established. ⊙The purpose of involuntary hospitalization is treatment, not punishment. The provision for commitment rests upon the supposed "necessity for treatment of the mental condition which led to the acquittal by reason of insanity." Absent treatment, the hospital is "transform[ed] . . . into a penitentiary where one could be held indefinitely for no convicted offense, and this even though the offense of which he was previously acquitted because of doubt as to his sanity might not have been one of the more serious felonies" or might have been, as it was here, a misdemeanor.

Had appellant been found criminally responsible, he could have been confined a year, at most, however dangerous he might have been. He has been confined four years and the end is not in sight. Since this difference rests only on need for treatment, a failure to supply treatment may raise a question of due process of law. It has also been suggested that a failure to supply treatment may violate the equal protection clause. Indefinite confinement without treatment of one who has been found not criminally responsible may be so inhumane as to be "cruel and unusual punishment."

Impressed by the considerable constitutional problems that arise because "institutionalized patients often receive only custodial care," Congress established a *statutory* "right to treatment" in the 1964 Hospitalization of the Mentally Ill Act. The act provides:

◊ A person hospitalized in a public hospital for a mental illness shall, during his hospitalization, be entitled to medical and psychiatric care and treatment. The administrator of each public hospital shall keep records detailing all medical and psychiatric care and treatment received by a person hospitalized for a mental illness and the records shall be made available, upon that person's written authorization, to his attorney or personal physician.[5]

It appears that this provision . . . was intended to cover persons hospitalized under any statutory authorization. . . . That right necessarily extends to involuntary commitment under D.C. Code 24-301.

Moreover, the considerations underlying the right to treatment provision in the 1964 Act apply with equal force to commitment under D.C. Code 24-301. These considerations are reflected in the statement of Senator Ervin, sponsor of the bill in the Senate. He called mere custodial care of hospitalized persons "shocking" and stated that of all the areas in which reform is badly needed, the "right to treatment" was "perhaps the most critical." He further said:

Several experts advanced the opinion that to deprive a person of liberty on the basis that he is in need of treatment, without supplying the needed treatment, is tantamount to a denial of due process. [The Senate bill] . . .

embodies provisions which will ameliorate this problem whereas existing law makes no provisions for safeguarding this right.[6]

Regardless of the statutory authority, involuntary confinement without treatment is "shocking." Indeed, there may be greater need for the protection of the right to treatment for persons committed without the safeguard of civil commitment procedures. Because we hold that the right to treatment provision applies to appellant, we need not resolve the serious constitutional questions that Congress avoided by prescribing this right.

The Group for the Advancement of Psychiatry has urged that "provisions that safeguard the patient's right to good treatment as opposed to simple custody" are an essential element of commitment laws.[7] A right to treatment in some form is recognized by law in many states. The requirement in the 1964 Act that the hospital keep records detailing psychiatric care and treatment and make them available to the patient's attorney reinforces our view that Congress intended to implement the right to treatment by affording a judicial remedy for its violation.

The patient's right to treatment is clear. We now consider how violation of the right may be established.

According to leading experts, "psychiatric care and treatment" includes not only the contacts with psychiatrists but also activities and contacts with the hospital staff designed to cure or improve the patient. The hospital need not show that the treatment will cure or improve him but only that there is a bona fide effort to do so. This requires the hospital to show that initial and periodic inquiries are made into the needs and conditions of the patient with a view to providing suitable treatment for him, and that the program provided is suited to his particular needs. Treatment that has therapeutic value for some may not have such value for others. For example, it may not be assumed that confinement in a hospital is beneficial "environmental therapy" for all.

The effort should be to provide treatment which is adequate

in light of present knowledge. Some measures which have therapeutic value for the particular patient may be too insubstantial in comparison with what is available. On the other hand, the possibility of better treatment does not necessarily prove that the one provided is unsuitable or inadequate.

It has been said that "the only certain thing that can be said about the present state of knowledge and therapy regarding mental disease is that science has not reached finality of judgment."[8] But lack of finality cannot relieve the court of its duty to render an informed decision. Counsel for the patient and the government can be helpful in presenting pertinent data concerning standards for mental care, and, particularly when the patient is indigent and cannot present experts of his own, the court may appoint independent experts. Assistance might be obtained from such sources as the American Psychiatric Association, which has published standards and is continually engaged in studying the problems of mental care. The court could also consider inviting the psychiatric and legal communities to establish procedures by which expert assistance can be best provided.

Continuing failure to provide suitable and adequate treatment cannot be justified by lack of staff or facilities. Congress considered a Draft Act Governing Hospitalization of the Mentally Ill prepared by the National Institute of Mental Health and the General Counsel of the Federal Security Agency, which contained the following provision:

○ Every patient shall be entitled to humane care and treatment and, *to the extent that facilities, equipment, and personnel are available,* to medical care and treatment in accordance with the highest standards accepted in medical practice. [Emphasis supplied.]

The [italicized] language was omitted in the present Act. This omission plainly evidences the intent to establish a broader right to treatment. As the Fourth Circuit Court of Appeals said of the right to treatment under Maryland's "defective delinquent" statute, "[d]eficiencies in staff, facilities, and finances would undermine . . . the justification for the law, and ultimately the constitutionality of its application."[9]

We are aware that shortage of psychiatric personnel is a most serious problem today in the care of the mentally ill. In the opinion of the American Psychiatric Association, no tax-supported hospital in the United States can be considered adequately staffed. We also recognize that shortage cannot be remedied immediately. But indefinite delay cannot be approved. "The rights here asserted are . . . *present* rights . . . and, unless there is an overwhelmingly compelling reason, they are to be promptly fulfilled."[10]

. . . If the court finds that a mandatorily committed patient, such as appellant, is in custody in violation of the Constitution and laws, it may allow the hospital a reasonable opportunity to initiate treatment. In determining the extent to which the hospital will be given an opportunity to develop an adequate program, important considerations may be the length of time the patient has lacked adequate treatment, the length of time he has been in custody, the nature of the mental condition that caused his acquittal, and the degree of danger, resulting from the condition, that the patient would present if released. Unconditional or conditional release may be in order if it appears that the opportunity for treatment has been exhausted or treatment is otherwise inappropriate. It is unnecessary to detail the possible range of circumstances in which release would be the appropriate remedy.

The government says the record shows that appellant is receiving adequate treatment. Since the District judge found no right to treatment, he did not inquire into the question of adequacy. There was evidence that appellant voluntarily left group therapy several months before the hearing below. But there was no inquiry into such questions as the suitability of group therapy for his particular illness, whether his rejection of this therapy was a manifestation and symptom of his mental illness, and whether reasonable efforts were made either to deal with such rejection or to provide some other suitable treatment. Also, the government psychiatrist said that appellant was receiving "environmental therapy." But the suitability and adequacy of the "milieu" as therapy for *this* petitioner was not explored.

We think "law and justice require" that we remand for a hearing and findings on whether appellant is receiving adequate treatment, and, if not, the details and circumstances underlying the reason why he is not. The latter information is essential to determine whether there is "an overwhelmingly compelling reason" for the failure to provide adequate treatment. . . .

Cross v. Harris (1969)[11]

. . . The Sexual Psychopath Act filled a gap in the commitment law. It was intended to be a humanitarian alternative to punishment for mentally disturbed potential sexual offenders who, some thought, could not be civilly committed and who, under the M'Naghten Rule then in effect, could not even plead "insanity" to criminal charges arising from their uncontrollable misconduct. . . .

We attempted in *Millard*[12] to provide an analytical framework to guide lower courts in applying the conclusory term "dangerous to others." Without some such framework, "dangerous" could readily become a term of art describing anyone whom we would, all things considered, prefer not to encounter on the streets. We did not suppose that Congress had used "dangerous" in any such Pickwickian sense. Rather, we supposed that Congress intended the courts to refine the unavoidably vague concept of "dangerousness" on a case-by-case basis, in the traditional common-law fashion.

This does not mean, however, that the statutory language may be disregarded. To be "dangerous" for the purposes of the [D.C.] Sexual Psychopath Act, one must be "*likely to* attack or otherwise *inflict injury*, loss, pain or other evil on the objects of his desire." . . .

These determinations must be made on the basis of the record in the particular case before the court. The expert testimony will therefore be relevant to three questions of fact: (1)

the likelihood of recurrence of sexual misconduct; (2) the likely frequency of any such behavior; (3) the magnitude of harm to other persons that is likely to result.

Having found the facts, the court must then determine as a matter of law—in this case, as a matter of statutory construction—whether those facts provide a legal basis for commitment. Two questions must be answered in making this determination. The first is what *magnitude of harm* will justify commitment. It is clear that Congress did not intend to authorize indefinite preventive detention for those who have a propensity to behave in a way that is merely offensive or obnoxious to others; the threatened harm must be substantial. Thus, commitment under the Sexual Psychopath Act requires that a person be found likely to engage in sexual misconduct in circumstances where that misconduct will inflict substantial injury upon others.

The second question is what *likelihood of harm* will justify commitment. It may well be impossible to provide a precise definition of "likely" as the term is used in the statute. The degree of likelihood necessary to support commitment may depend on many factors. Among the particularly relevant considerations are the seriousness of the expected harm, the availability of inpatient and outpatient treatment for the individual concerned, and the expected length of confinement required for inpatient treatment.

It is particularly important that courts not allow this second question to devolve, by default, upon the expert witnesses. Psychiatrists should not be asked to testify, without more, simply that future behavior or threatened harm is "likely" to occur. For the psychiatrist "may—in his own mind—be defining 'likely' to mean anything from virtual certainty to slightly above chance. And his definition will not be a reflection of any expertise, but . . . of his own personal preference for safety or liberty."[13] Of course, psychiatrists may be unable or unwilling to provide a precise numerical estimate of probabilities, and we are not attempting to so limit their testimony. But questioning can and should bring out the expert witness's meaning when he testifies that expected harm is or is not "likely." Only when this has been done can the court properly separate the factual question—what degree of likelihood exists in a particular case—from the legal one—whether the degree of likelihood that has been found to exist provides a justification for commitment. . . .

[E]ven if appellant cannot show that his future acts of exhibitionism will be infrequent, he may nevertheless be able to show that they will be harmless. In light of evidence as to the character and size of the likely viewing audience and the harm it may suffer, the District Court will have to consider whether appellant's potential exhibitionism can be deemed a sufficiently grave danger to warrant an indeterminate commitment. . . .

Congress may legislate to protect many different interests—psychic and aesthetic as well as physical and economic. But while it may prohibit ugly billboards because they give offense, it may not lock up ugly people for the same reason. The power to control an evil does not remove all restrictions on the means that may be employed for that purpose. This principle is fundamental to the constitutional order.[14]

On the present record, confinement of appellant under the Sexual Psychopath Act would deprive him of his liberty indefinitely—and perhaps permanently—for a propensity to commit acts punishable by a fixed jail sentence. Moreover, confinement would ignore, and apparently frustrate, his treatment needs. Confinement for a mere propensity is preventive detention. Particularly when the act in question is commonly punishable only by a short jail sentence, indefinite confinement, even though labeled "civil," is preventive detention with a vengeance. . . .

The dissenting opinion is in large part an attack on *Millard v. Harris,* which controls our decision today.[15] But although it misreads the holdings and rationales of both decisions, it raises issues of such importance that with all due respect, we are constrained to address ourselves to some of the dissent's statements.

First. On remand, the District Court will have to determine whether appellant is "mentally ill" and therefore within the purview of the Hospitalization of the Mentally Ill Act. But if it determines that he is *not* "mentally ill," it cannot avoid determining whether he is "dangerous" within the meaning of the Sexual Psychopath Act. In light of this, it is difficult to understand the objection to defining the statutory concept of "dangerous" for the guidance of the District Court on remand. There is ample precedent for our action here, and principles of sound judicial administration require us to make our remand order intelligible to the court and parties below.

Second. The dissent apparently would construe the statute so as either to read out of it the word "likely" or to read into it an unascertainable congressional intent to confine all exhibitionists as "dangerous." Even if the statute were fairly susceptible of such a construction, however, a long and consistent line of authority would counsel us not to adopt it "unless no choice is left." . . . For a statute "must be construed with an eye to possible constitutional limitations so as to avoid doubts as to its validity." . . . This "principle of wisdom and duty" has so often been repeated that it should no longer need discussion. But the premature decision of constitutional questions against which the dissent so rightly inveighs could not be avoided if we were to follow its construction of the statute, which would require us to confront the constitutional questions directly.

Third. Opinions are written for explication and instruction. Neither function would be served if, having concluded that the statute must be construed to avoid constitutional doubts, we then made no mention of the doubts we sought to avoid. Neither here nor in *Millard* have we *decided* any constitutional questions. But crucial factors affecting decisions are not to be kept as secrets known only to the court. Bench, bar, and litigants alike would be ill served if we were to conceal the bases for judgment.

Fourth. The dissent apparently considers the constitutional questions we have sought to avoid deciding so insubstantial that their very mention occasions rebuke. "This is not," we are told, "a situation involving strictly preventive detention." By our construction of this statute we have done our best to make this statement true. But the dissent would read the statute to bring this issue into the clearest possible focus. Appellant has been "treated" at St. Elizabeths Hospital for fifteen years—his entire adult life. Both of the examining psychiatrists testified that further hospitalization will not improve—and may aggravate—his condition, while outpatient treatment offers some hope of a cure. Perhaps the consequences of his exhibitionism could be shown to present such a grave risk to the public that he may legally be confined indefinitely solely for their protection. But if this is to be done, we should *at least* acknowledge what we are doing. We are not confining an unfortunate man in order to provide him with treatment that will lead to his rehabilitation; we are locking him up for our own "protection," in direct opposition to his treatment needs. Awareness of this fact might impel us to approach the problem with greater humility and caution.

Fifth. The dissent takes us to task for giving insufficient weight to "the *possibility* of serious psychological harm which might result to small children" (emphasis added). We are not unaware of this possibility. But the statute says that commitment is justified only if the person to be committed is "*likely* to . . . inflict injury" on other persons. Whatever may be the requisite standard of likelihood, there is surely no warrant for reading "likely" as synonymous with "might possibly."

Sixth. One premise lies at the core of the dissenting opinion: that exhibitionism is necessarily dangerous, no matter what the circumstances. This assumption so pervades the dissent that it can flatly state, with no citation of authority whatsoever, that Congress has decided that exhibitionism is dangerous; consequently, the dissent strenuously objects to what it conceives to be our disregard of congressional intent. But the House Report on the bill, the Senate Report, and the *Congressional Record* are empty of any indication that Congress even considered the question, let alone answered it. Determination of the legislative intent is often difficult, and even careful examination of the legislative history may leave grounds for disagreement. At the very least, however, courts should determine the intent of Congress from the legislative record, and not simply infer it from general notions of proper policy.

Seventh. The dissent, in successive paragraphs, first attempts to remove this case from the sphere of "preventive detention" by focusing on appellant's past conduct, and next resurrects the tired cliché that "we are not here dealing with *penal* legislation." The first of these paragraphs of course ignores both the language and operation of the Sexual Psychopath Act, which requires neither a criminal conviction nor any showing, attended by the procedural safeguards constitutionally required in criminal cases, that the person to be committed has engaged in specific proscribed conduct. And the two paragraphs taken together will illustrate the willingness with which many of us deny the reality of preventive detention. All too often courts justify a punitive disposition by looking to past conduct, while simultaneously ignoring the procedural requirements of criminal cases by invoking the false promise of "nonpenal" treatment and rehabilitation. "Noncriminal" commitments of so-called dangerous persons have long served as preventive detention, but this function has been either excused or obscured by the promise that, while detained, the potential offender will be rehabilitated by treatment. Notoriously, this promise of treatment has served only to bring an illusion of benevolence to what is essentially a warehousing operation for social misfits.

Predicting future behavior and evaluating its consequences is a uniquely difficult, if not impossible, task. It must be forthrightly confronted, not avoided by sugar-coating reality. There is no way on the record that we can escape the reality that as "penal" incarceration would set appellant free in ninety days, while the dissent's "non-penal" solution would likely confine him for years, if not for the rest of his life. The record here contains uncontradicted expert testimony that appellant's continued confinement would not "benefit anyone," while outpatient treatment offers the best chance for improvement of his condition. Judicial speculation is no substitute for record evidence.

18

Protecting Old Values in the New Century[1]

One advantage—I sometimes think the best advantage—of being a judge has been the opportunity to meet and forge close friendships with persons in many disciplines. I exploited the wisdom and patience of some of these friends in preparing the following remarks on the occasion of the Bicentennial in 1976. I discovered that they fell into three categories.

The pessimists, when told I was to speak about the future of civil liberties, glumly muttered: "That's easy—civil liberties don't have any future." The optimists waxed eloquent, predicting changes that would make the Garden of Eden look bare. And the realists were brutally honest. They suggested: "Just tell them you don't know about the future—and sit down." This last suggestion was most tempting. Indeed, it reminded me of a classic commencement address attributed to the humorist Art Buchwald: "We of the older generation have given you a perfect world," he told the graduates. "Don't louse it up." And he sat down.

Seeking inspiration for my own address, I tried to imagine what predictions a speaker might have ventured in celebrating the Centennial. But I wondered how many commentators in 1876 would have anticipated things we now take for granted—for instance, the electronics, media, or transportation technologies that have revolutionized our world and altered our freedoms. None of this gave me much confidence in my crystal ball. The history of civil liberties illustrates the wisdom of the philosopher Heraclitus: the only constant is change.

These are perilous times for civil liberties and civil rights.

We do not have and never wanted a "pure democracy." A primary goal of the Constitution and the Bill of Rights was to protect individuals and minorities from the oppression of the majority. As Justice Brennan has said: "Unabashed enshrinement of majority will would permit the imposition of a social caste system or wholesale confiscation of property so long as a majority of the authorized legislative body, fairly elected, approved. Our Constitution could not abide such a situation. It is the very purpose of a constitution—and particularly of the Bill of Rights—to declare certain values transcendent; beyond the reach of temporary political majorities. The majoritarian process cannot be expected to rectify claims of minority right that arise as a response to the outcome of that very majoritarian process."[2]

The way to protect our values is to respect and practice the American penchant for questioning authority. For those in positions of some authority it is an especially important part of that authority to ask the toughest questions.

* * *

Civil liberties define the junction of governmental power and individual freedom. They do so by carving out a sphere of autonomy around each individual. This sphere has been defined in part spatially, by recognizing the sanctity of the home against unreasonable searches; in part procedurally, by limiting arbitrary actions of government; and to a great extent in terms of protected activities, such as worship, expression, travel, and child rearing. In protecting this sphere against invasions, with varying degrees of vigilance, we approach Justice Brandeis's ideal, which he termed "the most comprehensive of rights"—"as against government, the right to be let alone."[3]

Significant practical benefits flow to both individuals and social groups by recognizing these rights. Individuals are accorded latitude to develop in directions they choose. The resulting diversity facilitates an interplay of ideas that can lead to fruitful innovation. Moreover, recognition of these rights lays the groundwork for an order more secure than that imposed by repressive regimes. But while the pragmatic justifications for liberty are indeed impressive, the framers relied mainly on principle when arguing for the rights of persons. They found rights compelling not just as the means to an end, but as ends in themselves, not only in calculating costs and benefits, but also in recognizing certain rights reflected their moral principles; so too, court decisions defining the scope of these liberties are necessarily statements of our ethical bearings. This infusion of morality into law need not involve judicial overreaching. To give meaning to words like "cruel and unusual," "reasonable," or "due process," we must consider not only history and precedent, but developing morality as well.

This is not to say that by donning black robes, judges acquire mystical insight into ultimate truths. I recognize relativity as a law of metaphysics as well as of physics. But I believe we can take note of evolving notions of human decency; and we must reflect them in our decisions. Unless our law aspires to morality, its justice will not merit the name.

Although moral and pragmatic arguments in the long run may converge on the proper balance between the rights of citizen and state, in the short run they often appear at odds. Since the actions of individuals radiate outward, the freedom of each appears to conflict with the interests—especially the security interests—of all. This may be a free country, but I will be much happier in it if your freedom to swing your arms stops short of where my chin begins. Thus, even in tranquil times, groups attempt to constrict the protected spheres of others. In times of crisis, when passions color perceptions, exaggerated fears lead to overly harsh responses. Justice Brandeis wrote of such times: "Men feared witches and burnt women."[4]

The founders of the nation foresaw such dangers. James Madison wrote to Thomas Jefferson: "The invasion of private rights is chiefly to be apprehended . . . from acts in which the Government is the mere instrument of the major number of the Constituents."[5] Indeed, the framers enacted the Bill of Rights to insulate the delicate liberty/security balance from passing emergencies and political might. They looked to "independent tribunals of justice" to provide, in Madison's words, "an impenetrable bulwark against every assumption of power" by the branches of government that were closer to the political process.[6]

If the history of our first two centuries fails to justify fully the framers' faith in the judiciary, it certainly vindicates their fears for liberty. Time and again, in passing emergencies, majorities have attacked dissidents' freedom without much hindrance from the courts. The ink on the first amendment was dry only seven years when a Federalist government, fearing subversion by Jeffersonian Republicans, enacted the Alien and Sedition Acts, which outlawed the publication of malicious or scandalous statements directed at the government. In our century, government responded to fears of anarchism by passing new Sedition Acts and by sponsoring Attorney General Mitchell Palmer's Red Raids; Washington answered an alleged military necessity by locking over 100,000 Japanese-Americans in concentration camps; and government met a communist threat with loyalty oaths, blacklists, and McCarthyism. Intelligence agencies invaded the liberties of antiwar, civil-rights, and women's-movement activists whose only crimes seem to have been dreaming dreams that differed from the FBI and CIA versions of revealed truth. During these crises, the courts approved some of these responses and failed to face others; seldom did they say: "No."

Although instituted to preserve rights for all, the government has repeatedly seen its own preservation as its raison d'être, as "the highest duty," to quote from Justice Frankfurter's concurring opinion in *Dennis v. United States*.[7] But we should remember it is a revolution we celebrate today. Those who fought it took great risks to overthrow a government destructive of rights, and to establish one recognizing a right to change even the form of government itself. The great danger is that individuals who wield the power of government will confuse dissent with insurrection, and mistake preservation of government for preservation of the status quo and of their own power. Of course, freedom carries many risks, but we have learned that those risks are seldom as great as they seem when expanded by the heat of the moment.

Although we might wish otherwise, the challenge of protecting freedom is not merely a historical curiosity. New threats to security press in on us, and others, in unforeseeable forms, will succeed them, providing fresh fuel for the fires of repression.

Today street crime has replaced anarchism and communism as our cause for alarm. That concern is manifest in President Gerald Ford's warning that our legal system leaves the rights of the majority "sadly out of balance."[8] In the courts, we see an expansion of searches deemed "reasonable" and a contraction of those requiring a warrant, a loosening of the elementary prophylactic rules of *Miranda v. Arizona,* and far-reaching limitations on the opportunity to litigate questions of this sort.[9] In the legislatures, there is a clamor to adopt tougher sentencing provisions. The spirit of our responses to previous demons is now incarnated in our reaction to crime.

Of course the crime problem is neither illusory nor easy to solve. The civil liberties issues are not battles pitting forces of light against minions of darkness. To the contrary, the issues have become increasingly complex, and libertarians themselves frequently line up on both sides.

Consider, for example, the sentencing issue. Proponents of mandatory minimum prison terms for all persons convicted of violent crimes offer a lofty justification for their proposal— protecting the rights of potential victims.[10] Mandatory incarceration, they claim, would serve this worthy purpose by enhancing whatever deterrent effect punishment has and by removing dangerous persons from the streets. Advocates of determinate sentencing also make an appealing case for their suggestions.[11] They argue that the curtailment of efforts to tailor sentences to the criminal rather than to the crime would have three major positive effects: first, it would reduce the need for probation officers to probe into the private lives of offenders in preparing presentence reports; second, it would undermine the justification for compelling treatment and prolonging commitment until an offender is "rehabilitated"; and third, it would limit the unbridled discretion of judges and parole boards that has led to gross disparities in sentences.

But the cost of such proposals to liberty, while perhaps more subtle, is still significant. The great increase in violent behavior which has put us in fear is for the most part only a symptom of the frustration, desperation, and rage felt by many of those living in our rotting inner cities. The response most consistent with our libertarian tradition is not to get tough with those who manifest these symptoms, but to get tough instead with the deprivations that cause the disease. It is simply unjust to place people in dehumanizing social conditions, to do nothing about those conditions, and then to command those who suffer: "Behave—or else!" To save our hides, we lose our souls.

Mandatory incarceration, determinate sentencing, and other similar ideas are thus the first steps in a thousand-mile journey, but in precisely the wrong direction—towards repression. Locking up those who manifest symptoms does not cure—or even address—the underlying ill. If it reduces crime, it will do so only because repression and fear can be effective. Determinate sentencing is also an ostrichlike response; it expressly eliminates from the process any effort to learn about the circumstances that fostered the behavior of a particular offender. As a result, we forfeit an opportunity to learn what must be done to prevent him—and others like him—from committing future offenses.

Our best hope is to seek out the causes of the criminal act—to discover the cause of failure. To do that effectively, however, requires both a major commitment of resources to the production of presentence reports that permit critical insights and an erosion of the obdurate resistance of almost all judges to a systematic articulation of exactly what had been learned about the individual prior to sentencing and what reasoning led to the sentencing decision.

Of course, eliciting the information necessary to understand the forces that drive people to crime is not a solution to the problem of preventing crime; it is only a prerequisite to solving the problem. Once we improve our understanding, we will still need to decide whether the costs of grappling with the forces that cause crime are more than we are willing to pay.

That question must be addressed directly. Tackling the causes of crime admittedly will not be easy. Rather than conceding the inevitability of social injustice and seeking the serenity to accept it, we must recognize its intolerability and search for the strength to change it.

The crime crisis is illustrative of the pressures against liberty that have arisen—and will arise—in response to threats. We must meet any challenge to civil liberties, but our past performance does not give much cause for optimism. But institutional and doctrinal changes that will better insulate courts from those forces are possible. Just as statutes creating emergency powers usually are enacted before an emergency actually arises, so questions dealing with the legality and scope of these statutes should also be resolved before the crunch is on. Similarly, in adjudicating individual criminal cases, courts should articulate per se rules setting the bounds of both protected individual activities and prohibited government conduct, so that in emergencies there will be less need to strike ad hoc balances and less danger that the balancers will have their thumbs on one side of the scales.

A second challenge to civil liberties in the next century will grow out of developments in science and technology. By placing new tools at the government's disposal, technological advances enhance its power, and raise the question of when—if ever—the government may use these tools.

In recent years, we have asked the question with regard to various surveillance technologies, from X-rays and magnetometers to wiretaps and "bugs." It is now possible to intercept conversations through windowpanes with laser beams, and to eavesdrop on telephone discussions by monitoring microwave radio channels. The uses of these new technologies are so hard to detect that even if the courts articulate clear-cut rules, enforcing them will be unusually difficult. Yet, as our experience with surveillance technology teaches, if we are to preserve the freedoms the framers sought to guarantee, we must guard against much more than the specific evils they feared.

Although I cannot predict the technological developments of the next century, I foresee intractable issues looming in behavior and thought control. The emerging wizardries of chemotherapy, psychosurgery, behavior modification, and genetic engineering, with their "Clockwork Orange" overtones,

are not an unlikely source of moral dilemmas. We may therefore decide that these "cures" should never be used—at least
without informed consent, itself a complex issue. But like all
technological advances, these developments carry promise as
well as peril. The promise here is twofold: alleviating suffering, and protecting society from "dangerous" persons. Thus,
even if banning these wizardries should be the right decision—
and it may well be—we should not feel righteous about it.
After all, society always has shaped value-formation and behavior, and if socialization fails, we employ less subtle means—
caging those we find mentally or morally deficient and attempting to "rehabilitate" them with electroshock, psychotherapy,
and the like.

Restraining government is a holding action; it does not extend the frontiers of the individual's protected sphere. In the
future, we will undoubtedly recognize new interests as rights.
However, it is important to focus, not on defining new rights,
but on finding new ways to vitalize old ones.

Traditionally, we have guarded civil liberties with a "thou
shalt not" strategy, seeking to foster freedom by protecting
citizens from the state. Sooner or later we will have to consider
whether that strategy alone can make freedom meaningful.
Several factors suggest that if it was enough in the predominantly rural, open society of 1776—and perhaps it was not
enough even then—it is woefully inadequate today.

The first such factor is the increased power of private groups.
With the advent of huge corporations, powerful unions, and
sophisticated technology, government no longer holds a monopoly on the power to invade liberty on a massive scale. Individual scientists, for example, can perform experiments that
unleash forces capable of untold destruction. A single television network can limit free speech by denying air time to outsiders or by censoring its own reporters. Unless private power
is exercised responsibly, we will either have to suffer private
abuse or countenance increased public regulation.

The second factor tending to undermine the sufficiency of
our "thou shalt not" approach is the growth of government
and our heightened sensitivity to its presence. No wall of sep-

aration between government and protected activity can be inviolable in our complex society. Government intermingles with religion, for example, when it taxes or exempts church property. It affects freedom of expression by creating parks or sidewalks, by enforcing, or declining to enforce, antitrust laws against networks or newspapers, or simply by setting postal rates. And even with respect to the most basic freedom, freedom of thought, government plays an important role, contributing to socialization directly through decisions involving curriculum and schooling, and indirectly through almost everything it does.

These twin developments portend the need to complement our traditional "thou shalt nots" with a set of "thou shalts." Requiring government to affirmatively facilitate freedom is not free of costs. Augmenting the power of government always carries risks. But the risks can be minimized by vigilantly seeking the least intrusive strategies of affirmative protection.

Consider, for example, the problem of expression where effective means of communication are seemingly scarce. Government could simulate a laissez-faire position by randomly allocating radio and television frequencies and by allowing the fittest to survive, subject only to the tax and regulatory laws that are applicable to all businesses. This, however, would leave open the possibility of monopolistic suppression by those in control. To avoid that danger, government has compelled those who control these forums to open them up to a diversity of views. But deciding what is a "fair balance" of opinionated programming leads government knee-deep into regulating speech.

Perceiving this danger, the Supreme Court has struck down a "fairness doctrine" for newspapers, and in the future may well reconsider its approval of the FCC's fairness rule. A third alternative would require government to neutralize the influence of persons with access to those forums by limiting the amount of speech they are permitted to engage in; but this approach was rejected by the Supreme Court as "wholly foreign to the First Amendment" when applied to campaign expenses. Instead, the Court approved another option—subsidizing speech so as to equalize access.[12] This option could be supplemented by increasing the number of communication outlets like UHF, cable television, or subscriber broadcasting. These latter strategies are fully consistent with our constitutional values.

Treatment of the mentally disturbed provides another example of the need for minimally intrusive affirmative action. Many libertarians, reacting to total institutionalization, would end involuntary commitment altogether. But setting disoriented persons adrift in a hostile world is no more likely to make them free than is confining them in the back wards of a public hospital. If they are to gain more freedom, they must receive ample treatment and supportive services in the community. Adequate funding for such programs, however, would be costly indeed, and permitting the mentally handicapped to live in our midst would make many uncomfortable. Once again we confront the inescapable: freedom is never free. And once again we must decide whether these costs are more than we are willing to pay.[13]

Perhaps the most compelling case for a set of "thou shalts" lurks in Anatole France's observation that "[t]he law, in its majestic equality, forbids the rich as well as the poor to sleep under bridges, to beg in the streets, and to steal bread."[14] Our courts have begun—tentatively and hesitantly—to deal with the problems of assuring equal rights to both rich and poor. There was a time not too long ago when we accorded rich and poor an equal opportunity to retain counsel in criminal cases, or to buy their way to the ballot box. As our moral concepts evolved, however, we began to provide a floor under the most basic rights—court-appointed counsel, free trial transcripts, and voting rights. Unless we choose to tolerate inequality in the exercise of rights, we will have to provide more than just a floor.

The freedom of children in Appalachia or Watts can be no more than a meaningless abstraction if government's only action to implement that freedom is the inaction of leaving them alone. Babies need the chance to grow into healthy adults, capable of supporting themselves and contributing to society.

This requires minimum income, quality education, and adequate medical care as matters of right, not of grace. To protect equality, we must ask not only when government *may* take group differences into account, but when it *must*. To foster freedom we must define not only what the state may not do to its citizens, but what it must do for them.

Recognizing basic needs as rights would raise new problems of liberty, as our experience with income redistribution demonstrates. Too often welfare recipients pay for government help with their privacy and autonomy—suffering oversight of their shopping lists and undergoing searches which we euphemistically label "home visits." The intrusion of the IRS—the self-incrimination issues raised by self-reporting, the First Amendment problems present in deciding which charities are tax-exempt, and the potential for misusing tax returns as a lending library—need no recapitulation here. Such problems, however, are not endemic to income redistribution. Moreover, I detect a trace of irony in the argument that recognizing basic needs as rights would intrude on the privacy that the poor currently enjoy in overcrowded tenements among rats, roaches, junkies, and muggers.

Questions of government power and individual freedom have never been easy. In 1788 James Madison wrote to Thomas Jefferson: "[I]t is a melancholy reflection that liberty should be equally exposed to danger whether the Government have too much or too little power, and that the line which divides these extremes should be so inaccurately defined by experience."[15] Our subsequent experience has not made that line any easier to find. Continuing search for it in a changing world, with sensitivity to the enduring values and wisdom of the framers, is the ongoing task that lies before us.

Notes

Introduction

1. Letter from Thomas Jeferson to W. C. Jarvis, Sept. 28, 1820, reprinted in *The Writings of Thomas Jefferson,* ed. H. A. Washington (1855), 7:177, 179.
2. C. Vann Woodward, *Thinking Back* (LSU Press, 1986), p. 99.
3. Speech at Georgetown University (10/12/85), quoted in *New York Times,* Oct. 13, 1985.

I   THE DILEMMA OF CRIMINAL RESPONSIBILITY

1. *See* Comprehensive Crime Control Act of 1984 (P.L. 98-473). States attempting to abolish the defense include Idaho, Montana, and Utah. *See, generally,* B. Weiner, "Mental Disability and the Criminal Law," in S. J. Brakel, J. Parry, and B. Weiner, eds., *The Mentally Disabled and the Law,* 3rd ed. (American Bar Foundation, 1985), p. 707 *et seq.;* American Bar Association, Standing Committee on Association Standards for Criminal Justice, *ABA Standards for Criminal Justice,* 2nd ed., vol. II (Little, Brown, 1980; ch. 7, 1986).
2. *Ake v. Oklahoma,* 105 S. Ct. 1087 (1985); *Ford v. Wainwright,* 106, S. Ct. 2595 (1986).

1. Morality and the Criminal Law

1. This chapter is based on the J. Edgar Hoover Foundation Lectures delivered November 18, 1975, at the University of Southern California, as elaborated in two later articles, Bazelon, Morality and the Criminal Law: Rights of the Accused, 72 *Journal of Criminal Law and Criminology* 1143 (1981); and The Morality of the Criminal Law, 49 *U.S.C. L. Rev.* 385 (1976).
2. Personal note, 1959.
3. *See* Easterbrook, Foreword: The Court and the Economic System, 98 *Harv. L. Rev.* 4 (1984); Tribe, Constitutional Calculus: Equal Justice or Economic Efficiency? 98 *Harv. L. Rev.* 592 (1985); E. Spaeth, Where Is the High Court Heading? *The Judge's Journal* 10 (Summer 1985).
4. "Connoisseur of Chaos," in *The Collected Poems of Wallace Stevens* (Knopf, 1954), p. 215.

5. E. Pound, Introduction to F. Sayre, *Cases on Criminal Law* (1927), p. xxxvi.

6. "Nous promettons selon nos espérances, et nous tenons selon nos craintes." La Rochefoucauld, *Maximes*, ed. F. C. Green (1945), p. 61.

7. Pound, *supra*, note 5, p. xxxvii.

8. O. W. Holmes, *The Common Law* (1885), p. 45.

9. *United States v. Alexander*, 471 F.2d 923 (D.C. Cir.) *cert. denied*, 409 U.S. 1044 (1973). (*See* Chapter 7 for a discussion and excerpts.)

10. *Cf. Everett v. United States*, 336 F.2d 979 (D.C. Cir. 1964).

11. *See United States v. Moore*, 486 F.2d 1139 (D.C. Cir.), *cert. denied*, 414 U.S. 980 (1973); *Easter v. District of Columbia*, 361 F.2d 50 (D.C. Cir. 1966) (en banc).

12. *See United States v. Barker*, 514 F.2d 208 (D.C. Cir.), *cert. denied*, 421 U.S. 1013 (1975).

13. J. Q. Wilson, *Thinking About Crime* (Vintage Books, 1977), p. 197. *See also* Wilson and Herrnstein, *Crime and Human Nature* (Simon & Schuster, 1985).

14. H. Packer, *Two Models of the Criminal Process*, 113 *U. Pa. L. Rev.* 1 (1964).

15. Letter from Nicholas deB. Katzenbach to David L. Bazelon, June 24, 1965, reprinted in Kamisar, Has the Court Left the Attorney General Behind?—The Bazelon-Katzenbach Letters on Poverty, Equality and the Administration of Criminal Justice, 54 *Ky. L.J.* 464, 491 (1966). (See Section III for further discussion of these issues, and Chapter 11 for the Bazelon-Katzenbach letters.)

16. By 1986 the GNP had grown to $4 trillion.

17. *See* Wilson and Herrnstein, *supra*, note 13. *See also* Brenner, *Estimating the Effects of Economic Changes on National Health and Social Well-being*, study prepared for Subcommittee on Economic Goals and Intergovernmental Policy, Joint Economic Committee, Jt. Cmte Print, S. Prt 98-198, 98th Cong. 2d sess. (GPO, June 15, 1984).

18. Hughes, "Dream Deferred," in *The Panther and the Lash* (Knopf, 1967), p. 14.

19. *Novak v. Beto*, 453 F.2d 661, 672 (5th Cir. 1971) (Tuttle, J., concurring in part and dissenting in part), *cert. denied*, 409 U.S. 968 (1972).

20. Goldberg, Foreword—The Burger Court 1971 Term: One Step Forward, Two Steps Backward?, 63 *J. Crim. L. C. & P. S.* 463, 464 (1972).

21. C. Silberman, *Criminal Violence, Criminal Justice* (Random House, 1978), p. 41.

22. *See* Brenner, *supra*, note 17.

23. "Youth Speaks No Remorse," *Washington Post*, Dec. 14, 1980, p. A-1, col. 4.

24. E. Walsh and S. Saperstein, "Fuller Killers Bred by Mean Streets," *Washington Post*, Jan. 5, 1986.

25. R. Smith, *Justice and the Poor*, 3rd ed. (reprint 1972), p. 8.

26. Letter from Nicholas deB. Katzenbach to David L. Bazelon, reprinted in Kamisar, *supra*, note 15, p. 490. Today the terms of debate are radically different from the 1960s War on Poverty. If my views were seen as unrealistic then, they will undoubtedly seem so to many today. But ideals do not depend on how close or how far we may be from attaining them. (See Chapter 11.)

27. *Griffin v. Illinois*, 351 U.S. 12, 19 (1956) (opinion of Black, J.).

28. Address by Charles Evans Hughes to the 42d Annual Meeting of the New York State Bar Association, Jan. 17, 1919, in 42 *Rep. N.Y. St. B. Ass'n.* 224, 240 (1919).

29. T. Macaulay, *History of England* (Harper, 1849–61), 1:383, quoted in *United*

States v. Barrett, 505 F.2d 1091, 1115 (7th Cir. 1975) (Stevens, J., dissenting).
30. Silberman, *supra*, note 21, p. 108.
31. L. Hand, "Thou Shalt Not Ration Justice," 9 *Legis. Aid Brief Case* 3 (1951).
32. *See* Bazelon, New Gods for Old: "Efficient" Courts in a Democratic Society, 6 *N.Y.U. L. Rev.* 653, 654–57 (1971).
33. W. Douglas, *We the Judges* (1956), p. 443.
34. B. Cardozo, *Law and Literature* (1931), p. 130.

2. *The Insanity Defense: Symbol and Substance*

1. This chapter is based on Bazelon, The Dilemma of Criminal Responsibility, 72 *Ky. L.J.* 263 (1983–84); The Insanity Defense: Symbol and Substance, American Academy of Psychiatry and the Law, 15th Annual Meeting, Nassau, Bahamas (1984).
2. "Despite its failure to command significant formal support, *Durham* did much to spur discussion of what type of test could be devised for determining criminal responsibility which would avoid both the narrowness of the M'Naghten rule and the overbreadth of alternative formulations seeking to cure this defect." Barbara A. Weiner, Mental Disability and the Criminal Law, in S. J. Brakel, J. Parry, and B. Weiner, eds., *The Mentally Disabled and the Law*, 3rd ed. (American Bar Foundation, 1985), p. 711.
3. Attorney General's Task Force on Violent Crime, *Final Report* (DOJ, 1981), p. 54.
4. See Chapter 17.
5. H. J. Steadman, J. Monahan, et al., Mentally Disordered Offenders: A National Survey of Patients and Facilities, 6 *Law and Human Behavior* 31 (1982).
6. 214 F.2d 862 (D.C. Cir. 1954), *overruled, Brawner v. United States*, 471 F.2d 969 (D.C. Cir. 1972) (en banc). (See Chapter 3.)
7. American Psychiatric Association, Statement on the Insanity Defense, Dec. 1982, reprinted in *Issues in Forensic Psychiatry* (American Psychiatric Press, 1984); American Bar Association, Policies Adopted Feb. 1983, *discussed*, Standing Committee on Association Standards for Criminal Justice, *ABA Standards for Criminal Justice*, 2nd ed., vol. II (Little, Brown, 1980; ch. 7, 1986), pp. 7.3–7.15, 7.294–7.299; American Medical Association, Proceedings of the House of Delegates (Dec. 1983), pp. 57–8; Comprehensive Crime Control Act of 1984 (P.L. 98-473).
8. 128 Cong. Rec. S7243 (daily ed., June 22, 1983) (statement of Sen. Mattingly).
9. Quoted in the published version of the article, 72 *Ky. L.J.* 263, 264, without a citation.
10. *See* Bazelon, "The Durham Rule," *Guide to American Law* (West, 1984), 4:223. (See Chapter 4 for a more extended discussion of the *Durham* experiment.)
11. *United States v. Brawner*, 471 F.2d 969, 1010, 1012 (D.C. Cir. 1972) (en banc) (Bazelon, C. J., concurring in part, dissenting in part).
12. In 1985, the Supreme Court held that indigent criminal defendants are entitled to "psychiatric assistance" at the government's expense in certain situations. *Ake v. Oklahoma*, 105 S. Ct. 1087 (1985).
13. *United States v. Morgan*, 482 F.2d 786 (D.C. Cir. 1973).
14. 740 F.2d 1104 (D.C. Cir. 1984). (See Chapter 5 for a discussion and excerpts.)

3. Durham v. United States

1. *Durham v. United States*, 214 F.2d 862 (D.C. Cir. 1954). *See also* David L. Bazelon, "The *Durham* Rule," *Guide to American Law* (West, 1984).
2. See Chapter 16.
3. *Brown v. Board of Education of Topeka*, 47 U.S. 483 (1954), striking down "separate but equal" education and beginning the modern civil rights movement in the law.
4. T. Szasz, *Psychiatric Justice* (1965).
5. Letter to Justice Felix Frankfurter, Aug. 20, 1954, copy in files with transmittal note from Justice Frankfurter, Sept. 16, 1954.
6. *Ford v. Wainwright,* 106 S. Ct. 2595 (1986).
7. 36 F.2d 548 (D.C. Cir. 1929).
8. S. Glueck, *Mental Disorder and the Criminal Law* (1925), pp. 138–9, citing *Rex v. Arnold*, 16 How. St. Tr. 695, 764 (1724).
9. 8 *Eng. Rep.* 718 (1843).
10. I. Ray, *Medical Jurisprudence of Insanity*, 1st ed. (1838), pp. 47 and 34 *et seq.* "That the insane mind is not entirely deprived of this power of moral discernment, but in many subjects is perfectly rational, and displays the exercise of a sound and well balanced mind is one of those facts now so well established, that to question it would only betray the height of ignorance and presumption." *Id.*, p. 32.
11. B. Cardozo, *What Medicine Can Do for the Law* (1930), p. 32.
12. *Holloway v. United States*, 148 F.2d 665, 667 (D.C. Cir. 1945), *cert. denied*, 334 U.S. 852 (1948).
13. *State v. Pike*, 49 N.H. 399 (1870).

4. The Experiment: 1954–1972

1. 312 F.2d 847 (D.C. Cir. 1962) (en banc).
2. 390 F.2d 444 (D.C. Cir. 1967).
3. 471 F.2d 862, 1010 (D.C. Cir. 1972) (en banc), Bazelon, C. J., concurring in part, dissenting in part.
4. 252 F.2d 608 (D.C. Cir. 1957).
5. *United States v. Eichberg*, 439 F.2d 620, 624–5 (D.C. Cir. 1971) (Bazelon, C.J., concurring).
6. Model Penal Code Sec. 4.01, Comment at 159 (Tent. Draft No. 4, 1955) (emphasis added). See ALI Proceedings, 206–20 (May 21, 1955) (unpublished).
7. *Davis v. United States*, 160 U.S. 469, 484 (1895).
8. *United States v. Alexander & Murdock*, 471 F.2d 923 (D.C. Cir. 1972). (*See* Chapter 7.)

5. Reprise: United States v. Byers

1. 740 F.2d 1104 (D.C. Cir. 1984), (Bazelon, Sr.J., dissenting).
2. See Chapters 16 and 17, and references for those chapters.

3. *Estelle v. Smith,* 451 U.S. 454 (1981).
4. *Jones v. United States,* 463 U.S. 354 (1983).
5. *Barefoot v. Estelle,* 403 U.S. 880 (1983).
6. *Ake v. Oklahoma,* 105 S. Ct. 1087 (1985).
7. ABA, *ABA Standards for Criminal Justice,* 2nd ed., vol. II (Little, Brown, 1980; ch. 7, 1986). *See, generally,* Symposium on the ABA Criminal Justice Mental Health Standards, 53 *George Washington L. Rev.* 338 (1985).
8. *Id.,* Part VI, and particularly the Commentary.
9. Stephen H. Wells, the 1984 ABA Criminal Justice Mental Health Standards and the Expert Witness: New Therapy for a Troubled Relationship?, 13 *Western State U. L. Rev.* 79 (1985), at note 132.
10. *See ABA Standards, supra,* note 7, Part III. *See also* Bonnie & Slobogin, The Role of Mental Health Professionals in the Criminal Process: The Case for Informal Speculation, 66 *Va. L. Rev.* 427 (1980).
11. P.L. 98-473, Chapter IV—Offenders with Mental Disease or Defect (amending Chapter 313 of Title 18, U.S. Code).
12. The U.S. Supreme Court held in 1895 that in federal cases the prosecutor had the burden of proving the defendant's sanity beyond a reasonable doubt, *Davis v. United States,* 160 U.S. 469 (1895). In 1952, the Court found that this was a rule rather than a constitutional requirement. *Leland v. Oregon,* 343 U.S. 790, 797 (1952).
13. L. Callahan, C. Mayer, and H. J. Steadman, Insanity Defense Reform in the United States—Post-Hinckley, 11 *MPDLR* 54 (1987).
14. *See* Underwood, The Thumbs on the Scales of Justice: Burdens of Persuasion in Criminal Cases, 86 *Yale L.J.* 1299 (1977).
15. See *ABA Standards, supra,* note 7, Part III.
16. 451 U.S. 454, 464–5.
17. 384 U.S. 436 (1966).
18. (See Chapter 17.) *See* Bazelon, The Dilemma of Criminal Responsibility, 72 *Ky. L.J.* 263 (1984); Bazelon, "Should the Psychiatrist Have a Role in the Criminal Justice System?," in J. Brady and H. Brodie, eds., *Psychiatry at the Crossroads* (1980); Bazelon, The Role of the Psychiatrist in the Criminal Justice System, 6 *Bull. Am. Acad. of Psychiatry & L.* 139 (1978); Bazelon, Psychiatrists and the Courts, 8 *J. Nat'l Ass'n of Private Psychiatric Hospitals* 4 (Spring 1976); Bazelon, Institutional Psychiatry—"The Self-Inflicted Wound," 23 *Cath. Univ. L. Rev.* 643 (1974); *see, generally,* E. Goffman, *Asylums: Essays on the Social Situation of Mental Patients and Other Inmates* (1962); A. Stone, *Mental Health and the Law: A System in Transition* (1975); T. Szasz, *Psychiatric Justice* (1965), pp. 56–84.
19. *See* Institute of Society, Ethics and the Life Sciences, In the Service of the State: The Psychiatrist as Double Agent, *Hastings Center Report Special Supplement* (April 1978) (Statement of Arlene Daniels); *Who Is the Client?: The Ethics of Psychological Intervention in the Criminal Justice System* (J. Monahan, ed. 1980), pp. 2–8; Slobogin, Estelle v. Smith: The Constitutional Contours of the Forensic Evaluation, 31 *Emory L.J.* 71, 133 (1982).
20. *United States v. Grunewald,* 233 F.2d 556, 591 (2d Cir. 1956) (Frank, J., dissenting).
21. *Tehan v. United States ex rel. Shott,* 382 U.S. 406, 415 (1966).
22. 384 U.S. 436, 460 (1966).

23. *See* A. Freedman, H. Kaplan, and B. Sadock, *Comprehensive Textbook of Psychiatry*, 2d ed. (1975), p. 718.
24. Goldberg, Resistance to the Use of Video in Individual Psychotherapy Training, 140 *Am. J. Psychiatry* 1172 (1983).
25. 451 U.S. 454 (1981).
26. 388 U.S. 218 (1967).
27. 214 F.2d 862 (D.C. Cir. 1954). (See Chapter 3.)
28. 471 F.2d 969 (D.C. Cir. 1972) (en banc). (See Chapter 4.)

II THE ROOTS OF CRIME

1. Address by President Reagan to the International Association of Chiefs of Police, in New Orleans, Louisiana, Sept. 28, 1981.
2. Radio address, Feb. 15, 1986, quoted in Bernard Weinraub, "Reagan Is Pushing the Welfare Issue," *New York Times*, Feb. 16, 1986. His view coincides with the interpretation that the Great Society actually halted a decline in poverty already underway in the 1960s. Charles Murray, *Losing Ground* (Basic Books, 1984).
3. Daniel Patrick Moynihan, *Family and Nation* (Harcourt Brace Jovanovich, 1986), p. 135.

6. Avoiding Realities

1. This chapter is based on The Crime Controversy: Avoiding Realities 35 *Vanderbilt L. Rev.* 487 (1982).
2. Baccalaureate Address, 1974.
3. Address by President Reagan to the International Association of Chiefs of Police, in New Orleans, La., Sept. 28, 1981.
4. M. Royko, "Evil Hearts and Minds," *Chicago Sun-Times*, Oct. 1, 1981, p. 2, col. 1.
5. U.S. Dept. of Justice, *Attorney General's Task Force on Violent Crime: Final Report* (1981).
6. FBI, Crime in the United States, 1984, *Uniform Crime Reports*, July 1985.
7. *See* U.S. General Accounting Office, Impact of Exclusionary Rule on Federal Criminal Prosecution (April 19, 1979). This GAO study of federal prosecutions found that evidence was excluded because of illegal searches in only 1.3 percent of the cases. Similarly, another study concluded that the rule has "little impact on the overall flow of criminal cases after arrest." Institute for Law and Research, 1979, A Cross-City Comparison of Felony Case Processing, *discussed* in D. Gordon, *Doing Violence to the Crime Problem: A Response to the Attorney General's Task Force* (NCCD, 1981), p. 4.
8. Comprehensive Crime Control Act of 1984 (P.L. 98-473).
9. *See* Pretrial Release: An Evaluation of Defendant Outcomes and Program Impact: Summary and Analysis Volume (unpublished draft) (Washington, D.C., Lazar Institute, 1981), discussed in D. Gordon, *supra*, note 7, p. 3.
10. D. Gordon, *supra*, note 7, p. 7 (quoting Governor Thompson's comments at the August 17 press conference releasing the report).

11. *Supra,* note 5.
12. National Institute of Justice, U.S. Dept. of Justice, *American Prisons and Jails* (1978), 1:159.
13. Bureau of Justice Statistics, *Prisoners in 1984* (April 1985).
14. Van Dine, Dinitz, and Conrad, The Incapacitation of the Dangerous Offender: A Statistical Experiment, 14 *J. Research Crime & Delinq.* 22, 31 (1977).
15. Cohen, *The Incapacitative Effects of Imprisonment: A Critical Review of the Literature* (1978) (National Academy of Sciences study of incapacitation and deterrence), *discussed in* D. Gordon, *Toward Realistic Reform: A Commentary on Proposals for Change in New York City's Criminal Justice System* (NCCD, 1981), p. 5.
16. A. Newton, *The Effects of Imprisonment* (NCCD, 1980), p. 139.
17. See Chapter 14.
18. Attorney General, State of New Mexico, *Report of the Attorney General on the February 2 and 3, 1980 Riot at the Penitentiary of New Mexico* (Sept. 1980), prologue.
19. *See* Frank E. Manuel, *Utopias and Utopian Thought* (Beacon Press, 1967).

7. United States v. Alexander and Murdock

1. 471 F.2d 923 (D.C. Cir. 1973) (Bazelon, C.J., dissenting). For an excellent discussion of the case, *see* Wales, The Rise, the Fall and the Resurrection of the Medical Model, 63 *Geo. L.J.* 87, 100–3 (1974).
2. *McDonald v. United States,* 114 U.S.App.D.C. 120, 312 F.2d 847 (1962) (en banc).
3. The Supreme Court has recently held that indigent defendants are entitled to expert psychiatric assistance at government expense in certain situations. *Ake v. Oklahoma,* 105 S. Ct. 1087 (1985).
4. *McDonald,* 312 F.2d at 851.
5. For a recent discussion of the problem of post-acquittal custody relating to the insanity defense, *see* American Bar Association, Standing Committee on Association Standards for Criminal Justice, Chapter 7 of *ABA Standards for Criminal Justice,* 2nd ed., vol. II (Little, Brown, 1980; ch. 7, 1986).

8. Justice and Juveniles

1. This chapter is based on Bazelon, Whose Needy Children?, 8 *J. of Law Reform* 237 (1975).
2. See Chapters 16, 17.
3. See introduction to Chapter 9 and cases cited there.
4. ABA/IJA, *Juvenile Justice Standards* (Ballinger, 1980).
5. Juvenile Justice and Delinquency Prevention Act of 1974, 18 U.S.C. 5031 *et seq.*
6. Victor L. Streib, "Why Are We Still Executing Juveniles?," *Criminal Justice,* 1:3 (Fall, 1986).
7. Statement of A. S. Regnery before Senate Subcommittee on Juvenile Justice, March 6, 1986.

8. Moynihan, *Family and Nation* (Harcourt Brace Jovanovich, 1986), p. 124.
9. J. Knitzer, *Unclaimed Children* (Children's Defense Fund, 1982).
10. E. Walsh and S. Saperstein, "Fuller Killers Bred by Mean Streets," *Washington Post,* Jan. 5, 1986.
11. For recent contrasting views on this, *see* Charles Murray, *Losing Ground* (Basic Books, 1984), and Moynihan, *supra,* note 8.
12. *Id.* The problem has grown ever more serious in the ten years since this article appeared.
13. B. Russell, *Marriage and Morals* (1957), pp. 171–74.

9. Kent v. United States

1. *Kent v. United States,* 383 U.S. 541 (1966).
2. *In re Gault,* 387 U.S. 1 (1967).
3. *In re Winship,* 397 U.S. 358 (1970).
4. *Schall v. Martin,* 467 U.S. 253 (1984).
5. B. Flicker, *Transferring Juveniles to Adult Court for Trial* (Institute for Judicial Administration, 1983).
6. Burger, J., dissenting (No. 20,922, D.C. Cir., July 30, 1968).
7. 343 F.2d 247, 264 (D.C. Cir. 1964), Bazelon, *dissenting.*
8. No. 20,922 (D.C. Cir., July 30, 1968).

III EQUALITY UNDER THE LAW

1. Schaefer, Federalism and State Criminal Procedure, 70 *Harv. L. Rev.* 1, 8 (1956).
2. American Bar Association, *ABA Standards for Criminal Justice,* 2nd ed., 4 vols. (Little, Brown, 1980). Plans are now underway for wider dissemination and for an updated edition. Personal communication, Laurie O. Robinson, Director, Section of Criminal Justice, ABA, July 29, 1987.
3. *United States v. Leon,* 104 S. Ct. 3405 (1984). *See* Davies, A Hard Look at What We Know (and Still Need to Learn) About the "Costs" of the Exclusionary Rule, 1983 *A.B.F. Research J.* 611 (1983).
4. Interview on "Evans and Novak," Cable News Network, April 1985, quoted in *National Journal,* 17:2646 (Nov. 23, 1985).
5. *The Federalist,* No. 78, J. E. Cooke, ed. (Wesleyan University Press, 1961), p. 527.

10. Fair Play in Criminal Justice

1. This chapter is based on Bazelon, Morality and the Criminal Law: Rights of the Accused, 72 *Journal of Criminal Law and Criminology* 1143 (1981).
2. Spaeth, Where Is the High Court Heading?, *The Judges Journal,* Summer 1985.

3. *Robbins v. California*, 101 S. Ct. 2841, 2851 (1981) (Powell, J., concurring).
4. 101 S. Ct. 2841 (1981) [*Robbins*]; 101 S. Ct. 2860 (1981) [*Belton*].
5. *Robbins*, 101 S. Ct. at 2855 (Stevens, J., dissenting).
6. 442 U.S. 753 (1979).
7. *United States v. Ross*, No. 79-1624, slip op. at 2 (D.C. Cir. April 17, 1980) (*Ross I*); *id.* at 1 (Bazelon, J., concurring and dissenting), *vacated and rev'd*, 655 F.2d 1159 (D.C. Cir. 1981) (*Ross II*).
8. *Miranda v. Arizona*, 384 U.S. 436 (1966).
9. M. Kaus, "Abolish the 5th Amendment," *Washington Monthly*, December 1980, p. 12. *See also* Wilkey, The Exclusionary Rule: Why Suppress Valid Evidence? 62 *Judicature* 214 (1978).
10. *Rogers v. Richmond*, 365 U.S. 534, 541 (1961).
11. *See* Y. Kamisar, "Equal Justice in the Gatehouses and Mansions of American Criminal Procedure," in *Criminal Justice in Our Time* (1965), reprinted in Y. Kamisar, *Police Interrogation and Confessions* (1980), p. 31.
12. MacInnes, "The Criminal Society," in C. Rolph, ed., *The Police and the Public* (1962), p. 101, quoted in Y. Kamisar, *Police Interrogation and Confessions, supra,* note 13, p. 32.
13. Y. Kamisar, A Dissent from the Miranda Dissents: Some Comments on the "New" Fifth Amendment and the Old "Voluntariness" Test, 65 *Mich. L. Rev.* 59, 85 (1966), quoting Weisberg, Police Interrogation of Arrested Persons: A Skeptical View, 52 *J. Crim. L.C. & P.S.* 21, 44 (1961).
14. *United States v. Frazier*, 476 F.2d 891 (D.C. Cir. 1973) (en banc) (Frazier II), *cert. denied*, 420 U.S. 977 (1975).
15. 476 F.2d 891 (Bazelon, J., dissenting) (appendix).
16. *Id.* at 906.
17. 372 U.S. 335 (1963).
18. Bazelon, The Realities of Gideon and Argersinger, 63 *Geo. L.J.* 811 (1976).
19. *Foster v. Illinois*, 332 U.S. 134, 139 (1947).
20. *McMann v. Richardson*, 397 U.S. 759, 771 (1970). *See* Bazelon, *supra*, note 18, at 830.
21. *Id.* at 264.

11. The Bazelon-Katzenbach Letters

1. The correspondence was reprinted in Yale Kamisar, Has the Court Left the Attorney General Behind? The Bazelon-Katzenbach Letters on Poverty, Equality and the Administration of Criminal Justice, 54 *Ky. L.J.* 464, 486 (1966).
2. Press Conference, Feb. 22, 1984, quoted at 42 *Congressional Quarterly* 468 (2/25/84).
3. *Gideon v. Wainwright*, 372 U.S. 335 (1963), held that criminal defendants have a right to counsel regardless of their ability to pay. *Griffin v. Illinois*, 351 U.S. 12 (1956), held that indigents have a right to a free transcript of their trial for use in an appeal. *Coppedge v. U.S.*, 369 U.S. 438 (1962), held that appeal of a conviction is a matter of right and indigent defendants are entitled to assistance of counsel unless the claim is clearly frivolous. *Hardy v. United States*, 375

U.S. 277 (1964), held that counsel to an indigent defendant in an appeal is entitled to a free transcript of the trial.

12. Counsel and Conscience

1. This chapter is based on Bazelon, The Defective Assistance of Counsel, 42 *Cincinnati L. Rev.* 1 (1973).
2. 287 U.S. 45 (1932).
3. 372 U.S. 335, at 344 (1963).
4. 407 U.S. 25 (1972). *See Scott v. Illinois*, 99 S. Ct. 1158 (1979).
5. *Supra*, n. 2–4. *Argersinger* held that the right to counsel extends to misdemeanor defendants facing a possible loss of liberty.
6. Criminal Justice Act of 1964, 18 U.S.C. 3006A, *as amended* (Supp., 1972).
7. *Escobedo*, 378 U.S. 478 (1964), held that where an investigation has begun to focus on a specific person that person has a right to consult with counsel prior to questioning.
8. Bazelon, Law, Morality, and Civil Liberties, 12 *U.C.L.A. L. Rev.* 13, 22 (1964).
9. Burger, Has the Time Come?, 55 *F.R.D.* 119, 123 (1972).
10. ABA Project on Minimum Standards for Criminal Justice, Providing Defense Services (app. draft 1971). See *ABA Standards for Criminal Justice*, 2nd ed., vol. I, ch. 4 (Little, Brown, 1980). For a comprehensive review of the issues in this chapter, *see* particularly vol. I, chs. 3–6, and vol. III, ch. 14.
11. Robert Spangenburg, Executive Director, the Spangenburg Group, personal communication, March 3, 1987. See Spangenburg, "Why We Are Not Defending the Poor Properly," *Criminal Justice*, 1:3 (Fall, 1986).
12. *See State v. Joe U. Smith*, 681 F.2d 1374 (1984).
13. See S. Bing and S. Rosenfeld, *The Quality of Justice in the Lower Criminal Courts of Metropolitan Boston* (1970).
14. *Colson v. Smith*, 315 F. Supp. 179 (N.D. Ga. 1970).
15. *United States v. Burks*, 470 F.2d 432 (D.C. Cir. 1972).
16. *Hardy v. United States*, 375 U.S. 277, 288 (1964) (Goldberg concurring). A more detailed discourse on the subject of providing a transcript for an indigent appellate is presented in Bazelon, New Gods for Old: Efficient Courts in a Democratic Society, 46 *N.Y.U. L. Rev.* 653, 661–63 (1971).
17. *Cross v. United States*, 392 F.2d 360, 367 (8th Cir. 1968).
18. *United States v. Burks, supra*, note 15.
19. *Mitchell v. United States*, 259 F.2d 787, 796 (D.C. Cir. 1958).
20. *United States v. Katz*, 425 F.2d 928 (2d Cir. 1970).
21. *Daugherty v. Beto*, 388 F.2d 810 (5th Cir. 1967), *cert. denied.* 393 U.S. 986 (1968).
22. 475 F.2d 934 (D.C. Cir. 1973).
23. *United States v. Benn*, 476 F.2d 1127 (D.C. Cir. 1973).
24. *United States v. Frazier*, 476 F.2d 891 (D.C. Cir. 1973).
25. The use of pre-trial release programs has expanded in recent years. *See* D. E. Pryor, *Practices of Pretrial Release Programs: Review and Analysis of the Data* (Pretrial Services Resource Center, 1982); A. Hall et al., *Pretrial Release Program Options* (NIJ, 1984).

26. *The Challenge of Crime in a Free Society* (1967), p. 128, quoted by Justice Douglas in *Argersinger v. Hamlin*, 407 U.S. 25, 32 (1972).
27. E. Cahn, Law in the Consumer Perspective, 112 *Pa. L. Rev.* 1 (1963).

13. United States v. Willie Decoster

1. *United States v. Willie Decoster*, 487 F.2d 1197 (D.C. Cir. 1973) (Bazelon, C.J., dissenting).
2. *Powell v. Alabama*, 287 U.S. 45, 69 (1932).
3. *Griffin v. Illinois*, 351, U.S. 12, 19 (1956).
4. *Diggs v. Welch*, 148 F.2d 667, 669 (D.C. Cir.), *cert. denied*, 325 U.S. 889 (1945).
5. *Bruce v. U.S.*, 379 F.2d 113, 116–17 (D.C. Cir. 1962).
6. *American Bar Association Project on Standards for Criminal Justice, The Prosecution Function and the Defense Function* (App. Draft 1971). The ABA House of Delegates approved the second edition of the Defense Function standards on February 12, 1979. The new edition reflects the work of the ABA, its consultants, and representatives from approximately fifty nationwide groups interested in the improvement of American criminal justice. *See* Foreword, *American Bar Association Standards Relating to the Administration of Criminal Justice, Prosecution and Defense Function* (2d ed., approved draft without commentary 1979), and the published version, with commentary, *ABA Standards for Criminal Justice*, 2nd ed., vol. I, chs. 3–5, and particularly p. 5.7 at n. 1.
7. *Santobello v. New York*, 404 U.S. 257, 260 (1971) (Burger, C.J.).
8. *Lakeside v. Oregon*, 435 U.S. 333, 341 (1978). The government prosecutor is under no less of a duty to see that the trial conforms to constitutional standards:

    The United States Attorney is the representative not of an ordinary party to a controversy, but of a sovereignty whose obligation to govern impartially is as compelling as its obligation to govern at all; and whose interest, therefore, in a criminal prosecution is not that it shall win a case, but that justice shall be done. *Berger v. United States*, 295 U.S. 78, 88 (1935).

9. *United States v. Powe*, 591 F.2d 833, 846–47 (D.C. Cir. 1978).

IV WHAT IS THE QUESTION?

1. Editorial, *New York Times*, Oct. 18, 1983.
2. *See* Bazelon, Veils, Values and Social Responsibility, *American Psychologist*, vol. 37, no. 2, pp. 115–21 (Feb. 1982); The Impact of the Courts on Public Administration, 52 *Indiana L.J.*, 101 (Fall 1976); Science and Uncertainty: A Jurist's View, 5 *Harvard Environmental L. Rev.*, 209 (1981); Risk and Responsibility, *Science*, vol. 205, pp. 277–80 (July 20, 1979).
3. Fredrickson, A History of the Recombinant DNA Guidelines in the United States, presented at the COGENE/Royal Society Conference on Recombinant DNA, Wye, England, Apr. 3, 1979.

14. Correcting Corrections

1. S. Gettinger, "Accreditation on Trial," *Corrections Magazine*, February 1982. This article provides a comprehensive discussion of the issues raised here.
2. The Official Report of the New York State Special Commission on Attica (1972).
3. *Rhodes v. Chapman*, 452 U.S. 337 (1981) (double-celling not unconstitutional); *Hootowit v. Ray*, No. 80-3366 (9th Cir. Feb. 16, 1982) (rejecting "totality of conditions" approach: "The Eighth Amendment is not a broad basis for prison reform. . . . Any needed prison reform is not a proper judicial function."); *Wright v. Rushen*, 642 F.2d 1129 (9th Cir. 1981). *But see Ruiz v. Estelle*, Nos. 81-2224, 81-2380, & 81-2390 (5th Cir. June 23, 1982) (reading *Hootowit* "to say that conditions of confinement that in some circumstances would not be cruel and unusual may in other circumstances, when combined with other conditions, rise to that level.").
4. Commission on Accreditation for Corrections, 1980 Annual Report (1981), p. 3 [hereinafter cited as 1980 Annual Report].
5. Commission on Accreditation for Corrections, *Statement of Principles*, Principle IV, *reprinted in* 1980 Annual Report, *supra*, note 4, p. 2.
6. American Correctional Association, *Declaration of Principles*, Principle IX.
7. *Id.*, Principle VI.
8. CAC, *Statement of Principles*, Principles III, XI, *supra*, note 4.
9. *Id.*, Principle XI.
10. For example, critical information about Florida prisons that had been accredited by the Commission came to light only after James Lohman of the Florida Clearinghouse on Criminal Justice described various institutional practices in a letter to former ACA President Oliver J. Keller, Jr., who then urged the Commission's executive director to investigate the matter. It is precisely this sort of information that is essential for the Commission to have *before* an accreditation decision is made. In another case, I was disturbed to read in a visiting committee report that an audit team learned of a hunger strike in the institution they were inspecting only because a committee member happened to read of the strike in the local newspaper just before arriving. Apparently, the superintendent of the institution had no intention of informing the team about the strike.

    Consider also the observations of Robert J. Brooks, Chief of Project Development in the Connecticut Department of Correction and himself a former Commission auditor: "Although the possibility of [consulting with others before, during, and after an audit] has never been precluded in the rules, there has been scant encouragement of it and the established procedures of audits do little to make it possible." Letter from Robert J. Brooks to David L. Bazelon, Mar. 19, 1982.
11. *See* Minutes of Regular Meeting, Commission on Accreditation for Corrections, at 20–21 (May 16–17, 1982).
12. *Id.*, at 19.
13. *See* Minutes of Regular Meeting, Commission on Accreditation for Corrections, at 11 (Aug. 13–15, 1981).

14. Statement of Commissioner J. J. Enomoto, Minutes of Regular Meeting, Commission on Accreditation for Corrections, at 22 (May 16–17, 1982).

15. The Commission has also recently approved task force recommendations to "require that each agency post notice(s) of an impending standards compliance audit," and to "require Commission consultants to interview agency inmates/clients." *See* Commission on Accreditation for Corrections, *Task Force V: Guidelines for Applicant Agencies*, at 2 (1982); Minutes of Regular Meeting, Commission on Accreditation for Corrections, at 20–21 (May 16–17, 1982). These measures, too, are thoroughly inadequate. On the notice-posting requirement, where are the notices to be posted? How often? What is the sanction for failure to post or re-post? Delay of the audit until there is proper posting? Denial of accreditation? On the requirement to interview inmates/clients, how are the interviewees to be selected? Will anyone who desires to be heard get an audience? Will the interview be conducted out of the hearing of the applicant's staff? The Commission has left these fundamental questions unanswered.

16. Statement of Anthony P. Travisono, quoted in Rawls, "Plan to Open Prison Review to Public Is Rejected," *New York Times*, Jan. 25, 1982.

17. David L. Bazelon, Notes from Regular Meeting, Commission on Accreditation for Corrections (Jan. 21–23, 1982).

18. Statement of Robert H. Fosen, *Ramos v. Lamm*, 485 F.Supp. 122 (D. Colo. 1979), *aff'd*, 639 F.2d 559 (10th Cir. 1980), *cert. denied*, 450 U.S. 1041 (1981).

19. Interview with Oliver J. Keller, Jr. (referring specifically to issue of audit team composition), quoted in Rawls, *supra*, note 16.

20. Letter to David L. Bazelon from a member of the Commission who asked that his name be withheld, June 2, 1981.

21. *See, infra*, Memorandum from David L. Bazelon to Board of Commissioners, Commission on Accreditation for Corrections (August 4, 1981); Bazelon, The Hidden Politics of American Criminology, 42:2 *Fed. Probation* 3 (1978). *Cf.* Bazelon, Veils, Values, and Social Responsibility, 37 *Am. Psychologist* 115 (1981); The Perils of Wizardry, 131 *Am. J. Psychiatry* 1317 (1974).
    Consider also the words of G. K. Chesterton:
    > The more a man looks at a thing, the less he can see it, and the more a man learns a thing, the less he knows it. The Fabian argument of the expert, that the man who is trained should be the man who is trusted, would be absolutely unanswerable if it were really true that a man who studied a thing and practiced it every day went on seeing more and more of its significance. But he does not.

22. See, e.g., Letter from Robert H. Fosen to David L. Bazelon, July 22, 1981, p. 2.

23. Since January 1982, for example, the Joint Commission on Accreditation of Hospitals has included a member of the public on its twenty-two-member Board of Commissioners. It is also considering public representation on its professional and technical advisory committees. The Council on Postsecondary Accreditation now requires at least one member of the public on each of its boards, as well as on its regional and specialized accrediting commissions. It even often includes a public member on its visiting accreditation teams. The same is true of regional elementary and secondary school accrediting bodies. In fact, the North Central Association—which is responsible for accrediting

elementary and secondary schools in nineteen states—allows members of the public to participate even at the self-study stage of the accreditation process.

24. The Commission must also insure that internal criticisms are not hidden from the profession. There is reason to believe that when recently seeking state and federal grants, it did not make the granting bodies aware of its then-pending internal criticisms.

25. Robert J. Brooks, a former Commission auditor, has advised me that "[i]t seems likely that correctional administrators have already developed an informal network for communicating their appraisals of auditors as 'tough' and 'not so tough.' " Letter from Robert J. Brooks to David L. Bazelon, March 19, 1982.

26. *See* Steven Gettinger, Accreditation on Trial, 8 *Corrections Magazine* 7, 16 (February 1982). One inmate at Union Correctional Facility in Florida described the institution's pre-audit activities: "You may think I'm exaggerating, but in four days I saw them paint the whole institution, and plant shrubbery and grass everywhere. After that, the hell with it." *Id.* An inmate at Florida State Prison advised Gettinger that "[t]he food that week was remarkably good—roast beef, steaks, chicken. And everyone handing out food that week wore hats and plastic gloves, something that's never been done before or since." *Id.*

27. *Id.*

28. *Id.* at 51.

29. It is reported that, on a follow-up visit, the audit team reviewed Menard's file of correspondence with Dr. Lambert King, the special master, and reported its "impression that Dr. King is generally satisfied with the effort and progress being made by the institution." When he heard of this report, Dr. King protested to the commission that "[h]ad any effort [to contact me] been made, I can assure you that I would have been cooperative in providing considerably more detailed information concerning Menard than what was presented" to the audit team. *Id.*

30. I have long urged that deliberative bodies must fully ventilate their decisions in a public forum with public input and participation. See, e.g., *International Harvester Co. v. Ruckelshaus*, 478 F.2d 615, 650–3 (D.C. Cir. 1973) (Bazelon, C.J., concurring); Bazelon, Coping With Technology Through the Legal Process, 62 *Cornell L. Rev.* 817 (1977).

31. As noted above, the Commission's recent assurance that it will "consider" outside information brought to its attention misses the mark entirely. *See supra*, note 12, and accompanying text.

32. The Florida Secretary of Corrections was permitted to make an unusual personal appearance before the full Commission in a closed-door session last May. As a result of his appeal, the Commission voted to waive compliance with a number of standards. From this experience, it seems questionable whether the Commission has any criteria for determining *which* agency heads or representatives will be allowed to make personal appearances before it. If all who so request may do so, there is no problem. But if it is anything less than all, there must be clear standards.

33. Commission on Accreditation for Corrections, *Statement of Principles*, Principle IV, *reprinted in* 1980 Annual Report, at 12.

34. *See, infra*, Memorandum from David L. Bazelon to Board of Commissioners, Commission on Accreditation for Corrections (May 13, 1981).

35. *See, infra,* Memorandum from David L. Bazelon to Board of Commissioners, Commission on Accreditation for Corrections (Aug. 4, 1981).

36. For example, I had asked whether the Commission *recruits* auditors for diversity of opinion; the response simply provided assurances regarding the heterogeneity of the existing auditor pool. I had asked about the Commission's role in determining the content of the standards; the response merely stated that "[t]he preliminary and final drafts of each manual have been reviewed and adopted by the Commission." I had asked whether the auditors routinely interviewed inmates and the heads of all institutional departments; the response concerned interviews only with agency staff. The list goes on.

37. *See* Minutes of Regular Meeting, Commission on Accreditation for Corrections (Aug. 13–15, 1981).

38. *See, infra,* Proposals for Reform of the Accreditation Process (submitted by David L. Bazelon, Jan. 20, 1982).

39. *See, supra,* notes 16–17, and accompanying text.

40. *See* Minutes of Regular Meeting, Commission on Accreditation for Corrections, at 4 (May 16–17, 1982).

41. 1980 Annual Report, *supra,* note 4, at 5.

42. *See* Gettinger, *supra,* note 26, at 9. Indeed, as a result of this strategy, the Commission sometimes does not even follow its *current* standards. The Commission must not, as it did in the recent Florida appeal, waive its standards to conform to less demanding judicial decrees. Such decrees only set constitutional minima, and they cannot take the place of the Commission's "aspirational" standards. The Commission must have the courage to follow its own standards and its own conscience.

43. *See, generally* Gettinger, *supra,* note 26, at 8–10, 16–18.

44. A task force recommendation to institute this practice was rejected at the Commission's last meeting. *See* Commission on Accreditation for Corrections, *Task Force VIII: Quality of Life,* at 2–4 (Apr. 30, 1982).

45. *See* Commission on Accreditation for Corrections, *Task Force VI: New Format for Plans of Action,* at 1 (Apr. 30, 1982).

46. The Commission recently rejected a proposal for conditional accreditation. *See* Minutes of Regular Meeting, Commission on Accreditation for Corrections, at 15 (May 16–17, 1982). The reasons it gave for this action are striking. For example: "no criteria for granting a 'conditional' accreditation award have been adopted by the Commission." This logic is circular: getting the Commission to adopt such criteria was what the proposal was all about. In addition, it was argued that manpower and money are insufficient to monitor adequately all conditions; that "if our monitoring is less than stringent, agencies are not always motivated to comply in a timely fashion"; and that "the policies governing the withdrawal of accreditation do not provide for immediate withdrawal based on an inadequate response to a condition attached to an accreditation award." Far from supporting the Commission's action, these "reasons" illustrate once again that its investigatory and deliberative processes are unreliable.

47. San Quentin was denied accreditation in May 1982, "the first such action ever taken by the Commission." *See* Robert Fosen, *Director's Monthly Letter,* June 1982, at 2.

48. Gettinger, *supra,* note 26 at 18.

49. *Id.*

50. It should be noted that the Commission does not seem to be in any hurry to fill vacancies that occur in the six slots reserved for outside organizations.
51. David L. Bazelon, Notes from Regular Meeting, Commission on Accreditation for Corrections (Jan. 21–23, 1982).
52. *Id.; see also,* Rawls, *supra,* note 16.
53. *See, generally,* Gettinger, *supra,* note 26, pp. 8–10, 16–18. *See also* Editorial, "Sham on Prisons," *Miami Herald,* Feb. 20, 1982, p. 24A, col. 1.

15. The Soviet Parallel

1. *Special Report: The First U.S. Mission on Mental Health to the USSR,* PHS Pub. No. 1893 (NIMH, 1969).
2. S. Bloch and P. Reddaway, *Psychiatric Terror* (Basic Books, 1977), p. 290.
3. Ad Hoc Committee on the Use of Psychiatric Institutions for the Commitment of Political Dissenters, *Report to the Board of Trustees,* American Psychiatric Association (1972); Statement of Chief Judge David L. Bazelon to the President of the American Psychiatric Association, the Board of Trustees of the American Psychiatric Association, and the members of the Ad Hoc Committee on the Use of Psychiatric Institutions for the Commitment of Political Dissenters (1972).
4. Bloch and Reddaway, *supra,* note 2 at 293.
5. *See* Institute of Society, Ethics, and the Life Sciences, In the Service of the State: The Psychiatrist as Double Agent, *Hastings Center Report Special Supplement* (April 1978), p. 2.
6. *Id.*
7. Walter Reich, "The World of Soviet Psychiatry," *New York Times Magazine,* Jan. 30, 1983.

16. Institutions and Adversaries

1. This chapter is based on Bazelon, Institutionalization, Deinstitutionalization and the Adversary Process, 75 *Columbia L. Rev.* 897 (1975).
2. S. Brakel, J. Parry, and B. Weiner, *The Mentally Disabled and the Law,* 3rd ed. (American Bar Foundation, 1985), p. 1, and generally. The leading regular source of information on legal developments in this field is the *Mental and Physical Disability Law Reporter* (MPDLR), published by the American Bar Association Commission on the Mentally Disabled. *See,* e.g., the *Developmental Disabilities Assistance and Bill of Rights Act* (P.L. 94-103), as amended, and the *Protection and Advocacy for Mentally Ill Individuals Act of 1986* (P.L. 99-319).
3. *Rouse v. Cameron,* 373 F.2d 451 (D.C. Cir. 1966) (see Chapter 17); *Lake v. Cameron,* 364 F.2d 657 (D.C. Cir. 1967).
4. *See,* e.g., President's Commission on Mental Health, *Report to the President* (GPO; 1978); A. A. Stone, *Law, Psychiatry and Morality* (American Psychiatric Press, 1984); *Issues in Forensic Psychiatry* (American Psychiatric Press, 1984); J. I. Klein, J. E. Macbeth, and J. N. Onek, *Legal Issues in the Private Practice of Psychiatry* (American Psychiatric Press, 1984).

5. 344 F. Supp 373 (M.D. Ala. 1972), holding that institutionalized patients have a constitutional right to treatment.

6. *NYSARC v. Carey,* 393 F. Supp. 715 (E.D.N.Y. 1975), holding that institutionalized mentally retarded persons have a right to protection from harm.

7. *O'Connor v. Donaldson,* 422 U.S. 563 (1975). For a review of the Supreme Court's decisions in disability law, see 8 *MPDLR* 502 (1984) and 9 *MPDLR* 2 (1985).

8. *Dixon v. Weinberger,* 405 F. Supp. 974 (D.D.C. 1975).

9. *See,* e.g., J. Monahan, The Prediction of Violent Behavior: Toward aSecond Generation of Theory and Policy, 141 *American J. of Psychiatry* 10 (1984).

10. Article 31B, Annotated Code of Md. (1951). *See Sas v. Maryland,* 344 F.2d 406 (4th Cir. 1964) for a description of the Patuxent program. The defective delinquent law was later repealed.

11. 418 F.2d 1095 (D.C. Cir. 1969). See Chapter 17.

12. "The best clinical research currently in existence indicates that psychiatrists and psychologists are accurate in no more than one out of three predictions of violent behavior over a several year period." Monahan, *supra,* note 9.

13. *Id.; see also* B. Ennis and T. Litwack, Psychiatry and the Presumption of Expertise: Flipping Coins in the Courtroom, 62 *Calif. L. Rev.* 693 at 724-29; J. Monahan, *Predicting Violent Behavior: An Assessment of Clinical Techniques* (Sage Publications, 1981).

14. *Overholser v. Russell,* 282 F.2d 195 (D.C. Cir. 1960).

15. *Lake v. Cameron,* 364 F.2d 657 (D.C. Cir. 1966) (en banc), *cert. denied,* 382 U.S. 863 (1966), *on remand,* 267 F. Supp. 155 (D.D.C. 1967).

16. 373 F.2d 451 (D.C. Cir. 1966). (See Chapter 16.)

17. Federal legislation, and more important, most state codes, now recognize this. Whether it is implemented in practice is doubtful. *See* sources cited *supra,* note 2.

18. *Donaldson, supra,* note 7.

19. Donaldson wrote a book about his long struggle. He said of the Supreme Court victory: "After thirty-two years of fighting for my right to be a free man, I had won vindication. Gratifying, yet somber too in the thought of the fellow sufferers who had already perished. The cameraman had to ask me to smile. When the microphone was thrust at me, I said: 'It is a victory for common sense.' Speaking from the heart, I then said that I was proud of my country. Proud that we had a system that could work to right a wrong." K. Donaldson, *Insanity Inside Out* (Crown, 1976), pp. 327–8.

20. *United States v. Alexander and Murdock,* 471 F.2d 923 (D.C. Cir. 1973, *cert. denied,* 409 U.S. 1044 (1973) (Bazelon, C.J., dissenting). [*See* Chapter 6.]

21. The ABA addresses this question in American Bar Association, *ABA Standards for Criminal Justice,* 2nd ed., vol. II, ch. 7 (Little, Brown, 1980; ch. 7, 1986). (See Chapter 17 at note 2.)

22. See Chapter 15.

23. In 1986, see the pages of any local newspaper.

24. The new panacea of "outpatient commitment" raises this issue graphically. For a discussion, *see* Mental Health Law Project, Community Services: The Second Half of the "Deinstitutionalization" Mandate, 19 *Clearinghouse Review* 1041 (Jan. 1986); National Task Force on Guidelines for Involuntary Civil Commitment, *Guidelines for Involuntary Civil Commitment* (National Center for State Courts, 1986), at 233 *et seq.*

17. Not Guilty by Reason of Insanity: The Right to Treatment

1. For example, S. Brakel, J. Parry, and B. Weiner, *The Mentally Disabled and the Law*, 3rd ed. (American Bar Foundation, 1985).
2. In 1983 the Supreme Court upheld the D.C. statutory scheme that allows hospitalization of a defendant found NGRI "until such time as he has regained his sanity or is no longer a danger to himself or society." *Jones v. United States*, 103 S.St. 3043, 3052 (1983). The American Bar Association's project on Criminal Justice Mental Health Standards thoroughly explored this issue. The standards adopted an automatic temporary commitment for evaluation, and a dual system for longer-term commitment for treatment. Defendants found NGRI for a dangerous crime would be subject to commitment under a slightly easier standard than ordinary civil commitment; the maximum duration of confinement under the special procedure is the maximum sentence for the crime charged; after that, the person would have to meet ordinary civil commitment criteria or be released. Defendants found NGRI of lesser crimes would be handled under ordinary civil commitment criteria in the state. This section represents a thoughtful and creative attempt to balance the requirement that all criminal defendants and all insanity acquittees be treated equally, with concern for both community safety and public perceptions of fairness and danger. American Bar Association, *ABA Standards for Criminal Justice*, 2nd ed., vol. II, ch. 7 (Little, Brown, 1980; ch. 7, 1986).
3. The right to treatment has been recognized by some but not all courts. It remains a controversial subject. *See*, e.g., *Wyatt v. Stickney*, 344 F. Supp. 373 (M.D. Ala. 1972); *Halderman v. Pennhurst State School and Hospital*, 446 F. Supp. 1295 (1975), *aff'd in part, rev'd and remanded in part*, 612 F.2d 84 (3d Cir. 1979), *rev'd in part and remanded*, 451 U.S. 1 (1981); *Youngberg v. Romeo*, 457 U.S. 307 (1982). The attorney appointed to represent Rouse, Charles R. Halpern, later was one of the lead attorneys in the Wyatt case and a co-founder of the Mental Health Law Project, which has litigated many of the seminal cases in mental disability law.
4. *Rouse v. Cameron*, 373 F.2d 451 (D.C. Cir. 1966).
5. D.C. Code 21-562 (Supp. V, 1966). This law was at that time one of the most advanced in the nation. It has not changed significantly in the years since, despite a virtual revolution in mental health law.
6. Hearings before the Subcommittee on Constitutional Rights of the Senate Committee on the Judiciary on a Bill to Protect the Constitutional Rights of the Mentally Ill, 88th Cong., 1st Sess. 12 (1963).
7. Group for the Advancement of Psychiatry, Laws Governing Hospitalization of the Mentally Ill 157 (Report No. 61, 1966).
8. *Greenwood v. United States*, 350 U.S. 366, 375 (1956) (Frankfurter, J.).
9. *Sas v. State of Maryland*, 334 F.2d 506, 517 (4th Cir. 1964).
10. *Watson v. City of Memphis*, 373 U.S. 526, 533 (1963).
11. *Cross v. Harris*, 418 F.2d 1095 (D.C. Cir. 1969).
12. *Millard v. Harris*, 406 F.2d 964 (D.C. Cir. 1968).
13. A. Dershowitz, "Psychiatry in the Legal Process: 'A Knife That Cuts Both

Ways,'" Address Delivered at the Harvard Law School Sesquecentennial Celebration, Sept. 22, 1967.

14. In 1975, the Supreme Court said in *O'Connor v. Donaldson*: "May the State fence in the harmless mentally ill solely to save its citizens from exposure to those whose ways are different? One might as well ask if the State, to avoid public unease, could incarcerate all who are physically unattractive or socially eccentric. Mere public intolerance or animosity cannot constitutionally justify the deprivation of a person's physical liberty." 422 U.S. 563 (1975). This was the first Supreme Court decision in this century involving the rights of civilly committed mental patients.

15. Our colleague [Judge Warren Burger] suggests that courts ignore "the dicta of *Millard*" and "the wide-ranging dicta of today's majority opinion." Even if our construction of the statutory definition of "dangerousness" in *Millard* and here could fairly be considered dictum, the suggestion would be open to considerable doubt. . . . But in fact the dissent's reference to "the dicta of *Millard*" and of today's opinion can be read only as an invitation to trial courts to ignore the *holdings* of both cases. . . . When there has been an "application of the judicial mind to the precise question," . . . decision of the question is the holding of the case. *Cohens v. Virginia*, 19 U.S. (6 Wheat.) 264, 399 (1821) (Marshall, C.J.). But we need not rest on so broad a ground. Our colleague has disagreed with the result in *Millard*, but since the result in that case rests solely on the construction of "dangerousness," that construction constitutes binding precedent. Any suggestion that trial courts disregard it violates sound judicial administration.

18. Protecting Old Values in the New Century

1. This chapter is based on Bazelon, Civil Liberties—Protecting Old Values in the New Century, 51 *N.Y.U. L. Rev.* 505 (1976).
2. Speech at Georgetown University, Oct. 12, 1985, quoted in *New York Times*, Oct. 13, 1985.
3. *Olmstead v. United States*, 277 U.S. 438, 478 (1928) (dissenting opinion).
4. *Whitney v. California*, 274 U.S. 357, 376 (1927) (concurring opinion).
5. Letter from James Madison to Thomas Jefferson, October 17, 1788, in B. Schwartz, *The Bill of Rights: A Documentary History* (1971), 1:616.
6. Address by James Madison Before the House of Representatives, June 8, 1789, in Schwartz, *supra*, note 5, 2:1031.
7. 341 U.S. 494, 519 (1951), *quoting* The Chinese Exclusion Case, 130 U.S. 581, 606 (1889).
8. Address by President Ford, Federal Bar Association Dinner, Miami, Fla., Feb. 14, 1976, in 12 *Presidential Documents* No. 8, at 218 (Feb. 23, 1976).
9. 384 U.S. 436 (1966); *see, e.g., Michigan v. Mosley*, 423 U.S. 96 (1975); *Michigan v. Tucker*, 417 U.S. 433 (1974); *Francis v. Henderson*, 96 S. Ct. 1708 (1976); *Estelle v. Williams*, 96 S. Ct. 1691 (1976); *Davis v. United States*, 411 U.S. 233 (1973); *cf. Stone v. Powell*, 96 S. Ct. 3037 (1976).
10. *See, generally,* E. Van den Haag, *Punishing Criminals* (1975), pp. 153–81; J. Wilson, *Thinking About Crime* (Vintage Books, 1975), pp. 162–83.
11. *See, generally,* A. von Hirsch, *Doing Justice: The Choice of Punishment* (Hill and

Wang, 1976); Twentieth Century Fund Task Force on Criminal Sentencing, *Fair and Certain Punishment* (1976).

12. *Buckley v. Valeo*, 424 U.S. 1 (1976). For a more comprehensive statement of my views regarding regulation of the broadcast media, *see* Bazelon, FCC Regulation of the Telecomunications Press, 1975 *Duke L. J.* 213 (1975).

13. See Chapter 14.

14. A. France, *Le Lys Rouge*, Calmann-Levy ed. (1910), pp. 117–18.

15. Madison's Letter, *supra*, note 5, at 617.

Index

A NOTE ABOUT THE AUTHOR

David Lionel Bazelon was born in Superior, Wisconsin, in 1909, and received his law degree from Northwestern University in 1931. After practicing law in the state of Illinois for a number of years, he was appointed in 1946 Assistant Attorney General of the newly created United States Land Division. In 1949 President Truman nominated him to the United States Court of Appeals for the District of Columbia, making him the youngest jurist ever appointed to that court. He served as its chief judge from 1962 through 1978, remaining on the bench as a senior circuit judge until his retirement in 1986. A man who has immersed himself in interdisciplinary thought, Judge Bazelon has been a lecturer in law and psychiatry at The Johns Hopkins University, the University of Pennsylvania, and the Menninger Clinic, and he was the only non-psychiatrist included in the first U.S. Mission on Mental Health to the USSR, in 1967. Among the numerous other organizations in which he has been active are the National Advisory Mental Health Council for the United States Public Health Service (1967–71); the Advisory Committee for Child Development for the National Research Commission (1971–78); the Commission on Accreditation for Corrections of the American Correctional Association (1980–82); and the American Orthopsychiatric Association, which he served as president (1967–70). As a member of the National Institutes of Health's Advisory Commission, Judge Bazelon has been considered one of the key architects of the proposed guidelines for genetic engineering, and he has served on the board of trustees for the Salk Institute for Biological Studies since its inception. An honorary fellow of the American Academy of Sciences and of the American College of Legal Medicine, he holds honorary Doctor of Law degrees from Georgetown, Syracuse, Northwestern, Boston University, the University of Southern California, Colby College, and many other institutions. He lives in Washington, D.C., with his wife, Miriam.

A NOTE ON THE TYPE

This book was set in a film version of a typeface called Baskerville. The face itself is a facsimile reproduction of types cast from molds made for John Baskerville (1706–1775) from his designs. Baskerville's original face was one of the forerunners of the type style known as "modern face" to printers—a "modern" of the period A.D. 1800.

Composed by American–Stratford Graphic Services, Inc.,
Brattleboro, Vermont

Printed and bound by Fairfield Graphics,
Fairfield, Pennsylvania

Typography and binding design
by Dorothy Schmiderer

WHEN MEN KILL

WHEN MEN KILL
Scenarios of Masculine Violence

KENNETH POLK

Department of Criminology
University of Melbourne

 CAMBRIDGE
UNIVERSITY PRESS

Published by the Press Syndicate of the University of Cambridge
The Pitt Building, Trumpington Street, Cambridge CB2 IRP, UK
40 West 20th Street, New York, NY 10011-4211, USA
10 Stamford Road, Oakleigh, Melbourne 3166, Australia

First published 1994

Printed in Hong Kong by Colorcraft

National Library of Australia cataloguing in publication data

Polk, Kenneth.
When men kill: scenarios of masculine violence.
Bibliography.
Includes index.
1. Homicide – Victoria. 2. Homicide – Case studies. 3. Men –
Psychology. 4. Violence. I. Title.
364.152

Library of Congress cataloguing in publication data

Polk, Kenneth.
When men kill: scenarios of masculine violence/Kenneth Polk.
p.   cm.
Includes bibliographical references and index.
1. Homicide – Australia – Victoria – Sex differences. 2. Violence –
Australia – Victoria – Sex differences. 3. Masculinity (Psychology) –
Australia – Victoria. I. Title.
HV6535.A82V536 1994
364.1' 523' 081 – dc20   94-8969
                                                                              CIP

A catalogue record for this book is available from the British Library.

ISBN 0 521 46267 3 Hardback
ISBN 0 521 46808 6 Paperback

Contents

Table: Forms of victim-offender relationships in homicide,
    Victoria, 1985–89   23

Acknowledgements

This research was supported by grants from the Australian Criminology Research Council. Throughout, the work has depended upon the close collaboration of Dr David Ranson, a forensic pathologist with the Victorian Institute of Forensic Pathology, who was responsible for the effective access that was gained to the Office of the Coroner of Victoria for the homicide data studied here. Dr Ranson participated in all stages of the research and was the co-author of the early research reports. He prepared major sections of Chapter 2 of this book, specifically those dealing with the homicide investigation and the role of the forensic pathologist in this process. This work could not have been done without the support of both Dr Ranson and the Victorian Institute of Forensic Pathology.

Several colleagues have helped in reviewing early drafts. Professor Don Gibbons of Portland State University has read sections of the manuscript, and has provided valuable advice through the years this work has taken. Margo Wilson and Martin Daly have given careful reading to drafts of the manuscript, and have been patient in their attempts to convey their important view of homicide. The exchange of ideas with the staff of the Institute for the Study of Social Change at the University of California, Berkeley, has been most helpful, and appreciation needs to be expressed to its Director, Professor Troy Duster, and others in that Institute such as David Minkus, David Wellman and Deborah Woo.

There were many research assistants who helped in collecting data from the files of the Office of the Coroner; these include Nick Hartland, David Ballek, Maj-Britt Englehardt, Santina Perrone and Hillary Little.

I am grateful for the constant support of Dr Christine Alder throughout the course of this research.

Excerpts from Wallace (1986), Katz (1988) and Daly and Wilson (1988) are reprinted with permission.

CHAPTER 1

Introduction

This book is about masculinity and homicide. It is an exploration of various patterns whereby men take the lives of others. Its empirical data are drawn from records of homicide which occurred in Victoria, Australia, between 1985 and 1989. Victoria is a state of Australia with a population of 4.5 million; 3.2 million live in the radius of the capital city, Melbourne. Throughout, the focal point of the analysis will be on the relationship between the offender and victim, and following on from that an investigation of the social dynamics which resulted in the homicide. The basic method consists of an examination of the themes which emerge from a review of a large number of case studies of homicide. As such this research is fundamentally qualitative in that it is seeking to identify the elements of the masculine scenarios of violence which are being played out in the dramas found within the narratives of homicides surveyed.

Setting the stage

The information available suggests that the rate of homicide in Australia in recent years has been running at just under 2 per 100,000 (Wallace, 1986, reported a figure of 1.9; Grabosky *et al.*, 1981, report a figure of 1.8, per 100 000; the National Committee on Violence, 1990, and Strang, 1992, show that the average figures for the past two decades would fall between 1.8 and 2.1 per 100 000). While a number of problems are encountered when comparisons are made between countries, these levels are well below the exceptionally high rates reported in nations such as Guatemala (with a rate of 63.0 per 100 000), or the high rates observed in the United States (9.1 per 100 000) (Wallace, 1986:

1

22). On the other hand, the observed rates tend to be higher in Australia than in such European countries as the Federal Republic of Germany (1.1 per 100 000), the Netherlands (0.8 per 100 000) or England and Wales (also 0.8 per 1000) (Wallace, 1986: 22). This 'middling' position of the homicide rates of Australia has also been confirmed by the recent report of the National Academy of Sciences in the United States (Reiss and Roth, 1993).

In general, Australia's homicide rate has tended to remain relatively stable over recent years, with the rate in most years falling between 1.7 and 2.1 per 100 000. As Wallace (1986: 24) points out, this stands in sharp contrast to the situation in the United States which between 1960 and 1980 experienced an increase of almost 100 per cent in the level of homicide. Of further interest is that fact that in one State in Australia, New South Wales, there were sharp drops in the level of homicide observed after the opening decade of the century, that is, the highest rates of homicide were observed prior to 1920 (Wallace, 1986: 24). There was probably much more, not less, murder on a per person basis in the 'good old days'. Certainly, the frequent assertion found in media accounts in Australia that 'violent crime is rising' does not appear to apply to homicide, especially if one takes a longer view of the time dimension.

The picture of persons who commit this offence in Australia tends to conform to observations in overseas research. The studies uniformly show that unlike property offences which involve predominantly younger offenders, slightly more than half of the offenders will be over 25 (Law Reform Commission of Victoria [LRCV], 1991; Wallace, 1986; Grabosky et al., 1981). In Australia, as elsewhere, homicide offenders are not likely to come from backgrounds of economic privilege. In both Victoria and New South Wales, where occupational data are available, less than 5 per cent of those who take the life of another come from occupations at the professional, managerial, or semi-professional levels (LRCV, 1991: 24; Wallace, 1986: 47). Quite often, these offenders are in fact unemployed, as was found among just over half (54 per cent) of the Victorian homicide offenders (LRCV, 1991: 22) and roughly one-third of the New South Wales offenders (Wallace, 1986: 47).

Turning to the circumstances of the offence, about half the time the offence occurs in the home (of either the victim or the offender), it is somewhat more likely to occur on weekend nights, and is highly likely to occur in evening hours (Strang, 1992; LRCV, 1991; Wallace, 1986). In sharp contrast to the United States where a majority of homicides will involve the use of guns, in Australian jurisdictions guns are involved in one-third of homicides or less (23 per cent in the recent national study, Strang, 1992), with knives and fists/feet accounting for

significant proportions of the remainder (Wallace, 1986; LRCV, 1991; Strang, 1992).

One major difference between Victorian homicide and that seen overseas, especially in the United States, concerns the variable of race. There are few residents in Australia whose origins are from Africa, so that this important component of homicide in the United States (for example, see Reiss and Roth, 1993: 51) will not be found in the present investigation. While in Australia overall the Aboriginal population contributes a disproportionate amount to the total number of homicides (21 per cent of all homicides, with the national homicide rate for Aboriginal males being 52 per 100 000, in contrast to the overall rate of 3.6), in Victoria the Koori population is much lower, and they made up only 5 per cent of homicides reported in 1990–91 (Strang, 1992).

The victim-offender relationship

In much of the research on homicide, in Australia and elsewhere, a major focal point has been the relationship between the victim and the offender. This flows out of the recognition that homicide is fundamentally a social act, and therefore it is important to explore the relationships that exist among the key actors in the event. Wolfgang's (1958) early research has played a major role in establishing the basic understandings and categories within which research on victim-offender relationships is carried out.

Wolfgang (1958) argued that a weakness of much of the criminological work that existed at the time was it examined either offenders, or victims, separately, rather than as interdependent participants in an inherently social event. Drawing upon the observations of von Hentig (1948), Wolfgang urged that the homicide scene be examined within a 'duet frame of crime', where the victim can be seen as 'shaping and moulding' the offender as the homicide unfolds.

This central idea that homicide research should examine the victim-offender relationship continues to echo in the current literature, as in the recent observation of Silverman and Mukherjee (1987: 37) that murder is a social event involving at least two actors in a 'social relationship that plays a dynamic role in the way that the homicide unfolds'. Luckenbill widens this somewhat when he observes that: 'By definition, criminal homicide is a collective transaction. An offender, victim, and possibly an audience engage in an interchange which leaves the victim dead.' (Luckenbill, 1977: 176)

One of the major observations which has emerged, first, from Wolfgang's investigation, and then others which have followed, is that homicide is not commonly an event involving people who are unknown

to each other. In the 1958 Philadelphia study, for example, only 12 per cent of the homicides involved persons who were strangers to each other (Wolfgang, 1958: 207). Later studies in the United States have suggested somewhat higher levels of 'stranger' homicide, such homicides accounting for 28 per cent of all homicides in the report of Zahn and Sagi (1987), and 32 per cent in the work of Hewitt (1988), although data prepared for the more recent National Academy of Sciences report on violence suggest a level of 'stranger' homicide in the range of 19 per cent (Reiss and Roth, 1993: 80). In Canada, 26 per cent of all homicide victims in 1979–83 were strangers to the offender (Langevin and Handy, 1987).

As is the case in the United States, homicide in Australia is not likely to occur among strangers. In South Australia, stranger homicides made up only 9 per cent of all reported homicides (Grabosky et al., 1981: 40), a figure close to the national 6 per cent observed by Strang (1992), although in New South Wales it was somewhat higher at 18 per cent (Wallace, 1986: 83). The figures were even higher in a recent study in Victoria, where 29 per cent of all homicides were reported to be 'stranger' homicides (LRCV, 1991: 16). Possibly these last figures are higher because the other two Australian states used police reports as their source of data, while the Law Reform Commission of Victoria investigation picked up the cases at the point of prosecution.

To put the matter properly, in Australia as elsewhere; homicide is an event most likely to involve some form of close relationship between the victim and the offender. As Wallace comments:

> Homicide in New South Wales is a crime which typically occurs between intimates; four out of five victims knew their attacker, and in a majority of cases, their relationship was a close one. The family was the most common venue for these homicides.   *(Wallace, 1986: 93)*

This information hardly provides an explanation for homicide, however. Knowing that homicides take place among people who share some amount of intimacy helps to locate the problem, but it only carries us part of the way to understanding the dynamics of violent behaviour. To go farther, it is necessary to go beyond the valuable foundation found in the work of writers such as Wolfgang, Luckenbill or Wallace. The present investigation will proceed from the assumption that a primary focus of exploration should be the relationship between victim and offender. It will be argued, however, that there are important limits to what can be explained from the use of such terms as 'stranger', 'friend/acquaintance' or 'family' to describe the bond between offender and victim. Such terms in fact provide few clues as to why the

homicide has occurred. Knowing, for example, that the offender and victim were bound by a family or friendship tie, or even that they were previously unknown to each other, by itself does not suggest what has provoked the killing. A major thrust of this research is methodological, and argues that it is time to re-enter raw data on homicides to establish more effective ways of describing victim-offender interactions that are richer in theoretical content.

But at the same time, there is a clear theoretical orientation of this research. Previous investigations suggest two major social vectors that run through homicide data. The first of these is social class. Writers from Wolfgang (1958) onward have pointed out the distinctive lower- and working-class distribution of violence in general, and homicide in particular. In the New South Wales data, for example, 5 per cent or less of all offenders, and all victims, were drawn from professional and managerial backgrounds (Wallace, 1986: 38). Explanations of why that should be the case have been less than compelling. Wolfgang and Ferracuti (1967) advanced a potentially helpful set of ideas in their discussion of the role of a 'subculture of violence' in supporting behaviour which could result in homicide.

Messerschmidt (1986) has opened up some interesting lines of inquiry in his discussion of the linkage between class, gender and violence. What such a discussion contributes is an explicit recognition of the second vector, gender, which is an important feature of homicide data. While there are some differences between Australia and countries such as the United States in terms of variables related to homicide (such as weapon use), one uniform finding across jurisdictions is that homicide is a masculine offence. Homicide offenders in Australia are predominantly male, the proportion of males being 86 per cent in a recent Victorian study (Naylor, 1993), 83 per cent in New South Wales (Wallace, 1986), and 90 per cent in South Australia (Grabosky et al., 1981) and in recent national data (Strang, 1992). These figures are comparable to the 90 per cent of males reported being arrested for homicide in the United States as a whole in 1991 (Bureau of Justice Statistics, 1992: 442), or such figures reported in individual studies as the 88 per cent reported for two up-state New York counties (Falk, 1990) or 82 per cent in Wolfgang's (1958) early study in Philadelphia.

It then follows that an important theoretical task is to account for why homicide should be such a distinctively masculine matter. The present investigation will draw heavily upon the work of Daly and Wilson (1988) in terms of their conceptual framework describing the role played by masculinity in homicide. It is their observation that across time, and across cultures, it has been established firmly that homicide is fundamentally masculine.

Daly and Wilson go well beyond this simple point, however, and describe a number of different ways that masculinity becomes played out in homicide data. One obvious dimension is that where the violence arises out of sexual intimacy. Certainly, other writers have pointed out the contribution of sexual intimacy to homicide (Silverman and Mukherjee, 1987; Easteal, 1993), and Wallace (1986: 83) was led to conclude that 'the marital relationship provides the context for some of the most violent encounters in our society'.

As important as such observations are, it also needs to be emphasised that a large proportion of lethal violence involves situations where both the offender and the victim are male. Wallace (1986), for example, reported that 54 per cent of all homicides were male-on-male.

One of the contributions of Daly and Wilson (1988) is that their account includes a description of major forms of such male-on-male violence, such as confrontations over 'honour' and the risk-taking involved in robbery homicides. Their work is important because it: (1) provides specific directions regarding particular forms of victim-offender relationships that might be explored; (2) identifies the critical gender basis of such relationships; and (3) argues for a diversity of forms of masculine violence.

There are, of course, a wide range of other sources which can be drawn into the present analysis. Katz's (1988) imaginative analysis of homicide within his framework of the 'seductions of crime' raises theoretical and methodological issues that are difficult to ignore. Especially relevant for the present analysis is his urging that we examine the 'foreground' of crime which gives emphasis to the 'lived experience of criminality' (Katz, 1988: 4). Gottfredson and Hirschi (1990) also advance hypotheses about homicide which, if not entirely accurate, nonetheless help point to directions which analysis might follow. Specifically, they identify elements of 'typical homicide' which are helpful in focusing data collection and analysis.

There are several large sets of homicide data that help set the context for the present work, including the reports of Wolfgang (1958), Wallace (1986) and Strang (1992). Wolfgang's study was carried out in one city, Philadelphia, and constitutes the starting point for contemporary analyses of homicide. In addition to opening up the discussion of victim-offender relationships, the Philadelphia data contribute a number of helpful concepts which continue to add to our understanding of homicide. Wolfgang's notion, for one example, the importance to some males of what to others are 'trivial altercations', is one that will feature in the present analysis of male-on-male homicide.

Wallace's (1986) investigation of homicide between 1968–81 in New South Wales provides one of the soundest compilations of statistical

data on homicide available in the research literature. Time and again it will prove useful as a source of comparative statistical information. As well, it contains a number of important theoretical insights, especially into the nature of masculine violence toward female sexual intimates. As a helpful backdrop of national Australian data, the work of Strang (1992) will be drawn upon at several points to help set the statistical context of homicide.

Other analyses of large data sets will contribute to the present analysis as well. Maxfield (1989) has carried out an extensive analysis of the victim-offender relationships information available in the vast Supplementary Homicide Reports collected as part of the Uniform Crime Reporting system maintained by the Federal Bureau of Investigation in the United States. Similarly helpful, especially for insights and comparisons regarding the form of the analysis of victim-offender relationships, is the study of homicide in up-state New York conducted by Falk (1990), and the analysis of the Canadian national data by investigators such as Langevin and Handy (1987).

In summary, the present research will continue the well established tradition which calls for a focus of homicide research on the nature of the social relationship between offender and victim which leads up to the killing. Consistent with such writers as Wolfgang (1958), Luckenbill (1977), and Silverman and Mukherjee (1987), the assumption is that this relationship is a dynamic one, with the victim and the offender often moving through complex social manoeuvres such that a description of the role of both parties is essential to understand the nature of the homicide. In many respects, the present analysis will follow the model of Lundsgaarde (1977) who has provided in his investigation of homicide in 'Space City' a rich source of case study material valuable for contrasts with the case study material of the present research.

More substantively, given that homicide overwhelmingly involves lower- or working-class males as offenders, this investigation will specifically probe into the scenarios of masculine behaviour involved in homicide. Empirically, it will attempt to establish the major patterns which indicate how men become caught up in lethal violence. It will then move to the much more difficult theoretical question of why it is that such violence is so distinctively lower class and masculine in character.

CHAPTER 2

Procedure, data and method

Since this is an empirical study of homicide, a number of matters have to be dealt with to enable the reader to make sense of the data as they unfold. In particular, it is essential that we: (1) clarify what we mean by the term 'homicide', (2) provide specific information on the body of data to be used in the study, and (3) review the particular approach to be used in the investigation.

Homicide defined

It is possible to define homicide, as a dictionary might, simply as 'the killing by whatever means of one human being by another'. Such a definition captures the spirit of what is inherent in the general understanding of the term. There are, of course, complications that arise as we proceed from this common sense interpretation of the concept to a more precise meaning which provides the focus for research analysis.

One of these is the issue of criminality. While there is some tragedy that lurks in all homicides, it has long been recognised that there will be a few killings that are either lawful or justifiable (most killings in war, for example, or those where it is possible to claim legitimate self-defence). Some investigations exclude these and focus exclusively upon those homicides which are unlawful. For an important example, Wolfgang (1958) in the very title of his landmark study, established the scope of his work as 'criminal homicide'.

While it is a matter of some interest to examine in the data which follow the conditions under which some homicides are deemed justifiable (as in cases where it is decided that the killing was in self-defence), as an empirical matter it is often difficult to discern how or why such

8

decisions are made by police, prosecutors or courts. As Daly and Wilson (1988) argue, if our aim is to study the behaviour of victims and their killers rather than decisions made by officials at one point or another in the criminal justice system, it is necessary to enter the problem at the earliest juncture, notably where the police have identified a case where a victim, or victims, have been killed by another person or persons.

The definition offered by Daly and Wilson, and which appears appropriate for purposes of the present research, is that the term homicide refers to: 'those interpersonal assaults and other acts directed against another person (for example poisonings) that occur outside the context of warfare, and that prove fatal' (Daly and Wilson, 1988: 14).

A number of implications follow from the statement of this approach. For one, in the pages which follow little attention will be paid to examining differences between murders and manslaughters. Central to the distinction of murders from manslaughters, from the viewpoint of legal process, in most instances will be the issue of intent, as found in the phrase 'malice aforethought' laid down early in English law. In actual practice, of course, other matters arise to cloud this distinction, including the process of plea or charge bargaining. As such, the ultimate designation between murder and manslaughter provides important information about how the justice system has responded to a killing. The focus here will be on the killing itself, and as such throughout this text the appropriate term will be homicide, rather than such terms as murder or manslaughter which are the eventual results of complex legal processes. This is in no way intending to minimise the importance of the issues raised in legal discussion of homicide (for example, see the lengthy account of Fisse, 1990: 25–130, or of Ashworth, 1991: 227–74). It is rather that, for present purposes, the mental and physical elements that are important for determining the meaning of murder and manslaughter are not central to the empirical task of examining how it is that people come to the point where one takes the life of another.

A further implication of the definition to be employed here, as Daly and Wilson (1988) are careful to point out, is that it implies an entry into the events at an early point, specifically at the police investigation stage. As such, quite different data result than if the focus were limited only to individuals who had been convicted of murder in a criminal court. In a strict legal sense, only those so convicted can be treated as 'murderers'. Yet, data after conviction are notably biased because of the various social factors that are involved both in the killing and the response of the justice system to that killing and its circumstances. As Daly and Wilson (1988: 15) establish in their discussion, data restricted to convictions in Detroit would result in the conclusion that wives are

much less likely to murder husbands than are husbands to murder wives, when in fact in that city (at least in 1972, the year being examined) more wives killed husbands than husbands killed wives.

The focus of the present research, as was that of Daly and Wilson, is on the dynamics of the killing itself, rather than the complicated, and certainly important, response of the justice system to that killing. As such, the entry point will be at an early point in the investigation, rather than drawing upon data much deeper in the justice process, such as files based on either murder convictions or murderers sent to prison.

A further implication of this approach is that some cases will be treated as homicide even where an offender ultimately may be found not guilty of a killing in the courts. For a number of reasons, a large proportion of cases where killers have been identified will not proceed through the criminal courts, such as instances where persons have committed suicide, or where the homicide is deemed lawful. Even in some cases where the preponderance of evidence lead the police or coroner to conclude that a person is responsible for the death, the exacting requirements of proving a case 'beyond reasonable doubt' may not be met.

Again, since our interest is in the killing itself, and not the complications that arise in the legal processes, here we will accept the conclusions drawn jointly by the coroner and the police as to the events relating to the homicide. As such there may be a few errors, but in no instance will accounts be considered if there is not a plausible case to be made from the case study that we are dealing with a homicide. The few inaccuracies that may result are much to be preferred to the gross distortions that would result if convicted killers were the only focal point of the investigations.

Finally, it should be obvious that homicides which go undetected or unreported cannot be considered. There are a number of ways this might happen. Some killings are carefully planned, and part of the plot may consist of disposing of the body in such a manner that its discovery is unlikely. The few illustrations within these files of bodies accidentally found in disused mine shafts, or which bob to the surface of water months or years after being killed, hint that there are more which remain successfully hidden from view.

There are, as well, homicides that take place within family circles that do not become part of the official record. At one end of the age continuum, death may result from 'elder abuse' and be recorded as an accident. At the other end of the continuum, examples can be found where babies died of horrific injuries not consistent with an ordinary household accident, and where the subsequent autopsy revealed indications of previous similar injuries which had healed (a pattern

consistent with battered children which in other cases are prosecuted as homicide), all of which suggest homicide, yet from the information available the death is classified as an accident.

Deaths at work which result from extreme negligence of employers by law in Victoria and most English-speaking jurisdictions might be treated as either murder or manslaughter, and have been in some cases in the United States (Reiner and Chatten-Brown, 1988) or the Netherlands (Field and Jorg, 1991). In Victoria, however, these events are not investigated by either the homicide squad or by other trained police investigators, and to date even if there has been an investigation (usually conducted by a government department such as the Department of Labour), the matter has not been carried forward to successful prosecution as homicide by the Director of Public Prosecutions. This is not for want of cases (see Polk, Haines and Perrone, 1993), but rather a consequence of a legal process which elects to deal with these in a different manner (where prosecutions are sought, they are likely to fall under sections of the *Occupational Health and Safety Act*, so that it is the violations of safety regulations, rather than the death, that becomes the focal point of the charge). Despite the examples of death at work resulting in convictions of employers either for manslaughter or murder, in none of the current systems of classifying homicide (including the Supplementary Homicide Reports which are part of the Uniform Crime Reports of the US Federal Bureau of Investigation) are such killings considered as a form of homicide.

In homicide, as in other forms of crime, then, there is no easy way to resolve this problem of the 'dark figure of crime', and answering the question of how much homicide 'really' exists. What can be pointed out, however, is that of all offences, homicide is the one taken most seriously both by the community and the justice system. There are examples, including instances among our case studies, where individual victims were identified even in circumstances where the body has not been discovered. In other circumstances, the homicide is uncovered after relatives of the victim have complained to the police, and it was this complaint that resulted in the discovery of both the crime and the body. While some unknown and unknowable number of killings, presumably small in contemporary Australian society, go unreported, of all forms of crime homicide is probably the one best approached through study of official data.

Homicides in Victoria 1985–89

This investigation will draw its data from files of the Office of the Coroner for the State of Victoria and utilises information on all cases of

homicide reported in the years 1985–89. In Victoria, the law provides that a death is reportable to the Coroner if it is appears to have been unexpected, unnatural or violent or to have resulted directly or indirectly from accident or injury. Among these will be deaths due to car and work accidents. Those deaths that occur during an anaesthetic, or occur as a result of an anaesthetic, and are not due to natural causes, will also be reported, as will be the death of a person who immediately before death was a person held in care or custody. Reportable deaths, further, include deaths of persons whose identity is unknown, and deaths where a death certificate has not been signed by a legally qualified medical practitioner. Finally, all cases of suspected homicide must also be reported to the Coroner.

More specifically, the *Coroners Act* (Vic.) of 1985 makes an inquest mandatory in cases of suspected homicide. There are a number of steps which are undertaken which lead up to this inquest. The likely sequence of a homicide investigation will begin with a report of the death to the police, followed by the police investigation, the analysis by forensic specialists, including the forensic pathologists, an autopsy, with the results of all of these brought together in the inquest conducted by the Coroner.

The police investigation

Although a dead body may be found in a variety of ways, the reporting of the suspicious circumstances of the death is usually made directly to the police either to a police station or to a Central Police Control Room. In either event it is the Central Police Communications Room that takes the first steps initiating the investigative process. While some discretion is left to the senior officer controlling the communications room, the usual scenario would be for the Senior Communications Officer to instruct a local uniformed police unit to attend at the scene and to report its findings. The local police who respond are responsible for completion of a 'Report of Death' form ('Form 83') which provides a brief summary of the events as these appear at the time, and information on the deceased including name, address, age, and when last seen alive.

The Communications Officer will, under most circumstances, also notify the Coroner of the death and an investigation crew from the local Criminal Investigation Branch. If the case appeared suspicious, the detectives would make arrangements for the Homicide Squad to be contacted and to take over the investigation.

The Homicide Squad officers are divided into a series of crews comprising approximately half a dozen police officers who work an

on-call rota system. They would attend the scene and be briefed by both the uniformed officers and the local Criminal Investigation Branch officers and make arrangements with the local police for preservation of the scene and control of access to the scene. At the same time, the various specialist investigatory teams will be contacted and will arrive at the scene to be briefed by the Homicide Squad officers. Such specialist teams include the scene photographers, the crime scene examiners, the specialist scientific staff of the State Forensic Science Laboratory in the appropriate area (ballistics, for example). At the same time, the Coroner's Office would make arrangements for a pathologist from the Victorian Institute of Forensic Pathology to attend at the scene and to assist in the investigation of the death.

Whilst the role of the police in this investigation is to investigate the death in relation to any criminal activity that may have taken place, the Coroner's duty is to investigate all aspects of the death explicitly excluding issues of direct criminal liability. As part of the Coroner's investigation it would be normal practice for the Coroner to attend at the scene of death, personally accompanied by a pathologist from the Victorian Institute of Forensic Pathology and perhaps other members of staff from the Coroner's Office. The role of the pathologist at the scene is to gain first-hand knowledge of the circumstances surrounding the death and the environment in which the body was found. The pathologist also assists in the general process of investigation by providing medical expertise regarding the issues of mode and time of death to the Coroner and the investigating police officers. The remainder of the specialist work at the scene includes the analysis and examination of the body in situ together with its environment with a report being compiled by the crime scene officer regarding the body at the place of death.

The autopsy

When all evidence has been examined at the scene, the body is removed to the mortuary at the Coronial Services Centre in Melbourne and a full autopsy performed, with photographic evidence of all injuries regardless of their immediate relevance to the death. The autopsy examination will include all portions of the body and will normally involve x-ray examination of the body as well as detailed section of not only internal organs but the skin and subcutaneous tissue. During this process, officers from the Homicide Squad will attend the autopsy to obtain information regarding the circumstances and cause of death from the pathologist in order to assist them in the investigation of the death.

The significance of the information arising out of the autopsy is often not fully appreciated. The identification of the cause of death is the one area of expertise that is generally recognised and yet it usually represents one of the simplest of tasks for the pathologist. It requires but little skill to recognise that a man with his head disrupted by a shotgun wound has a fatal wound and will have usually died following a 'gunshot wound to the head'. If the forensic pathologist is to assist in the investigation and subsequent prosecution of the offence it is at this point that the real detail of the work begins.

It has been long recognised by forensic pathologists that wound patterns are not random but that both the type and site of wounds play an important part in reconstructing the events surrounding the killing. In this way a body of expertise has developed that has been accepted and applied by the courts which often have little else but such medical evidence to use in order to arrive at a conclusion regarding the scenario surrounding the killing. In the past such medical opinion has gone towards elucidating individual elements of the physical interaction surrounding a killing that has resulted in macroscopic or microscopic injury. At a general level, pathologists have observed that different patterns of injury are not only associated with different specific physical interactions but also with the type of social relationship or interaction between the parties to the killing. Little qualitative or quantitative research has been carried out in this area, and this study with its unique source of data provides an opportunity to compare injury patterns with the social interaction patterns surrounding a homicide (for an overview, see Ranson, 1992).

In cases in Victoria, upon completion of the autopsy a full report is prepared by the forensic pathologist, and this is added to the file of the case to be considered by the Coroner at the inquest. In addition, various samples are obtained, and sent to the State Forensic Laboratory, and the resultant toxicology reports also become part of the file prepared on the death.

The police prosecution brief

It is the responsibility of the police to prepare a thorough report, a 'prosecution brief', of the various investigative steps regarding the homicide. Included in this report will be numerous witness statements, including lengthy transcripts of interview with individuals close to the victim, those who know the offender, and perhaps even the offender where such are available. The focus of these, of course, is on the circumstances which surround the death in question. As well, this report usually includes statements from forensic scientists and crime scene

examiners regarding specialist investigation of evidential items removed from the scene and at the time of autopsy. These components of the investigation are collated together by the police responsible, most often members of the Homicide Squad, with the statements from any suspect or individual subsequently charged with a criminal offence in relation to the death. The completed brief of evidence is then summarised by one of the investigating officers from the Homicide Squad and the total brief of evidence is then placed into the judicial process of prosecution and following this process, before the Coroner's Court for a coronial finding.

The inquest

As indicated previously, the law specifies that an inquest by the Coroner is required in all cases of suspected homicide. A Coroner's inquest occupies a unique niche in the structure of Anglo-Australian law since its proceedings are intended to establish the facts relating to the death, and its procedures are defined as inquisitorial, rather than adversarial (for an overview, see Selby, 1992). The inquest considers statements from relevant witnesses, police reports (including the Police Prosecution Brief), testimony regarding the autopsy, and if relevant, specialist testimony which throws light on the circumstances of the death. The report of the findings of the Coroner is relatively brief, in most cases roughly half a page in length. It states the identity of the deceased, the location of the death, and the causes and circumstances of the death. Regarding the circumstances, a typical entry might read:

> At approximately 8.55 pm on the 27th February 1988 the deceased, a Tattslotto Agent in Bourke Street Melbourne was shot by an unidentified person at his residence ... A quantity of money of approximately $8500, being the days takings from the Agency was removed from the deceased's premises by the person who shot the deceased. *(Case No. 839–88)*

In another case, the Coroner found that:

> the death occurred on or about 11.11.1988 ... [cause of death] ... gunshot wounds to the head and chest in the following circumstances. The deceased and R.H. had an argument and a confrontation in the loungeroom ... R.H. picked up a gun which the deceased had brought to the house and shot the deceased once and then several more times. And I further find that R.H. contributed to the cause of death. *(Case No. 4950–88)*

This report then becomes a part of the records on the homicide maintained in the Office of the Coroner.

The files

These various investigations and inquiries carried out in Victoria for cases of homicide result in a set of documents which constitute the files available in the Office of the Coroner. In most instances, the individual files will consist of the following source documents: (1) a form prepared by the initial attending police officers which reports the death (Form 83), this document providing a source of information about selected social characteristics of the victim, as well as a brief initial statement of the circumstances surrounding the killing; (2) a report of the autopsy performed by the forensic pathologists, this document providing a detailed description of the physical state of the deceased, including for present purposes a medical assessment of the cause of death; (3) a Police Prosecutor's Brief, which in most cases is an extensive document containing transcripts of interviews conducted with various witnesses relevant to the event, including in many cases transcripts of interviews with the offender; (4) the report of the Coroner's inquest, which provides a summary finding from the Coroner regarding the cause of death and who was responsible for the death; and (5) reports of toxicology and other relevant tests conducted upon the victim.

By their very nature, these files provide data about victims of homicide. Other points of entry, such as court records, are likely to be made up of data on offenders. Victim files can be expected to be somewhat more extensive than offender files, because there will be some instances where there is a known victim, but the identity of the offender cannot be determined. Further, there will be instances where a homicide occurs, but the authorities decide for one reason or another not to prosecute an offender.

A further characteristic of these files on homicide in Victoria is that all cases officially known to the police (by virtue of the processing of Form 83) will also be known to the Coroner. The situation in Victoria is unlike that in Philadelphia, where Wolfgang (1958: 12) observed that Coroner's records 'lack details of the offence which police files possess'. In contrast, in Victoria the Coroner's files will have most of the information contained in official police files, especially since it is the responsibility of the police to prepare the Prosecutor's brief which provides much of the data considered by the Coroner at the inquest. Unlike the Philadelphia records, however, these Coroner's files do not contain a record of the trial outcome, and these had to be obtained separately through the Director of Public Prosecutions (DPP).

One of the early tasks in reviewing these files was that of removing those cases which had been referred to the Coroner as homicides, but

where the death did not result from the act of another person, at least in the judgment of either police or the Coroner. Some bodies are found in what might be suspicious circumstances, but where further investigation shows the death to be the result of self-administration of drugs.

In other cases, persons have died from wounds which might have been inflicted by others, but where the circumstances suggest that a reasonable case could be made that the death was a result of an accident. For an example, a body of a well-known chronic alcoholic is found in the park with wounds to the head. These might have resulted from a fight, but the wounding is also consistent with an accidental fall, and the latter is the conclusion of the authorities in the absence of any other information. Similarly, there are cases where infants die from wounds where the circumstances are remarkably similar to the battered child syndrome, yet the authorities ultimately conclude that the death was accidental. Further information might have led some of these to be treated as homicide, but the preponderance of the available information suggests that for now the deaths are best treated as accidental, and thus they are excluded from further consideration in the present research.

Preparation of case studies

Each case of homicide for the period 1985–89 was examined, and a working file was prepared which pulled together the information from these various sources of information. From these working files, a case study was written for each case. The central focus of these case studies was the dynamics of the interaction between the victim and offender. In some cases, little would be known, particularly in some of the unsolved killings. Thus, the entry might consist of a brief observation that a body was found late at night at a service station, with a bullet wound to the head, with the homicide apparently occurring in the course of an armed robbery. In other cases (as can be seen in the sections which follow) much more information is available, and an extensive narrative can be developed which can run to several paragraphs. In all cases, names have been altered to protect the privacy of those involved.

At times, it appears that a reasonably accurate accounting of the events is possible, including many of the utterances which passed between victim and offender in the events leading up to the killing. This occurs because in the great bulk of the cases homicide is emphatically a public and social act, and the tragedy is played before a social audience who afterwards are able to provide an account where the various participants agree as to what was said. The multiple grievances that lead to lethal violence are frequently spread through time,

and relatives and close friends have a clear view of the precipitating events.

While in virtually all cases some narrative account can be prepared, some problems in the procedure need to be recognised. A major difficulty is that in homicides the viewpoint of the victim is not available afterward to provide an interpretation of what transpired, except in the few cases where the victim lingers for a period of time after the fatal wounding. In most instances it is possible by means of witness statements to obtain a reasonable account of what the victim apparently did and said in the precipitating events. Often strong advocates of the victim's point of view are present, such as their close friends or relatives, who may have seen the playing out of the whole tragedy.

Nonetheless, victims obviously cannot have the opportunity of the police interview, the Coroner's inquest, and the trial itself to tell the tale from their point of view. Furthermore, there are at times inherent conflicts in the homicide scene which carry over into the interpretations which follow. In some cases, the homicide results from conflict between two groups, each of which has a vital stake in selling a view as to who initiated the violence. In other cases, perhaps because of high levels of alcohol intake during the lead up to the homicide, the offender or other witnesses may not provide a clear account of what happened.

In the preparation of the case studies which provide the basic data for the present study, it is recognised that there are likely to be distortions in the accounts that are available. As much as possible, an attempt has been made to bring in viewpoints from those close to the victim. In the great majority of the cases, in fact, most observers available after the fatal wounding appear to agree on the basic outline of what happened. Where that is not the case, within the case study itself it is indicated that the interpretation of the events is open to some amount of confusion.

The study actually proceeded in two stages. The first stage was an investigation of general patterns of homicide, and was designed as part of a national initiative concerned with violence (Polk and Ranson, 1991a), and examined data for 1985 and 1986. The second stage evolved as a result of the emergence in the initial phase of the masculine scenarios of violence, and called for a further exploration of these by adding the data for the 1987–89 period.

An approach to the study of homicide

There are two important features of the approach to be followed in this book. First, the procedures are fundamentally qualitative in

nature. Specifically, the investigation focuses on a detailed thematic analysis of case histories which are prepared for all homicides in the files. Second, these case studies are prepared to throw light on the particular dynamics which characterise the interactional dynamics which link victims and offenders. In criminology the investigation of homicide is unique in its persistent emphasis on the critical role of the social interaction between victim and offender. Few have put the matter as well as Wolfgang (1958), who set criminologists off on the chase for an understanding of such social relationships when he argued that:

> homicide is a dynamic relationship between two or more persons caught up in a life drama where they operate in a direct, interactional relationship. More so than in any other violation of conduct norms, the relationship the victim bears to the offender plays a role in explaining the reasons for such flagrant violation. *(Wolfgang, 1958: 203)*

In virtually all sociological studies since that time, close attention is paid to what transpires between victim and offender. As a consequence, each researcher has developed an approach to the analysis of particular forms of relationship which are found between the victim and offender prior to the homicide.

If there is agreement that such a focus should guide research, there is little consistency in dealing with the question of how such analyses should proceed. It is interesting that over thirty years ago, at the beginning of this long line of investigation, Wolfgang could comment that: 'The usual difficulties of incomparable classifications are met when the distribution of victim-offender relationships is compared with other research.' (Wolfgang, 1958: 217)

It is a matter of empirical fact that in the ensuing period this problem of 'incomparable classifications' has not only continued, but arguably has worsened. None of the major investigations following the Philadelphia research has maintained the system of classification suggested by Wolfgang. Some writers follow a path of parsimony, as did Hewitt (1988) in reducing the scheme to but three categories, while others have gone for a more exhaustive listing, as found in the Supplementary Homicide Reports (Maxfield, 1989) where over thirty categories are employed. More important, of course, is the unfortunate diversity in the content of the categories. Most, in fact, suggest one or another form of relationship which is unique. Of Wolfgang's (1958) original list of eleven categories, subsequent researchers have tended to ignore such forms of relationship he proposed as 'paramour, mistress, prostitute', 'enemy', or 'innocent bystander'. Wallace (1986) employed

a grouping referring to a 'residential' relationship not mentioned by others, Maxfield's (1989) lengthy list proposed 'employee' and 'employer' relationships which are not found in other classifications, while Falk's (1990) category of 'neighbors' similarly appears to be unique.

In fact, among the many investigations on homicide carried out over the years, it would be fair to say that each tends to employ its own description of victim/offender relationships so that it is highly likely that no two lists will be the same. There may be agreement regarding what should be done (that is, analyse the dynamics occurring between victim and offender), but there is no clear agreement regarding how such analyses should proceed.

One should be careful not to overstate this case, however, since a review of the various classification schemes shows some minimum amount of consistency. Using the term 'relational distance' suggested by Silverman and Kennedy (1987), it is reasonable to argue that all of the classification schemes pose an underlying continuum which ranges from the most intimate relationships at one extreme, to the most distant (strangers) at the other. This idea of relational distance is brought into sharp perspective in the briefer of the classification schemes, such as Hewitt (1988) where provision is made for three groupings: 'relative', 'known' and 'stranger'; or Zahn and Sagi (1987) with their suggested 'family', 'acquaintance', 'stranger felony' and 'stranger non-felony' groupings.

For all that, the various classification schemes are more diverse than they are consistent. It can be argued that the reason for the diversity rests in the nature of the task itself, and the inadequacy of the common terms to carry us very far in understanding what is happening between offender and victim.

It is for this reason, of course, that many researchers have turned to another grouping, one which deals more directly with the particular conditions which produce lethal violence. Here, again, a starting point is Wolfgang (1958), who proposed a classification of 'motives' of homicide consisting of thirteen categories (which begins with his particularly well known 'altercation of trivial origin', which accounted for 35 per cent of all homicides in Philadelphia).

The consistency of this grouping fares even worse as we look at subsequent investigations. As a matter of fact, in the research which has followed there has not even been agreement regarding what it is that is being classified. For example, the Supplementary Homicide Reports used by Maxfield (1989) provided thirty separate groupings of what are termed 'homicide circumstance' (rather than motive), with only minimal overlap with the list suggested by Wolfgang.

A different approach is employed in the Chicago Homicide Project (Block and Block, 1992) which identifies various 'homicide syndromes', including homicides which are 'expressive' (where the immediate goal is to hurt, maim or kill, this grouping including 'competitive confrontations', neighbour or work-related killings, bar-room brawls, child abuse, elder abuse, revenge killings, etc.), those which are 'instrumental' (robbery homicide, burglary homicide, arson for profit, etc.), those which involve rape, or are street-gang related, one residual category designated as 'other', and a second residual grouping in which are placed cases involving some 'mystery' (including homicides which are unsolved or in which there is no evidence of motive).

The fundamental problem with existing codes of either relationships or motives/circumstances is that as these stand they do not provide enough information to inform theoretical analysis of why people kill. Knowing that persons are related by marriage provides a possible hint as to why the homicide occurs, since it would appear reasonable that the source of the violence resides somewhere in the marital bond. It does not speak to why either the husband or the wife has killed, however. Even more critical is a category such as 'stranger', since it becomes an enormous puzzle to determine what would generate the exceptional emotions most often found in a homicide when the people involved are previously unknown to each other.

While these various approaches to classifying either forms of relationship or motive may have some descriptive value, it can be argued that they are not of much use in helping to direct theoretical analysis of homicide. As Daly and Wilson put it:

> the prevailing criminological conception of motives in homicide is a woolly amalgam of several potentially independent dimensions: spontaneity versus premeditation, the victim-offender relationship, and only a relatively small dose of those substantive issues that murder mystery and ordinary speakers of English mean when they speak of 'motive' ... Violence arises from conflicts *about something*, difficult though it may be to pinpoint exactly what, and notwithstanding that the bones of contention may be multiple.
>
> (*Daly and Wilson, 1988: 173–4*)

It is the present contention that while there is some minimal amount of value in existing classification procedures, it is time to re-examine the actual data of homicide to observe if it is possible to obtain more concise and theoretically meaningful groupings of homicides. Such categories, it will be argued, should make reference not simply to the relationship between the individuals, but what it is that has transpired to bring the victim and the offender to the point where lethal violence is employed. In the terms used by Daly and Wilson immediately above,

it is assumed that the conflict was 'about something', and the task of the present research is to see if it is possible to obtain a better understanding of what constitutes such events.

Such a view starts from a similar point to that of Luckenbill (1977), who argued for viewing homicide as a 'situated transaction'. The aim of the analysis will be to identify the various themes which govern such social transactions, in order to see if an ordered and small set of groupings emerge.

The present investigation is not completely blind in carrying out such an analysis. Daly and Wilson in their work have emphasised the masculine character of homicide, pointing out that across time and across cultures homicide is a masculine matter. These writers have identified at least three dimensions of masculine violence which can help point the way for the present study. It is their view that males are more likely than females to employ violence: (1) in sexual relationships as a form of reproductive control, especially around the issue of jealousy; (2) in killings arising out of sexual rivalry; (3) in altercations involving 'honour'; and (4) in the situation of 'robbery homicides' (Daly and Wilson, 1988).

The present case studies were analysed in order to identify the major themes of victim-offender interaction in scenes of lethal violence. Each of the case studies was reviewed in terms of the key elements in the scenario of violence which unfolded. These were then grouped into those which seemed to share common themes. Thus, the process was fundamentally qualitative (in that it focused on the emergent themes of interaction based on case history accounts) and inductive in that the defining themes, or key elements of the scenarios, emerged from the close reading and then grouping of the individual case studies.

As the patterns began to emerge, guidelines, or a set of check lists, were developed to guide the coding. For each particular form of homicide, in other words, a series of questions could be used to provide for the accurate placement of cases into the various categories. It must be emphasised that the process was a highly emergent one, and the process gradually unfolded, with some types being altered as new data were added. The resulting set of groupings are discussed briefly below, and in the chapters which follow. In a chapter dealing with methodological issues, some of the specific issues which arise in the process of classification of homicide are addressed.

In general, the themes which emerge are consistent with the forms suggested by Daly and Wilson, although somewhat more clusters emerged from the present case studies. The various groupings will be discussed briefly here in order to establish the overall pattern, with a more detailed description of the major patterns to be elaborated in the

Table 1: *Forms of victim-offender relationships in homicide, Victoria, 1985–89*

Homicides in the context of sexual intimacy	(N=101)			
Female victim/male offender (Chapter 3)		73		
Jealousy/control			58	
Depression/suicide			15	
Male victim/male offender (Chapter 3)		13		
Sexual rivals			13	
Homosexual killings			0	
Male victim/female offender (Chapter 7)		12		
Provoked by violence			8	
Control/other			4	
Female victim/female offender (Chapter 7)		3		
Sexual rival			2	
Homosexual killing			1	
Homicides originating in family intimacy (Chapter 7)	(N=40)			
Children victims		31		
Victims of trauma			13	
Battered children				7
Victims of shooting, other				6
Victims of parental suicide			9	
Neonaticides			8	
Victims of neglect			1	
Other family victims		9		
Sister victim/brother offender			2	
Parent victims/son, step-son offender			5	
Other (in-law, grandparent victims)			2	
Confrontational homicides (Chapter 4)	(N=84)			
Homicide originating in other crime (Chapter 5)	(N=61)			
Double victims		31		
Reverse victims		18		
Killed by police			11	
Killed by citizen			7	
Professional killings		5		
Police killed		5		
Prison killings		2		
Conflict resolution homicides (Chapter 6)	(N=38)			
Victims of mass killers (Chapter 7)	(N=15)			
Unsolved (and unclassifiable) (Chapter 8)	(N=22)			
'Special' cases (Chapter 8)	(N=18)			
Mercy killing (Chapter 8)	(N=1)			
Total	(N=380)			

chapters which follow. Clearly, from the present data a large proportion of homicides have their origins in matters concerning sexual relationships. Just over one-fourth of all homicides (101 of 380, or 27 per cent) evolved in one way or another in the context of sexual relationships (Table 1).

In examining this major cluster, however, it became apparent that it was necessary to differentiate the cases by gender of both victim and offender. There were a total of 86 cases where males were the offenders. In the largest proportion of these (73 of the 86), the victim was the female partner of the male. Most of these female killings resulted from the attempt of the male to assert control over the behaviour of his partner through the use of violence (58 of the 73 female victims of male offenders), often in the context of jealousy. A significant proportion (15 of the 73), however, were in a situation where the male was extremely depressed, and the homicide was part of the planned suicide of the male. Masculine violence in cases of sexual jealousy is not limited to females, so that in addition, there were 13 cases where males killed their male sexual rival. Among these case studies there were no cases of homicide arising out of sexual jealousy among male homosexuals, although a longer time span would be likely to produce examples of such homicides.

Women were much less likely to kill in the context of sexual relationships. There were in all 15 such cases, of which 12 were made up of males being killed by their female sexual partners. Most of these (8 of the 12) were females killing in response to the violent behaviour of the male partner. Only 3 killings arose out of an attempt of the woman to exert possessive control over the partner's behaviour (there were no cases where the woman killed her male partner because of jealousy), and there was one case where a woman and her lover contracted for another male to kill her husband so that the two could live together. There were 3 cases where women killed women because of sexual relationships, 2 of these representing the removal of a sexual rival, while the remaining case was an instance of a killing with its origins in homosexual jealousy.

A second major pattern consisted of distinctively masculine 'confrontations' arising out of defence of honour. There were 84 of these homicides (accounting for 22 per cent of all killings). A major characteristic of these is that in most cases they emerged quickly out of some exchange, often involving insults, sometimes nonverbal gestures. The events would move rapidly and spontaneously from these initial events, often starting with a fight, then leading to the fatal injuries. Virtually all of the individuals engaging in this scenario were male, but there were four examples (5 per cent of all confrontational killings) where this pattern involved women as both offender and victim.

A third pattern involved homicides which arose out of other criminality, which accounted for 61 (or 16 per cent of the total). Most common here were double victims (31 of the 61) who were the victim first of some crime such as robbery or burglary, and then became the victim of homicide. In another 18 of the 61 cases, the ultimate homicide victim was an offender in an original crime (11 of these 'reverse victims' were killed by police, the remainder, 7, by the victim of the original crime). Included here as well are 5 professional killings, 5 police killed while on duty, and 2 cases where the death occurred in prison.

A fourth pattern involved what is termed here 'conflict resolution' homicides, where the killing resulted from the planned and rational intention to employ violence to resolve some form of personal dispute, over such issues as debts, shared resources or the like, between victim and offender. Most often this pattern, which accounted for 38 homicides (or 10 per cent of all homicides) involved persons well at the boundaries of conventional society, such that their close ties to a criminal way of life closed off any possibility of the use of conventional conflict resolution procedures.

While the present analysis will focus on four scenarios of masculine violence that can be derived from the major patterns reviewed up to this point, there are, of course, other forms of homicide. A further pattern, for example, involves multiple homicides. Within the present data, we found 2 examples of mass killings which contributed a total of 15 victims. There were no examples of the serial killings in this time period that feature so prominently in the analysis of homicide in the United States.

Killings within the boundaries of family relationship contributed another 40 cases (making up 10 per cent of all homicides), with most of these being 31 cases of children killed by parents. The largest group of these child killings were made up of deaths resulting from trauma (13 cases), with smaller numbers where the death was part of the suicide plan of a parent (9 cases), where the death was a neonaticide (8 cases) and there was one child who was a victim of parental neglect.

There was one case of a 'mercy killing' which could not be placed within any other category.

There were, in addition, 18 cases which were so odd, bizarre or different that it was impossible to trace an easy interpretation from the relationship to the killing, and these have been grouped together and placed within a category of 'special' killings and are discussed in Chapter 7. This same chapter will provide an analysis of the 22 killings which were both unsolved and unclassifiable within the other categories.

As analysts such as Wallace (1986) or Daly and Wilson (1988) have argued, gender is a fundamental issue which projects through these

figures. From the hypotheses sketched out by Daly and Wilson, the first three of the masculine scenarios of violence might have been expected, these consisting of the masculine use of violence around issues of sexuality and sexual control, the use of violence in the confrontational scene as a defence of masculine honour, and the masculine willingness to take risks involved in engaging in crime which threatens life. The fourth pattern, homicide as a form of conflict resolution, emerged inductively out of the present analysis. It is the task of the following pages to round out each of these four scenarios of masculine violence, and to provide the case study material which illustrates the empirical content of such patterns. After this, a brief discussion of the other forms of homicide will help to set the context for these four scenarios.

CHAPTER 3

Scenarios of masculine violence in the context of sexual intimacy

Homicide is most likely to occur between people who not only know each other, but in fact share some form of close relationship. In the words of Wallace (1986: 93), homicide 'is a crime which typically occurs among intimates'. Similarly, in their study of 'intimate homicide', Silverman and Mukherjee commented that lethal violence often occurs in relationships that initially were forged 'on the basis of some positive attachment'. (Silverman and Mukherjee, 1987: 37)

Among the many forms of intimacy, the one which accounts for the largest share of these homicides is that arising out of sexual relationships. In the analysis of national patterns, Strang (1992) observed that 21 per cent of homicides in Australia took place between 'spouses', a figure close to the 23 per cent observed in Wallace's (1986) study of New South Wales. As is true of homicide generally, the dominant picture, at least in Australia, is one of masculine violence. Wallace observed that:

> Marital murder in New South Wales is, as it was 100 years ago ... , a practice largely confined to men: 73.3% ... of the marital murders were committed by husbands; 26.7% ... were committed by wives. Thus, women were three times more likely than men to be killed by their spouse. Both numerically and proportionately, more women than men were killed by their marital partner. *(Wallace, 1986: 84)*

How is it that what begins as a relationship of closeness and intimacy can turn in such a direction that exceptional violence is provoked? The case study data enable us to draw out the threads that run through this particular scenario of masculine violence. For present purposes, it will be presumed that intimacy refers to couples who have established a

27

sexual relationship, so that this will include persons who are married, persons involved in a de facto relationship, as well as persons who have been going together to the point where a sexual relationship has been established. There were 73 homicides where males took the lives of their sexual intimates (accounting for 19 per cent of all homicides). There were, in addition, 13 homicides where a male killed what he presumed was his sexual rival, a form of homicide which also derives from some initial sexual intimacy. In total, then, there were as a consequence 86 homicides where males killed and where a sexual relationship provided the bond with the victim (23 per cent of all homicides).

There appear to be two distinct major sub-patterns to the homicides where men kill women, one concerned with sexual possession where violence is employed as a control strategy, the other with a pattern of suicidal masculine depression which also encompasses the female partner in a control process, but to quite a different end. The elements of these patterns can be seen in the various case studies which follow.

The theme of masculine possession

Wallace (1986) in her study of homicide in New South Wales observed that either separation (or its threat) or jealousy were the major precipitating events of homicides where men took the lives of their spouses. This, she argued, was a reflection of the ultimate attempt of males to exert 'their power and control over their wives' (Wallace, 1986: 123). In all, among the present case studies 58 of the homicides (15 per cent of all homicides) could be considered as a reflection of male use of violence to control their sexual partners.

It is commonly the threat of separation, and the feelings of jealousy aroused by such a separation, that prompts the violence. Daly and Wilson (1988) have argued that sexual jealousy and rivalry are the dominant motives in homicide involving women as victims and men as offenders. This arises, they postulate, out of the inherent desire of men to control women and their reproductive capacities: 'we find it highly significant that *men the world around think and talk about women and marriage in proprietary terms*' (Daly and Wilson, 1988: 189, emphasis in the original). They observe that jealousy and sexual ownership constitute the major 'dangerous' issue in marriage (Daly and Wilson, 1988: 200). Rasche (1989), in support of this observation, reports that the single most important motive for murder among intimates was the inability of the offender to accept the termination of the relationship.

Certainly, the theme of jealousy and control run consistently through the many case studies of intimate homicide. Consider the following account:

Some six years previously, Rita B. (age 39, home duties) after a divorce had formed a de facto relationship with G.K. (who was born in Cyprus). In the last few months of her life, this relationship turned stormy and violent. Her son later observed that: 'I was aware that there were many arguments between them ... I was aware of injuries received by my mother which I know were inflicted by G.K. I have seen G.K. physically strike my mother. I have seen bruises and she has complained of sore legs and back.' The son also stated that he: 'heard G.K. threaten to kill my mother. G.K. had been away for a while and my mother was going out with another man, a butcher from Kew.' The son testified that when G.K. found out about her other relationship, he again threatened his mother, saying: 'if I can't have you, no one will ...'.

Because of these assaults and threats, the police were called, and G.K. was subsequently charged with assault. Rita attempted to solve her problems by moving out. She made every attempt to keep her new address a secret, even pleading with the removalist not to divulge her address to anyone. The removalist later stated that Rita had told him that 'if anyone comes looking for me, don't tell them where I live because if he finds out he will kill me.'

Rita was correct in her assessment of G.K.'s intentions, but underestimated his inventiveness. When G.K.'s attempts to find Rita were unsuccessful (he did contact that removalist, who refused to provide the new address), he then hired a private detective who was successful in identifying the new address.

Shortly afterwards, Rita's mother received a call from her terrified daughter. G.K. had just called and said he was coming over to kill her. The mother told Rita to call the police immediately, which she did. By the time the police arrived she was already dead, having been killed by multiple gun-shot wounds to the head. G.K. immediately left Australia, and has not yet been found and brought to trial.   *(Case No. 1731–85)*

This male was obsessional in his desire to maintain control over his sexual partner. He would destroy his intimate 'possession' rather than let her fall into the hands of a competitor male. In addition, in this account a deep level of premeditation can be observed. The killing is not the spontaneous outgrowth of an argument which gets out of control. This male planned carefully, including going to the extraordinary lengths of employing a private investigator to locate the residence of his victim. Such elaborate steps are common in these intimate homicides:

It was just at the end of the working day, 5 pm, when A.L. walked into the Laverton Police Station and announced 'I have just shot my wife'. Police went to A.L.'s house, and found Clara L. (age 43, home duties) dead of multiple gunshot wounds. In the interview which followed, A.L. explained how he had purchased a percussion revolver (a 19th century weapon) from a gun shop by claiming he was a collector of antique firearms some two months prior to this, then taking the weapon home and testing it to make sure he knew how to make it work.

A.L. then related how he had carefully studied his wife's movements, and knew which train he could expect her to travel on after she finished her

shopping (she had moved out some three months before). As she stepped down from a train carrying her to her new home, A.L. approached Clara, and talked her into coming with him to his residence. As she was putting the kettle on to fix him a cup of tea, he fetched his revolver from an adjoining room, and shot her in the head. He said that he 'just had enough of her', and when questioned about his motives, he said that 'she's been sticking it to me for many years ... she's had a number of different men'.

Subsequent questioning of Clara's friends revealed a different story. They related that they knew her well, but, as one put it: 'I have been in close contact with Clara and she never had an interest in other men, nor was she having an affair with anyone.' This same friend related how Clara had been mistreated by A.L., including occasions where her face was so severely cut and bruised that several stitches were required to close the wounds. Finally, 'She couldn't stand A.L. because he was beating her up and tormenting her', so she moved out of the marital household. After she left, Clara received several telephone calls from her husband, calls which were abusive and threatening. A.L. then obtained the weapon, and successfully plotted her death. After the crime, A.L. showed no remorse over the killing, expressing instead a sense of relief.   *(Case No. 3858–85)*

Here, too, can be seen the careful planning which led to the homicide. The wife's movements were plotted, and the difficult steps were taken to obtain the murder weapon (hand guns are controlled weapons in Victoria). In both this and the first case, there is the presence of considerable violence prior to the homicide, that violence being a major factor in the decision of the woman to try to separate from the male.

The careful tracking of the movements of the victim as part of the plan illustrates the intentioned character of many of these homicides. When the rage has reached the point where the male is ready to kill, he often scouts out the movements of his victim, determining where and when she will be vulnerable to attack:

In April 1987, Vicki (age 25, kindergarten teacher) ended a four-year de facto relationship with P.L. The breakup was impossible for P.L. to accept. He began to harass her in various ways, including constant telephone calls (it finally reached the point where co-workers would refuse to put telephone calls through to her at the school). One Monday, P.L. was successful in reaching Vicki by telephone, and insisted that she stop by the next day to return some crockery which he thought was his, and for her to pay him money for the car she was driving (which P.L.'s delusions drove him to believe he was owed). She ignored the request. Vicki's failure to show up Tuesday night tipped P.L. over the edge. The following morning, he armed himself with a knife and at 7.30 arrived at the school parking lot, awaiting Vicki. He had left plenty of time to make sure that he would be there before her. When Vicki arrived shortly after 8 am, P.L. confronted her, an argument developed, and he then stabbed her several times with the knife. Afterwards he stated that when Vicki told him to 'fuck off', he 'snapped', and that he remembered little of what happened after that.   *(Case No. 3732–87)*

These killings, however, are not sudden outbursts of violence pro-voked by an argument or other moment of passion (in the above account, for example, P.L. may claim that he 'snapped', but as well he plotted Vicki's movements, arranged to be where he knew she would be, even arriving early, and he brought the weapon with him). While the degree of intentionality varies, it is possible in close to two-thirds of these cases (37 of the 58, or 64 per cent) to find some clear element of prior planning in the events leading to the death. To be sure, they may not all 'stalk' their victims as found in these previous cases, but in most these are planned homicides rather than a swift upswelling of passion-ate rage.

Another element common to this scenario of masculine violence is the delusional character of the masculine response (as in P.L.'s conviction that Vicki owed him money, or A.L.'s belief that his wife had been having affairs with other men). A more convoluted form of such delusions is found in the following case:

After some twelve years of marriage, mounting financial pressures meant that Natalie H. (age 33, process worker) had to take a job to help support the household and two children. At the factory where she worked she met a man with whom she struck up a friendship that widened into a sexual relationship. Eventually she decided to leave her husband, A.H., leaving to move in with her new lover.

The husband, who had migrated from Yugoslavia some twenty years previously, still clung to some of his old world values, and found himself unable to cope with the breakup of the marriage. As they were arranging the formal details of the separation through their solicitors, Natalie mentioned to her new partner that A.H. had threatened to kill her. A.H. had experienced a transitory sexual encounter with a prostitute immediately after the initial separation. Curiosity led him to look through the handbag of the woman, where he said he found a picture of himself. He then constructed an elaborate fantasy whereby his wife and her boyfriend had arranged for the prostitute, whom he convinced himself had AIDS, to infect him with AIDS in turn so that he would die and they could inherit his property.

As this fantasy became more fixed in his mind, and as he began to detect (in his imagination) the symptoms of AIDS, A.H. decided to murder his wife. He illegally purchased a hand gun through connections in St Kilda (a Melbourne suburb). He began to plot his wife's movements. One day when he knew she would be shopping, he decided to act. He took the gun and searched the shopping centre until he found her, an argument started, and he shot her in the head with the pistol, killing her instantly.

When asked by the police what had happened that afternoon he replied:
A.H.: 'Something cross my mind, I am not a man any more because of my health' [referring to the AIDS].
Q: 'Had you made up your mind that you wanted to shoot her?'
A.H.: 'Yes, I have in the mind, that is why I buy the gun.'
Q: 'When did you make up your mind to shoot your wife?'

A.H.: 'When the pain getting worse and I can't sleep, probably three weeks ago.'
Q: 'Why did you shoot her?'
A.H.: 'Because I have to die and I never do anything wrong with her, never look at another girl, and I look to keep the family going and because she go the other way. She meet another person and go to New South Wales and gamble. I believe she must die, too ...'
Q: 'Do you feel any regret that your wife has now died?'
A.H.: 'I don't know. I just worry for the kids. She no worry for me when she leave. I worry for the kids only.'

One of the witnesses who helped apprehend A.H. as he attempted to flee from the scene of the killing testified that A.H. had said: 'She's my ex-wife ... she deserved it.'   *(Case No. 231–86)*

Fuelled by the jealous rage, delusions can build in the minds of these men tormented by the thought of their lovers moving out of their control and into the arms of another man (for a more detailed account of the role of 'morbid' jealousy in homicide, see Mowat, 1966). This goes to the lengths in this case where the male became convinced that an elaborate plot had been concocted to infect him with a fatal illness, even to the point where he imagined the symptoms of the disease. Consumed by jealousy which strikes deep at his manhood, driven by his delusional pain, he decided that since he was dying, she 'must die, too'. This exceptional jealousy is a common thread through many accounts of masculine, intimate homicide:

Terri (age 32, machine operator) had been married to Mack (age 43) for fourteen years. Over the past couple of years, Mack had become increasingly jealous of his wife, making many unfounded allegations that his wife was having affairs with other men. His controlling behaviour edged into the extreme when it reached the point where he forbade Terri to leave the house without him. At one point (a year before the homicide) he threatened Terri with a gun.

In June 1988 Mack and Terri had an argument because Terri wanted to visit her grandmother in a nearby town, and Mack stormed out of the house. Terri packed the children in the car and began the journey toward her grandmother's. Mack was waiting for them, parked by the side of the road. As his family passed, Mack pulled a shotgun from the boot of his car, and began to pursue them. Terrified, Terri pulled into a rest area and asked people there to call the police because she feared that Mack would shoot her. Seeing him approach, she took off in her car. Mack followed, and was able to force her off the road. He came up to the car and yelled: 'You've got to come home. You have to stay inside the house, and you are not to see your parents any more. You're going to be all right, because I'm going to control your life.' Terri pleaded with Mack, saying 'I'm not doing anything, I'll come home.' Mack pushed the gun through the window, and shot and killed Terri. He then reloaded the weapon, and killed himself.

It was established afterwards that Mack had been seeing a psychiatrist, who had observed that 'his main concern was his perceived loss of control of his

wife ... if she continued in the same way, he would get his gun and shoot his wife and then himself.'   *(Case No. 2474–88)*

This male wanted virtually to lock his wife away, and his inability to exert this extraordinary level of control was a feature of his jealous rage. While for some men it is the threat of separation that generates masculine rage, in this case the woman's desire was simply to see her family, which the husband found literally intolerable.

It is hard to estimate the full level of delusional behaviour among these males, but a reading of the case accounts indicates that in one-third (19 of the 58, or 33 per cent) there is evidence that the male alleges sexual misconduct which others in the scene (family and friends of the victim) deny. While the male in some cases might have been correct, the point here is that many close to the victim allege that the male had deluded himself into believing that his partner was unfaithful, and the weight of the evidence suggests that males are too ready to not only believe in their partner's infidelities, but to react to these with violence. In some instances, as these previous case histories demonstrate, these delusions can go to rather extraordinary lengths.

It is not uncommon that males, trapped by the heat of the anger, express feelings of relief as with A.H. in the account above, rather than remorse, in the time immediately following the killing. The lack of remorse is captured in other accounts as well:

> After going out with Michael (age 25, bouncer) for several months, Eileen (age 26, secretary) began to attempt to withdraw from the relationship. Michael found this difficult to accept, and began to utter threats concerning Eileen's growing independence (Michael had a history of violence with previous girlfriends). His jealousy grew, and resulted in such actions as his attempt to break into Eileen's flat early one morning (Michael had managed to convince himself, without foundation, that she was sleeping with someone else).
>
> The crisis came on Christmas day. At the holiday gathering of Eileen's family the relatives noted an air of tension between the two. A minor incident flared when Eileen was, in Michael's view, overly friendly with other male guests at the party. When it came time for Michael to leave, Eileen went with him, indicating that she would return shortly. The couple parked their car in Errol Street, North Melbourne, and were overheard to argue. Police were summoned to the scene shortly afterward, and found Eileen dead (she had been strangled). When asked what happened by the police, Michael stated: 'I strangled the bitch, that's all.' When told that she was dead, Michael stated further: 'Fucking good, the bitch deserved it ... I wasn't going to let her hurt anyone again. I knew I had to do it ... I just lost it, she wasn't going to hurt me or anyone else again.'   *(Case No. 5524–88)*

The words 'the bitch deserved it' convey how far the mind's journey of these men has carried them. Their 'loved one' is now dead, but

rather than remorse at the awesome act of killing, the men had convinced themselves that their partner deserved to die, that the fate was a justifiable one. The power of this rage to push out any feelings of remorse is also found in the following case:

> After living for a few months with T.K. (originally from Yugoslavia) in a de facto relationship in Melbourne, Hanna M. (age 46) decided to move to the country with T.K. to establish a dairy farm. The move, the economic stresses, and other factors brought unexpected pressures into their relationship. T.K. began to drink heavily and the couple began to fight. A young Yugoslav who worked as a hand on the farm, and who lived there, commented that they began to fight all the time, and that T.K. would: 'push Hanna, he push her into walls, doors, all the time. He kicked her in the bum. When he did this he called her names. She would never hit him back, he was too big. She was scared of him.' Hanna's daughter testified that she had seen bruises on her mother several times, while another friend commented that Hanna had told her that T.K. had even tried 'to kill her on numerous occasions'.
>
> Late one afternoon events seem to boil over. First, T.K. started after Hanna with a hammer. When the young farm hand intervened, T.K. backed off, only to return a few minutes later carrying an axe, leaving little doubt that he intended to use it on both Hanna and the farm hand.
>
> Hanna, the hand, and the girlfriend of the hand made a quick exit from the farm. They approached the police, but were told there was little that the police could do. When the young farm hand explained that they had no place to spend the night, he said that the police told him: 'You go to motel or friends.'
>
> Lacking money, and having no friends in the country area, the three made the mistake of returning to the farm after dark. They attempted to sneak into the bungalow at the back of the property which was the residence of the farm hand, but were discovered by T.K.
>
> The young hand and his girlfriend indicated that they did not want to stay. Hanna decided that she would be able to remain there safely, at least for the night. The farm hand stayed long enough to be assured that she would be safe. T.K., when he came into the bungalow, said: 'Don't scream, I don't want to touch you.' The farm hand surreptitiously looked on for a few minutes, then left, since, as he said he: 'didn't hear any screaming . . . I thought it was the same as before. One minute scream, one minute quiet.'
>
> While somehow Hanna and T.K. managed to get through the night, the police were called to the scene the following morning. They found T.K. covered in blood, and Hanna dead from knife wounds. When asked what happened, T.K. answered: 'I grabbed her and told her that I will not let her leave . . . She begged me not to kill her because she said she still loved me, but I said it was a lie, she did not love me any more . . . I only wanted to destroy her . . . I wanted to get rid of her then I can go to the jail and stay in peace.'   *(Case No. 3028–86)*

In this account the anger is manifest, and in these immediate utterances can be found an expression of a sense of relief after the killing has been accomplished (and, certainly, no sense of remorse). The

death freed the male so that he then could live 'in peace'. We see in this narrative a further issue, the ineffectiveness of the justice system when called upon by potential victims. The absence of police action is found in the following narrative as well:

> Diane B. (age 32, on mother's pension) had met T.Y. (age 21, originally from Lebanon) at a disco a few months after she had broken up with her husband. The relationship went in fits and starts for about a year and a half. Finally, Diane cooled altogether and decided to call the relationship off.
>
> T.Y. became enraged. First, he called her and abused her, then threatened to kill her. He then came over to her flat, banging on doors and windows, brandishing a shotgun. Diane stayed hidden, and successfully deceived T.Y. into thinking that she was not at home. T.Y. then went to the house of her sister, threatening the sister and her husband with the gun, demanding that they tell him Diane's whereabouts. The couple was able to calm T.Y. down, and when he left he seemed to have himself under control.
>
> A few days later, however, he was again after Diane. This time he had lain in wait until he spotted her car, and then forced her off the road. In the argument which followed, TY.. said that he desperately 'wanted her back', and that 'if he couldn't have her, no one else would'. This time, though, as they talked T.Y. gradually calmed down and finally left.
>
> After this episode, Diane sought help from the police, informing them that she had been threatened with a gun. Their advice was that she should move, and cease further contact with T.Y. The police made no attempt to apprehend T.Y., and no formal record of Diane's complaint was made by the attending officers.
>
> One day shortly after, T.Y. again went to Diane's flat, this time being successful in gaining entry. What happened is not clear, but T.Y. first fired two shots from the shotgun into the ceiling of the flat, then one shot to the head which killed Diane, then turned the gun on himself, the result also proving fatal.   *(Case No. 1026-85)*

A repetition can be seen here of the attempt to claim exclusive rights over the intimate partner. A fact which stands out in this account is that the intentions of the male were well established. The unwillingness of the police to take action is notable, especially given that both witnesses and the victim made clear that the male had made threats with a gun.

Even if the police take aggressive action, however, they may not be able to contain the violence of the male:

> Iris H. (age 33) had lived for some years with G.R. (age 48), and the couple had one child together (an older boy from Iris's previous marriage lived with them as well). G.R. became progressively more violent toward his de facto wife, and she finally decided to move out. At the same time, she struck up a close relationship with an older workmate of her oldest son. This male friend later recounted that the boy (age 14) had told him that G.R. often threatened him and his mother, including threats 'to kill them and burn the house down'. The friend became very close to the mother, since 'she was

under severe stress and looked to me to talk to and seek advice about her domestic situation'.

G.R. broke in on the two while the two friends were having one of their chats, and proceeded to assault the male whom he saw as a rival, accusing him of 'back-dooring his missus'. The man told the police that: 'I defended myself but he was acting like a crazy person ... he threatened to kill me and Iris.' The police were called, and it was clearly established that the two had not been in bed together. The police were able to calm G.R., at least for that day, and he left.

Iris continued to be apprehensive, and sought help and advice from both police and the Salvation Army. Early in the evening a week after the previous incident, the police received a call from a woman saying that she had suffered a gunshot wound to the chest. Police arrived to find Iris on the floor, with her 3-year-old child kneeling beside her. She claimed that G.R. had shot her, but 'at least I saved my baby'. She died in hospital as a result of shock and haemorrhage due to multiple gun shot wounds. G.R. committed suicide after he shot his wife.   *(Case No. 1979–86)*

In this account, the police attended, and to all appearances had brought calm into the situation. Further, there was no indication to the police that the male had a deadly weapon in his possession. As in other of these cases, this male could not tolerate the separation of his sexual partner, and the images his mind created of her sexual activity with other men. There is, also, the background of prior physical violence that so often is responsible for the decision of the woman to leave her spouse.

In another account, the police gave the woman the good advice to remove her self well away from the scene, that advice was followed, but then the woman made the unfortunate mistake of returning for some goods she had left behind:

Polly K. (age 25, home duties) had been living in a de facto relationship with Abe R. (age 48) for ten years, with the couple having two children in that time. In recent months, the two had experienced what the police reports referred to as 'serious domestic difficulties' (that is, reports of physical assault of Abe on Polly).

Polly decided finally that it was time to make a break, accepting police advice that she remove herself from the home. She left the house for a few days, hiding with friends in a country area well removed from their Melbourne home. Abe became frantic, searching out all of Polly's known haunts, making various threats of what he would do when he found her.

After being away for a few days, Polly returned home for the purpose of gathering up her things. Abe happened to be home, and Polly made the mistake of attempting to negotiate a separation. An argument developed, which was followed by an assault by Abe on Polly. After the argument had cooled a bit, Polly collected some bedding and clothes, according to Abe's testimony, and retired to the caravan which was parked at the back of the house to get away from Abe.

Later that night, Polly was found dead in the caravan. A single shot had been fired into her body at close range. Abe claimed that she had committed suicide, but the police found the story unconvincing, and he was charged with the murder of his de facto wife.   *(Case No. 99K1–85)*

The police in this case had offered advice which might have avoided the final clash. Neither the police nor the woman were able to predict, however, the lengths to which this male would go when gripped by his possessive rage.

From these accounts one can draw the pessimistic observation that the justice system can offer little real protection from the jealous rage of a male determined and set on the course of homicide. Even when orders are issued explicitly restraining the male from further violence, the protection offered can prove sadly inadequate:

The de facto relationship between Sally (age 31, shop assistant) and Richard was complicated, difficult and littered with a history of violence. The two had begun their relationship in early 1986, but separated after four or five months. For a brief period, Sally reunited with her first husband, and Richard in turn initiated a new de facto relationship with another woman. Neither of these new relationships worked, and in the middle of 1987 Sally and Richard once again resumed living together.

The new pattern was a repeat of the old. The relationship became progressively more violent, and to friends Richard stated that he was considering killing Sally. The couple split again on 1 January 1988. On 4 January Sally went to the local police station, alleging assault and stating that Richard had indicated his plan to take her life. A restraining order on Richard was issued on 6 January.

That same day, Sally became fearful of Richard's mounting anger, and his capacity for violence, and approached a male friend and asked for protection. The friend agreed to stay with Sally at her house. That night, Richard broke into Sally's house, and bludgeoned both Sally and her friend to death. He then dragged her body out of the house, and disposed of it in a place which has still not been uncovered.   *(Case No. 2290–88)*

In this narrative there is again the theme of persistent physical assault prior to the final outburst. Unlike some of the previous accounts, the woman attempted to extricate herself from the danger posed by the relationship, seeking help both from the justice system in terms of the restraining order, and from a male friend. As is common, the separation itself served to escalate the violent anger of the male. Neither the restraining order, nor the help of a friend, served as a barrier to this determined and violent male. A similar pattern is found in the following case:

After enduring many years of humiliation and violence in the marriage, Dorothy (age 35, textile worker) finally separated from her husband Harold

(age 38) after police had been called to the marital home because of a
domestic dispute. At first she moved with her two children to a nearby
refuge, returning to the home after a few days in the hope that Harold had
cooled down. A court order was obtained restraining Harold from bothering
Dorothy, and because of the difficulties it was arranged that the turnover
point for Harold's access visits to the children would be the local police
station.

It was only a matter of days before Harold violated the court order, and as
a result he was arrested and spent eight days in gaol. The police then applied
for a more restrictive restraining order, and also cancelled his firearms
licence, and all of his firearms were seized after the order had been issued.

Dorothy continued to be fearful of her husband, and asked for and
received further assistance from the police. The police undertook initiatives
to gather evidence on Harold's threats, and spoke to him about the potential
consequences of his behaviour. Harold was persuaded to see a psychiatrist on
a voluntary basis, and began a course of treatment, including taking various
medications (mostly tranquillisers).

One evening, after consuming both a large dosage of drugs and a large
quantity of alcohol (his blood alcohol level was later measured at 0.23), he
broke into his wife's home. When the wife and the children arrived at the
house later, they were confronted by Harold, armed with a shotgun. They
attempted to evade him by running into a bedroom and slamming the door.
Harold shot through the door, wounding one of the children. He then broke
into the bedroom, and shot his wife, killing her instantly. Following this, he
went into the kitchen, reloaded the gun, and then killed himself.

(Case No. 4541–89)

In many ways, this might appear to be a textbook case of proper
management of a domestic dispute on the part of the justice system.
When called, the police did intervene. Arrangements were made to
remove the woman initially to a refuge. As a result of court orders, the
male was prohibited from having unauthorised contact with the family,
and his firearms were seized. He was persuaded, successfully, to begin a
course of psychiatric treatment. Still, the rage of the male was so
overwhelming that all of these protections were brushed aside in the
final burst of lethal violence. It is worth noting that early on in this case,
during one of the first of the police interventions, the male had told
police: 'If that bitch takes the kids, I shoot her and then myself, I don't
care if you lock me up, if it takes weeks or months or years, I get a gun
somehow and shoot her and then myself.'

It was clear afterwards how serious he was. Since the state employed
virtually all of its preventive powers in this account, what this makes
obvious is how vulnerable a woman can be to the calculated anger of a
determined male, and how ineffectual the protections offered by the
state can be. There were in these files at least six homicides in which at
some point the woman had obtained a restraining order of some kind
on the male, and this is probably an underestimate since this

information might not have been recorded in all cases. In all, 23 of the 58 show some contact with the legal system (police, court, solicitor) prior to the homicide.

At times, there arise human ambivalences that reduce the power of the courts to extend even what limited protection might be available:

> After many years of marriage Sally (age 41, process worker) arranged an amicable separation from her husband. Shortly after, she met Larry (age 45) and the two began a de facto relationship. This was not a successful relationship, and within six months Sally had taken out an interim intervention order to prevent Larry from 'contacting, harassing, molesting or assaulting' her, and he was further ordered to surrender all firearms. Within a week, Larry had persuaded Sally to let him return, and as a consequence the police had no choice but to allow the order to lapse.
>
> Larry began to feel personal pressures mounting as a result of financial pressures (he was unemployed) and the fact that he was facing court charges on other matters. In addition he was drinking heavily, and was suffering from alcoholic hepatitis. The arguments of the couple began to build in intensity. Finally, once again Sally told Larry to leave. Two days later, he broke into the house, shot and killed Sally with a .22 rifle, and then took his own life.
>
> *(Case No. 3468–89)*

These relationships are complicated. Women may find themselves caught in a crossfire of conflicting emotions, among them some residue of close attachment to the male, or perhaps economic and psychological dependence. Feeling the pull of such forces, they allow themselves to be swept back into the cycle of violence which in the above case proved lethal.

There are other instances where court events themselves provide a spark for masculine violence. In one case (4032–89), the husband broke into his wife's house (they had been separated for about a year and a half) and shot her in the early morning of the day on which family court proceedings had been scheduled. A similar response is found in the following narrative:

> Carol (age 28, antique-shop owner and prostitute) and Keith (age 41, unemployed) had lived for a number of years in a violent relationship (she had suffered black eyes, a broken nose, broken jaw, as well as multiple bruising). Carol had been running an antique business, but found it hard to support her two children and her unemployed husband. As the bills began to get out of control, Carol began working as a prostitute. With the passage of time, Keith became more withdrawn and obsessive. Carol found the strains of managing work as a prostitute with the other demands of her life difficult, and decided to give up the work as a prostitute (a decision which Keith resisted).
>
> Finally, Carol had enough of the difficulties in their married life and separated from Keith, filing for a divorce. A few days after, Keith came by

Carol's new residence to mind the children while she went to see her solicitor. When she returned, Carol showed Keith the Family Court documents relating to the divorce proceedings. Keith left the room to fetch a .22 rifle which he had brought with him earlier in the day, returned to the room and shot Carol three times, killing her instantly.   *(Case No. 5055–87)*

While emphatically not the cause of the death, in this narrative the issue of the court proceedings provided the spark which triggered the final violence. It was as if the documents themselves epitomised the act of separation, an act which was simply not to be tolerated by this male. There are other stories in which the court or justice system plays some background role in the violence:

After a number of years of marriage, Joan (age 34, factory worker) and Carl (age 39) separated and obtained a divorce. Carl retained custody of their child, with Joan having weekly access visits. Carl became concerned with Joan's behaviour during these access visits (his daughter had told him of seeing naked men, and of men sleeping with her mother during her visits). On five different occasions, Carl returned to the Family Court to attempt various modifications of the visitation rights, but was unsuccessful in all such attempts.

Despite the difficulties between them, Carl apparently still wanted Joan to return to him and to resume their married life. On one occasion, he took both the daughter and his ex-wife on a long holiday to Adelaide in an attempt to re-establish their relationship. This failed, and Carl was left with the impression that Joan had been using him financially and otherwise (she was born overseas, and their marriage had been the factor that had allowed her immigration into Australia).

Shortly after the Adelaide trip Joan visited Carl at his flat. According to his account of events, he offered her all the money he possessed ($10 000) if she would remove herself from his life. He stated that she laughed, saying 'Is that all you're going to give me?' Carl's anger flared, and he said that at this point he pushed her. Joan in turn used her long fingernails to scratch his throat and chest. The two fell to the floor, with Carl grabbing her about the neck. He continued to apply pressure to the neck, and Joan died of strangulation.

(Case No. 2856–89)

There were, from Carl's point of view, two possible options. He would have preferred his ex-wife to return to the marital home, and for them to resume married life. Failing that, he apparently would be content only if she were to be completely out of his life. The courts, it seems, would not grant him this second option, and Joan's behaviour closed off the first. From Carl's point of view, the inability of the Family Court to come to grips with what he defined as the unacceptable behaviour of Joan would be a major factor leading to this killing. In terms of both the law and the facts, of course, there would be little choice available to the court other than the one that it chose. And, when all is said and done,

the underlying issue was Carl's inability to cope with his wife's separation and divorce. It was not the Family Court that wrapped its fingers around Joan's throat.

A point demonstrated by this case, however, is that not all of these intimate homicides show the pattern of careful premeditation. There are instances where the anger does flare suddenly (although in most cases there is a well-established base of masculine resentment, if not prior violence). As in the case involving Carl, the violence can erupt suddenly when the female partner openly challenges the male, especially around issues of sexuality:

Alice N. (age 38, home duties) had been married to G.N. for twenty years. Their relationship had begun to crumble after the death of their 10-year-old daughter in a traffic accident in the previous year. Alice had become extremely frightened of her husband because he regularly beat and threatened her. As one neighbour said: 'Alice ... was frightened of G.N. She would tell me that he carried a gun and that he had pointed it at her and at the children. G.N. had often given Alice a belting ... earlier this year, G.N. gave Alice a belting in the driveway out the front of their house. He was kicking into her and she was lying in the driveway.'

Family had also become worried, including Alice's sister who explained 'when Alice would come to my place after these fights, she would be a nervous wreck ... I told her to leave him, but she was too scared of what he would do to her. He was a very jealous man and he had a very bad temper ... At one time, I recall Alice saying to me that she was frightened G.N. would kill her.'

Alice had approached police seeking help, but seemed indecisive when it became necessary for her to act in order to have the police take action. Things took a rapid turn for the worse.

G.N. became convinced that Alice was having an affair with one of his best friends (other family and the friend deny this). One morning Alice and G.N. had another argument. G.N. alleged to his son that when he had confronted Alice with the fact the affair had been going on for weeks, she replied to him 'For weeks? ... it's been going on for seven months!' G.N. stormed into his room, picked up his hand gun, came back and shot Alice as she sat on the couch in the loungeroom. G.N. then dashed over to the house of the friend whom he suspected of having the affair, and shot him as well. G.N. then fled, and some six days later turned himself in to a local police station in the company of his solicitor. Alice's wounds proved fatal, but the friend, although severely wounded, lived. (Case No. 3247–85)

It can be seen in this narrative that a challenge on sexual matters can provide a spark for the flaring of sudden violence. It must be added, however, that there was a solid base of hostile violence which had been constructed over time, and the presence of the hand gun, and the seeking out of the sexual rival, suggest that the argument had provided the pretext for actions which the offender had given prior

contemplation (although, to be sure, on the basis of the available evidence this cannot be considered a planned homicide). As well, there is in this case study an illustration of the indecisiveness in the woman that can be caused by a high level of violence, when there is fear that there might be an escalation of risk if a separation is threatened. The victim did attempt to reach out for help, both to family and to the police, which proved ineffectual apparently because of the profound level of tension and fear of potential consequences that any steps might provoke in the male.

In a similar case, a woman had separated for a few days from her de facto husband, and when confronted on the night that she informed him she wanted to terminate the relationship completely and announced that she had begun a sexual relationship with another man. The man flew into a rage and bludgeoned his partner to death (later committing suicide in a police cell). (Case No. 2985–88)

In another case, it was the husband's demand for sex and the refusal of the partner to comply (coupled with the fact that he felt he was losing control over her), which provoked the violence:

Mary T. (age 34, bank teller) had been married for some years to V. when the marriage began to cool for her. She began to move outward and establish a life outside the marital home, away from her husband and two children.

For the husband, this became difficult to bear when it involved Mary initiating a sexual relationship with another man. Mary finally approached a solicitor, instructing him to draw up the arrangements for a separation and divorce from V. This was a difficult period, and Mary's new lover later testified that Mary had told him there had been several heated arguments with V., and there had been instances of sexual assault.

Mary chose to stay in the marital home during this troubled time. On her birthday the lover sent flowers and a card to Mary, which provoked a major argument between husband and wife.

Later that night, according to V.'s testimony to the police, he attempted to make love to his wife. She refused to have anything to do with V. Angered, the husband persisted but Mary continued to resist. As his rage grew, V. began to use physical violence to force his wife to comply with his sexual demands. Mary began to scream, and V. put some clothing over her face to stop her from crying out. This resulted in her death through suffocation.

In an attempt to conceal what had happened, V. placed his wife's body in a car, poured petrol over her, and set the car alight. This clumsy attempt to disguise what had happened was penetrated by the police within a short time. When confronted, V. broke down, saying: 'I did it, I did it, I loved her so much, I loved her. I didn't mean it, I loved her.'   *(Case No. 3062–86)*

Some of these cases, then, fit a pattern of rage which boils over to the point where the homicide results. As in most such cases, however, a foundation of marital discord has been laid down, including previous

threats to separate on the part of the female, and prior violence on the part of the male.

It is also the case that the violence may spring from the desire of the woman to separate, regardless of whether the woman has become involved with a sexual rival:

> Tommy had been living with Jill and her three children for three years, but what had started as a good relationship had gone very sour. Tommy was a heavy drinker, and friends described him as drunk and a 'no hoper'. When Tommy would drink heavily (which he did often), it would lead to violent arguments with Jill, with friends commenting that this would result in Jill evidencing visible bruises and black eyes. As time passed, Tommy's violent behaviour increased and became more and more bizarre. On one occasion when Jill and the children were visiting at a friend's house, Tommy poured petrol around the outside of the house and threatened to burn the house down. On another occasion, he discovered that his teenage daughter was going out with a boyfriend, and he started slapping her around. When Jill intervened, he went outside, and started hitting the outside of the house with an axe, and would not stop until the police came and took him away. Some time after this episode, one night when Tommy came home drunk, Jill informed him that she was going to separate. His first response was to point to a short piece of rope and say that he was going to hang Jill and her children with it. Some time later, he went out into the shed, found a fishing knife, returned and stabbed Jill fatally.   *(Case No. 2191–89)*

Rather than jealousy, the issue in this case is sheer possessiveness. The threat of the separation, especially given the history of violence, was enough to push this male to the point where lethal violence resulted. The following is similar in the inability of the male to accept the fact of separation:

> Holly L. and R. had been going together for four years, but Holly had come to the conclusion that their relationship should be finished. R. had difficulty accepting this, and for a while Holly vacillated back and forth, but finally decided that it had to be terminated. R. took it badly, began drinking heavily, and commented to a woman friend that he planned to kill himself. He began to follow Holly around, and would plead with her to return. One night Holly and her friends were at a pub where R. was also present. One of Holly's woman friends went over to R. and asked him why he had been following Holly, and tried to tell him that the relationship was over. R. then approached Holly, and she, too, again told him that he had to accept that what they had was finished. Friends say that she was gentle in her language. He left the pub early in the evening: R. then went home and picked up his rifle. He returned to the pub, and waited some hours for Holly and her party to leave. When she came out, R. approached, and a scuffle broke out between him and one of Holly's woman friends who tried to intervene. He shoved her aside, and shot Holly at close range. Holly was killed instantly.
> *(Case No. 2959–87)*

For some men, then, it is sheer possessiveness that drives them, and faced with the loss of the partner their response is violence. The power of the male to control is demonstrated by the very act of destruction of his 'possession'.

Masculine depression and homicide followed by suicide

In several of the preceding accounts, the powerful motives of jealousy and loss of control resulted in the male taking his own life as well as that of his sexual partner. There is another pattern involving sexual relationships which evolves out of a theme of control mixed with exceptional depression. In these events, the male is going through some form of depressive crisis which is severe enough to lead him to consider suicide. These events revolve, then, around the decision of the male to take his own life, with the killing of the woman being a secondary consequence of this decision. These males are not primarily focused on the destruction of their partner, but reach the point of insisting, after they have concluded that their own lives must end, that their partner should be a part of this decision as well. In these files there were 15 such homicides, these making up 20 per cent of the cases where males killed their female sexual partner. A major differentiating characteristic of these cases is that the major focus is on the suicide of the male:

> One afternoon, the telephone operator of the Victorian Ambulance Service answered the telephone, and the following conversation ensued:
>
> A male voice, later identified as F.M. began: 'Ambulance, can you send an ambulance to (he gave his address in Carnegie, a Melbourne suburb)?'
> O: 'What's happened there?'
> F.M.: 'There's a couple of gunshot, gunshot, ... ah ... mmm, or people with gunshot wounds to be picked up.'
> O: 'And, who's got the shotgun?'
> F.M.: 'There's no shotgun.'
> O: 'But you just said there's been a couple of shotgun wounds.'
> F.M.: 'I said there's been gun shot wounds which is definitely small calibre.'
> O: 'But, who's ... who's ... who's got the gun?'
> F.M.: 'I've had the gun.'
> O: 'And, who have you shot?'
> F.M.: 'I've shot my wife, and I am about to shoot myself.'
> O: 'You are going to shoot yourself in Carnegie?'
> F.M.: 'That's correct, yes.'
> O: 'Right, can I talk you out of this?'
> F.M.: 'Well, I don't think it's possible ... It's a case of euthanasia and all ... as far as I'm concerned, it's double euthanasia, and, ah, I've made up my mind ... we've reached the end of the road.'
>
> By that time, a physician had come on to the line in an attempt to help the operator. They were not successful in their attempt to keep the telephone conversation going. By the time the ambulance arrived at the address, the

officers found both F.M. and his wife, Bonnie M. (age 47, pensioner) dead from gunshot wounds to the head.

The couple were both married for the second time, and had met in a psychiatric hospital in Shepparton where each had been undergoing psychiatric treatment. The husband had experienced exceptional depression in recent weeks. The wife had expressed the fear to neighbours that F.M. might take her life, since he threatened her previously with a rifle. One of the neighbours reported that she had said that F.M. 'was very depressed and she feared she would be killed and that F. would also kill himself.'

(Case No. 1499–86)

There is no jealous rage in this account, no threat of separation, in fact no anger or particular animosity toward the woman. While the woman expressed fear of the possible violence of her husband, that violence is of a fundamentally different quality to that in homicides provoked by jealousy or separation. In some of these cases, the depression appears to be brought on by various effects of the aging process which begin to accelerate upon retirement:

Helen H. (age 67, retired pensioner) had been married to F.H. for forty years when the husband retired from work. The period after the retirement had been difficult for the couple, with both being treated for serious medical and psychiatric problems. In the case of F.H., this included a history of deep psychological depression, such that for many days on end F.H. would spend virtually all day in bed, rising only for meals.

Helen was quite close to her son, whom she would generally call two or three times a day. She expressed to her son concerns for her safety, confiding to him that F.H. had attempted to strangle her on at least two occasions. She told him that F.H. 'did not want to live, and he wished that they could both go together'.

One afternoon the son received a call from his wife saying that she had just had a call from F.H. and that he 'was acting strangely'. The son immediately called his father, who tried to assure him that 'mum's all right, everything is all right'.

Still, the son found the tone and manner odd. He decided he had better go and have a look for himself. When he arrived at his parents' house, he found his mother dead from strangulation on the couch. Hearing water running in the bathroom, he went in where he found his father, also dead, had stabbed himself in the bath.   *(Case No. 859–85)*

In this narrative, the element of masculine control can be seen in the husband's view (not shared by the wife) that the couple should 'both go together'. There is some indication of the possibility of lethal violence, but the prior indications have a different quality to those originating in jealous rage. In some of the cases involving older couples, the impact of rapid breakdown in health contributes, and there are sometimes hints that the decision to end life is a joint one:

Molly H. and A.H. were both in their seventies, and retired pensioners. Two years previously, they had sold their family home (in which they had lived for thirty years) and bought into a property which they shared with their son and his wife.

Over time, Molly and A.H. became increasingly unhappy over the new arrangements. They were now several miles from their friends, and as their health started to fail it became increasingly difficult for them to maintain contact with friends. A.H. became convinced that his son had coerced him into buying the property, and that they were trying to force them out of the house, even though the couple owned a half interest in the property. In fact, the son was trying to set them up in their own self-contained unit on the property (which the couple refused), and had even offered to buy out their half interest so they could return to their former community (also refused).

The health of the two began to fail drastically. Molly had several operations on her abdomen, and had reached the point where she had to be assisted to get up from bed and to go to the toilet. A.H. had been diagnosed as having cancer of the prostate, and was beginning to suffer from severe bleeding of the bowels. Both were suffering from obvious signs of depression as well, but when advised by both friends and the son to consult a psychiatrist, A.H. replied that 'They can't do anything for us now ...'

On 11 May, the son and his wife went out for the evening, and then off for a couple of days to see other relatives. As they were leaving, the son reported that his mother clung to his wife, 'and thanked us for Mother's Day and for the present. Mum was upset and crying ... Dad just remained at the table and glanced at me ...'

Early the next morning a friend called the house, and A.H. answered. The friend reported that: 'He was terribly agitated, and kept saying "it's all my fault" over and over again. He stated that Molly couldn't come to the phone, and kept repeated that "he'll have to go", whereupon he then abruptly ended the call.' Their bodies were found when the son and his wife returned home the next day. The Coroner found that Molly had died from a gunshot wound inflicted by her husband, and that the husband had then died from the effects of a self-inflicted gunshot wound.   *(Case No. 1388–86)*

This pattern of physical deterioration and mutual agreement to end life was repeated in another account where the note left behind stated: 'My head hurts more and more. I am very sorry, but it's all too much' which was signed by the husband, with the words 'ditto' written in and signed by the wife. (Case No. 5141–87)

Couples confronting their final period together under conditions of physical deterioration may see few options open to them in terms of maintaining adequate care and dignity in their lives:

Nellie M. (age 74) and C.M. (age 75) had been married for fifty-three years. Nellie had suffered severe strokes and epilepsy, and was totally dependent on C.M. since she was incapable of leaving her bed (she was also virtually blind). If anything, C.M. was in worse medical condition, having previously had a cancerous larynx removed, and more recently two operations for lung cancer. C.M.'s increasing loss of weight and debilitation was making it more

and more difficult for him to manage the household chores. When neighbours called in to check on the couple early one June day, they found Nellie dead from a rifle wound to the head, and C.M. dead from self-inflicted gunshot wounds.   *(Case No. 2337–87)*

For these two who faced almost complete physical breakdown, the choice of homicide and suicide might be viewed as their way of maintaining some control over their lives. When couples are younger, the theme of depression can run through the homicide-suicide, with the source of that depression being the press of economic circumstances:

D.L. (age 42) had been a highly successful owner of a car dealership, but had been out of the business for several months. In late 1987 he purchased a new car dealership expecting to continue his pattern of success, only to run head-on into the consequences of the economic downturn. Instead of making money, the losses began to mount rapidly, and gradually built up to debts totalling hundreds of thousands of dollars. Friends noticed that he was deteriorating both mentally and physically. Arguments broke out between D.L. and his wife Joan (age 42, homemaker).

On 11 February, D.L. attempted to enter several hospitals, finally finding one which assessed him as having a major depressive illness. The hospital agreed to admit D.L. the following day when a bed became available. Instead, on 12 February, D.L. first shot and killed his wife, shot his mother-in-law (who survived) and then turned the gun on himself.   *(Case No. 669–88)*

When the male is younger in these depressive suicide/homicide cases, the provocation appears from these case studies to be found in economic breakdown as well as, or instead of, an erosion of physical health. In the following case there was a mix of economic and health factors which contributed to the ultimate decision of the husband to take both his wife's and his own life:

For many years I.K. (age 49) had been an ideal parent and husband. He was known to be a hard worker, and made a good living as an independent builder. Then, in early 1985 he underwent a dramatic change. He became moody and depressed, and began to go from doctor to doctor seeking medication and help. He began to take heavy doses of tranquillisers. He stopped work.

As money began to dry up, and economic stresses mount, arguments began to develop between I.K. and his wife Kathy K. (age 47, home duties). No violence between them was observed. As one daughter said: 'My father never hit or struck my mother, and I didn't think he was capable of doing anything like that. With a sound, rational mind, I don't think my father was capable of doing anything violent.'

Then one day, an argument with Kathy over money seemed to trigger I.K. Perhaps it was that during the argument Kathy had asked for her half of the money which she was entitled to as a result of a recent sale of a residence,

and she obviously intended to use the money to begin to function more independently of I.K.

The next morning, as one of the daughters was leaving the house for work, he called her back, gave her $50, and kissed her. This was so different from the normal pattern that the daughter recalled afterwards: 'It was on my mind that he might commit suicide.'

A friend called in later that day and found Kathy dead in the kitchen. She had been strangled with a bit of rope. A few minutes later I.K. was found, also dead, in a shed at the back of the house where he had hanged himself.

(Case No. 1144–86)

As is true in the other cases within this pattern, there is no indication of jealousy, nor any signs even of prior attempts at violence in connection with suicide. Trapped by the closing down of the economic dreams, this male saw no option but to commit suicide, but also to 'protect' his family from the fate that would befall them without his sources of support. There is one account in which physical injury, financial pressures, and cultural differences are woven together in the factors which produce the final tragedy:

T.P (age 34, factory worker) had arrived in Australia from Vietnam with her husband, V.P., some five years previously. Apparently their married years in Vietnam were stable and happy, as were the first four years in Australia, according to later testimony from the family. V.P. had sustained an injury at work which apparently brought about a significant change in his outlook and behaviour.

Lacking a job, under financial stress, V.P. began to worry about money and became noticeably depressed. To one of the family members, who thought it was a joke, he had said he might have to kill his wife.

It was the couple's two young children, the eldest being only 5, that can provide an account of the event leading up to the homicide. The child indicated that there had been some violence between the couple on earlier evenings: 'Daddy would hit mummy. Mummy would hit him back, then stop.' One night the daughter heard her father say: 'If I die, you'll die as well.' The mother replied that she did not wish to die. A struggle broke out on the couple's bed. T.P. attempted to fight V. off, but V. was too strong, and he was able to strangle his wife, using a chain.

The daughter, who observed these events, recalled that: 'Daddy told me to go back to bed, saying "your mother must die, your father must die. We cannot live." ' The father then went into the lounge room and managed to strangle himself using rubber bands.   *(Case No. 415–85)*

The common themes running through these accounts are masculine control coupled with depression. These cases require a careful reading to distinguish this particular pattern from other situations where males take their own lives after killing their sexual partner. There were, in fact, almost an equal number of males who killed their wives out of a sense of possessiveness or jealousy and then committed suicide, as there

were males who fitted this pattern of depression-homicide-suicide (14 compared to 15). The key element of the sub-pattern identified here is that a reading of the case narrative indicates that it is profound depression which has pushed these males to the point where they contemplate the step of committing suicide. Their primary goal is self-destruction. In a way analogous to that of jealous males, these husbands view their wives as possessions which should be carried along in this final journey. Their female partners are not to be left behind and alone. In contrast, most of the masculine killings of women in the context of sexual intimacy are primarily about the destruction of the women, then when that goal is accomplished some of the males (14 in all) took their own life.

Some other cases

While a high proportion of cases where men take the lives of women with whom they are sexually involved are characterised by themes of jealousy and manifest possessiveness, or perhaps of depression/suicide, it needs to be recognised that there are some cases which do not fit easily into either of these two moulds. In the broadest sense, these cases fit into a pattern where violence is a distinctively male form of control, or attempt to extend control, of the sexual partner. It needs to be recognised, however, that empirically the patterns are diverse. Indeed, Easteal (1993) was led to conclude, regarding patterns of spousal homicide that:

> The findings have confirmed that there is no one simple cause and effect formula to be found. On the contrary, not only do most of these cases appear to represent the climax of numerous factors intermingling but they also show that those factors vary somewhat depending upon gender, ethnicity, and age.
>
> (Easteal, 1993: 91)

While there is complexity in these narratives, at the core most demonstrate a willingness of males to employ violence as a way of controlling the life of the woman. There is, for example, the following case in which the male used homicide as the device for discarding a partner who was no longer wanted:

> The homicide of Rose M. (age 30, home duties) is unusual in many respects. For one, the death was a result of strychnine poisoning, the only poisoning homicide that is found in these files. Rose was found dead at her suburban Bayswater home, seated in a chair in the kitchen, after a call from her husband, Ken M. (age 33) had alerted a neighbour that something might be wrong since Rose was not answering her telephone. The attending police noted that there 'were no signs of violence. There are no suspicious circumstances ...'

So the matter stood for three months, until the toxicology report revealed that the cause of death was strychnine poisoning. The obvious suspect, Ken, denied any responsibility for the death. There are several signs that point to his being responsible. For one, he had in recent weeks established a close relationship with another woman which had been observed by many witnesses (and the woman, in fact, moved in with him after the death of the wife). Rose had complained to her friends that her husband had been noticeably cool towards her, and had cut off all sexual relations with her. Witnesses also established that Ken had said he would not pursue another divorce (Rose was his second wife), since his first divorce 'had cost him $94 000.'

There were, as well, several suspicious inconsistencies in his statements to the police. Finding no other person with motive or opportunity, and rejecting the notion of suicide, the police eventually charged the husband with the homicide of his wife.   (*Case No. 21–86*)

So, in this little house in Bayswater we encounter one of the few true mysteries in these files. One obvious factor which emerges from this is that the reality of criminal justice procedure is far removed from what one reads in mystery novels. It is difficult to trace the trail of a suspected homicide when it has taken three months to determine the key fact that the victim was, in fact, murdered. The case demonstrates, however, that jealousy or the threat of separation is not always the motivation which drives males to take the lives of their spouses. The case might be made, of course, that in the eyes of the husband his wife was a disposable possession, to be cast away when a new love entered his life. In such a scenario, the wife is still viewed as property, but property which can be cast off when so willed by the male, and thus the killing is an ultimate expression of control.

In another case, the issue was the attempt to exert sexual control. A young woman (age 18) had been friendly with a male co-worker. The male become progressively more eager to press his attention on the girl, who became increasingly concerned with his advances. One night he convinced her that he could give her a ride home. What happened at the point is not clear, since the male tells a story that the girl attacked him, which the police and courts chose not to believe. What seems most likely is that the male pressed his attentions too vigorously, the two fought, and somehow the male lost his head and stabbed the girl to death (Case No. 1041–85). While technically this is not a case where a relationship had been established, the two had known each other, the early moves toward a sexual relationship had been made, and it appears that it was the young woman's resistance to the male's sexual advances which resulted in her death.

What this does is to underscore again the fact that there are diverse threads running through this material, and there are many ways sexual

bonds can result in homicide. In another of these different cases, the victim was a child with whom the male had struck up a sexual relationship, and the homicide was a crude attempt on the part of the male to fend off the consequences of public disclosure of the relationship:

R.L. (age 46, unemployed) had not had great luck in his life. A police report described him as having: 'a long criminal history including offences relating to violence and dishonesty ... He appears to be a person of little education, with an alcohol abuse problem extending over a long period of time.' From 1983 to 1985 he served a term in prison.

Over recent years R.L. had formed a friendship with the C. family (both of the parents of the C. household had lengthy criminal histories themselves). Upon his release from prison, the attachment with the C.'s was close enough that for a period of time R.L. rented a bungalow located at the back of their residence.

Isolated from other kinds of contacts with women, R.L. over the months and years developed a close relationship with a daughter of the household, Tammy C. (age 12). This had developed into what the police in their subsequent report described as an 'unhealthy relationship', that is, the two became sexually involved.

This was a dangerous game to play because of its potential consequences, and perhaps to protect himself, R.L. moved away from the C. household. He continued to see the family, including Tammy, however.

The peril was increased when Tammy became pregnant, a fact which was discovered when she suffered a miscarriage. Tammy refused to reveal the identity of the father to her mother. She did, however, tell two of her young friends that R.L. was the father, and further, that he had threatened to kill her if she revealed that he had been involved with her sexually.

Apparently becoming apprehensive that the whole affair was coming unstuck, R.L. called Tammy while she was having her birthday party. He asked Tammy to come over later because he had an additional present. When Tammy arrived, he produced a shot gun and shot her once in the head, killing her instantly. R.L. then called Tammy's mother, and asked her to come over as well. Upon her arrival, he held the gun to her head, threatening to shoot her and the rest of the family as well. R.L. then attempted to choke Tammy's mother to death, but she was able to break away and alert the police.   (Case No. 1199–86)

This narrative not only indicates the diverse threads by which sexual intimacy can be tied to homicide, but as well the problems of developing adequate schemes of classification. In this account there is sexual intimacy which links the male with his female child victim, but also it could be seen as a form of homicide which is the outgrowth of another crime (in this case, the illegal sexual relationship with a child), or even a form of conflict resolution (involving the silencing of a witness), both of which shall be covered in later sections of this book. It is included within the present scenario because it was the sexual intimacy which provided the essential link between offender and victim, and became

the cause of the behaviour which followed. It also serves to emphasise the difficulties in presuming that only jealousy, the threat of separation, or even depression are the driving factors in masculine homicides arising out of such intimacy. Instead, this killing appears to constitute a last, desperate bid on the part of this socially incompetent male to control the young person and to prevent disclosure of the relationship which had come to pose a great threat to him.

A further illustration of the diversity of motives in settings of sexual intimacy is found in the following case:

A.B., a retired bank manager, and his wife Nancy B. (age 56, retired school teacher) were having difficulty adjusting to retirement. Previously, their lives had been busy, and by all accounts the marriage was a stable and comfortable one. The children report that to their knowledge, there were no instances of violence in the marriage.

With the retirement, however, the two seemed to get on each other's nerves. A.B. in particular, seemed especially edgy. To complicate matters, he had constructed an elaborate delusion that he had contracted AIDS as a result of an incident some four years previously involving one of the young women working at the bank. The woman expressed amazement when asked about this later, denying emphatically that there had been any sexual contact between them (there was an age differential between them of over forty years). She did note that at a bank outing there had been one occasion where there took place something which she took to be a 'sexual advance' on A.B.'s part, but it consisted of no more than 'him pushing his body against me'.

One afternoon, the married couple were driving back to their suburban home from Melbourne. A.B. became especially agitated. He had convinced himself that one of his daughters had discovered the secret of his AIDS, and that she was going to confront him when they arrived home. He felt he had to discuss the matter with Nancy before they returned to their home.

By the husband's account, he then stopped the car so they could 'have a talk'. The problem was that his wife didn't want to engage in any such discussion. A heated argument broke out. What happened then can be taken from the later transcript of the police interview:

Q: 'What made you upset?'

A.B.: 'It was a build-up of things during the day, and the fact that I thought there was going to be a confrontation with the family. I knew they weren't happy ... '

Q: 'When you say you got upset, do you mean emotionally or otherwise?'

A.B.: 'Yes, emotional ... always emotional. I suppose I was a bit wild, too. I possibly got upset with Nancy, and then it was the end of Nancy.'

Q: 'The end of Nancy?'

A.B.: 'Yes, you know, in all those years of marriage I'd never hurt Nancy.'

Q: 'And, did you strangle Nancy?'

A.B.: 'Yes, I could see myself losing her, you know ... '

Q: 'Well, do you recall actually grabbing Nancy around the neck?'

A.B.: 'I've thought about that quite a few times. I recall putting my hand over her mouth to stop her crying out.'

Q: 'Do you remember why she cried out?'

A.B.: 'Because I had my hand on her throat. I mean, I'm not a killer, I've never even killed a dog or a cat ... '
Q: 'Why did you kill Nancy?'
A.B.: 'I thought there was going to be a big discussion when we got home that night.'
Q: 'Did you go to that area with the view of strangling Nancy?'
A.B.: 'No, I was going to talk to her ... '
Q: 'Was there any premeditation on your part in Nancy's death?'
A.B.: 'No ... no ... but, normally she would listen to me ... but, she wouldn't listen ... she was saying no, no, no, we better not.'

After killing his wife, A.B. picked up a piece of glass and slashed himself on the throat and wrists. When after some time it became clear to him that this attempt at taking his life was unsuccessful, he then deliberately collided with another car. While unsuccessful in bringing about his death, A.B. was injured. During the course of treatment in the hospital, A.B. developed severe psychotic symptoms.   *(Case No. 3999–86)*

There is in this tale no consuming anger, fuelled by jealousy, nor profound depression pushing the male toward suicide. There are no warning symptoms in terms of any prior violence. There is agitation on the part of the male, there is an argument (over whether or not there should be a discussion), and it could be said that the woman has resisted the will of the male. It was, to be sure, the male who killed, and probably at the core was the resistance of the woman to allow the male to control the situation.

Some of these cases approach the bizarre. In one, the female victim and her husband first attended a party with friends, where the woman consumed a large quantity of both beer and wine. She became so drunk that she had to be helped to the car for the return home. After arriving at home, she consumed more wine (her blood alcohol level was established at autopsy to be 0.27). Apparently the woman and the man began to engage in sex, and the woman requested bondage. Her husband handcuffed her wrists, tied her feet with rope, then gagged her with pantyhose, then proceeded to engage in sexual intercourse, first administering several blows to her body. The woman died some time during the encounter. (Case No. 5261–87)

In another of these cases, the woman victim and her husband became involved in an argument (apparently provoked by the male's drinking) on their patio. Blows were struck, dishes and food thrown at each other, and then the two grappled, became entangled, and fell, with the heavier male falling on top of his wife. The woman died from injuries sustained from this fall (Case No. 5436–87). A further case involved a woman whose aggression and abuse had been a persistent problem to family and neighbours (the police had been called to the house because of her behaviour on a number of occasions) who

apparently was killed when she became involved in yet another abusive argument with her husband, when she placed a belt around her neck and taunted her husband to pull it tight. The two then fought, and the woman died from the injuries sustained. (Case No. 1034–89)

Some caution, then, is essential in terms of examining the scenarios of masculine violence when men kill when influenced by themes of sexual intimacy. While some scenarios predominate, notably those deriving either from jealousy/possessiveness or depression/suicide, there are some killings in situations of sexual intimacy where it is not easy to trace and categorise the male's motivation. These eight cases constitute the group of such cases, with most of the remaining fitting into patterns where the homicide arose out of classic themes of jealousy, possessiveness and control. Even in the few cases which differ from the general pattern, the violence is masculine, and the death is of a female sexual intimate, and to some degree the violence has been a mechanism for controlling the behaviour of the woman.

Masculine control/jealousy violence which reaches other victims

While the major and obvious target for violence generated by jealousy or control will be the female sexual partner, in some instances others in the scene become victims either as well as, or instead of, the woman. There were, in all, twelve cases where the violence of the male reached out to the sexual rival of the male, and represents one form of what Daly and Wilson (1988) refer to as 'killing the competition':

R.L. had been living with V.L. (age 46) for some twelve years. In recent months, R.L. had become progressively more violent toward V. so she decided to leave.

Eddie K. (age 56, pensioner) had been a close friend of both for a number of years, and V. decided to move in with him. V. was uncertain how to proceed, since she still felt some warmth toward R.L. In fact, one week after moving in with Eddie, V. returned to R.L., but, as she said later, 'it didn't work out' and she went back to Eddie.

After a few weeks, however, R.L. could take the state of affairs no longer. He wrote to V. stating that if she did not return he would do something 'he did not want to do.'

A few days later these words were translated into action. During the day one weekend, R.L. entered Eddie's house and punched him several times, finally being restrained by onlookers. R.L. left, but as he did so he screamed at Eddie: 'I will get you, I will kill you.'

At 6 pm that night R.L. returned with a shotgun, but was seen 'sneaking around the house'. The police were called, and when they couldn't find him around Eddie's house, they went to R.L.'s house. They questioned R.L. but he denied possessing a gun or being near the house. Meanwhile, Eddie filed assault charges against R.L. with the police.

Early the next morning R.L. surprised Eddie as he left the house, shooting him with the shotgun. Eddie ran into the house, pursued by R.L. who fired a second and fatal shot to the head. He also shot V., although she survived. Shortly after, R.L. committed suicide by driving his car into a tree.

(Case No. 4169–86)

As has often been true in these accounts, there were clear warnings of the lethal violence to come. Police were alerted that violence with a gun had been threatened, but the response proved ineffective in averting the use of that weapon in the homicide which followed. The themes of the case are similar to others involving jealousy. The woman, his possession, was not just slipping out from under his control, but even worse she was taking up with a new sexual partner. In this instance, the offender selects as the target for his jealous rage his sexual rival, and then takes his own life afterwards. The male did attempt to take the life of his woman partner, but the wounding did not prove fatal. In a comparable case previously discussed, a male took the lives of both his sexual partner and a male friend who had been sought out to help protect the woman. The female victim was worried, correctly, that the restraining order she had obtained from the police would not be sufficient to guard against further and more intense violence. (Case No. 2997–88)

The next of these cases displayed the same element of jealousy, but differs both in that the male offender showed no prior signs of violence either toward his estranged wife or towards her new lover who became his victim in the homicide, and further, he confined his violence to his sexual rival:

Debbie had been married to A.P. (age 39) for some seven years. She had previously been married, and the 12-year-old son from that marriage lived with the married couple (and had, in fact, been legally adopted by A.P.). While A.P. was from all accounts a quiet man with few friends and a limited social life, he enjoyed a close relationship with his adopted son.

After six years in which the marriage from all accounts went reasonably well, the relationship between Debbie and A.P. deteriorated. The two had begun to live separate lives, and Debbie initiated an affair with Bob F. (age 39) whom she had met at work. Shortly after, Debbie announced her intention of leaving the marital household to live with Bob. Since it was the Christmas season, Debbie agreed to put off her departure for a few weeks.

This period was a frustrating one for A.P. Debbie was spending most of her nights away with Bob, while A.P. would remain at home with the son. Responding to A.P.'s pleas for reconciliation, the couple went off for an island holiday, but the attempt failed and the couple returned to Melbourne.

Upon arrival, Debbie immediately telephoned Bob, then left to spend the night with him at his flat. Somehow, the next day A.P. was able to lure Bob to his house. He apparently first sat with him and had a drink or two (Bob's

blood alcohol level was found to be 0.016), and then came up behind him
and shot him once in the back.

The police found a note at the scene written by A.P. intended for his wife.
In it he claimed that Bob had destroyed all of their lives, and argued that it
was necessary for him to kill Bob in order to save his wife and son. In
particular, he stated that Bob would neglect the son and soon tire of Debbie.
A close friend of A.P.'s claimed that A.P. had told him that Bob 'was a con
man, shifty, and wouldn't look after [the son] properly and end up using
Debbie and dumping her'. He also commented on the jealousy, saying that
A.P. 'couldn't stand being at home while his wife was out with this other
person', and, ominously, that 'This guy will be fixed up.' A.P.'s car was found
abandoned on the Great Ocean Road but no trace of A.P. has been found. It
was presumed that A.P had committed suicide.   *(Case No. 3969–86)*

While the jealousy of this male is shared with many of the other male
killers reviewed here, what is different about this case is that the anger
is aimed exclusively at his sexual rival. Clearly, in playing the delaying
game wavering between the two households, the wife had underestimated enormously the capacity of her husband for violence.

Conclusion

The use of lethal violence arising out of sexual relationships, for whatever reason, is distinctly a masculine matter. Of the 102 homicides that
involved a sexual bond, only 16 involved women offenders. In a typical
year roughly one in five homicides will involve male offenders whose
victim is linked to them in one way or another by virtue of a sexual
bond. The overriding theme that runs through these killings is masculine control, where women become viewed as possessions of men, and
the violence reflects steps taken by males either to assert their domination over 'their' women, or to repel males who they feel are attempting to take control of their sexual partner.

Daly and Wilson have observed that in looking at many of these cases
it is important that the conception of the problem be wider than the
obvious sexual jealousy that is often found, observing that:

> a better label might be *male sexual proprietariness*. It is manifested in the
> dogged inclination of men to control the activities of women, and in the
> male perspective according to which sexual access and woman's reproductive
> capacity are *commodities* that men can 'own' and exchange. This proprietary
> point of view is furthermore inextricably bound up with the use or threat of
> violence in order to maintain sexual exclusivity and control.
>
> *(Daly and Wilson, 1988: 182)*

What has been found in the present scenarios, of course, is that there
are actually two dominant forms of sexual ownership. One is the form

that Daly and Wilson identify, where violence, and rage fuelling that violence, is aimed at generally younger women and is in response to the attempt of the male to control the reproductive capacities of the woman. These data are consistent with the pungent observations of Bean: 'Murder is the final irrevocable step, the ultimate expression of men's control over women. For some men, the need for control is not satisfied until this irrevocable step is taken.' (Bean, 1992: 43) In a common variant of this scenario of jealousy, the action shifts to encompass the male competition in the sexual triangle.

The second scenario is no less proprietary, since in many of the accounts where the homicide is part of the male suicide plan the woman is clearly seen as a possession, or commodity, which the man must dispose of prior to his own death. In these cases as well, the killing represents the ultimate control of the man over the woman (there were no cases where a depressed woman killed her male partner as part of her suicide plan).

Across these scenarios, the final act of violence in a large proportion of the case studies has not occurred as a result of a domestic argument which has spontaneously overheated (although this happened in some of the cases). Instead, in a majority of cases these reflect a calculated and planned homicide in which males exacted their final and terrible price of violence on the women they once loved, or on the males they deemed to be sexual rivals.

CHAPTER 4

Confrontational homicide

While it is generally well known that males typically account for over 80 per cent of homicide offenders (for example, Wolfgang, 1958; Voss and Hepburn, 1968; Wallace, 1986; Falk, 1990; Strang, 1992), it is less well known that at least half of all homicides involve incidents where males play the role of both victim and offender. Consistently, empirical studies such as that carried out in New South Wales by Wallace (1986) show that a slight majority of all homicides (53 per cent in Wallace's research) involve male offenders taking the lives of male victims.

Classifying these male-to-male homicides has always provided something of a problem. Whereas an overwhelming proportion of male offender-female victim homicides take place within some bond of intimacy, male-on-male homicides tend to be spread across a range of relational categories, including 'strangers', 'acquaintances', 'friends'. Rarely are they found in relationship bonds of family intimacy (an exception would be a stepfather killing his infant son). Put another way, the existing groupings of 'relationship to victim' in homicide research are unlikely to provide much in the way of insights regarding the social dynamics that have brought these actors to the point when a killing results where both victim and offender are male.

Since such killings account for over half of all homicides, it seems appropriate that we begin to seek ways of grouping such homicides that are both descriptive and theoretically helpful in accounting for the 'behavioural transactions' (to use Luckenbill's, 1977, term) that result in homicide. Our method, once again, is to read through the individual accounts of homicide in order to identify the dominant scenarios which describe this masculine violence.

58

What is immediately striking in the analysis of these accounts is the role of what seem to be spontaneous arguments between males in lethal encounters. In appearance, these are similar to what Wallace (1986: 155) described as 'interpersonal disputes':

> Interpersonal disputes formed the basis of the majority of killings outside the domestic sphere. A large number of these quarrels were unpremeditated events that erupted between strangers or acquaintances, usually while socializing in or around a club or hotel, or in the home of either victim or offender. The content of the disputes in these circumstances may be less important than the male context in which they occurred.*(Wallace, 1986: 155)*

Such disputes are comparable to some degree to what Wolfgang (1958: 191) classified as an 'altercation of relatively trivial origin, insult, curse, jostling, etc.', this category making up the largest in volume of the 'motives' of homicides in Philadelphia (accounting for 35 per cent of all killings). Observing the importance of 'altercations' in the general picture of homicide, Daly and Wilson comment on the kinds of typical homicides that are found in American statistics:

> Most of the victims were men, and almost all were killed by men. Most of the victims, like most of the offenders, were nobodies: unpropertied and unmarried, little educated, often unemployed. Most of the homicides were not committed in the course of robbery, but instead arose out of arguments or insults or rivalries. Most of the victims were acquainted with their killers. Only a handful were related to them.   *(Daly and Wilson, 1988: 124)*

It is the anatomy of these masculine disputes that will be the focus of the present chapter. There were, in all, 84 of these confrontational homicides (this scenario accounting for 22 per cent of all homicides). Daly and Wilson underscore the point that in these killings, the underlying issue is 'honour'. Yet, honour among these men often is triggered, if previous accounts are correct, by what may appear to the outsider to be the most 'trivial' of altercations. What is it that provokes males in these circumstances to the point where they kill? Understanding how these events, which often seem to proceed from what appear to be relatively minor starting points, but then flare into lethal violence, is fundamental to the development of any theoretical understanding of the nature of homicide. To seek that understanding, and to identify the basic interactional dynamics of such killings, we now return to our case studies.

Some case studies of confrontational homicide

In the first of these accounts, it can be seen how conflict can build spontaneously to the events which result in a killing:

Gabe W. (32, soldier) boarded a train at Flinders Street Station (the main city commuter railway station) after an evening of drinking with his friends (his blood alcohol level was subsequently established to be 0.224). When Gabe attempted to take a seat, Mike M. ordered him, 'offensively,' to move on to another seat. Challenged, Gabe refused, and attempted to force his way on to the seat. Mike leaped up and struck Gabe, and the two fought. Although Gabe received a number of blows, and was kneed in the face, he finally managed to pin Mike down.

Witnesses relate that at this point Gabe said: 'If you don't stop now, I'll break your neck.' Then, believing that Mike would stop, Gabe released him. Mike instead produced a knife, stabbing Gabe three times in the chest. One of the blows penetrated the heart. Gabe collapsed and died in the aisle.

(Case No. 4714–86)

In many respects, this is a classic form of confrontation. The violence evolved quickly between males who had never met previously. We cannot know what the initial non-verbal cues were that flowed between the protagonists. The two males, however, knew that this was a contest of honour. In essence, Mike was saying this is my space, and you challenge my claims at your peril. For Gabe, the public nature of the confrontation could not be ignored. The altercation took place in a definitively public arena in front of a social audience whose presence would have to be felt by the combatants. In this case, the whole set of events, from start to finish, occurred within a few minutes. As is characteristic of such skirmishes, the combatants did not anticipate at the onset that a death would result. Their intent as they entered into the exchange was to defend their honour by means of the fight.

In the next account similar features are found, except that the direct role of peers is more obvious in the confrontation:

Late one Saturday night, Anthony N. (age 19, unemployed) was walking back with friends towards their home after attending a local 'Octoberfest.' They had enjoyed a pleasant evening of drinking at that event (Anthony's blood alcohol level was later established at 0.08). In a small park, they met up with another group, including Don B. (age 18, unemployed) and Peter. T. (unbeknown to Anthony and his group, this second group had armed itself in advance with broken billiard cues and knives).

One of the young women in Anthony's group was part of the triggering of the confrontation between the two groups when she asked if she could ride Peter's bike. He replied: 'You can have a ride if I can ride you.' Insults and challenges began to flow back and forth between the two groups. At one point, Anthony is recorded as having said to Don: 'You're a bit young to be going to Octoberfest, aren't you?' Don responded with: 'Don't call me a kid.'

The exchanges escalated into pushing and shoving. Anthony said: 'If you want to have a go, I'll have a go back.' Don then threw a punch at Anthony, and the fight was on. At first it was a general group scuffle, and at one point Anthony broke a beer stein (obtained at Octoberfest) over the head of a member of Don's group.

The main group conflict began to simmer down, but Anthony and Don sought each other out and continued their personal dispute. At first Don was armed with the broken pool cue, but Anthony was able to take it off him. Peter then handed Don a knife. Witnesses agree that at this point, Anthony kept repeating to Don: 'I'll kill you, I'll kill you.' Don was able to come in close to Anthony, however, and slashed out with his knife, stabbing Anthony in the left thigh, right hand, and finally the left side of his chest. By now all eyes of the groups were on the two. They saw Anthony stagger, and he began to bleed profusely. The two groups broke off the fight, each going their separate ways.

One of Anthony's friends asked if he was feeling all right, to which he replied: 'I think I have been stabbed.' The friends helped him to a nearby house and called an ambulance, but Anthony died before medical help arrived. Don had no idea of the seriousness of the injuries he had caused, and was said by his friends to be 'shocked' when he was informed the next day of Anthony's death.   *(Case No. 3661–85)*

Here, again, the males were quick to take up violence in defence of their honour. In this account, one of the provoking comments ('You're a bit young') would fit into the pattern that Wolfgang (1958) termed 'trivial altercation', where the nature of the provocation would hardly warrant setting off a scuffle which would have lethal consequences. A fundamental characteristic of such confrontations is that initially the intent is to defend masculine honour by means first of words, then the fight. The killing is not a planned event, but flows out of the more spontaneously developing fight.

As before, it is a public setting (in this account a park), and in this case the friends of both of the principals play an important supportive role in the conflict (including providing the weapon at a crucial point in the encounter). Peers here provided more than a passive social backdrop to the encounter, as the combat widened to include what had initially been an audience. The intent at the onset was to fight, and even afterwards the parties, including the offender, were unaware of the extreme consequences of their conflict. As in the first instance, alcohol lurks in the background as a feature of such events.

In some incidents, the spark which provokes male aggression consists of actions toward women friends:

One weekend night, Tommy F. (age 29, unemployed) and his friend Charlie began their round of drinking, first at the Crab Cooker restaurant, then gravitated to the Bowling Green Hotel where they remained, drinking, for several hours. Another group came in much later in the evening, including Mike D. (age 26, assembly worker), Pete, and Rog, who was a boyfriend of Jennie (a waitress at the pub).

At closing time, as Tommy and Charlie were leaving, they passed Rog and Jennie in the hallway. In passing, Tommy made a comment to Jennie which Rog took to be an insult. An argument developed between Rog and Tommy

which led to a fight between them on the sidewalk outside. Tommy was punched to the ground, and the fight broke up with Tommy and Charlie withdrawing to their car which was parked nearby.

Shortly afterwards, Rog, Jennie, Mike and Pete came out of the hotel to head for home. Tommy and Charlie had waited for them, and the two once again approached and proceeded to confront and challenge Rog. When the other males joined in, Tommy pulled a knife and backed away to his car.

Mike and Pete gave chase to the car. Mike picked up a piece of timber, and began to hit the car repeatedly. Tommy suddenly leaped out of the car, and stabbed Mike with his knife. Badly hurt, Mike fell to the ground. Tommy kicked him several times in the head, then jumped back into the car and drove off. The knife had penetrated Mike's heart, and he was dead when the ambulance arrived (his blood alcohol level was 0.05).   *(Case No. 3264–86)*

In addition to the initial impetus being provided by an incident involving a woman friend of one of the males, this narrative shows how confused the roles may become, since when groups are involved the person killed may have been peripheral to the initial events which led to the fight. The fatal events involved, in other words, a member of the initial social audience who became swept up in the fight, from background to foreground of the action, and died as a consequence. The scene of the initial conflict is a pub. The combatants were previously unknown to each other.

All of the previous events occurred relatively quickly, proceeding from initial insult to the fatal wounding within a matter of minutes. In other cases, the time dimension is more extended:

Keith R. (age 27) and his close friend Stan J. had been drinking through the late evening hours of Friday and on into the early hours of Saturday morning. Somewhere along the way, they had managed to insult the sister of a bouncer in one of the clubs they attended, Gabby R. As the two friends, very drunk, were leaving their local football club at 5 am, Gabby decided to settle the score of the insult to his sister, and picked a fight with Stan.

Being a bouncer, Gabby was very fit, and Stan was drunk. In no time Stan was down and receiving a severe beating. Keith attempted to intervene to pull Gabby off his friend. At this point, Gabby's friend, and another bouncer, Sam B. turned on Keith. Witnesses say that he not only punched Keith, but after Keith was down he was kicked repeatedly and savagely in the lower back.

Keith seemed winded and shaken by the beating he had taken. He took a taxi home. A few hours later, his wife found him moaning with pain, and took him to the hospital. His condition worsened steadily over the three days he was in the hospital. Doctors decided finally to operate, and found that his kidney had been severely damaged by the beating he had received. After the operation, Keith's condition suddenly deteriorated, and he died some six hours afterward. Despite the evidence of a brutal beating, and testimony regarding the kicks by the bouncer, the Coroner found in this case that the killer was 'acting in self defence'.   *(Case No. 446–85)*

As in the previous accounts, there is in this narrative a mix of masculinity and alcohol. Unlike the previous cases, rather than moving rapidly from insult to fatal injury, the event was extended over several hours. The first altercation had taken place in a pub, then some hours afterwards the affair was concluded outside a football club.

The pub looms as a recurring locale for masculine violence. In a few instances, the fight, and killing, take place in the pub:

> Dennis (age 23, unemployed) and a group of three friends had been celebrating the birthday of one of the group when they stopped in the Doutta Galla pub at 9.30 in the evening. Fred (age 31) was there drinking alone. The initial provocation for a fight was the challenging eye contact between Fred and one of Dennis's friends. The friend said: 'I don't like this arsehole Turk [Fred was born in Turkey] ... he looks sleazy.' Fred then approached the friend and said: 'What are you staring at?' To which the friend replied: 'What are you on about?' Fred then claimed: 'You're staring at me', to which the friend replied 'Get out of here.' One of the other members of the group attempted to intervene at this point, and Fred told him: 'Fucking keep your head out of it.' In reply, the one who had attempted to intervene said: 'Well, fuckin' cop this', and punched Fred in the head.
>
> An all-out bar room brawl developed. Fred produced a knife, and slashed his attacker across the stomach, and followed this by stabbing his opponent of the staring contest in the leg. Dennis and his friends, and other patrons in the bar, armed themselves with billiard cues and surrounded Fred, who then sought shelter behind the bar. When Dennis reached over to pull him from behind the bar, Fred stabbed him in the chest. One of Dennis's friends, known in the pub as 'Dogsbody', pummelled Fred several times over the head with a cue. Fred twisted around and was able to stab his attacker twice in the body. Patrons then started shouting: 'Let's kill him, he's stabbed Dogsbody, let's kill him.' Fred attempted then to seek shelter in the pub office behind the bar, where the barman was counting the night's takings. Fred locked the door, and pleaded: 'Don't let them get me, they're going to kill me.' Several men kicked at the door until they were able to break it down. Fred then grabbed the barman, and held a knife to his throat, threatening to kill the barman if the group approached any closer. Someone yelled 'The Turkish cunt has got him', and the group started throwing bottles at Fred to make him release the barman. When the barman was able to break free, Fred was showered with an avalanche of bottles. The police entered at this point, and the fight subsided. Dennis was found, dead, on the floor (his blood alcohol was 0.309). Fred denied the stabbing, but acknowledged that he 'was running for my fuckin' life, I was, mate'. Fred's blood alcohol level was found later to be 0.047. *(Case No. 3631–87)*

In another illustration of the minor provocation that can set these events in motion, the initial invitation to fight in this account came in the form of the non-verbal 'eyeing off' between two males. In this case, the whole event takes place in the pub itself, rather than having the final confrontation spill out into the nearby streets. There is, as well, a

hint that ethnicity played some role in the conflict, as the aggressor in the precipitating events, and the eventual killer, was Turkish and epithets thrown referred to his origins.

It is probably more common for the lethal violence to occur outside the pub:

> Leonard (age 23, labourer) and John finished work and went to the nearby Shamrock and Thistle pub, arriving at 5.30 and drinking heavily through the evening (Leonard was later found to have a blood alcohol level of 0.227). In the course of the evening the two exchanged insults with a number of the bar patrons, and one of them later alleged that Leonard had made a sexual pass at his girlfriend.
>
> At one point, John went off to the toilet. Another patron came roaring out of the pub later, alleging that John 'was a poof, he put the hard word on me'. He then approached Leonard, and a fight broke out between Leonard and this patron, who broke a billiard cue in half and hit Leonard several times over the head with it. At about this point, Leonard and John were told: 'You don't even drink here, it's not your pub, get out.' The two were asked by the barman to leave, and they did.
>
> Another of the patrons alleged that at this point he went outside and found Leonard vandalising a car, including pulling off the radio aerial, which he used to strike the patron (although the police could find nothing to verify this part of the story). This patron then went inside and sought the help of a friend. The two of them then carried out a vicious assault on Leonard and John, first holding each and punching them until they fell to the ground, then kicking each of them alternately in the body. For good measure, they jumped up and down on Leonard several times. The two then went back inside to continue their drinking. Leonard died from the effects of a lacerated liver. *(Case No. 4795–87)*

This illustrates what is probably the more common scenario of a confrontation which begins in the pub or disco, with the final lethal violence occurring in the street immediately outside. In this case, the two were seen as outsiders to the others who were in their 'local'. Further, as has been seen in other of these accounts, a fight which begins by one person, may be finished off by somebody else.

A similar case of violence starting in the drinking establishment, and finishing in the streets is found in the following account where the confrontation began in a nightclub.

> Daniel (age 34, sales representative) went into a well-known King Street nightclub, and began drinking with a female friend (who was a member of the Victoria Police). The friend asked Daniel to hold on to some of her things for the night, including her police badge. Somewhat later, another patron, Les (age 23) was observed causing trouble for other patrons. Daniel went over to the bouncer, produced the police identification, stated he was a policeman, and asked that Les be thrown out because of the trouble he was causing. The bouncer, having no reason to doubt Daniel's legitimacy as a policeman, asked Les to leave.

When Les found out that a police officer was responsible for having him ejected, he became enraged. He was overheard to say: 'Are you going to let a cop tell you how to run fucking security? ... Bring him out, I'll punch the shit out of him.' He also stated: 'It's a cop who's been trying to con my girl.' Les nearly got into a fight with the bouncer, but was dissuaded from that. He then got into a taxi with four other people, and offered to pay $10 if he could use the cab and cruise around looking for Daniel. A short time later the search proved successful, and Les leaped out of the taxi, chasing after Daniel shouting: 'Keep running, you cunt! I'm going to bash your brains in.' When he caught up with Daniel, he began to 'pile drive' punch him, and then when Daniel fell to the ground, kicked him viciously, again and again, yelling: 'You bastard, you bastard, you don't do that.' Les then returned to the nightclub, where he was heard to say: 'That guy copped it, I knew I'd get him ...' Daniel died from the head wounds received during the kicking (his blood alcohol level at autopsy was found to be 0.178). *(Case No. 4024–88)*

While having many of the central elements of other confrontations, one of the unusual features of this account is that the victim was in occupational and lifestyle terms, clearly of middle-class background (this is one of the very few cases where either victim or offender are from middle or higher class social positions). It shows, again, how an initial dispute begins in a bar where the offence to masculine honour is laid down, with the actual violence taking place in the public space outside the drinking establishment. In this, and the following account, the potential of exceptional violence in these encounters is demonstrated:

On the night of Boxing Day, Martin O. (age 33, cleaner and maintenance worker) decided to go out for a few drinks with his sister and other family. They went first to the Bricklayers Hotel, and then after it closed, to Regines Disco. At about 2 am the rest of the group decided to head for home, but Martin decided to stay on 'for a while'.

Martin stayed until the disco closed at 4.30, and began to walk home. By this time, Martin had consumed a considerable quantity of alcohol (his blood alcohol level was found later to be 0.232). At the same time, Jamie T. and Paul B. also left the disco and headed up the same street. Martin and the other two exchanged insults and taunts. Then, Paul and Martin started to fight. Without warning, suddenly Jamie entered into the fight, giving Martin a savage kick which knocked him over. Jamie followed this with several more kicks to head and body while Martin was down. At one point, Jamie reached down and ripped open Martin's pockets and wallet, taking what money he could.

Paul alleges that he ran off at this point, since he felt that Jamie was out of control. As he was walking away, he saw Jamie pick up a large rock, and drop it several times on Martin's head. When police arrived on the scene a few minutes later, they found Martin dead of what the autopsy determined was traumatic brain damage resulting from massive fracturing of the skull.

(Case No. 4995–86)

From available records, it is hard to fathom what provoked the extreme viciousness of this attack. In this narrative a sub-theme of 'other crime' enters in, given the theft of the wallet. Since the events leading to the death appear to fit the general pattern of masculine conflict and confrontation, this has been considered here rather than Chapter 5. The theft here seemed to be an afterthought, rather than the major motivation on the part of the offenders. Unlike some of the previous accounts, it appears that while both victim and the offenders had been drinking in the pub, the precipitating events seemed to occur in the streets themselves. There was no evidence that the conflict in the streets was a continuation of some earlier dispute in the disco.

This pattern of confrontations taking place in the streets after leaving a pub is not uncommon:

> Alfredo (age 66, pensioner) was known to the police as one who occasionally would 'partake in alcohol' and as a result had developed what police records referred to as a 'minor police history'. On this summer's day, he had spent many hours in the local pubs of Northcote where he was well known (his blood alcohol was later established to be 0.164). He set off for home, first taking a tram to the bus terminus in Queens Parade to wait for the Hoddle Street bus. Apparently his foreignness (he was speaking at times in his native Italian) and his tipsy state annoyed a young man at the stop. The young man began an argument, which was broken up by others waiting at the stop. The bus arrived, and Alfredo and the young man both climbed aboard, with Alfredo taking a seat toward the front. As the bus was nearing his home, Alfredo got up and moved to the rear exit of the bus. At this point, the argument with the young man was renewed. When the bus came to a stop, the young man flung Alfredo backwards out of the bus, with the result that he hit his head on the curb, resulting in fatal head injuries.
>
> *(Case No. 433–88)*

As in the previous case, the whole of the confrontational events occurred after the victim had left the pub (and there is no indication that the offender had been drinking, although this cannot be stated with certainty since the young man was never identified). There is, as well, a mix of the ethnic conflict theme that has been seen in some of the previous cases.

At times, the violence in or around pubs involves bouncers:

> It was a long day of drinking for Paul (age 30, a construction labourer) who began early in the afternoon at the Morwell Hotel. He continued to drink there until 10, becoming along the way both drunk and abusive to other patrons. Around 10 pm Paul then shifted to a local club, and continued his earlier behaviour. After about an hour one of the waitresses complained to the manager about Paul's abusiveness. In turn, the manager asked Jim (known as 'The Gentle Giant') to keep an eye on Paul. Jim stated that he told Paul to 'Stop swearing or I will throw you out.' Jim had to speak to him two or

three more times, and finally told him that 'he had had enough to drink and he had better go home'. Jim then went into the kitchen for a cup of coffee, to allow Paul to cool off a bit and hopefully leave of his own accord, which he did.

The doorman, who knew Paul, reported that about 12.30 Paul 'walked past me and straight into a wall next to the entrance door to the hotel'. He heaved himself up, and weaved his way away from the hotel. Apparently still angry, Paul started kicking cars along the street. Jim was called out to the scene, along with another bouncer and the manager.

Paul apparently was convinced that someone had stolen his car (he had, in fact, come to the club in a taxi), and was yelling out things like: 'I'll kill the cunt who stole me car.' When the group from the club was unable to pacify Paul, or to convince him that he had left his car at home, the manager went back to his office to call the police.

Paul, however, continued to yell and kick cars. Jim again tried to calm Paul, but then Paul made the mistake of attempting to throw a punch at Jim. As a reflex, Jim stated, he countered with a left hand to Paul's jaw. Although it did not have great force, Paul's head snapped back, his knees buckled, and he fell backwards hitting his head with great force on the roadway. Paul died later in hospital as a result of traumatic brain damage.   (*Case No. 1458–87*)

Through account after account, the role of pubs and alcohol in confrontation is found. It is consistent with what has been observed elsewhere regarding the role of violence in and around licensed premises. (Homel and Tomsen, 1993: 61)

At times, in fact, the scenes are so clouded by the excessive intake that it isn't possible to trace with any accuracy what happened:

One Friday afternoon, Gary F. (age 43, labourer) collected his pay packet and set off for a night of drinking. People who knew him well said that Gary often drank a lot, but that generally drink made him quiet and friendly. That night, he spent most of the evening in the Railway Hotel. During the course of the evening, he met up with Calvin T. (age 26, railway labourer) and the two had several drinks together. They were, in fact, the last to leave the pub at closing time.

By then, both had consumed a large quantity of alcohol (Gary's blood alcohol was established later to be 0.296). They had walked only a short distance when an argument broke out between them (Calvin later was unable to remember what the dispute was about). The argument led to a fight. Calvin quickly was able to get the better of Gary, and when Gary was down, he was kicked and beaten ferociously about both head and body. Calvin finally stopped, then wandered off and continued his drinking, giving various accounts of the fight to people he met. He also was spending freely, and it was later suspected that it was Gary's money he was spending, since Gary's empty wallet was found beside him when police arrived to investigate.

An ambulance was called when a passer-by found Gary unconscious by the footpath, and Gary was taken to hospital where he died early next morning as a result of the beating he had received.   (*Case No. 1121–86*)

No amount of further investigation was able to penetrate the alcoholic confusion of these events to piece together what precisely had triggered the violence which resulted in Gary's death. It is not always possible to trace the fine details of these events if they end late at night, in deserted laneways, after a long night of drinking. What can be known is that the death resulted from a fight between two males, who before they set off from the pub had apparently been getting on well. Whatever set them off, it happened quickly.

There is through many of these accounts the persistent report of alcohol use by one or more parties involved. In fact, alcohol or drug use is reported in just under 90 per cent (76 of the 84) of the confrontational homicides. A similar finding of a high level of alcohol involvement in 'expressive' homicides involving 'confrontational competitions' in male-to-male violence was reported in Chicago by Block and Block (1992). There is, of course, a frequent link reported between violence and the use of alcohol (Gerson, 1978; Gibbs, 1986; Tomsen, Homel and Thommeny, 1991; Strang, 1992; Victorian Community Council Against Violence, 1992), although the nature of that connection is not easy to untangle. Obviously, there is some possibility that alcohol has a direct effect in terms of increasing aggression among some men (Boyatzis, 1974). Of greater relevance to the encounters observed here, however, is the nature of social settings in which large amounts of alcohol are consumed.

These scenes, including pubs, parties, barbecues (and the public venues available immediately afterwards, such as streets, public transport locales, parks, etc.) provide the open and leisure settings where working or lower-class males come together, most often for simple relaxation and recreation. Alcohol use tends to be a feature of such settings, obviously in pubs, but also at parties, barbecues and similar locations. But these are also contexts where males can 'eye each other off', where insults can be exchanged, where an audience provides an important social backdrop, increasing the importance of defending one's masculinity and honour (in a similar way Toch, 1969: 149–51, refers to the role of the 'chorus' in violent encounters). It is suggested here, then, that the major significance of drinking lies in what it tells us about the settings in which masculine contests of honour are initiated and sustained. Thus, while there may be some contribution of a physiological effect of alcohol on aggression, it could be hypothesised that at least of equal importance is the social context of leisure, where males flow in and out, which encourages and supports the taking up of violence in support of masculine honour.

Breaking from the scene to fetch a weapon

One feature which has been found in a few of these accounts is that one or another of the parties breaks off the immediate conflict, to bring a weapon into the scene:

Mick F. (age 36, unemployed) started his drinking at the house of a friend late in the afternoon, and then the two of them moved off to their local, the Victoria Hotel. They continued drinking 'shout for shout' for some time (Mick's blood alcohol was later found to be 0.147).

In the middle of the evening, the group was approached by Jimmy S. (age 53), another of the pub regulars. Jimmy, also feeling the effects of alcohol (some hours later, his blood alcohol was still found to be 0.197), upbraided Mick for some insulting comments he had made toward his 'missus' (observers commented that a trivial exchange had occurred between the two earlier in the day, or at least in their view the comments were trivial). There were mutual insults and challenges, and finally Mick hauled back and struck Jimmy, a short fight ensued, with Jimmy being rather badly beaten. Hurt as well as drunk, Jimmy needed help from bystanders to make his way out of the pub.

Mick and his group settled back to their drinking, when they were interrupted by Jimmy's de facto wife, who proceeded to abuse Mick for his beating of Jimmy. Then, Jimmy himself re-entered the bar. Without a word he walked up to Mick, pulled out a knife, and stabbed him once in the chest. As before, Jimmy was set upon, this time by the friends of Mick. Jimmy was assisted out of the pub by his de facto spouse. Help was summoned for Mick, but the knife had penetrated his heart and he died before he could reach hospital. *(Case No. 3778–85)*

This narrative pulls together many of the themes seen in earlier cases. The action takes place in a pub, the major protagonists had been drinking heavily, and the encounter takes on special meaning when the challenge to masculine honour takes places in front of peers. One difference is that there was a break in the action when the offender left the scene to search out the murder weapon. A further element that is somewhat different here is that the initial violence is taken up by the ultimate victim of that violence, this fitting the pattern which Wolfgang (1958) has termed 'victim precipitated' homicide.

In some accounts, the break to fetch a weapon is short when the weapon is close at hand:

It was a pleasant spring afternoon, and a group of mostly teenagers gathered at the home of Mel B. (age 17, unemployed) for a barbecue. By 5 pm the party had run out of beer, so Mel, as host, gathered up a couple of friends and they went to a local pub to replenish the supply of drink.

When they returned, Mel noted that Avery B. (age 17, unemployed) had consumed two cans of beer from the private stock of Mel's father. Mel had

explicitly instructed Avery not to touch that beer, and an argument developed. Witnesses stated that the two had been at each other earlier in the day, and on previous occasions as well. By then, both had consumed a fair quantity of alcohol (Avery's blood alcohol level was later found to be 0.133).

Fed up with Avery's attitude, Mel ordered Avery to '... get out'. Avery then punched Mel with a fist to the face, and the two began a minor scuffle which was broken up by friends.

The friends managed to calm the two down a bit, and Avery moved off a short distance, then again threw some taunts Mel's way. Mel went into the house, picked up a knife, and returned outside. Mel then lunged at Avery, stabbing him in the abdomen. Avery staggered a few steps, then collapsed. His friends took him by car to a nearby hospital, where he died a few hours later (from massive blood loss).

When approached in the evening by police, who indicated that they were trying to clarify the circumstances of the stabbing, Mel said (according to the police report): 'So what? I was stabbed once and the police didn't do anything about it.' When pressed further by the police who informed him that Avery was in a 'serious condition' (this was before the report came through that Avery had died), Mel became irate, repeating: 'The police didn't do anything when I got stabbed. I don't know why you are here now.'
(Case No. 3211–85)

In this case, the interruption of the confrontation was brief as the weapon was close at hand. This constitutes, as well, another of the accounts where the offender, after the termination of the encounter, remained quite unaware of the seriousness of his attack. When the weapon is a gun, the effects are more immediately apparent:

Jim M. (age 52) and Mrs S. had been neighbours for some years. In recent months, there had been several disputes between them over problems that took place when Mrs S. watered her garden. As she watered, apparently she would wet the side of the house of Jim. This angered him, and he finally started watering her house in retaliation. Mrs S. alleged that the two had heated exchanges over this, and that Jim had previously assaulted her over the matter (Jim denied the allegation).

On the evening of the Melbourne Cup, Mrs S. was working in her yard when Jim returned home after several hours of drinking in a few local pubs. Mrs S. stated that as he turned up his walkway, he kicked at the fence between their properties, and then spat at her. An argument between them ensued, as it heated up Jim leaped over the fence and assaulted her.

Hearing the argument, her male friend, Paul T. (age 59) came out of the house to come to her defence, holding a small axe in his hand. The two males scuffled, with Jim wrestling Paul to the ground. Mrs S. then came into the fray, hitting Jim over the head with rocks and the axe. This brought the fight to an end, with Jim subsequently returning to his own house.

He reappeared moments later with a shotgun, and fired a shot which severely wounded Paul. Jim went back into his house, but as Mrs S. was summoning the police, he came out of his house again and fired yet another shot into Paul. The second shot was fatal. Afterwards, Jim claimed that he was affected by alcohol to such an extent that he recalls little of what happened.

While Jim's blood alcohol level could not be established, Paul, the victim, was found to have a blood alcohol level of 0.16. *(Case No. 3459–85)*

Again the weapon was close at hand, although this offender was unlikely to decamp the scene unaware of the severity of the injuries. In another case, what started out as a fight at a party became, in a similar fashion, a homicide when the male who was defeated in front of an audience broke out of the scene to go to his home to fetch a gun, and then return to use the gun to restore his honour:

It was the beginning of summer, and George W. had an 18th birthday party at the back of his parents' home in a bush area of country Victoria. There were about fifteen to twenty young people in attendance, mostly drinking, talking and doing a bit of dancing.

Late in the evening a fight broke out between Billy E. (age 17) and Darren L., apparently over Darren's advance to a girlfriend of Billy's. The two had gone off into the bush for their fight. Richard B. (age 23) waded in and stopped the fight. In the process, he and Billy first exchanged heated words, then Richard punched him a couple of times to make sure the fight stopped. Despite feeling the effects of alcohol (Richard's blood alcohol was later determined to be 0.12), Richard had no trouble getting the best of Billy.

Billy was humiliated and angry, and left the party. Richard returned to the party, saying that: 'Billy reckons he's gonna shoot me ... he's gone home to get a gun.' It was established later that the two had a feud which had lasted for over two months, that started when Richard had also broken up a fight, punching up Billy in the process. The two had argued several times since.

A few minutes later Billy returned with a shotgun, hollering: 'Dinger, where are you?' When Richard walked out of the group towards Billy, Billy fired, killing Richard instantly with a shot to the head. Billy then turned the gun on himself. *(Case No. 4476–86)*

While it is not unusual for a weapon to be brought back into the scene, in these confrontational homicides in this Australian setting there are only a handful of cases where the weapon is a gun, and in none of these confrontational cases is there an instance where the weapon is a hand gun (in contrast to these kinds of altercations in the United States, as described in the case studies assembled by Lundsgaarde, 1977). This previous case is distinctive further in that it is the only case of confrontational homicide where the offender kills himself after killing his victim.

The male who has brought the gun into the scene may, of course, have that weapon taken from him, and he can become a victim of the violence which he has precipitated:

Gregor B. (age 24, machine operator) and his friend Ned set out one evening for a pub crawl. After many drinks, and while they were at their third hotel, Gregor went to the toilet. When coming out of the toilet, Gregor

became involved in an argument with a woman who, like him, had had too much to drink (Gregor's blood alcohol level was found later to be 0.120). The nephew of the woman, Albert S. (age 18), intervened, shoving Gregor away. The two pushed at each other, arguing heatedly. The pub bouncer came over, and ordered Gregor to leave the pub.

When Ned came out, he found Gregor waiting in his car. Gregor was furious, explaining that he had been bashed up and 'called a "wog" ' (Gregor was a recent migrant from Yugoslavia, and 'wog' is a general epithet applied to persons perceived to be ethnically different). Gregor then asked to be driven home so he could fetch his shotgun and bring it back in order to force his attackers to apologise. They went to Gregor's house to pick up the weapon. Gregor's wife pleaded with him to either stay home, or leave the gun behind, but he replied that this was 'something he simply had to do'.

Gregor and Ned returned to the pub just on closing time. As Albert and his group came out, Gregor threatened them with the shotgun, insisting that they all line up along the wall. They all stood quietly until Gregor turned to say a word to Ned, who was still in his car. At that moment Albert rushed Gregor, knocking him down and taking control of the gun. Three of Albert's friends began to beat and kick Gregor. Albert ordered Ned out of the car, and when Ned refused, smashed one of the car windows. Ned sped off. Albert then added his bit to the beating of Gregor, hitting him with the butt of the shotgun. He then pointed the gun at Gregor, and fired a shot which hit him in the neck, killing him instantly.

When apprehended a few minutes later, Albert said: 'He was going to shoot me ... I acted in self-defence. I know I acted rashly. Is the bloke all right, the bloke I shot? ... I wanted to shoot the tyres out ... When I first got the gun, I tried to shoot it in the air but it wouldn't go off ... I thought he wouldn't be hit ...' Circumstances suggest that Albert may not have intended to shoot when he did. Forensic tests revealed that the gun had a sensitive trigger. Further, Albert very nearly shot his own friends as well, one of them, in fact, receiving a burn mark on his jeans because he was close to the line of fire when Gregor was shot.   *(Case No. 2069–86)*

There is much here that fits the general pattern of this form of masculine violence. Gregor's sense of honour was offended by the argument (which started in a pub), the insult of being called a 'wog', and then by being thrown out of the pub. The fetching of the weapon in this case was explicitly about restoring Gregor's wounded masculinity since he at the time stated that it was his intent to use the gun to force his attackers to 'apologise'.

Race and ethnicity as elements of masculine conflict

Given the multicultural makeup of Victoria, with its large communities of migrants from Italy, Greece, Turkey, Lebanon, Serbia, Croatia, Vietnam and Southeast Asia (among others), it is not surprising that racial and ethnic identities provide dimensions along which masculine conflict can emerge, as in the previous case and some of the others

reviewed previously. There are several narratives of homicide in which the thread of racism winds through the encounter:

V. (age 27, unemployed) was originally from Vietnam but had lived in Melbourne for some time. He was planning to move to Queensland in a few days to accept a job offer. A group of his friends (all Vietnamese) decided to throw a party in his honour.

The group went along Racecourse Road to the local shops and pub to obtain the supplies for the party. While part of the group went into the Palace Hotel to buy beer, V. and a friend went across the road to buy some pizza. As they crossed the road, a battered green sedan pulled up with what the Vietnamese could only describe as 'western' males inside. These men alighted from their car and started verbally to abuse the two Vietnamese, following this with threats to use a chopping knife that one of the group produced. V. remained alone briefly while his friend went to summon help from their friends in the pub.

At the same time as the group of Vietnamese arrived on the scene, a further group of 'western' males poured out of the pub. A general melee developed, in which the Vietnamese group apparently threw beer bottles at their attackers in an attempt to defend themselves. Surrounded now by the original group augmented by those that had come from the pub, the outnumbered Vietnamese broke ranks and began to run to the safety of their flats further along Racecourse Road.

The green car followed in pursuit, grabbing and beating whatever stragglers they could reach. One of these was V., who was viciously beaten, including receiving a severe blow to his head. Found shortly later unconscious in the street, V. was taken to Royal Melbourne Hospital where he died three days later of brain damage from the head injuries.   *(Case No. 666–85)*

As is true of other confrontational homicides, there does not appear to be any element of planning in this homicide. One group was walking along the street, the other driving by in a car when the car stopped and words were exchanged the pressure built quickly to its lethal outcome. What is central in this account is that it was the simmering ethnic tensions which provided the focal point of the conflict. As well, this is another instance of how the audience of males can become thrust directly into the scene as participants in the violence.

In a similar case of group conflict between 'Old Australians' and Vietnamese, the victim in the end is in the 'Old Australian' group:

The dispute broke out between a group of 'Old Australian' and Vietnamese youths on St Kilda beach, just behind Luna Park. It had started, according to observers, when Donnie (age 16) and his friend Sam were walking up and down the beach 'looking for a fight'. They approached one young person and said: 'You fucking fat shit … do you want a fight?' The two apparently moved on after this boy backed off saying he didn't want to fight. Donnie and Sam as they moved away from the one encounter, found themselves amongst a crowd of Vietnamese young people.

In the jostling, the conflict shifted to the Vietnamese. Taunted, one of the Vietnamese boys kicked Sam 'in the guts'. The two Anglo boys drew out their knives and threatened the Vietnamese youths. This initial confrontation was broken by the girls in the Vietnamese group, and the two clusters separated. The Vietnamese group moved off some distance, while the Anglo boys stood around, playing with their knives, and showing off. One of the smaller Vietnamese lads walked over and offered his hand, trying to smooth things over. The Anglo boys responded by telling him to 'piss off', saying 'we'll keep on fighting'.

The Vietnamese group decided to leave. The boys went to the nearby changing rooms. Donnie moved up and challenged the Vietnamese youth who had kicked his friend, again pulling out his knife. The Vietnamese boy pulled out an even bigger knife. At this point, apparently, Donnie put his knife down with the intent of engaging in a fist fight to even things up. As he was doing so, Tan V. (age 14) slipped up from behind and stabbed Donnie once with his knife, then quickly dashed away. Donnie collapsed and died before medical help could be summoned.   *(Case No. 4189–86)*

This case had many elements that some would identify with 'pub violence', yet it took place in a public park area. In both this and the previous case, the initial provocation centres around racism of 'Old Australians' aimed at the recently arrived Vietnamese. Both involved conflict between loosely formed groups. Donnie's death, of course, provides another illustration of victim-precipitated homicide.

At times, the conflict which occurs takes place between two ethnic identities, as in the following narrative of a fight between Chinese and Vietnamese youths:

As was his usual custom, Edgar L. (age 19) left his suburban home to go into the China Town section of the city in order to take Kung Fu lessons. He met his friend Keith L. in Little Bourke Street, where they played some of the machines in the 'Tunza Fun' amusement parlour for a few minutes, then went off to their Kung Fu lessons.

Their class finished at 2.30 pm, and the two first had coffee with friends, then returned to the Tunza Fun at about 3.30, and started playing the Kung Fu Master machine which was their particular favourite. Suddenly, six Vietnamese youths approached and started to strike both Edgar and his friend. Edward then turned and challenged the group, saying (according to one witness): 'Come on, I'll do ya.' One of the Vietnamese groups came in close, produced a knife, and stabbed Edgar once in the chest. The Vietnamese group then quickly slipped away. Edgar staggered outside, and collapsed on the sidewalk, where he died a few minutes later (the knife had penetrated his heart).

The police investigation was able to pull together only scanty details of this homicide. They were unable to identify or locate any of the six Vietnamese young people involved. One of Edgar's friends recalled seeing the Vietnamese group sitting outside a Little Bourke Street restaurant earlier in the afternoon, and commented that this group had previously caused trouble for Chinese young people in the street. Further, there was some provocation on

Edgar's part, since earlier he and his friends had been yelling out anti-Vietnamese insults in Chinese as they had been walking down the street on their way back from their lessons.   *(Case No. 1047–85)*

In this narrative a distinction can be drawn between the victim providing some provocation for violence, and the more specific term of victim precipitation of violence. Edgar at no point challenged his attackers with deadly violence, but on the other hand his earlier behaviour served as the catalyst for the aggressive behaviour of his attackers. Ethnic differences, again, provide the source of the friction. The main setting where the acts of this homicide were played out were the city streets, with the final stages taking place in the amusement parlour.

Groups, gangs and violence

Several of the previous encounters involve groups of males which come close in appearance to what some might refer to as 'gangs', as in the following homicide:

The feud between a group of young men predominantly of Italian origin (but including some Greek and 'Old Australian' members) and a group of 'Skips' (Old Australians—from 'Skippy the Kangaroo') had been going on in Werribee (an outer Melbourne suburb) for some time. Months before, a group of Skips had crashed a party at the local Italian Social Club, insulting and taunting various young males in attendance until a fight broke out. One of the ringleaders of the Skips on this occasion immediately left town to search for work. When he returned months later, as far as he was concerned he was ready to pick up where he had left off.

Soon afterwards, there was another encounter between the two groups outside a local convenience store. In the confrontation, mostly verbal, one of the Skips produced a gun, and threatened the other group with it. This incident was reported to the police by the Non-Skips, but no action was taken.

The night after, the migrant group decided to take steps to settle the matter once and for all. Word went out, and a large group of them gathered together (about twenty in all), and set off for a local school hall where they knew the Skips would be gathered.

At the hall, when the Skips saw the large group outside, they became apprehensive since they numbered a bare half dozen. They quickly locked all the doors, but one of the migrant group managed to sneak in through an open toilet window. He threw open the door, the large group poured in, and a general brawl broke out.

At first, it went very badly for the small group of Skips. Suddenly, however, one of the band leaped into the brawl holding a rifle. He managed to fire several shots. Unarmed and unprepared for an attack with a gun, the invading group quickly melted away. The shots were not warning shots (witnesses commented later that the gunman had struck a Rambo-like pose as he fired). One of the attacking group (Barry S., age 19, bouncer) was struck in the heart and died before he could reach hospital. One other was badly wounded, but survived his injuries.   *(Case No. 3641-86)*

This has many common features with earlier accounts, but differs in the important respect that there were two groups involved whose conflict extended over time. The initial events, as best as these can be traced back to the confrontation in the Italian Social Club, involved some combination of masculinity and racism, a combination which took on lethal overtones in the final encounter.

There are examples of recognisable lifestyles that differentiate between groups of young people which then may provide the grounds for collective conflict, as in the following narrative:

> Colin (age 17) was a member of a loosely organised group known as 'Bogans', while Charles (age 19) was identified as a 'Headbanger'. Both were at a disco in a local tennis centre when a group of the Bogan males became involved in an argument with a group of girls who were hanging out with the Headbangers. After a brief exchange of taunts and insults, one of the girls punched Colin, who retaliated with a punch in return. Charles came over and attempted to pull the girl away. Colin called Charles a coward and a wimp, and began to throw punches at Charles. At this point, a general fight began between the two groups, involving ten to twelve people. Charles then pulled out a knife, and stabbed Colin several times in the chest and abdomen. Colin died shortly after (his blood alcohol level was found to be 0.079). *(Case No. 1931–87)*

In this narrative, the disco provides an open, public setting in which groups of males circulate, thereby opening up the possibility of conflict. Both groups involved are distinctively working-class, but set off from each other rather clearly in terms of such behaviour as clothing and hair styles. One issue seen in these events was the active role played by the female Headbanger, since it was her punching of the Bogan male that initiated the physical violence.

Given the group nature of the conflict found in these last accounts, a natural question which follows concerns the extent to which these findings indicate the presence of gang behaviour in Victoria. Assessing whether there is a 'gang problem' requires some clarity and agreement regarding the use of the term 'gang'. There is nothing new, obviously, about collective forms of trouble in Australia. Newspapers in Melbourne and Sydney complained of the 'larrikin' problem over a century ago, and somewhat before that there was the 'Kelly gang'.

In the United States, however, gangs and gang violence tend to be given a more specific meaning. One concise definition offered in the United States was:

> A youth gang is a self-formed association of peers, bound together by mutual interests, with identifiable leadership, well-developed lines of authority, and other organisational features, who act in concert to achieve a specific

purpose or purposes which generally include the conduct of illegal activity and control over a particular territory, facility, or type of enterprise.

(Miller, 1980: 121)

While other writers have disagreed about the particulars of this definition (for example, see Spergel, 1984: 201; or Sanchez-Jankowski, 1991: 28–9), it would seem that in the American scene the term 'gang' is likely to refer to a group that has a relatively high degree of organisation, with an explicit leadership structure, a defined territory which is part of the gang identity, and clear colours or other insignia which set them apart. Using these rough guidelines, it would appear that such formalised gangs are rarely encountered in Australian communities.

There are instances, as seen above, of collective violence among young males. What seems characteristic of the violence in Australia is that much of the conflict between groups seems to result from what can be seen as the 'social friction' that occurs as groups flow past each other in public space. When conflict between two groups took place which led to a homicide, it often happened outside the neighbourhood of both groups.

Walmsley (1986) has observed a similar form of group movement, friction, and confrontations over honour in the UK, which took place in a 'troublespot' in Newcastle in a small area where there were twelve pubs:

Groups of young people moved from pub to pub during the evening and this led, towards closing time, to friction between groups suddenly arriving at a pub ... Such situations produce violent incidents whether inside or outside the pub. Again violence sometimes occurs when large numbers of people leave rival establishments (eg. dance halls) at about the same time.

(Walmsley, 1986: 17–18)

This writer went on to describe violent incidents which had taken place late at night at burger stalls, where it was observed that: 'In each case "individual worth and identity were at stake, in front of other bystanders, in an impersonal setting". Provocative remarks were made, or something was seen by one party as provocative and the incidents escalated into violence.' (Walmsley, 1986: 18)

Such accounts are virtually identical with those described in the present case studies. It should be noted that the friction which occurs in the social space is probably highly concentrated in terms of the times when violence is likely to result. The space is often occupied in the daylight and early evening hours by groups of other conventional citizens, whose separate claims to the social character of the setting are likely to exert a dampening effect on violence. One is likely to fight in

front of an audience of masculine 'mates', and is inclined in other directions if in the audience is mixed aunties, younger sisters, grandfathers, or strangers occupying disparate age and gender roles.

What this also suggests is a different relationship involving space, violence and young males in Australia than in the United States. In the US it has been suggested that territoriality is one of the 'most important defining characteristics' of street gang behaviour, and this in turn is reflected in the way homicides are clustered in space (Block, 1993). In Australia, as perhaps is true in the UK as well, given the observations of Walmsley (1986), it is to be expected that there will be a much wider spread of the violence, although it must be emphasised again that when these group conflicts occur in Australia they are likely to occur in distinctly public settings.

Where group identities exist in Victoria (at least in the period being studied), such as 'Bogans', 'Headbangers', 'Wogs', or 'Skips', these are loosely defined and derive more from general and widely spread lifestyles, rather than membership in territorially based gangs. As indicated in the accounts above, group identities can nourish collective violence in Victoria, as seen in the pub encounter between the Bogans and Headbangers, or in the street clash between the Chinese and Vietnamese groups also previsouly described. The nature of that collective violence, however, seems tied more to issues having to do with the uses of public spaces, rather than to protection of home territory. As groups move through such public scenes as pubs, parties, streets, parks, or similar spaces, the frictional contact may result in contests of honour between males. The conflict, as can be seen in the case studies, may involve individuals or perhaps even groups. Without question, the collectivity of males is a central feature of the conflict, with group members on both sides providing both participants and social audience for the contest as it emerges and erupts into violence. In this, it is suspected that there is much in common with a large proportion of male violence in the United States, including homicides which become identified as 'gang violence' in American cities.

At the same time, while there is group violence, what is not present in the current Australian scene are formally organised and structured gangs. These Australian groups do not have a formal leadership structure, they do not wear insignia which sets them apart from other gangs, and there is not a clear identification with, and protection of, their local territory. Homicide in Australia can be seen to be an occasional consequence of group activity, but not as a feature of the ritualised and formalised gang conflict found in the larger cities of the United States.

Confrontational violence with innocent victims

In most confrontational events, the ultimate victim will be a major actor either in the initial dispute itself, or the social audience that provides the setting for the conflict. In some situations which are clearly confrontational in their character, the victim is a bystander whom ill fate casts in the role of participant in the events:

Elton C. (age 28, builder) had been drinking heavily for some time at the Bayswater Hotel. He was buying for himself and others a drink that consisted of a mixture of vodka, bourbon and tequila. After of a few of these, Elton became increasingly argumentative and difficult to control. Finally, after making unsolicited and unwelcome advances to a group of women in the pub, Elton was ejected by the bouncer. Elton was furious. He climbed into the van he used in his building business, and decided to use the vehicle as his instrument to 'get even'. He drove the van at high speed around the parking lot, weaving in and out, menacing pub customers as they left the hotel. One of the bystanders was Bob T. (age 29). Elton sped his van towards Bob at a high rate of speed, then swerved away at the last minute. The rapid swerving caused a ladder and some copper tubing attached to the roof of the van to shake loose, and Bob T. was struck with great force in the neck and chest by the copper tubing. The tubing caused deep cuts, causing rapid blood loss, which proved fatal.

Being quite unaware of the serious consequences of his earlier behaviour, after having first left the hotel, Elton returned a few minutes later to have another go at pub patrons in the parking lot, and he consequently was arrested by police who by then were at the scene. Elton's blood alcohol level was established to be 0.245, while that of his victim was found to be 0.211.

(Case No. 662–85)

The precipitating events for this homicide are to be found in what happened in the pub, the confrontation between Elton and the bouncers, and then Elton's reaction to the humiliation of being ejected. Elton's car then becomes the weapon of revenge, and Bob became the unfortunate victim of Elton's sense of being wronged.

This use of a car as a weapon is found in the following case as well:

It was early on New Year's morning, and two groups of teenagers were doing 'wheelies' and otherwise causing trouble with their cars in a car park near the Barwon River. Three men approached the cars, and 'told off' the teenagers, who allege that in addition the men had damaged their cars by breaking off their external mirrors. The men then walked off down the road in the direction of a nearby caravan park.

The youths decided that they wouldn't 'let them get away with that'. With a cry of 'let's show them', the two cars took off in pursuit. The two cars made a pass at the men, and insults were hurled back and forth. The cars went past, then turned for a second run at the men at very high speed. The three men were able to leap out of the way, but the leading car swerved on to the shoulder and the driver lost control. As the car spun well off the road,

Charles (age 17, student), who was walking home from a party with friends (and who had not been a party to any of the events which precipitated his death), was struck and killed instantly.   *(Case No. 35–87)*

Again, this is a scene of confrontation and honour. The teenagers were at first intimidated (one of the older males had claimed, falsely, that he was a 'narc'), but given some time to talk up their courage, responded to the challenge laid down by the older men. As in the previous case, it was ill fortune that put Charles in the scene of a masculine conflict in which he played no active part, other than to become the ultimate victim. Confrontational violence, then, may reach out to claim victims who have played no part in the escalating steps which produce a death in the final stages of the encounter. Nonetheless, the violence which produces the fatal injuries emerges out of a challenge to masculine honour, and the setting is one of confrontation, with the victim suffering the misfortune of having wandered close enough to the scene to be caught up in the violence.

Confrontations involving friends

While in the main these confrontations are likely to occur in public settings such as a pub, party or in streets, and as a result involve participants who are either strangers or at best acquaintances, at times the rapid flaring up of argument and violence can involve persons who are well known to each other, as is found in the following case:

Murkha G. (age 46, unemployed on worker's compensation) and Eddy C. (age 48) had been close friends for fifteen years. They had been neighbours for ten of those years, and visited each other's house frequently. Both were unemployed on worker's compensation. Eddy had been involved in a car accident the previous week, and according to his wife, was 'rather depressed'. One day, both of the families went to a traditional Turkish religious ceremony attended by roughly 300 guests. It was an event associated with joy and celebration, and there was much drinking. The two friends had managed to consume virtually a whole bottle of raki (a powerful form of spirit alcohol) between them, and a new bottle was placed on their table. While both had been drinking heavily (Murkha's blood alcohol level was later established to be 0.05), Eddy was visibly intoxicated. His friend decided that to protect him, he would keep the bottle away from him for the rest of the party.

Throughout the night, Murkha would keep repeating when his friend asked him for more to drink: 'You've had enough', to which his friend would reply: 'I can take it.' Later on, when once again Eddy asked for a drink, Murkha suggested that he: 'have some lemonade, you've had enough to drink'.

Eddy took this as an affront to his honour. He was enraged, and according to witnesses he 'turned white'. He threatened Murkha with the lemonade bottle, then 'stormed' out of the hall.

He was followed by both his wife and Murkha. His friend caught up with Eddy just after he had opened the boot of his car. The wife saw the two 'grab' at each other, went up and pulled Eddy away to break up the fight. In fact, Eddy had stabbed Murkha in the neck. Murkha collapsed on the road outside the hall. An ambulance was summoned, but Murkha died before he could receive medical attention.

Questioned at the station afterwards, Eddy said: 'It must be me, but I can't remember. I was drunk ... [regarding the knife] I don't remember getting it out ... I remember we fight, that is all ... Things are mixed up. Murkha was laying down. I thought I pushed him ... I remember pushing him, but I don't know why.' *(Case No. 3128–86)*

This has much in common with other of the confrontational encounters. It involves two males, both of whom were under the influence of alcohol, caught in an honour contest in front of what is for them an important social audience. While the initial spark that set off the confrontation might appear trivial when placed alongside its eventual consequences, for the males involved it was serious enough to set in motion the steps which escalated to the killing. A similar encounter involved a group of Chileans who were members of a soccer club:

A group of club members sat around drinking for several hours after one of the regular Saturday matches, including the club secretary, Sal (age 48), the club president Max, and a supporter Julio. It seems that over recent months Sal and Max had had several disagreements over the running of the club. On top of this there were political disagreements, which surfaced on this particular day as Max and Sal began to argue. As the dispute heated up, Sal became agitated and punched Max. Max did not retaliate, telling Sal not 'to be stupid', and Sal backed off and apologised. Later, another argument developed, this time between Sal and Julio over the use of a telephone, blows were struck, and Julio then grabbed a billiard cue and hit Sal over the head with it. Sal then said he was leaving, and was followed outside by Julio. Julio returned after a short time, and continued to drink with the others in the room (starting another fight in the process).

When the group finally closed the club and left, they discovered Sal lying unconscious on the footpath. The group took Sal home, where his wife cleaned him up and put him to bed. When he did not regain consciousness in the morning, an ambulance was called and he was taken to a hospital where he died a few days later as a result of complications which developed from the severe beating he had endured. *(Case No. 3864–87)*

This account is similar in many ways with the previous one. The scene was one where heavy drinking was taking place, involving persons well known to each other. One distinctive feature in this set of events was that the initial fight involved two persons well known to each other, with the eventual deadly assault pulling in a third party who was more peripheral to these initial persons and their relationship.

Among men, when these quarrels occur, the setting can be a pub which has provided the focal point for their meeting:

> David (age 46, builders labourer) and Richie were part of a group who drank regularly at the Junction Hotel. David, who was described as a 'happy-go-lucky type of guy' by his friends, had been drinking for several hours prior to joining his regular group at the Junction (his blood alcohol was later found to be 0.390). He was sitting with the group at a large table, when after having a few more drinks, he called over to a woman friend at the other end of the table, saying: 'Come down and have a drink with me.' Richie, it transpired, had just left the woman friend to go to the bar to buy some more drinks (a barmaid estimated she must have served Richie over a dozen rum and cokes). After a few minutes, Richie came over to the two of them, put both hands on the table and said to David: 'I'm telling you, you'll never do that again.' David mumbled some reply, provoking a challenge by Richie: 'Come out the front and I'll show you ... I'll teach you a lesson.' When David got up, the woman friend said: 'Come on, Davie, sit down and don't be stupid. You are full.' David replied: 'I'm all right, leave me alone, just watch me jacket.'
>
> Richie's account of what happened outside was that David threw a punch at him, and that he then hit David once, and then David fell backwards and hit his head on the road. When Richie tried to lift David, David fell back and hit his head again. Another friend came over (also drunk), and tried to help, but the two of them continued to have trouble managing to keep David up. A third observer to these events noted that: 'His head would have been probably four or five feet off the ground when he fell back. I think he would have done that about three times.' An ambulance was called and took David to the hospital where he died a short time later of the serious head injuries he had sustained.   *(Case No. 3465–88)*

This pattern of exceptional drunkenness, and then a lashing out at a person with whom the offender had previously been friendly, is repeated in several other accounts. There were, in all, thirteen homicides (15 per cent of the 84 confrontational homicides, in other words) where the victim and offender knew each other reasonably well prior to the killing. While the nature and intensity of these friendships varies considerably, it is obvious that the friendship bond by itself does not serve as a barrier to prevent individuals (nearly always males) from becoming caught up in a contest over honour or reputation.

Some deviant cases: confrontations involving women

While this analysis has proceeded with the presumption that confrontational homicides are definitively male behaviour, there were among these cases some in which the central actors were female:

> Carol (age 31, single mother) was walking to the local supermarket near the council flats where she lived, when she became involved in an argument with

Donna (age 21) and Tricia. The two women apparently felt that Carol had insulted them, and was responsible for graffiti alluding to their lesbian relationship. As the argument heated up, Donna suddenly punched Carol, grabbed her by the hair, and threw her on the ground. Since Carol had her 6-month-old baby with her, she thought that a defensive response was called for, and she managed to break off the conflict and run with her child back to her own flat.

Carol then armed herself with a small wooden baton, and had two male friends drive her so that she could 'go down there to get them two bitches.' The men stood by the car while Carol went to the front door of Donna and Tricia's flat, calling out: 'Now, come on out and fight me.' Tricia came to the door, and alleged that Carol hit her across the face with the baton. Tricia then woke Donna who had been napping. Donna grabbed a knife and went outside. When she saw the weapon, Carol said: 'Hey, you don't have to use the knife.' Carol then backed off, and started running for the car. Donna followed, shouting 'I'm going to fuckin' kill you.' Donna lunged forward, and stabbed Carol in the chest. Carol's right pulmonary artery was cut, and she bled to death at the scene. It was later established that Donna had a long history of violence, and had previously stabbed Tricia during one of their domestic disputes.   *(Case No. 4202–88)*

There is much in common with the other conflicts which have fatal outcomes. Insults are exchanged, a fight breaks out, the action breaks off and one of the parties leaves to fetch a weapon, and then returns to a scene where the final violence takes place. It differs, and remarkably so, in that it involves women. In another case, an argument at a barbecue breaks out, and a killing follows:

Ruth (age 42) is an Aboriginal woman with a long history of physical abuse by males and alcoholism, and had previous arrests for assaultive behaviour. She had begun the day of these events consuming two bottles of methylated spirits in the morning, followed by considerable wine in the afternoon (even five hours after the fatal injuries, she still had a blood alcohol level of 0.17). In the afternoon, a group assembled around the barbecue, where Ruth was preparing sausages and other meat. Apparently an argument broke out between Ruth and one of the males. Ruth picked up a knife and began to lunge at her antagonist. A mutual friend, Billy, moved in between them in an attempt to smooth things over. Trying to continue the fight, Ruth swung the knife wildly, trying to get around Billy. Instead, she struck Billy once in the arm, and once in the chest. Billy collapsed shortly after, and died before help could arrive.   *(Case No. 1234–88)*

In this narrative we can see the pattern of extensive alcohol use so common in other confrontational homicides: a provocative exchange (lost now in the confusion of alcohol) and then sudden resort to violence. A distinctive feature of this account is that while the offender was female, the victim was male. This case provides another illustration, as well, of how once violence is set in motion its effects may touch actors

not central to its precipitation. In another case, similar in the sense that the individuals had known each other and had been drinking heavily, a woman and a man sitting around a bush campfire began an argument over some stolen cigarettes. The woman started beating the man, who pleaded with another male for protection. The woman became even more enraged, and finally picked up a knife and stabbed the male in the back. (Case No. 3200–89)

The final case involves women both as offender and victim:

> Kylie (age 29, unemployed) and Sally (age 26) had been friends for many years, both growing up in the Broadmeadows area, and both had just recently been in Fairlea (the prison for women in Victoria). Kylie was living with her sister in her sister's flat. While in prison, Kylie had started a correspondence with Larry, which she stopped after leaving prison. Sally, whose sentence continued for some time, then took up and continued this letter-writing to Larry (Kylie was unaware of this).
>
> One afternoon the three were sitting around after sharing drugs (Kylie was later found to have traces of diazepam, nordiazepam, oxazepam and morphine in her body), when Kylie looked through some of Sally's letters and found the letters from Larry. An argument developed between the two. After hurling abuse back and forth the two began to scuffle (Kylie's sister stated later that Sally was 'off her head on drugs'). Sally then went into the kitchen, brought back a knife, screamed 'You reckon I'm a cunt do you?' and stabbed Kylie twice in the chest.   *(Case No. 2174–87)*

The precipitating events for the fatal injuries in this account consist of the same kinds of provocative insults that account for many masculine confrontations. The violence follows in a sudden burst, and a friendship of long standing is in a matter of an instant torn apart by the death of one (and a further stay in prison for the other).

While there are too few cases to begin to make anything approaching firm conclusions, it is distinctive that in all four of these events involving women, while the basic interactional dynamics were similar to the male confrontational homicides, the women knew their victim reasonably well. Thus, when this form of spontaneous swelling up of provocation, rage and violence occurs involving women in the offender role, it is not likely to occur in those kinds of settings where the potential victim would be unknown. These four deaths, at least, are not the sort that occur in the 'social friction' of movement through public space that is part of so many of the male-on-male homicides.

These handful of cases require, of course, that we be clear about what we mean when we refer to this pattern as a masculine scenario. Virtually all (80 of the 84, or 95 per cent) of the confrontational homicides involve males as both offender and victim. The handful of female offenders represent a small proportion both of confrontational homicides, and the

homicides where women are involved as offenders. There are 43 of these homicides in all where women are offenders, so that the four confrontational offenders represent just under 10 per cent of the homicides accounted for by women offenders (most women killers restrict their violence to a close circle involving either sexual partners or their children, see Chapter 7). The script of confrontation is one which can be read and played out by women, but this is a rare event, especially when placed up against the greater frequency of males to become involved in this form of violent behaviour. Over 95 per cent of confrontation homicides involve males as both victims and offenders. The dynamics of confrontational violence, in other words, are overwhelmingly masculine in character.

Luckenbill's six-stage model of conflict

Luckenbill (1977) argued that homicide can be viewed as the outcome of a dynamic interaction involving a victim, an offender and the audience in front of whom these actors play. He observed that such interactions can be seen as moving through six stages. The first stage consists of an 'opening move' performed by the victim and defined by the offender as an offence to 'face'. This opening move could be a direct, verbal expression by the victim, it might consist of the refusal of the victim to cooperate or comply with the requests of the offender, or it might consist of some physical or non-verbal gesture which the offender subsequently defines as offensive.

The second stage where murder was involved resulted when the offender interpreted the victim's opening move as offensive. Luckenbill makes clear that it may not be the victim's intention to be offensive. What is at issue is the interpretation on the part of the offender.

In the third stage the offender, rather than excusing or ignoring the provocation, or leaving the scene, responds with a 'retaliatory move aimed at restoring face and demonstrating strong character' (Luckenbill, 1977: 181). In most cases, this consisted of a verbal or physical challenge being issued to the victim. In a small number of cases, the interaction ends at this stage, since the offender in issuing the challenge actually kills the victim.

In the fourth stage, the victim has been placed in a problematic position by the challenge laid down by the offender. A range of options potentially are available at this juncture. An apology might be extended, the behaviour perceived by the offender as offensive might be discontinued, or the victim might leave the scene. Instead, when a killing took place the victim stood up to the challenge, and entered into a working 'agreement with the proffered definition of the situation as one suited for violence'. (Luckenbill, 1977: 183)

In the fifth stage, the offender and victim are committed to battle. Fearful of 'displaying weakness in character and consequent loss of face', the two evolved a 'working agreement that violence was appropriate' (Luckenbill, 1977: 184). In some cases, the parties sought out and secured weapons to support their verbal threats and challenges.

In the sixth stage, after the victim had fallen, there were three ways that the situation was terminated. In over half of the cases reviewed by Luckenbill (1977) the offender fled the scene, while in the remaining cases the offender either voluntarily remained or was held for the police by members of the social audience.

There are many of the male-to-male homicides, especially the brief confrontational killings, which seem to fit particularly well with the model of conflict posed by Luckenbill. It is in these encounters that it is possible to trace the movement from the initial move by one of the actors, through the stages which result in the lethal violence. Toch (1969: 131), noting a similar phenomenon, has commented on how violent encounters can be 'cumulatively created' by the individuals involved. Consider the initial case study of this section, in which a soldier and a young male begin an argument in a railway carriage, which results in a fight, and then the death of the soldier from a knife wound. In this account, the opening move (in our terms, the challenge to masculine honour), is made when the young man, Mike, tells the soldier, Gabe, to find another seat. Stage Two follows when Gabe interprets the move as offensive, and then Stage Three occurs when Gabe, rather than looking for a seat elsewhere, challenges Mike by attempting to take the seat. Mike in moving to Stage Four then 'must stand up to the challenge' which he does by springing up, fists ready, which then leads to the actual fight (Stage Five), and then Gabe's fatal stabbing. Mike then left the scene, and was apprehended later by police (Stage Six).

While the escalating steps in the confrontation of this narrative correspond to those specified in the model, it became clear as an attempt was made to apply the six-stage model to other homicides that there were apparently some differences in the Victorian data and those available to Luckenbill. Despite the fact that the records were reasonably extensive, at times it simply was not possible to trace all of the stages, even in confrontational homicides. The data simply are not available in some instances to trace through the steps from some initial provocation, the various stages leading up to the killing itself.

One persistent problem was that posed by the homicides whose events were extended in time. There was one account, for example, where the only information available was that P.C., a male, walked up to P.K., another male, who was drinking in pub, and shot him with a rifle

(Stages Four and Five of the model). P.C. then fled, and was appre-hended later by the police (Stage Six). While P.C. alleged that P.K. and some of his friends had 'set him up' some time in the past, the specific form of Stages One, Two and Three, the opening moves, could not be determined from the Coroner's files. In another account, reviewed above under the section on collective violence, two groups of young males had been feuding for many months. The death resulted when one group finally decided to corner a small number of members of the other group at a meeting hall where they were practising martial arts. When the group broke into the hall, a collective fight began. One of the members of the group being attacked broke out a rifle, firing a number of shots which wounded several members of the attacking group, one of whom was fatally hurt. Here the problems with the model are multiple. For one, the origins of the feud (the initial Stages One, Two, Three) have been lost in time. For another, given the group character of the conflict, whatever the original stages were, they may not have involved those who played major roles in the final stages of the drama. While the groups could be seen as moving through a series of stages in building up to the lethal encounter, the specific individuals who became victim and offender may have had limited roles in the stages prior to the final lethal encounter.

There were other cases which moved through developmental phases, but the ultimate victim played no part in the evolving interactions. There were two cases reviewed above where the ultimate victim had little to do with the escalation through the steps of violence, other than to become the victim. In the case of the man who became the victim of Elton's wild driving of his car in the parking lot of the pub where he had just been ejected, there were initial stages to the event, and it is certainly possible to trace the steps that resulted in Elton's rage and consequent behaviour. In a manner well outside that of the model posed by Luckenbill, however, the victim played no role in these early stages.

Finally, there is the claim by Luckenbill that these six stages char-acterised all homicide cases regardless of such factors as 'age, sex, race, time and place, use of alcohol, and proffered motive' (Luckenbill, 1977: 186). In the present study the greatest applicability seems to be in the forms of masculine violence which are the focus here. While possibly relevant in some accounts of intimate violence, these stages would not be found in cases involving sexual intimates where the extremely depressed male plans suicide, to be preceded by the homi-cide of his female partner. Nor would it apply to cases of infanticide, where the offender is engaged in a complicated denial of the existence of the victim.

It is the present general conclusion, therefore, that while of some heuristic value, the observation of Luckenbill that his model fits all homicides cannot be confirmed. Despite the extensive data in the present case studies, there are a number of narratives where it simply is not possible to identify each of the six stages in the model. Furthermore, in several of the patterns of homicide found here, the dynamics clearly do not unfold in the stages laid down by Luckenbill.

In many of the killings, however, especially those confrontations which move quickly to the point where it becomes lethal in its consequences, it is possible to identify a developing dynamic that has some correspondence to Luckenbill's model. In these situations, we can agree with Luckenbill when he asserts:

> homicide does not appear as a one-sided event with an unwitting victim assuming a passive, non-contributory role. Rather, murder is the outcome of a dynamic interchange between an offender, victim, and, in many cases, bystanders.   *(Luckenbill, 1977: 185)*

The issue of class, gender and economic marginality

Perhaps the most important failing of Luckenbill is that while he describes an important pattern of interaction, and points out that both victim and offender may play significant roles in that interaction, the model does not provide any clues as to why the offender and victim become involved in what proves to be a homicide. Luckenbill (1977: 186) comes close when he underscores the importance of the role of 'maintaining face and reputation and demonstrating character', language which implies a masculine motivation for the violence. As his description stands, however, it provides a potentially helpful description of the interactive dynamics that make up a confrontational encounter, but it does not address either the gender characteristics or the economic marginality that feature so strongly in male-to-male violence.

It is the present contention that it is important to see confrontations as 'contests of honour' in which the maintenance of 'face' or reputation is a central matter. Further, these are seen as quintessential masculine matters. This agrees, then, with Daly and Wilson (1988) who have argued that it is males who become involved in violence around the issue of reputation:

> A seemingly minor affront is not merely a 'stimulus' to action, isolated in time and space. It must be understood within a larger social context of reputations, face, relative social status, and enduring relationships. Men are known by their fellows as 'the sort who can be pushed around' or 'the sort that won't take any shit', as people whose word means action and people who

are full of hot air, as guys whose girlfriends you can chat up with impunity or guys you don't want to mess with. In most social milieus, a man's reputation depends in part upon the maintenance of a credible threat of violence.

(Daly and Wilson, 1988: 128)

The theoretical account provided by Daly and Wilson is one of the few that recognises the diverse forms of masculine violence that make up contemporary homicide patterns. It is their argument that the general thread of masculinity that runs through homicide reflects forms of male aggressiveness which can be accounted for by evolutionary processes of adaptation. While their formulation is helpful in moving us towards an understanding of the masculine character of violence, in its present form it needs some expansion to encompass the class elements of this form of homicide. The lethal violence being examined here is defined both by its class and gender characteristics. It is predominantly male and working/under-class behaviour. How is it that we can account for these two features of confrontational homicide?

It is the defence of honour that makes what some might consider a 'trivial' provocation become the grounds for a confrontation which builds to a homicide. Wolfgang was one of the early observers of the phenomenon of the apparent triviality of the events which provoke some homicides:

> Despite diligent efforts to discern the exact and precise factors involved in an altercation or domestic quarrel, police officers are often unable to acquire information other than the fact that a trivial argument developed, or an insult was suffered by one or both of the parties.   *(Wolfgang, 1958: 188)*

It seems clear, however, that what is trivial to a firmly respectable observer may be quite central to the marginal actor's sense of masculinity. Daly and Wilson (1988) have argued along similar lines, that for some men it is important that to maintain their sense of honour they not allow themselves to be 'pushed around', that they maintain a 'credible threat of violence' (Daly and Wilson, 1988: 128). Such perceptions are actually consistent with Wolfgang's observations. After the sentence noting the apparently 'trivial' character in some of the disputes leading to homicide, Wolfgang went on to observe:

> Intensive reading of the police files and of verbatim reports of interrogations ... suggest that the significance of a jostle, a slight derogatory remark, or the appearance of a weapon ... are stimuli differentially perceived and interpreted ... Quick resort to physical combat as a measure of daring, courage, or defense of status appears to be a cultural expectation, especially for lower class males ...   *(Wolfgang, 1958: 189)*

Further, Wolfgang (1958: 189) is explicit in his statement that it is the observers in the criminal justice system who, drawing upon middle and upper-class values which have influenced the shaping of legal norms, have seen the disputes which lead to homicide as trivial in origin. For the lower-class players in the homicide drama, the challenge to manhood is far from a trivial matter.

Putting it together: the structure of confrontational homicide

In the common schemes for classifying relationships between victims and offenders, these confrontational clashes between males would be split pretty evenly between homicides involving 'strangers' or 'friends/acquaintances'. In terms of the common 'motives' for homicide, many would fit into the grouping of 'altercation of relatively trivial origin' (Wolfgang, 1958). Certainly, there are many of these killings where the precipitating incidents seem negligible when placed alongside the final outcome. A case can be made that in both his substantive text and in the presentation of case studies, many of the homicides described by Wolfgang correspond to the present grouping of confrontational homicides (for example, see Wolfgang, 1958: 226–7).

What is at issue here is how best to capture the social dynamics of the relationship between the victim and offender in these circumstances. Obviously, the statement either that the parties were 'strangers' or 'friends-acquaintances' which would come from common classifications of such 'relationships' would be empirically correct, but would be useless in terms of actually describing the nature of what has transpired. In some accounts the individuals have not known each other, while in others they have a passing acquaintance (as in some confrontations that begin in pubs). The form of the confrontation is the same, regardless of these circumstances. Accordingly, groupings such as 'stranger' or 'acquaintance' are inadequate to express the nature of the interactional dynamic occurring between these males.

What is fundamental to the confrontation scenario is that it is the altercation itself which defines the relationship between the parties. The two have come together, and become known to each other, through the fight itself. Whether they are friends, acquaintances or strangers, the dynamics of male confrontation are played out within a set of mutually recognised expectations regarding how the encounter is to proceed. In these accounts (except those few where the ultimate victim truly was an innocent bystander) the victim as well as the offender was actively involved in the encounter. In many the victim actually initiated the violence. In most of the remainder, the victim was a willing participant in the encounter.

This form of homicide has been identified in the work of Daly and Wilson where they refer specifically to 'confrontational disputes' arising in a 'field of honour', arguing that homicides arising out of 'trivial altercations' are essentially affairs of honour bearing a strong resemblance to honour contests observed in other cultures:

> The precipitating insult may appear petty, but is usually a deliberate provocation (or is perceived to be), and hence constitutes a public challenge that cannot be shrugged off. It often takes the form of disparagement of the challenged party's manhood: his nerve, strength or savvy, or the virtue of his wife, girlfriend or female relatives. *(Wilson and Daly, 1985: 69)*

It is, of course, the essential masculinity of this form of homicide that is of central theoretical interest, both in the present case and the works of Daly and Wilson. This is the most common of the scenarios of violence observed in the present data where, in the main, the principals are male, although it has been noted that four cases (5 per cent of the confrontational homicides) did involve women. The script defining the various moves which make up this pattern is one which is drawn upon nearly always by men, but is on rare occasion followed out by women.

To summarise, this form of homicide involves behaviour which is essentially a contest of honour between males. In the initial stages of the encounter, what the participants in a confrontational killing intend is first to argue, then to fight. The argument which produces that fight is spontaneous, as are the events which follow. These conflicts typically occur in leisure scenes, especially scenes where males predominate. The venue most often is a public setting, including in and around pubs, in streets or laneways, in public parks or reserves, parties or barbecues, and in public transport settings such as bus stops, railway stations, or even on the train carriages or buses themselves. In most such settings, an active role is played by the social audience, particularly male peers. The social nature of such scenes is reinforced by the role of alcohol, whose use has been found to be a feature of a great majority of these homicides.

The lethal violence is not premeditated, at least at the starting point of the conflict. Some confrontation scenes move rapidly to the point where deadly violence is employed, as where the parties begin with a fist fight, then raise the stakes by pulling knives. Others are more complex, however, and may involve one of the parties leaving the immediate scene to return a short time later with a weapon. In some instances the conflict may become elaborated into a feud which simmers for weeks, or months before the lethal violence results.

Through it all resound the joint themes of masculinity and lower social class position. Extreme violence in defence of honour is defini-

tively masculine and lower or underclass in its makeup. But, not all such males feel compelled to defend their reputation or status with violence. Why it is that some males pursue violence to secure their reputation or status, while others avoid such challenges, constitutes a major question for further research and theoretical discussion.

CHAPTER 5

Taking exceptional risks:
homicide in the course of other crime

There are some circumstances where a person will carefully plot the taking of another person's life. In many situations, however, the killing results from events which initially are about something else. One such situation, as we have seen, is that where two males begin an argument, and their words lead to blows and then a death. Upon setting themselves out to fight, the males in confrontation are knowingly exposing themselves to some risk, since there is always the known danger of losing a fight and being physically beaten. What most are not likely to know is that the fight will lead to the death of one of them.

In the next scenario, however, the individuals are thrusting themselves typically into a much greater risk situation, either in terms of the threat to the lives of potential victims, or ultimately to their own lives. When individuals set out to commit a serious crime such as armed robbery, they do so recognising that the threat of violence employed may, in fact, become real violence. And, that this threat is real is demonstrated in the accounts which follow.

Homicide which occurs in the course of other crime contributes a significant proportion to the total amount of homicide observed in the present research. In the five-year period, there were a total of 61 such homicides (16 per cent of all homicides). Four distinct sub-themes were identified within this general homicide scenario.

The first variation: double victims

The first major variation on this theme is made up of those cases where the victim in the initial crime becomes the victim in the homicide as well (31 of the 61). Most often, the offence where this double

victimisation occurs is armed robbery. In some cases since the offender was not apprehended the details of the event are scanty:

> D.Z. (age 24, night watchman) was employed by Metropolitan Security Services as a night patrolman. On Saturday 2 March, between 12.30 and 1 am he was seen in the vicinity of Salty Street, Altona, in his marked company car. Shortly after, people in the vicinity of the nearby K-Mart Store in the Altona Gate Shopping Centre heard the sound of a shot. D.Z. failed to answer his car radio after 12.30 am. At 3.30 am his car was found with its headlights on. His body was found a short distance away, near a time-clock checkpoint at the west end of the store. He had been shot with a .22 rifle. There was evidence of tampering with the door adjacent to the time clock. No offender has been identified in this death.   *(Case No. 599–85)*

Despite the sparse nature of this account, there is enough information to make the reasonable guess that the victim had been killed during the course of an armed robbery. Little more can be known about what happened between victim and offender to provoke the killing in the course of that robbery. Even less is known in the case of A.S.:

> Shortly after 8 pm, an unknown person (or persons) entered and robbed the service station where A.S. (age 24) worked. At 8.10 pm, A.S. was found, unconscious, on the floor with a gunshot wound to the head. He was taken to hospital where he died ten days later without regaining consciousness. No other details have been uncovered in this case.   *(Case No. 1837–86)*

Again, the specific dynamics of provocation are unknowable in cases such as this where a person has been victimised in a situation where all that is known is that either a robbery or a burglary has also taken place. Some of these unsolved, double-victim crimes involve elderly victims:

> There had been three attempted break-ins to houses in Drummond Street, Ballarat, on that New Year's Eve. At midday on the following day, relatives who had come to visit Karen S. (age 70, pensioner) became alarmed when she did not answer her door. Finding the door unlocked, they entered only to find the woman dead in her bed. She had been struck over the head several times with a ceramic jug. The house had been ransacked.
> *(Case No. 11–88)*

In some of these double-victim cases more is known, as in one where the offenders were drug users in search for money to support their habits:

> Paul and Amy, both heavy users of heroin, decided to travel to Reservoir (a Melbourne suburb) to do a burglary. At the time, Paul was using 3 to 4 grams of heroin a day, and since he was unemployed relied on burglaries to support

his use of drugs. They first approached the house of Samuel (age 88, retired) and when they told him they had forgotten an address, he invited them in to check the telephone book. They then left his house, and tried unsuccessfully to break into two other homes. By this time it was dark, and Paul decided to break into Samuel's house. He first knocked on the door. When there was no answer, he then went around the back, and broke a window to gain access through the back door. According to Mark, at that point Samuel jumped him from behind. Mark punched Samuel several times, then tied him up and put him on a bed. Paul then ransacked the house, finding $200 in cash and a $300 watch. When Samuel's son came the next day, he found that Samuel had died during the night of complications resulting from the beating he had sustained. *(Case No. 1885–88)*

In another case, because the victim lived for a short time, somewhat more detail is available although the offenders have not yet been identified:

After a work accident, S.G. (age 44, unemployed), a recent migrant from Rumania, moved to a block of land in the country. One night, a neighbour observed S.G.'s house on fire. Driving up to the house, the neighbour saw S.G., suffering from severe burns, attempting to climb into his car. The friend put him in his own car, and drove him to the nearest hospital which was in Ballarat. S.G. told the neighbour during the drive that two men had tried to steal money from him. Failing to find any money, the two poured petrol over him, then lit a match and set him alight. S.G. was first treated in Ballarat, then transferred to the Burns Unit of the Royal Melbourne Hospital where he died two days later. His murder remains unsolved.

(Case No. 2353–85)

In other cases where the homicide was solved, it is possible to sketch out more details of what took place:

It had been a long day for J.R. (age 43, mechanic, part-time taxi driver). He had left home for work at 5 am, and had told his previous taxi customers at around 11 pm that he intended to go home. Shortly after 11 pm, S.D. (age 22) climbed into his taxi while it was parked at a service station in Hampton. S.D. first asked to be driven to a street in Brunswick were he dropped a Christmas present off for his son. He then asked to be driven north along Sydney Road, then into a deserted area near Campbellfield.

S.D. then asked J.R. to stop. He produced a .22 sawn-off rifle which he had concealed in a bag, and ordered J.R. out of the car. After taking about $150 from J.R., S.D. forced him into the boot of the car, closing the lid firmly. After a few minutes, he opened the boot again, and shot J.R. several times with the rifle. S.D. then drove off in the taxi, stopping to dispose of the body outside the country town of Finley, and to throw the gun out somewhere north of Shepparton. He then drove until the taxi ran out of fuel just north of Jerilderie. S.D. then fled to Queensland where he was apprehended one month later.

S.D. was unable to provide any motive for the killing. His family regarded him as a violent individual with a short temper. He had threatened to kill his

ex-wife, and had previously been involved in a stabbing incident. He had a previous record with the police, including offences of violence.

(Case No. 5036–86)

Even with the information that is available, it is difficult in this narrative to account for why the offender felt he had to kill his victim. In another case, the armed robbery led to a death which occurred some time after the initial crime:

> M.H. and K.H. were unemployed and addicted to heroin. One of the methods they employed to obtain money for drugs was armed robbery (although they later stated that it was never their intent to harm anybody).
>
> One night the two armed themselves with knives and entered a milk bar at Templestowe (a Melbourne suburb). The proprietor, H.H. (age 65), came out from the residential portion of the premises to serve them. Seeing them armed and masked, H.H. put up minor resistance, which stopped when one of the robbers cut him on the hand.
>
> The two took the money out of the till, then forced H.H. back into the residential quarters, insisting that H.H. tell them where the rest of the money was hidden. Fearing for their lives, H.H.'s wife told their attackers where they could find the rest of the money (about $1300). The intruders grabbed the money and ran out of the milk bar.
>
> A few days later H.H., who had a history of lung and heart problems, collapsed and died. Drawing upon medical testimony, the Coroner concluded that 'the stress suffered by the deceased in the armed robbery resulted in prolonged emotional disturbance and physiological change … resulting in heart failure …' finding that the death 'was substantially caused by the unlawful, dangerous and intentional acts' of M.H. and K.H.
>
> *(Case No. 2732–85)*

The lethal effects of taking exceptional risks, as found in this account, may take a form quite unanticipated by the criminal offenders. Two of the cases where armed robbery leads to murder involve attacks on homosexuals:

> J.S. (age 55, part-time cleaner) was known to be a practising homosexual who frequented Footscray Park (which had a reputation as a homosexual meeting place, particularly at night). One night when he was in the park, R.H. (age 36), who had just had an argument with his girlfriend, came into the park and sat down on one of the benches to simmer down. While on the bench, R.H. overheard a conversation in which he believed that J.S. had $1500 in his possession.
>
> R.H. decided to take the money from J.S. He went back to his car and took from it a sawn-off .22 rifle. In order to frighten off others who were in the park, R.H. went up to them, first attempting to frighten them by shouts and insults, finally firing his gun into the air.
>
> When the others had dispersed, R.H. began to stalk J.S. J.S. apparently attempted to run away, R.H. was able to catch him. A witness who remained said that J.S. attempted to push the gun away from his head, and R.H. then

fired the weapon at J.S. J.S. screamed and limped a couple of steps away, then fell. R.H. then fired another shot into his body.

R.H. then took his victim's wallet and fled. A little while later, he inspected the wallet and found that it contained only $40. R.H. then returned to the scene and searched his victim's body for the money. Finding none, he took his car keys and then searched his victim's car. There was no further money to be found. Immediately after, R.H. left the state, and was arrested some three weeks later in New South Wales. *(Case No. 3925–85)*

In this case, the homosexuality of the victim was peripheral to the decision first to rob, then kill his victim (although it might have contributed to the level of violence in the encounter). In another case, the armed robbery was part of a group's harassment of homosexuals:

The Lagoon Pier Changing Rooms in Beaconsfield Parade, Port Melbourne, had developed a reputation as a meeting place for homosexuals, especially in the early hours of the morning. This reputation reached the homophobic community as well, attracting the attention of a group of young men who engaged in the attacks on homosexuals known as 'poofter bashing', although they also intended to rob their victims as well.

After first spending the late hours of the night in various pubs, the group then went to the changing rooms to beat up homosexuals. At 3.30 in the morning they jumped on their first victim, but after being grabbed and beaten he was able to squirm out of their grasp and flee.

A short time later, B.C. (age 30) arrived. There is no evidence that B.C. was a homosexual. He had been out with his wife and friends to dinner earlier that evening. Afterwards, he and his wife had an argument, resulting in B.C. packing a bag and leaving. He left home at 2.30, and stopped by the changing rooms at 3.30. When he walked into the men's toilet, he was jumped on by the waiting group of young men. He was beaten and kicked savagely, and afterward robbed by his attackers. When police were called to the scene at 5.15, they found B.C. dead on the floor of the changing room. Severe head injuries were the cause of death. *(Case No. 920–86)*

In this incident involving 'gay bashing' there tends to be combined dual motivation of robbery as well as a homophobic dispensing of punishment aimed at the gay lifestyle.

In the following case, the 'other crime' is a combination involving drug dealing, robbery, and possibly revenge for a previous robbery:

Jenny D. (age 32, pensioner) frequently had obtained heroin from D.K. ('American Dave') for the past four years. On 3 December 1986 Jenny called American Dave to arrange a drug deal at a suburban railway station. The real purpose of the meet was to lure American Dave out of his house, which a boyfriend of Jenny's successfully robbed while American Dave was away. Jenny received a share of the $1000 that was taken.

Two days later, Jenny needed more heroin and once again arranged to meet American Dave. Her friend who had conducted the robbery warned

her that American Dave would 'know you set him up'. Jenny replied that
there was no problem, since '... I have got him once or twice before'. The
friend gave her an extra $100 for her to buy him some heroin as well.

Jenny left and did not return. Jenny's boyfriend and two women went to
American Dave's house, and inquired what had happened to Jenny. He
denied seeing Jenny, abused and hit the women, and then chased them from
his house with a pistol.

Jenny's body was found later that same day in the gutter of a country road.
She had head injuries consistent with being beaten with a pistol, as well as
bruising to the face and arms. American Dave was charged with Jenny's
murder. While on remand he confessed to another prisoner that he had
killed Jenny, stating that she had owed him 'a lot of money'.

(Case No. 4677–86)

Here is a complex situation where a deviant lifestyle, and the participation in a cluster of criminal offences (robbery, drug use, fraud),
become part of the lethal violence.

A similar mix of drug dealing and robbery is found in the following
narrative:

Police received a call to attend at 65 Hoddle Street (in inner Melbourne) at
2.17 one morning, arriving within ten minutes to find the body of T.P. (age
29, unemployed) on the floor near the rear door with a knife buried in his
stomach. Death was caused by multiple stab wounds.

The police investigation pieced together the following observations. T.P.
for some time had been making his living dealing in drugs, especially heroin.
One of his regular customers was D.P. (age 23, unemployed). Although T.P.
was his regular lifeline for drugs, D.P. had become antagonistic towards him,
with D.P. making several threatening telephone calls to T.P. Because of his
dependence on drugs, D.P.'s life had become increasingly chaotic. Lacking a
job he had no source of regular income to support his drug habit. His lack of
money had forced him to move from place to place because of his non-
payment of rent.

On the night of the murder, T.P. and some of his friends were drinking
and chatting in T.P.'s home. D.P. came by and joined the group. At the time,
several thousand dollars were spread over the table along with a large supply
of drugs. T.P. offered a free shot of heroin to D.P., which he accepted. About
half an hour before the police received the call summoning them to the
scene, the friends left to go to a nearby disco for drinks, leaving T.P. alone in
the house with D.P.

D.P. claims that the killing was done by two masked men who broke into
the house in order to rob T.P. However, this does not explain where D.P.
suddenly had the money to pay cash for several days of expensive hotel
accommodation and restaurant meals. Further, he had arranged with some
friends to give him an alibi for crucial times (when the friends found out that
a murder was involved, they provided full details to the police). The police
concluded that D.P., having a history of discord with T.P. anyway, murdered
T.P. to obtain both the money and a supply of drugs.   *(Case No. 273–85)*

One characteristic of the previous two events is that the victim and
offender were known to each other. That is, unlike many of the other of

these killings which flow out of the commission of other crime, these were not 'stranger killings'. This situation, where the victim and offender are known to each other, was found in the following case as well:

Alice (age 42, nurse) had employed Mark (age 30) to paint her house several months previously. Being short of money one late November day, Mark first went to the house of another previous customer who owed him $3000, and when he found no one at home, broke in and vandalised some of the furniture. He then went to a nearby pub and had several drinks. Afterwards, he decided to burgle Alice's house, because by his accounting she owed him $200 for the work he had done on her house. When he arrived at the house, he knocked at the front door, and was surprised when Alice answered (she had been on a late shift the previous night).

As he told the story, Mark then pushed his way into the house, demanding his $200. When she refused to pay, he tied her up and gagged her, then proceeded to rummage through the house for items to steal. At one point he had observed that the gag had caused Alice to collapse, so he loosened both the gag and the bindings. At that, Alice then started screaming and hitting him. Mark then subdued her, tied her up again, and then stabbed her to death (she was stabbed a total of eleven times). He then left (taking a few items of jewellery), locking the door behind him.

Later that afternoon, Mark called the police and informed them of the murder. Mark became upset at the reports distributed to the media by the police which indicated that Alice had been sexually assaulted (which Mark denied). Mark then called a local television station, and arranged to meet them at the Jolimont rail footbridge so that he could tell his side of the story. When he arrived for the interview, he was arrested by the police, with the proceedings being filmed by a television crew.   *(Case No. 5156–87)*

In the most common situation it might be presumed that, most often where an offender sets out to commit a crime such as robbery, it would involve an unknown person, but in some instances the knowledge of the person and perhaps the presence of money is an important feature of the crime, and also likely to be tied to the thought processes that lead to the killing.

A rather different set of circumstances involving persons known to each other can occur when the crime is attempted sexual assault, as is found in the following case:

W.J. (age 33, unemployed) and his girlfriend R.M had come to Victoria seeking work. One day, they met up with a circle of amiable friends in Melton (an outer Melbourne suburb), and began to arrange and plan for work. The group had a pleasant afternoon, drinking at a local pub and shooting pool. As it became evening, the group retired to the house of G.M., continuing to drink and also to smoke marijuana.

They continued this well into the evening. By all accounts everyone was getting along. When it became late, it was clear that W.J. was too far gone on drugs and alcohol to drive. G.M. offered to let W.J. and his girlfriend use the

extra bedroom in his house. The offer was accepted and the couple retired to bed.

Later, R.M. was awakened when she felt that someone was in the room, touching her arm. It was G.M., who was naked. R.M. pleaded with him to leave, to which he replied: 'Are you going to do it? ... or I'm going to, you know, start a drama or something like that.' When she refused, G.M. then upped the ante, saying: 'Are you going to do it? ... or I'll get the gun and shoot both of you.'

R.M. again refused. G.M. then left the room, returning with his shotgun. He pointed it first at R.M., then W.J., repeating what he had said. R.M., terrified, attempted to waken W.J. who had slept through these events. Finally, he woke up, saw G.M. with the gun, saying: 'What are you doing? Leave us alone.' G.M. replied: 'Take that', and shot him. *(Case No. 4580–86)*

This was the only case in this five-year period involving a double victim where rape (or the intent to rape) was the initial offence. It is to be anticipated that with a longer time span, or a large set of data, cases would emerge in which there are women victims who are first sexually assaulted, then killed, but none such are found within the present case studies.

In another case, again involving offenders known to each other, the offender argued that the homicide was a result of what was originally intended as an assault:

Lynne C. (age 25) made her living as a prostitute. She had managed to arouse a deep anger in Kylie S., allegedly because Lynne had both 'dobbed in' her brother to the police, and also set him up for a bashing. She arranged to pay Lynne for services provided to a male friend to whom Kylie owed some money.

It was arranged for her to meet her client at a suburban motel. After the two had been in the room for a few minutes, Kylie and a male friend broke in. They bound and gagged Lynne, and started to beat her. During the course of the beating, Lynne died of asphyxiation because her mouth was tightly sealed and she was unable to breathe through her nose. Kylie and her two friends then took the body and dumped it several kilometres away in some vacant bushland.   *(Case No. 1264–86)*

An unusual feature of this case is that it is one of the few where the original offender involved was a female. There is another case in these files where the death apparently resulted from an assault:

Len C. (age 21) had accumulated a total of seventeen offences prior to the events which resulted in the death of Arnie B. (age 72). Earlier that day, he had knocked at a door, and assaulted two young men, totally unknown to him, because he believed that they had assaulted his brother (it turned out that a previous occupant at the address was responsible).

The facts of the death are difficult to establish. All of the physical evidence suggested that Arnie had been struck several times with a blunt instrument

while seated, watching television. Len's story was that Arnie had approached him in the toilet of a nearby pub. Len alleged that in the toilet Arnie had come up to him and attempted to touch his penis, which Len says he 'brushed off'. Len states that he then followed Arnie through a fence and up the back stairs to Arnie's council flat. As he was climbing the stairs, Len stated that Arnie set his small dog on to him. Len then punched Arnie, and pushed him into his flat. Len was apparently surprised when he was informed that Arnie was mute and deaf.   *(Case No. 2919–85)*

This case is murky in terms of what transpired and how it should be classified. On the basis of the information available, it appeared that the offender had a history of exceptional violence, and that in all probability the above events were part of a pattern of assaultive violence, perhaps with the intent to rob.

A number of factors stand out in these and other case studies of double victims. First, most of these cases involve offenders who are highly marginal and willing to take great risks with their own lives and the lives of their victims. Second, where known, most of the offenders are male. There were five cases where females were involved in the offence, two involving women only in the homicide (prostitutes who turned on their clients), and three involving women as accomplices in the killing. Men offenders accounted, putting it in other terms, for 25 of the 31 double-victim homicides.

The second variation: the offender as victim

There are times when the tables turn suddenly on criminal offenders. One of the hazards of serious crime, in other words, is that the offender may find himself (in most cases) the victim of lethal violence (becoming what has been called a 'reverse victim', Maxfield, 1990). There were, in all, 18 such reverse victims found in these files. In some of these cases, the victim of the initial crime turns the tables and becomes the offender in the homicide (7 of these 18 reverse victims were where the killer was a civilian victim of the initial crime):

Late one night, two intruders, M.F. (age 25) and P.E. (age 22) broke into the house shared by the brothers N.T. and T.T. According to the story the brothers told the police, their attackers carried a gun and attempted an armed robbery. The brothers managed to divert the robber with the gun, there was a general struggle, and the brothers killed both robbers with knives (the autopsy established that both of the intruders had died of multiple stab wounds, and that they had both been drinking heavily). The Coroner found at the inquest that the 'wounds were justifiably inflicted' while the brothers 'were acting in self defence.'   *(Case Nos. 2083–85 and 2084–85)*

In a similar account, the initial crime consists of attempted theft of a
motor car:

For most of the evening, D.A. (age 28, car driver) had been drinking in a
suburban hotel a few kilometres from his home. Without a car, perhaps short
of money, he attempted to solve his transportation problem by breaking into
a car. As D.A. was in the process of hot-wiring the car, the car owner, R.T.,
came on to the scene. D.A. then made his second mistake of the night by
taking a swing at R.T. R.T. had the advantage of not being intoxicated, and
was further exceptionally fit. It was a short fight. While D.A. was able to land
at least one blow which caused a slight cut to R.T.'s face, R.T. quickly got the
best of him, hitting him several times to the face and body. D.A. suffered
severe injuries to his face, including facial fractures.

While serious, these wounds by themselves were not fatal. Five days later,
D.A. underwent surgery for treatment of the fractures under general anaesthetic. Upon completion of the surgical procedures, the drug Naloxone was
administered. The consequences were rapid and fatal. D.A. developed acute
pulmonary oedema, and died shortly thereafter. The Coroner found that the
Naloxone was 'reasonably and properly administered', and the observed
fatal effects in D.A.'s case are 'extremely rare though documented in medical
literature.'

Further, with respect to R.T., the Coroner found that during the fight he
had continued to strike D.A. 'where a reasonable person with comparable
high fitness and strength ... would have known or ought to have known that
to continue striking the deceased after the second strike could or would
result in serious injury'. Nonetheless, it was held that the sequence of events
were such that R.T. could not 'reasonably be held responsible either in
causation or degree of proximity', and the death, therefore, was declared to
be 'accidental'. Although clearly marginal, the case has been kept in these
files because the initial chain of events was set in motion by the attempted
auto theft, and the fatality itself was an outcome, even if indirect, of the
beating sustained in the course of that theft.   *(Case No. 2017–85)*

In these cases, the original offender has taken the risk of engaging in
a serious crime, creating a scene in which the stakes run high. Citizens
may fight back, and at times the result may be the death of the original
offender. In a slightly large number of cases (11 of the 18), it was police
who were responsible for the killing. Among such cases are those in
which the death results from police intervention in the course of an
armed robbery:

C.B. (age 27, unemployed) had first met his partner-in-crime, F.H., in prison.
C.B. was a regular user of drugs, especially opiates. After release, C.B. and
F.H., in order to obtain money, had been engaging in a series of armed
robberies of small chemist shops, focusing on those which were sub-agencies
of the State Bank of Victoria.

These robberies had been frequent enough, and concentrated in a small
enough area, to allow the Armed Robbery Squad of the police to make
reasonable guesses regarding where they might strike next. Several such

shops were staked out, including one in Huntingdale Road, Chadstone (a Melbourne suburb).

This was the shop that the two had selected for the next robbery. At 9.30 one morning, the two, armed with cut-down .22 rifles and wearing cut-up jumpers for hoods, entered the shop. Witnesses inside said that the pair were 'very polite' and kept repeating that everyone should 'stay quiet and nothing will happen'. Another reported them as saying: 'Do as you're told and nobody will get hurt'.

After taking money and drugs from the shop, the two ran to their car. The waiting police identified themselves and called out for them to stop. An instant later, several shots were fired, wounding F.H. and killing C.B. The Coroner found that under the circumstances, the death of C.B. was 'justifiable homicide'.   (*Case No. 242–85*)

Several of the persons who can be classified as 'offender victims' were killed by police in the course of making an arrest. Some of these involved shoot-outs, where the victim as well as the police fired a weapon during the encounter:

Milton M. (age 22) had been under police surveillance for some time as a suspect in several robberies which had been at gunpoint (including discharging of the gun). Based on information they had obtained, the police stepped up their watch on Milton, since they anticipated that another robbery was about to occur. Milton was observed leaving his house, with 'what appeared to be a firearm tucked down the front of his pants.' He drove to a nearby car sales yard, where he switched cars.

Apparently Milton became aware that the police were following him, since he pulled an abrupt U-turn, and headed directly for the police car, veering away at the last minute. The police then pursued Milton, turning on their lights and siren. The car was intercepted, and the police jumped out of their car with their weapons drawn. Observing that Milton had drawn his weapon, the police fired a number of shots at the car. Milton appeared to slump on the passenger side of the car. The police then called out: 'Police: get out of the car', and fired a further warning shot into the air.

Milton decided to make a run for it, opening the passenger side door, and fleeing down the street. As he was running, he half-turned and pointed his revolver at the police over his left shoulder. The police then fired more shots, one of them hitting Milton in the back of the head, killing him instantly.

(*Case No. 1269–87*)

Another of these cases where police were confronted with an armed suspect involved a person suspected of killing one of the security guards who also is found in these files as a 'double victim':

George (age 33) had a long history of criminal offences. Police had located him and made an attempt to arrest him for suspected murder in the car park of a shopping centre. As they approached his car, police allege that George produced a firearm, and pointed it at police as he attempted to drive away. Police fired three shots at him as he sped away. When his car crashed into a

pole a short distance down the road, it was found that one of the shots had
gone through the car's rear window, and into the back of his head.

(Case No. 4364–88)

In some circumstances, the offender was killed in the course of an
armed robbery when he was not, in fact, carrying a lethal weapon
himself:

> Over thirty armed robberies had been committed on service stations and
> convenience stores in the bayside suburbs of Melbourne, provoking the
> police to saturate the area with a large number of police, including assigning
> police officers to surveillance duty at specific stations. After several fruitless
> days, the more experienced Armed Robbery Squad officers at the Beach
> Road Solo service stations were replaced by two young constables from the
> local East Bentleigh uniform branch.
>
> Just after 9.30, Arnold G. (age 25) entered the station wearing a full
> balaclava and overalls. He went over to the counter, grabbed the attendant by
> the throat, and thrust his hand into the till. The attendant then fell to the
> floor. Coming up from behind Arnold, the two constables were unable to see
> that Arnold was not armed. One of the constables called out: 'Police here …
> stop.' When Arnold turned to face the officers, both opened fire, and Arnold
> was killed.   *(Case No. 4394–87)*

There were as well in these years, some other cases which were less
clear-cut in terms of the dynamics of the police behaviour:

> Glen A. (age 24) had been suspected by police of being involved in the kill-
> ing of two police in what became known as the 'Walsh Street Killing.' Fearing
> for his safety (and knowing that he was a suspect), Glen, in the company of
> his solicitor, surrendered himself to police. He was formally charged over a
> previous arson, but not detained regarding the police shooting.
>
> Glen was granted bail on the arson charge on the conditions that he
> report to the Coburg police every week, and that he live with his parents.
> While Glen was careful to report regularly, he was violating the bail condi-
> tions by continuing to live in his Carlton flat. Police discovered this location,
> and as part of the massive effort to locate the police killers, placed his flat
> under 24-hour supervision.
>
> The listening post established for the flat was abandoned on the day that it
> was determined that Glen was going to move from the flat. As Glen was
> driving his car, he was stopped and questioned on another matter (con-
> cerning a hit-and-run involving the son of a policeman). For some reason, at
> this point the police took Glen back to his flat for further questions. When
> they entered, Glen stood by, according to the police account, as they
> searched the ground floor of the flat. The group then went upstairs, where
> Glen was alleged to have gone over to a pile of clothes and pulled out an
> imitation pistol. One of the police then pulled his gun, telling Glen to drop
> the pistol. When Glen did not drop the gun, it was said, the officer then fired
> six shots from his pistol into Glen. His gun being empty, the officer then took
> another gun from a fellow officer, and fired another shot (into the back of

Glen's head). Glen died later in hospital from the effects of the bullet
wounds.   *(Case No. 2060–89)*

This case has provoked considerable controversy, and ultimately led
to the prosecution of the police officer on a charge of murder, but the
jury returned a verdict of not guilty. In a similar case:

Gary S. (age 36) was a known criminal and drug user, currently out on bail
for the murder of a drug trafficker. Police decided to raid his house having
been tipped off that he was dealing in heroin and that he was in possession of
a firearm. When they approached the house, they apparently made enough
noise to alert Gary that someone was approaching. Since Gary was apparently fearful of reprisal for the previous murder, he armed himself with a
baseball bat and went to the back door. The police stated later that when they
burst into the house, they thought he was armed with a gun, rather than a
bat. Police fired several shots at Gary, following him into the house, with the
final shot being fired into the back of Gary's head. Gary died at the scene.
                                                     (Case No. 695–88)

In the five-year period of this study, there were in all ten homicides
where the police were responsible for the killing. The circumstances of
some of these cases has been a source of public concern, and a special
inquest has been carried out by the Coroner on some of these events (a
report was released in December 1993). In July 1993, in fact, several
police were charged with murder over the deaths in two of these
accounts (Case Nos 4364–88 and 2060–89).

Even more clearly than in the previous variation, there is a strong
theme of masculinity in these cases where the offenders in the original
crime become the victim of the homicide. Further, all of these reverse
victims are exceptionally marginal in both an economic and social sense.
It takes extreme conditions to push persons to the point where their own
lives become exposed as a consequence of their criminal activity.

The third variation: professional killings

One further and rather specialised variation consists of professional or
contract killings. While these contain elements distinct enough to
occupy, perhaps, a theme by themselves they are included here
because, as is true of the rest of such accounts, the link that ties the
victim and the offender goes backward to other crimes. The rationale
which leads to the killing, in other words, is to be found in the
connection of the victim with his or her earlier criminal activity (often
difficult to piece together). There were five such cases in these files.
The first of these cases, involving two victims, involves alleged contacts
within the criminal underworld:

It was the routine of Mrs B.P. to clean the Lygon Street flat in Carlton every Friday morning. When she arrived at the flat on 31 May 1985, she found its two occupants on the floor, dead. Both had been shot in the head in 'execution' style. As is typical in professional killings, which the police concluded this was, the story could be only partially pieced together.

One of the victims, A.C. (age 24, student) was an innocent victim who had the misfortune of becoming the flatmate of a person involved in the drug trade. The other victim, B.W. (age 23) was known to police as a result of his drug dealing, and his involvement with escort services. The limited information that the police could assemble suggests the possibility that 'hit men' from New Zealand were hired to 'damage' B.W. (that is, beat him up) as a warning because his behaviour had become erratic and threatening to the wider criminal organisation of which B.W. was a part. The police believe that when the two hit men went to the Carlton flat, they expected to find only one person. Upon finding two, the killers decided, according to the police report 'to kill both of them so there would be no witnesses.' The case remains unsolved. *(Case Nos 1584–85 and 1585–85)*

In another case involving two victims, both were apparently involved in the complex set of criminal activities that ultimately led to their deaths:

Lynnette G. (age 29) was a heroin addict who formed a de facto relationship with Robert P. (age 30) in August 1986. Shortly afterwards, the two moved into a private hotel, Purnell's, that had become the front for a crime business involving importation of drugs, armed robbery and standover debt collection. Robert became involved in the dealing of drugs, while Lynnette's role most often was on the importation side as a courier.

Robert and Lynnette played relatively minor roles in the operations of the group, which was alleged to be bossed by Peter G., Gary M. and John F. It is not clear why, but over time Robert's role in the group became problematic. Some of the troubles hinged around the arrest of one of the other couriers in the group, with whom Robert had developed a close relationship (it was alleged that the arrest of the courier was, in fact, engineered by Gary). At any rate, the three leaders became apprehensive of Robert, especially when he went on his own to Pentridge to speak with the arrested courier.

As a result of his contacts with the courier, Robert arranged to go into a bush location with Lynnette to pick up a supply of heroin left there by the arrested courier. Peter, Gary and John suggested that they all go and make a day of the trip, including a picnic. When Robert told a friend about the new arrangements, the friend tried to warn him about the possible dangers involved. Robert indicated that he thought there was no cause to worry. Robert and Lynnette set off on the picnic, and have not been seen since. Their bodies have not been recovered, but police have alleged that Peter, Gary and John arranged for their deaths, and then were able to dispose of the bodies in a fashion so that they would not be discovered.
(Cases Nos 1325–88 and 1326–88)

A common characteristic of these deaths is that it is impossible to state for certain what has happened. The victim has been known to be

involved in criminal activity (or connected with someone who was), and the death gives every indication of being a 'contract' or professional killing. The scenario is brief, and the events seem to connect back to an earlier pattern of criminality which is presumed to account for the circumstances which provoked the death.

A fourth variation: prison killings

Included within this cluster are cases which involve killings which took place inside prison walls. These pose a particular problem for classification because of the scant information which tends to be available. The first of these is brief:

M.A. (age 33) had a criminal history extending back to adolescence, and had experienced several stays in prison. One afternoon when the inmate count at Geelong Prison was one person short, during the resultant general search of the prison M. A. was found in a cell, dead as a result of multiple stab wounds to neck and chest. At inquest, the Coroner found that 'Despite continuing investigations the identity of the person or persons involved in the death has not been discovered.'   *(Case No. 2868–87)*

In common with such killings, no information could be obtained from other inmates which threw any light on the offenders in this homicide, let alone the social dynamics which resulted in the killing. This silence is found even where more of the specific circumstances are known, as in the following account:

Allen T. (age 41) was serving his time in Pentridge Prison. As Allen and a prison officer were delivering meals in 'H' Division, upon entering a yard the officer observed one of the inmates holding a homemade knife. Following standard procedure, the officer retreated to the doorway, calling for help. The door was then slammed shut from the inside. From a vantage point on the wall, another prison officer observed C.H. (a prisoner) strike Allen several times over the head with what appeared to be a white bag (which had been filled with weights). As well, when the officers were able to reach the scene, Allen was found to have suffered stab wounds (his death, however, resulted from the head injuries).

While Allen had earlier written to the State Ombudsman complaining that threats of violence on him were being ignored by the prison authorities, there was no indication of any motive or animosity involving C.H. (who was one of those convicted of the Russell Street bombing, in which a central police station was bombed, and one police constable killed, see Case No. 1133–86 below). None of the prisoners present in the yard provided information in the course of the investigation.   *(Case No. 3261–88)*

One of the common characteristics of the killings originating in the criminal culture is that little is actually known about the concrete

circumstances of the deaths. The offenders, as is common with the general scenario, are all male. The available evidence suggests strongly that the deaths are related to the criminal activities in which the victims have been participants. The bonds of the criminal culture, however, make it difficult to assess in most of these the specific provocation that has resulted in the killing. Even when a conviction results, the story of the homicide itself will most often be unclear. Again, what is clear is that the two victims, and their attackers, were all male.

The final variation: police as victims

Police work can be risky, involving as it does the responsibility for apprehension and control of individuals who under the right circumstances may be willing to resort to lethal violence. In the five-year period there were four such police victims, the first of these involved a police officer who interrupted two persons as they were in the process of stealing a car.

> Policeman M.M. (age 34) was on night duty during the early hours of a Saturday night in a small country town. After returning from patrol, he drove the police vehicle alone to his house to fetch some milk for coffee. On the way home, he came across R.N. and M.L. who were attempting to steal a car. They had successfully broken into the car, but when they had hot-wired it they found the battery was flat. As M.M. came across them, they were trying to push-start the car.
>
> M.M. parked the police car and after talking with the two for a moment, radioed back to the police station for details about the car. R.N. was, in fact, well known to the police and had an extensive record. He also harboured considerable resentment toward the police because of his perception of their harassment.
>
> When M.M. returned to the car to continue his questioning of the two suspects, a struggle broke out between R.N. and the policeman. R.N. gained control of the policeman's gun. M.M. shouted: 'Don't, R., don't do it.' R.N. answered back: 'I'm going to kill you', and fired five shots into M.M.
>
> (*Case No. 3589–86*)

In this account, the circumstances are of a classic type where a police officer encounters offenders as they are engaging in criminal activity, and then becomes a further victim of the crime. Some of the cases in Victoria where police are killed, however, result from a deep antagonism between police and members of the criminal underworld. Included among these is the death which resulted from the 'Russell Street Bombing':

> At about 12.30 pm on 27 March, 1986, a two-tone Holden Commodore was seen being parked on the kerb at Russell Street just outside the door of

the Police Complex. At 1 pm a large explosive device that had been placed in the car exploded, destroying the car, causing heavy damage to the police building, and injuring a large number of persons. One of these, Constable Angela R. Taylor died later in hospital from burns received in the explosion.

This set off one of the most extensive and exhaustive investigations in the history of the Victoria Police. Forensic examination of the explosion scene was exacting, and was able to establish that the device consisted of: (1) a 'Diamond' brand alarm clock; (2) an 'Everready' battery; (3) a block of wood (which was later identified as having been sawn from a post at the property of one of the accused); (4) 50 mm flat-head nails (which were identified as coming from a box of nails in the possession of another of the accused); (5) a galvanised metal strap (which was identified as coming from the lid of a 'Willow' brand rubbish bin owned by one of the accused); and (6) wires. Other items identifiable at the scene and later linked up with various of the accused included fragments of a rug and tool fragments.

The various files on this case run into hundreds of pages. Five persons were ultimately charged with the bombing. The complex story of the bombing works its way through several other crimes, including armed robberies of banks, a burglary of a milk bar, several car thefts, and armed robbery and burglary of a dwelling, a brutal sexual assault, and other offences. All of these offences weave in a complex pattern toward the gradual escalation of the motivation for the bombing, and the accumulation of the various bits and pieces of paraphernalia which were brought together in the construction and concealing of the explosive device. The five charged were all known offenders, and had done time in prison. Numerous witnesses later were able to testify to the 'intense hatred' of police by two of these in particular, and their 'desire to kill as many police and court staff as possible'.

(Case No. 1133–86)

This was the first of two well-known cases involving deliberate and planned killing of Victoria police. The second became known as the 'Walsh Street Killings':

Constables S. Tynan (age 22) and D. Eyre were on patrol when they were called upon to investigate a report of an abandoned car in the middle of the road in Walsh Street, South Yarra. As the two constables left their divisional van to approach the vehicle, they were gunned down by a number of men who had been waiting in nearby bushes.

Shortly after the killings, the Victoria Police began to piece together the story. Their informers in the underworld of Melbourne indicated that the shootings were in response to the gunning down of their friend who was a suspect in a homicide connected with an armed robbery (Case No. 4364–88, above). Following their leads, the police were able to identify a number of potential suspects and accomplices. Two of the suspects were subsequently killed by police in the process of apprehension (see Case No. 2060–89, above). Two individuals close to the remaining suspects were placed in protective custody after agreeing with police to testify against the remaining four individuals who were alleged to have taken part in the killings, and who were placed under arrest.

The case of the Crown relied heavily upon testimony of the two persons held in protective custody, but the testimony of these two collapsed during the course of the trial. In this case, unlike the Russell Street bombing, the police were not able to assemble a large body of persuasive forensic evidence to substantiate their case. The four defendants were acquitted after a lengthy trial. After the finding of the court, the Victoria Police took the unusual step of formally closing the file on the case.   *(Case Nos 4369–88 and 4370–88)*

There are a number of features which stand out in this account. One is that it shows how interconnected criminal events can be, since the initiation of these was a first killing involving an armed guard, which apparently then led to the attempted apprehension and shooting of the suspect of this killing (described above in Case No. 4364–88). In retaliation, the two police constables in the previous account (Case Nos 4369–88 and 4370–88) were allegedly chosen at random by underworld killers attempting to 'even the score'. In turn, this was followed by the police killing of two of the suspects of these Walsh Street shootings (Case Nos 2060–89 and 4949–88, this last not included in the text). It is not certain at this point if we have seen the end of this tragic trail of death. Police resentment is deep over the murder of the two constables, and the unsuccessful prosecution of the case laid against their alleged killers. In turn, friends in the criminal world who were close to those killed by the police also feel frustrated by the failure of the case against the police officer tried for killing Glen A. (Case No. 2060–89), as well as antagonism aimed at those who became witnesses for the prosecution in the Walsh Street killings. This potent mix of anger and frustration could easily lead to further violence and bloodshed.

Homicide during the course of crime: concluding observations

Thousands of crimes are committed every year in Victoria. Only rarely do these lead to a death. In some cases, the fact that a death results requires a bizarre turn of fortune, as in the case of the unsuccessful and probably drunken car thief who died in hospital as a result of a reaction to a drug used to treat the injuries he received at the hands of the owner of the car he attempted to steal (Case No. 2017–85 above).

One observation that can be made in most of these cases is that exceptional risks are being taken by the offender of the initial crime. One indication of this is the common role that guns play in these crimes. These are offenders who, in engaging in the initial offence such as armed robbery, are committed to a more desperate course of action than others who contemplate serious crimes. Many of these offenders are either firmly caught up in an established criminal career, as in the cases of police killer M.M. (and those involved in the Russell Street

bombing) or S.D. who shot a taxi driver, or they are enmeshed in heroin addiction, as in the cases of American Dave, or D.P. who killed his drug dealer. With their bonds to conventionality greatly attenuated, they are, thereby, on top of the risks taken in the commission of the initial crime, more ready to take desperate measures if something goes wrong during the course of that crime.

Closely related is the fact that this linkage of marginality and exceptional risk taking is to a large degree masculine behaviour. The offenders in 56 of the 61 cases where a death is attributable to the course of other crime are males. Women, like men, find themselves in desperate economic circumstances, and sometimes take risks as a result. When marginal women act, however, their actions are unlikely to place others, or themselves, at risk of violence, especially in terms of violence instrumental in the course of some criminal activity.

This form of homicide has been identified in most other studies of homicide. Wallace (1986: 160) in her Australian study found that 'instrumental' violence in the course of crime, or apprehension-intervention with respect to crime, accounted for 21 per cent of all homicides in New South Wales in the 1968–81 period. A slightly lower proportion was observed in the 1975–85 US data by Maxfield, who found that 16 per cent of homicides were in one way or another related to the commission of another crime (Maxfield, 1989: 675).

A feature of both of these studies is that they are based on very large numbers of cases. As a result, they provide some estimate of the levels of the specific types seen here. Both, for example, report that when the homicide is a situation of the 'double victim', that is, the victim of the homicide was also the victim of the other crime, robbery or theft account for a larger proportion than does sexual assault (these trends were more sharply pronounced in the United States, see Maxfield, 1989: 675, contrasted with Wallace, 1986: 159). Both researchers use the term 'instrumental' to highlight the link of these homicides with some other on-going criminal activity, and the same usage is suggested by Block and Block (1992) in their identification of instrumental killings as a form of 'homicide syndrome'. Maxfield (1989) uses the term 'reverse felony' to cover the situation where the criminal in the initial crime becomes the victim of the homicide, such events making up 3.3 per cent of all homicides in his US data. He reports that the police or citizens are found in roughly equal proportions as the killer in these events.

At a more theoretical level, Daly and Wilson (1988, and Wilson and Daly, 1985) have identified the general issue of masculine competitiveness, and employed the concept of 'risk taking' to cover the hazards posed when persons engage in behaviour such as serious criminality.

As such, they are able to place this specific pattern of homicide within a general theory which sees masculine proclivity for violence as part of more general strategies of coping with the competitive situation which exists between males.

A final observation of these cases is that in a large proportion of the cases the victim and the offender are unknown to each other (this is especially true in those involving double victims). In the more common classifications of homicide research, these would be considered 'stranger' homicides. Examination of data on 'stranger' homicides in other research, in fact, shows that a majority of these take place in the course of some other crime. In the national study of stranger homicide in Canada, for example, Langevin and Handy (1987) report just over three-fourths of all stranger homicide fit this pattern, with the largest proportion (44.4 per cent of all stranger homicides) taking place during a robbery, with a smaller proportion happening as a result of sexual assault (21.1 per cent), with the remaining taking place in a category described simply as 'during other crime' (10.3 per cent). Wallace (1986) turns the analysis around, reporting that in the case of homicides that occur in the course of robbery or theft, almost three-fourths (72 per cent) involved situations where the victim and offender were 'strangers'.

In the present research (using an approach similar to that of Wallace, 1986: 159, with respect to these forms of homicide), the fact that the parties are strangers to each other is deemed to be an ancillary feature of the dynamic which links offender and victim. The definitive feature of their relationship is the nature of the crime which is what brings them together, rather than the fact that they are strangers.

Putting the matter another way, it is suggested that in thinking about the 'relationship' between victim and offender in situations where the killing results from the course of other crime, the category that is developed should refer explicitly to that pattern of criminal activity. The relationship which produces the death is the crime itself. In some cases the individuals know each other, in other cases they do not. If they know each other, they may have been friends at one time, or it may just be a passing acquaintance. It is not the relationship of friend, acquaintance, or stranger which defines social dynamics that result in the killing. It is, in fact, the criminal behaviour. As such, that criminal behaviour should provide the central focus of attention in the way these homicides are classified, and in the theorising about this risk-taking behaviour.

CHAPTER 6

Homicide as a form of conflict resolution

Disagreements and conflicts are an inevitable feature of social life. What varies widely are the procedures employed to negotiate such discord. For many, the thought of violence, or even direct confrontation with others, is repugnant. Elaborate mechanisms are called upon to rationalise and drain away the tension of potentially threatening scenes. As an extreme measure, the civil law serves as an ultimate bureaucratic process of dispute resolution. In some circumstances, however, these non-violent alternatives are rejected, and more direct, and violent, methods are employed to settle the disagreement.

A review of the present case studies indicates that among the masculine scenarios of violence is found a persistent theme where violence is taken up as a planned device for the resolution of conflict. Such a tactic is not to be undertaken lightly. The risks are great, since in the course of the resulting conflict there will often be a fight involving deadly weapons, with the consequence that the initial perpetrator of the violence becomes its victim. Afterwards, the rational and premeditated character of the killing may expose the killer to the full weight of prosecution for a charge of murder. How it is that some males are willing to take such enormous risks is a puzzle that can be resolved only by review of the texts of several accounts of this form of homicide. There were, in all, 38 of these conflict-resolution homicides, these making up one in ten (10 per cent) of all homicides.

Cases of violent conflict resolution

Most of the accounts of conflict resolution involved individuals who at an earlier point in their relationship had been reasonably close, that

113

closeness indicated by a willingness to share such resources as money or living accommodation. What would then happen is that the very sharing of these resources provided the core of a dispute between the two which would not go away, but could not be ignored. Debts, in particular, can be difficult to negotiate:

> Gregory R. (age 25, unemployed) and Ken S. (age 24, also unemployed) had been close friends since primary school. Neither had regular full-time employment, and evidence suggests that they were well enmeshed in the local drug scene.
>
> A recent rift had developed between them, arising out of a $600 loan Ken owed Gregory (Gregory had lent the money as part of a drug deal, but Ken had used the money to buy drugs for himself). Ken also had reason to believe that Gregory had been informing on him to their motorcycle gang ('The Immortals').
>
> Deciding to bring the matter to some sort of a head, Ken obtained a gun and persuaded a friend to drive him around looking for Gregory. They tried a number of addresses, including a party where Gregory had been earlier. The two ultimately found Gregory back at his home. Ken went up to the door carrying his gun. Gregory, apparently having been forewarned that trouble was afoot, and met Ken at the door holding a sawn-off shotgun in his hands. An argument ensued, leading to a struggle in which glass panels of the door were broken. Ken's gun fired, striking Gregory in the head and killing him instantly.   *(Case No. 175–86)*

In many respects, this represents almost an ideal type of conflict-resolution homicide. Both of the individuals are enmeshed in a lifestyle of unemployment and drug use that places them well at the boundaries of ordinary community life. The dispute is about a matter, money lent over a drug deal, that cannot be brought within the boundaries of legitimate dispute-resolution procedures.

The two individuals have known each other for some time, and within some homicide-relationship typologies (for example, Wolfgang, 1958; Wallace, 1986) this would be considered as a homicide among 'friends'. There is a reasonable amount of planning in this particular account, such that the violence is a considered and intentional device for dealing with the conflict over the debt. It could be argued, of course, that Ken did not necessarily mean to kill Gregory. What is certain, however, is that a scene was created where the threat of what could be lethal violence was contemplated as a way of bringing a conflict to some end.

In the previous case, the issue was that of a debt, a matter that can easily set these forces in motion, as is illustrated by the next narrative as well:

> Ben was a well-known drug dealer in the country town of Bairnsdale, and Gary had been buying marijuana from him for years. Some months before,

Gary had made a $200 purchase from Ben, but had been unable to pay because money was tight. As time went on, Ben became increasingly insistent about repayment, and began to make threats of violence. The threats became increasingly abusive, and at one point led to a fight between the two. Ben followed this with telephone calls, threatening the life not only of Gary, but also his wife and children. Deciding that Ben was serious, one night Gary gathered up his shotgun, dressed himself in black, and went to Ben's house. Peering through the window, Gary saw that Ben was watching TV. Gary fired several shots at Ben, killing him on the spot. Gary then set the house on fire in an attempt to confuse the investigation, but the fire was put out before any serious damage was done.   *(Case No. 1127–87)*

One comes to know one's customers over time, in the drug world as in any other business. Conventional and unconventional transactions are based in part on the building up of trust between buyer and seller. For the person in a conventional business, however, there are a number of options open in the pursuit of a slow paying customer that are closed to one who trades in an illegal commodity. Pushed to the extreme, the grievance of this seller became progressively surrounded with violence, reaching a climax with the lethal outcome.

When thieves fall out: coping with friends who steal

The more heavily the participants are involved in criminal activity, the more difficult it becomes to settle disagreements within conventional frameworks, as indicated in the following:

The trouble between Del (age 33, plumber) and George came to a head over the Christmas holidays. The two had first become friends when Del was a customer of the shop where George worked as butcher. What was especially attractive to Del were the drug deals that George offered as a sideline to his regular fare. Del over time gradually became involved in the drug business with George, and for some period the drugs were kept at Del's house since it seemed safer to keep them there. At one point, George and Del together raided a competitor's marijuana crop, taking the spoils to Del's house where it was packaged and stored until it was sold.

Gradually, however, the friendship cooled, and George in particular came to distrust Del. At first George was apparently ill at ease with the control that Del started exerting over what he thought was his business, but he then became convinced that Del was stealing from him, this reaching the point where George became convinced that Del was responsible for a burglary to his house. Just before Christmas, George confided to a friend that he had purchased a hand gun, and was going to 'take care' of Del. Two days after Christmas, Del arranged to do a deal for drugs with George, giving George an advance of $2000 on a transaction that was to total $8000. Later that day, George called Del, telling him that he could come to the house to collect the drugs. When Del arrived, George stepped up behind him, and shot him several times, killing him on the spot.   *(Case No. 5447–89)*

If you are both a thief and a drug dealer, how do you handle the problem of a partner who is stealing from you? Bound tightly together because of business and friendship networks, it becomes progressively more difficult to ignore the perceived problem of the partner's dishonesty. George in his view found himself worked into a corner where in order to sever the working relationship, he had to take the step of killing the distrusted partner.

There is a similar account in which the individuals originally became involved with each other as a result of friendship forged in prison:

> The badly decomposed body of Mitch B. (age 32, unemployed) was under a heavy growth of weeds at the back of a block of flats in mid-1988. Three years later Harold M. and Jim M. were charged with the death on the basis of information supplied by a prison informer. The three had been close as a result of time spent together in gaol, but they fell out because of allegations that Mitch had been stealing from Harold's wife. Unable to deal with the matter any other way, Harold and Jim obtained a pistol and solved their problem by killing Mitch.   *(Case No. 1792–88)*

Again we see here the problem of persons enmeshed in the criminal subculture confronting the problem of theft. In a way similar to the previous account, the individuals in this narrative found that their options narrowed swiftly to the use of lethal violence. In a similar case study, the planned use of violence against one who was thought to be stealing from the group suddenly turned back on to those initiating the violence:

> Everett (age 32, unemployed) was a chronic alcoholic and user of amphetamines, with a history of violence. Michael (age 17) also was a heavy user of amphetamines, and used Everett as his source of supply. Since he was unemployed, Michael would steal goods and trade them with Everett for drugs.
>
> Everett and two of his friends were drinking at a hotel in an outer eastern suburb, and as they became more and more drunk (Everett's blood alcohol level was later established at 0.238), they decided that they would give Michael a 'hiding' because of his alleged theft of a camera from a neighbour and of some marijuana plants from Everett.
>
> When Michael arrived at the hotel later that afternoon, Everett and two of his friends offered to drive Michael to a place where he could sell the camera. They took Michael to a secluded area in the Dandenongs, and started to bash him up in the car, telling him that they were going to 'bash him up and cause serious injury'. and that 'This would be your last ride'. All the while, Michael (who had thought that Everett was a friend) kept asking what he had done wrong.
>
> Everett then ordered Michael out of the car, and was helped when one of his friends grabbed Michael by the hair and jerked him out of the car. At this point Michael produced a knife. When the attackers crowded around him, he slashed out, stabbing Everett in the neck, and another of the group in the

chest. Michael then took to his heels, and was able to make his escape. Everett died from his wounds before he could obtain medical aid. When questioned by police, Michael stated that he had acted in self-defence, arguing: 'What else could I do?' *(Case No. 745–88)*

The turning of the tables on those who initiated the attack provides an illustration of how the odds can turn quickly in these events, and is another example of 'victim precipitated' homicide (Wolfgang, 1958). What it serves to underscore is the important point that the decision to use violence is one which involves great risks, including the possibility that equally or more extreme violence may be thrown back upon the person who initiates the violence. In this case, and in others as well, what is at issue in the scenario is the willingness of some involved to set themselves off on a course to use violence to settle a dispute. It is not always clear how that violence will be negotiated, and who becomes the ultimate victim.

Other matters: the problem of shared space

There are a number of sources for the conflicts which set the forces in motion. Another can be that these persons often share the same space, and out of that closeness disputes can arise which do more than erode the friendship:

Jimmy Z. (age 37) rented a house in Kensington (an inner Melbourne suburb). Since the house was close to their work, his two friends Tommy S. (age 21, factory labourer) and Daryl W. (age 22) settled into a routine of staying at his house. This continued for some weeks despite the fact that Jimmy and Tommy became more and more hostile to one another.

As Daryl tells the story, Jimmy woke him at 9 am one morning, asking: 'What am I going to do?' Since his friend was clearly distressed, Daryl agreed to walk up to the local shops with him to buy 'smokes and a drink'. On the way to the milk bar, Jimmy asked Daryl if he could obtain a gun. Daryl said that he wouldn't be able to, but then asked why Jimmy needed a gun. The reply was: 'To kill Tommy'.

Daryl states that at this point he argued that this seemed an extreme reaction. Jimmy indicated that he was fed up with Tommy, that he was tired of the constant niggling, and that they had had an argument the previous night in which Tommy had threatened him with a knife.

When they returned to the house, Jimmy asked Daryl to close a connecting door that would close off an area where a handyman was doing some house repairs. Jimmy then picked up a hammer, and walked over to where Tommy was sleeping, and began to hit Tommy repeatedly about the head. Not knowing what to do, Daryl ran out. When he returned an hour or so later, Jimmy was covered with blood, the hammer was broken, and Tommy was dead. *(Case No. 1005–86)*

Unlike the previous accounts, in this narrative the violence was not provoked by debt or theft, but rather seemed to be an extreme response to gradually accumulating, mutually provocative acts between flatmates which had begun to include threats of violence. The question 'What am I going to do?' captures the problem faced by these individuals. In marginal groups, cut off from the protection represented by police and the law, the threat of violence may be especially disturbing. In their view, they may see little recourse but to take up even greater violence as a way of coping with the looming threat.

At the same time, one other rather odd case study indicates that the factors which cut people off are many, and can include cultural differences as well:

> Eduardo and Austin were both Africans who had been sharing a flat for several months. Their original friendship had deteriorated, and the two had been bickering for some time. Austin's complaints included the fact that Eduardo refused to pay his share of either rent or food, and in addition kept removing Austin's property (including TV and video). Eduardo was also, in Austin's view, continually making noise at inconvenient hours. The arguments became more heated, and reached the point where the two were challenging each other to fight. Austin told a friend of his that he was a 'commando' and that he was going to kill Eduardo.
>
> One morning, Eduardo got up early, and made his usual amount of noise while taking a shower. Austin was awakened, and again complained to Eduardo. Both decided, according to Austin's account, that the time had come to settle their differences. They both went to their rooms and dressed for the fight, which took place in the driveway outside. Austin quickly got the better of Eduardo, and after he had punched him several times, Eduardo fell to the ground. Austin then grabbed him by the hair and banged his head several times on the concrete. After a few minutes, when Eduardo did not regain consciousness, Austin threw a bucket of water on him, thinking that would revive him. When Eduardo did not respond, Austin went to a neighbour, who summoned an ambulance. Eduardo, however, died of massive brain injuries before medical assistance arrived.   (*Case No. 2256–89*)

Austin and Eduardo had been close enough at one point to be willing to share accommodation. As their mutual grievances accumulated, the two apparently had no way to vent the hostility, given their view of themselves as males, but to use their fists. While in other circumstances this might have led to a kind of mutual resolution of the problem, the exceptional violence of Austin assured a lethal end to this form of masculine dispute arbitration.

Violence as a counter to violence

With these groups caught outside the world of conventionality, one common feature of the accumulation of dispute and misunderstanding

is that escalation leads to threats and displays of violence, then provoking the use of violence as a form of protection, as in the case of Jimmy seeking a way of dealing with Tommy in Case No. 1005–86 above. This use of violence as a counter to threats is seen in the following narrative as well:

In June 1988 two timber cutters exploring a mine shaft in country Victoria discovered a badly decomposed, headless body. Documents on the body established that it was that of Phil H. (age 35, unemployed), better known to his friends as 'Rhino'. The story the police were able to piece together indicated that for some time Rhino had been a source of trouble for his friends.

On the day he was killed, Rhino had engaged in a heated argument with Perry H. (age 20, unemployed). Partly the argument was because Rhino had earlier broken into the house of Perry's sister, stealing a video and stereo. Also, Perry was certain that Rhino had stolen some pills from one of the rooms in his house. In response, Rhino was said to have threatened not only Perry, but Perry's children, and was seen to have struck one of the children.

The group (several lived at the house) then calmed down a bit, and settled into some serious drinking. After a few hours, most had gone to sleep. One of the residents of the house stated that Perry then came up to him and said: 'Let's kill the scumbag.' The two then finished off about half a bottle of whisky, and by then 'were in an aggro mood'. The two went out to Rhino's truck, where Rhino slept. Perry went in through the passenger's door, his friend went in on the driver's side. The friend stated that at this point Perry said 'something like, how you goin'?' and Rhino turned to the friend and said: 'G'day'. The friend states that at this point he told Perry to forget about it, but that as he was turning away he heard a couple of 'thumps' and then heard Rhino gurgle. The friend returned to the truck, and looking at Rhino told Perry that he was dead, but Perry still stabbed Rhino two or three more times in the chest.

The conspirators first disposed of the body by burying it in a shallow grave in nearby bushland. Becoming apprehensive that it would be discovered, they returned later to dig the body up and then dispose of it down the mine shaft. At some later point one of the co-defendants returned to the scene and cut the head off the body and buried it in isolated bushland some distance away.

When questioned later, Perry said that: 'I wouldn't have done it if he didn't threaten the people I love.' (*Case No. 2329–88*)

What methods are available to handle personal threats within close personal circles? For others caught more firmly in the conventional world, such situations might be dealt with by a call to the police, perhaps some technique of avoidance, or calling on friends or neighbours to help out in solving the problem in some non-violent fashion. These males choose a violent path. The killing, further, is not a spontaneous event, but comes after a period of reflection and planning, somewhat abbreviated (and not notably astute). This combination of marginality,

the building up of violent exchanges, and then an ultimate intentioned homicide is found in the following account as well:

> Joe A. (age 28) was shot down early one morning just after he had started at his job as a cleaner in the local post-primary school. He had a prison record, and a history of violence combined with a reputation for a bad temper. He was known to be a good street fighter, and had worked as a bouncer at a number of local pubs and discos.
>
> He had previously been a close friend of Mike S. (they had met in an Office of Corrections Attendance Centre). According to police, in addition to socialising with Joe at parties and discos, Mike had also been involved with him in committing crimes. Mike also had a reputation for violence.
>
> The two tempers ultimately clashed, and a fight resulted in which Joe hit Mike with a spanner. Mike had become convinced that Joe had informed on him while he was in gaol, and that he also was responsible for firing shots at his house. When police were called as a result of the shots, Mike told them not to worry as he himself 'would fix things up'. Shortly afterwards, when Joe went out from the school where he was working to check on a report that someone was tampering with his car, he was fired at by a man the police believe to be Mike. Joe attempted to run, but was cut down by the bullets. His killer walked up to him and fired a final shot into his head before jogging off to a waiting car.   *(Case No. 291–86)*

In this account is found the interesting phenomenon of the coming together of the two worlds, one legitimate, the other illegitimate, when the police became involved over the shots which were fired just prior to the final episode. The informal rules of the culture in which many of these individuals live dictate, however, that conventional mechanisms for deflecting conflict away from a violent and deadly course were closed off. In the local language, one becomes a 'dog' if he 'dobs in' a fellow member of the culture. Here, police offered to help but Mike elected to 'fix' things himself, with a gun.

Dead men (or women) tell no tales: killing to silence

There are three cases where a friend has become a potential threat in terms of possible testimony to either police or courts. The offender then protected himself by killing the victim who is seen as posing the threat. The homicide in such cases, in other words, is motivated by the intent to destroy critical evidence. In the first of these cases, the victim had early on willingly agreed to participate in the cover-up of a crime, only to come under increasing pressure as the successive interrogations wore down the concocted story:

> Peter S. (age 15, student) had been present when his older brother and Don C. (age 26) were involved in stealing a car. When Peter's older brother fled to

Queensland, Peter became the key witness whose story would either convict or acquit Don. Don was greatly agitated by the prospect of going to prison, and offered to buy Peter a trail bike if he would change his story to protect him. This Peter apparently agreed to do, and Don bought him the trail bike.

As the investigation developed, however, Peter's story became unstuck when he realised that if he continued with his story he would be tripped up in its inconsistency and also throw the whole blame on to his brother. For a while, Peter wavered between two different stories, but finally broke down and told the true story which implicated Don.

Don was furious, telling his friend George E. that 'the little bastard dobbed me in'. Don and George decided the way that Don could avoid prison was to kill Peter. They approached a friend to borrow a dinghy which they would use to drown Peter, telling the friend what they intended to do. The friend refused the request.

Their next plan was to take Peter on a hunting trip, and to shoot him. This was easy to arrange since Peter thought of Don as a good friend, and enjoyed their hunting trips together. They planned the trip for a weekday, saying to one of their friends: 'Peter is going on a one-way trip on Thursday. It's all arranged because he is going to wag school and nobody will know where he went. His mother won't miss him because he's done it before.' The friend was unsuccessful in explaining that what was planned was 'stupid', and that Don would, at most, be at risk of a good behaviour bond since the alleged offence was his first, but Don's reaction was: '... yeah ... but this way I would be sure.'

Late on that Thursday, Don arrived back at his friend's house, saying: 'Well, I'm glad that's over.' He then recounted in detail how he and his friend had carried out the shooting. There seems to be a strange sense of unreality in this case, since Don told other friends the story as well. The friends thought that Don was simply telling tall tales, until the TV news broadcasts reported the finding of Peter's body.   (*Case No. 1606–86*)

In this case, other friends attempted to warn the offender away from the violent path he had set for himself, but he persisted. The successful removal of the certain threat of the former friend's testimony came only at the price of the graver peril posed by the charge of murder which was entered against him.

As odd as this trade-off may seem, this was not an isolated case. Another similar account involves a group of persons all of whom had been in prison:

Richard M. (age 21, unemployed) was a passenger in a car being driven by Paul R. (age 19) when there was an accident. Since Paul had a prison record, was drunk, and was not licensed to drive he prevailed upon Richard to claim that he was driving when the accident took place. Being 'good mates' Richard agreed.

Richard was not fully aware of the consequences of his act of friendship. Tension began to build between Richard and Paul as it became clear that Richard was going to face serious traffic charges in magistrates' court (where his prior prison record would spell trouble), as well as a bill for $5000 damages which Paul could not pay.

Paul became convinced that Richard was going to break under the pressure. About four weeks after the accident, Richard arrived home from work in the company of two friends. Paul and two others drove up. Richard went over and chatted for a couple of minutes, returning to his friends saying that if he did not return; 'they would know what to do.' Then one of Paul's friends came over to the two, saying: 'You haven't seen me here tonight, boys.'

Later that night, Paul woke up a friend asking if he could leave a car at his house overnight, saying that he would return the next day to 'clean the blood out of it.' The friend observed that Paul had blood on his hands and clothing. Paul returned the next day, and cleaned out the car, recounting to this friend in detail how he and his other two friends had carried out Richard's killing. Having left so many persons in possession of the knowledge of what the three had done, the Coroner had no trouble finding that Richard had died from wounds 'to the throat, chest and abdomen which were unlawfully and maliciously inflicted by . . . ' Paul and his two friends.

(Case No. 2951–85)

In this case, the cluster of individuals involved, including both victim and offender, had extensive criminal records including serving time in prison. Perhaps because of the common prison experiences, there was a heightened level of anger over what was perceived as the potential breach of loyalty in informing on a friend, this in part accounting for the brutality shown in the actual homicide. The final of these cases involved an individual who had just been released from prison:

Kenny I. (age 32) was released from prison at midday on a Tuesday, and immediately set about making plans for the elimination of Val W. Apparently Val, a prostitute who had, according to police testimony, 'a long criminal history', was a potential witness in a case against some of Kenny's friends in prison.

That evening, Kenny picked up his friend Lenny C. (age 26, unemployed and also with a recent prison record), and the two of them went by Val's flat to pick her up. While at the flat, Kenny, Lenny and Val 'shot up' some heroin. As Val went into the bathroom to inject herself, Kenny told her flatmate that Val had 'to be put off.' The two women, Kenny and Lenny then drove off.

The group were at the time in the northern suburbs of Melbourne, and drove along a deserted street close to the Campbellfield shopping centre. The flatmate in her testimony to the police alleged that at that point Kenny, Lenny and Val got out of the car, supposedly to 'do a drug deal' according to the story which they told the unsuspecting Val. A few minutes later, the woman stated that she 'heard a bang', and the two men then jumped in the car and said: 'Let's go', saying to her: 'You've seen nothing, heard nothing, and know nothing.'

The three then went to a nearby fast food outlet, and made themselves conspicuous to the attending staff. This was part of the tale they concocted which was to include them dropping Val off to do a drug deal, with them returning to find her killed by some unknown drug dealer. Unfortunately,

the woman friend yielded under police interrogation, providing an account of the events which resulted in Kenny and Lenny being charged for the murder of Val. The woman disappeared prior to their trial, and it seems highly likely that she, too, fell victim to this form of protective violence.

(Case No. 4740–86)

If possible, this group of individuals appear to fall even farther beyond the boundaries of conventional life than the other groups we have examined. Deeply enmeshed in a criminal culture, which partly originated in prison, there was on the one hand scarce regard for informers, while on the other there was operating an equation which gave little value to the life of the victim in comparison to the threat of testimony which might send one of their mates to prison. Neither dead men, nor dead women, tell tales, and without such tales it is often impossible to mount a prosecution. In these last three accounts, the disagreement which is resolved through violence involves a triangular pull between the two parties (victim and offender) and the justice system.

Homicide and conflict resolution among more conventional males

While in general this pattern of conflict resolution appears to involve persons whose lifestyle is well removed from conventionality, there were a few whose patterns of living were, in fact, closer to mainstream existence:

Sam M. (age 46, property developer) and his wife were keen gamblers, travelling regularly to various casinos in Australia. On one of their visits to South Australia, they met Arnold through mutual friends. Sam and Arnold then started going to casinos together, often gambling against each other at backgammon. In late May 1989 Sam and Arnold played backgammon against each other at Adelaide, and Arnold ended up owing $17 000 to Sam.

Arnold was unable to pay the debt on the spot. A month later, in late June, Sam arranged for Arnold to come to Bendigo to bring at least some money to reduce the debt. Prior to leaving for Bendigo, Arnold obtained eight sticks of gelignite from a friend, telling the friend that he needed it to blow up a stump. The friend commented that Arnold seemed concerned at the noise and smoke made by a conventional burning fuse, and had asked for instructions on the obtaining and use of an electronic detonator.

Arnold then left for Bendigo, being met at the airport by Sam. The two men began playing backgammon that night, and were still playing late at night when Sam's wife went to bed. When the wife returned home from work the following day, she was surprised to find that Arnold was still there, and that he and Sam were continuing to play backgammon. The wife commented that she thought Arnold had planned to go home that day, and he replied that there had been a problem in transferring the money from his wife's account. Sam said that the money wasn't that important, and offered to drive Arnold to the airport if he wanted to go home. Arnold insisted that he would

stay. At some point in the night she was told that Arnold had won back $5000 of the money he owed.

When Sam's wife arrived home the next night, she found once again that Arnold was still there, and that the two were continuing their backgammon game. The wife reported later that Sam seemed agitated, and assumed that this was because of the troubles that Arnold said he was having in transferring the money that was owed from the out-of-town account.

The wife went to bed at about 11 pm, and the men were still gambling. Before she went to bed she went downstairs to assure herself that all the locks were fixed on the security doors. She was unable to recall when her husband came to bed, noting only that it was quite late. Arnold later stated that the two had quit at about 2 am, and that he had then gone to his bed in a back bedroom.

Just after 6 in the morning, there was a large explosion in the couple's bedroom which was at the front of the apartment. The wife was able to stagger out on to a balcony, where she was rescued by a neighbour. When she had last seen her husband, he was unconscious and on fire. He died at the scene, with the cause of death being multiple injuries as a result of the explosion.

Arnold later stated that he had won back the money that he was owed, but Sam's wife disputed this claim, pointing out that the score sheet was not tallied in the manner that her husband used. The police became suspicious when Arnold's evidence became inconsistent over time, and when it did not fit with other witness accounts or with the forensic evidence. Arnold was charged by the police with both murder and attempted murder.

(Case No. 981–89)

This case represents a qualitatively different scenario from some of the other accounts. While the violence is clearly masculine, and it involves persons who could be considered friends, the principals are not deeply involved in a life of social marginality. The killing appears to be more an act of desperation by a person pushed to the wall by a large debt. A similar account is found in the following:

Ken P. (age 45, independent trucking contractor) was a hard-working 'truckie' who owned his own truck and was generally known to be a hard businessman where money was concerned. Three years previously he had formed a business partnership with John M. (age 40), but the partnership broke up after disagreements developed over money matters. Ken claimed that John owed him in the range of $35 000 from the proceeds of the part-nership. Business and personal failure loomed over John. His wife left him, and his personal behaviour became noticeably erratic. It was his view that Ken was cheating him, and taking away trucking jobs that were rightfully his.

One night as Ken was loading his truck at a truck depot in country Orbost, a shot was heard, and upon investigation Ken was found on the ground beside his truck, with a bullet wound in his side. He died some three weeks later of complications from the wound which was established to be from a .303 rifle. John M. was later apprehended and charged with the homicide.

(Case No. 1314–85)

These last two narratives share with others the common theme of masculinity, friendship, and argument of debt, and violence, but differ in that the offenders cannot be seen to be deeply mired in a life of exceptional marginality. When pushed to extremes, it appears that some conventional males will call upon unconventional violence as a way of resolving what are seen to be desperate circumstances, as illustrated in the following as well:

Ross D. (age 50, maintenance officer) had been working for a couple of years with the Ministry of Housing in Pascoe Vale. He had become progressively frustrated with his work situation. He had indicated to witnesses that he felt frustrated by what he saw as inadequate and inefficient work practices, and by his inability to change them. Over time, his resentment towards his workmates began to build, especially in relation to his supervisor, Graham S.

Things reached a head when a tenant's dispute resulted in a complaint against Ross, which in turn led to Graham filing a report on Ross. In reply, Ross alleged that there were various incidents of corruption among his workmates.

One evening late in August, Ross's parents (with whom he lived) reported that Ross appeared 'unresponsive and vacant'. He was 'abrupt and grumpy' toward his father, and spent much of the evening sitting at a table writing. After that, he appeared restless, and was, according to his mother 'like a caged lion, up and down.' He left the house at 10 pm, refusing to tell his parents where he was going, other than saying he was 'going for a drive'.

Shortly afterwards, neighbours of Graham heard cries for help and moans, and saw a car fitting the description of Ross's car driving off down the road. A few minutes later, another neighbour found Graham unconscious in his driveway, covered with blood. From the forensic evidence, it was clear that Graham had been attacked in the loungeroom of his home, and had attempted to flee, travelling only as far as the driveway (where he died). Ross committed suicide by driving into a semi-trailer on the Goulburn Highway the following morning (there were five suicide notes left behind, which were what Ross had been writing the night before).   (*Case No. 3113–89*)

Conflicts at work can be vexing, but most find other ways of dealing with such situations that fall well short of violence, let alone lethal violence. On occasion, money matters can push conventional as well as unconventional individuals to exceptional action, as found in the following:

Alex (age 52, farmer) and John were neighbours and farmers. Running into severe financial difficulty, John decided that the solution to his problems would be to subdivide his property. This required the submission of plans to local council for approval. That approval was not granted, primarily because of objections filed by neighbours, the principal of these being Alex.

The pressures on John began to mount. In his view, it was the stress of their stretched financial circumstances which led to his mother's death from cancer. Finally, the bank informed John that unless the subdivision went ahead in the immediate future, they would be forced to foreclose.

John's story at this point was that he had heard gunshots coming from Alex's property. He had previously spoken to Alex's son about similar incidents. This time, John stated that he went to Alex's house to sort the matter out, taking with him a loaded .303 rifle. John stated that he knocked on Alex's back door, and that when Alex came out he ordered John off the property. According to this account, the two then began to wrestle over the weapon, and while he was unclear over the details, he admitted that Alex was shot while he was on the ground trying to rise from a prone position (Alex died from a 'close range gunshot wound to the head', according to the autopsy report). John then went home and changed and burned his clothing. He also went to a nearby jetty and dropped the rifle into Corio Bay (where it was later recovered by police). John was charged with murder by the police.   *(Case No. 2971–89)*

Of the total group of conflict-resolution homicides (41 in all), there were four of these cases where it could be said that the males involved were respectable in terms of their work and social lives. In these accounts, the violence as in other narratives is masculine and aimed at the resolution of a long-standing dispute. These four offenders could not be seen, however, as being tied to unconventional lifestyles or patterns. There are a few cases, in other words, when what appear to be relatively commonplace males are pushed to some extreme they call upon exceptional violence as a reasoned device for the resolution of personal friction. This was not common, however, since roughly only one in ten (4 of 41) of the conflict-resolution cases in these files involved individuals who could be seen as relatively conventional in terms of their lifestyles.

There was as well one further case where the violence represents a collision of conventional and unconventional worlds:

Rick was a self-taught, self-employed motor mechanic who made a living by reconditioning motor cars and engines. In May 1987 he advertised a V8 Valiant engine for sale in the *Melbourne Trading Post*. Phillip (age 35, unemployed) bought the engine from Rick and fitted it to his car. When he was unable to start the car, he called Rick to complain. Rick went to Phillip's house, and in order to attempt to start the car, supplied a starter motor at no cost. When the car still wouldn't start, Rick towed the car back to his garage and stripped the engine down. He found that the engine, which had been in perfect shape when he sold it, had twice the required amount of oil, and, as well, there was sand in the oil.

When Rick informed Phillip of the problem, Phillip began to show the first signs of aggression (Phillip had a long history of criminal offences, including arrests for assault). When Rick was unable to fix the car to Phillip's satisfaction, he began to make threats toward Rick, including threats of shooting up his house and 'blowing off his knee caps'.

When these threats became persistent, Rick's wife went to the police, returning to the police some five days later when the harassment continued (this time accompanied by Rick).

Drawing again upon the *Trading Post*, this time as a buyer, Rick purchased a .22 semi-automatic rifle, and taught his wife how to use it. The rifle was then kept stored, fully loaded, in the wardrobe of the couple's bedroom.

Phillip had decided it was time to take action regarding his threats. At about 5 one evening, Rick and his wife heard Phillip pounding on the back door. When they did not let him in, Phillip began to break down the back door. Rick called out several times telling Phillip to leave the house, but Phillip ignored these requests, and finally succeeded in forcing his way in through the broken back door. By then Rick had gathered up the rifle from the bedroom, and as Phillip entered the house, Rick shot him five times. Phillip staggered out of the house, and collapsed near the back gate. He was conveyed to the nearby Dandenong Hospital where he died three days later.

(Case No. 2622–87)

While the individuals in this account were far from friends, in many respects the account shares much in common with the earlier narratives of conflict resolution. Persons with greater resources and a different understanding of the legal system might pursue more conventional avenues to redress a problem arising out of what is perceived as a failure to live up to contractual obligations. On Phillip's side, his background of marginality and aggression provided him with a set of experiences such that the effective way to resolve conflict was direct physical violence. While Rick was perhaps less marginal, he, too, had a criminal history and as well was inclined to deal with Phillip's violence by the counter ploy of violence (although Rick and his wife had made at least an attempt to seek out conventional procedures to solve the problem). Ultimately, the two males were reduced to a situation where violence was met with violence, with fatal consequences.

Discussion

The categorisation of homicide found in previous research has not identified in explicit terms this particular pattern of killing as a mechanism of conflict resolution. In the most common of the 'social relationship' classification schemes based on relational distance, these conflict-resolution homicides never involve strangers, nor in the present instance are family members involved. The nature of the conflicts dictates that the parties involved have developed some amount of personal knowledge of each other (in order for the conflict to develop out of that relationship), so definitively most often these would fall within the boundaries of homicides between 'friends' or 'acquaintances'.

While such a classification is technically correct, by itself it tells us little about why the homicide occurs. In fact, in the first attempt to organise these themes (from the 1985–86 Victorian data), most of these homicides were placed within a grouping of killings occurring in a

relationship of intimacy, that intimacy being friendship (see Polk and Ranson, 1991b). This classification changed as more data emerged from the second phase of the research (when the 1987–89 data were considered). What this form of internal replication showed was the inherent weakness of the traditional classification methods. People do not kill each other because they are friends. Something has to happen to push friends to the point where the previous bond of intimacy is transformed and violence becomes possible.

In the replication phase, it became clearer that there were two patterns by which persons who have been friends reach the point where extreme violence between them became possible. One, it was necessary to recognise that friends, as well as strangers and acquaintances, can find themselves in a situation where one lays down a threat to honour or reputation which is seen as requiring a violent response (for an exploration of why this might occur, see Polk, 1993). Two, under some conditions, persons who previously have been friends may reach the point where a disagreement between them festers over time and is seen by one or another of the parties as requiring violence in order to bring the matter to a conclusion. In any case, consideration of these themes allowed the development of ideas about how and why the homicide had occurred which is richer in information than the simple observation that the individuals involved had at some point been friends.

It is less clear where these homicides would be placed in the second vector of classification schemes concerned with either 'motives' or the 'circumstances' of the homicide. Wolfgang (1958) had as one of his motives of homicide 'altercation over money', which appears virtually identical to 'arguments over money' found in the Supplementary Homicide Reports of the Uniform Crime Reports (Maxfield, 1989), but such a term would describe only a portion of the homicides reviewed here, since many of the killings were generated by issues other than money. Falk (1990) reported as motives of homicide 'business dealings' and perhaps 'drug dealing' which similarly would mesh only partially with the grouping suggested here.

In the typology of homicide suggested by Wallace (1986), there is some overlap with what was referred to as homicides among 'people who shared home or work environment' or a special category provided for killings among 'criminal associates'. Regarding this last grouping, Wallace noted the same theme of premeditation observed in most of the conflict resolution homicides: 'These killings were always quite deliberate and premeditated; the victim's movements had been observed and he was usually shot in or around his house as he arrived at or emerged from his home.' (Wallace, 1986: 154) At the same time, the small number of this last category reported by Wallace (only 12

homicides out of a total of over 1300), and the fact that many of the events included in the first ('home and work') category are more confrontational, suggests that the present category is rather different in its makeup than what was intended by Wallace.

The general conclusion is that the particular grouping of homicide as a form of conflict resolution is quite different to that found in other classifications. This pattern of homicide is suggested for consideration in future classifications groupings since it constitutes a significant proportion of all homicides (roughly one in ten in the present investigation), and the nature of the terms describing the grouping provide a description which should mesh more neatly into theoretical frameworks attempting to account for homicide.

Only additional research will establish whether the scenario found here will bear up in other settings. This particular pattern was progressively refined as the investigation evolved. For purposes of replication, it is possible now to explicate the major defining features of this scenario. Conflict-resolution homicides are those where, first, the victim and offender have known each other for a considerable period, most often being friends in the early stages of their relationship. Second, conflict between the parties also begins to build over time, such that the dispute is clearly not a spontaneous outgrowth of an argument which suddenly flares up to the point of lethal violence. Third, one or another of the parties then reaches a point after the disagreement has built up where violence is elected as a method of resolving matters. As such, the case should show some evidence of planning regarding the use of violence to cope with the problem faced by one of those involved.

It may not be demonstrable that homicide was the intended outcome in each case, although it would be expected that the anticipated level of violence was extreme. In the present accounts of 'victim-precipitated homicide', for example, what the ultimate victim (who is the one who can be said to have planned the use of violence) intended may have been a high level of violence that fell short of homicide.

Given these three major criteria, it becomes relatively straightforward to make a distinction between most conflict-resolution homicides and those which occur within the confrontational scenario by virtue of the analysis of the themes which were found in the individual case studies. In the confrontational situation the precipitating events are spontaneous and involve a challenge to the honour of one of the parties, either in the form of a verbal insult, a gesture, or perhaps a jostle. The confrontation thereby lacks a history of a particular tension between victim and offender, particularly one which evolves out of what was previously a friendship. While most confrontations occur over a very short time span, even where there is a break in the action (most often

for one of the actors to fetch a weapon), that break is relatively short, involving in most circumstances minutes or hours, rather than the weeks, months, or even years, for the dispute to emerge that leads to the conflict-resolution homicide.

Further, in most cases the conflict-resolution killings are readily differentiated from the other major male-on-male scenario, that involving homicides arising out of the course of other criminality. Thus, homicides where there is an ongoing robbery or armed burglary, where the initial victim of the robbery or burglary becomes a homicide victim (what can be termed 'double victims'), are easy to differentiate from the conflict-resolution homicides. Such a distinction is also straightforward in cases where the ultimate victim of the homicide is the initial offender (what can be termed 'reverse victims') in the crime that leads to the killing (as where police waylay an offender in the course of an armed robbery).

In the case of the present scenarios, employing the three criteria enabled a relatively direct determination if the case involved the commission of a crime such as armed robbery or burglary. Further, when the violence flared quickly, had no prior history, especially if it involved persons who knew little or nothing of each other prior to the encounter, it could be assigned readily to the confrontational scenario. While there was some possibility of difficulty in examining killings which occurred between males who had known each other for some time, in most instances it was relatively clear if the violence erupted suddenly (thereby being considered as a confrontational event), or whether the violence resulted from a previous set of disputes and displayed some evidence of planning on the part of some of the participants (thereby falling within the boundaries of the conflict resolution scenario).

At the same time, one of the characteristics of raw data is that, as schemes of classification begin to form, cases emerge which pose problems of 'fit'. Consider the following case:

Keith (age 26, unemployed) had met Charles while serving time in Sale Prison. After drifting around for a few weeks after his release from prison early in 1988, Keith met up with Roger, who was the brother of Charles, and from this meeting renewed his friendship with Charles. For some time, Keith had been seeing Roger, Charles and his de facto wife, and Dan, another friend of Charles.

The relationship between this group and Keith became somewhat tense, in part because of concerns expressed by Keith about the presence of stolen goods in Charles's house (Keith had voiced anxiety that discovery of the property might result in his return to prison). Insults began to flow between the various individuals, including Dan reporting to Charles that Keith had called him a 'dog' because of the time that Charles had spent in protective

custody while in prison. Keith also alleged to Dan that Charles had 'lagged somebody in' while serving time.

Dan, as a result, argued to Charles that they ought to 'knock' Keith, but at first Charles said that he had replied: 'Look, don't worry about it, you're crazy, just don't do anything.' One evening shortly after, Charles, Dan, Keith and the de facto wife of Charles were in the car when an argument broke out between Keith and Dan. They pulled the car over, and the group tumbled out on to a nearby reserve, and a brawl began involving Dan and Charles fighting with Keith. A knife was produced and Keith was stabbed a few times in the thigh.

The group then got back into the car, with Keith being thrown into the back seat. They then drove to Roger's house, and when Roger came out to the car, he too, entered into the violence against Keith. At this time Roger said to the others: 'Well, we've just got to get rid of him.' Keith at this point said: 'No, come on, you know it's bullshit' and then, 'fair enough, all right, all right, I done it, I done it, fair enough.'

The group then drove the car out into the country. At this point, Keith began to scream and beg for his life, saying things like: 'I'm sorry, I apologise' and 'You're not going to kill me are you?' When the car stopped, Roger reached over and cut Keith in the throat. They pulled him out of the car by his hair, and Dan kicked and then stabbed him, calling him a 'dog'. Close to death, Keith started to moan. Roger then said 'Well, I'll finish it' and stabbed Keith one final time hard in the back of the neck. One of the party later commented that in order to retrieve the knife, Roger had to stand on Keith's neck. The offenders went to great lengths to conceal the crime, thoroughly cleaning the car, replacing the seat covers and seat belts, and throwing out their clothes.   *(Case No. 1193–88)*

In this account, the final acts of the drama began with the fight between the main players. The continuation of the violence, and carrying that violence to the lengths of the killing, on the other hand, were a result of the earlier base of arguments and tensions between Keith and the rest of the group. Thus, the group had been considering for some time the possibility of silencing the victim, and the fight provided the opportunity to accomplish this end.

This narrative suggests the possibility that in some cases there may be a blurring at the edges of the 'confrontational' scenario (which springs spontaneously out of masculine disputes over honour), and the conflict-resolution scenario (where there is an element of planning to the violence). In this case study, the death itself was the direct outgrowth of a fight which sprang up between the offenders and victim. At the same time, there had been a long-simmering dispute which had led some of the offending group to conclude well before the homicide that they should kill the victim.

Where does this homicide fit? Answering this question depends a bit on the direction of the research strategy. If a proposed system of grouping is to meet minimum standards of reliability, a set of rules

should be present which allow the accurate classification of the case, that accuracy being gauged by the degree to which different coders produce the same judgments. With respect to the case study at hand, a problem is posed because it obviously contains some elements of two scenarios. If it is necessary to classify the case so that it fits either a confrontational or a conflict-resolution scenario, the rule might be proposed that homicides should be placed within the scenario where they fit most closely to the features on the checklist.

In this particular narrative, the individuals had known each other for some time, there had emerged a long-standing dispute such that killing the victim had been suggested earlier, but it would not appear that the actual killing was the result of a considered plan. At the same time, the triggering event for the killing was a fight which appeared to some degree to be a spontaneous event. A significant break in the action took place, however, after the initial fight when the victim was thrown in the car and taken back to the residence of one of the offenders. It was only then that the offenders took up the question regarding whether the victim should be killed, and they then made an explicit and considered decision to 'knock' him.

On the basis of a 'closest' rule, guidelines could be written so that this case, and others like it, would be placed in the conflict-resolution category, since on the one hand the participants knew each other, there was a long-standing dispute, and at a certain point the offenders explicitly decided to kill the victim. The reason for not inclining the case toward the confrontation scenario (despite the central role of a fight) is that in a large proportion of the confrontation scenarios there was no particular inclination on the part of the offender at any point explicitly to kill the victim. In fact, often offenders leave confrontational scenes convinced that they have only injured, perhaps not seriously, the victim.

There are of course other options, such as creating categories which explicitly recognise that scenarios may mix, as can happen where two males meet in a pub, they argue outside after leaving, a fight ensues, and then after the fight the offender robs the victim (this showing elements of scenarios involving confrontation and of occurring within the commission of another crime). Further, continual reading of additional cases in other jurisdictions could identify new themes in case studies which might require the specification of additional scenarios of violence. It is likely, for example, that if this work were extended to the United States it would be necessary to provide room for a scenario concerned with gang violence.

Emergent from the patterns found within these case narratives of homicide is a major scenario of violence that evolves around the

readiness to use violence as a way of resolving some form of personal dispute. This pattern of violence, and its defining elements, emerged over the course of the investigation, with the shape changing between the first and second phase. In the initial 1985–86 analysis (Polk and Ranson, 1991a), these had been classified as homicides occurring within the relationship of friendship. In the second phase, which served much like a replication, a number of facts became clear. One was that some of the conflict-resolution killings involved people who had known each other for some time, but clearly could not be considered friends. The second was a problem that as long as friendship was the central matter, a handful of confrontational killings involving friends also had to be included in the grouping (these now have been shifted to the confrontational scenario since they fit that pattern more closely). As a logical matter, the further analysis indicated that the focal point of this scenario was not that the persons were well known to each other (although that is true for all of these cases), but that as a result of some matter evolving between them, a persistent dispute had emerged which one or both of the major actors felt had to be resolved through the use of violence. The emergent criteria, in other words, evolved around homicides where the parties had known each other well over a period of time, and where there was a demonstrable issue (often concerned with a debt, or similar matter) which the parties were unable to negotiate, which then became a matter to resolve through the planned use of violence.

Up to this point discussion has focused primarily on the form of the social dynamics that describe how conflicts emerge between victim and offender which become resolved through violence, but there were, as well, two dominant social variables that were found in most of these conflict resolution killings. The great majority (roughly 90 per cent), of these involve individuals who live close to the margins of conventional society. While the specific factors vary, in most of these killings the participants are likely to have criminal histories, often including spending time in prison, they are likely to be unemployed, and they may be involved in the use of illicit drugs.

It is a common observation that homicide in general is most likely to be predominantly a lower or under-class phenomenon (Wolfgang, 1958; Wallace, 1986). The findings here suggest at least a partial reason why this might be the case.

Persons tied more firmly to routine lifestyles, who possess financial and social resources, can be argued to be more likely to be able to confront such disputes by means other than violence. Obviously, even among the well-positioned, friends can become enemies as disputes emerge around such issues as money, property or even reputation.

Economic and social resources permit the well-positioned to cloak their disputes in the rational garb of legal or other arbitration systems, and thus vent disputes through channels that drain away the potential for violence.

If one's social position in the criminal community makes resort to the justice system a life-threatening matter, or if one is unable to pull together the large amounts of money that lawyers and other agents of arbitration may require, then alternative mechanisms must be sought. Put another way, one of the costs of extreme marginality is denial of access to the formalised system of justice. For the men in these case studies, the alternative has been the planned use of extreme violence. This pattern, as such, would appear to be close to what Black (1984: 1) referred to when he claimed that much of 'crime is moralistic and in-volves the pursuit of justice'. Black contended that crime can function as a form of social control, and is often provoked, as among these offenders, by the behaviour of someone else who is defined as 'deviant', although here it is acknowledged that the boundaries around the term are rather distinctively drawn. For these individuals, however, violence certainly becomes an ultimate form of exerting (or attempting to exert) social control.

A second common social thread that runs through all of the narra-tives reviewed here has been the distinctive *masculine* willingness to resolve disputes through the use of violence. There were some events, however, where women were involved. There were two cases where women were the victims in conflict-resolution scenes, including one of the cases where the victim was killed as a way of destroying evidence. There were two cases where women were peripheral participants in violence that primarily involved males (as in the case immediately above, where a woman was involved in the group that helped dispose of Keith's body). There was as well one case where a conflict developed between two prostitutes, one of whom thought the other had informed on her brother to the police, so with two male confederates she lured the victim to a motel room. There the victim was bound and her mouth gagged firmly, and then beaten. Since her nose was completely blocked, the woman died from suffocation (Case No. 1264–86).

These data require only a slight alteration of the observation regard-ing the masculinity of this scenario, since there was no case where a woman acting alone was the offender (although it is highly likely that the addition of more cases might produce such an occurrence). Women are involved in the social world of marginality and crime as sexual partners, friends, and participants. As such, they can be swept up in the events where violence becomes employed as a way of dealing with conflict. At the same time, their role tends to be either peripheral or

passive, and it is exceptionally rare that women are the central, aggressive actors in this scenario. The use of violence as a device for conflict resolution is emphatically a masculine phenomenon.

It needs to be recognised that virtually all homicides involve some form of conflict, and thereby the killing can be seen as a resolution of that conflict. In the present analysis, a distinction is being made which flows roughly along the instrumental-expressive continuum. Some homicides are clearly events which are initially about something else, such as an exchange of insults, an unanticipated reaction during a robbery, or a heated domestic argument, which then boil over quickly and the consequent violence takes a lethal form. In other cases the violence is more instrumental in character, and there is evidence of some amount of thought given to the use of that violence as a solution to a dispute which has emerged. What is at issue here, then, is the question of why males are more likely to take the considered risks that are inherent in a tactic whereby violence is employed in a planned way to bring disputes to a conclusion.

Accounting for the masculine willingness to resort to violence in such circumstances becomes a more specific aspect of the general question posed by writers such as Daly and Wilson (1988) regarding why homicide generally is so distinctively male. To this can be added the further dimension that conflict resolution homicide involves males found at the outer boundaries of conventional life. Exactly why this scenario involves marginality and masculinity poses a conundrum which only further thinking, and more data, can answer.

CHAPTER 7

Rounding out the picture of homicide

Up to this point, this investigation has focused on major forms of homicide that are distinctly masculine. It is clear, however, that the four major scenarios do not exhaust either all forms of homicide, or even all forms of masculine homicide. The purpose of the present section is to take up the task of examining other forms of lethal violence, in part to round out the general description of homicide, but also thereby to make a case for the differentiation of the previously discussed scenarios of masculine violence.

Multiple homicides

Within any large set of homicide data, it is to be expected that there will be found two main forms of homicides where there are large numbers of multiple victims. In the five-year time period of this limited study, there were two dramatic examples of mass killings, the first of the two groups of multiple homicide. Mass homicide involves what Holmes and De Burger (1988) refer to as a 'murder spree', which they describe as follows:

> Victims of a murder spree typically are selected by chance; they tend to come into contact with their killer purely by accident ... A murder spree is characterised by the death of several victims over a rather short time span ... at the hands of a relatively reckless assailant who kills thoughtlessly upon impulse or expediency. *(Holmes and De Burger, 1988: 18)*

The first of the present case studies of this form of homicide consisted of what came to be known as the 'Hoddle Street Massacre':

136

After having a few beers at the Royal Hotel in Clifton Hill, Julian Knight left the pub at around 8.30 pm and walked home. He had been back in Melbourne for about a month after resigning from the Royal Military Collage, Duntroon. Arriving home, he went about gathering up two rifles, a shotgun, and ammunition. He crossed the railway line to gain access to a knoll where there were some trees. Knight knelt down, aimed one of the rifles at on-coming cars, and started his shooting spree. The criminologist Kapardis describes what followed: 'He pulled the trigger, then again, and again and again ... This was it – COMBAT; aiming at real targets, shooting at people and seeing them 'drop'. This was the real thing – killing people ... He was enjoying it, killing was giving him pleasure, and he kept on shooting, indiscriminately at people in passing cars ...' (Kapardis, 1989: 10–11). At the end a few minutes later, there were seven people fatally injured, and 19 others who had been less seriously wounded.

(Case Nos 3436–87, 3438–87, 3440-3443–87, and 3622–97)

This outburst of lethal violence put Knight in the record books as Australia's worst mass murderer, but he was not to remain there for long. Before the year was out, Melbourne reeled under the shock of another of these rampages:

Late in the afternoon of an early December day, Frank Vitkovic entered the Australia Post Building in Queen Street, Melbourne. He went to the fifth floor, and approached the counter where he asked to see his friend Tasos. The friend had not seen Vitkovic in months, and had no reason to think that there were not still on good terms. Vitkovic, on the other hand, had been through deep troughs of depression in recent weeks, and had come to blame others for his many personal difficulties, focusing blame especially on Tasos. When Tasos came up to Vitkovic, he pulled out a rifle, aimed it at Tasos, and pulled the trigger. Barely comprehending what was happening, but realising that Vitkovic was trying to shoot him, Tasos fled, crying out for other staff to call the police (which they did). Vitkovic then leaped the counter, and tried to stalk Tasos. Unable to find him, he then began to shoot other workers, first on the fifth, on the twelfth, then the eleventh floors. Finally, one of the office workers managed to grab him from behind, and the gun was finally taken from him. Vitkovic managed to shrug out of the grasp of his captors, and leaped out a window to his death on the footpath below. Eight people lost their lives in this killing spree. *(Case Nos 5346-53–87)*

The two acts accounted for fifteen homicides, or 5 per cent of the total number of homicide victims found in the five-year period. It can be pointed out that in these cases, the victims were previously unknown to the offender. As such, these constitute a cluster of 'stranger' homicides. While this is a feature of these killings, it is the present argument that it is not as central as other matters to understanding the character of this homicide. There are a number of factors, not understood at this time, which trigger the horrific violence of these offenders (Lunde, 1975; Kapardis, 1989). The fact that victim and offender are strangers

to each other is not particularly germane to the analysis of this, or even other, forms of homicide (see the next chapter).

Serial murder

A second major form of multiple homicide, serial killings, did not occur in Victoria to our knowledge within the five-year period. While mass homicide takes the form of a sudden outburst of killing which involves several victims, serial homicide involves the killing of separate individual victims with a time interval, most often weeks or months, between victims, often in a different geographic location (Egger, 1984, 1990). Holmes and De Burger (1988) have defined serial murder as consisting of repetitive killings, which are one-on-one killings with rare exceptions, where the relationship between victim and offender is that of stranger or slight acquaintance, where the killer is motivated to kill (these are not crimes of passion) and yet apparent or clear-cut motives are lacking.

It is exceptionally difficult to establish the rate of serial killing. Holmes and De Burger (1988) have estimated that in the United States there are between 3500 and 5000 serial killings a year. This is a large number indeed, and if accurate, it would mean that such killings account for up to 20 per cent of all homicides in that country in a given year, a number which others view as exaggerated (Egger, 1990; Kiger, 1990). The nature of serial killings, involving at times long time intervals between homicides, and different geographic locations (and therefore a record in a different place), and the fact that many of the bodies are successfully hidden, all combine to make it difficult to assess the size of the problem.

In the present study which covers a five-year period in Victoria, there were no known cases which fitted this pattern. There were relatively few homicides where the offender was unknown and the circumstances were unclear regarding the nature of the homicide. Among these, at most a handful could even conceivably fit common patterns of serial killing as identified in the literature (Holmes and De Burger, 1988; Egger, 1990). There were two cases of women which constitute true 'mysteries' (one found dead at the spot on the beach where she routinely sunbathed in the nude, another found dead as a result of a stab wound in her bed – in neither of the cases was the victim sexually assaulted), but even these did not conform to the pattern of most serial killings. There may be, of course, cases of missing persons whose bodies may be found later, which conform to the pattern. As matters stand, however, it would appear in Victoria at least that among known homicides serial killing is exceptionally rare.

By 1993, however, it had begun to appear that a pattern of serial killing of women may be developing in the Seaford-Frankston area of Victoria (these homicides not falling within the present study). A suspect has been charged with these killings, but only time will determine if the arrest has brought this series of deaths to an end.

Multiple homicide: observations

There is one sense in which multiple homicides reported here and elsewhere conform to a major focal point of this research: this involves males as perpetrators. It has not been included as a major scenario form for two reasons. First, these killings are infrequent, so much so that it is difficult on the basis of present data to describe any meaning-ful pattern. Secondly, where the motivations for such killings have been described, they have tended to focus on psychopathological interpretations (Lunde, 1975; Holmes and De Burger, 1988: Vetter, 1990), rather than on the systematic features of masculinity which are part of the present analysis. The horror and public outrage provoked by these dramatic forms of homicide assure that these will be on the agenda of criminological analysis (for an illustration, see Kapardis, 1989). In all likelihood, however, research on multiple killings will require data which spans across time and jurisdictions in order to generate enough cases for systematic analysis as accomplished in the United States by Hickey (1990). For present purposes, however, the data are too scanty to provide a base on which to construct a meaningful analysis of the interplay between masculinity and violence in multiple homicides.

Family killings

There is a second general area where killings are similarly infrequent and yet masculine, these consist of killings that occur in family relation-ships other than spouses or children. Despite the claim made by some that violence is endemic in family relationships, in fact, outside the immediate relationships of sexual partners and children (as victims), homicide is exceptionally rare. Among the 1373 victims found in Wallace's (1986) study of homicide in New South Wales between 1968 and 1981, only 96 (or 0.7 per cent) were the mother, father, brother or sister, in-law, grandparent or other family relation (other than spouse or child) of the offender. Similarly, in the present more limited time period, there were but nine such homicides within the family network, these making up 2 per cent of all homicides.

As is true of many other forms of homicide, these are again distinctively male homicides. In New South Wales, among offenders who were some form of 'other family' relation to their victim, 90 of the 96 were male, and in the present study, all 9 of the offenders were male. Little is known about these homicides involving other family relations. Regarding one form, Wallace (1986: 135) observed that 'there seems to be very little written on parent killings', and she adds a few pages later that 'Very little is known about violence between siblings in Australia, or elsewhere for that matter' (Wallace, 1986: 139).

The few cases available in the present analysis means that there is little that the present research can add. Among the nine victims, five were parents killed by their son (two fathers, one step-father, and one case where both parents were killed), there were two sisters killed by their brothers, there was one case of a victim who was the mother-in-law of the offender, and a final single case where the victim was the grandfather of the offender. While distinctively masculine, these homicides provide too small a base to begin to build any form of systematic analysis. It can be noted that a common element running through many of these, as observed by Wallace, is a theme of exceptional mental illness, with many of these verging on being classified within the 'special' grouping (Chapter 8).

What can be said, of course, is that these forms of homicide are distinctive in terms of their scarcity. This allows some speculation about the view that the family has become a setting where high levels of violence are common. In contrast to the image of the family as a source of comfort, warmth and harmony, there is a growing perception that the family instead can be a major source of pain. The National Academy of Sciences report commented that: 'Recently we have come to realize that our homes may be as dangerous as our streets' (Reiss and Roth, 1993: 221). Another observer has commented:

> The veneer of the family as a harmonious, gentle, and supportive institution is cracking from increasing evidence ... that the family is also the scene of varying degrees of violent acts, ranging from the punishment of children to slapping, hitting, throwing objects, and sometimes a homicidal assault by one member of the family on another.   *(Gelles, 1987: 20)*

What the present data suggest is that while it may be true that there is an unacceptably high level of violence within the circle of the family, lethal violence tends to be restricted to particular bonds, namely those involving marital partners, or perhaps to children who become victims of parental violence. Outside these two specific dyads, homicide is, in fact, so rare within the family circle that this fact itself is worth mention.

The killing of children by their parents

When the focus is shifted within the boundaries of family relationships to children who are victims of their parents, two differences emerge. First, these killings are more frequent. In Wallace's study in New South Wales, child victims of parental violence accounted for 8 per cent of all homicide victims, a figure identical to the present Victorian study where there was a total of thirty-two such victims (if we include for purposes of this analysis one 'special' case involving a woman offender, thus making up 8 per cent of all homicides).

Second, this is one form of homicide which is not distinctively masculine. In New South Wales, 59 per cent of the parental killers were, in fact, women. Overall, among the child victims in Victoria, fourteen were killed by their fathers (or step-fathers), fourteen by their mothers, there were two where the parents were deemed jointly responsible for the death, and there was one case where it could not be determined who had caused the death. From these figures, then, the offending parents were evenly divided between males and females, a striking distribution when compared with other forms of homicide.

It is also important to note that child victims are most often killed by their parents. There were no examples in the five-year period in Victoria where a child was killed by a stranger, although such killings have occurred since 1989. In Wallace's (1986) larger body of New South Wales data, in only 5 per cent of the cases was the child a victim of a stranger, and, in fact, in 85 per cent of the cases the child had been killed by either natural parents (68 per cent of victims) or step/foster parents (17 per cent). Children, in short, when they are killed are likely to be the victims of those with whom they have the closest social bonds.

There are four important sub-themes within the group of child killings. The most frequent grouping involved deaths by some form of traumatic injury, where there were thirteen cases in all. Of these, seven involved the classic pattern of battering (four where the father/step-father was deemed responsible, one where the mother was the offender, one case where the injuries were seen as joint responsibility, and one case where it could not be determined), while six involved other forms of killing (all with male offenders, these frequently involving somewhat older children).

The next largest group of child victims, nine, are found in the situation where the child's death is part of the parent's suicide. In some of these cases, especially where the perpetrator is a woman, the killing is seen as an attempt to protect the child from the harm they might suffer without their mother. Often in these murder/suicides, the offender has a history of deep depression.

Connie H. (age 24) had been married to George. H. for six years. It was a marriage marred by tragedy. When their eldest child was only 4 months old, he suffered severe head injuries in a traffic accident, resulting in extensive brain damage. The child was quite disabled, and did not respond to treatment in Australia. The couple travelled to the United States on three occasions to seek further treatment.

The two in fact did not have the finances to cover the costs of the medical treatments, although they did receive help from volunteers and public appeals. The financial pressures mounted, and this was compounded by the fact that the exceptional disability was not showing significant improvement, and required a high level of care. The birth of the second child created further demands on their time and resources. Both parents began to feel immense stress. Both underwent courses of psychiatric treatment, with George being admitted to mental hospital once, and Connie three times. Connie had attempted to commit suicide twice, and had herself admitted to hospital on the third occasion because she began to hit the children and feared she might injure them.

After two brief attempts at separation, George decided that it would be best for all if he left the household. Connie felt an exceptional sense of isolation. She refused to discuss her problems with a psychiatrist, because she feared being committed again to psychiatric hospital. She felt that George's parents were constantly interfering in family matters, and that her own parents (from Europe and firmly opposed to divorce or separation) did not care.

One night George came over to see the children. Connie asked him to spend the night, but he refused. A day or two later, he informed her that he intended to move into a flat with a fellow worker who was female. This was enough to tip Connie over the edge. She confided to the baby-sitter that she intended to commit suicide, and that she 'loved the children too much to leave them behind.' The baby-sitter spent hours with her attempting to calm her down, and even offered to spend the night with her if that would help. Connie appeared calm and reassured, however, and said that wouldn't be necessary.

After the baby-sitter left, Connie wrote out several long suicide notes. She left extensive instructions regarding their funerals, stating she wanted her son buried to her left, the daughter to her right. She had purchased new clothes for the children's funerals, and laid them neatly on the couch. Connie carefully labelled all the drawers in the house, so that George would be able to find things.

In the note to her parents, Connie wrote: 'I don't feel I am murdering my children, but saving them from sorrow and pain without their father ... it's the only way out ... all I ever wanted in life was a happy marriage and happy, healthy children ... I have tried very hard ... I cannot leave my children behind ... At least with God there will be peace and happiness and no pain, so I will take them where they will be happy, and I will be there to care for them.'   *(Case No. 2886–85)*

These three deaths represent a profound tragedy, one which has sources and elements far removed from the overt external aggression found in much of masculine homicide. Wallace has commented how these have an appearance close to mercy killings:

Altruistic intentions appeared to motivate the offenders to take the lives of the children when they suicided – altruistic in the sense that regard for the well-being of the child was a primary concern ... The primary feature was overwhelming depression and mental anguish in the offender rather than any hostility toward the victim. For various reasons, largely unrelated to the children ... the parents contemplated suicide. But they could not face leaving their dependants behind, defenceless and unprotected (in their view) to face the world alone.   *(Wallace, 1986: 132)*

While there are too few cases for much in the way of conclusive observations, the present data are consistent with other research (Wallace, 1986) which suggests that homicides/suicides involving a parent and children are different for women and men. The following is consistent with accounts of the masculine variant:

In an instance of homicide of a woman caught up in a sexual relationship with an exceptionally jealous and violent male, the evidence pointed to the conclusion that the de facto husband, Bill S., had started off on a purported 'holiday' after he had decided to end their marital relationship by killing his wife, Val, and taking his own life. After travelling from Adelaide to a point where he was just inside the Victorian border, he shot his wife with a gun, set their camper alight, and finally shot himself. The two had a long and stormy relationship, with Val attempting to leave several times, only to return to face Bill's escalating violence.

In a further twist of this story, Bill faced a decision regarding what to do with his stepdaughter (age 11) and his own son (age 15). Despite the fact that there had been frequent arguments with the son, Bill elected to leave the boy behind as they set off on the 'holiday'. He insisted that the stepdaughter join them, however. The consequences were that the son survived, while Bill in his moody, possessive rage killed the stepdaughter as well as his wife.   *(Case No. 8612–86)*

The homicide in this account involving the wife shows many of the common features of homicides resulting from masculine jealousy and control, and has been classified as one of the killings considered within that scenario (Chapter 3). For present purposes, it demonstrates how children can become unfortunate pawns in the violent games played by their parents. A feature demonstrated here is that when husbands kill children, they may also include the spouse, whereas with women this pattern is rare. In the present case studies where the death of a child was part of the parental suicide, six of the offenders were women, four were men.

Almost as frequent was neonaticide (the killing of an infant within the first 24 hours of birth), where there were eight victims (seven known women offenders, one additional case where the offender was never identified but where it is presumed that the mother was involved

in the death). Most of these involved a pattern of exceptional denial
which seems to be characteristic of this form of homicide:

> Except for a brief period at college, Joan M. (age 29) had lived in one small
> country town all her life. She worked as a clerical assistant at two part-time
> jobs. With the coming of the new year in 1985, several of the townsfolk sus-
> pected that Joan was pregnant, but she denied such allegations (the towns-
> folk had held the same suspicion in 1980).
>
> One day in early February, Joan came home from work, and as usual
> started to watch TV. She had felt 'fine' throughout the day. Feeling
> uncomfortable, she retired to her room, and then went into labour for an
> hour and a half. As soon as she gave birth, she covered the baby with a towel
> and put it in a plastic bag, and hid it in her clothes basket. Joan then changed
> and washed her bedding, had a shower, and then started reading a book.
> Later that night Joan's housemate noticed that Joan had almost completely
> lost her voice.
>
> Five days later, friends found the body in Joan's room. She had unsuccess-
> fully tried to conceal the smell with air-freshener. They notified the police.
> When the police officer carrying out the investigation approached Joan and
> stated: 'I've checked your bedroom and I've seen what's inside the basket',
> Joan's response was: 'Yes, what's wrong?' The police described her as
> 'extremely confused' and she indicated that the incident had occurred 'a
> long time ago'. When asked why she did not tell anyone about the preg-
> nancy, she replied: 'I didn't think it was true', saying at another point that
> she 'just hoped it would go away.'
>
> Joan volunteered that a similar death had taken place some five years
> previously. She stated that she had placed a pillow over the child's face, and
> then buried it in the back yard. As with the first death, Joan had little
> recollection of the event. She did not notice the sex of either baby. When
> asked by police if she wanted the babies to die, she stated: 'I don't know if I
> did nor didn't ... I didn't know what else to do, I suppose. I was worried
> about what the people in town would have said ...'   (Case No. AG96–85)

The psychological pressures on the women who are caught up in this
pattern are extreme, and result in psychological confusion and an exceptional capacity to deny to themselves and to others that the pregnancy is
real, even when confronted with the birth itself. Wallace (1986) has
observed the extraordinary levels of denial in this form of homicide:

> Without exception, the neonaticides were accompanied by the concealment
> both of pregnancy and of the birth itself. All of the women had their babies
> alone, most commonly in their own bedroom or bathroom – even, in some
> cases, when others were present in the home at the time. That these women
> could successfully conceal their pregnancy and the ordeals of childbirth
> from others close to them may appear somewhat incredible, but once again
> is a typical feature of neonaticides reported elsewhere.   (Wallace, 1986: 118)

In the previous narrative, the young woman was unable to face what
'the people in town would say', and she then followed the path of

denying the pregnancy, these mental processes being strong enough to carry her through the birth itself. The fact that this happened twice to this young woman makes these facts even more striking. As observed by Wallace, in the present narratives the women experience childbirth either in their bathrooms or bedrooms, often with others present in the house at the time. This pattern, clearly, is a distinct form of homicide, being hugely different in content and meaning from the major forms of masculine violence that account for the bulk of homicides.

The final form of child homicide, which involved one case, is a case of neglect where the death occurred when the child was place on a lengthy fast in the belief by the parents that this would result in a cure of the illness suffered by the child. The child was otherwise carefully tended by the parents, but because of the extended starvation, the child succumbed to the effects of malnutrition. Both parents (trained nurses) were deemed to share the responsibility for this death, which was deemed to constitute criminal homicide (the parents were both convicted of manslaughter).

What these data tell us is that the killing of children is very different to other forms of homicide. It tends to be almost exclusively a matter which takes place within close relationships, with the great proportion of offenders being parents. The gender distribution of offenders is distinctive, although it is also clear that the proportion of women offenders varies in terms of the particular form of child killing. Such killings overall, however, are certainly not an exclusive domain of masculine violence.

Women as killers

While the major purpose of this investigation is to examine scenarios of masculine violence, the data on children provide but one indication that women, too, can kill. In general, of course, women are responsible for lethal violence much less often than men. In New South Wales, 15 per cent of all offenders were women (Wallace, 1986), while the figure from Wolfgang's (1958) Philadelphia data was 17 per cent. In the present case study data, in 11 per cent of the cases a woman was involved in the killing as offender or accomplice, while women alone were offenders in 9 per cent of the lethal violence.

More important than these numbers is the issue of why women kill. It was possible in an earlier time to argue for a view that women are 'more perfidious by nature' (Rasko, 1976: 398). This was been expressed in what is perhaps an extreme form in the writings of Sparrow:

> Women being different from men in their mentality, thought-processes, intuition, emotional reactions and in their whole approach to life and death,

when they murder, do the deed in a way that a man often would not contemplate. Their crime does not bear the mark of Cain, it is stamped with that
characteristic subtlety and horror that has distinguished the rare evil women
of all times.   *(Sparrow, 1970: 8)*

This view of women's crime as more subtly evil has been called into
question by more recent research in Australia and elsewhere (Naylor,
1990). Certainly the homicides of women take a different form to those
of men. Empirically it has been found that when women kill, it is more
likely to involve a family member than is true for men. Wallace (1981),
for one, reported that the victims of women killers were overwhelmingly family members (81 per cent), whereas for men the family victims
accounted for roughly only one in three homicides (36 per cent,
Wallace, 1986: 74). Equally important is the fact that there are different
reasons for the family violence of women (Wilbanks, 1982).

When women kill within the family circle, in roughly half the cases
the victim is likely to be the spouse of the offender (Wallace, 1986). In
their examination of incarcerated women who had killed their spouses
or boyfriends, Bacon and Lansdowne (1982) reported that in fourteen
of sixteen cases the woman had been assaulted by the man she was
subsequently accused of killing. Thus, the violence of these women can
be viewed as both reactive and defensive. In an important way, what it
represents is violence mirrored back on to precipitating behaviour
which has its origins in the willingness of males to use violence in their
attempt to control the actions of women. Consistent with this view is the
finding of Wallace that: 'Women killed their husbands against a background of violence; they killed in response to and because of violence
perpetrated by their husbands on them and/or other members of their
family.' (Wallace, 1986: 108)

Conforming to this finding, in the present case study data just over
two-thirds (71 per cent) of women took the lives of a victim that was
close to them, the victim being either a male sexual partner (12 cases,
these making up 29 per cent of women's homicides) or the child of the
woman (16 cases, or 38 per cent of homicides where the killing involved women). When women killed their sexual partner, most often it
was in direct response to the violence of the male (8 of the 12 cases).
Several of these narratives where women had experienced violence
suggest a pattern of consistent violence raised in commentary on what
has come to be known as the 'battered women's syndrome' (Browne,
1987; Gillespie, 1989; Easteal, 1993). In only two cases was the killing a
response to the threat of the male to leave (one other followed an
argument), and there were no recorded examples in this five-year
period of a woman killing her male partner because of jealousy. There

was one case where a woman and her lover contracted with another male to kill the husband in order for the two to be free to start a new life together. In this limited period, when jealousy was a factor in the killing by a woman, the victim was another female. In two cases, the victim of the woman killer was the sexual rival, while in one other case the victim was a lover who provoked a jealous rage in her lesbian partner. The vast majority of lethal violence around the theme of possession, jealousy and control is emphatically masculine in it makeup, and when women kill within sexual relationships, it is most likely to be a defensive reaction to prior male violence.

From these data it is clear that the pattern observed in Victoria regarding the ratio of female/male to male/female violence is quite different to that observed in the United States. In cities such as Chicago or Detroit, it has been reported that the number of women killing their husbands is roughly equal to the number of men killing their wives (Wilson and Daly, 1992). The present data casts the net a bit wider by including all forms of sexual intimacy, and within that bond men are emphatically much more likely to kill their woman partner (73 such cases) than are women to kill their male partner (12), with the ratio of women killers to men killers being 16. This figure is comparable to the 'sex ratio of killing' (that is, the homicides perpetrated by women per 100 perpetrated by men) observed in cases of spousal killings in England and Wales (23), lower than that found in Canada (31), and significantly lower than that observed in Chicago (102) or Detroit (119).

As such, these data do not support the hypothesis of the sexual symmetry of spousal violence (McNeely and Robinson-Simpson, 1987; Straus and Gelles, 1990) which argues that wives and husbands behave alike in assaults. More importantly, the patterns observed here provide confirmation of the contention made by Wilson and Daly (1992) that it is critical to observe the differential pattern of motives in violence of males as distinct from females (see also Dobash et al., 1992). The violence of women toward men observed in the present case studies arises from fundamentally different sources than does the violence of men toward women.

As indicated above, women may be involved in the killing of their children, although most often it involves either neonaticide (8 of 16 cases where women were involved in the killing of their children), with most of the others being killed as part of the suicide plan of the mother (6 cases), and relatively rarely were women responsible for traumatic deaths of children (there were no cases of shooting, and only one case where the woman alone was responsible for a battered child, while in another case the woman was held jointly responsible).

As seen in previous sections, women are rarely involved in the distinctly masculine scenarios of violence. Women rarely kill in a desire to control their male sexual partners (only two cases, and as observed above, in sharp contrast to male sexual violence, no male lost his life to the jealous rage of his woman partner). There were no cases where a profoundly depressed woman killed her male spouse as part of her suicide plan. In confrontational violence, over 90 per cent of offenders were male (4 of the 84, or 5 per cent, of confrontational homicides being committed by women), with comparable figures being found where the violence occurred in the course of other crime (5 of 61, or 8 per cent, of offenders being women) or in conflict-resolution situations (2 of 38, or 5 per cent, of offenders being women). Further, in these last two situations, most women if they were involved, were accomplices of males who were likely to have played the dominant role in the death. Only one of the homicides in the course of other crime involved women (two co-defendants) acting alone, and in conflict-resolution scenes, both cases involved women as accomplices rather than as sole offenders in the death.

There is a strong stamp of intimacy, in other words, on women's violence. This has been captured in the following observations:

> While murder in general, is a very personalised crime, ... female murder appears to be an especially intimate act. That is, women are more likely than men to murder another family member ... particularly a husband or child; outside of husbands and children, the only significant choice for women appears to be a lover.   *(Blum and Fisher, 1978: 192)*

Masculine aggression is broad ranging, and lethal violence reaches out across a range of social situations as victims. Female lethal violence is much narrower, is focused on a close circle of intimacy, and is often reactive to the breakdown of that intimacy. There is tragedy in these killings, and often a long period of great personal hurt, but there is little here to support the view of women as subtle, vicious and evil killers.

Pulling it together

Homicide can take many forms, and flow out of a multitude of motivations. Not all homicide is a playing out of the themes of masculinity described within the four major scenarios identified in the previous sections of this book. Women, too, can kill, although often when women kill their sexual partners they are responding to prior violence of the male, so at least some of these can be seen as spinning out of

masculine violence as well. Men can kill for reasons other than the four major themes that are identified here. For all that, it is also true that over two-thirds of the present homicides result from the playing out of the four masculine scenarios identified here (269 of the 380 homicides, or 71 per cent of the total). Further, while other forms of violence are significant and merit further investigation, within the present body of data there are too few cases upon which to build an analysis. One, serial homicide, in fact, is totally absent from these data, at least as far as can be seen from information based on these known and solved homicides. What is striking in looking at the overall patterns, then, is the degree to which lethal violence in general is masculine, and from a theoretical point of view how much of it can be subsumed within a coherent view of masculine scenarios of violence.

CHAPTER 8

Problems in the study of victim-offender relationships

The task up to this point has been to distil from the various case studies the major themes, or scenarios, which describe the relationships between homicide victims and offenders. It is possible now to shift the analysis to the question of the implication of this thematic method for the more general study of victim-offender relationships in homicide.

There are significant barriers to the development of schemes of classification of such events which need to be acknowledged. Some derive from the initial sources of data. At least three issues are paramount: (1) the problem of unsolved homicides; (2) the issue of homicides where the motivation cannot be assessed from the existing information; and (3) the problem that in any case the voice of the victim is likely to be absent.

Unsolved cases

One of the useful components of the suggested 'syndromes' of homicide of Block and Block (1992) is their use of the term 'mysteries' to cover those circumstances where it is not possible to distinguish the nature of the interaction between homicide victims and offenders. The first of these concerns those cases where the offender cannot be identified, since in such cases it follows that it may not be possible to specify the dynamics which link the unknown assailant with the known victim.

In some instances, despite the fact that the specific offender is unknown, it has actually been possible in the present research to make some presumption about the nature and character of the events which led to the homicide. There were a number of present case histories, for example, where the unsolved homicide could reasonably be presumed

to have evolved out of other criminal activity. In one of these, an attendant was found dead from a gunshot wound, late at night at the service station were he worked, and the till had been broken into. In a second, a security guard was found dead, also from a gunshot wound, late at night, with the physical evidence suggesting that he had come across an armed burglar during the course of his nightly rounds. In both of these (and two similar cases) all of the evidence points to the homicide arising out of the course of another criminal act, and these thereby can be classified within these scenarios.

There were additional cases where the death resulted from a masculine confrontation, but where the offenders had not been identified. In one of these, a young Chinese male had wandered down the main street of Melbourne's Chinese quarter shouting insults to Vietnamese in Chinese. Shortly afterwards he was attacked and killed by a group of young Vietnamese who remain unidentified. A similar case involved a fight among a group of Vietnamese men where the lack of language and cultural skills on the part of authorities meant that an offender could not be identified. A third case also concerned a Vietnamese, but in this instance the victim was one of a group of young Vietnamese males who were attacked by a group of whites (who remain unidentified) as they were outside a pub waiting for friends who had gone inside to buy beer. In all three of these accounts, the known facts point to a masculine confrontation between the known victim and the unknown killer which began initially as a fight or disagreement. As such, despite the fact that the homicides remain unsolved, it is possible to place the killing within the scenario of masculine confrontation.

Other cases, however, are more troublesome. These are made up of accounts where the offender was unknown, and where it was not possible on the basis of the scanty facts to determine the nature of the relationship between the victim and offender. Two of these unsolved cases involve women victims:

At the time of her death, Inga Mayer (age 47, part-time garment worker) was living in a caravan park in Rosebud (a seaside resort in outer Melbourne). She had been through two marriages, and was considered to be a 'free spirited' person who had relationships with a number of males. She was one of those persons who was known to 'love life' and in the phrase of the police, had 'no known enemies'. There was no evidence of any recent antagonism with any specific male friend.

Her daily routine consisted of doing a bit of work in the morning, then (since it was summer) at 11 am she would drive her car to a nearby beach, and then walk to an isolated spot well removed from the more frequented beaches, where she would sunbathe in the nude. The day of 13 February began as had many others. The last time Inga was seen alive was as she drove away from the caravan park at 11 am. She was found by a passer-by at

3.30 pm, who alerted police. Inga, who was nude when she was found, had been beaten about the head with a piece of wood. She was not sexually assaulted. The police were unable to establish either a motive for the crime, or an offender.   *(Case No. 445–85)*

This is clearly a case of homicide, but from the facts available no assessment can be made regarding the nature of the motivations of the offender and the role played by the victim in the homicide. The investigation was unable to reveal known male associates with whom sexual intimacy might be presumed to provide a basis for the homicide. Forensic evidence did not support the hypothesis that the victim had been sexually assaulted. She had not been robbed. In short, no motive could be established which might explain why this homicide occurred, nor was it possible to place the killing within one or another of the homicide scenarios.

Similar circumstances are echoed in the following case:

Inez Watson (age 26, nurse) had just decided to return to her career as a nurse after recovering from a long period of emotional stress connected with the death of her husband from cancer. When her neighbours noticed that they had not seen her for a few days, and that her mail was piling up at her letter box, they entered her house and found her dead, in her bed.

Subsequent investigation revealed that she had been stabbed to death, but very little else. She had last been seen some five days before, when a male friend had dropped her off at her door after they had been out to a pizza. Inez was due to return to work that night, but did not appear. Investigation revealed that a male friend, a physician, had actually been by to see why she had not shown up to work. This friend had entered the apartment, and found her body. In his statement he said that he had 'panicked, and didn't know what to do'. He was unable to provide an explanation of why he didn't report the death to the police, other than to say that he was 'in a state of shock'.

The police were unable to establish any motive or possible offenders of the crime. Inez had not been sexually assaulted. At the time of the inquest, the police noted that the death 'was still being investigated', and the Coroner found that he was 'unable to say whether death resulted from unlawful and malicious conduct or otherwise'.   *(Case No. 879–86)*

The Coroner was being unusually cautious in his conclusions, since a death by stabbing would appear almost certainly to constitute a case of criminal homicide. As in the previous case, factors which are most likely to account for the victimisation of women (sexual intimacy or sexual assault) cannot be established. There was no evidence of either robbery or burglary as possible explanations for the homicide.

Another three cases illustrate killings involving individuals firmly enmeshed in a marginal world of drugs, crime and unemployment:

Paul 'Mouse' Atwater (age 19, unemployed) was described by police as a 'young unemployed person who appears to have led a nomadic lifestyle. Although relatively young, he had appeared before various courts on seventeen separate charges including burglary and assault. He was a member of a city gang known as the 'Westside Sharps', with whom he frequented the Flinders Street Railway Station steps, inner-city hotels, and the nearby banks of the Yarra River. Police allege that this group was 'regularly involved in assaulting and robbing public transport travellers and assaulting and robbing homosexual persons in the city area'.

The last certain sighting of Mouse was by one of his friends, who stated that Mouse had left him at midnight two days before his body was found. Mouse had indicated that he intended to go 'home', although the meaning of that term is not exactly clear since Mouse had no fixed address. His body was found half a kilometre from the highway in a remote country area. He had been shot several times in the head with a .22 rifle (using hollow point bullets). Mouse had consumed considerable alcohol before his death, as his blood alcohol reading was 0.215. Once again, the Coroner concluded that he was 'unable to say whether death was by unlawful and malicious conduct or otherwise'.   (*Case No. 1125–85*)

Since the nature of the wounds and the location of the body appear to rule out either suicide or accidental death as explanations, once again for present purposes there is no need to be as cautious as the Coroner since the facts point to the death of Mouse as constituting a homicide. What cannot be established, however, is who was responsible, and what provoked the unknown offender to employ lethal violence.

Similar circumstances are found in the following case:

The movements of Jim Lane (age 24, unemployed) were varied on the weekend of his death. On Saturday night he attended a large party run by the Coffin Cheaters Motor Cycle Club in Bayswater, and he was seen leaving that party with an unidentified girl in the early hours of Sunday morning. On Sunday night, Jim picked up his regular girlfriend at 7.30, and they went to his place where they watched videos and had dinner.

Several telephone calls were received by Jim that night; at just after 11 he told his girlfriend that he had to go out for about an hour, but that she should remain because he would definitely be back. He said that he had to first make a stop, and then go to his friend, Jerry's, place. He never returned. The next morning, Jerry called and asked where Jim was, saying that he had not shown up as they had agreed (it was later established that their meeting involved a drug deal). Jim's body was found on a remote beach near Port Campbell the following day. His death was caused by a gunshot wound to the left chest. The identity of the offender could not be established.

                                                    (*Case No. 17–85*)

These themes of a marginal existence, involvement in criminal activity, and an unsolved death take a slightly different twist in the final unsolved case:

George Sams (age 22, unemployed) had spent the day with his friends at
the local hotel where he hung out much of the time. Earlier in the day, he
and his friend 'Mousey' had scored some drugs, and then gone to the home
of a friend where they shot up (George had a history of drug use which went
back several years, and was suspected to have been an occasional dealer
as well). Later that night, George told Mousey that he was going off that
night to 'do a job', which involved a task somewhere in the bush where he
was to 'burn or blow up something for insurance'. He confided to Mousey
that his confederate in the arrangements was the bouncer in their local pub.
Before he left, as if he had some misgivings, he gave his bank book to
another friend, saying that if anything should happen, he should 'use it for
the kids.'

George left at about 8.30 that night, saying that he was late for 'the job'.
His body was found next morning, several kilometres away, near Kilmore. He
died from multiple wounds which included stab wounds to the body, and
fractures to the skull, ribs and fingers. While it was suspected that George's
long history as a drug user and dealer was involved, the homicide was
unsolved. The Coroner classified this as murder inflicted by a person or
persons unknown.   (*Case No. 12—85*)

In all three of these last cases it seems likely that the homicides were
related to the other criminal activities of victims. All were participants
in a subcultural world well at the boundaries of conventionality. It was
not possible to establish definitively, however, who was responsible for
the homicides, and the specific bonds that linked these victims with
their offenders.

Such unsolved cases constitute one of the major problems of victimology research where the analysis proceeds outward from the relationship between victim and offender. In this investigation 6 per cent of the
total cases (22 of 380) must be excluded from the analysis because the
basic data are not available from the case studies. This level of residual,
unknown cases compares reasonably well with that observed in other
investigations. In the work of Maxfield (1989) slightly more than one-
quarter (28.6 per cent) of all cases were classified as 'unknown relationship.' In his early research in Philadelphia, Wolfgang (1958: 204)
reported a lower rate of unsolved cases, his 6.8 per cent approaching
the figure observed here. In the national study in Australia, Strang
(1992) found that no suspect had been identified in 45 of 323 homicide
incidents in 1991/92, a rate of unsolved homicides of 14 per cent.

From these figures, three points can be made. One, it is likely that
data collected by many justice system agencies (such as the Uniform
Crime Reports in the United States) will show a very high proportion of
missing data because the routine bureaucratic procedures are often not
sensitive to the requirements of accurate classification of victim/
offender relationships. Where the researcher is forced to rely on the
agency to make the classification, in other words, a high degree of

'unknown' cases is likely to result. Two, with good quality data (such as original case files of homicides), and research procedures which call for the investigator to enter the files to make the classification, it is possible to reduce the number of 'missing data' cases to somewhere in the range of 5 per cent or less. Three, under the best of circumstances it is still inherent that research on homicide which requires information on both victims and offenders will suffer to some degree from missing data, because it is inevitable that some homicides will remain unsolved.

To be sure, in at least some of the unsolved cases a scenario can be drawn from the physical evidence available which allows enough of a classification of the relationship for the analysis to proceed, most commonly when the victim has been part of the scene of another crime such as robbery, burglary or rape. Wolfgang (1958: Chapter 16), for example, did a separate analysis of unsolved homicides and reported that 60 per cent of these cases involved robbery-homicides. Wolfgang went on to establish that there is internal complexity in the unsolved cases. He argued that from a technical point of view there will be four types of unsolved cases, including those where: (1) a suspect is identified, brought to trial, but not convicted; (2) a suspect is identified by the police, but not brought to trial; (3) a suspect is known to police but has escaped arrest; and (4) no suspect has been identified by the police (Wolfgang, 1958: 286).

In the first three of these instances, despite the fact that an offender has not been convicted, his or her identity will be known. Further, the circumstances of the homicide in most can be clearly established. There are numerous instances in the present files where the offender committed suicide, for example, and thus will not be brought to trial. In another case in the present files, a jealous male killed his female partner and then fled the country. For purposes of the present investigation, therefore, such cases need not be treated as 'unsolved'.

Wolfgang similarly concluded that, while technically falling outside the boundaries of solved criminal homicide, these cases can be included in an investigation of homicide. He suggested a more limited definition which provided that an 'unsolved homicide' consists of those killings where the Coroner's inquest determines that the perpetrator or perpetrators are unknown in a case of criminal homicide (thus excluding justifiable or excusable homicides) and where the police are unable to identify a person 'sufficiently suspect' to result in his or her arrest, if they could be located (Wolfgang, 1958: 286).

While Wolfgang's approach provides a starting point, the present study can be even more restrictive. Since in some instances it is possible to make a classification of the social dynamics which link offender and

victim even where the specific offender is not known, the unsolved cases can be limited to those for which no scenario can be drawn which links the victim and the unknown offender into a clear pattern of relationship. The group of cases excluded from the analysis can thereby be reduced to a minimum. As a result, the residual group constitutes only a small portion of the total cases which are unsolved in a technical sense of the term. These cases are not so much unsolved as they are unclassifiable within a meaningful scheme of victim/offender relationship.

For all that, it is inherent in the nature of homicide that a pool of cases will remain for which it will not be possible to describe a relationship between the victim and offender because details remain unavailable since the case is unsolved. It is perhaps indicative of the seriousness with which homicide is treated that, in fact, the ultimate number of these unsolved and unclassifiable homicide cases is so low, falling in the range of something under 5 per cent. This is also a reflection of the nature of the event itself, since in most of the homicides reviewed the violence was played out in front of a social audience who were able to provide vivid testimony of the events which led to the death. Even where the murder has been, in essence, 'behind closed doors', the facts of the homicide in most cases were clear in terms of what had transpired between an offender and the victim. There were, in reality, few mysteries in these files.

The problem of 'special' cases

In the grouping of homicides suggested by Block and Block (1992) they suggest a category of 'mysteries' which, in addition to unsolved cases, includes those accounts where an offender can be identified but where there is 'no evidence as to motive'. In any body of homicide data, there is likely to be a special group of cases that will confound any attempt to classify the killing on the basis of the social dynamics which link offender with victim, precisely because these dynamics cannot be determined on the basis of the information available, even when at times that information is vast indeed.

In the case studies of masculine homicide analysed up to this point, it has been possible to find a rationale in the critical relationship between victim and offender which gives meaning to the lethal events that evolved. The observer can read these accounts and 'understand' how it was that a jealous husband came to kill his wife, or how a male's protection of his 'reputation' led to a fatal confrontation with another male. The various scenarios have a coherence (based on the nature of the victim-offender relationship) which permits their classification with other homicides which seem to share central themes and elements.

In the case of those bound by close personal relationships that have been classified here as deriving from sexual intimacy, the male offender and the victim are often attending explicitly to the breakdown of the bond of intimacy as events lead them into lethal violence. In confrontational homicides, victim and offender are likely to have a relatively clear idea of the step-by-step 'transaction' which will lead them to physical conflict (although they clearly do not expect this to be a lethal conflict). In an armed robbery, a scenario can be described in which the victim and the offender each act and react to the other's behaviour during the course of, first, the robbery, and then the fatal violence which results (the 'duet' of crime which Wolfgang, 1958, called attention to in his early work).

There are a handful of cases, however, where this coherence breaks down. It turns out that the assumption that it is useful to classify homicides by virtue of the victim-offender interaction is deceptively complicated. For example, when it is recorded that a homicide involves an offender husband and a victim wife, it is presumed that identifying this relationship tells us something about the homicide in that it provides an initial clue as to such possible underlying issues as possessiveness and jealousy which might be played out in the marital relationship. Establishing the relationship becomes a starting point for the building up of a more elaborate analysis of the specific themes that operate in the given case, and in cases which share with it more general themes and elements.

There are a few cases encountered in these files where what happens between the key actors is so odd, bizarre, or unusual that there is a disruption of the connection between the identification of a particular social relationship (for example, husband as offender, wife as victim) and the building up of an analysis about the homicide. What is common in these cases is that knowledge of the nature of their particular relationship, at least as revealed by the present files, does not lead easily to developing a reasonable account which is able to trace the homicide back to the nature of the bond between victim and offender.

Perhaps the best way to understand this problem is by confronting an example. In the first of these cases, the homicide victim was a wife killed by her husband:

Just before midnight on 2 April 1986, H.S. (age 41, invalid pensioner) came into the South Melbourne Police Station and informed the attending officers that he had killed his wife. In the interview which followed, H.S.'s answers to questions led the investigating police to believe that he 'may have been suffering from some mental disability at the time'. Both H.S. and his wife (W.S., age 31) had long histories of mental illness, including lengthy hospitalisation.

Q: 'What happened between you and W.?'
H.S.: 'I murdered W.'
Q: 'How did you do that?'
H.S.: 'With a knife.'
Q: 'What do you mean by that?'
H.S.: 'I stabbed her.'
Q: 'Why did you do that?'
H.S.: 'To kill her.'
Q: 'Why did you want to kill her?'
H.S.: 'I don't know.'
Q: 'Did you have an argument?'
H.S.: 'I'm not sure.'
Q: 'Where was she when you stabbed her?'
H.S.: 'In bed.'
Q: 'Was she asleep or awake?'
H.S.: 'I'm not sure.'

. . .

Q: 'What were you doing just before you got the knife?'
H.S.: 'I was in bed with W. and then I got up and then got the knife. Then I went back and stabbed her.'
Q: 'Did you decide to kill W. before you got the knife?'
H.S.: 'Yes.'
Q: 'When did you decide to kill her?'
H.S.: 'I don't know, it just sort of happened.'
Q: 'Do you remember why you killed W.?'
H.S.: 'No.'

. . .

Q: 'Did you have an argument during the day at all?'
H.S.: 'No.'
Q: 'Had you planned to kill her before you went to bed?'
H.S.: 'No.'

. . .

Q: 'Did you do anything after you stabbed her?'
H.S.: 'Yes.'
Q: 'What?'
H.S.: 'I kissed her.'
Q: 'Did you do anything else to her?'
H.S.: 'Yeah, I put my arms around her.'

. . .

Q: 'Do you fully understand that you have killed your wife?'
H.S.: 'Yes.'

. . .

Q: 'The only thing you haven't been able to tell me is why you killed her, can you tell me now?'
H.S.: 'I don't know why.'   *(Case No. 965–86)*

What provoked this homicide? When pressed by police in the interview immediately after the event, even the offender professed no understanding of what he was up to, or what led him to murder his wife. In all other cases of intimate homicide involving sexual partners

where the victim was female and the offender male, the available information indicated that there was a 'rationale' on the part of the offender whereby the outside observer could see the nature of the mental processes that led the offender to kill his partner. Even where these processes are delusions, as in the case of A.H. who developed the erroneous notion that his wife had arranged for a prostitute to infect him with AIDS (Case No. 231–86), the observer can work through the nature of the dynamics that ultimately led to the killing.

In the case of the invalid pensioner H.S., from these files no such interpretive rationale exists. The wife was not suspected of having affairs with other men, nor had she threatened to leave (the events that provoke the intense possessiveness that leads so many men in intimate sexual relationships to take, ultimately, the steps toward lethal violence). At this point, at least, there was no indication of the deep depression that leads some men to kill their wives as part of their own suicide plans. Even when pressed several times by the police, the offender could advance no reason for him to have killed his wife.

In the mechanical, quantitative data sets on homicides, this killing would pose no problem in terms of how it would be classified. Since by definition the two individuals were man and wife, it would be considered as one of the many which fall within 'spousal' or perhaps 'domestic' homicide. The present research, however, has evolved with the fundamental assumption that classification of a homicide in terms of the relationship between the victim and offender can be justified only if this informs us about the nature of the lethal event. In this 'special' account of homicide among sexual intimates, it was possible to locate the offender and victim in terms of *who* they were within a social relationship (that is, husband and wife), but it was not possible to answer the question of *why* the interaction within that relationship led to homicide.

There is in this account considerable evidence of mental disturbance on the part of both the wife and the husband. Both had experienced long periods of hospitalisation in mental institutions. While this suggests that this might be a case of 'murder through madness', even if it were true that the offender was psychologically disturbed, and thus looked out at the world through a set of lenses which, to our view, were distorted, there still should be some thread of interpretation which leads the individual through the events which provoked his action. What makes this case so special at this point is that the husband repeatedly was asked why he committed the offence, and each time could give no satisfactory answer.

Fortunately, it was possible to round out this account by obtaining supplementary information from another official source. After cases

have moved into and through the trial phase of the criminal justice system, including the sentencing and appeal stages, a large file has accumulated and is retained in the office of the Victorian Director of Public Prosecutions (DPP). These files contain a number of documents that are potentially useful for gaining further understanding of this and similar cases. This includes material relating to the trial, as well as psychiatric reports prepared both prior to the trial and prior to sentencing, and the pre-sentence reports prepared by a social worker.

In the case of H.S., it was the psychiatric reports that were particularly revealing. Consistent with the record of interview prepared by the police, the psychiatrist who saw the defendant immediately after the event observed: 'I have no knowledge what the prisoner says regarding the alleged offence as he says nothing.'

When interviewed many weeks later by another psychiatrist, however, a tentative picture begins to emerge. This psychiatrist noted that the defendant said to him that at the time of the offence:

> He felt 'racey', … He said he was not able to think logically, he couldn't control his thoughts.
> The report went on to note regarding the married couple that:
> They had previously contemplated suicide ... the homicide ... was going to be a 'suicide/murder combination'. He [the defendant] said he had intended to jump off the balcony.

A third psychiatrist, also examining the defendant much later, supported these observations of the possibility that suicide was contemplated, noting that the husband said that:

> He stated that around 10.30 pm he decided to jump off the balcony of their flat. He removed himself from bed, and started looking down at his wife feeling very sorry. He related that they had an understanding that his wife would be unable to live without him. He stated: 'I could not commit suicide and leave her.'

Both of the last two psychiatrists concluded that the husband was, in fact, seriously unbalanced mentally. One concluded: 'I have no doubt that this man was actively psychotic at the time of the commission of the alleged offence.' Similarly, the other was of the view that 'by virtue of defect of reason, occasioned by mental illness … that he would not have been capable of appreciating the rightness or wrongness of his act'.

This offender was moving through life at the pace of a drummer hidden from our view. He was mentally ill to the point where he qualifies under the stringent requirements of the M'Naghten Rules of not being

legally culpable for his act in bringing about the death of his wife. That does not mean, however, that the homicide was without motive.

There is here, assuming the psychiatrists are correct in their report of the intended suicide, evidence that this husband was acting in a manner similar to some of the depressed older men observed in the section on intimate homicide (Chapter 3). Such men, suffering from depression and at the same time having a proprietorial view of their wives, decide to take the life of their partner as part of their suicide plan. Mentally ill this offender may be, and perhaps the theme is distorted by that illness, but in the relationship between this male offender and his female victim there may have been a form of the possessiveness that is a dominant feature of homicides committed on women by men.

This can only be advanced as a tentative hypothesis, however. The dimensions of this case remain basically unclear. While a possible interpretation is hinted at from the additional records, it remains the case that a definitive interpretation can not be offered which links the interaction between the offender and his victim. Given that fact, this account should still be kept apart from the main body of case studies as a 'special' case.

Another case, which involves brothers as victim and offender, was similar in that the case study as prepared from the files of the Coroner yielded a homicide with no apparent explanation:

A.G. (age 23, qualified electrician) had been living with his parents and brother, I.G. (age 20) for the three weeks since he had been discharged from the army. Over the past few months, A.G.'s behaviour had become increasingly erratic. He had been in the army from 1983 to 1986, when his odd and disruptive behaviour led him to first be subject to disciplinary action, and eventually to psychiatric and psychological examination and discharge from the army on psychiatric grounds. A.G. returned to the family home, apparently burning with resentment towards the army and the company sergeant-major (whom he had vowed to kill).

One day, some three weeks after his discharge, the two brothers spent a quiet Saturday at home, watching television and videos. They had a few drinks together, and nothing in the accounts available suggests that the day had been anything but pleasant and easy.

In the middle of the evening, I.G. decided to take a shower. A.G. stated later that at this point he began to think upon his resolve to kill his company sergeant-major, and he decided to fetch a bullet from a back shed at the rear of the family home to work on it to make it more 'potent'.

In his testimony to the police, A.G. states that he began to wonder 'what it was like to kill someone.' To find out, he decided to kill his brother. I.G. came back into the bedroom after his shower in order to dress. A.G. placed some earplugs in his ears, raised the gun, sighted on his brother's head, and pulled the trigger. The one shot was instantly fatal. He fled from the house, surrendering to police within a few hours. He could offer no motive for the crime.   (Case No. 4155–86)

As was true in the previous case, here there was no clear motive for the crime. There was no argument between the two brothers as occurred in another case in these files where a brother killed his sister after a series of events and disputes led to an argument between sister and brother, and then the final steps where a gun was fired and the sister killed. That killing can be traced step-by-step from initial disputes to the final violence. In the account of what happened between these two brothers there was nothing in the reported interaction between them that provides any clue as to why the death occurred. The offender himself could offer no motive, other than he wanted to know what it was like 'to kill someone'.

Once again, the files of the Director of Public Prosecutions were consulted to see if a rationale could be found for the homicide. In this case, a number of psychiatrists had seen the offender, and by and large they remained mystified when it came to why the act had occurred. One found that the killer 'specifically denies any resentment towards his brother', another found that 'He is unable to explain why he killed his brother', while another observed that: 'The offence remains apparently motiveless, evidently this man having a good relationship with the victim, his brother.'

No less than four psychiatrists agreed that madness was not apparent in his makeup, and was not a factor in the crime. One commented that there were 'no active psychiatric symptoms present', another that there was 'no evidence of significant psychiatric disturbance at present', while another found that there was 'no formal mental illness'.

The records here cannot provide a definitive reason, then, why this individual, who does not suffer from mental illness, would be moved to kill anyone, let alone his brother. Although not admitted by the offender, one possible reason did emerge in the volume of material available. Some months previously the life of the offender was transformed by a serious motor car accident. He was hospitalised for several months, underwent several operations, and was left with significant facial disfigurement as a result. It was after this accident that his psychological makeup seemed to change, and he began to act in the aggressive manner that ultimately led to his discharge on less than honourable grounds from the army. The driver of the car in that accident was his brother, the victim of the homicide. Was the homicide motivated by a desire to get back at the brother who had caused so much suffering? On the basis of evidence available at this time, we cannot know. At no time did the killer offer this as a motive for the homicide, even when questioned closely by the psychiatrists. In the trial, however, the defence did offer this as a possible explanation for the homicide. It cannot be stated here with any certainty, however, that this was the reason why he was moved to take up his rifle against his brother.

The safest conclusion is that at the moment no clear reasons emerge which account for this killing. What is known is that it was a homicide between brothers. It is not possible at this time to provide a reason why this relationship resulted in the homicide. This case study is placed, therefore, in the category of 'special' homicides because it has not been possible to identify what it was about the relationship itself that contributes to an explanation of the homicide.

Two of the other 'special' cases involve persons who might otherwise be considered as bonded by friendship:

> Three days before Christmas, at a few minutes before midnight, S.S. (age 19, invalid pensioner) arrived by taxi at the Russell Street Police Station, where he went up to the desk and announced that he had stabbed someone. Police and ambulances were directed to the address he provided, where they found M.G. (age 75, pensioner) on the floor of his flat, dead as a result of a single stab wound to his abdomen.
>
> Police investigators found that S.S. had been born to parents who had migrated from Yugoslavia when he was 6 years old. After leaving school, S.S. had travelled from State to State working as a labourer. While in Darwin some five years before these events, he had been placed in a mental institution where he was diagnosed as being schizophrenic. He subsequently received psychiatric treatment in Sydney and Melbourne. At the time of this incident, he was being treated for paranoid schizophrenia, including heavy medication.
>
> When asked why he had stabbed the old man, who had befriended S.S. and asked him to his flat several times, S.S. replied that: 'He said I had hands like a female, and said I was a poofter because I wasn't married ... and, he kept talking about Hitler.' S.S. had several times been invited to visit with M.G. and use the TV, as S.S. did not own one. At another point in the interview, when S.S. was asked again if M.G. had called him a poofter, S.S. replied: 'No, he was Austrian and he made me watch German movies all the time. My grandfather had been killed by Germans in the war. I had just had enough.'   *(Case No. 3954–85)*

The interaction between the victim and offender as described by the offender were such that the nature of the rationale offered makes little sense. The offender offered a fragment of a motive ('he made me watch German movies all the time'), but this motive, and the others advanced ('he said I had hands like a poofter', or 'he kept talking about Hitler'), were quite unlike the motives of other homicides. Assuming that even the mentally ill have some rationale, however different that might be, for their homicides, it was decided to probe deeper into this case as well. As in other accounts involving offenders where mental illness played a role, before and after the trial the offender was seen by a number of psychiatrists. An important feature of this homicide were the 'voices' heard by the offender. As one psychiatrist observed: 'When asked why he killed the man, he said he heard voices telling him to kill

the man. He was deluded that he was the Angel of Death.' A second noted that the offender 'believes that he is the Angel of Death and that God commanded him to kill'. Another put it slightly differently: 'The voices were from the Angel of Death. They said to kill him.'

These psychiatrists all agreed that this was extreme mental disturbance, one finding that at the time of the murder the offender 'was suffering from a psychotic illness and had no real control over his actions'. Responding to the specific legal requirements of the case, a second stated that 'In my view ... he was insane within the M'Naghten Rules at the time of the commission of the alleged offence.' If this case were to be classified within the victim/offender categories employed here, it would be considered as a murder between friends. The actual facts of the homicide, however, require that it receive special treatment. Understanding this homicide dictates that circumstances be considered which go well beyond the nature of the relationship between the disturbed offender and the unfortunate victim who had befriended him. This account has little in common with the other cases where persons tied at one time by the intimate bond of friendship experience the breakdown of that bond to the point where one murders the other in order to resolve their differences.

While there are signs in the brief biographical sketches of some of these special cases that mental illness on the part of the offender plays either a major or minor role in the homicide, this does not always appear to be the case:

Tommy M. (age 19, metal cutter) and Colin E. (age 19, metal cutter) seemed to all outside appearances to be quite friendly. They both worked at the same place, and other workers described them as getting on quite well.

On the Friday before Christmas they both attended work as usual, finishing early, collecting their pay, then attending a company barbecue. The two seemed to be in good spirits, eating and talking together for the three to four hours of the barbecue. Afterwards, they went together to the Excelsior Hotel for a few more Christmas drinks in the public bar.

Before leaving the bar together at about 7 pm, Colin obtained a pocket knife from an acquaintance in the bar, saying: 'I just want to get some money.' His friend gave him the knife, thinking, he said later, that Colin was 'all talk'.

The two left the hotel and headed for home. They proceeded to walk along a nearby creek for a short distance, when Colin suddenly turned on his friend and began to stab him in a frenzy. Tommy sustained over 100 stab wounds, from his eyes to his groin as well as defensive wounds to his hands.

Colin then removed Tommy's pay packet containing some $198 and returned to the pub. He then proceeded to tell the patrons of the bar what he had just done. At first, no one would believe him. In the words of one witness, we thought, 'no, Colin would be bullshitting'. As proof of his claim, Colin then produced Tommy's pay packet. Finally, the patrons believed him.

Their reaction was to assault Colin and drag him out the door of the pub, taking the stolen money from him and giving it to the pub manager. Colin wrenched himself out of the grasp of the group and fled the hotel. He was arrested a few days later and charged with Tommy's murder.

(Case No. 3940–85)

This account is placed among the 'special' homicides because upon reading the case study it is not clear how the killing could be connected to what had previously happened between the offender and his victim. On the basis of information from the files of the Director of Public Prosecutions, it appears that the psychiatrists determined that mental illness did not provide an explanation for the homicide.

The defence, however, advanced the argument that the offender was heavily addicted to stimulating drugs, and at the time of the homicide had been routinely taking very large dosages of 'speed'. There were two effects of this heavy use of the drug, according to this argument. First, it tended to confuse the judgment of the defendant, especially when used in combination with large amounts of alcohol, as was true on the day of the homicide (while it was some time before the offender was apprehended and therefore his blood alcohol level at the time could not be measured, the victim, whom in all accounts had been matching him drink for drink all afternoon, was found to have a blood alcohol reading of 0.229). Second, its costs put the defendant under heavy financial pressure.

The defendant claimed in a pre-sentence statement that 'At the time I was in a bad way with drugs', and referring to the events immediately before the killing stated:

I do remember at the pub worrying about how I was going to cope for money ... I also remember thinking about pinching T.'s money. It's all a bit of a fog, but I remember thinking I needed the knife to scare him.

One of the witnesses testified that the offender was very drunk in the time just before the killing. After stumbling into their table, he apologised and started up a conversation (the witness was a complete stranger to the defendant):

He said that a guy had $1000 holiday pay on him and that he was going to stab him. I then remember saying, 'where's the knife?' and he said 'Here', and tapped his pocket. He kept talking about stabbing this guy for his money, but I heard someone say that they worked together and I thought he was only talking.

This case might be classified under at least three of the categories used in previous sections of this report. First, the two might have

engaged in a spontaneous masculine confrontation, but there is no evidence of any argument between them. Second, the murder was apparently motivated by Colin's desire to 'get some money', which resulted in the robbery of his friend, but the facts of the case do not suggest this as anything like a typical armed robbery. Third, since the two had been close mates, it is possible that some rift had developed between them, and that the violence was a method of resolving their dispute. The nature of the homicide indicates, however, that whatever transpired lacked the essential planning and premeditation that is so distinctive among the conflict-resolution killings.

The police investigating the crime asked several questions of people who had observed the two both prior to, and on, the day of the murder, and were unable to establish any indication of conflict between the victim and his attacker. One cannot work one's way from a breakdown of the friendship into the homicide, and more specifically, there is no indication of emergent conflicts within the friendship which impelled the offender to employ violence as a mechanism of conflict resolution. The distinctiveness of this case is preserved, thereby, by placing it among the group of 'special' homicides.

In another case, we find again a combination of a background of psychological disturbance and a set of confusing events which result in homicide:

Kenny D. (age 20) had an extensive history of mental illness. His behaviour attracted psychological attention early in life during his primary school years, where he was diagnosed as 'hyperactive' and placed on medication to slow him down. Kenny was expelled from high school for 'being uncontrollable'. Shortly after that, he was in children's court for charges of sexual assault involving a number of young girls.

After a further offence involving throwing a rock at another boy which caused serious head injuries, Kenny was placed in a mental institution. There followed other offences of violence which led to him being hauled back to court, then back into the mental institution.

Staff involved there in his most recent treatment seemed to feel that progress was being made. Kenny was able to move into a residential program, and he even found and held a job. He was then established in his own flat in Carlton (an inner Melbourne suburb).

Kenny had met Lorrie M. (age 19) while both were patients at the residential facility in Parkville. Lorrie, who was diagnosed as schizophrenic, later became an outpatient, returning to live with her mother in the council housing flats in Carlton.

Kenny had not seen Lorrie for a couple of months, and decided to stop by her flat 'just to see how she was going'. During the visit, Lorrie apparently asked if she could go with him to his place for tea. Lorrie's mother later recalled that Kenny: 'wasn't enthusiastic but he agreed'.

In his later testimony, Kenny's account was that they returned to his place, listened to music and spent some time 'kissing and cuddling on the couch.'

He then fixed tea. After the meal, Lorrie started 'screaming out something, I don't know ...' Kenny asked her to calm down, and he said that he 'even tried to ask her what was wrong, but she started to carry on even worse.' She then went into the bedroom, saying she was going to take a nap.

Somewhat later, Lorrie woke up, and began screaming again. Kenny said that: 'I pleaded with her to be quiet. I then went back into the kitchen and she continued yelling. I went to a drawer in the kitchen, got out my handcuffs and some masking tape, thinking I might be able to shut her up that way.'

Kenny then went into the bedroom, according to his account, first handcuffing her, then winding the 'masking tape around her head and covering her mouth'. Kenny's narrative stated that then: 'She became quiet and I went back to the fridge and had some coke. She must have ripped the tape off, and started yelling again ... I then assembled my crossbow, to try and scare her into being quiet ... I went into the bedroom, and told her to be quiet or leave. I just went off my head. I just couldn't take it any more, and I fired the crossbow ... I had just blown my temper.'

The story doesn't stop there. Kenny went on to relate: 'I put down the crossbow, and realised what I had done. I could see that she was still alive. I took advantage of the situation. I realised what big trouble I was in by shooting her with a crossbow, so I decided to rape her. She tried to fight me off with her arms ... I thought I was in enough trouble as it was, and it couldn't be any worse for me.'

Kenny then gagged her, and left her, still alive, in the flat. He called Lorrie's mother to assure her that Lorrie was all right, then wandered about the city, eventually going to his parents' house to spend the night. Later in the week, he eventually tried to flee, flying to Tasmania under a false name. He was found on the following Sunday in a youth shelter in Launceston, confessed, and was returned to Melbourne to face charges of murder.

(Case No. 3645–85)

As was true with the other special cases, it was difficult to penetrate the rationale offered by this offender. Strapping a person to a chair, and then taping the mouth, are unusual techniques, to say the least, of pacifying a sexual intimate. The rape of the victim, after the fatal wounding, and the rationale offered for the rape, make this case stand apart.

Little additional information was revealed when the files of the Director of Public Prosecutions were reviewed in an attempt to round out this account. These files reinforced data previously obtained which indicated that the offender had a background of behaviour in which violence and mental disturbance were combined. The offender was unable to offer much to attending psychiatrists in the way of an explanation for the homicide, seeing it in his terms as a form of an 'accident'. The psychiatric reports, while commenting on the history of mental illness, did not find that the behaviour of the offender in committing this crime fell within the boundaries of insanity as legally defined.

Because of the extraordinary violence and its rationale, this case does not seem to fit well within the other forms of homicide which have been identified. While the record of the trial indicates that according to the evidence the two had been sexually intimate prior to the homicide, it is not clear what it was about their intimacy that was in any way responsible for the death. In other cases of homicide involving sexual intimacy between the partners, that intimacy (and often its disintegration) can be seen as a central theme which runs through the events which result in the killing of the victim. In this case, while there was intimacy, and certainly exceptional violence, it is not possible to say what it is that connects the two. There is in particular none of the obsessive jealousy or control themes that have featured so prominently in the scenario of masculine violence towards female sexual partners. Accordingly, this case, too, is set aside among the group of 'special' offences.

Some of the same themes of brutality, bizarreness and incomprehensibility are found in the case of Linda G.:

Homicide files will contain many brutal killings, but few found in Victoria were as savage as the homicide of Linda G. (age 21, invalid pensioner). Linda was mildly handicapped intellectually. After spending much of her younger years in an institution for the mentally retarded, she had recently moved in with her mother. Friends and family described her as having a 'lovely and childlike manner'.

A few months before, mutual friends had introduced Linda to Charlie S. (age 29), but they seemed to dislike each other. Charlie often called her a 'dog' and when he saw her would 'bark at her'. Despite this antagonism, Charlie alleges that he had a casual sexual relationship, and would, as he put it, call on her when he 'felt like a root'.

There is some dispute about the set of events that led to the actual murder. There is a suggestion that Linda was angry with Charlie and his brother Arthur, and that she was going to confront them about their harassment of a girlfriend of hers. Charlie's story is that he called her and invited her out.

The story the offenders tell is that they took her to a spot along the Merri Creek, where they all had several drinks (Charlie said that he drank a considerable amount of Southern Comfort during the course of the night). They allege that Linda then stripped, and engaged in various sexual acts with both men simultaneously.

They at first were content with beating her, but at some point, the two decided that 'We'd knock her.' They then moved on and engaged in perhaps the most savage acts that exist in these files. The two engaged in vicious sexual mutilation, gouged out one of her eyes, broke off a piece of wood and forced it up her sexual organs, among other acts.

This case is bizarre also in the way the two responded after the act. Both brothers bragged not only to friends, but even to the investigating police, about what they had done. Arthur said to the police afterwards: 'I'm glad I done it, I don't care what anyone thinks of me. I haven't slept better since I done it. I feel really great. She was a nobody, anyway.' When asked by his

sister why he had done it, Arthur replied that it was 'just something to do'. Charlie told the police that: 'We were scared she would call in the coppers ... she was a lowie ...' Both provided graphic details to the police of the numerous sadistic acts they had committed on Linda's body.

(Case No. 1606–85)

As was true with the previous file, this case seems to fall outside the boundaries of other categories of homicide we have reviewed, although in some ways it might initially seem to fit in at least two. There was a prior sexual relationship between one of the offenders and Linda, but the steps leading to the homicide were completely unlike the dynamics of 'intimate sexual' relationships between offenders and female victims of the age of Linda. There was no indication of jealousy or a sense of 'possessiveness' which was threatened by Linda.

A better case might be made that this was an instance of homicide which occurred in the course of another crime, in this case, sexual assault. The initial problem with this interpretation is that the sexual activity engaged in by the woman was apparently voluntary (and this aspect was not questioned by the prosecution during the trial).

Both to see if there was some better explanation for the crime itself, and for the exceptional brutality shown, the files of the Director of Public Prosecutions were obtained for this case as well. Two specific bits of additional information emerged from these records. First, there were some clues regarding the source of the brutality. Further testimony revealed that the brother responsible for initiating and carrying out the greater part of the savage violence had been unable to perform sexually, as found in this exchange from a record of interview:

Q: 'Did you have sex with her at any stage?'
A.S.: 'I tried to ... but it just wouldn't work ... I couldn't get it up.'
Q: 'Did she make any comment about your inability to get an erection?'
A.S.: 'She said, "Have you been giving it to that sheila you're now with?"'
Q: ... 'Was that remark about your inability to get an erection?'
A.S.: 'I can't be exactly sure, but it was to do with that or about the sheila.'

In the accounts of both of the brothers, it was immediately after this that the one brother lost his head, and began to beat her, saying then that they should 'knock her' (that is, kill her). When asked why he had gone to fetch the knife, the same brother replied: 'I was worried that she was going to yell out rape and for the assaults.' [*Q:* 'In order to prevent her from going to the police?'] 'Yes.'

It seems likely that the extraordinary brutality towards the young woman was a response to her challenge of the masculinity of the leading offender. While bizarre, it therefore has elements that perhaps

require it being considered under the issues of gender role that have emerged so strongly in the section on intimacy. The unique features of these events, however, suggest that for present purposes its distinctiveness should be preserved by setting it aside in the category of special cases.

One other of these cases seems to hinge on mental incompetence of the offender, although at a level not recognised by the courts:

> The life of Georgie Hunter (age 19, unemployed) had not been easy. He was retarded both mentally and physically. Throughout his young life, he had been exceptionally clumsy, constantly stumbling and falling off bikes. He had become such a butt of teasing and jokes that he had reached the point where he would do his best to avoid social scenes where he would meet people.
>
> Through a casual contact, he had met Mrs Campbell, a neighbour in the suburb, a week before the murder occurred. Mrs Campbell was highly regarded by her friends and neighbour, and was known for her friendliness. The week after found Georgie in her street again, when upon seeing a group of other young people he became fearful. He went up to her door seeking the safety of her house.
>
> Mrs Campbell let him in. Through the distorted mirror of Georgie's confusion, the sequence of events from this point is hard to establish. Apparently at one point he asked to go to the bathroom, and while there pulled out his knife, which he then used to stab and kill Mrs Campbell. When asked why he stabbed her, Georgie said: 'I dunno. I just got frightened. I only wanted to be friends.' When asked why he had taken the knife out of his pants pocket, he replied: 'I was worried she would see me.' He was then asked: 'Why did this worry you?' to which he replied: 'I dunno. I was thinking in the bathroom that I should have stayed home.' Later in the same interview, Georgie stated that 'I went to the house to make a friend because I was lonely and I haven't got many friends.'   (Case No. AG 870656)

In this account we have a confused young male, possibly both mentally retarded and to some degree mentally ill, who first sought the friendship of his elderly neighbour. He became frightened, and convinced that Mrs Campbell was going to do him harm, he struck out. Consultation of additional files found that psychological assessment ruled out insanity as a defence. It was acknowledged that Georgie had a history of odd behaviour, in which he was easily provoked to bursts of violence. In this case it is not easy to identify a relevant category of victim-offender relationship. There has been no need to use the term 'acquaintance' or 'neighbour' for classification in the present study. Since the offender states that what he was seeking was friendship, then it might be so classified, if it were necessary to force each homicide into some such framework. To do so, however, would seem to serve little analytical purpose.

Homicide and the 'special' cases

This research has proceeded from the assumption that a key to understanding the nature of the events that make up homicides rests in an appropriate classification of the different motivations that link offenders and victims. In most of the cases reviewed in previous sections, the events constitute something like the 'duet' in the metaphor first used by von Hentig (1979). Thus, the major participants, including the offender and victim, move together through a complicated set of moves, each influencing the other, ultimately resulting in lethal violence. Knowing the particular form of victim-offender relationship in most cases will provide a good clue as to the nature of these duetlike moves. Where the victim is the sexual partner of a male offender, at issue is likely to be power, control and masculinity. Similarly, honour or reputation is likely to be central to masculine confrontations which result in homicide, and where the individuals have been bound together in friendship, the dominant pattern that has emerged is one of the readiness of some males to employ violence as a technique of dispute resolution.

The 'special' cases, of which there were 18 in the present investigation (or 5 per cent of all homicides), prove to be a problem for standard forms of analysis of victim and offender relationships in homicide. Each of the special cases on technical grounds would have been classified within forms of victim/offender relationships typically found in studies of homicide. Two involve what might be classified as homicide between friends where the killing is a form of conflict resolution, one is a homicide within the family involving two brothers, while in another three there was some form of sexual bond (however brief) between the male offenders and their female victims, and the final case is a homicide between persons known to each other as acquaintances.

Consider the case where the mentally ill young man was prompted to kill his elderly friend because his 'voices' told him he was the Angel of Death. This event is unlike any of the other homicides involving friendship where the homicide is a form of conflict resolution. While it technically shares with these other killings the fact that the individuals involved were friends, it is radically different in terms of the social dynamics of the relationship between the victim and the offender, especially in terms of the different rationality offered here to account for why the killing took place.

In some of these special accounts, the offender either was clearly mentally ill, or could be considered as functioning in a mentally abnormal way at the time of the homicide. It is not the intent here,

however, to shift the analysis away from the interactions between offender and victim onto the mental state of the offender. Instead, in each of these cases the investigators have attempted to isolate as clearly as possible what the circumstances of the relationship were between the two parties. It is this dynamic which has been termed here 'special', rather than the mental state of the offender.

It may be, of course, that the addition of more cases would suggest that a separate category be created for homicides where the violence has its origins in the mental illness of the offender. There is, for example, a persistent theme of offenders motivated by 'voices' which runs through some of these 'special' accounts. Whatever happens, the suggestion for the present analysis is that in these circumstances the ordinary and routine classification of homicide by virtue of the relationship between offender and victim is difficult indeed.

The points to be made from these special cases are twofold. First, it is highly likely that such distinctive events are inevitably part of the events which lead to homicide both here and elsewhere. In investigations of homicide, the materials that provide the base for analysis of the victim/offender relationship ought to be reviewed carefully, in other words, before events are classified simply as, say, an instance of husband/wife, or brother/brother killing. Such a classification may be technically correct in a narrow sense, but as the above accounts suggest, it may not be an accurate reflection of the particular events of special cases.

Second, these cases demonstrate that there are ultimate limits in what can be done in analysing homicide through the victim/offender relationship. In a handful of cases, there may not be enough material available to make clear what it was that was going on between the two parties. Where some interpretation cannot be made regarding the nature of the interaction which has taken place between victim and offender, simply classifying the event along one or another of the standard categories of victim/offender relationship will not prove theoretically or empirically meaningful.

The approach which focuses on this relationship as the major vehicle for the analysis of homicide presumes that it is possible not simply to classify such accounts, but to provide some meaning for what has transpired between the parties. It is suggested here that even where the body of data is reasonably good, as the present set tends to be, in a few cases the nature of the events may be hidden from view by mental confusion on the part of the offender, the absence of accurate accounts of those events, or even the obvious deliberate twisting and misstating of these events on the part of those who survive the homicide.

Put another way, building up an understanding of homicide by focusing on the critical relationship between the victim and the offender

inevitably will lead to some classification of such relationships in order to reduce the observations to meaningful conclusions. In the various themes and variations reviewed in previous sections the accounts tended to share common features not simply in the objective relationship observed between offender and victim (for example, women victims of male sexual intimates), but in terms of the factors within these cases which led the events down a path towards homicide (such as sexual proprietoriness and jealousy). A distinctive feature of the special cases is that while they might share with other cases an objective classification of the relationship between victim and offender (wife and husband), the essential facts of these cases are quite unlike the other accounts within the category.

There is, in short, something distinctive about these events which sets them apart. The interactions, motivations and dynamics of other cases simply do not fit for these 'special' events. Accordingly, we are arguing here for a procedure which places these cases in a category of their own, where their distinctive features can be preserved. These are properly considered, in the term suggested by Block and Block (1992), as true homicide mysteries.

The issue of the missing voices

There is as well the problem that the development of any narrative, such as a case study or a police file, on a killing will be a social construction based on available evidence from which some voices will be absent, and others either deliberately or inadvertently less than well-focused. It is an elementary fact of social psychology that the same act viewed by different observers, even under laboratory conditions, may yield substantially different accounts. This will be no less true with the real life circumstance of a killing, especially since the voice of one of the most central parties, the victim, is absent in nearly all cases (there are a few instances where the victim lingers before dying). Further, there are some circumstances where the different observers have oppositional and partisan points of view. If the killing involved a collective argument between two groups of young people, they may give vastly different accounts of who 'started' the violent encounter.

There is no simple way out of this problem. Fortunately, most homicides are definitively social events, where most available accounts agree on the steps which led to the homicide. Often, there will be available either relatives or close friends of the victim who can provide their memory of the actual words of the victim before the homicide (memories which frequently can be cross-checked with other witnesses).

For all that, there are cases which pose significant problems for the external observer. There are a small number of cases where the actual killing was not observed, and where the alleged offender denied the killing. In one case which took place in San Remo (a seaside holiday resort), a woman was drowned after walking along a dock with her husband, from whom she had recently separated. The couple had many violent arguments in the days immediately before the death, the man expressed to friends his rage that his wife had moved in with another man, and he had further said that he was going to 'do her in'. When the wife, who was a good swimmer dies, is it reasonable to presume that he had pushed her into the water and caused her death?

In a similar case, a woman is found shot dead in the family home, and her husband is found tied up in the boot of the car outside the house. It was the man's story that the couple had been set upon by a group of thieves, who had shot his wife and bound him and placed him in the car. The couple, it transpired, had experienced great difficulties in the marriage, including the woman taking a lover. The police were able to uncover a great number of inconsistencies in the story of the husband.

Both of these accounts demonstrate the problems that can arise as a consequence of lack of access to the missing voices which might round out the story of what 'really' happened. While the police argued that both of these men were guilty, in fact, while the second husband was convicted of murder, in the first narrative the husband ultimately was not brought into court for the death of his wife.

There are other ways that these events can become clouded and uncertain. In more than a few cases, the available witnesses, and per-haps even the offender, have ingested such exceptional levels of alcohol that no amount of probing can reveal a very clear account of the death. In one illustrative case, an infant was found battered to death after it had been in the care of a rather large family grouping. The accounts given agree that all of the adults present at the party that night were exceptionally drunk, and none of the group admitted responsibility for the beating. No charges were laid in this case.

For all of these reasons, the unknown cases, the special circumstances where the motivations of the killing are not easy to assess, or because of the limits imposed when voices are absent or distorted, the investigator who sets out on the important task of unravelling the interactions between homicide victims and offenders must recognise the limits of what that analysis can achieve. Some homicides must remain outside such an exploration because the available information is not sufficient for appropriate classification. Others, even where it is known what the static social relationship between offender and victim is (such as

husband-wife, or brother-brother), should be excluded because in fact the reasons for the killing remain hidden from view.

Despite these limits, with a reasonably rich body of data it is not unreasonable to expect to be able to describe meaningful narratives in close to 90 per cent of cases of homicide. Where cases can be reviewed in detail, and where the inquiry is directed by explicit theoretical interests, it should be possible to describe reasonably coherent scenarios which capture the basic patterns which run through such data.

On the study of homicide

Having now examined the present data on homicide scenarios, what implications do these raise for how studies of homicide are conducted? A review of existing literature will show rather distinct differences between traditional approaches to the investigation of victim-offender relationships, and the present analysis of scenarios of homicide. Typically, previous investigations, drawing upon the pioneering work of Wolfgang (1958), have tended to focus either on relationships defined in terms of the nature of the social bonds between the participants, or on the motives which bring and hold the individuals together.

The first of these deals with a dimension of social relationships which ranges from intimate familial roles at one end of a continuum, to those involving strangers at the other end. These can vary from relatively sparse schemes, which pose an intimate category such as 'family', an intermediate category involving 'friends/acquaintances', and then a more extreme category of 'strangers' (Hewitt, 1988, and Huong and Salmelainen, 1993). Many others attempt to fill out such schemes, posing a number of other categories, most of which will round out the possible forms of known or intimate relationships (spouses, boyfriend-girlfriend, mother-child, etc.). Among these is the eleven-category list proposed by Wolfgang in his original study, and the even more extensive list of the Supplementary Homicide Reports which calls for more than two dozen specific categories (Maxfield, 1989). Silverman and Kennedy (1987) have pointed out that the theoretical content of such schemes is based on notions of 'relational distance', where the social bonds range from those involving close relationships of family intimacy to the extreme of strangers where the link is the most distant.

The category problem: 'stranger homicide' as an illustration

While the approach of Silverman and Kennedy has proven insightful in its treatment of available secondary data on homicide, there are a number of problems with this form of treatment of 'victim-offender

relationships' which can be thrown into sharp perspective by a brief examination of the concept of stranger homicide. Though the notion of stranger homicide looms large in media accounts of contemporary crime, and has even been the target of a number of recent accounts of homicide (Kapardis, 1990; Langevin and Handy, 1987; Zahn and Sagi, 1987; Silverman and Kennedy, 1987; and Reidel, 1987), it is significant that at no point in the grouping of the scenarios of homicide from the thematic analysis of the present case studies was it necessary or relevant to make use of the term 'stranger homicide'.

Every single one of the nearly 400 homicides could be grouped into a meaningful scenario or the important residual categories without giving primary emphasis to whether the event involved strangers in contrast to persons known to each other. There were no killings that could be described within a scenario which would be labelled 'stranger homicide'.

The reasons for this finding are straightforward. Put simply, people don't kill each other because they are strangers. Homicide tends to involve exceptional tensions and emotional extremes. With rare exceptions (to be discussed below), these tensions are not found among people who remain totally unknown to each other. There were homicides which involved persons who were not known to each other. The great majority of what are called stranger homicides elsewhere, however, are to be found in two of the present masculine scenarios of homicide. Many will be where the homicide occurs in the course of another crime, for example, during the course of armed robbery. Another large number will occur as a result of a masculine honour confrontation. It is the present conclusion that the thematic material within the scenario provides a better description of the ongoing dynamic between the parties in the homicide than does the designation that the event is a 'stranger homicide'.

In masculine confrontations, for example, it appears to be quite irrelevant whether the persons know each other or not in terms of the basic dynamics of the emerging dispute over honour. It is a social game played out by understood rules, most often by willing participants, which may involve persons known or unknown to each other. Put another way, if they haven't been acquainted before, they come to 'know' each other by virtue of the confrontation itself. If it is necessary to preserve a category of 'stranger homicide', it would follow that there would be two groupings of confrontational homicides, one for those involving persons previously known to each other, and one for those involving strangers. Since there appears to be no difference between the two, the present suggestion is that there is no need whatsoever to retain the term 'stranger homicide' as a major indicator of the social relationship between victim and offender.

Homicides do occur between strangers. Large numbers of confrontational killings, and those which arise in the course of other crime, will involve persons previously unknown to each other. Mass killings, discussed previously, also would fall into this category.

At issue, ultimately, is the theoretical importance of the underlying dimension of relational distance, as expanded by Silverman and Kennedy (1987). While of some use for particular arguments, as in its connection to notions derived from 'routine activities' approaches (see Kapardis, 1990), this conception of 'distance' is exceptionally static. While descriptions of relationships such as those involving persons tied together because they share family bonds, or those linked by friendship, or strangers, define a social status between victim and offender, the content of these relationship categories provides few clues as to why the homicide has occurred. Thus, it is a commonplace observation in criminology to point out that a majority of victims of homicide know the person who took their life. While this is an empirically verifiable observation, it adds little information to our knowledge of why that homicide has taken place.

On the motivations muddle

It is partly to address these kinds of problems that investigations attempting to unravel the dynamics of victim-offender interaction have also probed what are referred to as 'motives' (Wolfgang, 1958) or 'circumstances' (Maxfield, 1989) of homicide. In some respects, such classifications come closer to the present scenario approach, at least in the sense that these give explicit attention to the fact that homicide can result from circumstances concerned with the commission of another crime. Thus, in Wolfgang's (1958) groupings there is recognition that homicide can result from 'robbery', the 'halting of a felon', or as a consequence of an attempt at 'escaping arrest'. The Supplementary Homicide Reports (Maxfield, 1989) provides a much more extensive list and includes specification of homicides as an outcome of the commission of 'instrumental' felonies (for example, rape, robbery), 'property' felonies (burglary, larceny, auto theft), or 'other' felonies (including arson).

Other aspects of such lists have been unsatisfying. It is here that Wolfgang (1958) included his well-known notion of 'trivial altercations' as a motivation for homicide, as well as such categories as 'domestic quarrel', 'jealousy', 'altercation regarding money', or 'revenge', among others. While helpful and an important starting point for research which has followed, obvious problems with such a list emerge from close reading of homicide files, including the fact that an event can

involve a significant mix of jealousy and a domestic quarrel, yet at the same time start from an immediate apparently trivial argument (put in other terms, the categories are not mutually exclusive). Further, from present findings it would seem that many male confrontational encounters appear from the outside to be the kinds of events that Wolfgang was aiming at in his use of the term 'trivial altercation', yet in that early research he does not narrow this term to identify fundamentally masculine violence.

While much more recent, even less satisfying is the treatment of a large category of 'conflicts' within the Supplementary Homicide Reports (Maxfield, 1989). While within these 'conflicts' are provided more specific forms which include 'lovers' triangle', 'brawl under alcohol', 'argument over money', and a rather odd inclusion in this context with the label 'killed by baby-sitter', in fact the vast majority of conflict homicides reported within the Supplementary Homicide Reports are found in a residual grouping of 'other arguments' whose content is unspecified and unclear. While many masculine brawls involve alcohol, some which are virtually identical in form do not. Arguments over money may be spontaneous, but many involve definitively premeditated and calculated homicides. In sum, there are many like things that are not placed together in this scheme, there are many unlike things that are grouped together, but most homicides in this scheme fall into the residual categories, either of 'other' (and therefore undefined) arguments, or those where the circumstances are 'unknown'.

Close in many important ways to the present use of scenarios are the various 'syndromes' of homicide suggested by Block and Block (1992). These investigators propose a general grouping of 'instrumental' homicides that encompass most of the specific forms of homicide which have been grouped in the present investigations as homicides consequent to the commission of other crime, these 'instrumental' homicides including killings resulting from robbery, burglary, arson for profit, or contract and gangland deaths (rape is provided for in a separate category). Block and Block provide a distinct grouping for street-gang killings (which would not emerge in Victoria given the absence of formally structured street gangs), and a residual for such 'other' homicide syndromes as murder-suicide pacts and mercy killings.

Particularly problematic for present purposes is a broad band of killings which are grouped as 'expressive' homicides, and include 'neighbour or work-related killings', 'bar-room brawls', 'spouse abuse', 'child abuse', and 'elder abuse', among others. From the present data, despite the utility as a general classification scheme for homicide, there are important theoretical, logical and empirical problems with this

form of grouping. Probably most important is that there is no separation of homicides by gender, most critically in the treatment of killings between spouses. Quite different scenarios of violence hold when men kill their sexual partners (at issue most often is some form of masculine control over the life of the woman), than when women kill their sexual partner (where commonly they are responding to the often extreme violence of the male, and very rarely are such killings motivated by jealousy – the common male motive). Further, the deep and long-term planning involved in some of the killings by men of their women partners stretches in uncomfortable ways the implications of the term 'expressive' homicide.

There are, as well, questions regarding the comprehensiveness of the groupings suggested by Block and Block (1992). The present data would suggest that the term 'bar-room brawl' is much too narrow, since the masculine confrontations involved in such killings can occur in streets, in parks, at parties, or in public transport settings. It is, further, not clear where killings which are a form of planned, rational dispute resolution would fit, since these could hardly be considered 'expressive' in the common understanding of that term.

In general, whether the focus is on the static dimension of social relationships, or whether the issue is motivation or circumstance, it would be hard to argue with the assertion of Daly and Wilson (1988: 171–2) that the existing methods of grouping the events which link homicide victims and offenders are a conceptual 'hodgepodge'. One indication of the absence of coherence is that over the many studies it is virtually impossible to find two which have the same list of either relationship forms or motivations.

On the classification of homicide

While the main purpose of the present analysis has been to probe and explore in a highly inductive fashion four particular scenarios of predominantly masculine violence, as a prior step (as indicated in Chapter 2) it was necessary to evolve a way of grouping all homicides (see Table 1, Chapter 2). It must be emphasised that this form of grouping was definitively emergent and it resulted from the attempt to read and identify coherent patterns for clustering each of the 380 case studies. As the study evolved, the following kinds of guidelines were used to establish the groupings.

A starting point was: did the killing develop out of a sexual relationship (marital, de facto, boyfriend-girlfriend) among the participants? If so, what was the gender of the offender? If the offender was male, and the victim female: (a) was the offender using violence as a result of

jealousy or in an attempt to control some behaviour of the woman, such as to keep her from separating, to control her sexual behaviour, or perhaps to conclude a fight?; or (b) did the offender exhibit a pattern of profound depression, and was the killing a part of the offender's planned suicide?; or (c) had the offender initiated a new sexual relationship, and was the killing a way of discarding an unwanted partner? If the offender was male and the victim was male, was the victim a sexual rival or was the victim involved in a homosexual relationship with the offender, and did the killing represent an attempt to control the behaviour of the victim?

If the offender was a female, and the victim was male, was the killing in response to prior violence of the male or an attempt to control the behaviour of the male (for example, to prevent his separation), or a way of discarding a no longer wanted sexual partner?

In confrontational killings, the key questions concerned the origins of the conflict. These occurred in male-on-male (or in a handful of cases, female-on-female). The critical question would be whether or not there was any evidence of the violence being precipitated by an insult, jostle, or other form of unplanned exchange. Did the violence proceed spontaneously from an insult to the honour of the participants?

In homicide in the course of other crime, most cases could be classified easily by simply asking the question: did the homicide result as a direct consequence of the commission of a crime? Was the victim the victim of the original crime (a double victim) or did the offender in the original crime become the ultimate victim? If a reverse victim, was the offender either a member of the police force, or a citizen? In some cases (such as killings of police) the cluster is expanded by asking the question: was it some other crime, or another crime pattern, that led to the commission of this homicide?

Conflict-resolution homicides are somewhat troublesome because virtually all homicides can be seen as the last state of some conflict. The scenario here is reserved for those cases which can be reached by the following kinds of questions: was the killing a planned and intentional device for resolving some long-standing personal dispute between the victim and offender? Were there factors present which indicate that it was not possible to resolve the dispute in other ways? Is it clear that the homicide was not spontaneous?

The above guidelines would address the four major scenarios examined in detail here. The other forms can be addressed as follows. Regarding multiple homicides (those involving three or more unrelated individual victims), the guide would ask whether or not the events were part of a 'murder spree' or separated in time and therefore evidence of serial killing (Egger, 1990).

Cases of homicide arising out of family relationships (other than spousal bonds) show considerable internal complexity. If the victim is a child, and the offender involves one or both of the parents, then the questions need to address whether the child was a victim of trauma (what form?), the parent's suicide plan, neonaticide, or neglect. Relatively few homicides involve family dyads other than spouses or children killed by parents, and while not theoretically satisfying, for a complete scheme of classification it will be necessary to answer the simple question regarding the nature of the relationship between victim and offender.

While all of the present homicides, save the one mercy killing, could be classified in the above groupings and questions, there were two kinds of remaining categories. One consisted of the 'special' cases where the relationship information could not produce a meaningful explanation of the homicide (previously discussed). The second consisted of the unsolved homicides where not enough information was present to provide a meaningful classification (also discussed previously).

Since these categories are emergent, and derive from a relatively small number of homicides, it is highly likely that attempts at replication would lead to modifications. Certainly if employed in the United States it might be necessary to add a grouping for gang homicides, and perhaps a category that makes specific reference to conflicts flowing out of drugs.

It needs to be acknowledged that raw homicide data are exceptionally diverse, and developing any systematic form of clustering is difficult. While there are many cases, for example, which come close to the ideal types within the scenarios described above, there are other, more troublesome cases which may either fall somewhere between two groupings, or perhaps in its own unique space.

For an illustration, there was the instance of two young males who had been close friends for years. They had enjoyed the outdoors together, and spent much time camping and hunting. One of the men was involved in a motorcycle accident, and became a quadriplegic. After many months, he became deeply depressed and decided to take his own life. The only method available to him was to refuse sustenance. The young man was returned to hospital, and was kept alive through alternative feeding procedures over which he had no control. His depression continued, and with it his desire to terminate his life. He finally was able to convince his young friend to kill him with a hunting rifle, after which the friend committed suicide.

There is no question of this not constituting, as well as a great personal tragedy, criminal homicide, since the acts involved were fully intentional. But it clearly stands apart from most other forms of

homicide observed, making up the one example in this time period of mercy killing.

Most often, however, the problem lies not in the fact that the case stands alone, but that it contains elements of two scenarios. There were two instances where men met in a street after drinking, insults were exchanged, a fight started, a participant was felled, and then afterwards one of the offenders relieved the victim of his money. While the inter-action contained some elements of homicide during the course of another crime, both of these were classified as confrontational homi-cide since the dynamics which produced the killing fitted the elements of that scenario, and the robbery came after the fatal injuries had been inflicted.

There were specific problems noted with the 'conflict-resolution' grouping. There were a few instances where cases could be considered as having elements of both that scenario and homicide arising out of the course of other crime. This is in part because one of the major factors that puts individuals outside the system of conventional arbitra-tion procedures is their participation in a criminal way of life. An argu-ment over a drug debt, for example, is both a conflict which cannot be negotiated by the legitimate legal system, and also arises out of partici-pation in criminal activity.

Similarly, there were some instances where conflict-resolution homi-cides displayed elements of confrontational homicides, especially in the sense that the final episode might contain a fight. There are no easy ways out of these problems. What the classification scheme can do is be clear about what the guidelines are for classification. Where a case has elements of both types of homicides, in the present circumstance it has been classified in the grouping where it shares the most elements. If the procedures are tried in a replicative analysis, especially if there are many more cases, it may be necessary to create sub-categories which recognise the shared features.

Putting this another way, while the use of clear criteria should result in the differentiation of most homicides into the three predominantly male-on-male scenarios, some small amount of overlap is likely to occur, because it is the nature of the phenomena that elements may mix and fuse. Individuals whose lives revolve around drug use and sale, and other criminal activities, may have a long-standing disagreement about a debt that provokes one party to consider the use of violence to settle the matter, but that decision may be acted upon in a leisure setting where the two encounter each other and begin to argue. What is important is that the account be described so as to preserve the critical elements which evolve around the masculine readiness to call upon violence as a way of responding to particular social stimuli.

It also can be noted that occasionally it is necessary to step outside the literal relationship between the specific offender and victim to determine the nature of the scenario. This occurs in such cases as those where the victim by accident intrudes into a scene which has been set in motion by other forces. The man who walked out of a pub and became the victim of another man's violence in the parking lot of a pub was just as much a victim of a confrontation (much of which had taken place earlier in the pub between the offender and the bartenders) as other victims who perhaps participated more directly in confrontational violence. Understanding a scene, in other words, may give a deeper and richer meaning to situations which would not otherwise be revealed by such static terms as 'accidental' victim or 'father-daughter' homicide.

One further factor that became clear as this analysis proceeded was that it was much more complicated in terms of the diversity of elements than was anticipated at the beginning. Originally a plan was established to qualitatively analyse the thematic material in each case study (which was done), and then after writing out the summary, to utilise a set of 'key words' which could apply across the cases.

The problem that emerged very quickly was that the different scenarios each require a distinct set of questions. The essential features of one pattern are quite irrelevant to another. In cases of homicide arising out of sexuality, where the offenders are male, the investigator would be interested in knowing what evidence there was of violence as a control technique, of prior violence on the part of the male, whether or not that violence had been reported, if it was reported, what action was taken, or whether there was evidence of profound depression on the part of the male, and if that led to a plan for suicide.

In cases of confrontational homicide, the specific features which round out the scenario concern the nature of the initial provocation (insult, gesture, jostle, etc.), the location of the events (pub, party, street, park, etc.), the role of peers, the presence of alcohol, and perhaps the role the victim played in precipitating the violence.

In cases of conflict-resolution homicide, the pattern dictates an examination of the nature and length of the bond between offender and victim, the nature of the intended use of violence (for example, was it the victim who first used violence?), the factors that restricted access to other forms of conflict resolution (criminal history of offender, the source of the conflict – such as a drug debt, etc.).

In narratives dealing with homicide in the course of other crime, the primary focus of the narrative would be on explicating the nature of the pattern of criminality that resulted in the homicide (armed robbery, burglary, etc.), how that set up the scene where the homicide

occurred, and the particular role of victim and offender (double or reverse victim, for example).

The point is that the enterprise needs to be seen as leading to a complex logical tree that quickly branches out into unique sets of data, each requiring a distinctive set of questions in order to round out the pattern. There is no single protocol, or simple set of questions, which apply across all cases uniformly which can produce much in the way of useful data.

It must be emphasised that the whole inductive and exploratory thrust of the investigation indicates that further and future work may alter to some degree the patterns reported here. This happened, in fact, even as this work progressed. In an original formulation, for example, drawing upon earlier work, there was an attempt to preserve a category of homicide which took place within the intimate bond of friendship. As the work evolved, and especially when 1987–89 data were added to the 1985–86 collected in the preliminary phases, it became clear that this category was not appropriate. Careful reading, and the development of tighter case study guidelines, indicated that this grouping actually contained two different forms of homicide. On the one hand, there were homicides between friends that were identical in content to confrontational homicides, and these should be so classified. On the other, what further analysis demonstrated was that what was at issue between friends who became involved in homicide was some conflict that they were unable to resolve through conventional means.

This illustration of how these conceptual schemes evolve and change provides recognition that it is likely further exploration will dictate further modification of the overall set of groupings. This should not detract from the importance of the present work, and its attempt to differentiate the major scenarios within which masculine violence is carried out. These are compatible with case study narratives in other accounts, and flow along the lines suggested in the theoretical writings of writers such as Daly and Wilson (1988).

Conclusions

The present review of case study data raises serious questions about what can be achieved through secondary analysis of some of the large-scale data sets such as the Supplementary Homicide Reports in the United States. The individual groupings within which such data report information on either relationship or motivation have been revealed to be of limited usefulness in describing the nature of the social dynamics that have transpired between victim and offender. In individual circumstances, homicides may be pressed into categories of relationship

even when further analysis would demonstrate that knowing that relationship reveals nothing about why the killing has taken place. Throughout, the exceptionally large residuals, the unknown or unclassifiable cases, raise important questions about the general quality of information available. In the Supplementary Homicide Reports, for example, 28.6 per cent of the relationship data are 'unknown', and in the case of the 'homicide circumstance codes' overall 16.7 per cent are classified as unknown, and within the data recorded as 'conflict' 32.8 per cent (of all homicides) are recorded as 'other argument' (Maxfield, 1989: 675–7).

In general, the weight of the present analysis raises several questions about the common schemes for classification of homicide data. On the one hand, the major underlying dimension of social distance throws up categories ('family', 'friends/acquaintances', 'stranger') that are static and devoid of much in the way of theoretical content. On the other hand, these do not preserve the important dimension of gender which has been found in the present instance to be essential in reviewing homicide data.

In the hands of inventive investigators, secondary analysis of large national data sets may reveal some amount of useful information. From the present data, it can be suggested that such research will be sharpened by clear differentiation by gender in its earliest stages. It would appear much more likely, however, that advances in an understanding of the social dynamics of homicide will be revealed by original data collection from files which are sufficiently detailed in information regarding behaviour of both victim and offender.

The weight of the exploratory analysis of masculine scenarios of homicide which has been undertaken in the present investigation comes down on the side of substantiation of Wolfgang's (1958) claim that an important feature of homicide research should be an untangling of the social dynamics linking victim with offender. What this discussion has raised are the general limits of that analysis, including those imposed by the maintenance of previous categories of analysis which appear of negligible value in guiding present day research. Further advances in understanding homicide are likely to require new categories, sharpened theoretical directions, and original data sufficiently abundant in data regarding the 'duet' of interaction between victims and offenders. Even with that, however, analysts must initiate such work with a clear understanding of the forces operating in the data which will set boundaries on what can be achieved.

One final issue along these lines concerns the overall ability to generalise about the findings observed within these scenarios. Are the conclusions reached here limited to Victoria, or can the patterns be

inferred to have wider applicability? Some of the data speak to the caution that must be considered in making any simple inferences to a country like the United States. The overall homicide rate in Australia is much lower (Strang, 1992; Reiss and Roth, 1993), certainly in Australia there is not found the dense Afro-American ghettos that so clearly have impact on the picture of homicide in America (Reiss and Roth, 1993), and there is a much lower level of use of hand guns in homicide than in the United States, firearms contributing to 23 per cent of homicides in Australia in 1990–91 (Strang, 1992: 14), compared with 64 per cent in the United States in 1990 (Bureau of Justice Statistics, 1992).

There are some issues that arise specifically with respect to the playing out of the scenarios as well. For one example, it is clear that the ratio of wives killing husbands to husbands killing wives is much lower in Australia than in the United States (Wilson and Daly, 1992), although the Australian ratio is roughly in the range of countries such as the United Kingdom.

Despite these differences, it can be argued that the general patterns isolated within the scenarios do generalise across national boundaries. The use of violence as a technique of control of women by men has been widely commented on in the research commentary (for an analysis, see Daly and Wilson, 1988), and the phrase uttered in Victoria by a violent male 'If I can't have you no one else will' echoes through literature in the United States and England (see Campbell, 1989; Rasche, 1989, or Mowat, 1966).

The notion of violence as a defence of masculine honour derives from considerable overseas research and thinking as well, in particular the work of Daly and Wilson (1988). The readiness to use violence to defend masculine reputation was commented on specifically by Wolfgang (1958: 188), and features clearly in a number of the case studies observed by Lundsgaarde (1977). This scenario is hardly unique to Victoria.

Most other research provides a specific place for the analysis of homicides which occur in the course of other crime (for example, Wolfgang, 1958: 238–44; Maxfield, 1989; or Block and Block, 1992). In the Philadelphia data, for example, roughly 12 per cent of the homicides took place in the course of other crime (Wolfgang, 1958: 207 and 240), in comparison to the slightly large 16 per cent in the present study. What the present study contributes is a conceptualisation of this particular scenario as deriving from the exceptional *masculine* willingness to take risks which is argued for as a way of looking at this pattern of homicide. This readiness to engage in highly risky criminal behaviour is hardly unique to Victoria, nor is its masculine quality. In fact, all of the 'felony-homicides' (the term employed by the author) in the Philadelphia investigation were male (Wolfgang, 1958: 241).

While the final scenario, involving violence as a form of conflict resolution, has not explicitly been addressed in previous research, it is hardly a new phenomenon. The homicides that occur between various groups within the organised crime networks in the United States would represent this pattern, since these, too, arise often as the final mechanism for resolving competing claims over territory or control of criminal activity. In a way, what the specification of this scenario enables is a sharpening of terms employed in previous research, such as where homicide is viewed as arising out of 'arguments' (Maxfield, 1989) or 'altercations over money' (Wolfgang, 1958: 191). The present usage sets the violence more directly into a theoretically relevant context, and also specifies its masculine content.

Looking at the patterns overall, then, it would seem that the present data are in fact consistent with what has been observed in other settings, although of course there has been a distinctive shaping of the data into the suggested scenarios. There is widespread agreement among the various available studies that homicide is predominantly masculine and lower or under-class in character, and what this book has advanced are particular ways of looking at such violence that appear generally consistent with homicide data across a wide range of previous investigations.

CHAPTER 9

Towards a theoretical analysis of homicide

Roughly 4.5 million people currently live in Victoria. Among these, only a handful, somewhere in the neighbourhood of seventy persons a year, will find themselves in the extraordinary position where they take the life of another person. What is it that pushes individuals to this extremity? Answering this as a theoretical question must be central to any serious discussion of homicide. From the case study material reviewed here, as well as previous research, there appear to be two factors of particular significance in understanding homicide: masculinity, and under or lower-class position.

There is a wealth of literature that establishes the indisputable proposition that homicidal violence is masculine in its makeup (Wolfgang, 1958; Wallace, 1986; Daly and Wilson, 1988). Males overwhelmingly account for most offenders, and to a slightly lesser degree, most victims in homicide. Even where women kill men, it has been demonstrated that the major reason is that the women are defending themselves against prior, and extreme, violence on the part of their male sexual partners (Blum and Fisher, 1978; Gillespie, 1989; Polk and Ranson, 1991b; Easteal, 1993).

The purpose of the present investigation has been to address the particular forms that such masculine violence can take. Throughout, there is strong support for the general proposition that a theme of masculine competitiveness runs through homicide. It is males who feel compelled to compete for resources, for status, for dominance and control of sexual partners, and who are willing to employ violence against other males if called upon in order to assure successful competition. Four specific scenarios of masculine violence have been identified.

The first general scenario consists of the use of lethal violence as a feature of the control over the behaviour of sexual partners. Essential to this scenario is the idea that men view women, to use the apt concept employed by Daly and Wilson (1988), in proprietory terms, where women are seen as possessions over which the male is expected to have exclusive rights. In some situations, the male perceives that the woman is moving out from under his control, as when there is an attempt to break away and form a sexual liaison with a new partner. In such instances the competitive theme is direct and paramount, and the male will feel challenged, as a test of his maleness, to bring the woman 'under control', including, if necessary, the use of violence. In extreme cases, of course, the male announces to the woman and to the world, 'If I can't have you, no one will', in essence destroying the woman to deny the attempts of a competitor to gain authority over the disputed property. Another variant of this theme, where the issue is control of the sexuality of the woman, is where the violence is aimed directly at the sexual rival, with the homicide taking the form of the challenged male taking the life of the male he perceives to be his sexual competition.

Equally proprietory are the cases where depressed males take the lives of their sexual partners as part of their suicide plan. Here again, the woman is viewed as a commodity, over which the male has rights regarding the proper disposal. For such men, it is inconceivable that the woman should be left alone to fend for herself.

What is noteworthy in the present data is the dramatic asymmetry of these major variants on this first scenario. There were no women who killed their sexual partners out of jealousy, and no women killed their husbands prior to their own suicide. This willingness to call upon lethal violence as a feature of sexual control is distinctly and definitively masculine in its makeup. In form and substance, the thematic materials which have emerged from the present case studies are consistent with the ideas of sexual proprietoriness laid out by Daly and Wilson (1988).

The remaining three scenarios all relate to forms of what are mostly male-on-male violence. One such scenario, again drawing closely on the ideas of Daly and Wilson, has been termed 'confrontational' homicide. These are killings which begin in some form of honour contest between males. These tend to start spontaneously from some form of exchange which to an outside observer may appear to be 'trivial' (Wolfgang, 1958), and can be started by an affront to the male, perhaps disrespect to a female companion or a family member, even by simply what is seen as an insulting glance or look ('eyeing off', for an example). A distinctive feature of this scenario, in other words, is that when it begins, what is initially intended is the defence of honour, and the participants may not in any way intend that the violence ultimately take lethal form

(evidence for this can be found in the fact that quite commonly it is within this scenario that we report 'victim precipitation', to use the term suggested by Wolfgang, 1958, where the person who becomes the victim is the one who precipitates the actual violence).

A further distinctive feature of this scenario is that, with rare exceptions, the parties are relatively willing participants in the escalation of violence, in that they actively engage in the combat that leads to the death. Accordingly, the terms 'victim' and 'offender' when applied to this form of homicide may not convey the willing involvement of the various parties in the escalating violence. The social audience plays a crucial role in this form of homicide, providing not only social supports for the violence as it emerges, but in many accounts those who are initially part of the audience may become directly involved in the violence itself, ultimately becoming either offender or victim of the homicide.

Another of these masculine scenarios, again most often male-on-male, consists of violence arising out of the course of other crime. Here the essential feature seems to be the exceptional marginality which leads some males to take extraordinary risks with life.

The final scenario is one where violence becomes employed as a device for resolution of conflict. Males caught beyond the boundaries of conventional life find themselves in a bind when it comes to disputes over such issues as unpaid loans, since the ordinary mechanisms of arbitration, including legal remedies, are closed off. Violence, in such circumstances, becomes an ultimate arbiter of the dispute.

These scenarios are all distinctively masculine. Women rarely attempt to control their sexual partners through the use of violence, are unlikely to deal with threats to their honour through violence, nor are they prone to either risk life in the course of other crime, or to feel it necessary to resolve a dispute by killing their opponent in the conflict.

At the same time, especially in terms of the male-on-male scenarios, the use of lethal violence is definitively working- or under-class behaviour as well. Middle- or upper-class males rarely become involved in confrontations which become lethal, nor are they likely to engage in street forms of criminality which result in the loss of life, nor do they commonly employ violence as a form of resolution of conflict.

What might account for the patterns observed in these case studies? There are a number of theoretical traditions that might be drawn upon. Two recent formulations have attempted to delineate general theories of crime, proposing that a common thread of elements runs not only through forms of homicide, but virtually all crime. Other formulations are more specific to homicide, and are focused on such issues as its gender or class makeup.

A general theory: seductions of crime

One view of homicide which has provoked considerable discussion is Katz's *Seductions of Crime* (1988). Katz in an analysis of what was termed 'righteous slaughter' raised the following questions: (1) what is the killer trying to do in a 'typical homicide'? (his phrase); (2) how does he understand himself, his victim, and the scene at the fatal moment?; and (3) with what sense and in what sensuality is he compelled to act? He then develops the notion of 'righteous slaughter', in which he argued that the typical homicide:

> is an impassioned attempt to perform a sacrifice to embody one or another version of the 'Good.' When people kill in a moralistic rage, their perspective often seems foolish or incomprehensible to us, and, indeed it often seems that way to them soon after the killing. But if we stick to the details of the event, we can see offenders defending the Good, even in what initially appears to be crazy circumstances.
>
> *(Katz, 1988: 12)*

Katz then reviewed several case studies of homicide, drawn from writers such as Lundsgaarde (1977), many of which have elements similar to the cases reviewed in the present study. From these, Katz argued that the 'typical homicide' has the following features (Katz, 1988: 18–19). First, such a homicide is a 'self-righteous act undertaken within the form of defending communal values' (Katz, 1988: 18). Second, the 'typical homicide' is characterised by its 'lack of premeditation'. The third characteristic is a bit more cumbersome. What he is concerned with is the fact that the actual killing may not be what is intended in the homicide: it is artificial to take a 'killing' as the act to be explained. What the non-predatory assailant is attempting to do is more accurately captured by the concept of sacrifice: the marking of the victim in ways that will reconsecrate the assailant as Good. The victim's *death* is neither a *necessary* nor a *sufficient* element of the assailant's animating project (Katz, 1988: 18).

With these characteristics assumed as the attributes of typical homicides, Katz then moved on to develop notions about the role of humiliation as it contributes to the rage which leads to homicide, saying in a typical paragraph:

> When the assailant suddenly drops his air of indifference, he embraces and creates his own humiliation. He then makes public his understanding, not only that he was hurt by the victim, but that he was falsely, foolishly, and cowardly *pretending* not to care. In this double respect, the once-cool but now enraged attacker acknowledges that he has already been *morally* dominated just as he moves to seek *physical* domination. He becomes humiliated at the same time and through the same action in which he becomes enraged.
>
> *(Katz, 1989: 23, emphasis in the original)*

Katz spent several more paragraphs on the question of how humiliation interacts with rage to set the stage for the homicide, as for example:

> when a person becomes enraged, he confirms his humiliation through transcending it. In rage, he acknowledges that his subjectivity has been overcome by implicitly acknowledging that he could not take it any more. But now the acknowledgment is triumphal because it comes just as rage promises to take him to dominance over the situation.   *(Katz, 1989: 26)*

The language is richly textured, the argument complex, but how accurate is Katz's work as an account of homicide? Given that he builds his analysis from the three observations about the 'typical homicide', its value can be partly judged by the degree to which these observations correspond to reality.

Initially it can be pointed out that Katz is in immediate trouble when he employs the phrase 'typical' homicide. He explicitly excludes 'predatory homicides' from consideration, but one must presume that all others are contained within his concept of the 'typical homicide'. Does this mean that the various forms of intimate homicide (sexual or familial), confrontational homicide, conflict-resolution killings, or even negligent work death (all of which legally can be defined as criminal homicides), will fit within the boundaries of his term 'typical homicide?' Since this seems obviously not the case (given the substance of his discussion of humiliation and rage), then Katz might help by providing a little clearer guidance regarding what is, or is not, a typical homicide.

After expending the effort in the preparation and analysis of the present case studies, as well as reading many other accounts of homicide contained in the works of investigators such as Lundsgaarde (1977), the present analysis would not be as bold as Katz and suggest that there is a 'typical' homicide. None of the specific scenarios identified constitute a distinct majority of all homicide cases, and most of the individual forms of homicide themselves have features which are distinctive enough to set them well apart from the others.

Granting Katz for a moment the use of the term 'typical homicide' for purposes of discussion, problems develop quickly when one asks how well his three features of 'typical homicide' bear up when compared across a set of homicides. First, there are many homicides that are not 'self-righteous' acts whose purpose is the upholding of the communal good. Neonaticide is characterised by a form of extreme denial of the pregnancy, the birth, and then the act of homicide, and as such falls far outside the criterion held out by Katz. The depressive, elderly males who kill their wives before they commit suicide would not seem

to be likely candidates for consideration as 'righteous' individuals up-holding the common good. The bungling criminals who kill their friends in order to destroy evidence against themselves for other and more minor crimes are clearly acting out of self-interest rather than any interest in the wider 'good'.

Second, there is the question of premeditation. This is an important issue in the argument developed by Katz, since it is the rapid and spontaneous shift from humiliation to rage that provides the core of his conception of the typical homicide. Here, again, the data are not kind. It has been found that a majority of men who kill their wives have given careful thought to the murder they are going to perform (although often the accounts display an exceptional level of rage). Certainly, the criminals who kill to destroy evidence also have given considerable thought to what they plan to do.

In discussing what happens after rage has overcome humiliation, and then resulted in a killing, Katz observes that:

> After their lethal attacks, killers often retrospectively acknowledge a determining sense of compulsion. They frequently say, 'I got carried away'; 'I didn't know what I was doing'; 'I wasn't myself'. These are not only face-saving devices or ploys to reduce punishment, since, as was already mentioned, killers often do not attempt to escape or spontaneously call the police and confess. At times, the urgency with which they bring in the authorities and condemn themselves seems to be an attempt to prove that they have regained control of themselves – that they are typically rational and that the killing was an aberrant moment that disrupted their characteristic state of moral competence. Thus, the killers may be truly disturbed by the question, 'Why did you do that?'   *(Katz, 1988: 25)*

Some killers in the present files utter such phrases, but many do not. Many husbands who kill their wives know exactly what they are doing, and if anything express a sense of relief once the goal, the wife's death, has been attained. In many of the cases of confrontation, the killers left the scene quite unaware of the seriousness of what they had done, but certainly not in a state of mind such that they would say they didn't know 'what they were doing', or that they 'weren't themselves'.

Katz's third characteristic is a bit harder to examine, since his unique use of language makes it difficult to divine precisely what he means. It can be presumed that what is at issue is that the homicide in his view should serve the effect of establishing at its conclusion a situation where the offender is seen as a defender of the 'Good', then again events such as neonaticide (where the homicide is denied in the consciousness of the offender) or elderly suicide/murders provoked by extreme depression would not seem to fit. When criminals kill friends

to destroy evidence against themselves, it is not likely they would see such acts of self-interest as a defence of the common 'Good'.

Within each of the specific variations of homicide that have emerged from the present data, many killings do not fit the formula which Katz describes as constituting a 'typical homicide.' This creates a peculiar bind in the assessment of Katz's formulation. It seems likely that much of the problem arises out of the method employed by Katz in his analysis. What Katz apparently did was first to theorise about the nature of homicide, then selectively enter the available volumes of case studies (such as can be found in Lundsgaarde, 1977) to isolate those cases which 'verify' his idealised conception of how the act proceeds.

Certainly some homicides can be found, both in other studies and in the present one, that correspond to Katz's notion of a 'typical homicide'. Many confrontational homicides show some correspondence to what Katz seems to have in mind, but there are simply too many examples of homicides which do not fit the patterns described by Katz to conclude that his account is an accurate description of homicide in general.

Also, it must be granted that in some homicides there appears to be a strong interplay between humiliation and rage. When the middle-aged drunk confronts a younger and fitter male over comments made about the older man's de facto wife, the beating the older man received in front of both his wife and the male onlookers was deeply humiliating (Case No. 3778–85). When his wife left him, the 'old-country' husband was humiliated to the point where he said: 'I am no longer a man' (Case No. 231–86).

In these cases, and several like them, the humiliation boiled over into a lethal rage. What is important, however, is that the subsequent violence was most often far from the spontaneous variety described by Katz. There was a clearly premeditated, intentional quality in these homicides which at a minimum meant that the person left the immediate scene to fetch a weapon, and in many of the other cases (especially involving sexual intimacy) this was accompanied by a rather complex plan for the actual killing.

In fact, if one examines closely the dynamics of the homicides most closely corresponding to Katz's notion of 'spontaneous' homicide, which would appear to be confrontational homicides, it is not clear whether there is a good fit of the humiliation-rage model. One male challenges the honour of another as a start to the sequence of lethal violence, that much is clear. But in an exact sense, is it true that one has 'humiliated' the other? Is it not the case in many of these situations that what the fight is about, and the masculine rage, is the *attempt* of the initiator to humiliate? Often it would seem that it is the fight, that is the violence itself, which will determine who is to be 'humiliated.'

There are some confrontations where the initial steps of the confrontation have, as a matter of fact, resulted in one of the parties being publicly humiliated in front of peers. It is specifically these events which are followed by the humiliated party leaving the immediate scene to return at some later time with a weapon. Thus, Katz seems to be wrong on two counts. First, in those homicides which are most 'spontaneous', while it is clear that there is a threat of humiliation present, it cannot be said that experienced humiliation is what provokes, through some 'spontaneous' transcending experience, a rage which results in the killing. Second, when one of the parties has experienced successful humiliation (that is, he is beaten in a non-lethal fight), this may be followed by a build-up of rage which results in a complex set of events whereby a weapon is brought back into the scene, but the time interval is great enough so that Katz's notion of 'spontaneity' does not apply.

Even in those cases where his analysis might fit, his conception of humiliation, rage, sacrifice and marking is curiously empty of its critical gender content. Despite the fact that Katz concludes his discussion of righteous slaughter with a section which comments on the significance of gender in homicide, his discussion of the basis of humiliation and rage does not treat the concept of masculinity. Instead of commenting on why homicide is so distinctively a male phenomenon, Katz (1988: 48–9) makes a few comments on the scarcity of homicide by women, and makes a few conjectures on why this might be so. He does not reflect, however, on what it is about masculinity that provokes 'righteous slaughter'.

What is at issue are the grounds for the humiliation and rage that are so central to Katz's analysis. The view that has been advanced here is that in scenes of sexual intimacy, males may feel rage when their woman partners begin to move out from under their control, especially if this involves sexual activity with another male. When the conflict is with another male, however, the provocation to rage may rest with an insult to masculine face, status or pride. From a theoretical point of view, Katz's elaborate logical construction is found to be unsatisfying because it is empty of any substantive reference to masculinity as providing the fundamental basis for that humiliation and rage.

There is much innovative and provocative thought presented in the description given by Katz of what he terms righteous slaughter. The present work, certainly, would support an argument for examining the 'foreground' of crime, and, in fact, that is why the analysis has engaged in a close reading of actual narratives of homicide. Perhaps if it were possible to know more precisely what he meant by a 'typical homicide', and it could be assured that such homicides behaved by the rules he

described, and perhaps if his conception of humiliation and rage
treated the masculine basis for that rage, then the account might be
more compelling. The task of accounting for the wide range of homicides found in this present study, has led to the conclusion that the
homicides show greater diversity than can be encompassed in Katz's
idealised conception of the typical homicide. Further, it is difficult to be
satisfied with a set of notions that purport to provide a theoretical
framework to understand homicide that does not in its basic structure
treat the dominant theme of masculinity which runs through account
after account of homicide in Victoria.

Those familiar with Katz's work will realise that he included as well
comments on what he termed 'cold-blooded, "senseless" murder' (Katz,
1988: Chapter 8, 274–309). The present work can throw little light on
that analysis. What he does is select from major non-fictional accounts
three dramatic case histories of 'senseless' killing, and then subjects
these to his own unique exploration. Unfortunately, while he makes
clear which homicides are not 'senseless' (those which result from 'situ-
ationally emergent rage', serial killings, killings where the killer 'goes
berserk', that is, mass killings, and killings in the course of robbery
because of the resistance of the victim) he is less than clear which
homicides meet the criterion of being senseless. As a result, it is not
easy to determine which narratives among the cases in this study might
fit within his category.

In examining the text of his argument, it would seem that few, if any,
cases would meet his criteria. Consider, if you will, his concern for
'cosmological control' where he argues that:

> First, there is a cosmological contingency. The primitive god reigns as master
> of the universe, throwing thunderbolts from on high or speaking through
> the silence of the prophet's thoughts. When he sends a message, it will boom
> forth like thunder or stun a man's awareness, as might the sudden burning
> of a bush. Thus, if one is effectively to mobilize the form of primordial evil,
> he needs a situation structured for cosmological transcendence.
>
> *(Katz, 1988: 304)*

Katz, in his search for conditions which 'endow the situation with
privileged meaning' (Katz, 1988: 305) is reading a level of higher order
mental functioning than seems to be available in the present 380
homicides in Victoria. Some of these involve acts of gruesome horror,
but where there is evil one is struck by how mundane it is. There may be
in Katz's search for cosmological significance a transformation of acts
which viewed through other's eyes demonstrate, quite to the contrary
of the visions of Katz, the banality of much of the evil found in
homicide.

Homicide viewed within a general theory of crime

A quite different view of homicide is advanced in the recent theoretical writing of Gottfredson and Hirschi (1990). What these writers propose is a general theory of crime, one which they argue can embrace such diverse acts as auto theft, burglary, robbery, rape, embezzlement, drug offences, and among these, homicide. Crime, in their view, in its various forms requires little in the way of planning or effort, it offers few long-term benefits, it provides excitement and thrills, and it causes pain and discomfort for the victim.

In making their case, Gottfredson and Hirschi (1990) review various forms of crime, describing for each a 'typical' or 'standard' form. As might be expected, these descriptions tally with their conception of the existence of a general category of 'crime'. When it comes to homicide, they begin with an assertion which may come as a surprise to readers of these pages, since they argue that contrary to popular and scholarly opinion: 'homicide is perhaps the most mundane and, in our view, most easily explainable crime' (Gottfredson and Hirschi, 1990: 31).

After providing a couple of pages of 'facts' about homicide, Gottfredson and Hirschi then assert that homicide comes in 'two basic varieties':

> people who are known to one another argue over some trivial matter, as they have argued frequently in the past. In fact, in the past their argument had on occasion led to physical violence, sometimes on the part of the offender, sometimes on the part of the victim.   *(Gottfredson and Hirschi, 1990: 33)*

The individuals then find themselves in the present situation, in which: 'one of them decides that he has had enough, and he hits a little harder or with what turns out to be a lethal instrument. Often, of course, the offender simply ends the dispute with a gun.' (Gottfredson and Hirschi, 1990: 33)

The second of their varieties consists of a crime such as robbery which can alter and change when for some reason:

> (sometimes because the victim resists, sometimes for no apparent reason at all) the offender fixes his gun at the clerk or store owner. Or, occasionally, there is a miscalculation during a burglary and the house turns out to be occupied. Again sometimes because the victim resists and sometimes for no apparent reason the offender clubs, or shoots the resident.
>
> *(Gottfredson and Hirschi, 1990: 33)*

It would seem here that Gottfredson and Hirschi have fallen into the same trap as Katz of starting with preconception of typical crime, and

from that evolved a view of a 'typical homicide' which is rather removed from reality. To be fair, some homicide fits the pattern they describe.

Regarding the first of their types, however, a relatively small proportion of homicides fits a pattern of people who know each other well, who have argued in the past, and then on this occasion the argument goes out of control. This happens in a few cases of domestic homicide, perhaps most noticeably in the one or two cases where a woman offender is defending herself against the violence of her male partner. A very large percentage of homicides involving sexual intimacy where males kill females are clearly planned in advance (including cases where elderly males commit suicide afterwards), and thus do not correspond to this portrait of a 'typical' homicide. The great bulk of confrontation homicides are not situations where people know each other and have argued previously (although this is true of a handful of such killings).

From the characteristics of typical homicide given by Gottfredson and Hirschi, it can be estimated that, at most, about one-third of all Victorian homicides (and this is an outside limit) come close to fitting within the boundaries of the term they propose. What seems to have happened is that Gottfredson and Hirschi, like Katz, have begun their analysis by first developing a highly crystallised notion of typical crime. From that derived notion, and a selective reading of the literature on homicide, they deduce a view of what constitutes 'typical' homicide. They have then committed the fundamental error of entering the data on homicide, and selecting from the accounts of homicide a portrait of homicide consistent with their preconception (and thus with their general theory of crime).

Unfortunately for their theory, in reality most homicide becomes, thereby, not 'typical'. By itself, this is not sufficient to shake the logical foundations they have established for a general theory of crime. This problem, however, appears to apply equally to other forms of criminality they embrace within the general theory. For example, their claim that white-collar crime fits the general pattern seems even more flawed (Gottfredson and Hirschi, 1990: 180–201). Such crime as insider trading is hardly spontaneous, can hardly be said to involve meagre long-term benefits (when major offenders are able to pay civil penalties which run literally not just into millions, but hundreds of millions of dollars), and clearly requires extensive skill and planning (for example, arranging for off-shore trading through foreign merchant banks in order to protect the participant's identity, see Stewart, 1991).

These are not trivial points for the complicated structure created by Gottfredson and Hirschi. They posit as a focal notion the idea of 'crime in general'. Central to their theory is a particular description of 'typical crime', of which 'typical homicide' or 'typical white-collar crime' are

merely sub-types. If such forms of crime empirically do not correspond to crime as they define it, the implications for the theory are serious indeed. The logical structure of their formulation proposes that there are certain conditions (the explanatory variables) which are tied in a particular way to general crime (the dependent variable). If the empirical data suggest that their account of the dependent variable is flawed, then the theory itself becomes untenable.

To be fair, some homicide (like some white-collar crime, or some robbery) fits neatly into the general theory of crime espoused by Gottfredson and Hirschi. These writers, however, have not titled their book 'A General Theory of Some Crime'. They argue that it is a theory of 'typical' or 'standard' crime (the terms are exactly theirs), across a range of specific offences, including homicide. If most homicide (white-collar crime, rape, robbery, etc.) falls outside the boundaries of what these writers see as 'typical', then questions must be raised regarding whether the empirical reality of crime bears a close enough correspondence to their conception of general crime for the theory to merit serious consideration. One is left wondering how it can be that homicide is, as they assert, so 'mundane' and 'easy to explain' when their conception of homicide fits so little of real-world homicide.

Accounting for the masculinity of homicide

Daly and Wilson (1988) have developed a comprehensive framework which is explicitly concerned with accounting for the masculine character of homicide. Men's killing of wives, in their view, is a reflection of the mechanisms which have evolved whereby men strive 'to control women and to traffic in their reproductive capacities' (Daly and Wilson, 1988: 189).

These writers recognise that homicide is diverse in its forms. Observing that males more often kill males than females, they then offer a view that such male-on-male homicides also evolve out of mechanisms which can be interpreted as a process where males are 'killing the competition', arguing that these can be interpreted as:

an assay of competitive conflict. In every human society for which relevant information exists, men kill one another vastly more often than do women. Lethal interpersonal competition is especially prevalent among young men, which accords with many other aspects of life-span development in suggesting that sexual selection has maximized male competitive prowess and inclination in young adulthood.   (Daly and Wilson, 1990: 83)

It is their argument that an evolutionary view can also account for the masculinity of robbery homicides:

Men's minimum needs for survival and sustenance are hardly greater than
those of women, and the men of Detroit are certainly no more likely to be
desperately poor than their female counterparts. But in a paternally invest-
ing species such as our own, males gain reproductive success by commanding
and displaying resources that exceed their own subsistence needs. We suggest that the chronic competitive situation among males is ultimately
responsible for that sex's greater felt need for surplus resources with which
to quell rivals and attract mates.   *(Daly and Wilson, 1988: 179)*

Up to this point, the Victorian data have been consistent with the
hypotheses advanced by Daly and Wilson in the large body of their
works. Males predominated as offenders in homicides where the social
bond was based on sexual intimacy, and the social mechanisms that
emerged from case history after case history is that of masculine sexual
proprietoriness.

Certainly, the masculinity that virtually defined confrontational
homicides and homicides in the course of another crime conforms to
the ideas advanced by Daly and Wilson. They have explicitly treated
both of these forms of lethal violence in their discussion of homicide,
and the present case studies are entirely consistent with the portraits of
these which they provide (Daly and Wilson, 1988: 123–36, and 178–9).
Without some elaboration and expansion, however, the formulations of
these writers seem less well-adapted to accounting for the class characteristics which in the present data rival the gender characteristics of
homicide, and for some help in this domain it is necessary to turn to
another form of thinking about violence.

Homicide and the subculture of violence

One well-established theoretical position is that homicide can be explained by the existence of a 'subculture of violence'. This thesis claims
that the life circumstances of particular social groups generate violence
as a common outcome of routine social interaction. One of the first
statements of this view is contained in the early work of Wolfgang
(1958)):

A male is usually expected to defend the name and honor of his mother, the
virtue of womanhood ... and to accept no derogation about his race ... his
age, or his masculinity. Quick resort to physical combat as a measure of
daring, courage, or defense of status appears to be a cultural expectation,
especially for lower-class males of both races. When such a culture norm
response is elicited from an individual engaged in social interplay with others
who harbor the same response mechanisms, physical assaults, altercations,
and violent domestic quarrels that result in homicide are likely to be
relatively common.   *(Wolfgang, 1958: 188–9)*

This argument was expanded in the later work of Wolfgang and Ferracuti (1967), where they argued that a subculture of violence does not completely oppose the dominant culture, nor does it require that violence be a response in every situation. What the subculture does is to promote a number of social conditions under which violence is likely to be either expected or required. The carrying of weapons, for example, is viewed as a willingness to either expect or participate in violence, and to be ready for quick retaliation should a threat of violence emerge. In some situations, non-violence may not be a choice, as occurs when a male is expected to defend his masculine identity or lose the respect and friendship of his male peers. Thus, as Wolfgang and Ferracuti (1967: 161) state: 'Violence can become a part of the life style, the theme of solving difficult problems or problem situations.'

The subculture of violence thesis has faced wide-ranging criticism (for reviews, see Gibbons, 1992; or McCaghy and Cernkovich, 1987). Some have argued that poverty is a better predictor of homicide than a subculture of violence, while others have contended that within the types of lower-class communities which are supposed to support such a subculture, research has not been able to establish a higher level of support for violence than is found in middle or upper-class communities.

At the same time, the description of actual homicide posed by Wolfgang (1958) or by Wolfgang and Ferracuti (1967), in fact, has stood the test of time. As the present data on confrontational homicide demonstrate, there are those situations where males stand ready to use lethal violence in defence of their honour, and these situations involve distinctively males in working- or under-class contexts. As Wolfgang noted in Philadelphia in the quotation immediately above, so too in Victoria, Australia, there are situations where violence is a 'cultural expectation'.

McCaghy and Cernkovich (1987: 137–8) argue that rather than simply reject the notion of a subculture of violence, it might be better to examine closely the specific conditions which contribute to homicide. In their thesis of a 'subculture of lethal violence' McCaghy and Cernkovich suggest that some conditions which encourage violent behaviour include placing an emphasis on masculine honour and physical prowess, victim precipitation, alcohol use and weapon availability.

Thoughts on masculinity, vulnerability and violence

A starting point in a theoretical attempt to link up these complex phenomena is to emphasise the fundamental masculinity of lethal violence. Gender stands out as a persistent feature of homicide. Most offenders

are male, in the present and in other research (for example, Wolfgang, 1958; Wallace, 1986; Falk, 1990). Males accounted for all but 5 per cent of the cases of confrontational homicide. Males made up virtually all of the original offenders in homicides in the course of another crime (five cases involved women, in four of these the women were accomplices of men who were the principal offenders). Males were the killers in scenes of conflict resolution (two such cases involved females as accomplices, however).

The source of this masculinity can be seen as resulting from inherent competition between males, and in the willingness of males to employ violence as a feature of that competitiveness. Daly and Wilson argue that violence evolves as a device of effective, if high risk, competition among males:

> Competition among males is more intense than that among females in a simple objective sense: the variance in male fitness is greater than the variance in female fitness. Among men as compared to women, the big winners win bigger ...   *(Daly and Wilson, 1988: 140)*

Quoting another writer, they then go on to conclude: 'as a general consequence, the entire life history strategy of males is a higher-risk, higher-stakes adventure than that of females' (Daly and Wilson, 1988: 140).

At this point a conundrum is posed by the finding that violence, especially confrontational and risk-taking violence, is exceptionally rare among economically well-off males. If violence among males can be seen as a feature of successful competition, there would seem initially to be a puzzle posed by the empirical finding that the most successful in the competition for desirable mates are, in fact, the least likely to feel called upon to employ violence. Why are privileged males so unlikely to 'kill the competition', since as the greatest winners, according to this formulation, they would have the most to lose?

One possible line of argument is that while males are competitive with other males, both for attainment of the limited economic resources and for controlling the reproductive capacity of desirable females, in contemporary society that competition has been expanded to widen the devices available to achieve success to include such dimensions as class, wealth, status and power. At the same time, physical prowess has waned in importance. The mature male of established class position, with wealth, recognised status in the community, and power to influence the political mechanisms of community governance, has less need to resort to physical prowess either to subdue his competition or to control his female partner.

Both economic and sexual competition may be problematic. Material insecurity, and jealousy, may be as much a part of privileged life as anywhere else. Thus, the male may feel he has to fight off challenges to his economic position, as well as to insulate his female partner from male competitors. How that insecurity is dealt with, however, may differ according to the resources available.

A possible helpful line of argumentation has been advanced recently by the anthropologist Gilmore (1990). In reviewing data on masculinity across a number of cultures, Gilmore concluded that there were three essential features to masculinity: 'To be man in most of the societies we have looked at, one must impregnate women, protect dependents from danger, and provision kith and kin' (Gilmore, 1990: 223).

In many societies, these 'male imperatives' involve risks, and masculinity can be both dangerous and competitive:

> In fulfilling their obligations, men stand to lose – a hovering threat that separates them from women and boys. They stand to lose their reputations or their lives; yet their prescribed tasks must be done if the group is to survive and prosper.   *(Gilmore, 1990: 223)*

At this level, the argument is consistent with that of Daly and Wilson. Can these ideas be expanded to include the under-class character of this violence as well? A possible line of reasoning is established in Gilmore's argument about the impact of differential social organisation on masculinity:

> The data show a strong connection between the social organization of production and the intensity of the male image. That is, manhood ideologies are adaptations to social environments, not simply autonomous mental projections or psychic fantasies writ large. The harsher the environment and the scarcer the resources, the more manhood is stressed as inspiration and goal.   *(Gilmore, 1990: 224)*

If Gilmore is correct, it would seem reasonable to argue by extension that the contemporary male who possesses economic advantages is able to provide the base for the procreative, provisioning and protective functions through his economic resources, and these same resources provide the underpinnings for his competition with other males for a mate. In other words, physical prowess and aggression no longer become necessary for the economically advantaged male to assure his competence in reproduction, provision or protection.

For males at the bottom of the economic heap, however, the lack of access to economic resources has the consequence of rendering these issues, and therefore their sense of masculinity, as problematic. For

such males, the expression and defence of their masculinity may come
through violence. Messerschmidt, for one, has argued along these lines:

> Some marginalized males adapt to their economic and racial powerlessness
> by engaging in, and hoping to succeed at, competition for personal power
> with rivals of their own class, race and gender. For these marginalized males,
> the personal power struggle with other marginalized males becomes a mech-
> anism for exhibiting and confirming masculinity.   *(Messerschmidt, 1986: 70)*

There are deeply rooted aspects of culture which place men in competition with other men in terms of their reputation or honour. Assuming that Gilmore (1990) is correct in his assertion that the bases of
masculine rivalry derive from competition regarding mating, provisioning and protecting, males who are well integrated into roles of economic success are able to ground their masculinity through methods
other than physical confrontation and violence. For economically
marginal males, however, physical toughness and violence become a
major avenue by which they can assert their masculinity and defend
themselves against what they see as challenges from other males.

It can be argued that part of the adjustment to contemporary life has
been the translation of the general problem of maintenance of masculine control into its economic and political forms, relegating physical
violence to a background role in the maintenance of social control for
those who can make some claim to economic and political resources.
For some, of course, physical violence remains as a potential weapon to
be employed when other devices appear to fail. Looking at the control
of women, this view is derived in part from feminist observations of the
nature of male dominance and power. As Stanko has argued:

> Power, prestige, and credibility ... are awarded on a gender basis: men, as
> men, have greater access to the benefits of power, prestige and credibility. It
> is likely that female children, as part of growing up in an unequal, thus-
> gendered position, learn that they are less valued and have less prestige than
> their male counterparts.   *(Stanko, 1985: 72)*

Thus, part of the control of men over women is derived from their
power. While this extends across the broad range of social relationships
(including the world of work), it intrudes specifically into the domain
of sexuality. As Stanko puts it: 'Women learn, often at a very early age,
that their sexuality is not their own and that maleness can at any time
intrude into it ... male sexual and physical prowess takes precedence
over female sexual and physical autonomy' (Stanko, 1985: 73).

This dominance, Stanko (1985: 70) argues, is such that as part of
'typical' male behaviour women come to expect, as routine, sexual

intimidation and violence. In this view, as expressed by Alder (1991): 'male violence against women in male dominated societies is an expression of male power which is used by men to reproduce and maintain their status and authority over women' (Alder, 1991: 168).

Power, however, derives from a number of sources, and it is argued here that some males are able to maintain their status and authority by means of their economic and social status and the mechanisms which these provide. Males who have an array of resources may be able to maintain their position with respect to their women and other men without recourse to violence. In the first instance, women as wives, secretaries, clients, patients, students, party workers and similar roles, are 'kept in their place' by laws, regulations, ethics, economic sub-ordination, and social expectations. Married women, in particular, are particularly constrained by law and custom, as Scutt has argued:

> Within *his* own four walls any man can do as he chooses – and any women must submit ... Protestations that marriage is a partnership and women and men have equal rights within it are empty in the face of a primitive allegiance to a belief ... that a man is head of *his* household.
>
> *(Scutt, 1983: 279, emphasis in original)*

For persons of established privilege, available resources are powerful enough so when men feel that intimidation of women, or other men, is necessary, steps short of lethal violence are likely to be available. It may be, however, that when those males who possess fewer of these resources are placed in a position where in order to maintain their 'masculinity' in the face of challenges to their status from their female partner, or other males, violence, including ultimately lethal violence, may be called into play.

Occasionally even among those of privilege, the female partner's behaviour may not be brought under control by other techniques, and violence may follow, including ultimately homicide. As we have seen from the present data, relationships involving sexual intimacy is one social context where in the present Victorian case studies instances were found of homicide involving some men of established social position (for example, a bank manager, a primary school principal, and the owner of a car dealership).

In male-to-male lethal violence, including confrontational homicides, the absence of males of privilege either as offenders or victims suggests that the most successful competition among males is waged on economic and social fronts, rather than relying on direct physical assaults and violence. The real winners in the male world of class, wealth, status and power are able to establish their dominance by virtue

of their economic and social position in the market place, in the world of work, on bureaucratic ladders, in corridors of power, or perhaps in extreme forms of rational conflict, in the courts.

Those at the bottom of the economic heap, however, will have fewer such resources available. For them, a major vector along which masculinity can be defined and, and the issues identified by Gilmore (1990) negotiated, is that of physical prowess and violence. They may not have much in the way of money, their voices may count for little in City Hall, but they are ready to beat the stuffing out of anyone in the public bar at the Victoria Hotel that 'gives them lip' or 'mouths off.'

Similarly, males who experience extreme economic marginality, with their ties to conventional society grossly attenuated, are more open to taking exceptional physical risks. Such males are willing to expose others, and themselves, to the danger of lethal violence in order to wrest away some of the economic resources of the more privileged. Armed robbery, in other words, can be viewed as a form of competition where males with scarce resources are willing to take enormous risks to seize the riches accumulated by others. In the form of homicide termed here 'conflict resolution on the margins', males who are at the far boundaries of the society, when they become embroiled in heated conflict with a friend (also a member of the under class), may feel that they have little recourse but to engage in physical violence as a way of settling the competitive battle.

The description of the present themes as scenarios of violence folds well into conceptions of subcultures of violence (Wolfgang and Ferracuti, 1968). The scenarios can be viewed as established scripts which are available to guide masculine action. As scripts, these are, in fact, widely known. For one example, middle-class as well as under-class males will know a variety of scenarios that might be acted out when confronted with an insult from another male in a public or leisure scene, including the ones that can lead to an honour contest, confrontation and violence.

What is important at that point is which scenario is drawn upon to determine the action to be followed. What a subculture of violence does is to set the stage for violence, to create the conditions under which males feel impelled toward direct confrontation or physical aggression. Scenes of potential violence are highly conditional, in other words. There are many features which may be operating to create restraining judgments (to use the term suggested by Athens, 1980) to deflect behaviour in the direction of non-violence. Some settings, however, are socially constructed in such ways that violence is likely to be a central feature of the script that is to be played out, and it is here that a subculture of violence is central in providing the essential supports for

directing action down a path toward violence. Caught in a situation where the script calls for violence, surrounded by a social audience pushing the action in that direction, the males involved may see little choice but to play out the violence dictated by the scenario.

Segal has argued along similar lines, pointing out that there are widely shared images, or fantasies about violence and masculinity:

> The aggressive masculine style which lower working-class men are more likely to value and adopt is not exclusive to them, of course. It is part of the fantasy life, if not the lived reality, of the majority of men enthralled by images of masculinity which equate it with power and violence (where would Clint Eastwood be without his gun?).   *(Segal, 1990: 265)*

In a way similar to the present discussion, Segal then goes on to puzzle out why it is lower-class males are more likely to act upon these definitions of masculinity:

> Many social mediators – from school, jobs, friends, family, religion and politics – effect the way fantasies may, or may not, be channelled into any active expression ... It is the sharp and frustrating conflict between the lives of lower working-class men and the image of masculinity as power, which informs the adoption and, for some, the enactment, of a more aggressive masculinity.   *(Segal, 1990: 265)*

The images of aggressive masculinity are widely spread through male fantasy life. In the mind, across social classes men know the content of the scripts which guide Dirty Harry or James Bond through their violent encounters. Some men, however, are restrained from acting within these scripts, those males being those who have other alternatives for establishing themselves along the needs of protecting, provisioning and providing, especially men who have resources of money, status and power. Lower- and under-class males, however, may find themselves in a position where violence provides a major vector along which they can anchor their masculinity.

The present findings suggest diversity in the patterns of both the masculinity and the class character of the violence observed. The violence associated with masculinity assumes different forms in the sense of resulting in violence to control women, the defence of honour, the willingness to take risks, or the readiness to call upon violence to resolve personal disputes. Similarly, a tentative hypothesis can be advanced that the scenarios may tap into somewhat different points in the class structure. While more data are needed to substantiate the observation, it would appear that the exceptional risk-taking where violence occurs in the course of other crime, and at least some of the

conflict-resolution violence, is found among those males farthest from the boundaries of conventional community life. In these forms the sheer physical risks are great, and the course appears to be taken up only by those with the least to lose. This does not mean that the more economically advantaged do not take risks. Rather, as James Stewart's (1991) account of the insider trading and other financial manipulations of the likes of Dennis Levine, Ivan Boesky and Michael Milken in the United States in the 1980s suggests, when the well-positioned take risks: (1) they are able to confine those risks to activities with a low potential for violence (although there is the interesting tale of how one of the circle of traders implicated by Boesky armed himself with an array of weapons only to be arrested as he set off to kill Boesky, described by Stewart, 1991: 366); and equally important, (2) they make a lot more money when they do take risks.

Confrontational violence, while fundamentally lower and under-class in its makeup, would seem to tap into a slightly less extreme part of the class structure. While those involved may draw upon scripts of violence when the subcultural cues indicate that defence of honour is called for, some of those involved would not seem to be positioned as far from the boundaries of conventional lower-class life as those willing to become involved in the risk-taking of engaging in violent crime. If anything, the subcultural supports for violence as a device of males in the control of women would seem to be spread even wider into conventional culture. The present case studies can only hint at this possibility that these scenarios connect up in somewhat different ways to the class structure, however, and further work would be needed to both clarify and substantiate these links between masculinity, class and violence.

Some thoughts on policy

Despite its public prominence, its very rarity makes it difficult to provide easy solutions when it comes to homicide. Still, from the information obtained here, some initial pathways can be established. A first level of concern might be directed at the complicated issue of gun control (Strang and Gerull, 1993: 197–228). While the limits of such a policy need to be recognised, an argument can be made for the continuation and even extension of Australia's existing controls on firearm ownership. Such policies, in all probability, would have their greatest impact in limiting the harm in those situations where the violence escalates rapidly, as in many of the confrontational encounters. There is a form of a subculture of violence in Australia, as found in the description here of the playing out of confrontation violence found in locations such as pubs (Tomsen, Homel and Thommeny, 1989). In the American scene, as

found in the accounts provided by Lundsgaarde (1977), where males have ready access to hand guns, these disputes can easily become lethal. The general spontaneity, however, means that any barrier placed between the combatants and deadly weapons, such as laws placing guns out of easy reach, will translate into the saving of many lives.

Realistically speaking, the effects would probably not be great in situations of some of the conflict resolution killings, or in the carefully premeditated spousal homicides. In such situations the offenders are willing to expend considerable resources to obtain weapons, and at least in the immediate future, it is likely that illegal sources of supply would be available. There are recognised limits, in other words, to what can be achieved by gun control strategy.

A more medium-range strategy is suggested by the very term 'scenario'. Many of the situations which turn lethal are relatively easy to translate into dramatic scripts defining the most obvious steps in the duet of interaction that leads to the killing. For at least the jealousy-control and confrontational scenarios, these might be transformed into scenes which could be presented to adolescents as they move into their late adolescent years. In particular, it might be possible to create a variety of 'role playing' situations, in which adolescents take turns in playing both the central actors and members of the social audience. These scripts could be written so that young people learn to play out, both as central actors and members of the social audience, non-violent endings to potentially violent encounters. The intent of these would be to involve in a direct and active way males (in both secondary and primary school) in role-playing experiences which convey that violent and controlling masculine behaviour is unacceptable. In a similar manner, Toch (1969: 232) has suggested the use of such techniques as psychodrama and 'test situations' which allow participants to explore alternative courses of action and their consequences.

While one should not overstate what might result from such an educational process, it is clear that many actors caught up in potentially violent situations are inexperienced with violence. They thereby lack a repertoire of established technique for deflecting the interaction down a non-violent path. Educational efforts which role play such techniques need to emphasise both the roles of the central protagonists and members of the social audience, since the audience can exert considerable influence on the immediate interaction, and also because often as the violence escalates it is one of the members of the initial audience who gets swept in to the point where he becomes the ultimate victim of the lethal violence.

Most importantly, of course, there is the persistent issue of economic marginality that must sooner or later be addressed in societies with a

minimal commitment to social justice. It is inconceivable, at least writing in the 1990s, that it would be possible to eliminate the economic and social stresses that push some persons to the point where they are willing to risk, or even plan, lethal violence. At the same time, most developed economies have allowed economic conditions to evolve which assure a large, and relatively permanent, under-class population. Unfortunately, solutions to this problem are difficult to come by. Much of this under-class problem is a direct result of structural economic changes which have rapidly closed off entry positions to viable careers in the lower occupational levels. This has been most obvious in the rapid closing down of manufacturing activity in developed nations, but it also includes the disappearance of lower positions which in the past were the entry points to positions of relatively high status, such as clerks in banks, file clerks in offices, or stock boys/girls in retail firms. Economists, especially those close to governmental policy makers, tend to argue for solutions to cyclical downturns in the economy, partly because these would show quick returns for any effort expended (often because they have been slow to recognise, or acknowledge, the structural changes which are taking place).

The result is that governments, whether dominated by left or right economic policies, tend to generate solutions which, if they have any effect at all, have an impact on the most advantaged of the unemployed, leaving virtually untouched the least advantaged among us. Few government pronouncements today speak directly to the issue of the large under-class populations that are bubbling under the surface of the domestic peace of developed economies. The result is a very large population of highly marginalised males, drifting the city streets of Australia, Canada, the United States, the United Kingdom, and the other countries of the western world. In this drifting process, the conditions are ripe for countless scenes in which both confrontation and conflict-resolution scenarios are played out.

Providing the economic alternatives directly aimed at reducing these large under-class populations certainly should serve to reduce the essential conditions for these forms of violence. Jobs, wages, family roles, political roles, and other social involvements would serve to pull many who are currently floating along in disconnected, under-class ways of life into what should prove to be more conventional and acceptable ways of behaviour, including a reduction in the willingness to use, and the need for, masculine violence. Accordingly, it is argued here that a society which is serious about the reduction of violence should look above all else to its economy, and to ways of providing for the deflection of individuals from the economic traps involved in under-class life.

Conclusions

There will be no single theory which accounts for the exceptional diversity of homicides. A conclusion based on the homicide data derived from the present case studies, however, is that some theories seem less adequate than others in explaining the nature of lethal violence. Both Katz (1988) and Gottfredson and Hirschi (1990) have developed a theoretical account which presumes a form of 'typical' homicide which does not appear to correspond to anything close to a majority of homicides. Since most homicides are well outside their description of the 'typical', the resultant theories at best will have limited utility.

In contrast, the virtue of the idea of a 'subculture of violence' (Wolfgang and Ferracuti, 1967) rests first and foremost in its enduring accuracy in capturing empirically a portion of homicide. The notion that there are social contexts in which violence, including at times lethal violence, becomes virtually a required response in the legitimate defence of masculine honour, holds in the present data which are far removed in geographic space and in time from the original observations of Wolfgang (1958) or Wolfgang and Ferracuti (1967).

At the same time, that description applies only to a specific group of homicides. The value of the thesis advanced by Daly and Wilson (1988) is that it reaches across the major forms of homicide. By entering the argument first with the proposition that much of homicide is dominated by gender, and then branching outward from that to discuss situations of masculine control over the sexuality of women, masculine competition for status among themselves, and masculine competition for scarce resources, a conceptual framework follows which embraces the scenarios of homicide which have emerged from these case studies.

Homicides of males where their female sexual partners are their victims appear to be motivated fundamentally out of the view of women as masculine possessions. As such, the violence can be seen as an extreme of the more general pattern of male dominance, including physical intimidation, which feminists argue is a feature of men's control of women. As has been seen, much of homicide where men are the victims of women results from masculine attempts at physical intimidation, since these women in most instances take up violence as a method of coping with the assaultive behaviour of their partners.

Homicides of males where their victims are other males are likely to derive from male competitiveness. Lacking the access to power in economic and social arenas that might allow the competition to take other forms, confrontational violence in lower- or under-class social positions thus becomes their way of maintaining honour or reputation

in the face of a challenge from another male, with the resultant violence, according to Daly and Wilson (1988), serving as a device whereby the males are able to destroy their competitors.

The predatory violence which occurs in the course of another crime similarly derives from competitiveness, in this case when economically marginal males pursue crime as their method of gaining access to economic resources. Persons with more resources may be pressured out of masculine competitiveness to take some of the risks involved in engaging in criminal behaviour, but are likely to channel these into various forms of elite crime. It can be argued that white-collar crime has the dual advantages of offering to those whose status is high enough to engage in this form of criminality the opportunity for much higher gains, and at certainly much lower risk in terms of the potential that their own lives might be taken in the course of the criminal behaviour.

The present investigation, thereby, provides a tentative empirical base for theories of homicide which focus on questions of the ways by which masculinity in general is an over-arching feature of homicide, and where masculinity combines with working- or under-class position for some of the specific forms of lethal violence. While the data are limited to a small group of homicides over a five-year period in one state in Australia, this book has attempted to raise theoretical issues which have a broad potential sweep in terms of their implications for further qualitative and quantitative research. Hopefully, the present findings will help serve as a guide to that research.

References

Alder, C. (1991) 'Socioeconomic determinants and masculinity', pp. 161–76 in
D. Chappell, P. Grabosky and H. Strang (eds) *Australian Violence:
Contemporary Perspectives*. Canberra: Australian Institute of Criminology.

Ashworth, A. (1991) *Principles of Criminal Law*. Oxford: Clarendon Law Series.

Athens, L.H. (1980) *Violent Criminal Acts and Actors*. London: Routledge &
Kegan Paul.

Bacon, W. and Lansdowne, R. (1982) 'Women who kill husbands: The battered
wife on trial', pp. 67–93 in C. O'Donnell and J. Craney (eds), *Family
Violence in Australia*. Sydney: Longman Cheshire.

Bean, C. (1992) *Women Murdered by the Men They Loved*. Binghampton,
New York: Haworth Press.

Black, D. (1984) *Toward a General Theory of Social Control—Selected Problems*,
(Vol. II). Orlando: Academic Press.

Block, C.R. (1993) 'Lethal violence in the Chicago Latino community',
pp. 267–342 in A.V. Wilson (ed.) *Homicide: the Victim/Offender Connection*.
Cincinnati, Ohio: Anderson Publishing.

Block, R. and Block, C.R. (1992) 'Homicide syndromes and vulnerability:
Violence in Chicago community areas over 25 years', pp. 61–87 in *Studies
on Crime and Crime Prevention*. Vol. 1, No. 1. Stockholm: Scandinavian
University Press.

Blum, A. and Fisher, G. (1978) 'Women who kill', pp. 187–97 in I. Kutash *et al.*
(eds) *Violence: Perspectives on Murder and Aggression*. San Francisco:
Jossey-Bass.

Boyatzis, R.E. (1974) 'The effect of alcohol consumption on the aggressive
behavior of men', *Quarterly Journal of Studies on Alcohol*
35: 959–72.

Browne, A. (1987) *When Battered Women Kill*. New York: The Free Press.

Bureau of Justice Statistics (1992) *Sourcebook of Criminal Justice Statistics – 1991*.
Washington, D.C.: United States Government Printing Office.

Campbell, J.C. (1989) 'If I can't have you, no one can: Power and control in
homicide of female partners', paper delivered at the annual meeting of
the American Society of Criminology, Reno.

Daly, M. and Wilson M.(1988) *Homicide*. New York: Aldine de Gruyter.

Daly, M. and Wilson, M. (1990) 'Killing the competition', *Human Nature* 1: 83–109.

Daly, M., Wilson, M. and Weghorst, S.J. (1982) 'Male sexual jealousy', *Ethology and Sociobiology* 3: 11–27.

Dobash, R.P., Dobash, R.E., Wilson, M. and Daly, M. (1992) 'The myth of sexual symmetry in marital violence', *Social Problems* 39: 71–91.

Easteal, P.W. (1993) *Killing the Beloved: Homicide Between Adult Sexual Intimates.* Canberra: Australian Institute of Criminology.

Egger, S.A. (1990) *Serial Murder: An Elusive Phenomenon.* New York: Praeger.

Egger, S.A. (1984) 'A working definition of serial murder and the reduction of linkage blindness', *Journal of Police Science and Administration* 12: 348–57.

Falk, G. (1990) *Murder: An Analysis of Its Forms, Conditions, and Causes.* London: McFarland & Company.

Field, S. and Jorg, N. (1988) 'Corporate liability and manslaughter: should we be going Dutch?' *Criminal Law Review* 791: 156–69.

Fisse, B. (1990) *Howard's Criminal Law.* Sydney: Law Book Company.

Gelles, R.J. (1987) *The Violent Home.* Beverly Hills, California: Sage.

Gerson, L.W. (1978) 'Alcohol related acts of violence: Who was drinking and where the acts occurred', *Journal of Studies on Alcohol* 39: 1294–6.

Gibbons, D.C. (1992) *Society, Crime and Criminal Behaviour,* 6th edn. Englewood Cliffs, NJ: Prentice-Hall.

Gibbs, J.J. (1986) 'Alcohol consumption, cognition and context: Examining tavern violence', pp. 133–51 in A. Campbell and J.J. Gibbs (eds) *Violent Transactions: The Limits of Personality.* New York: Basil Blackwell.

Gillespie, C.K. (1989) *Justifiable Homicide: Battered Women, Self-Defense, and the Law.* Columbus, Ohio: Ohio State University Press.

Gilmore, D.D. (1990) *Manhood in the Making: Cultural Concepts of Masculinity.* New Haven: Yale University Press.

Gottfredson, M.R. and Hirschi, T. (1990) *A General Theory of Crime.* Stanford, California: Stanford University Press.

Grabosky, P.N., Koshnitsky, N.S., Bajcarz, H.D., and Joyce, B.W. (1981) *Homicide and Serious Assault in South Australia.* Adelaide: Attorney-General's Department.

Hewitt, J.D. (1988) 'The victim-offender relationship in convicted homicide cases: 1960–1984', *Journal of Criminal Justice* 16: 25–33.

Hickey, E. (1990) 'The etiology of victimization in serial murder: An historical and demographic analysis', pp. 53–71 in S.A. Egger (ed.) *Serial Murder: An Elusive Phenomenon.* New York: Praeger.

Holmes, R.M. and De Burger, J. (1988) *Serial Murder.* Newbury Park, California: Sage.

Homel, R. and Tomsen, S. (1993) 'Hot spots for violence: the environment of pubs and clubs', pp. 53–66 in H. Strang and S. Gerull (eds) *Homicide: Patterns, Prevention and Control.* Canberra: Australian Institute of Criminology.

Huong, M.T.N.D., and Salmelainen, P. (1993) *Family, Acquaintance and Stranger Homicide in New South Wales.* Sydney: New South Wales Bureau of Crime Statistics and Research.

Johnson, C.M. and Robinson, M.T. (1992) *Homicide Report.* Washington, D.C.: Government of the District of Columbia, Office of Criminal Justice Plans and Analysis.

Kapardis, A. (1990) 'Stranger homicide in Victoria, January 1984–December 1989', *Australian and New Zealand Journal of Criminology* 23: 241–58.

Kapardis, A. (1989) *They Wrought Mayhem: An Insight into Mass Murder.* Melbourne: River Seine Press.

Kapardis, A. and Cole, B. (1988) 'Characteristics of homicides in Victoria, January 1984–June 1988', *Australian Police Journal* 42: 130–2.

Katz, J. (1988) *The Seductions of Crime: Moral and Sensual Attractions of Doing Evil.* New York: Basic Books.

Kiger, K, (1990), 'The darker figure of crime: The serial murder enigma', pp. 35–52 in S.A. Egger (ed.) *Serial Murder: An Elusive Phenomenon.* New York: Praeger.

Langevin, R. and Handy, L. (1987) 'Stranger homicide in Canada: A national sample and a psychiatric sample', *Journal of Criminal Law and Criminology* 78: 398–429.

Law Reform Commission of Victoria (1988) *Homicide* (Discussion Paper No. 13). Melbourne: Law Reform Commission of Victoria.

Law Reform Commission of Victoria (1991) *Homicide Prosecutions Study.* Melbourne: Law Reform Commission of Victoria.

Levinson, D. (1989) *Family Violence in Cross-Cultural Perspective.* Beverly Hills, California: Sage.

Luckenbill, D.F. (1977) 'Criminal homicide as a situated transaction', *Social Problems* 26: 176–86.

Lunde, D.T. (1975) *Murder and Madness.* Stanford, California: Stanford Alumni Association.

Lundsgaarde, H.P. (1977) *Murder in Space City.* New York: Oxford University Press.

McCaghy, C.H. and Cernkovich, S.A. (1987) *Crime in American Society*, 2nd edn. New York: Macmillan.

McNeely, R.L. and Robinson-Simpson, G. (1987) 'The truth about domestic violence: a falsely framed issue', *Social Work* 32: 485–90.

Maxfield, M.G. (1989) 'Circumstances in Supplementary Homicide Reports: Variety and validity', *Criminology* 27: 671–96.

Messerschmidt, J. (1986) *Capitalism, Patriarchy and Crime: Towards a Socialist Feminist Criminology.* Totowa, N.J.: Rowan & Littlefield.

Messerschmidt, J. (1993) *Masculinities and Crime: Critique and Reconceptualisation of Theory.* Lanham, Maryland: Rowman & Littlefield.

Miller, W.B. (1980) 'Gangs, groups and serious youth crime', in D. Sichor and D. Kelly (eds) *Critical Issues in Juvenile Delinquency.* Lexington, Mass.: Lexington.

Mowat, R. (1966) *Morbid Jealousy and Murder.* London: Tavistock Publications.

Naylor, B. (1990) 'Media images of women who kill', *Legal Services Bulletin* 15 (February): 4–8.

Naylor, B. (1993) 'The Law Reform Commission of Victoria homicide prosecutions study: the importance of context', pp. 93–120 in H. Strang and S. Gerull (eds) *Homicide: Patterns, Prevention and Control.* Canberra: Australian Institute of Criminology.

National Committee on Violence (1990) *Violence: Directions for Australia.* Canberra: Australian Institute of Criminology.

Polk, K. (1993) 'A scenario of masculine violence: confrontational homicide', pp. 35–53 in H. Strang and S. Gerull (eds) *Homicide: Patterns, Prevention and Control.* Canberra: Australian Institute of Criminology.

Polk, K. and Ranson, D. (1991a) 'Patterns of homicide in Victoria', pp. 53–118 in D. Chappell, P. Grabosky and H. Strang (eds) *Australian Violence: Contemporary Perspectives*. Canberra: Australian Institute of Criminology.

Polk, K. and Ranson, D. (1991b) 'The role of gender in intimate homicide', *Australian and New Zealand Journal of Criminology* 24: 15–24.

Polk, K., Haines, F. and Perrone, S. (1993) 'Homicide, negligence and work death: the need for legal change', pp. 239–62 in M. Quinlan (ed.) *Work and Health: The Origins, Management and Regulation of Occupational Illness*. Melbourne: Macmillan.

Ranson, D. (1992) 'The role of the pathologist', pp. 80–126 in H. Selby (ed.) *The Aftermath of Death*. Annandale, NSW: Federation Press.

Rasche, C.E. (1989) 'Stated and attributed motives for lethal violence in intimate relationships', paper delivered at the American Society of Criminology, Reno.

Rasko, G. (1976) 'The victim of the female killer', *Victimology* 1: 396–402.

Reidel, M. (1987) 'Stranger violence: Perspectives, issues and problems', *Journal of Criminal Law and Criminology* 78: 223–58.

Reidel, M. and Zahn, M.A. (1985) *The Nature and Pattern of American Homicide*. Washington, D.C.: United States Government Printing Office.

Reiner, I. and Chatten-Brown, J. 'Deterring death in the workplace: the prosecutor's perspective', *Law, Medicine and Health Care* 17: 23–31.

Reiss, A.J. Jr. and Roth, J.A. (eds) (1993) *Understanding and Preventing Violence*. Washington, D.C.: National Academy Press.

Sanchez-Jankowski, M. (1991) I*slands in the Street: Gangs and American Society*. Berkeley, California: University of California Press.

Scutt, J. (1983) *Even in the Best of Homes: Violence in the Family*. Ringwood, Victoria: Penguin.

Segal, L. (1990) Slow Motion: Changing Masculinities, Changing Men. London: Virago.

Selby, H. (ed.) *The Aftermath of Death*. Annandale, NSW: Federation Press.

Silverman, R.A. and Kennedy, L.W. (1987) 'Relational distance and homicide: the role of the stranger', *Journal of Criminal Law and Criminology* 78: 272–308.

Silverman, R.A. and Mukherjee, S.K. (1987) 'Intimate homicide: An analysis of violent social relationships', *Behavioral Sciences & the Law* 5: 37–47.

Sparrow. G. (1970) *Women Who Murder*. New York: Tower Publications.

Spergel, I.A. (1984) 'Violent gangs in Chicago: In search of social policy', *Social Service Review* 58: 199–226.

Stanko, E.A. (1985) *Intimate Intrusion: Women's Experience of Male Violence*. London: Routledge & Kegan Paul.

Stewart, J.B. (1991) *Den of Thieves*. New York: Simon & Schuster.

Strang, H. (1992) *Homicides in Australia 1990–91*. Canberra: Australian Institute of Criminology.

Strang, H. and Gerull, S. (eds) (1993) *Homicide: Patterns, Prevention and Control*. Canberra: Australian Institute of Criminology.

Straus, M.A. and Gelles, R.J. (1990) *Physical Violence in American Families*. New Brunswick, N.J.: Transaction Publishers.

Toch, H. (1969) *Violent Men: An Inquiry into the Psychology of Violence*. Chicago: Aldine.

Tomsen, S., Homel, R. and Thommeny, J. (1991) 'The causes of public violence: Situational vs. other factors', pp. 177–94 in D. Chappell, P. Grabosky and H. Strang (eds) *Australian Violence: Contemporary*

Perspectives. Canberra: Australian Institute of Criminology.

Vetter, H. (1990) 'Dissociation, psychopathy and the serial murderer',
     pp. 73–92 in S.A. Egger (ed.) *Serial Murder: An Elusive Phenomenon.*
     New York, Praeger.

Victorian Community Council Against Violence (1990) *Violence in and Around
     Licensed Premises.* Melbourne: Victorian Community Council Against
     Violence.

von Hentig, H. (1948) *The Criminal and His Victim: Studies in the Sociobiology of
     Crime.* New Haven: Yale University Press.

Voss, H.L. and Hepburn, J.R. (1968) 'Patterns of criminal homicide in
     Chicago', *Journal of Criminal Law, Criminology and Police Science* 59: 499–508.

Wallace, A. (1986) *Homicide: The Social Reality.* Sydney: New South Wales
     Bureau of Crime Statistics and Research.

Walmsley, R. (1986) *Personal Violence.* (A Home Office Research and Planning
     Unit Report). London: Her Majesty's Stationery Office.

Wilbanks, W. (1982) 'Murdered women and women who murder: A critique of
     the literature', pp. 151–80 in N.H. Rafter and E.A. Stanko (eds) *Judge,
     Lawyer, Victim, Thief: Women, Gender Roles, and Criminal Justice.* Boston:
     Northeastern University Press.

Wilson, M. and Daly, M. (1985) 'Competitiveness, risk taking and violence:
     The young male syndrome', *Ethology and Sociobiology* 6: 59–73.

Wilson, M. and Daly, M. (1992) 'Who kills whom in spouse killings? On the
     exceptional sex ratio of spousal homicide in the United States',
     Criminology 30: 189–215.

Wolfgang, M. (1958) *Patterns of Criminal Homicide.* Philadelphia: University of
     Pennsylvania Press.

Wolfgang, M. and Ferracuti, F. (1967) *The Subculture of Violence: Towards an
     Integrated Theory in Criminology.* London: Tavistock Publications.

Zahn, M.A. and Sagi, P.C. (1987) 'Stranger homicides in nine American cities',
     Journal of Criminal Law and Criminology 78: 377–97.

Zimring, F.E., Mukherjee, S.K. and Van Winkle, B. (1983) 'Intimate homicide:
     A study of intersexual homicide in Chicago', *The University of Chicago Law
     Review* 50: 910–30.

Index

Please remember that this is a library book,
and that it belongs only temporarily to each
person who uses it. Be considerate. Do
not write in this, or any, library book.

DATE DUE

MAR 3 0 1995			
AP 27 '95			
NOV 1 1 2001			
NO 1 '05			

Demco, Inc. 38-293